EMPIRES OF INTELLIGENCE

The publisher gratefully acknowledges the generous contribution to this book provided by the Ahmanson Foundation Humanities Endowment Fund of the University of California Press Foundation.

EMPIRES OF INTELLIGENCE

Security Services and
Colonial Disorder after 1914

MARTIN THOMAS

UNIVERSITY OF CALIFORNIA PRESS   Berkeley   Los Angeles   London

University of California Press, one of the most distinguished
university presses in the United States, enriches lives around the
world by advancing scholarship in the humanities, social sciences,
and natural sciences. Its activities are supported by the UC Press
Foundation and by philanthropic contributions from individuals and
institutions. For more information, visit www.ucpress.edu.

University of California Press
Berkeley and Los Angeles, California

University of California Press, Ltd.
London, England

Reproduction of images in this book is by permission of The
National Archives, London. Some of the chapter sections draw on
articles that have been published before: "Bedouin Tribes and the
Imperial Intelligence Services in Syria, Iraq and Transjordan in the
1920s," *Journal of Contemporary History* 38, no. 4 (2003): 539–62.
Copyright by Sage Publications and the editors of the *Journal of
Contemporary History;* "Colonial States as Intelligence States: Security
Policing and the Limits to Colonial Rule in France's Muslim
Territories, 1920–40," *Journal of Strategic Studies* 28, no. 2 (2005):
1033–60. Copyright by Taylor and Francis and the editors of the
Journal of Strategic Studies; "Economic Conditions and the Limits to
Mobilisation in the French Empire, 1936–1939," *Historical Journal*
48, no. 2 (2005): 471–98. Copyright by Cambridge University Press
and the editors of the *Historical Journal.*

Library of Congress Cataloging-in-Publication Data

Thomas, Martin, 1964–.
    Empires of intelligence : security services and colonial disorder
after 1914 / Martin Thomas.
        p.   cm.
    Includes bibliographical references and index.
    ISBN: 978-0-520-25117-5 (cloth : alk. paper)
    1. Intelligence service—Middle East—History—20th century.
2. Intelligence service—Africa, North—20th century.
3. Intelligence service—Great Britain.   4. Intelligence service—
France.   5. Middle East—Colonization.   6. Africa, North—
Colonization.   I. Title.
UA832.T46   2008
325'.3—dc22   2006032565

Manufactured in the United States of America
15   14   13   12   11   10   09   08
10   9   8   7   6   5   4   3   2   1

This book is printed on New Leaf EcoBook 50, a 100% recycled
fiber of which 50% is de-inked postconsumer waste, processed
chlorine-free. EcoBook 50 is acid free and meets the minimum
requirements of ANSI/ASTM D5634-01 (*Permanence of Paper*).

CONTENTS

ILLUSTRATIONS

MAPS

FIGURES

ACKNOWLEDGMENTS

This book has been a long time in the making. The research and writing of it, though in some ways a rather solitary occupation, was in others very much a collaborative one. Archivists and library staff pointed me in the right direction in the search for documents and private papers. Generous colleagues listened indulgently to "work in progress" conference papers, commented helpfully on draft chapters, and swapped ideas about the relationship between intelligence gathering and the colonial state. University committees and other grant-giving organizations made the entire process feasible by offering financial support and that most precious commodity of all, time. Finally, family members put up with someone who was all too frequently distracted and more absentminded than usual. I wish to express my sincere thanks to all of them here.

Access to government records, especially those of security services and police agencies, is sometimes a delicate business. That this was not generally the case for me in Britain owes much to the advice and patience of the staff at the National Archives, Kew; the British Library's India Office Archive; and the St. Antony's College Middle East Centre and the Rhodes House Library, both in Oxford. My work in French archives was made a good deal easier by the personnel of the Centre des Archives d'Outre-Mer in Aix-en-Provence; the Foreign Ministry archives at the Quai d'Orsay and in Nantes; the Service Ministry archives at the Château de Vincennes; the Paris Prefecture of Police archives; the French National Archives; and the Aude department archives in Carcassonne. I am especially grateful to the staff of the Vincennes Fonds Privés who allowed me to consult French security service files so soon after these records had been repatriated from Moscow.

I also wish to thank the trustees of the following private paper collections for granting me access: Fernand Gambiez; Henry de Jouvenel; the First

Baron Killearn; Louis-Hubert Lyautey; Georges Mandel; Viscount Alfred Milner; Marius Moutet; Paul Painlevé; Joseph Paul-Boncour; Gabriel Puaux; Albert Sarraut; and Maxime Weygand. It also seems only fair to record the more constructive attitude toward the release of colonial intelligence records held by British government ministries since the early 1990s. There are echoes of this greater openness in France, too. In both cases, it is much to be hoped that government and public will recognize the value of shedding light on policies and actions in far-off places regardless of how they reflect on a violent colonial past whose consequences are still very much with us all today.

Exeter University's School of Humanities and Social Sciences gave me sabbatical leave to complete the writing of the book. I owe much to excellent colleagues in Exeter's Department of History as well as in the Institute of Arab and Islamic Studies and the Centre for the Study of War, State, and Society. Their suggestions helped shape my own thinking about intelligence and empire. Several organizations gave me opportunities to present findings and discuss other useful lines of inquiry. These groups included the Society for French Historical Studies, the French Colonial History Society, the American Political Science Association, the Study Group on Intelligence, the Centre for Intelligence and Security Studies at the University of Wales, Aberystwyth, and the British International History Group. More fundamentally, none of the research for this project could have been completed without the generous funding support of the Leverhulme Trust and the U.K. Arts and Humanities Research Council.

For their sound advice, countless references, and good company, my thanks go to Robert Aldrich, Martin Alexander, Andrew Barros, Antony Best, Mathilde von Bülow, Kent Fedorowich, Chris Goscha, Bill Hoisington, Talbot Imlay, Simon Kitson, Mark Lawrence, Fred Logevall, Joe Maiolo, Bob Moore, Kim Munholland, Christian Ostermann, Rogelia Pastor, Len Scott, and Neville Wylie. I am deeply indebted to Peter Jackson, who has supported this venture from first to last and whose insights on intelligence and policymaking have been invaluable. At the University of California Press, Niels Hooper, Rachel Lockman, and, before them, Monica McCormick have all been unfailingly helpful. Suzanne Knott managed production of the book and Madeleine B. Adams copyedited the manuscript, both of them with great patience and skill. Finally, to Suzy, as ever, thanks for everything.

ABBREVIATIONS

AEMNA	Association des étudiants musulmans nord-africains: North African Muslim Students Association, founded in Paris in December 1927
AHC	Arab Higher Committee, founded to coordinate Palestinian protest, April 1936
AOF	Afrique Occidentale Française
APO	Assistant political officer
BCR	Bureaux centraux de renseignement: French regional military intelligence centers
CGT	Confédération Générale du Travail: French trade union confederation, founded in 1895
CGTT	Confédération Générale du Travailleurs Tunisiens, founded in 1924
CGTU	Confédération Générale du Travail Unitaire: Communist-backed French labor confederation, founded in 1922
CID	Criminal Investigation Department
EEF	(British imperial) Egyptian Expeditionary Force
ENA	Étoile Nord-Africaine: the North African Star, the first Algerian nationalist party, led by Messali Hadj and founded in 1926
JIC	Joint Intelligence Committee
MHC	Mediterranean high committee, senior civil-military advisory group on French North African and Levant affairs, founded in 1935
PCA	Parti Communiste Algérien
PCF	Parti Communiste Français: French Communist Party, established in 1920
PO	Political officer

POW   prisoner of war

PPA   Parti Populaire Algérien: Algerian Popular Party, Messalist Algerian nationalist party, founded in 1937

PSF   Parti Social Français: French Social Party, ultrarightist party, founded in 1937

RAF   Royal Air Force

RG   Renseignements Généraux: Paris-based political police

RIC   Royal Irish Constabulary

SCR   Section de Centralisation du Renseignement: French War Ministry intelligence analysis center, the main recipient of BCR reports

SEL   Section d'études du Levant: Beirut military intelligence assessment center

SG   Sûreté Générale (renamed Sûreté Nationale in 1934)

SIS   Secret Intelligence Service

SNS   (Palestine) special night squads

SPS   Sudan Political Service

SR   Service de Renseignements: French military intelligence

SSC   Secret Service Committee, established as a British Cabinet sub-committee, January 1919

SSO   Special service officer

TJFF   Transjordan Frontier Force

NOTE ON TRANSLITERATION

In most cases, 'ayns (') and hamzas (') are the only diacritics included in the transcription of Arabic names and terms. I have used commonly accepted Anglicized versions of Arabic words and place names elsewhere. For simplicity, certain personal names are transliterated on their first use and are then rendered in an Anglicized transliteration without diacritics.

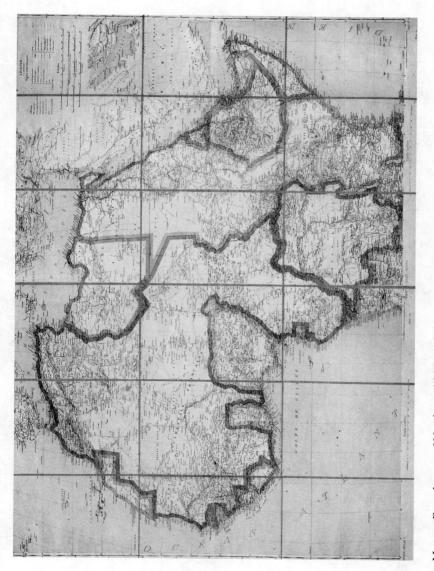

Map 1. French map of Northern Africa and the western Middle East.

INTRODUCTION

Exploring Intelligence and Empire

The Intelligence State

This book is about the process, aims, and results of government information gathering in the quasi-colonial states that spanned the North African Maghreb and the Middle East from the start of the First World War to the start of the Second.[1] It is a study of intelligence gathering as a primary weapon of occupying powers. Overall, the book tries to answer a simple question: When colonial governments faced choices about the treatment of subject populations, how did they decide what to do? Political beliefs, racial assumptions, and the intellectual formation of those in positions of power all played their part. Monetary constraints and strategic factors were also influential. But so were uniquely local considerations: the expressed wishes of trusted local allies, the views of political and religious leaders, and the probable reaction of the wider indigenous community. The most salient factor of all, however, was the intelligence available to those in authority.

My aim then is to compare the information-collection practices and intelligence-assessment methods of the French and British imperial security services, placing them within the wider framework of imperial policymaking and administration. On the French side, the focus extends from the three Maghreb territories of Morocco, Algeria, and Tunisia to the Levant mandate of Syria. On the British side, security service activity is assessed in the mandates of Iraq, Palestine, and Transjordan, and the linked territories of Egypt and Sudan. What follows is the first comparative study of colonial intelligence gathering in the early twentieth century, and a story with powerful resonance in an era of continuing foreign occupation of Middle Eastern territory.

In part, the chapters that follow explore the role of covert intelligence agencies in colonial policing and, more specifically, the containment of early anticolonial nationalism. In part, they examine the role of specialist Arab affairs officers in French and British territories as pivotal links between indigenous urban elites, tribal communities, and migratory Bedouin on the one hand, and central administration on the other. As a whole, the book suggests a new model for the colonial states of the interwar Arab world as what may be termed *intelligence states*. A note of caution should be struck here. The label *intelligence state* is not meant to imply that intelligence and power were one and the same. As John Ferris, one of the first historians to integrate intelligence into the analysis of state policy, warns us: "Intelligence is not a form of power but a means to guide its use, whether as a combat multiplier, or by helping one to understand one's environment and options."[2] It is this last aspect of intelligence as an aid to policy formation that was pivotal to the survival of colonial states.

Most operations of government were ultimately dependent on the quality of information received about the socioeconomic activity, customs, laws, and political attitudes of dependent populations denied basic rights and freedoms. With limited coercive means at their disposal, the French and British authorities from Morocco to Iraq relied on this broad array of incoming information to provide advance warning of any threats to imperial authority. Much of this data was routinely gathered in the course of day-to-day administration. To use a modern term, it was predominantly "open-source" intelligence, or "osint," and ranged from demographic and economic statistics to reports on village meetings, district court proceedings, and religious ceremonies. Its providers were just as likely to be regional colonial officials as specialist intelligence analysts. In many cases, they were one and the same.

Intelligence assessments were conditioned by the accumulated experiences of district officers, tax and education inspectors, regional governors, and central government administrators. But the world of colonial intelligence gathering was never an entirely European one. Much of the most prized intelligence about public behavior derived from locally recruited personnel who worked with security services in numerous ways as informants, interpreters, and covert operatives, or as soldiers and police deputies. We shall thus be dealing not only with open-source intelligence but also, to use another technical term, with "all-source intelligence," information of all types derived from both overt and covert sources. European officials inevitably relied on indigenous bureaucracies and established status groups to make sense of the cultural practices observed in colonial society.[3] And, with the notable exception of Palestine, in the Middle East mandates the European powers built their administrative structures, fiscal regimes, and juridical regulations on the preexisting Ottoman regulatory system.[4]

As Colin Newbury argues, the resulting interactions between Western officials, established elites, and indigenous appointees are better understood as a patron-client relationship than through the generic descriptor of indirect rule.[5] To attribute the remarkably long lifespan of colonial systems to the selective delegation of limited authority to the most trusted members of established local elites is too reductive an explanation of colonial state governance in the particular circumstances of North Africa and the Middle East. Admittedly, imperial government in these regions survived because its senior representatives strove to reconcile their economic, strategic, and political requirements with the local interests of the dominant indigenous hierarchies. These shared interests might originate in land ownership, commerce, or some other common economic activity. They might be a combination of these and other, more cultural factors: family or clan lineage and religious attachment, for instance.[6] What emerged might be described as a partnership of sorts between colonial rulers and established local elites. The colonial state formation that resulted was as much the product of the endogenous social hierarchy as of the exogenous decisions of imperial powers.[7]

Such systems of political clientage could, and did, persist for decades. But they were rarely stable, not least because the patron-client relationship at their heart remained asymmetric. Imperial clientage was ultimately a system of rulers and the ruled rather than a genuinely collaborative partnership.[8] Even the most trusted indigenous supporters of the colonial state sought greater political influence, enhanced status, or more privileged access to resources at the expense of their European rulers. In other words, even those who collaborated with the colonial state as its indigenous intermediaries—whether as ceremonial leaders, municipal governors, Muslim judges, or junior functionaries—were always likely to challenge a political system that confined them to an inferior position, thus eventually reversing the loss of status that accompanied the original imposition of European control.[9] As a result, the patron-client model of colonial state authority was predisposed to generate political conflict because it was subject to renegotiation as the limits of what was politically possible and financially expedient for imperial authorities and their indigenous client elites changed over time.[10]

To these discrete sources of political instability we must add other, deeper social changes that helped place intelligence assessment at the center of government. The pressures of population growth, urbanization, and proletarianization in the late nineteenth century also drove European states to take a closer interest in the family lives of their citizenry. The line between public hygiene and private behavior was increasingly blurred. Ideas of national efficiency and social Darwinism, positivist faith in technological progress, and growing official interest in the emerging social sciences encouraged governments to believe that the nation—and its colonies—could be improved through the judicious application of state power. Emile Durkheim's sociological theories were particularly popular among colonial officials.[11] His benevolent view of bureaucratic surveillance as a logical administrative response to the demands of government in structurally complex societies appealed to colonial service personnel eager to justify their work.

Seen in this light, state surveillance was an outgrowth of scientific modernism, not just an instrument of repressive control.[12] Domestic arrangements, personal morality, and, above all, reproductive behavior were more explicitly linked to issues of social stability, public order, and policing. This connection also existed in colonial territories. Perhaps the strongest evidence of increasing state surveillance of domestic life was the official concern with mixed-race progeny born as a result of relationships between European men and local women in colonial societies (equivalent relationships involving European women remained rare). As Ann Stoler has argued, this signified the creation of new "racial frontiers" between rulers and ruled—frontiers that, like any other, had to be policed.[13]

The need to penetrate indigenous society in order to monitor and control it returns us to the problem of consensual rule. Colonial states could never govern by popular consent because their foundations rested on concepts of racial hierarchy at variance with genuine popular inclusion.[14] Racial exclusion, and the assumptions of Western cultural superiority that underpinned it, introduced a violent and self-destructive dynamic to colonial empire.[15] As Patrick Chabal points out, colonial systems of government could not put down secure foundations because they did not develop organically from within indigenous civil society.[16]

Instead, the effort to coopt those elements of civil society willing to work within the colonial system remained a high priority for imperial administrators. Cost considerations were critical to the responses of colonial governments to preexisting institutions and hierarchies. On the one hand, it was economical to rule through indigenous political and judicial structures where possible. On the other hand, it was imperative that these institutions remain subordinate to colonial authority.[17] This remained the case in those Muslim states where the European rulers scrupulously avoided all mention of the dread word *colony* and made extravagant claims of political pluralism, if not representative democracy. It was frequently asserted by French and British authorities alike that imperial governance respected the communal composition and ethnic differences of subject populations while binding them into a cohesive "national" polity, albeit one not yet fully fledged and capable of self-rule. Whether federal or unitary, this was colonial nation building at its rawest.

Yet it would be wrong to dismiss indigenous involvement in colonial government as merely the cooption of elites and the recruitment of junior auxiliaries by European officials. Neither could supplant the other. Nor were government and society entirely distinct from one another. Drawing on the work of the French sociologist Pierre Bourdieu, analysts of state formation in the modern Middle East have suggested that the state may be understood as a political field in which competing interests—imperial governments, commercial elites, urban notables, tribal confederations, and political parties—sought influence and material concessions.[18] Reviewing this literature in the context of tribal power in the Transjordan mandate, Yoav Alon describes the concept nicely, "If the state is to be understood as a framework or arena for political contest, a 'political field,' it is easier to grasp why tribes can co-operate with this political arrangement. Acts of resistance, as occurred in many tribal societies . . . , can be understood in the light of this principle, as an attempt not to overthrow the state, but to influence it and compete for resources from the central government."[19]

There are limits to this model of imperial pluralism. No matter what the elaborate administrative structures of shared authority between imperial rulers and ostensibly sovereign indigenous administrations, interest groups, or ethnic communities, only Ibn Saud's Saudi Arabia developed beyond European colonial, or neocolonial, control. The limited life expectancy and international scrutiny inherent in the mandate concept certainly imposed limits on the extent of British or French political domination and economic exploitation of the states in question.[20] But, like the protectorate system, mandate governance was closer to colonialism than to a genuine power-sharing arrangement between European advisers and indigenous authorities. The Moroccan sultan's *makhzen* administration, its Tunisian beylical counterpart, the Egyptian monarchy, the Hashemite regimes of Iraq and Transjordan, and the emirates of the Persian Gulf, even the thousands of junior administrators—or *effendiyya*—across the Middle East, were all manipulated by the French and British authorities in situ.

Where do the security services fit into these administrative structures of imperial clientage? The answer is threefold. First, the native affairs services in rural areas and the police agencies of urban districts stood at the interface between European imperial authority and indigenous elite opinion. In several of the territories studied here, it typically fell to military intelligence officers and policemen to report the preliminary indications of a collapse in the patron-client relationships on which local government administration was based. Second, intelligence providers, whether dedicated security service personnel, indigenous informants, or civil administrators, advised imperial government of the day-to-day workings of the clientage system. Their reports on the constant cycle of competition for influence, resources, and power between an alien administration and its indigenous auxiliaries were integral to the capacity of the colonial state either to forestall violent conflict or to suppress it quickly. Third, the security services were also adjuncts of the apparatus of imperial policing. Intelligence of organized dissent—furnished by Sûreté personnel in Morocco or Algeria, by British political officers in Anglo-Egyptian Sudan, or by special service officers in the southern desert of Transjordan and Iraq—was the first stage in the process of force redeployment and repression. Security services were the colonial state's early warning system. If they failed to predict unrest, or if their intelligence of it was ignored, the resultant "warning failures" imperiled colonial authority.[21]

The security services also played a more active role than merely gathering, analyzing, and disseminating intelligence within the state apparatus—the classic "intelligence cycle."[22] They strove to control political participation, sometimes using their powers of arrest and detention for the purpose. They regulated public political conduct by enforcing restrictions on freedom of association or prohibitions on political or trade union organization. And they manipulated the local political process by covert surveillance and coercive intervention when the colonial order appeared to be under threat.[23]

In practice, colonial security services struggled to separate their roles as intelligence providers and agencies of state violence. Often, they conflated the two. Aside from the ethics of such behavior, the use of intelligence as the basis for repressive measures against individuals or entire communities, whether conducted within legal parameters or not, inevitably compromised the effectiveness of future intelligence gathering by alienating the targets of this repression. Hannah Arendt's well-known theories about the state's use of political violence to achieve purely instrumental goals suggested that such violence was typically employed by regimes fearful of losing their grip on power.[24] As Jock McCulloch has noted, the absence of consensual authority in colonial states necessarily placed state violence at the very heart of colonial systems of social control.[25] Jim House and Neil MacMaster have shown in the context of French police killings of Algerian nationalists in 1961 that one logical, if appalling, endpoint of this repressive colonialism could be the descent into "state terror." There was always a risk that security force intelligence might be exploited by unscrupulous officials, not just to contain anticolonial opposition, but to eliminate those identified as opponents of the state.[26] The point is that colonial intelligence providers operated in political environments where arbitrary and sometimes extreme violence by policemen, soldiers, company foremen, farm overseers, and native auxiliaries was habitual. Time and again, it fell to colonial security services to perform a dual role here, both preempting the application of such violence by early intelligence warnings, and recommending the use of coercive force when intelligence indicated imminent dissent. It was a tall order.

The metropolitan reaction to the shooting of hundreds of Indian civilians by British imperial troops at Amritsar in April 1919 suggested that, during the interwar period, press and public opinion in Britain—and France as well—would question wholesale killings of dependent populations on a scale comparable to the initial phases of colonial occupation in the previous century.[27] The fact that Middle East mandates were subject to a form of international scrutiny through the League of Nations mandate commission acted as a further constraint on the use of state violence to maintain order. As Gil Merom argues, the greater the capacity for the democratic expression of opposition to brutal methods of external political control in dependent societies, the less feasible it becomes for colonial states to employ unlimited force to uphold their power. Merom frames his argument in terms of a "normative gap" between the expectations of educated opinion and the capacity of a colonial state to employ unlimited violence against a subject population.[28] Put crudely, the use of unrestricted state violence against colonial civilians was increasingly intolerable to domestic opinion in Britain and France. Greater restraint was called for. In these changed circumstances, intelligence agencies had to ensure that force was targeted efficiently, either to prevent the outbreak of more widespread violence or to ensure that order was restored as quickly as possible.

Intelligence and the Colonial State

Military historians describe intelligence effectively used as a force multiplier. Information about enemy dispositions, imminent threats, or potential subversion may add substantially to the capacity of states, armies, or police forces to achieve their desired results in policy, battle, or the maintenance of order.[29] Historians of empire have not tended to view in comparable terms the information acquired by colonial states about dependent populations.

One reason for this may be that, as we have seen, constitutionally and conceptually, colonial states occupied a shifting middle ground between domestic and foreign, between statehood and dependence on an external power. There was inherent organizational tension between colonies without recognized national status as subordinate components of an imperial system and the European nation-states at the heart of that system. Furthermore, colonial governments struggled to transcend their origins as occupation administrations. A territorial presence was but the necessary prelude to the cultural, legal, and social transformations that signified the imposition of meaningful political control.[30]

The murky status of the colonial state was clouded still further by four additional factors. First, colonial states, although confined by their relationship to the metropolitan imperial power, retained some autonomy as political actors. Second, the modern international system may have recognized colonial territory as British or French (or elsewhere Belgian, Dutch, Portuguese, American, or Japanese), but the vast majority of colonial populations were assuredly "foreign" in terms of ethnicity, culture, and political allegiance. This raises the third problem. Colonial states were not bound together by the common interest of the general population and the central authority that governed them. Indeed, the growth of national political communities was something that colonial authorities generally strove to avoid until the eve of decolonization.[31] Across Europe, popular identification of the state with the nation became more commonplace as ethnically based concepts of nationalism and self-determination took root in the post-1919 international system. This was anathema to colonial state authorities, which necessarily denied any equivalence between the two.

It remained both an operating assumption and an ethical imperative for imperial governments to belittle the national aspirations of colonial populations. Here we arrive at the fourth key factor. Colonies may have exhibited both the defined territoriality of a state and a single, central authority, but they lacked any voluntary associational basis between rulers and ruled to help underpin the state.[32] Crawford Young takes us to the heart of the matter. His analysis of the internal dynamics of African colonial states has a particular resonance for the European protectorates in North Africa as well as the Middle East mandates established after World War I: "The colony as a subspecies of state had several distinctive characteristics. It was a dependent appendage of an externally located sovereign entity, alien to its core. Its inner logic was shaped by the vocation of domination. The very success of its hegemonic project constituted a civil society that over time was bound to reject its legitimacy."[33] If governors and governed did not agree on the idea of a national community, there was correspondingly little basis for the development of a moral economy of the colonial state based on a common understanding of rights, laws, and the obligations of community membership.[34] Instead, colonial subjects were unlikely to accept their subordination to external authority indefinitely, making the relationship between the imperial power and its overseas territories fundamentally unstable. Such instability prohibited the kind of interstate partnerships founded on the voluntary limitation of hegemonic power, or "strategic restraint," and limited recognition of client state interests that G. John Ikenberry describes in relation to the postwar orders of the nineteenth and twentieth centuries.[35] Clientage between imperial overlords and indigenous colonial elites developed below the horizon of interstate activity for the obvious reason that colonies were denied the sovereign attributes of a state.[36] But what would happen when one of the partners in this relationship articulated its political demands in terms of "national" rights? It was this that colonial security services were expected to foresee and to forestall in the decades after 1919.

Investigating Intelligence and Empire

The chapters that follow examine various aspects of this intelligence power in the colonial states of the Arab world after 1914. Chapter 1 traces the nature and development of intelligence gathering and security policing in imperial territories across the Arab world between the two world wars. It explores the connections between senior imperial administrators and their imperial security services, suggesting that the providers of political intelligence quickly established themselves as a bridge between government and subject populations. Put simply, imperial administration could not function without the security services and, in tribal society especially, intelligence officers were the most familiar face of central government. The chapter dwells on the social background, the training, and the field experience of security agency personnel, both military and civilian. It argues that in each of the territories studied, homogenous intelligence communities existed, bound together by common problems, shared practice, and, in certain cases, a growing opposition to European settlement, capitalist enterprise, and the sectarian interests of the indigenous urban commercial elite.

Chapter 2 examines the role of past precedent in shaping the "official mind" of imperial security services in Muslim societies. Constant reference to earlier experience shaped the perception of early Arab nationalism—whether secular and leftist or Islamic and traditional—as inherently destructive of colonial order and elite authority. The incompatibility of Arab nationalism and colonialism is obvious. But the effect of security service reading of the Arab nationalist threat on the development of French and British colonial states has not been examined through the eyes of the intelligence officials involved.

The second chapter also investigates the movement of security agency personnel within the French and British imperial systems, focusing, in particular, on the adaptation of administrative practice from older colonies to the Middle East mandates after the First World War. In this chapter, I suggest that the development of the North African and Middle East territories into intelligence states after 1919 owed much to prevailing ideas of governance, popular control, and racial hierarchy among officials and Arabist specialists charged with the imposition of colonial order. Four past precedents of key significance are examined in some detail, two from the British Empire and two from the French. In the British case, there are the "lessons" of policing the North-West Frontier in British India, and the role of the Sudan Political Service in the containment of intercommunal rivalry in the Anglo-Egyptian Sudan.[37] Britain's imperial intelligence specialists made much of the accumulated experience of policing and counterinsurgency in the Indian subcontinent and, more recently, Ireland. Britain's long-standing tradition of collaboration with Muslim princely states in India, Malaya, and Arabia, and its wartime support for Sherif al-Husayn's revolt against Ottoman suzerainty also played a central role in shaping the attitudes of intelligence practitioners toward the differing forms of indigenous opposition they encountered in the Arab world.[38] In the French case, the Algiers government and the North African Residencies, as well as the native affairs specialists and military commanders stationed in the Maghreb and the

Levant, took pride in their anthropological approach to understanding Muslim societies in contrast to the crude mercantilism of their British rivals. The experience of the *bureaux arabes* in early colonial Algeria, and the success of the "Lyautey method" of pacification and indirect rule in the Moroccan protectorate are investigated by reference to their subsequent application in mandatory Syria.

Chapter 3 focuses on France's Muslim territories to investigate security responses to differing forms of indigenous opposition. It focuses, in particular, on two distinct sources of anticolonial thought: pan-Islamist teachings and Communist ideology. The threat perceptions of the French intelligence communities in the Maghreb and the Levant indicate a profound mistrust of Islamic engagement in colonial politics and a tendency to exaggerate the dangers of Communist subversion. If the Communist challenge was overblown, the power of Islamic mobilization was not. And this, in turn, confronted French colonial authorities with a dilemma, born of the fact that imperialist doctrine asserted France's unique sensitivity to the patchwork of Islamic observance, Sufi religious orders, and tribal custom in North and West Africa.[39] But official efforts to classify Muslim social groups were distorted by specious racialist theory and misinterpretation of Islamic customs and social status.[40] And the fact remained that, in North Africa especially, Muslim civil society proved both resilient and resistant in the face of creeping European colonialism. As George Joffé has argued, "the urban elite tended to accept colonial control to the extent that traditional Islamic political structures were retained, and to condemn it insofar as they were not."[41] For every Muslim official or cleric willing to acknowledge French authority in Algeria as in other Muslim territories, the silent Muslim majority remained hostile to French infractions against sacred spaces, Muslim religious observance, and Islamic juridical authority.[42] In these circumstances, the impenetrability of Islamic society fostered the proliferation of intelligence agencies and security surveillance.

Chapters 4 and 5 analyze the performance of British and French imperial security agencies confronted with violent unrest and communal rebellion. Chapter 4 focuses on early challenges to British imperial authority in Arab territories in the years immediately following World War I. The effectiveness and growing influence of Britain's colonial police and military intelligence agencies in central administration is examined in connection with a series of revolts immediately after the war ended. The role of intelligence information is considered in the following case studies: urban protest and the 1919 Zaghlulist revolt in Egypt; the long-running unrest in Iraqi Kurdistan; the rebellion across Shi'ite Iraq in 1920; and the disorders in 1920s Sudan that produced fundamental change in the administrative structure of the territory. In Egypt and the Sudan, security responses to nationalist disorder placed the intelligence services at the heart of imperial power. So, too, in the Iraq mandate, where communal dissent was especially bitter and containment of Kurdish revolt was an intractable problem. In practice, the security agency intelligence network and the paramilitary police force deployed in northern Iraq were all that prevented Kurdish secession. In northern and southern Iraq, increasing use of air power to coerce dissenting tribes was no substitute for local policing. But state reliance on ethnically recruited irregular forces stored up communal hatreds that spilled over into recurrent violence between Kurds, Assyrians, and Arabs.

The fifth chapter is a partner to the fourth. It holds a mirror to the activity of the British security agencies by considering the operations of their French counterparts in Morocco and Syria. Outside the confines of the major urban centers of both territories, the constitutional prerogatives of French imperial rule were disputed among differing ethnic communities, tribal clans, and religious groups. The chapter investigates the role of French security agencies first in containing rebellion, and then in limiting dissent in two regions: the Moroccan Rif and the Syrian Jabal Druze. The picture that emerges is that the policing of rebellion in the 1920s catalyzed the development of imperial intelligence states throughout the Arab world.

Chapter 6 compares another aspect of Franco-British security service activity—the policing of itinerant Bedouin populations in the southern deserts of Syria, Iraq, and Transjordan. Long colonial frontiers, many of them arbitrarily laid down in defiance of local topography or ethnic distribution, were impossible to police thoroughly. Efforts to improve the effectiveness of state control over the movement of colonial people and goods thus became inseparable from the process of acquiring information about the nature of the environment through which this human and commercial traffic passed. Intelligence frontiers broadly corresponded to the frontiers of settlement, but in territories with large nomadic populations, effective government required an information stream from these nonsedentary populations in the desert interior. Detailed knowledge about viable overland communications routes, navigable waterways, reliable sources of water and grazing, meteorological and epidemiological data, and, most important, the economic connections among differing communities, offered the best guide to where, when, and how colonial subjects were likely to migrate in search of income. The chapter addresses the causes and consequences of tribal control policies, usually implemented by security agency personnel. It uses the example of Bedouin populations to draw out the similarities of French and British practice. Each followed established Ottoman precedent in encouraging the sedentarization of nomadic tribes. Sedentarization was accompanied by increased restrictions on nomadic freedom of movement. The chapter argues that this attempt to "domesticate" migratory tribes amounted to an attack on the very fabric of their culture.

Although intelligence personnel and imperial policing agencies were fundamental to the imposition of central government authority in the countryside, their role in developing strategies of urban policing is better known. Chapter 7 delves deeper into the operational aspects of security surveillance and intelligence gathering in urban settings throughout France's Arab territories during the interwar years. It examines the day-to-day work of the French security agencies—the Service de Renseignements military intelligence service and the policemen of the Sûreté Générale—reviewing their methods, and their effectiveness as seen by central administration. Intelligence gathering and imperial policing are examined through various case studies of urban disorder in French North Africa and the Levant mandates. This chapter investigates security service work in "the Arab street" of the interwar period, linking urban policing to colonial urbanism as facets of social control.[43] It devotes particular attention to three aspects of security agency work: the legal proscription of nationalist groups and the confinement of their leaders; the infiltration of nationalist meetings and the uses made of the intelligence thus accumulated; and, finally, the politicization of the security agencies in response to the growing radicalism of Arab nationalism.

The interplay between repression of nationalist protest and the accretion of intelligence power in colonial states is further examined in chapter 8. Here the focus spans the entire interwar period, linking the growth of organized Arab protest in the Palestine mandate to the widening role of security agencies in imperial policing during the 1930s. This chapter is a study in misperception and failure: the mistaken assumptions made about the security of mandatory control, the exposure of chronic weakness in the British system of intelligence gathering, and the failure of security strategies based on a "minimum force" doctrine of imperial policing.

In chapter 9 we turn our attention to the late 1930s. Scholars of decolonization wrestle with the theoretical problems inherent in any concept of a transfer of power from a colonial state to a postcolonial nation. The idea of any such transfer as an orderly, finite process, or the symbolic relinquishment of authority by agreed stages has long been discredited. Nevertheless, colonial historians must address the questions of when, where, why, and how imperial authority broke down. This chapter relates these problems to intelligence gathering and colonial policing in the Arab territories on the eve of the Second World War.

This chapter suggests that intelligence assessment and surveillance of subject populations were often collaborative ventures between the local authorities and trusted indigenous intermediaries. It investigates a specific period—1936 to 1939. The reasons for this are threefold. First is the coincidence of two quite separate but equally significant events for the French and British security agencies in the summer of 1936: the election of the

Socialist-led Popular Front coalition in France, and the outbreak of the Arab revolt in Palestine. The promise of Popular Front colonial reform transformed the nature of social protest and intelligence gathering in French Arab territories. And the Palestine revolt, which is analyzed in chapter 8, hastened the development of a shared sense of Arab identity in opposition to European rule. A second reason for the specific chronological focus is that official efforts accelerated in 1936 to renegotiate the terms of the French and British imperial presence in Syria, Lebanon, Egypt, and Palestine. This shift in policy affected every facet of security agency activity in the territories concerned. The third justification for the focus on 1936 to 1939 is the conjunction of the growing threat of world war and attempts by the security agencies to consolidate working relationships with trusted local subordinates in order to maintain order at minimal cost. These policy shifts are examined in the context of a limited "transfer of power," ultimately frustrated as the likelihood of war increased.

The conclusion ties together the discussions of the preceding chapters by addressing the book's central theme of colonial states as intelligence states. It revisits the nature of the security agencies established in North Africa and the Middle East after the First World War, and retraces their increasing administrative role as the challenges of interethnic violence, communal rebellion, and organized nationalist protest undermined the stability of imperial systems throughout the interwar Arab world. A further theme revisited in the conclusion is the security agencies' increasing preoccupation with the penetration of imperial authority in rural society. Bringing the growing challenges of organized urban opposition and rural disorder together, the conclusion focuses once again on the main currents in the discourse of security service reportage and policy advice, tying these to the concept of the intelligence state that underpins the book as a whole. We are thus brought full circle to the issues raised in this introduction. Just as covert intelligence was for many years a "missing dimension" of international history, so, too, its importance in colonial history is only gradually emerging.[44] Intelligence and empire were inextricably linked in a symbiotic relationship, the growth of one nourishing the consolidation of the other.

THE DEVELOPMENT OF INTELLIGENCE SERVICES AND SECURITY POLICING IN NORTH AFRICA AND THE MIDDLE EAST

Our purpose in this first chapter is twofold: to explain the types of intelligence gathering conducted in French- and British-controlled Arab territories after World War I, and to trace the development of the security agencies that conducted it. The task looks simple, but identifying the various military, police, and intelligence agencies that comprised the imperial security services in the Arab world between 1918 and 1939 is less straightforward than one might imagine. The reason is, in large part, one of boundaries: jurisdictional, administrative, and racial. Colonial administrations were more animated by problems of internal security than were the metropolitan governments they served. Administrators outside the security services thus were integral to the process of information collection and analysis. Colonial states were intelligence states insofar as the entire bureaucratic apparatus of imperial administration in Muslim territories contributed to state surveillance of the subject population. It is therefore important to bear in mind that, while distinct security services existed in each of the territories studied here, they made use of funds, information, and personnel supplied by branches of the civil administration with no formal connection to the police or the armed forces.

The demands of wartime government between 1914 and 1918 stimulated greater bureaucratization of colonial states, especially military and police agencies, and colonial intelligence gathering against enemy powers became more institutionalized once war was declared. French and British civil and military intelligence staffs gathered information about colonial subversion sponsored by the central powers and, of course, planned subversive operations and propaganda offensives of their own.[1] Wartime administrative expansion added to the pool of qualified individuals available for colonial service in the Arab Middle East after the war. The early 1920s witnessed a general retrenchment of colonial security services, however, as imperial governments tightened their budgetary belts. In common with their metropolitan equivalents, the imperial bureaucracy of the secret services shrank in the early 1920s before expanding markedly in the subsequent decade.[2] In the French mandates of Syria and Lebanon, the military intelligence service remained an elite organization of less than one hundred personnel.[3] For much of the period studied here, colonial security services thus comprised a numerically small community of specialist police and military intelligence officers. Many of the latter were dispatched to the provinces or the desert interior, either as regional governors or as native affairs advisers. In all the colonial states investigated here, this distinct security service network was intimately linked to civil administration, feeding information to it and relying on its prompt intervention to maintain order even in the remotest locations. In the broadest sense, the entire administrative apparatus of the colonial state was an intelligence community, the colonial state an intelligence state.

Intelligence and Colonial Order

After 1918, problems of imperial authority in the Arab world stemmed above all from the gathering popular pressure for greater rights, freedoms, and cultural autonomy. Simply put, the rising force of Arab nationalism and other forms of indigenous opposition to European rule precluded the maintenance of stable imperial systems in the Middle East.[4] Indeed, the very imposition of European political control in territories across the Middle East catalyzed the development of national identities defined in opposition to this external authority. At one extreme, Palestinian Arab identity, while linked to wider Muslim religious affiliations and the specific issue of Jewish immigration, was also shaped by the imposition of mandatory rule.[5] With "nation building" in Palestine came oppositional Palestinian nationalism. So too in Syria, where the diffusion of nationalist ideas based on an inclusive populist nationalism gained huge momentum in the brief period of Amir Faysal's republic from 1918 to 1920.[6] At the other extreme, the Iraq mandate welded together from former Ottoman *vilayets* and governed in conjunction with a Sunni elite posited a form of nationalism acceptable to the British and the Hashemite authorities in Baghdad.[7] In Toby Dodge's words, Iraq was a nation "invented" by the mandate.[8] Not surprisingly, this artificial Iraqi nationhood sharpened the communal loyalties of its principal victims: the Shi'ite majority of the south and the Kurds of the north. In these circumstances, security intelligence assumed critical importance in preventing, curbing, or suppressing explosions of public discontent.

Protectorates and mandates may not have been colonies properly defined in constitutional terms, but the security service activity within them

Figure 1. Inventing a British Iraq I: British imperial troops
commemorating the armistice at the Baghdad memorial
to General Maude, one of the first architects of the Iraq
Mandate. TNA, AIR 23/7386. Crown copyright, reproduced
courtesy of the National Archives, London.

was assuredly colonial in its fundamental purpose: to solidify imperial rule.
Colonial intelligence gathering thus straddled the boundaries of conventional military intelligence, which focused on gathering and analyzing information about foreign powers, and internal security intelligence, which was
devoted to political policing of the domestic population. First and foremost,
surveillance of colonial populations targeted internal subversion. Clearly,

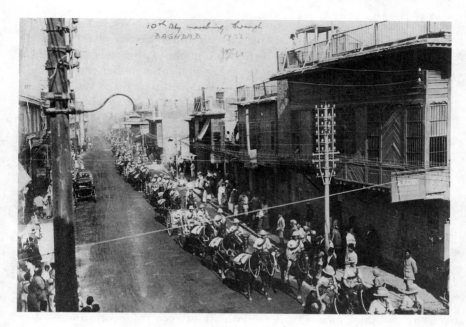

Figure 2. Inventing a British Iraq II: British army column staging a march-past through central Baghdad, 1922. TNA, WO 305/1933. Crown copyright, reproduced courtesy of the National Archives, London.

subversion was a loaded term. As understood by colonial security agencies, it embraced every manner of political activity deemed a potential focal point for organized opposition to colonial authority.

That said, we *can* afford to be somewhat more reductive. Emergent anticolonial nationalist groups dominated security policing in the two decades after 1919. Paradoxically, this preoccupation with internal subversion led to the retention of a certain foreign focus, more akin to the concerns of military intelligence.[9] As we shall see in chapter 3, colonial security service surveillance of German and Ottoman efforts to foment dissent in British- and French-ruled Muslim territories in the First World War persisted into the 1920s with only a slight change of emphasis to foreign support for pan-Islamism, the caliphate movement, and even anticolonialism itself.[10] And the persistent tendency among police and military intelligence agencies to exaggerate the connections between Communist egalitarianism and anticolonial nationalism underlined the fact that colonial intelligence gathering was as much about foreign threats as domestic ones.[11]

Another distinctive feature of security services was that their knowledge about the dependent population was primarily acquired for the purpose of social control by an endogenous ruling elite, and only secondarily for the improvement of indigenous people's lives. Little systematic effort was made in the colonial setting to persuade dependent populations that state authorities acquired information about them for their ultimate benefit.

This state of affairs was not surprising. For one thing, there was less direct correlation in the colonies between the information acquired and the benefits conferred by the state than in Britain or France. Colonial tax collection, identity checks, military obligation, and police record keeping were tailored to the requirements of the imperial power, not those of the subject population. Colonial fiscal regimes were designed to meet the costs of administration itself, not to fund social spending beyond the requirements of administrators and settlers themselves. Additionally, colonial budget surpluses were generally the product of export trade in primary goods rather than taxation revenue, making it still less probable that state expenditure would be devoted to the welfare of colonial subjects.[12]

Identity cards restricted internal and external economic migration according to the wider interests of the colonial authorities rather than the local needs of the migrants themselves. The cataloguing of personnel records contributed to the criminalization of the colonial poor, the principal target of these measures. Armed with these records, security forces often worked from the presumption that vagrants, the unemployed, and economic migrants were most likely to transgress European and customary law and to become repeat offenders.[13] By 1918, colonial military service meant, first and foremost, defense of the metropolitan power or of the empire, not the immediate local protection of kith and kin. Police intelligence gathering, whether undertaken for the retrospective punishment of rule breakers or as a preventive measure to enforce control, was racially framed and applied. In sum, the colonial state amassed information about subject populations to guarantee its monopoly over the use of force and to impose its authority on a subject population designated to play arduous but subordinate parts in a European-dominated economic system.

As we can see, because colonial rule was not rooted in consent, self-determination, or popular will (indeed, it stood in complete opposition to them), colonial security intelligence was intrinsically different from the security intelligence practiced "at home" by the imperial powers. By the start of World War I, the centralized accumulation of information about British subjects was not only integral to state intervention but popularly accepted as such. This data collection process had, of course, begun much earlier, even though the Treasury proved consistently reluctant to fund it. Home Office and Board of Trade officials were quicker to see the utility of such statistical information gathering.[14] As Edward Higgs puts it in relation to late Victorian England, "The creation of a more centralized and pluralist state, the need to increase national efficiency, and the relative eclipse of moralism, can be seen as leading to the increased generation of data to inform central intervention in local government and society."[15] In France, resistance to such state information gathering lasted longer, and a comprehensive fiscal system also developed more slowly.[16] Nonetheless, by 1914 in France, as in Britain, taxation, military obligation, welfare provision, and civil and criminal law were all informed by data systematically acquired by the state through census records, income data, identity registration schemes, criminal profiling, and social surveys.[17]

The Great War therefore accelerated changes already underway. Societal mobilization in 1914–18 proved beyond doubt that the very survival of the nation-state demanded an unprecedented level of administrative control.[18] The concept of state bureaucracy as a rationalized information-gathering system became more deeply embedded as a feature of modern industrial society.[19] Indeed, social scientists have gone further, suggesting that state efforts to categorize, stratify, or remold the citizenry to meet ideological objectives or defined policy criteria are a benchmark of modernity itself.[20] Widening spheres of state intervention, whether for positive motives of improved living standards and welfare provision, or more negative ones of repression and coercive control, are thus indicative of this shift toward greater bureaucratic domination over society.[21] Greater regulation of public behavior, economic activity, internal population movement, and fiscal exaction may not be inherently new, but such regulatory power is inescapably modern.[22]

Types of Intelligence

Throughout the territories investigated here the boundaries between overtly political or criminal intelligence and more generic government information about a subject population were always blurred. Security intelligence was not entirely a matter of reporting seditious behavior and political activity. As suggested earlier, colonial government also required less contentious information about local demography, economic activity, and the institutions of civil society in town and countryside. The success of this colonial "information order" rested, in turn, on the degree of economic development in individual territories. The quality of infrastructure and internal communications systems determined the speed with which all intelligence could be transmitted to the central power.[23] Road systems and postal and telegraph networks augmented the scale and speed of governmental activity, enabling politicians and officials to take a welter of diverse up-to-date information into account as part of the daily cycle of decision making and policy planning.[24]

Environmental Intelligence

The importance of infrastructure to intelligence transmission reminds us that an understanding of the physical environment was critical to the imposition and maintenance of colonial rule. This may be more readily appreciated if one thinks in terms of maps—both cartographic and cognitive. British and French mapmakers, many of them employed by their military intelligence departments, traversed African and Arab territories in the late nineteenth and early twentieth centuries.[25] Some produced the first cartographic information available to Western officials charting the topography of colonial territories.[26] Roads, railways, harbors, cables, and telegraphs followed, their lines of advance revealing the progress of colonial expansion in general, and the advice of military intelligence experts, surveyors, and crown agents in particular.[27] Some focused on human geography and social anthropology, compiling ethnographic surveys of tribal concentrations and migratory patterns.[28] Others produced revised intelligence assessments that updated or corrected previously available information about water sources and rainfall, tribal migrations and agricultural activity, topography and communications.[29] Some updated previously available environmental intelligence as threat perceptions of the strategic value of particular ports, bases, and other key locations altered.[30] Still others tried to learn from local populations how best to adapt to physical conditions, and placed social behaviors as diverse as childrearing, marriage codes, and funeral rites in their environmental context. Whether maps, anthropological surveys, or sociological studies, these assessments were pivotal to military strategy in the Middle East and East African campaigns of the First World War and the frontier delimitations that followed in the 1920s.[31] In perhaps the clearest example of the application of specialist ethnographic data to assist the implantation of external rule, French native affairs administrators in the Middle Atlas region of the Moroccan protectorate were assigned to compile a database of information on the composition, distribution, and customs of the region's Berber tribes. This was what one analyst has dubbed "strategic knowledge in the service of the colonial system."[32]

The gathering and recording of ethnographic information was subjective, loaded with the values and presumptions of its practitioners. Factors such as education, racial prejudice, a scientific understanding of the natural world, political outlook, or religious affiliation informed the ways in which ostensibly empirical evidence was recorded. Mental maps were never simply about geography. They also represented the cognitive recognition of what was deemed important in any particular environment.[33] It was through this accumulation of written record and personal experience that colonial policymakers built up their mental maps of the territory and society under their authority.

This brings us back to the role of environmental intelligence. Taken together, this material represented a constantly updated archive of colonial geography—physical, human, political, and economic—intended to facilitate governmental decision making and promote inward commercial investment.[34] Information about climate, meteorology, river systems and water sources, demographic distribution, farming, and livestock conditions helped officials to construct a cognitive map of the local economy. Public spending priorities reflected this environmental intelligence, as did the development of taxation systems that focused on the subject population's most valuable assets, typically livestock, land, and labor rather than wage income or capital savings.[35] There were, for example, at least four distinct agricultural taxes in rural Algeria before the First World War, and local variations in taxation were commonly applied to reflect the predominant crops grown in a particular region.[36] Knowledge about scarce natural resources was essential to measure human and livestock pressure on land and likely competition for access to grazing or water. Communal rivalry over land possession added complexity to the problem.[37] Only with reliable intelligence about recurrent epidemics, famine, or other medical crises could a viable public health strategy be devised and "foreign bodies," whether human or bacterial, be contained.[38] In colonial societies that retained strong ties to the land, and whose economies were linked to the agricultural cycle, environmental intelligence was therefore integral to colonial governance.

The well-known role of geographical societies and anthropological survey groups as agents of popular imperialism in Britain and France make more sense in light of this. Georges Hardy, the one-time director of education in Senegal and Morocco who was appointed head of the École Coloniale in 1926, was, for example, quick to see the link between geographical research and successful colonization. In 1933 he penned a book on the subject in which he noted, "Whether it is a matter of European settlements or the simple indigenous environment [encadrement], the occupation of a populated country, or taking possession of a deserted land, colonization would essentially seem to rely upon the transformation of a region that has been retarded or neglected in the development of human potential. It therefore requires above all, a perfect knowledge of the regions to be transformed."[39] Historians have considered the connections between colonial expansion and the development of geography, ethnology, and anthropology as academic disciplines in Europe.[40] Taking environmental information seriously as part of the intelligence apparatus of colonial states, however, is something that few scholars have yet addressed.

Human Intelligence (Humint)

An essential feature of the modern nation-state is its capacity to integrate incoming information quickly into its decision-making processes. Distillation and exploitation of information about local conditions, physical as well as political—not to mention intelligence of perceived internal or external threats to authority—enhances the state's capacity to make reasoned policy choices about how best to use the security forces at its disposal. Modern forms of information transfer are one part of this equation. Another is the growth in administrative personnel. Greater bureaucratization of government and a system of record keeping for rapid data retrieval were essential to enable senior officials to act on a manageable volume of all information reported. In this sense the increasing sophistication of intelligence gathering fit a broader pattern of technological advance that underpinned imperial conquest and consolidation.[41] Much of this information fits the conventional demarcation between differing types of intelligence. But it is also important to remember the predominance of human intelligence (humint) sources in the array of information available to colonial security services. Typically gathered from controlled sources, often agents, informants, or local officials in the pay of the security services, humint enabled colonial governments to evaluate indigenous responses to state action.[42]

Signals Intelligence (Sigint)

Colonial intelligence agencies before 1939 generally derived more information from humint than the more technologically advanced panoply of signals intelligence (sigint). Information derived from the interception and cryptanalysis (code breaking) of electronically transmitted messages was rare outside the realm of interstate relations. Anticolonial groups did not often communicate with one another electronically or in code. That is by no means to suggest that sigint was irrelevant. After 1920, mandate and protectorate governments were increasingly equipped with the means to send and receive electronic messages. Comintern agents also communicated in telegraphic cipher. Foreign missions, including those hostile to Britain and France, did so too. And local politicians sent and received telegrams that were subject to interception. So, before discussing the broader role of humint in colonial security policy, it seems sensible to comment on the extent of sigint received.

Colonial policymakers were privy to large quantities of signals intelligence. After 1919, the bulk of sigint material either acquired by or relayed to the French and British authorities in the Arab world derived from intercepts of diplomatic and military correspondence from Kemalist Turkey. Some of these intercepts were en clair dispatches, but most were transmitted as coded ciphers that required dedicated code-breaking staffs to decode them. Where telegraphic or cable facilities were made available to local, indigenous governments, as in Egypt, Iraq, and Syria, the issuing imperial authorities ensured that they could listen in to the resultant messages transmitted. From time to time, the imperial authorities even supplied personnel to encode sigint traffic on behalf of the local governments, and thus monitor outgoing material. In addition, French and British imperial officials made efforts to intercept one another's cipher traffic. Ironically, sigint was also sometimes shared between them, notably when it related to German or Soviet penetration of Arab territories or the activities of pan-Islamist groups that spanned French and British overseas possessions.[43]

Signals intelligence was therefore pivotal to attitude formation among the policymaking elites in these territories. It commanded respect because it represented information gathered direct "from the horse's mouth." But decoded signals rarely determined short-term policy decisions. There were several reasons for this. Much intercepted cipher traffic was not fed into the policymaking process swiftly enough to affect the courses of action adopted. Even en clair sigint required translation, reprint, and circulation, a bureaucratic process that took time and required specialist personnel. Taken alone, sigint was insufficiently comprehensive to allow informed policy choices to be made. Sigint's importance to the colonial states studied here lay in what it revealed about longer-term trends in policy and opinion, potential flash points, and organized opposition to imperial rule.

Signals intelligence was also integrated into threat assessments compiled by intelligence staffs, diplomats, and senior colonial advisers. It helped intelligence analysts measure the intentions of political opponents, but it was less useful as an indicator of these opponents' capacity to mobilize support in opposition to colonial rule at any given moment. Only the patient accumulation of humint among indigenous communities could fill this gap. Taken in combination with such humint, signals intelligence helped shape the threat perceptions of imperial policymakers. If sigint's impact on colonial security policy may be registered in these deeper, more intangible terms of attitude and "the official mind," the fact remains that, in peacetime conditions, colonial governments did not develop bureaucracies capable of exploiting incoming sigint on a day-to-day basis.

Image Intelligence (Imint)

Much the same could be said of image intelligence (imint), which refers primarily to two types of visual information: aerial photography by military reconnaissance flights and the production of accurate topographical intelligence for use by officials.

Developed before the First World War, the use of imint after 1919 became closely tied to strategies of rural policing, frontier surveillance, and tribal control. Aerial photography provided essential intelligence about tribal raids and deployments of hostile forces in otherwise inaccessible terrain such as the Moroccan Rif, Syria's Jabal Druze, the hill country of Kurdistan, or the vast interior of Sudan. It also provided valuable evidence about movements of people and animals, everything from hajj traffic, cross-border infiltration, and nomadic migration to livestock grazing, water sources, and locust infestations. In addition to this imint, pilots and their observers typically submitted written summaries of reconnaissance flights that either supplemented aerial photography or rendered it superfluous.[44] Use of aircraft thus extended the range of situational intelligence gathering, literally providing a view of events in the rural interior sometimes simultaneously, or even in advance, of intelligence information relayed at ground level by telegraph, land line, or courier by district officers, Arab affairs specialists, or police outposts. Imint also affected long-term policy formulation, not least because aerial photography intersected the ongoing work of colonial mapmakers, geologists, and archaeologists. By the 1920s, aerial surveys had revolutionized the working practices of military staffs and civilian specialists whose decisions demanded accurate information about topography and climate, agriculture and water distribution, or sites of archaeological interest.[45]

The Supremacy of Humint

The exploitation of human intelligence was altogether different. Among Western European states in the early twentieth century, the balance between the generation of sigint and humint gradually tilted in favor of the former.[46] In colonial states, however, the opposite applied. Acquiring information about the dependent population was always fundamental to colonial rule, as much for the purposes of fiscal calculation, social policy, and resource allocation as for the needs of political surveillance. The administrative apparatus of social control was an admixture of European regulation, customary law, and long-established practices of commerce, social exchange, and intercommunal relations only slowly affected by changes in central government. Colonial legal systems, for example, varied from territory to territory, but often developed from the interaction of European administrators and local elites anxious to circumscribe the imposition of Western regulation of civil law, land ownership, and criminality.[47] In this administrative field, as in others, the state's accumulation of information about dependent societies was a gargantuan intelligence-gathering exercise.

Here we confront a problem. To treat humint as any information derived from contact with a subject population is to render the term meaningless. But, in the colonial settings analyzed here, humint comprised far more than specifically political intelligence drawn from local informants. Covert surveillance of political meetings and religious gatherings, and the monitoring of protonationalist secret societies and illicit contacts between anticolonial organizations, inevitably attracted most comment among security service analysts. But more prosaic, open-source intelligence about popular behavior was more important in the long term. Amassing information about the daily lives of the local population enabled colonial security services to evaluate more sensational intelligence about subversion and disorder. Only by amassing such low-grade intelligence about social conditions could security services assess the significance of higher-grade humint on oppositional activity.

Put simply, human intelligence represented both specific information about threats to the colonial order drawn from native milieus and a more diffuse range of evidence about social structure, customs, and beliefs. The weight attached to the former was measured by reference to knowledge of the latter. Demographic surveys, economic data, and sociological analyses of tribal organization not only assisted government in determining taxation levels, commercial priorities, and communal policy, they influenced the intelligence culture—denoting the shared outlook and operating assumptions—of the imperial security services. Seen in this light, humint pervaded all facets of security service policy.

Information and Colonial Rule

Those same agencies of the colonial state that amassed information about indigenous populations also sought to control the movement of knowledge within local society. Their aim was to mold popular opinion, or, at the very least, shape the views of influential elites. Colonial security required a measure of control over the ebb and flow of political debate. It was just as essential to know what was being discussed in mosques, bazaars, communal wash-houses, tribal conferences, and village meetings as it was to uncover the plans of nationalist organizations operating at the margins of legality. Only then could local authorities set about influencing these differing forums of opinion to European advantage. Legislative proscription of subversive groups was too blunt a weapon. If used indiscriminately it was likely to undermine those institutions of civil society—tribal and village councils, debating clubs and meeting houses, professional associations, trade guilds, and business networks—that Western rule claimed to promote. Governments required information from within such forums in order to anticipate the causes of dissent.

Intelligence of this kind informed the daily actions and executive decisions of colonial states in North Africa and the Middle East. There is an analogy here with the British experience in colonial India, as revealed in C. A. Bayly's pioneering work. Good colonial government in the British Raj, in the sense of unchallenged imperial authority, relied in large part on what Bayly terms an "information order." This represented the exploitation of state intelligence gathering to regulate indigenous means of social communication, or, to use Bayly's terminology, "an empire of information" to control a distinct "empire of opinion." The maintenance of colonial order exploited the formal, increasingly bureaucratized information systems of the colonial state to exert influence over autonomous networks of social communication in Indian society—local language media, religious forums and mass social gatherings, indigenous marketplaces, and meeting places of the indigenous elite.[48]

By the same token, bad colonial government, evinced by disorder and rebellion, signified a breakdown in the state's intelligence about indigenous society. When this occurred, colonial officials and settler communities frequently succumbed to "information panics," filling the void left by intelligence gathering with unsubstantiated rumor.[49] The credence attached to these rumors reflected racial or class prejudice, compounded by varying degrees of paranoia born of the closed, undemocratic structure of colonial society.[50] As previously discussed, in all contexts in which European intelligence providers formulated threat assessments about non-European colonial subjects or regional rivals, prevailing racial attitudes inevitably affected intelligence analysis. The operating assumption of "threat" in intelligence analysis implies that an individual or group exhibit both the intention to act and the capacity to do so in ways prejudicial to state security. Yet intelligence analysts had little truck with detailed consideration of changing levels of support for hostile political groups. More sweeping generalizations took precedence instead. British and French colonial threat assessments assumed that political disorders were likely to begin in urban or tribal settings. It was further calculated that the peasant majority in the countryside was easily led into dissent by their own community leaders or, more simply, by a sense of having little to lose. Furthermore, a common security service belief that Muslim subjects were predisposed to religious fanaticism or political extremism obviated the need for careful evaluation of their grievances. Since these complaints were typically a product of colonialism itself—racial exclusion, economic marginalization, and affronts to culture—it was perhaps inevitable that colonial intelligence analysts were, on occasion, deaf to them. Put simply, intelligence assessments characterized colonial subjects as putty in the hands of shrewd political manipulators, whether European or indigenous.

The result was that alarmist colonial threat assessments could gain credibility without much corroborative evidence. In French Africa, for instance, the return of tens of thousands of ex-servicemen from the Western Front after 1918 generated widespread concern among colonial authorities.[51] It was widely feared that resentful Africans with direct experience of life in France would upset the colonial state's cultural construction of France as unquestionably superior to and different from African society.[52] Fear of disorders linked to colonial demobilization stimulated employment schemes for Algerian veterans based on the allocation of low-grade public sector jobs to returning servicemen.[53] Meanwhile, ethnographers worked in conjunction with French West African administrations in the 1920s to reinforce concepts of difference between French culture and the ingrained traditionalism of African society.[54] Colonial control over social communication began from the proposition that indigenous subjects could be persuaded to believe what officials chose to tell them about their rulers.[55]

In the Asian context, official fears of pan-Asianism, Islamic "fanaticism," multinational support for the caliphate movement, and memories of the "yellow peril" literature of the early twentieth century all colored evaluations of anticolonial movements.[56] Ironically, however, a paucity of intelligence— even crudely racist intelligence—compounded the tendency among European populations to paint subject races in lurid colors. As Bayly puts it, "The basic fear of the colonial official or settler was, consequently, his lack of indigenous knowledge and ignorance of the 'wiles of the natives.' He feared their secret letters, their drumming and 'bush telegraphy' and the nightly passage of seditious agents masquerading as priests or holy men."[57] Information panics in nineteenth-century India over *thuggi* armed gangs and, most significantly, the spread of mutiny in 1857, illustrated how momentous the disruption of an empire's information system could be. These intelligence failures were often described as vital precedents from which the colonial state had to learn if it was to survive.[58]

Such information panics highlight the dilemmas confronted by all colonial security services striving to assure imperial authority over subject populations denied basic rights and freedoms. In societies where verbal communication among the illiterate majority remained the principal means for the transmission of political ideas, colonial security forces had to find ways to learn what was being whispered about them or planned against them. The fundamental iniquity of colonial rule, however, made it especially hard for agents of the colonial state to penetrate indigenous society in order to anticipate rebellion or unrest. Not surprisingly, policemen, political and military intelligence analysts, and district officers found it easier to gather useful intelligence about the literate, urban indigenous elites close to the centers of imperial power than to take account of the opinions of the illiterate masses in town and countryside. On those occasions when the authorities did learn of planned sedition, demonstrations, or strike actions, the propensity to use force made it harder still to acquire such information in the future. Colonial officials, afraid that their tenuous control over a resentful population might collapse, applied disproportionate force to contain unrest in the short term, which only heightened the likelihood of more widespread dissent in the long term.[59]

It was no coincidence that the writ of imperial authority was weakest in distinct theaters in which accurate information about social behavior and public attitudes was hardest to obtain. Colonial frontier regions stood out in this respect. Whether the frontier in question was administrative, ethnic, or international, regions at the furthest margins of colonial conquest and settlement were policed in a distinct frontier style. The military played a leading role in local administration, the transition to civil policing was usually slower than in urban centers, and in many cases such a transition never occurred at all.[60] Obvious examples include the Moroccan Rif, Syria's Jabal Druze, Iraqi Kurdistan, the land frontier of the Aden protectorate, the southern desert of the Fertile Crescent, and the upper Nile reaches of southern Sudan. In these instances, geographical inaccessibility combined with strong communal affiliation either to frustrate the accumulation of accurate human intelligence or to prevent its rapid transmission to central government.[61] Comparisons may be drawn between these "unruly" regions and similarly remote areas of British South Asia, such as Waziristan and Burma, in which imperial government proved unable to use intelligence to prevent disorder.[62]

In urban settings, too, the colonial authorities often struggled to acquire reliable, usable information about discrete sections of the community. Mosques were increasingly monitored by informants and regulated by restrictive legislation on the content of religious ceremony. Market centers and ports were also subject to close surveillance because these were primary points of contact between a local community and the wider world. Industrial workplaces were another key site of state surveillance as urbanization and the emergence of an organized colonial proletariat gathered pace. Surveillance alone did not constrain the political processes being observed. Sometimes the objects of state interest were not aware they were being watched. More often they were, and adjusted their behavior accordingly. Whichever the case, religious, commercial, and industrial gathering points remained forcing grounds for organized opposition. Moreover, entire arenas of indigenous society were beyond the reach of state surveillance. British and French colonial authorities singularly failed to amass information about the social lives and political opinions of Muslim women. The colonial authorities appreciated that public segregation of the sexes in Islamic society was no barrier to the politicization of women. The widespread emergence of women's movements and the strong presence of women protesters in public disturbances from food riots to nationalist demonstrations after 1918 only confirmed the point. But at no stage did the colonial states of North Africa and the Middle East develop viable channels of communication with leaders of female opinion. Households, women's bathhouses, the reserved spaces of mosque prayer halls, even the first classrooms for trainee women professionals, remained outside the intelligence-gathering system. Political surveillance was an overwhelmingly male occupation in terms of both the watchers and the watched.

Civil Administration and Intelligence Specialists

Much of the day-to-day work for those gathering information about dependent populations was routine, a cycle of clerical record keeping and statis-

tical returns, provincial tours, meetings with local dignitaries, and the arbitration of minor disputes. These accumulated tasks were typically registered
in summary reports of past activity. Details of public works inspections,
meetings with settlers, traders, and mission staff, discussions with lowly village headmen or chiefly rulers: all were distilled into written records.[63]
Individual events, discussions, or observations of particular importance
might justify a letter, telegram, or telegraphic dispatch to the governor's
office or the local military headquarters. But this was the exception, not the
rule. In general, the more prosaic records of local administration were the
stuff of intelligence assessment. The paper chain of regional bureaucracy
passed up the line of imperial authority was the raw material of the colonial
information order.

Across colonial territories this summary information was codified in similar ways. District commissioners' monthly or weekly reports, regional governors' summaries of local conditions, or more specialist departmental surveys of policy options typically divided their analyses of the colonial situation
into what could be classified as administrative intelligence, environmental
intelligence, and political intelligence.[64]

Administrative intelligence related to matters such as taxation systems,
judicial proceedings, public health, economic migration, and tribal affairs.
Environmental intelligence was primarily a matter of communications and
agronomy. It described the state of the internal infrastructure, soil conditions, the crop cycle and pests, market prices and foodstuff shortages, meteorological data and water resources, and the size and condition of national
livestock herds. Political intelligence reported local disputes, the reaction of
community leaders to policy changes or significant political developments,
and the activities of organized political groups, whether parties, tribal confederations, or labor organizations. Where comments on public opinion
were made, they were typically deduced by reference to issues of the day in
the vernacular press and any major public gatherings whether oppositional,
ceremonial, or commercial.[65]

The proportion of incoming reportage devoted to administrative matters
remained broadly constant, a reflection of the perennial nature of the
issues discussed. Taxes, criminal proceedings, and variable public health
were permanent preoccupations of colonial government. By contrast, the
volume of reportage on environmental topics and political affairs varied in
response to the most pressing concerns of the colonial authorities at the
time. District officials and garrison commanders paid closer attention to
severe agricultural problems such as harvest failure, drought, labor shortages, or crop infestations because of their adverse impact on the local economy and society. And political intelligence was most fulsome when dominated by "bad news" of local violence or mounting threats to the colonial
state.[66]

The obverse was that in more tranquil political conditions, district commissioners, police captains, and even regional governors were content to pass over the local political scene with little comment. Prevailing assumptions about the corruptive potential of urban politics on otherwise compliant peasant cultivators and tribal populations compounded this tendency to report on rural political developments in terms of the disruptive presence of external elements from the towns, whether politicians, absentee landlords, 'ulamā, or effendi administrators.[67] It was a stock feature of British political intelligence especially to write extensively on political issues only in response to tangible evidence of local instability provoked by such "outsiders." In more placid conditions, political officers simply noted that there had been no important developments in the period under review.

In the French case, too, the native affairs officers who collated incoming local and regional intelligence reports often interpreted political developments in a reductive fashion. In the first few months following the First World War, the native affairs division (*direction des affaires indigènes*) in the Algiers government-general made a sharp distinction between the colony's urban centers, where Muslim civil society merited close analysis, and rural Algeria, where oppositional politics was still viewed as a by-product of prevailing economic conditions rather than as an indicator of emergent popular nationalism.[68] As we shall see in chapter 7, this rigid distinction between town and countryside would continue throughout the interwar years. It is thus incumbent on the researcher to stress that, for all the intelligence reports filed on colonial dissent, there is also an abundance of more mundane evidence regarding places and periods in which, according to the officials involved, nothing much seems to have happened—or at least nothing much thought to be worth reporting.

Reportage of administrative, environmental, and political intelligence was ultimately reflected in the policy advice of more senior colonial administrators, too. In August 1917, Sir Percy Cox took office as Britain's civil commissioner for Mesopotamia. Once in the post, he filed a series of periodic reports on British prospects in what was by then known as Iraq to the India Office Political Department and the interministerial Eastern Committee in Whitehall. Throughout Cox's tenure in Baghdad the nature and extent of British political control over the three Iraqi *vilayets* remained uncertain. Faced with the challenges of reconstruction, Cox's early reports were inevitably dominated by administrative matters: the role of Arab notables and former Ottoman officials in government and judicial affairs, the establishment of an Iraqi police force, and the distribution of food supplies to the major towns. Environmental intelligence from army political officers in the Iraqi interior also figured large. It was clear, for example, that repair of roads and communications networks, and extensive irrigation projects along the Tigris and Euphrates were essential if social order were to be maintained after the war ended.

Another concern was the regulation of Bedouin migration. Large-scale population movements complicated British efforts to ensure adequate food distribution to the major population centers in and around Baghdad, Kerbala, and Basra.[69] The accent on state building lent extra weight to information gathering about infrastructure, economy, and demography to the virtual exclusion of purely political intelligence.[70] During 1918–19, Curzon's Foreign Office and the British administration in Iraq also monitored the army officers that dominated the Arab political clubs, which were so influential in articulating the demands of the Sunni elite grouped around Amir Faysal's administrations, first in Damascus and then in Baghdad.[71]

Cox's disdain for the installation of a Sherifian ruler in Iraq was widely known, but the information he received from political officers, technical advisers, and Mesopotamia Expeditionary Force officers during 1917–19 was dominated by the short-term requirements of civil administration. Cox's reports to London and Delhi duly reflected this information flow. What, in hindsight, was portrayed by Cox's admirers, Gertrude Bell prominent among them, as dispassionate British pragmatism at its best, was little more than the hand-to-mouth existence of a tenuous imperial administration reliant on the advice of its intelligence community to determine its immediate policy choices.[72] These initial surveys acquired additional importance because the government of India had shelved plans, put forward by Cox himself in May 1917, to establish a Mesopotamia study commission to advise on political conditions in the Iraq *vilayets*.[73]

There are a number of parallels between the priorities in intelligence reportage in the Iraq mandate and those in the first phase of French control in the Levant. High Commissioner General Henri Gouraud and his principal government ally, Prime Minister Alexandre Millerand, conceded that intelligence gathering had to fill the gaps left by the weakness of overstretched imperial forces in Syria, Lebanon, and Cilicia.[74] Much like the Baghdad High Commission, French officials in Beirut also amassed information on the Levant's ethnic and religious communities, Bedouin migratory cycles, and tribal allegiances in order to consolidate French authority.[75] The ethnic composition of Syria and Lebanon was every bit as complex as that of Iraq, but in contrast with the construction of the Iraqi state, which rested on the enforced unification of previously disparate regions, the partition of Ottoman Greater Syria was shaped by the French determination to consolidate a separate, Christian-dominated Lebanese state and by the creation of the neighboring British mandates in Palestine and Transjordan. It is simplistic to argue that French administration amounted to a system of divide and rule. Gouraud's staff, regional commanders, and the urban governments of Syria's four main towns—Damascus, Aleppo, Homs, and

Hama—did exploit information on communal politics to entrench French authority at the expense of the Sunni Arab majority, however. Gouraud was quite explicit about this in the months preceding the French confrontation with Faysal's Damascus regime in July 1920:

> The objective is to restore regional order, calm and confidence, protecting the population against troublemakers [*fauteurs de troubles*]; and, to that end, pursuing political ends while limiting the use of force to cases of absolute necessity. . . . In order to dissociate elements of the Muslim population that tend to unite over religious matters, we will need to favor particular minorities, different nationality groups such as Kurds, Assyrians, Circassians, etc., that are all amenable to constituting a defense against external threat, provided that we know how to attract them to us.[76]

Intelligence gathering thus fulfilled two pressing administrative needs at the outset of French mandatory control. First, it identified potential flash points of political violence, enabling the Beirut high commission to allocate limited military and police resources to greatest effect. Second, it accumulated data on the ethnic, confessional, and economic composition of Syria and Lebanon that laid the foundations for regional policymaking for the next twenty years. The pattern of information collection set in the first years of the French mandate remained remarkably consistent throughout the interwar years. In November 1935, the Levant Army's military intelligence service (Service de Renseignements—SR) defined its work in the following terms:

> Foreign military intelligence services in Syria and Lebanon, as in general throughout the Near East, gather less purely military intelligence than they do political and economic information. Detailed knowledge of the country, its communications and access routes, the diversity of its social and religious composition as well as the reasons that pit one group against another (tribal organization and rivalry, [ethnic] minorities, pan-Arab movements, etc.), may, in effect, seem both more important and more difficult to acquire than knowledge of military organization, [which is] often a matter of numbers and strengths.[77]

The Levant SR was not alone in seeing itself as integral to the machinery of government. Civilian police agencies and the army officers of the Muslim affairs bureau conceptualized their role in broader terms than criminal investigation, rural administration, or military security. Each recognized that the information order of which they were a part was the bedrock of governance. After all, French mandate administration was not the product of a long gestation, but the abrupt creation of an externally imposed peace settlement and the crushing military defeat of an Arab regime. Detailed knowledge of potential sources of opposition to mandatory control remained critical throughout the quarter century of French rule.

The Sûreté and the Service de Renseignements

In the Syrian mandate, much like the Moroccan protectorate, the combination of a well-developed urban civil society and coherent tribal communities hostile to European control ensured the security services' pivotal role in French efforts to impose their imperial power.[78] We shall be considering these cases at length in chapter 5, but at this stage it is worth dwelling on the organizational structures of the security agencies concerned: the Sûreté and the Service de Renseignements. The French secret police acquired greater importance during World War I. By 1914, it was subdivided into the Renseignements Généraux linked to the Paris Prefecture of Police and a dedicated special branch, the police spéciale of the Sûreté Générale (SG), which tracked seditious activity in France. Both worked under Interior Ministry control.

The wartime activities of the French civil and military security services were highly politicized, something that fit a longer tradition of politically motivated intelligence operations. In common with secret police forces across Europe, by 1900 covert policing in France was synonymous with dirty tricks, secret blacklists, agents provocateurs, and the interception of mail, variously employed to weaken groups or individuals considered threatening to the state.[79] After war broke out, the SG, in particular, increasingly pursued a political agenda of its own, at variance with the conciliatory, Union sacrée–inspired ideals of its ministerial chief, Louis Malvy. During 1917 the SG and army intelligence staff worked in unison to foment a conspiracy theory linking foreign espionage, antimilitarism, and senior politicians willing to contemplate a negotiated peace. Their aim was to divert public and press attention from the flawed military strategy that precipitated the 1917 mutinies. This meshed with a longer SG campaign to oust Malvy from his post as interior minister, thereby lending support to Georges Clemenceau as leader of a more resolute right-wing coalition. By tracing the development of this conspiracy theory, David Parry has shown that the French intelligence community could unseat certain ministers and ruin the reputations of others in pursuit of its preferred policies. We need to bear in mind that the politicization of security service surveillance was an accomplished fact long before the armistice.[80]

In 1915, the SR, the principal intelligence-gathering agency of the French general staff, was tied more closely to the Sûreté Générale. (The latter was renamed the Sûreté Nationale in 1934.) The military intelligence analysts of the service ministry deuxième bureaux, who processed and assessed incoming SR material, were also privy to increasing quantities of SG reports. On 28 May 1915, a research center was established by ministerial order within the Paris Prefecture of Police, which was paralleled by a military Section de Centralisation du Renseignement (SCR) attached to the army's deuxième bureau within the War Ministry. This SCR received reports from—and coordinated the activities of—the local military intelligence centers (Bureaux centraux de renseignement—BCR) within each French military region. BCR staff worked in liaison with their civilian partners in provincial Sûreté offices and functioned independent of the municipal police forces across France.

From December 1915, the intelligence-gathering functions of the SR and SCR were linked to a newly established War Ministry cinquième bureau that was also responsible for the dissemination of propaganda, postal control, and liaison with Allied military intelligence services. This wartime demarcation between the activities of the SR and the SCR persisted in the interwar period. The former collected intelligence on foreign powers and formulated policy advice on the basis of the information gathered. The latter devoted itself to counterespionage and surveillance of seditionist threats within metropolitan and imperial territory.[81]

By the war's end the SR had become a core element of French military planning. Its survival—if not its budget—assured, the SR was again tied to the deuxième bureau rather than to the wartime expedient of the cinquième. Henceforth, the central bureaucracy of the "deuxième bureau SR-SCR" became embedded in a number of War Ministry properties in Paris. Senior military intelligence analysts worked in the suitably academic surroundings of the rue de l'Université, just off the boulevard Saint Germain. This was also the location of the army staff's deuxième bureau headquarters. From the rue de l'Université, raw SR intelligence was passed on to the deuxième bureau offices around the corner, where it was collated with incoming reports from military attachés and synthesized into assessments distributed to staff officers and the service ministers concerned.

Meanwhile, in its counterespionage activities, the SCR had closer ties to the police spéciale and to individual Prefectures of Police, which, as civil policing agencies, remained attached to the Ministry of the Interior. For the Paris prefecture, in particular, this surveillance work became integral to the growing workload of the capital's police immigration service.[82] Since 1899, the War Ministry had focused its intelligence gathering on foreign army activities abroad. Civil authorities retained responsibility for counterespionage in France, in Algeria, and throughout the empire. Counterespionage work was initially added piecemeal to the caseload of the Sûreté and the gendarmerie nationale, but army involvement was inevitable because effective counterespionage served the military interest. The intelligence amassed about potential enemies assisted general staff planning, mobilization preparations, and military deployments. Hence the importance attached to the SCR.[83]

Counterespionage work was laborious, time-consuming, and highly specialized. Reorganized by decree a year before World War I began, counterespionage operations in France were brought under the overall jurisdiction of the Interior Ministry by a decree of 24 November 1924. The Sûreté's role as coordinating agency for counterespionage was replicated in imperial territories, meaning, in practice, that military intelligence officers were required to liaise with the Sûreté in all matters affecting state security against foreign subversion. In several colonial capitals the central Sûreté office was the main repository for the files routinely used in counterespionage work: criminal data, travel and visa documentation, and the personnel records of all public sector employees, both civil and military.[84] Among the tasks included in this ordinance were the monitoring of frontiers and any militarily sensitive areas such as bases, munitions stores, armaments factories, and testing ranges. Despite their close cooperation, the SCR and the Sûreté retained their distinct military and civilian identities and neither formally took precedence over the other. The autonomy and parity that each enjoyed was thus intended to encourage cooperation without jurisdictional rivalry.[85]

Inevitably, there was some duplication of effort between the military intelligence analysts of the SR/SCR and the detectives of the Sûreté, but French colonial authorities accepted this as a minor inconvenience next to the benefits of shared expertise and information exchange. Moreover, the theoretically rigid distinctions between military intelligence and civilian policing blurred in colonial societies where political violence typically required the combined efforts of army and police to contain it. Time and again, SR and Sûreté personnel extended their inquiries into one another's domain, with military intelligence interesting itself in subversive political groups and the Sûreté monitoring any signs of seditious attitudes among colonial garrisons.

In colonial towns and cities during the interwar years, most Sûreté surveillance operations sought out four main targets: local Communist activists, strike organizers among colonial workers, nationalist groups, and colonial student bodies. Although the relative emphasis on these targets differed markedly among territories, the cycle of police transfers between colonies and metropolitan France encouraged homogeneity in Sûreté operations across the empire as a whole. From the Interior Ministry, the Direction de la Sûreté Générale maintained overall responsibility for its subordinate units across the empire and further ensured a certain uniformity of practice. One instance of this was the surveillance of Maghrebi immigrant workers in the Paris region coordinated from the capital's main police headquarters, a practice emulated in provincial cities such as Lille, Marseilles, Strasbourg, and Toulouse, and similarly copied in French North Africa.[86] As we shall see in chapter 7, immigrant workers from Kabylia, the densely populated Berber heartland of Algeria, were therefore monitored by police agencies during their stay in France, and by equivalent police units once they returned home.[87]

Within France and its empire, police officers still held the leading role in monitoring urban sedition, typically sending monthly or even weekly reports to local prefects. The prefectures, in turn, prepared intelligence summaries, which were then transmitted to the Ministry of Interior or the Ministry of Colonies as appropriate. As the scale of security policing increased, so too did reliance on indigenous personnel. During the 1920s, larger numbers of local Muslim applicants were taken on as Sûreté agents as central government pressed colonial police services to make additional posts available to ex-servicemen. In Algeria, the posts of *inspecteur de la police mobile* and *agent de la police départementale* were also sometimes reserved for Muslim ex-servicemen after 1918. In rural communes, army experience, rather than police training, determined the recruitment of local auxiliaries. Greater numbers of Muslim ex-servicemen, most of them long-service professionals, joined rural police forces during the 1920s and were typically assigned more low-grade positions than their settler counterparts as village policemen or farm guards.[88] The predominance in postwar Sûreté reports of humint gathered by indigenous agent informants could be read as a sign of strength or weakness. On the one hand, local informants with close ties to their local community were best placed to provide reliable information about Muslim opinion. On the other hand, colonial security services were, at best, dependent on the quality of the information provided by their indigenous intelligence providers and, at worse, open to manipulation by them.

New Intelligence Developments: Sigint and the British Example

There was no British security service in the Arab world with quite the same esprit de corps as the French SR, or quite the same numerical strength as the Sûreté, but Britain's imperial intelligence providers were every bit as important to imperial rule. The use of signals intelligence (sigint) in Britain's Middle Eastern territories underlines the point.

Before 1914, the employment of sigint in colonial conflicts and imperial policing was still in its infancy. Yet, as John Ferris has clarified, the use of such intelligence for the surveillance of regional rivals and movements of hostile, or potentially hostile, military forces at the margins of imperial territory was becoming widely established before the war in Europe spread to the Ottoman Middle East.[89] The usefulness of sigint was a function of the speed with which it could be translated, analyzed, and exploited. Hence the development of dedicated cryptographic departments, of which the Admiralty's Room 40 has drawn the greatest historical attention. Code breaking, deciphered wireless transmissions, intercepted letters and cable communications, as well as diplomatic and commercial correspondence were all facets of the security apparatus of the British imperial state prior to the expansion of Britain's power into the heart of the Arab world after 1914.

On the eve of World War I, humint from diplomats, businessmen, tourist travelers, and agents was the main source of covert information on the Ottoman Middle East available to the British authorities in Egypt. By the time Ottoman Turkey entered the conflict, however, sigint was fast catching up with more traditional forms of humint as a source of strategic information. Unprecedented access to Ottoman prisoners of war (POWs) and defectors in the first years of the conflict meant that the relative importance of humint grew next to the more modern forms of technical intelligence available—from aerial reconnaissance to the interception and decryption of enemy wireless transmissions.[90] This did not, however, alter the fact that sigint was becoming a vital element of strategic planning and tactical decision making.[91] Yigal Sheffy's meticulous evaluation of the use of intelligence in the Palestine campaign concludes that humint made only a marginal contribution to British military success. Reconnaissance and, above all, wireless intelligence were more central in key theaters, particularly in the Hijaz, where Ottoman military reliance on wireless transmissions was greatest.[92]

Furthermore, one of the less well advertised facets of the entente cordiale in action was the liaison between British imperial cryptanalysts and their more experienced French military counterparts in the army's commission of military cryptography. Ferris points out that George MacDonogh, the head of the War Office Intelligence Department, sought close ties with his French colleagues from 1912, a development emulated by the British Secret Service, which shared MacDonogh's respect for French intelligence expertise.[93] In the eastern Mediterranean theater, the regional naval commands spearheaded Anglo-French intelligence cooperation. Information was exchanged and joint operations planned between French intelligence staff attached to their naval squadron in Egypt and the British Eastern Mediterranean Special Intelligence Bureau. Both organizations placed agents in the Levant from 1915 onward and shared the intelligence gathered on Ottoman troop movements and strategic intentions.[94]

The government of India's Political Service, staffed largely by Indian Army officers, also maintained a watching brief on the Arab territories of the Ottoman Middle East and the Persian Gulf area.[95] In 1906, the Indian general staff created a Special Section of its Intelligence Branch devoted to cryptographic work against the czarist regime and Russian commanders in territories from Persia to Manchuria. In 1907, a dedicated code-breaking bureau supplanted the Special Section entirely. Understaffed and sometimes overlooked by policymakers, these code breakers nonetheless exploited the Indian government's control of the international communications cables passing through India's soil. Control of this communications network offered unprecedented access to the military telegram traffic of foreign states, Russia and China especially.[96] Meanwhile, between 1914 and

1918 Indian police intelligence focused on disaffected Hindu leaders in Bengal, Har Dayal's revolutionary Ghadr party, and India's Muslim population. The government of India watched for signs of sedition among these groups, fired by German and Ottoman propaganda calling for pan-Islamic solidarity with the Turkish caliph. In fact, Ottoman propaganda in India and among British imperial forces in Egypt, Palestine, and Mesopotamia was singularly ineffective. The subversive activities of the German Foreign Ministry's Intelligence Bureau for the East headed by Baron Max von Oppenheim posed a more tangible threat. But Oppenheim's efforts always foundered on the lack of credible Indian leaders with whom to cooperate. German sedition among the tribes of southern Persia proved a more dangerous menace to British interests than Berlin's support for Indian revolutionaries.[97]

By the end of World War I, the focus of British imperial, and indeed metropolitan, sigint surveillance of rival powers had shifted from Germany to Soviet Russia, a less familiar and therefore a less well understood intelligence target. It bears emphasis that much of the confusion and persistent exaggeration surrounding alleged Communist intrigue and support for pan-Islamism in the British Empire mirrored similar uncertainties at home.[98] The British secret services were reorganized between 1919 and 1923 to focus primarily on Soviet sedition. In January 1919, the Cabinet established a Secret Service Committee (SSC) dedicated to surveillance of Communist sedition in Britain. This was the harbinger of a more thoroughgoing reorganization of Britain's Secret Intelligence Service (SIS) marked by greater centralization of incoming information—both sigint and humint, covert and open-source—regarding revolutionary sedition sponsored by the Soviet Union. By the end of that year the Government Code and Cipher School was providing both the SSC and the SIS with decrypts of Bolshevik communications decoded by a former czarist cryptographer, Ernst Fetterlein. As ever, British colonial interest in Russian subversion centered on India, and many in the British intelligence community seemed inclined to view Soviet activities there as just the latest stage in the endless "Great Game" of Anglo-Russian imperial rivalry in South-Central Asia.[99]

British Security Policing and Administration

They may have made use of the same developments in intelligence techniques, but the security agencies in British imperial territory during and after World War I nonetheless differed from their metropolitan counterparts in other key respects. Differences between homeland and empire become more apparent when one considers the issue of security policing.

Britain's colonial police forces typically were armed and upheld internal security alongside locally garrisoned troops. The distinctions between the two sometimes became blurred. By the late 1930s, colonial police units from Palestine to Kenya bore more resemblance to an army—an alien presence in a local community, equipped with rifles, battle dress, and armored cars—than to the unarmed officer on the beat more familiar in Britain. Existing police stations acquired reinforced doors and windows; new police buildings were designed as barrack-style accommodations, deliberately isolated from the surrounding population to be policed.[100] Even rural police outposts resembled fortified installations. The militarization of police forces in Egypt and Britain's Middle East mandates highlighted another key facet of colonial policing: the absence of public consensus about the proper role of police agencies. This, in turn, nurtured the official assumption of popular hostility to a local police presence. The involvement of colonial police in tax collection and the movement of people and goods within states and across frontiers, and their accumulation of records on the dependent population distanced them from the community as a whole.[101] At the same time, the security services' centrality to the administrative life of the colonial state helped ensure that military and police bodies would be among the foremost "national" institutions forged by colonial powers, particularly in those territories, such as Transjordan, with no recent history of independent national existence and markedly different patterns of settlement from province to province.[102]

The British Residency in Cairo was acutely conscious of the growing public mistrust of the police after the March 1919 uprising led by Sa'd Zaghlul (discussed in chapter 4). The problem was compounded by officials' inability—or reluctance—to disaggregate criminal behavior from political protest. Year-on-year increases in murder and robbery in 1919, 1920, and 1921 were ascribed to the tense political situation rather than to the diversion of more police resources to political repression at the expense of the prevention and detection of capital offenses and crimes against property. The strength of the main city police forces was much augmented after the 1919 disorders. Residency statistics for 1921 revealed thirty-one European officers in Cairo and twenty-nine in Alexandria, with a further 131 and 199 European constables working in the two cities. Taking into account the additional 162 Egyptian police officers and 4,263 Egyptian constables in Cairo and Alexandria, the police presence in Egypt's two main urban centers was considerable. Most were assigned to crowd control, policing demonstrations, and combating "mob violence," to the exclusion of more "normal" police work.[103] Furthermore, the backbone of Egypt's provincial police, a locally recruited *ghaffir* (village police) force some fifty thousand strong, was entirely supported by the hated *ghaffir cess:* an arbitrary tax levied on each village, which hit the poorest in the community especially hard. In these circumstances, the most visible expressions of public animosity toward the police were attempts to evade tax payment and refusal to divulge any information to *ghaffirs*. Compelled to operate without "the slightest assistance" from the general public, the Egyptian police in the aftermath of the 1919 uprising increasingly represented an alien occupation force, not the community protectors they claimed to be.[104]

In several colonial states, police efforts to maintain public order superseded criminal detection as official fears of disorder grew. As a result, the covert aspects of police operations developed apace. Special Branch officers and even senior Criminal Investigation Department personnel increasingly devoted themselves to political—rather than criminal—intelligence gathering, often working alongside military intelligence staff. Use of native informants and undercover agents to provide information on political gatherings, industrial disputes, student politics, and urban opinion became commonplace. In those colonies such as Aden where a "native police" auxiliary existed, its activities were typically confined to rural policing and detection of minor criminal misdemeanors. In other colonial settings, such as India, reliance on native auxiliaries hastened the slide toward violent suppression of nationalist protest. Public revulsion at "police excesses" intensified in response.[105]

The British experience in Arab territories was slightly different. High commissions in Cairo, Jerusalem, and Baghdad did not create separate indigenous police forces, but instead recruited local personnel to fill the junior ranks of the Egyptian, Palestinian, and Iraqi police under the supervision of European officers and sergeants. But the ethnic composition of security forces in Britain's Arab territories was highly controversial and tightly regulated. The failure of colonial-style paramilitary policing to contain Irish insurgency from 1917 to 1921, and the prevalence of former Royal Irish Constabulary officers among colonial police forces thereafter, led to more systematic official consideration of colonial police training and operations, as well as the ethnic composition of police cadres.[106]

Iraq was a case in point. The progressive reduction of British influence over policing and, with it, intelligence gathering remained a critical issue for all sides in mandatory Iraq as the British edged toward withdrawal with the signature of two Anglo-Iraq treaties in January 1926 and December 1927.[107] These two accords prefigured the confirmation of Iraqi independence under a further treaty agreement signed on 30 June 1930, whose terms were to come into effect only with Iraq's admission to the League of Nations in October 1932. In the period intervening between the initial treaties and eventual Iraqi independence, the retention of British police inspectors and security advisers attached to the Baghdad Interior Ministry came to symbolize Britain's continuing hegemony.[108] Covert information gathering did not cease with Iraq's accession to independence. In December 1932, the Foreign Office decided to continue channeling security intelligence through the senior British adviser to the Iraqi Interior

Ministry, the long-serving Sir Kinahan Cornwallis.[109] The training and organization of the Iraqi Army, a force increasingly stratified along communal lines, was another focal point of contested sovereignty, particularly as army levies were largely assigned to the repression of internal dissent.[110]

But it was British reliance on Royal Air Force (RAF) squadrons to enforce order throughout Iraq through coercive bombardment of recalcitrant tribes, disaffected communities, and even urban strikers that remained the most salient feature of imperial policing in the mandate on either side of the 1926 treaty watershed.[111] Convinced that the air force had proven its capacity for economical colonial control in the "splendid training ground" of Iraq,[112] as late as January 1930 British commanders insisted that only imperial air policing could keep the peace:

> The view is held—not only by the Air Staff but by practically all competent authorities with personal experience of Iraq—that for a very considerable period the maintenance of law and order in that country cannot safely be entrusted to the Government in Baghdad. The area is too vast, the racial feuds are too bitter, the temper of the tribesmen is too truculent, to permit of adequate control by a local and largely sectional administration disposing of the police and military forces now available, or likely to be available within a reasonable time.[113]

The concession of RAF base rights in Iraq after independence, and the use of the hated Assyrian levies to guard them, compounded the suspicions of the Iraqi opposition.[114] Little wonder that the Baghdad government attached such importance to the concession of sovereign control over internal security policy at independence.[115] It was no coincidence that the British military mission created under the terms of the June 1930 treaty to help train Iraqi security forces was specifically prohibited from engaging in any intelligence-related activity.[116]

In some respects, British intransigence over imperial policing, as well as the choices made about the personnel employed, amounted to little more than an affirmation of long-established martial race theories and recruiting procedures for indigenous police and army personnel. These had long favored ethnic minorities and rural communities deemed to have a vested interest in an imperial presence to prevent oppression by a Sunni Muslim elite.[117] But colonial dissent rarely conformed to neat ethno-geographical lines. The spread of pan-Arab and pan-Islamic sentiment after 1918, the enduring appeal of radical leftist ideas, and the development of industrial proletariats in Middle East cities created new poles of political attraction that transcended ethnic or tribal identity. The growth in refugee populations in mandate territory stimulated both by the disruption of World War I and by the hostile Turkish attitude to Armenian, Circassian, and Assyrian communities, added another layer of complexity to the policing of local insurgencies. After the shock of the Egyptian uprising in 1919, doubts persisted among senior officials about the political allegiance and reliability of indigenous police and administrative personnel. These anxieties led to greater reliance on troops and European-officered native levies to crack down on political dissent and public disorder, a process that culminated in the deployment of regular army forces to contain the Arab revolt in Palestine between 1936 and 1939.[118]

From 1918 to the mid-1930s, French employment of Circassian irregulars to crush Druze resistance and British reliance on Assyrian Christian levies to suppress Kurdish separatism and Arab disorder in Iraq undermined the supposed impartiality of imperial policing.[119] Irregular force involvement in punitive operations against entire tribes or settlements, usually ordered on the basis of humint gathered by political officers in the field, stored up profound resentments. In the Assyrian case, these exploded into horrendous intercommunal violence and Iraqi Army retribution over the summer of 1933, events that underscored the failure of protracted efforts to settle the Assyrian refugee community in northern Iraq.[120]

Greater recourse to special powers and extraordinary legislation to curtail public expressions of opposition to the colonial state meant in practice that Egypt and Palestine in particular were, on occasion, subject to legal regulation virtually indistinguishable from martial law. In these extreme circumstances, the jurisdictional boundaries between police and armed forces in matters of internal security became even more fluid and ill-defined, much to the annoyance of those involved. Army commands were typically reluctant to become immersed in civil policing; police officers resented military interference in police matters, fearing an irreversible loss of public support for the forces of law and order. And disorder always exposed the extent of colonial reliance on locally recruited auxiliaries to do much of the dirty work of intelligence collection and counterinsurgency operations.

Fears about the trustworthiness of indigenous junior police recruits helps explain why political authority over colonial police forces was highly centralized. Governors, resident ministers, or high commissioners took a close interest in policing and habitually intervened in matters of manifest political importance such as the proscription of political parties, the detention of nationalist or religious leaders, strike breaking, and the policing of demonstrations. During the 1920s, police repression of labor unrest and nationalist organizations in Egypt, Palestine, and Iraq did more than anything else to politicize the security forces, both at the level of individual police personnel and in the eyes of the wider public.[121]

A similar process was at work in British India, where police "success" in containing civil disobedience in 1930–33 only heightened public hostility to the Indian police as an institution.[122] In the British Middle East, as in the Indian Raj, suppression of well-publicized dissent made police forces appear more ubiquitous than their limited numbers would otherwise suggest, encouraging popular identification of colonial rule as a "police state" reliant on the coercive power of security forces and intrusive regulation of social interaction to survive. Police personnel and their families became targets of anticolonial opposition and faced intimidation, violent assaults, and assassination. Even in these stressful conditions, money remained a more severe constraint on police activity than public antagonism. Throughout the interwar period, financial pressures imposed manpower limits and budgetary restrictions on the scope of police operations in Britain's Middle East territories. Not until the late 1930s did the British government create a supervisory body to regulate the activities of police forces throughout the dependent empire.[123]

Conclusion

Many of the officials who supplied intelligence to higher authorities in the imperial territories of North Africa and the Middle East did not regard themselves as part of a colonial security service establishment. Most were regional administrators, preoccupied with the daily tasks of local government. These tasks tied them, nevertheless, to the bureaucracy of colonial state surveillance. As Muslim opposition to imperial rule intensified, police forces became more identifiable with the colonial order, more an occupying force patrolling a hostile environment, and more an instrument of state coercion and intelligence gathering than a partner in the fight against crime. Much as the extension of British imperial control in World War I prompted the creation of new informational structures that reported back to the central government, so the greater demands for military information in war catalyzed the refinement of British cryptanalysis, a trend exemplified by the establishment of government cryptographic bureaus. Ironically, after campaigning began, Allied access to large numbers of captured POWs tipped the scales in favor of human intelligence once more.

Within French North Africa, sophisticated French counterintelligence operations and competition for the loyalty of tribal leaders, urban notables, and the general population was integral to state efforts to maintain control. The growing administrative obsession with Muslim opinion was driven by the emergence of mass political action in the imperial territories of North Africa and the Middle East. Imperial authorities always considered early indications of any shifts in public opinion fundamental to their capacity to maintain control. In one key respect, however, the surveillance of dependent populations in the Arab world was always less ambitious than its metropolitan equivalent. Within imperial territory, information on popular mood was generally used to uphold colonial power rather than to adjust policies to meet the demands of the indigenous population. The rigid confinement of indigenous staff to junior positions makes it difficult to speak of genuine Anglo-Arab or Franco-Muslim intelligence communities rather than European-controlled intelligence systems employing local subordinates. Greater reliance on these junior functionaries in the provision of agents' reports and in the maintenance of public order, however, altered the nature of intelligence gathering and assessment. The intelligence states of the interwar Arab world were thus in constant flux, reliant on indigenous intermediaries to sustain imperial control, but also looking to past precedents to help inform current decision making. It is to this more backward-looking aspect of empire surveillance that we now turn.

2

PAST PRECEDENTS AND
COLONIAL RULE

This chapter returns us to the question put at the beginning of the book. How did colonial governments make policy choices about the treatment of subject populations, particularly in circumstances where imperial security was at stake? The role of what might be termed "lessons from the past" in determining these choices is central to the answer. So, too, is the part played by intelligence providers, whose past experiences provided frames of reference for policy makers, shaping the ways in which these lessons were understood by politicians and senior colonial officials. The sections that follow thus connect past precedents and the dilemmas of colonial security in the interwar period.

The plethora of precolonial institutional and legal arrangements that European imperial powers confronted when consolidating imperial administrative control precluded any single model of colonial governance, particularly as colonial governors generally lacked the resources—financial and military—to act as they pleased.[1] The overlap among religious authority, political legitimacy, and legal structures in Islamic societies added a further dimension to this complexity, making it harder still to impose colonial rule in societies where political power, cultural interaction, and social identity were bound up with membership in the Muslim community, the *umma*.[2] Colonial authorities recognized the organizational power of Islam and the centrality of Shari'a law to Muslims' lives. Yet colonialism imposed requirements for political loyalty, as well as legal systems based on the ownership and sale of private property, that were at variance with customary practices and Islamic codes of behavior.[3]

British and French officials in North Africa and the Middle East drew on recent examples of "best practice" from other colonies in an effort to overcome these difficulties. Lessons learned about security agencies and policing, the movement of information in indigenous societies, and economical means of social control were an admixture of previous practice in other colonial settings, adaptation of existing administrative structures, and a good deal of trial and error. This was always two-way traffic. Metropolitan and colonial security services swapped ideas and exchanged personnel, each adapting the practices of the other to suit its local needs. The intelligence state of the interwar period was a borrowed model.

Borrowing from the Past: British Imperial Precedents

Long before the outbreak of war in Europe in August 1914, the British imperial authorities, the government of India above all, recognized the value of criminal, political, and military intelligence gathering at both a strategic and a tactical level. Foreign influences and imported methods of extremist violence were commonly cited to explain the subversive actions of Indian and Irish revolutionaries in particular.[4] Several of the features of colonial policing that would become commonplace after 1918 in Egypt, Sudan, and Britain's Middle East mandates were first developed by the Indian Police Service in the late nineteenth century. In the words of Peter Robb, faced with the growth of Indian nationalism, "it was in intelligence gathering and in the suppression of political violence of dissent that the professionalism of the police came to be concentrated."[5] Statistics on crime levels among distinct communities, extensive record keeping about individual suspects, and the use of paramilitary "special forces" to deal with outbreaks of political violence or to break colonial strikes were all practices familiar in British India before World War I.[6] All were adopted by the Palestine police in the 1920s, whose Criminal Record Office and Fingerprint Bureau both drew on profiling techniques developed in India.[7]

If intelligence practices developed in British India offered guidance to security services in Britain's Arab territories after 1918, the mounting costs of empire cast a long shadow over the Middle East in the years immediately after World War I. The Lloyd George coalition, Liberal-led but Conservative-dominated, and in office until October 1922, struggled to match Britain's extended imperial commitments to the imperative of postwar economic retrenchment. When Britain's acquisition of Middle East mandates was confirmed in 1920–21, the chief of imperial general staff, Sir Henry Wilson, voiced widespread military concerns about the extent of Britain's global obligations. The protection of empire and peacetime imperial policing duties seemed beyond British means. In Wilson's words, "in no single theatre are we strong enough."[8] Uprisings and violent unrest in Ireland, Egypt, and India in 1919 suggested that a global crisis of British Empire was in full swing, and that its perpetrators, whatever the physical distances and cultural differences that separated them, drew inspiration and succor from one another's struggles.[9] An effective security response demanded that police and army agencies follow the same pattern of borrowing, learning from the experience of counterinsurgency in other colonial theaters.[10]

Wilson was an Ulsterman. The devastating experience of the Anglo-Irish war illustrated the difficulties of counterinsurgency operations conducted among a largely hostile population.[11] British policing in Ireland was hardly a model of success.[12] To borrow Charles Townshend's memorable phrase, the selective application of martial law to those regions most affected by nationalist violence generated "the maximum odium for the minimum effect."[13] Yet the experiences of the Royal Irish Constabulary (RIC) and General Tudor's infamous "Black and Tans" auxiliaries provided the most recent example of British paramilitary policing.[14] Their ultimate failure had another effect: releasing large numbers of former RIC personnel for service in the empire.[15] The security lessons of the Anglo-Irish war rebounded through British imperial policing between the wars.[16] More recent Indian examples also resonated throughout British colonial security policy, in particular the ongoing operations on the North-West Frontier of Waziristan. Tim Moreman has illustrated the awesome scale of the tribal control problem along the North-West Frontier. By 1920, the Pathan tribes could amass a fighting strength of 419,243. Well over 100,000 of these fighters possessed breach-loading rifles. Worsening poverty compelled Pathan *lashkars* into more extensive raiding. They were only temporarily subjugated during a punitive Indian Army campaign in Waziristan conducted during 1919–20.[17] Operations were set to continue for years. The intractable pacification campaign along the North-West Frontier guided the strategies developed by the authorities in British India to deploy troops to uphold internal security "in aid of the civil power."[18]

Britain's increasing imperial security requirements before and after World War I were a catalyst to the expansion of centralized data collection by metropolitan security services. Obvious examples include the pioneering use of fingerprinting techniques by the mid-nineteenth-century Indian police force, and the use by MI5 and special branch units across Britain of surveillance techniques refined in Ireland from the 1880s onward.[19] It was a similar story in the Arab world. The administrators, policemen, and intelligence officers who staffed the governments, high commissions, district offices, and rural outposts of British imperial territory in the Middle East brought to their assignments the accumulated intellectual baggage of their previous training and earlier postings. In the British case, the Indian government civil service, the Sudan Political Service (SPS), the Egyptian High Commission, and its wartime Cairo cousin, the Arab Bureau, were among the most important for civilian officials.

From Sir Evelyn Baring's appointment as agent and consul general in 1882 until the imposition of a British protectorate in 1914, British administrative practice in Egypt was colored by the Indian training of its principal practitioners.[20] In turn, Egyptian specialists, such as Sir Ernest Dowson, who devised land registration and taxation schemes for mandatory Palestine and Transjordan, built on their previous experience.[21] Colonial pacification operations and more recent First World War campaigns were also forcing grounds for young security service recruits. After 1918 the Suez Canal garrison, the Egypt and Mesopotamia expeditionary forces, the Indian Army officer corps, and the first Royal Air Force squadrons sent to assist imperial policing along the North-West Frontier, in Aden, and in Mesopotamia provided a raft of military recruits to Britain's Middle East mandates.[22] Indian government Criminal Investigation Department staff formed the backbone of the Secret Intelligence Service station in Istanbul. In the years immediately preceding the Chanak crisis in September 1922, they focused on intelligence assessment of the twin threats of pan-Islamism and Bolshevik sedition in the Near East.[23] More famously, officers of the Indian police service and, above all, the RIC, shaped the training and ethos of the Palestine police.[24] At the end of the Mandate, Palestine police officers would, in turn, move on to numerous other British overseas territories, from Cyprus to southern Rhodesia, influencing patterns of policing in the final years of empire.[25]

The Palestine example illustrates how bitter lessons of counterinsurgency policing learned by RIC officers during the Anglo-Irish war acquired added importance once significant numbers of former RIC personnel found reemployment in colonial police forces. Many had direct experience of intelligence gathering and knew its risks.[26] The new arrivals were likely to meet established police personnel already familiar with Ireland, as, from 1907 onward, intending colonial police officers usually underwent instruction at the Dublin depot.[27] As a result, police personnel and noncommissioned officers with recent experience of state repression in Ireland, before or after partition, dominated the auxiliary units and paramilitary security forces established by Britain's Middle East administrations. Former officers of the RIC, many faced with Catholic retribution in newly independent Eire, were omnipresent in the expanded Palestine police restructured by high commissioner Lord Plumer in 1926 (discussed in chapter 8).[28] The Royal Air Force armored car companies that patrolled the deserts of Iraq and Transjordan also drew recruits with recent experience as auxiliaries in Ireland. These men were the blunt instruments of colonial repression, but they also typified the cross-fertilization of imperial policing and intelligence gathering traditions in the interwar years.[29] It was hardly surprising that intelligence assessments and policy advice about the Arab mandates were an admixture of local hearsay, empirical observation, and "lessons from the past" in other, very different colonial or quasi-colonial environs. Civil administration in Palestine, for instance, brought together civil servants and colonial officers from as far afield as Cyprus, Malta, Sudan, Rhodesia, and Mauritius, not to mention the recruits from Ireland and the British military.[30]

These new arrivals still faced huge difficulties, however adaptable their previous career experiences might prove to be. Limited knowledge of local languages, customs, religious practices, tribal boundaries, and peasant economies fed uncertainty about the loyalties of recently subjugated peoples. Most of the British administrators deployed in Iraq and Transjordan after 1920 had only wartime experience to guide them in their assessment of sociopolitical conditions. Many had served in General Edmund Allenby's Egyptian Expeditionary Force (EEF) during the Palestine campaign of 1917–18.[31] Some could call on past imperial policing experience in two theaters where tribal rivalry and intercommunal conflict determined interaction with the British imperial state: the Indian North-West Frontier and the Anglo-Egyptian Sudan.[32] A privileged few had connections with the Arabist specialists of the Arab Bureau in Cairo, a Foreign Office outpost that was the principal Middle East peace-planning agency of World War I.[33] So important was the Arab Bureau's pioneering role as training center and model of intelligence administration that it deserves more detailed consideration before we move on to consider French imperial precedents.

Recent British Precedent: The Arab Bureau

The Arab Bureau was another information-gathering agency whose activities pushed it deeper into the realm of state surveillance. Its collection and analysis of sensitive political intelligence pointed the way to the integration of an "information order" into British imperial administration in the Middle East. The war effort compelled the British government to assume more central responsibility for the strategic coordination of imperial resources, and additional ministries became directly engaged in Middle Eastern issues. As a result, the government of India's imperial primacy over its "western sphere" in the Arab world faced stiffer competition from Whitehall departments and the burgeoning British military and diplomatic establishments in Cairo.[34] The military humiliations of the failed Dardanelles campaign and defeat after the protracted siege of Kut-al-Amara in central Iraq in 1915–16 provoked a reappraisal of wider strategy in the war against Ottoman Turkey, one outcome of which was that British officials in Cairo increasingly took charge of the planning and direction of the Arab revolt.[35]

The Arab Bureau was established in January 1916 as a coordinating body to provide political and military intelligence on regional politics, Arab opinion, and the war against Ottoman Turkey. Technically a section of the Sudan Intelligence Department under the Egyptian high commissioner, the Bureau was therefore answerable to the Foreign Office in London. Within months of its creation, however, the Bureau's role as an intelligence provider to government and military commands shaded into that of an autonomous policymaking agency.[36] The Arab Bureau could claim many parents, among them the Cairo Residency, the Foreign Office Eastern Department, and the military intelligence staff of the EEF. Despite its hybrid origins, the Arab Bureau was first and foremost a political intelligence department serving two masters—the Cairo Residency and the Foreign Office in London. Whatever its patrimony, the Bureau was shaped in the image of its staff, most of whom were Arab specialists, conversant with vernacular Arabic, and either familiar with the prewar security service apparatus of Egypt and Sudan or transferred to the Bureau from military intelligence postings with the British units operating in the Middle East by 1916.[37]

Bureau staff molded British perceptions of the Arab revolt, the nature of Arabism, and Arab nation-states.[38] As Bruce Westrate, the author of a key work on the Bureau, comments, only a "thin line" separated its informational role from its advisory one. The first Bureau chief, the former director of military intelligence in Egypt, Colonel Gilbert Clayton, and his closest superior, Sir F. Reginald Wingate, governor general and *sirdar* (commander) of the Sudan, clearly intended to use the Bureau for the advancement of their preferred Arab policies.[39] In 1917, Wingate's replacement as governor in the Sudan, Sir Lee Stack, lent the Bureau further support, bringing to bear his long experience as director of intelligence in Cairo from 1908 to 1914.[40]

During its four-year lifespan, the Bureau operated from a cluster of three rooms at the Savoy Hotel in Cairo. Although some of its staff, most notably T. E. Lawrence, were increasingly peripatetic, the Bureau's handful of Arab specialists accrued influence over British imperial policy, thanks primarily to their unique analytical perspective on Arab politics and society. Bureau membership represented the pick of the experienced Arabist specialists available among British diplomatic and military personnel in the Middle East. At any one time, the number of permanent staff typically ranged between ten and twenty. Some of these individuals, such as Gertrude Bell, were selected because of their recent experience in service intelligence agencies. Others acquired their specialist knowledge through colonial or military service in Sudan, Egypt, or India. It was an eclectic mix of field operatives, military officers, and more cerebral university types. Some of this latter group had put their academic expertise to use before the war as administrators, archaeologists, topographers, or social anthropologists. The Bureau's deputy director, Captain Kinahan Cornwallis, entered the SPS in 1906 after reading Arabic at Oxford.

David George Hogarth, Clayton's successor as Bureau chief, also had Oxford connections. Hogarth was a former curator of Oxford's Ashmolean Museum and a leading archaeologist of Arab antiquity. These individuals built up what Paula Mohs terms "an archive of instruction" to guide British

Middle Eastern policy.[41] What united these self-proclaimed "intrusives" was the conviction that accurate information gathering and shrewd analysis of the prospects for Arab self-rule held the key to long-term British supremacy in the Middle East.[42] As their highly partisan advice regarding the Sykes-Picot agreement indicated, Bureau personnel rarely held back their opinions regarding the complexion of future Middle East administration.[43] By 1917 the Arab Bureau had become "an office of advocacy in association with the Arab movement."[44] Its machinations continued after the Mudros armistice in October 1918. As the Bureau's historian notes, "The pilgrimage, the caliphate, and intertribal hostility were all viewed from the perspective of the anticipated confederation [of pro-British Arab states] and the installation of informal measures of control."[45]

The profile of Arab Bureau membership says much about British strategic priorities in the Middle East, but it is the expansion of Arab Bureau influence that concerns us here. The Bureau was not the sum total of Britain's intelligence capability in the wartime Middle East. Nor was it a great success. Until Bruce Westrate's revisionist treatment in 1992, historians were uniformly critical of the Arab Bureau's amateurism, political meddling, and pro-Hashemite duplicity.[46] But as a government agency uniquely created to make available local intelligence on the basis of which informed imperial policy would be devised, the Bureau was a signal precedent in the creation of Britain's imperial security agency network after World War I. Bureau staff never recognized, or at least never acknowledged, the supposed demarcation between political and military intelligence. Nor did they respect the boundaries between information provision, source evaluation, intelligence analysis, and policy advice.

The intellectualism of Arab Bureau staff, characterized by their shared interest in classical Arabic and the anthropological development of Middle Eastern societies, found echoes elsewhere. Sir Percy Cox's inner circle of policy advisers in Baghdad shared a similar outlook. Interest in social anthropology sustained the careers of intelligence officers and military commanders in Transjordan, much as it did among members of the SPS, perhaps the most "academic" of all the imperial bureaucracies in the Arab world.[47] Competition for entry to the SPS was intense and narrowly focused on recent graduates. In the mid-1930s, recruits were still exclusively sought from nine British universities. Year after year, the majority of successful applicants were drawn from Oxford or Cambridge, to which those fresh out of an undergraduate degree program immediately returned to complete a one-year course of "Tropical Study" built around intensive training in Arabic and law. (Mature students went instead to the London University School of Oriental and African Studies.)[48] Trained candidates then began a probationary period of anything from two to five years as assistant district commissioners in Sudan, during which they were required to pass further examinations in Arabic and civil and criminal law. This was typically followed by promotion to full district commissioner or transfer into one of the Sudan government's technical departments such as Agriculture and Forests, Health, Education, Public Works, or Finance.[49]

These initial years on assignment in provincial outposts seem to have encouraged a diversion of academic energy into the study of local populations, which was, after all, implicit in the political intelligence-gathering work of an assistant district commissioner. One SPS member, Harold A. MacMichael, better remembered as the British high commissioner in the latter stages of the Palestine revolt, established the journal *Sudan Notes and Records* in 1918 as a forum for SPS anthropological data on the Sudanese.[50] His book, *The Anglo-Egyptian Sudan*, published in 1934 after he had completed six years as civil secretary in Khartoum, became essential reading for SPS appointees.[51] Where the Arab Bureau and SPS led, others followed, embodying what would become a cardinal feature of imperial intelligence states: the conviction that only intelligence providers possessed the expertise necessary to make sound political judgments about indigenous social structure, colonial governance, and public order. At the root of this confidence lay a profound respect for lessons learned the hard way by earlier generations of colonial officials faced with similar challenges. This faith in the power of precedent would endure throughout the interwar years. In August 1936 one finds Major John "Pasha" Glubb, revered as the most innovative Bedouin control officer in the southern deserts of Iraq and Transjordan, quoting with approval the precepts of tribal policing laid down by Sir Robert Sandeman, the nineteenth-century pacifier of Baluchistan.[52]

French Imperial Precedents

France's self-image as a defender of Muslim interests built on the achievements of the *bureaux arabes* and their successors in nineteenth-century Algeria. Founded in 1844, the *bureaux arabes* were an army administrative service. Their members reported to a directorate of Arab affairs in Algiers and held responsibility for rural governance and the supervision of local intermediaries, whether chiefs, religious leaders, or judicial appointees. Junior-ranking officers of the *bureaux arabes* usually made the preliminary selection of which indigenous authorities to work with in each administrative region, or *cercle*.[53] Members of the *bureaux arabes* also remained active military personnel, an important distinction. By the early twentieth century, their closest counterparts in the British Empire—officers of the Egyptian Army who decided to put their expertise to use as district commissioners in rural Egypt or Sudan—had to apply for transfer to a civilian administrative service.[54] In French Algeria, however, the army's role in rural administration remained paramount, and its practitioners' approach to local government was always intelligence driven.

If the *bureaux arabes* provided the administrative model for French imperial intelligence providers, it was Morocco, rather than the established colony of Algeria, that offered more recent lessons in how security services might contribute to the consolidation of French rule. Methods of repression devised in the Moroccan Protectorate would be applied elsewhere in French North Africa until the final, bitter end of empire in the early 1960s.[55] During the first two decades of the twentieth century, the gradual extension of French political control over the sultanate's zone of administration, the *blad al-makhzen*, in northern and coastal Morocco, was predicated on a series of political bargains with tribal leaders, urban notables, and senior members of the Sharifian government. A protracted, violent affair, this imposition of French authority, part coercive, part negotiated, demanded astute intelligence reportage about the groups and personalities involved, as well as the prospects of securing their long-term compliance. This surveillance did not end with the formal establishment of the Residency government in 1912, but increased in scope and purpose in the two decades that followed. Outwardly, protectorate administration gave every appearance of an effective patron-client relationship between France's first resident general, Louis-Hubert Lyautey, and the sultan's central *makhzen* administration of royal court and Moroccan ministerial offices. In practice, however, the sultanate was increasingly confined to a ceremonial political role, retaining its most significant powers in judicial matters of Shari'a law. Lyautey's government scrupulously maintained the aura of limited intervention that belied the increasingly tight control it exerted over the appointments of municipal officials, district chiefs (*caïds*) nominated by tribal leaders, and the magistrates (*qadis*) that issued Shari'a judgments. By 1918, regional government, tax collection, and foreign and military affairs were all subject to stringent French regulation within the *blad al-makhzen*.

During the interwar years, Morocco's seven French regional governors assumed the trappings of their counterparts in the prefectures of Algeria, building up large administrative staffs with wide fiscal and policing powers. The civil-military authorities on both sides of the Morocco-Algeria border also pooled their intelligence more systematically. In May 1929, the two colonial governments agreed to rights of police pursuit across their common land frontier, both to control economic migration and to curtail the movement of dissidents across the frontier.[56] Meanwhile, in the high Atlas and southern Moroccan territories outside the traditional zone of Sharifian rule, French imperial consolidation rested on shifting alliances with the paramount *caïds* of the Marrakesh region, all of which required detailed intelligence about clan affiliations, caïdal politics, and the socioeconomic benefits to be derived from often protracted and costly military campaigning.[57]

For the Syrian administration, Lyautey's style of indirect rule in French Morocco was *exemple par excellence.* Officers of the army occupation corps in Morocco were prized as district officers and military intelligence analysts in the Syria and Lebanon mandates after 1920.[58] The physical proximity of Morocco, Algeria, and Tunisia promoted interchange of bureaucratic personnel among them, even though internal government in the three Maghreb territories differed in key respects.

In Tunisia, France's other North African protectorate, military intelligence officers serving as *contrôleurs civils*—effectively district officers with extensive political and judicial powers—also consolidated French political control. Their regulation of Arab society was more town-based, however, and demanded a careful handling of the competing demands of Muslims, French settlers, and the more established community of ethnic Italian colonists. During the 1920s, security intelligence work in the Tunisian interior focused on preventing the outward spread of urban nationalism.[59] Familiarity with urban intercommunal tensions made Tunisia's *contrôleurs civils* particularly well suited as appointees to serve in the towns and cities of Syria and, more especially, Lebanon, whose populations were even more heterogeneous than those of Tunisia. But interchange between police spéciale officers was far more common; Sûreté personnel transferred between imperial territories and inspectors were encouraged to accept temporary placements in the Maghreb. Both the Interior Ministry and the Foreign Ministry, the two government departments with juridical responsibility for the three North African territories, promoted this regular interchange of senior Sûreté staff.[60]

Police officers in colonial Algeria answered to the Ministry of Interior, and the Algiers Sûreté communicated with Paris far more than other French security agencies in North Africa or the Levant. To a degree then, the civil bureaucracy of Algiers government, departmental prefects, subprefects, and regional police offices was set apart from the administrative apparatus of the Morocco and Tunisia protectorates and the Levant high commission, between which personnel transfers were more commonplace. Whatever the constitutional differences, the distinctions among the security agencies in the French North African territories should not be exaggerated. They were always interdependent, their threat assessments were informed by the same preoccupations, and their styles of intelligence gathering and policing were not markedly different. Furthermore, in all three locations the army played a central role in the maintenance of internal order. The more martial flavor of French administration in its North African protectorates and Levant mandates also determined the movement of officials among territories. The Levant Army was largely composed of units of France's professional army in North Africa, the Armée d'Afrique, as well as French-officered detachments of the West African *tirailleurs sénégalais,* whose regiments formed part of the standing colonial army, La Coloniale. Widespread deployment of *tirailleurs sénégalais* in Arab territories was not the only connection with black Africa. The predominantly Muslim colonies of the French West African confederation, notably Senegal, French Sudan (Mali), and Niger, also provided a reservoir of Arabic specialists to serve north of the Sahara.

Intelligence specialists were part of a distinct imperialist milieu in the French Empire of the early twentieth century. The giants of French colonial expansion in the first decades of the Third Republic were the frontier imperialists who drove the process forward at the colonial periphery, rather than the Paris ministers, government advisers, and business leaders who debated policy options at the metropolitan center.[61] For years after its formal creation in March 1894 the Ministry of Colonies was overshadowed by more powerful government agencies. Over the next two decades the voice of the Ministry's foremost department—the political affairs division—resounded in the Council of Ministers (the French Cabinet) only when especially strong-minded ministers such as Théophile Delcassé or Gaston Doumergue fleetingly raised the profile of colonial policy.[62] More specialist Colonial Ministry sections, such as the inspectorates of public works and health, attracted highly qualified personnel but were starved of funding.[63]

Many of the leading administrators in French North Africa in the early twentieth century cut their teeth as colonial conquerors in sub-Saharan Africa, Indochina, and, above all, Madagascar in the late nineteenth century. The conquest of Madagascar proved an especially influential experience. During 1895, the invading French forces initially found malarial mosquitoes to be a far more lethal adversary than the indigenous population.[64] But once the French Army established itself in the island's populous heartland and imposed a protectorate treaty on the Imerina dynasty in October 1895, the civilian Residency and the military command were soon bitterly divided over the trustworthiness of Madagascar's political elite. In consequence, during 1896 the creation of a functioning military intelligence service in the island's principal towns became critical to the eventual French response to the outbreak of the so-called Menalamba rebellion.[65] Accustomed to the zero-sum game of imperial rivalry with Britain, the French colonial lobby and General Joseph Gallieni's military staff, newly installed in the Malagasy royal capital, Tananarive, were conditioned to view local political dissent as the product of outside interference. And since Gallieni's underlying purpose was to dispense with the inconvenience of the protectorate and establish full colonial control, questionable military intelligence regarding the factional politics of the Imerina royal court was quickly put to use to eradicate potential opponents of the French colonial project. In October 1896, the queen's uncle and her leading court official were duly executed after a sham trial.[66] Faulty and, in this case, falsified political intelligence was exploited to justify arbitrary imperial consolidation.

This sad episode reveals three points of relevance here. First, we should be aware that in a colonial context, the veracity of political intelligence was a secondary concern to those who exploited it. More important was its political utility in advancing colonial control. Second, the weight attached to intelligence material was likely to increase in inverse proportion to the specialist knowledge of the governing authorities. In crude terms, the less known about local life beyond the governor's palace, the more the opportunity for a colonial intelligence service to make its mark on policy. Finally, the Madagascan example reminds us of the need to treat the supposedly authoritative nature of intelligence material with a healthy skepticism. Though suggestive of specialist knowledge, intelligence material could be little more than a dressing up of rumor or the recapitulation of the flimsiest evidence for political ends.

Gallieni was far from duped by the intelligence information he received. The supreme theorist of colonial pacification and a shrewd republican political operator, Gallieni put political intelligence to its logical use—to play politics.[67] The general had spent four years as a prisoner of war after the 1870 conflict with Prussia. He used the time to learn German and study Prussian military tactics. His recognition that an understanding of one's opponent was the key to success informed his subsequent actions as colonial governor first in French Sudan (1886–88), then in Indochina (1892–94), and finally in Madagascar (from 1895).[68] Gallieni's pacification strategies in each location were based on control of communications, the colonization of indigenous administrative systems, and the measured display of military force for maximum public effect. Intelligence played a vital role in policy formulation throughout the process. Knowledge of local topography was essential to road construction and access to the urban centers from which rebellion was most likely to arise. A rudimentary grasp of the regional economy and its key commodities and markets was fundamental to the containment of unrest in societies where the majority of peasant cultivators relied on the sale of surplus agricultural produce to survive. Some understanding of tribal cultures, local elites, and precolonial systems of governance was essential to the parasitization of these administrations by French civil and military advisers.

As Paul Rabinow has shown, Gallieni and his foremost colonial patron, Jean-Marie de Lanesson, who was appointed governor general of Indochina in 1891, followed the racial tenets of France's leading social Darwinist thinker, J. B. Lamarck, in their pacification of colonized populations.[69] Much as Gallieni insisted that detailed intelligence about local geography was fundamental to successful military expeditions reliant on extended supply lines in hostile territory, so he and de Lanesson agreed that political control was facilitated by the manipulation of preexisting communal rivalries and economic tensions within the indigenous population. Gallieni made the point directly: "An officer who has successfully drawn an exact ethnographic map of the territory he commands is close to achieving complete pacification, soon to be followed by the form of organization he judges most appropriate."[70] These precepts were somewhat misleadingly termed a *politique des races:* a policy of racial domination certainly, but theoretically one mediated by the recruitment of administrative and military auxiliaries from favored ethnic groups among the colonized peoples. From 1895, colonial government in Madagascar followed this pattern, operating behind the facade of a Merina administration neatly subdivided into nine services. Beneath a layer of provincial government, French district administrators relied on small advisory committees of local notables (mainly settler farmers and businessmen) who became the main source of intelligence about social and political activity in their *cercle.* Reliable information from the countryside was always highly prized. In Indochina, Gallieni was even prepared to arm rural populations willing to resist the forced exactions of Vietnamese rebel groups in northern Tonkin.[71]

By contrast, French colonial officials and garrison commanders schooled in Gallieni's approach to local government were reluctant to allow settlers to play a more direct role in policing. This ran counter to the centralizing impulse of French colonial bureaucracy and, on occasion, mirrored an underlying antagonism between cultured civil administrators and supposedly brutish settler agriculturalists.[72] Far better to rely on trusted indigenous auxiliaries whose judicial authority among their own people was more likely to be respected. Again, the echoes of rural policing in mid-nineteenth-century France seem clear. The propertied classes and part-time rural policemen—colonial equivalents of the *gardes champêtres* or *gardes forestiers* that helped keep the peace in the French countryside of the 1840s and 1850s—were integral to the prevention of disorder and the administration of justice.[73]

It is perhaps fruitless to attempt a clinical separation of military and political intelligence in such contexts. Information about popular dissent might provoke a punitive military operation in the short term, but was likely to result in the construction of improved road links and permanent garrisons in the long term. Each action was intended to consolidate central government authority, whether by direct coercion or the threat of future sanction more swiftly administered. The economic benefits of improved infrastructure and assured security were far from incidental. Evidence of increased prosperity, improvements in public hygiene, and provision of a permanent water supply were more effective tools of colonial control than bayonets and prisons. The attendant transformation of military occupiers into administrators, supervisors of public works, and judicial officials marked what Paul

Rabinow tellingly defines as "the civilization of military life."[74] Pursued to its fullest degree in Lyautey's Moroccan protectorate after 1912, intelligence as information broadly defined was the wellspring of this creeping annexation of indigenous government apparatus.

Almost a decade after the arrival of French forces in Madagascar, Gallieni's chief protégé, General Lyautey, was again at the forefront of an aggressive enterprise in colonial pacification, this time as divisional commander in southwestern Algeria. Much encouraged by the Algiers governor, Charles Jonnart, the French war minister, General Louis André, and France's most forceful colonial lobbyist, Eugène Etienne, Lyautey defied the Paris government, and more particularly Foreign Minister Théophile Delcassé, in his determination to extend imperial control. Having seized the Berguent oasis just inside Moroccan territory in June 1904, Lyautey then insisted that the continued occupation of adjacent Moroccan territory was both strategically essential and morally justified on the grounds that French forces would afford better protection from marauding tribal bands to local inhabitants. As Kim Munholland has demonstrated, this was classic frontier imperialism—a rolling military pacification based on Gallieni's model of staged advance. Military authority crept forward inexorably, like an oil stain.[75]

Certain observations are pertinent from the perspective of imperial policing and colonial intelligence. In the case cited earlier, the military command exploited local disorder on the disputed Algeria-Morocco border to validate territorial expansion. Put another way, the extension of colonial control was justified as a policing imperative. On the other hand, it seems reasonable to extrapolate that Lyautey and his military superiors either manipulated or withheld detailed intelligence on the anarchic conditions along this frontier in order to disarm Foreign Ministry criticism of the army's action. That Lyautey could get away with a clear act of aggression just as Delcassé was attempting to consolidate French influence over the Moroccan sultanate by diplomatic means highlights the centrality of intelligence exploitation to empire building at the turn of the century.

Lessons from the Desert

For both British and French imperial security services there was another distinctive arena in which intelligence gathering posed unique challenges, as much environmental as cultural or political. This was the vast rural expanse of Muslim colonial states where small numbers of tribal control specialists bore primary administrative responsibility for the imposition of European regulation. But before any such regulation could be devised, much less imposed, colonial government required detailed information about the populations they claimed to rule. The intelligence-gathering techniques as well as the ethnographic studies and cultural assumptions of the intelligence gatherers involved in the early years of desert tribal control exerted a lasting influence over desert policing between the wars.

In March 1909, Harold A. MacMichael, a renowned officer of the SPS, submitted an ethnographic survey of the Kababish Bedouin to the Eastern District officer in Bahr El Ghazal. MacMichael, a future high commissioner of the Palestine mandate, was no mere dabbler in social anthropology. As mentioned earlier, he sat on the editorial committee of the semiofficial Khartoum government journal *Sudan Notes and Records,* which, after its establishment in 1918, quickly became the principal forum for the dissemination of ethnographic intelligence gathered by SPS administrators about the Sudanese population.[76] MacMichael also went on in 1923 to publish an influential study of Sudan's Arab-speaking population.[77] In 1909, he prefaced his analysis of the Kababish with a warning about the misapprehensions current among British officials in the SPS regarding the demarcation of tribes and the nature of tribal affiliation:

> The word "tribe" as commonly used generally implies, among other things, a closely homogeneous collection of families or individuals living together under a hereditary or elective sheikhdom, and largely distinct by race from other such communities. . . . The most obvious way of beginning any inquiry with a view to determining the origin of the various families composing any tribe is to find out from its members the name of every section and sub-section of the tribe, and then to inquire from members of other tribes the reasons for the distinctive names borne by each. By inference—a frequently misleading way is to inquire directly into the origins of the tribe from its own sheikhs. The reason for this is obvious: it is to the interest of the sheikhs to lay stress upon the unity of their tribe, and consequently they are loath to confess that their tribe was in the first instance formed by a coalition of different races, nor to admit that it has since been joined by many foreign elements. Rather, with specious candor they will answer one's questions by saying that their tribe traces its descent to one of the relations, or at least companions, of the Prophet.[78]

The intrinsic interest of MacMichael's observations is less significant to us here than the evidence of how he gathered tribal intelligence. Prior to visiting the Kababish, MacMichael studied accounts of their customs presented to the Royal Geographical Society in 1850 and to the London Anthropological Institute in 1887. But he relied on conversations with the Kababish and their near neighbors to inform his conclusions. As his comments suggest, MacMichael received conflicting accounts of tribal origins and affiliations. He had no objective criteria against which to measure these differing statements, so his assessment fell back on his own classical education and his broad understanding of the original Muslim Arab penetration of Sudan more than a thousand years earlier. His findings were therefore an admixture of earlier data, interviews in the field, and the educational background that informed his thinking.[79] This bears emphasis because

MacMichael's study of the Kababish community became a yardstick for SPS policy appreciations of the Bahr El Ghazal region. Yet MacMichael had made no secret of how tentative his conclusions actually were. In other words, colonial policymakers sometimes attached undue weight to tribal intelligence surveys simply because they were hard to come by. Their rarity and specialist nature conferred a respect that obscured their subjectivity.[80]

MacMichael's experiences are instructive in other ways. In the Anglo-Egyptian Sudan and the southern desert territories of Transjordan and Iraq, itinerant district administrators gathered the bulk of political intelligence: the SPS in the former case, special service officers in the latter. With so few staff available and such huge, and often inaccessible, areas to administer, it could not be otherwise. Inspection tours were substantially devoted to the acquisition of humint. Up-to-the-minute information from tribal sheikhs, Bedouin headmen, and merchants was especially prized. Such individuals were not only information providers but surveillance targets as well, owing to their unique ability to influence social communication among desert populations. Sheikhs, Bedouin, and merchant traders all traveled widely, often across district and intercolonial frontiers. Their connections with other communities and their sensitivity to local changes in economic conditions, market prices, and taxation rates guaranteed their place at the heart of desert intelligence gathering.[81]

Patterns of social communication and colonial surveillance in French desert territories were remarkably similar. Here, too, the combination of the assumptions about differing civilizations derived from a classical education and the lessons of recent experience in other desert colonies shaped the outlook of the information gatherers in the colonial interior. The architectural remnants of classical civilization in North Africa and the Levant gave extra stimulus to the parallels drawn with the Roman Empire in particular.[82] The tradition of specialist military administration of tribal lands also had a long French imperial pedigree, and, for Service de Renseignements (SR) officers, amounted to the purest form of associationism. In the pre-Saharan territory of southern Algeria, the Armée d'Afrique held responsibility for the administration, policing, and surveillance of nomadic clan groups. Further south, at the juncture of the Sahara and the West African Sahel, military administrators also regulated nomad societies in French Sudan and Niger throughout the colonial period. By 1918, the western Sahara was thus at two distinct interfaces: one between the colonial administrations of Algeria and the French West African federation, the other between the Saharan territories of southern Morocco and Mauritania that had yet to be pacified.[83] The administrative picture was different again in Chad. Nominally a colony of French Equatorial Africa, Chad's strategic location, forbidding desert environment, and low population density ensured its separate legal and fiscal status as a distinct army fiefdom.[84] Tribal control officers in North and West Africa never imposed outright colonial control on the nomad populations under their nominal authority. The land seizures, the ambitious integrationist projects, and, in black Africa, the forced labor characteristic of the civil administrations in Algiers and Dakar were largely absent from the Saharan territories.[85]

Across the Maghreb's desert south, small units of *spahi* cavalry, typically fifteen strong, patrolled the principal migratory routes used by nomadic herders. They tried to ensure that Bedouin groups kept to designated "migratory zones," both to avert clashes over the limited water and grazing available and to prevent large numbers of Bedouin from encroaching on areas of pastoral settlement. But as the boundaries of European and Muslim agricultural activity pushed southward in the early 1920s, desert policing in southern Algeria became more volatile. These *spahi* units increasingly patrolled an internal frontier between twentieth-century colonization and traditional Bedouin nomadism. In one sense this boundary was geographical, demarcating privately acquired farmland from customary Bedouin migration routes and grazing sites. In another it was cultural, imposing limits on the southerly penetration of pastoral agriculture in an effort to safeguard the established Bedouin lifestyle. But the intense pressure on grazing land inevitably provoked conflict between sedentary agriculturalists and nomadic Bedouin unable to move freely or find adequate pasture for their livestock. The result was a postwar escalation in livestock theft from other tribes, settler estates, and Muslim smallholders. Large estate owners increasingly employed armed guards, and desert policing became more clearly identifiable with punitive action against Bedouin livestock raiding.[86] Similar evidence of endemic postwar unrest emerged from nearby imperial territories with large well-armed nomad populations, southeastern Morocco and northern Niger, for instance.[87]

The 1920s were therefore part of a longer transitional period in French desert policing and intelligence gathering as priorities shifted from exploration, colonization, and pacification to legal regulation, sedentarization, and social control. It was in this context that the fullest post–World War I guidelines on desert policing were produced. Their author was General Laperrine, the first commander of the unified Saharan command established by Aristide Briand's government on 12 January 1917 to cope with the wartime drain on military personnel in the Saharan territories of French North, West, and Equatorial Africa. Jurisdiction over desert policing reverted to individual colonial authorities on 22 August 1919. Nonetheless, the wartime experiment in federal control was judged a success, thanks to Laperrine's thoughtful and innovative methods of policing and tribal control. The general summarized his reflections on tribal control policy in a 146-page document sent to the War Ministry's African Section on 27 July, a month before his Saharan command ended.

The main points of Laperrine's report merit closer examination because they became a benchmark for army intelligence officers' nomadic control measures for years afterward. Laperrine identified several governing principles to effective colonial rule of desert populations. First among these was the delineation of common policing regulations for all desert populations under a single colonial authority. It had to be recognized that local commanders would apply the rules as best suited local circumstances, but to equip them to make appropriate decisions on their own initiative, field officers had to be kept informed of the rationale for policy. Improved communications were essential. Laperrine identified more all-weather roads and a desert telegraph service as critical to population control, early notification of unrest, and dissemination of good practice among intelligence specialists. Not surprisingly, he also insisted that frequent tours of inspection and a permanent police presence along arterial communications routes were indispensable if order was to be kept. But Laperrine recommended a departure from past practice by rejecting actions likely to worsen intercommunal relations. The risks of intensified tribal raiding as a consequence of heightened enmity between tribes and other indigenous communities outweighed the benefits of a strategy of divide and rule. He was also well aware that most intelligence personnel policing the desert interior succumbed to a sense of acute isolation. Hence his final recommendation that instances of good practice be more widely shared between them. Weekly desert intelligence bulletins were to be compiled, summarizing events of political significance and the actions taken to achieve pacification.[88]

From his seat of government in Rabat, Resident General Lyautey was particularly impressed by Laperrine's recommendations. He recognized a kindred spirit who saw the key to lasting colonial control in information gathering rather than coercive power.[89] He was not alone. Laperrine's recommendations shaped the first Saharan policing directives issued to the governments of French Africa after the dissolution of his Saharan command. These directives located the SR at the heart of desert policing. It fell to the military intelligence service to ensure that all incoming intelligence from *méhariste* columns, local informants, loyalist tribal sheikhs, camel trains, travelers, and spies was systematically recorded, fully cross-referenced, and distilled into useful policy advice. Given the vast tracts of territory involved, such advice was geared to the optimum allocation of limited resources. Patrols could not be expected to cover huge distances overnight; aircraft were too few in number to reconnoiter or bombard sensitive areas; and the movement of nomadic populations had to be taken into account when deciding where units were best deployed.[90]

Admittedly, in Lyautey's case, Laperrine was preaching to the converted. The Moroccan Residency had, by 1919, created a detailed training program for its intending tribal control officers. Supervised by Colonel Henri

Berriau, Lyautey's most trusted adviser, entrants to the Moroccan native affairs directorate completed 140 hours of language training in Arabic and Berber. They attended a series of ethnographic classes devoted to the study of Arab society. Most read—and some contributed—to the *Revue du Monde Musulman,* a journal influenced by Durkheimian concepts of social organization, ethnography, and "race science."[91] These were soldier-researchers accustomed to viewing tribal organization in sociological terms. In their efforts to consolidate tribal loyalty to the French protectorate, these officers often helped clan leaders resist the encroachments of the sultanate and French settlers alike on tribal lands, customary practices, and the legal autonomy of the tribe. It was an article of faith among Lyautey's staff that socially cohesive Berber groups were better served by French than Arab rule. The French Empire as a whole was conceptualized in pseudoanthropological terms as a hierarchy of colonized races in which those nearest the top could aspire to a comparable level of "civilization" through careful imitation of French practice.

After 1920, French policing in Syria's southern desert drew on the experience of Armée d'Afrique native affairs specialists and camel-borne *méhariste* patrols in France's Saharan territories. The military intelligence personnel designated to police Bedouin populations in the Syria mandate saw themselves as the latest in a distinguished line of imperial pioneers. Judged on their official reportage alone, they attached immense significance to the distinction between conquest and pacification. Tribal control, in their eyes, was less about colonial mastery than the transformation of clan loyalties, preferably by persuasion and example rather than military force. The Levant Army's Contrôle bédouin were, after all, the only soldiers policing an entirely new French imperial frontier after World War I. Created by General Henri Gouraud's administration in 1920, this tribal control agency reported to Colonel Georges Catroux, the high commission delegate in Damascus soon to be appointed head of the Levant SR. Soldiers trained in Lyautey's native affairs administration in Morocco filled the Contrôle bédouin ranks. It was a background shared with their superiors. Catroux and his deputies in Aleppo and Latakia, as well as Robert de Caix, the first high commission secretary-general, had all worked with the resident general in Rabat. *La méthode Lyautey* was a formative cultural experience for all of them.[92]

These recent precedents provided a mental map to the first SR officers assigned to the Syrian desert, enhancing their influence in shaping French administrative attitudes.[93] Elizabeth Thompson classifies these military officials as one of the three pillars of French mandatory rule alongside the civil bureaucracy of the Beirut high commission and the local elites that served as intermediaries to the wider Syrian population.[94] At the juncture of security intelligence work and imperial policing, they wielded decisive political influence in the consolidation of mandatory power. The Syrian example was typical; indeed, the experiences of tribal control specialists in French and British territories pointed to a common conclusion. Desert policing was intelligence policing. Its first principle was that centralized analysis of diverse information was the sole means to impose imperial authority over extensive desert regions in which tribal violence remained endemic.

Metropolitan Precedents

The argument in this chapter thus far has suggested that intelligence states of North Africa and the Middle East were, to some degree, modeled on earlier colonial precedents. To stop here would, however, be to reveal only part of the picture. To color in the background more fully, we must turn to European, not imperial, soil. The intellectual borrowing that characterized the development of security service procedures also extended to practices adopted by European states in the decades before World War I.

Let us take the French example first. Nineteenth-century France had well-established cryptographic agencies—or *cabinets noirs*—dedicated to code breaking and the refinement of sigint techniques.[95] The police forces of the Third Republic also took a lead in amassing secret civil and criminal records of the metropolitan population. From the outset, this criminal profiling focused disproportionately on immigrants, casual laborers, and vagrants, the assumption being that data on these "rootless" elements of society comprised an archive of antisocial behaviors inimical to the security of the state.[96] The most significant aspect of this information gathering was also the most prosaic: the development of the so-called Bertillon system of record keeping that enabled the state to maintain detailed files on individual citizens. Named after Alphonse Bertillon, the chief of the Paris police identification bureau, the Bertillon system was introduced in 1882 to store identification records of offenders detained at the Palais de Justice. Refined and expanded thanks to the introduction of fingerprinting techniques and photographic identification, police record keeping kept abreast of the growth in urban populations and the higher incidence of recorded crime that accompanied greater industrialization in the Belle Époque.[97]

While one impulse behind state surveillance was civil, another was military. The crushing defeat in the Franco-Prussian war in 1870 made the French officer corps of the early Third Republic acutely aware of the need to match the Prussian efficiency that characterized the army of a newly unified Germany. The result was a greater professionalization of French Army organization and training, a corollary of which was the development of a military intelligence system that worked in liaison with French police agencies in the monitoring of foreign residents, immigrant workers, and potential spies. This process also reflected the predominant social mores of the day. The official tendency to single out distinct communities as "dangerous classes" (a term coined in 1840s France) was, in some ways, a by-product of contemporary bourgeois assumptions that linked crime with social instability and political extremism. The severity of army repression of the Paris Commune in 1871 brought home just how savage state reaction could be against any lower-class Parisian deemed to show "criminal" and therefore subversive propensities.[98] Police agencies and military authorities in the early Third Republic associated social exclusion with indigence and dishonesty, identifying the marginalized not as victims but as authors of their own misfortune. It was but a short step from equating criminality with social instability to targeting political opponents as seditionists.[99]

In the colonial context, race joined class and economic indigence as markers of "dangerous" political proclivities. The more racially codified state surveillance in the colonial empire still drew on metropolitan precedents of intelligence gathering and riot policing. From the late 1870s, the War Ministry's deuxième bureau and the Paris Prefecture of Police began working together to monitor potential "subversives" living across metropolitan France. By the late 1880s, the deuxième bureau's statistical section directed French counterespionage operations as well. In 1888 its director, Colonel Jean Sandherr, an Alsatian from Mulhouse, began compiling the infamous lists of suspects to be detained in time of war: Carnet A for the alien population, and Carnet B for French citizens suspected of espionage. Members of the Gendarmerie nationale, mainly ex-servicemen serving in rural districts, as well as better-trained Sûreté officers, assisted the process, feeding information to the Interior and War Ministries.[100] The extent of the lists is staggering. In April 1899, Sandherr produced Carnet lists for consideration by the Supreme War Council that projected 65,000 arrests in Paris alone. On the eve of the Dreyfus case in 1894, this figure had been narrowed down to some 30,000, the reduction attributable to the abandonment of plans to detain immigrant families in purpose-built camps. Some 100,000 arrests nationwide were envisaged nonetheless.[101]

Why should these remarkable facts matter to a student of French colonial intelligence services? The answer is again one of past precedents adopted by colonial state authorities. In 1913 the Interior Ministry advised the Rabat Residency to adopt the Carnet system, thus extending it to cover the newest of France's Muslim territories.[102] In May 1914, Lyautey's staff duly complied, beginning the surveillance of those suspects on the Carnet lists who had moved from France to the Maghreb.[103]

The use of troops as last-resort adjuncts to the police in maintaining civil order in France before 1914 was another practice that reverberated through the empire in later years. Colonial policing in the interwar period was particularly redolent of the techniques of state repression developed to counteract subsistence crises in mid-nineteenth-century France. There were several features common to both. These included a numerically small bureaucracy reliant on local intermediaries for information, overstretched police and gendarmerie forces, particularly in rural areas, and a greater capacity to maintain order in and around large settlements where garrison forces could be called out quickly to supplement local police personnel.[104] The army's role as an instrument of state violence in the nineteenth century peaked with the extrajudicial killing of thousands of Communards in 1870, the bitter aftermath of which lingered into the early decades of the Third Republic as soldiers and gendarmes repeatedly clashed with striking industrial workers.[105] In common with a pattern later discernible in imperial territories, the focus of security force repression in Belle Époque France gradually shifted from town and countryside to larger industrial centers. The same shift would take place in French-controlled Muslim territories during the interwar years.

In other respects, however, protest policing and riot control developed differently in France and its Arab empire after 1918. Before World War I, the policing of strikes and other forms of civil protest in metropolitan France was notable for the sheer number of uniformed men deployed.[106] As Anja Johansen suggests, this could be interpreted in a positive light as a measure intended to minimize the likelihood of confrontation.[107] Whatever the case, organized protest in France was policed rather differently after the war ended. Whereas regular troops were customarily deployed to police industrial disputes in France before 1914, the professionalization of a mobile gendarmerie force—the *garde républicaine mobile*—after the war resulted in more limited use of the army in an internal security role on French streets in the interwar years. By contrast, in the French North African territories, troops were still called out on numerous occasions after 1918 to supplement urban police forces. Use of a dedicated, specialist gendarmerie force in the Maghreb was more limited, largely due to cost considerations. In Algeria and Tunisia, the local gendarmerie was funded from the local budget, leaving little room for the creation of a distinct, more mobile element. Troops thus remained the preferred reserve for riot control. Morocco followed suit in 1927 after the War Ministry withheld funding for the protectorate's gendarmerie units.[108]

The racial dynamics of colonial control were also prejudicial to the growth of a mixed-race gendarmerie. The North African governors were reluctant to admit naturalized *indigènes* into a paramilitary police force, an expedient that would have enabled force expansion at minimum wage costs, because they feared that Muslim gendarmes garrisoned in Maghreb cities might not be reliable in the event of serious urban disorder. In such cases, it seemed better to trust the army, whose colonial troops were under iron discipline and were typically deployed to regions outside their own locality.[109] Furthermore, according to a senior official in the Rabat Residency cabinet, even loyal

Muslims allegedly lacked the qualities of "finesse, tact, and subtlety" required of a proficient gendarme. More to the point, Muslim recruits were likely to resent being paid less than French colleagues for the same work, while French gendarmes might complain about additional competition for coveted postings.[110]

In the French and British cases then, it was colonial, not metropolitan, policing that retained a strongly martial flavor after 1918.[111] An organizing principle common to all such internal security tasks was that colonial forces, civil or military, be deployed quickly enough to contain disorder. Intelligence gathering was pivotal to this. Whatever their differing policing styles, the British and French imperial systems were broadly comparable in the high priority they each attached to the acquisition of intelligence about sources of dissent.

Wartime Developments

The facility with which the military authorities across the French and British empires adopted sophisticated techniques of popular surveillance after 1918 clearly owed a good deal to the experience of war in Europe and the concomitant fears that national unity would break under the strain. The war prompted greater systemization of metropolitan civil and military intelligence gathering and state counterespionage work.[112] Signals intelligence analysis, the interception of official, private, and commercial mail, military censorship, and the use of informant networks were integrated into the apparatus of the state. All the major combatants developed large military bureaucracies assigned to the surveillance of political opinion, fighting capacity, and morale among their troops.[113] Spurred by evidence of flagging frontline morale, soon confirmed by the spring mutinies that followed General Robert Nivelle's disastrous April offensive, in 1917 the French military *commissions de contrôle postale* analyzed soldiers' letters and, in turn, provided raw material for periodic deuxième bureau assessments of the mood in the trenches.[114] From modest beginnings in 1914, at the armistice four years later British postal censorship staff numbered some 4,861. And, as in the French case, British military headquarters staff also compiled regular summaries of troop morale drawing on material gleaned from intercepted mail.[115]

The warring governments also paid closer attention to civilian loyalty at home. With Home Office approval, Basil Home Thomson, the head of the British Special Branch monitored British ex-servicemen's associations for any evidence of revolutionary disaffection among men whose military training and combat experience made them a particular cause for state concern.[116] The surveillance techniques learned in the war years were neither forgotten nor abandoned at war's end. The aggregation of information on the attitudes of a particular section of the community, whether frontline troops, servicemen returnees, factory workers, or families awaiting loved ones, and the assessment of public opinion, always a more elusive and nebulous phenomenon, had proved its worth. By 1918, the Allied Supreme War Council was fed a monthly diet of Interior Ministry reports on French morale.[117] Covert surveillance had become a fact of political life.

As the focus of state attention returned once more to the civilian population, intelligence agencies, government departments, and, in the French case, prefectures continued to monitor local opinion. In peacetime the Western democracies frowned on the routine interception of private correspondence. But the emergence of opinion polls and mass observation techniques during the 1930s owed something to the earlier official obsession with public attitudes. As Peter Holquist has argued, the consolidation of the "national security states" that emerged between the wars thus took root during the Great War. Although Soviet Russia and Nazi Germany might spring to mind in this regard, administrative capacity to monitor the civilian population was by no means confined to dictatorial regimes.[118]

The parallels with the increasingly detailed *bulletins musulmans* (Muslim affairs information reports) compiled after 1918 by deuxième bureau staffs in Arab territories are striking. Generally, these were prepared by officers trained as Arab affairs specialists, many of whom had been recalled to the Western Front. The anonymity and collective nature of these reports makes it difficult to trace the careers of their authors. It is apparent nonetheless that many had recent wartime experience with censorship techniques, press analysis, and the evaluation of military morale. Systematic monitoring of Muslim public opinion was thorough and it was widely read. Net intelligence assessments provided regional commanders, colonial governments, and the Paris War Ministry with detailed information on local opinion, political trends, and sources of potential disorder, and were usually submitted on a fortnightly or monthly basis.[119]

The central bureaucracy of Muslim affairs specialists in Paris paralleled its colonial equivalent. The Muslim affairs divisions of the Ministry of Colonies and the War Ministry produced monthly—sometimes weekly—bulletins compiled by regional officials and army intelligence officers, many of whom were closely attuned to Muslim concerns in North and West Africa, Syria, and Lebanon. The Ministry of Colonies' Muslim affairs section was originally an army intelligence agency, but from 1911 it was staffed by civilian personnel. Until its establishment was cut back in 1935, the section compiled thrice-monthly reports for the Ministry's political affairs division on political trends, contacts between Islamic groups, and the Arabic press both in French territories and the Middle East more generally. In addition, it was the Muslim affairs section that liaised with other departments—the Quai d'Orsay, the War Ministry, the Ministry of Interior, the Prime Minister's

Figure 3. A 1923 RAF aerial photograph of the British garrison command's Baghdad headquarters complex on the banks of the Tigris River. TNA, AIR 23/7386. Crown copyright, reproduced courtesy of the National Archives, London.

office at the Hôtel Matignon—about possible threats to French authority in Muslim territories. The War Ministry's Africa-Levant section, created in January 1922 by the fusion of two previously separate bureaus, performed much the same function for the army staff. Just prior to the Rif War, in December 1924 this section was further expanded, becoming an advisory department for all Muslim overseas territories. By the mid-1920s, the Paris governmental establishment had no shortage of Arab specialists.[120]

Their British equivalents in the early 1920s were equally impressive. British Middle Eastern intelligence summaries were compiled by intelligence officers attached to the major British Middle Eastern commands in Cairo, Baghdad, and Jerusalem, and were distributed even more widely than their French counterparts. At the height of the Arab revolt, the *Arab Bulletin* prepared by the intelligence staff of the Arab Bureau in Cairo combined field intelligence with summaries of regional politics and more lengthy appreciations of social conditions, public opinion, and Hashemite prospects. Inevitably, these bulletins reflected the academic backgrounds of most Arab Bureau staff and the scholarly ambience in which they worked.[121] If this set a precedent, the Arab Bureau's respect for human intelligence gathered by the "men on the spot" established another. Both the academic, semianthropological style of the Arab Bulletin and the prominence given to field operatives' assessments permeated the style of intelligence collated by the British imperial authorities across the Middle East after the war. Reports of this kind were soon a matter of routine and were widely read by policy makers in home and imperial governments. By 1921, fortnightly political intelligence reports prepared by the Royal Air Force garrison command in Iraq, for example, were sent not only to interested departments—service ministries and the Colonial and Foreign Offices—in London, but also to neighboring imperial authorities in Transjordan, Palestine, and Egypt, as well as to the government of India and British consular officers across the Middle East.[122]

Why did this intelligence gain such a wide official audience so quickly? One reason was the distinctive nature of the Middle East imperial settlement after 1919. Behind the rhetoric, a key motivation of colonial rule was to facilitate European economic exploitation. In newly acquired Arab territories this long-term objective was sometimes obscured by the primordial duty to construct modern nation-states from the former Ottoman provinces placed under League of Nations mandate. The terms of the mandates set limits to the scope and the theoretical duration of French and British authority in Arab territories. But, in doing so, they revalorized the transformational impulse of imperial rule by explicitly linking European authority with social, political, and economic progress. The "tutelage" of subject peoples in the Middle East was justified as the most efficient means to ensure that they ultimately shared the fruits of European civilization.[123] In other words, the mandate principle legitimated economic development alongside the establishment of functioning bureaucratic systems and parliamentary institutions, making all these elements measures of imperial rule.[124]

Another abiding priority of the administrations in Damascus, Baghdad, and Amman was to establish the exact territoriality of the mandates, itself an essential prerequisite to statehood. French, British, or Arab sovereignty over the Middle East successor states required a clear demarcation of geographical boundaries.[125] But there was much more to statehood than a redrawing of maps.[126] The mandate regimes required new administrative apparatus, national policing and security services, and a revenue base to fund their operation.[127] Only then could the local governments impose their authority, often by force. In a very real sense, the mandate authorities bludgeoned their way into the Middle East. Those Arab elites that chose to collaborate with these new masters were sure to be accused by their own communities of condoning brutal methods over which they had little control.

Conclusion

As their imperial reach extended after World War I, imperial authorities were remarkably confident that the lessons of intelligence gathering in more established colonies were at least relevant, if not directly transferable, to very different societies. Abiding beliefs in various race theories help explain this. So, too, does awareness of the commonly held conviction among colonial officials that Muslim communities shared similar views of Europeans, of state power, and of respect for authority. Taken together, these unspoken assumptions encouraged officials to conclude that intelligence practices that "worked" in one setting before 1918 could work in another after it.

The adaptation of metropolitan and past colonial practices was particularly apparent in colonial policing, helping to define the scope and priorities of local forces.[128] John Willis, for example, connects past precedents to the use of the colonial police in Britain's southern Arabian territory of Aden as an instrument of colonial state building and capitalist modernization: "The policing of the economy, the enforcement of morality, the regulation of labor, the monitoring of the urban poor and other undesirables had its origins in years of practice in London and the other colonies."[129] The formulation of security policy in colonial states therefore came laden with the intellectual baggage of its practitioners. Their shared experiences helped to mold them into distinct intelligence communities united by their shared approach to colonial governance. Sometimes failing, sometimes succeeding in their efforts to maintain imperial order, these communities of practice were at the heart of security policing throughout the interwar years.

Seen from the perspective of intelligence gathering, the similarities between British and French administrative styles outweigh the differences. British indirect rule and French associationism traded on colonial officials' understanding of tribal hierarchies, religious affiliations, and the political economy of peasant societies still adjusting to the demands of export-driven colonial economic policies. In each case, acquiring local knowledge was pivotal to effective governance. Studies of indigenous culture, agriculture, judicial regulation, and the settlement of disputes, many of them initiated before the consolidation of European rule, continued throughout the colonial period and often beyond it as well.

Once the British conceded national independence to mandate Iraq in October 1932, for instance, a network of Interior Ministry advisers, itinerant police inspectors, and regional consuls continued to report on their Iraqi protégés.[130] This more elastic intelligence gathering system persisted after the 1935 ascent to power of the former leader of the anti-British opposition, Yasin al-Hashimi, until the outbreak of World War II wrought more fundamental change.[131] Put simply, indirect rule, associationism, and even the looser arrangements of postindependence clientage as in Iraq required an information order to work effectively. This conclusion emerges more strongly when one takes account of the tiny numbers of district officers deployed throughout vast swathes of the British and French empires. Although based on a geographical area outside the scope of this study,

Anthony Kirk-Greene's exhaustive study of district commissioners in British sub-Saharan Africa is relevant to us here. He makes plain that the so-called thin white line of colonial administration was incredibly slender.[132] Staff of the SPS, for example, nominally administered almost a million square miles of imperial territory and yet never numbered more than 125 at any point.[133] French officials in West, Central, and North Africa were certainly far more numerous, but even their total deployment seems small when measured against the numbers of population and the size of territory they administered. The four-part formula that Kirk-Greene proposes as the key to British district officers' success in the early twentieth century—coercion, collaborators, confidence, and competence—was itself predicated on another essential ingredient: the quality of the political information they obtained.[134]

3

CONSTRUCTING THE ENEMY

Intelligence, Islam, and Communism

This chapter investigates imperial intelligence gathering about ideologically driven unrest. It is also intended to provide some background to central threat perceptions that informed intelligence gathering and security policing in the specific crises of colonial control examined in subsequent chapters. Islamic piety and atheistic Marxist-Leninism may seem poles apart, but, from the perspective of intelligence analysts, they had much in common. Both attracted committed adherents who abhorred Western materialism and imperialist social theories. Each held the capacity to mobilize mass support. And both rejected a capitalist international system predicated on the supremacy of white-ruled empires. It was this internationalist dimension to Islamism and Communism that preoccupied French and British security services because it suggested that, whatever the relative local weaknesses of pan-Islamist and Comintern-organized anticolonial groups, their real strength lay elsewhere: in their appeal to colonial subjects to unite across imperial frontiers in opposition to European control. The estimates made by imperial intelligence communities about the nature of the enemies they faced must also be taken into account. It is for this reason that the chapter begins by considering how opponents of Britain and France's Middle Eastern imperial ventures were viewed, first in popular culture, and second in terms of stereotype.

Intelligence and Popular Culture

Intelligence providers never worked in a vacuum. The priorities, targets, and objectives of security surveillance often mirrored prevailing attitudes "back home" about perceived threats to society. Prominent among these was the place accorded the "spies," "fifth columnists," "terrorists," and "religious fanatics" in the metropolitan popular culture of the time. Take the British case.

Imperial exoticism and patriotic adventure, combined with science fictional speculation about the nature of future warfare, were recurrent themes in popular fiction and the serialized novellas of the penny press in Edwardian Britain. Authors as diverse as Rudyard Kipling, H. G. Wells, Erskine Childers, and Herbert Strang embraced this literary style. Their writings made their mark on public perceptions of empire and the optimum means to protect it.[1] In the same prewar decade, public suspicion of German immigrants, and alleged foreign subversives more generally, intensified. Fed by the Anglo-German naval race, alleged invasion threats, and growing "spy fever," particularly in the coastal counties of southeast England, greater governmental sensitivity to seditious elements among the immigrant population was pivotal to the establishment of Britain's modern secret service and the legislative measures enacted against resident aliens both before and immediately after the outbreak of war in August 1914.[2] As Nicholas Hiley suggests, the early methodology and threat perceptions of Britain's internal security service, MI5, were conditioned by fictional stereotypes of the foreign spy and the seditious foreign immigrant.[3] Such images nurtured public support for tighter surveillance of continental immigrants, German workers above all, on the eve of war.[4] In its pre-1914 heyday, spy fiction played on middle-class fears of social breakdown and imperial decline, invoking civic duty and individual heroism as the only salvation for a nation under threat. Whatever kudos attached to Britain's fledgling security service had little to do with the mundane clerical administration and endless personnel filing that characterized the bulk of covert intelligence work.[5]

Widening interest in the use of air power in imperial defense, stimulated by best selling novels and the popular press, also reflected sharper public awareness of British imperial and national insecurity after the South African War. Pressure groups advocating the development of military aviation, such as the Aerial League of the British Empire (established in 1909) and its companion Women's Aerial League, blended commonsense advocacy of the strategic potential of the airplane with more populist fantasy regarding the miraculous capacity of air power to reinvigorate indigenous respect for colonial authority.[6]

The popular images of colonial peoples cowed into submission by displays of the newest Western technology, and of German spies prowling British defense installations, made their mark on colonial intelligence gathering as well. After the shock of the Indian mutiny in 1857, British officials had fewer illusions about the thin ice of imperial prestige that separated them from the chill waters of public disorder.[7] This was particularly true in Muslim territories where the unifying force of pan-Islamism, proclaimed in the late nineteenth century by the Ottoman sultan Abdul-Hamid II, was considered a potent source of popular devotion transcending ethnic, tribal, or national loyalties.[8] David French has pointed out that fear of Muslim dissent even constrained British strategic planning prior to and during World War I until the loyalty of Muslim troops in the Indian Army was bloodily confirmed on the Western Front.[9] The stereotypical subversive nationalist dedicated to terrorist methods to overthrow colonial rule and operating in a cosmopolitan environment of internationally planned covert operations was not entirely a creature of myth. MI5 was immersed in covert surveillance and infiltration of Irish nationalist organizations long before the Easter Rising of 1916.[10] By 1914, Indian Ghadr Party revolutionaries mounted terrorist campaigns in India from their bases of operations in North America and Europe.[11] And wartime Ottoman pan-Islamic propaganda played on the literary tropes of the colonial religious fanatic, the spy, and the terrorist, making it harder still to disaggregate fact from fiction.

In the event, German efforts to foster sedition in India, Persia, and occupied Arab territories, much of it coordinated by the Foreign Ministry's Orient Intelligence Office (Nachrichtenstelle für den Orient), proved just as unrealistic as the contemporary British fears of a coherent pan-Islamist threat sponsored by the Turkish caliph.[12] If anything, the tendency among French and British imperial officials to discern a guiding German, Turkish, or Bolshevik hand behind emergent nationalist protest fostered undue complacency about the organizational capacities of Arab nationalists acting alone.[13] British examples illustrate this point well. Arguments between British governmental departments over the significance of pan-Islamism persisted throughout the early 1920s as senior intelligence officers in the Middle East disagreed over the extent of local support for the caliphate movement. The India Office surrendered jurisdictional control over Iraq in 1921, but continued to insist that pan-Islamism threatened imperial security in South Asia and the Persian Gulf. By contrast, the Colonial Office took a more sanguine view, inspired by the influx of former Foreign Office and Arab Bureau personnel to its Middle East Department. The former Arab Bureau chief Sir Gilbert Clayton was particularly dismissive of pan-Islamism, accusing those who took it seriously of ignorance of Arab grievances. In October 1923, Clayton, by then attached to the Palestine high commission in Jerusalem, took aim at the Secret Intelligence Service (SIS). SIS reportage on Middle East security was widely circulated in Whitehall, and increasingly contradicted Clayton's monthly Palestine intelligence summaries.[14]

Whereas Clayton ascribed Palestinian unrest to Jewish immigration, Muslim hostility to Zionism, and economic pressures on the peasantry, SIS claimed that pan-Islamic propaganda, sponsored by the Ankara government, triggered the growth in nationalist sentiment among Palestinians and Arabs more generally. There was an obvious explanation for this disparity. The SIS intelligence effort in the Middle East was essentially a by-product of its monitoring of Soviet sedition and Turkish irredentism. Drawing on sigint and agents' reports, SIS analysts therefore tended to view local political developments from the perspective of international strategic rivalry.[15] So, too, did the interministerial Anti-Bolshevik Committee, a Cabinet advisory body known for its insistence that pan-Islamism was externally directed and controlled. SIS reportage and Anti-Bolshevik Committee discussions paid little heed to socioeconomic and interethnic factors of a purely local nature, reducing Arab populations to mere instruments of interstate competition. Clayton relied far more on humint from local informants, analysis of the Arabic press, and the distillation of situation reports from district officers and the Palestine police. His was the more rounded view. As he put it, "There is a tendency in purely Intelligence Agencies to be attracted towards mysterious and occult organizations spreading their tentacles all over the world. The 'Black Hand' is a very fascinating bogey but sometimes it is advisable to look nearer home for the real source of trouble."[16]

If the threat of jihad against the European infidel was overestimated—there being no early twentieth-century equivalent to 'Abd al-Qadir's long-running resistance in western Algeria during the 1840s or the Madhist uprisings in Sudan forty years later—the emergence of mass politics and party-based nationalism posed a greater, if less sensational, threat to Western imperial control in North Africa and the Middle East. Nor were colonial security analysts entirely confident that the ghosts of earlier times had been laid to rest. In the immediate aftermath of World War I, French officials in Algiers were shocked by the rise to prominence of Amir Khaled, grandson of 'Abd al-Qadir and the first figurehead of Algerian national resistance in the twentieth century.[17] During the 1920s, the Sudan Political Service was similarly unnerved by the recrudescence of Madhism in northwest Sudan, an area theoretically pacified twenty years earlier.[18]

Intelligence Gathering and Stereotyping

Colonial intelligence gathering was not everywhere a matter of misperception and chimerical fears. Security services in the British and French empires recognized local variations, cultural differences, and complex social strata in the colonies under their charge. But in times of acute political crisis, security service personnel reverted to a simpler typology. When the colonial order was under threat, indigenous subjects were more often viewed monolithically as potentially, if not actually, dangerous rather than as a differentiated, heterogeneous national population among which only a tiny minority of individuals harbored seditious ideas. This conflation of the dependent population into the category of potential enemy—a classic case of "othering," in the language of postmodernist scholarship—reflected the underlying structural weakness of colonial states.[19]

The propensity to stereotype suggests that additional sources of information and new intelligence bureaus to process it did not invariably mean better analysis of local social conditions. Reportage was inevitably subjective, often heavily loaded toward a particular conclusion. The greater prevalence of information gathering in colonial government sometimes resulted in the accumulation of intelligence that merely reinforced long-standing prejudices by providing allegedly definitive evidence to confirm them. Statistics on property crime and intercommunal violence, reports of tribal feuding, evidence of low productivity in colonial industry, teachers' and missionaries' laments about the differential aptitudes of settler and indigenous children, and informants' often sensationalist summaries of inflammatory speeches by imams or Muslim politicians were grist for the mill of conservative colonial officials reluctant to cede more autonomy to local elites.

Here, of course, one confronts ideas of orientalism as defined by Edward Saïd and scholars of colonial discourse. Was colonial intelligence gathering always doomed to fail because it derived from flawed Western assumptions about Islam, Muslim societies, and non-European culture more generally? Were the personnel of imperial security agencies stymied by racial prejudice and cultural arrogance, and therefore doomed to read things wrong? Could the many Arab specialists in colonial government that held genuine reverence for Middle Eastern cultures ever be more than outsiders looking in, constrained by the inescapable influences of their own cultural backgrounds? In short, was the process of colonial intelligence gathering little more than an exercise in "othering" dependent populations? If so, then its claims to objectivity and shrewd anticipation of sources of dissent were inevitably wrongheaded. In this reading of events, all intelligence assessment was skewed by the preexisting beliefs and cultural outlook of information providers, intelligence assessors, and policymakers. Surely, evaluations of ethnic minorities, tribal confederations, or political movements were similarly unbalanced by the tendency to define such groups through the prism of orientalist assumptions about Islam, Arabs, and other non-European races? If so, then any historical reading of imperial intelligence analysis in the interwar years is bound to reveal more about the cultural milieu of the intelligence gatherers than about the subjects of their reports.

The interpretative problems that arise from considering the "orientalist gaze" of some colonial intelligence analysts are essentially matters of degree. It is incumbent on any scholar of colonial societies to watch for evidence of stereotyping and crass misrepresentation of indigenous peoples in the evidential base they use. And it seems dangerous to dismiss all information gathered by colonial states because it is riddled with recurrent stereotypes, racist characterizations, and inherent bias. The fact remains that intelligence, even flawed and manifestly biased intelligence, was the raw material for security policy formulation and colonial decision making. Conversely, it seems equally dangerous to adapt Foucault's complex ideas about the connections between knowledge and power to colonial security agencies by asserting that the information imparted by intelligence providers automatically conferred power on the colonial authorities. These were never simple equations. High-quality intelligence assessment took into account the reliability of the source and the opinions of those individuals responsible for collating information. Yet even the most useful intelligence had its limitations. Some information had only transitory importance. Some could not be acted on for want of local resources or state sanction. And most of the information garnered by agencies of government acquired value only as part of a larger whole. The individual significance of the array of statistics, demographic surveys, police reports, policy advice, and intelligence decrypts collected by colonial states was not always immediately apparent, but was always more than the sum of its parts.

The shrewder intelligence analysts inside colonial governments knew that the best intelligence about prevailing opinion tended to be an accumulation of open-source humint inconspicuously gathered by the observation of social behavior and workaday conversations. Information acquired amid the informal cultural networks of social communication among Muslim men was especially valued. According to the Algiers military intelligence bureau, evidence accumulated in social milieus where men chatted freely was bound to be most reliable. Take, for example, the bureau's assessment of Muslim cafés:

> Throughout Algeria, in village settlements and tribal gathering points, one space is always reserved for communal discussion, something highly valued by this race of orators and political leaders. That space is the Moorish café (café maure). Neither the ministerial commissions of inquiry nor the tourist parties that take such an interest in the customs of these "primitives," nor even the investigators sent to discover the root causes of Muslim attitudes that settlers cannot explain, ever bother to stop in such establishments, which seem bland and uninviting. But long before the establishment of village councils (djemâas de douars), Muslim clubs in the major towns, or the development of an independent Arabic press, news, political ideas, and public opinion all took shape in the cafés' smoky atmosphere.[20]

It was perhaps an obvious point, but one that was often lost by more senior officials: to understand the indigenous population—and avoid the worst of stereotyping—one had to move among it.

World War I and Fears about Muslim Loyalty

For eminently practical reasons, then, imperial powers tried to turn the potency of local religious culture against their rivals while harnessing the power of religious devotion to the colonial system. Colonial states and their external enemies claimed to be committed defenders of Islam as each sought to gain advantage among Muslims living under Western rule. The high point of this process occurred during World War I and was bound up with the disintegration of Ottoman power in the Middle East, but the aftereffects of this competition for Muslim loyalty reverberated throughout the 1920s.[21] British colonial governments always monitored the connections between Islamic foundations, Sufi brotherhoods, and leading 'ulamā in all their Muslim territories.[22] By 1914, however, the Muslim population of British India consumed by far the most attention. Germany's support for Indian revolutionaries built on attachment to the Ottoman caliphate movement among Punjabi Muslims.[23] Both issues obsessed the British authorities in Delhi. Although primarily concerned by sedition within India, the governors of the Raj also fretted about support for pan-Asianism more generally. The marked growth of pan-Islamism in China in the years following the Xinhai revolution in 1911 therefore became an additional cause for concern.[24]

If India was Britain's main Muslim obsession, for France it was North Africa and, more particularly, its still-contested prize, the Moroccan protectorate. The massive expansion of German and, to a lesser extent, Ottoman support for Moroccan resistance to French rule occasioned by the outbreak of war in 1914 precipitated a commensurate growth in the protectorate's security apparatus. Settler pressure across French North Africa for state repression of reformist movements also mounted. Elite Muslim groups such as the Young Algerians faced more stringent surveillance. Their modernist aspirations and links with like-minded reformists from Egypt and the Ottoman provinces nurtured colonists' fears of a pan-Arab plot to evict European populations from the Maghreb.[25] From the rebellious Berber tribes of the Rif interior to the protonationalist and generally pan-Islamic supporters of the Young Turk movement, the war rekindled Muslim hopes that the consolidation of French imperial control could be reversed. The transfer of Armée d'Afrique divisions to the Western Front and the organization of a German network in neutral Spanish territory to foment disorder in Morocco placed unprecedented strain on the military intelligence service within the French protectorate.[26]

Lyautey feared that the pacification previously achieved would be swiftly undone by the withdrawal of military manpower. He was thus determined to conceal the actual fragility of colonial state power by proving that French prestige remained intact. This was no easy task. As he complained to Minister of War Alexandre Millerand in June 1915, it required immense effort to convince the sultan, loyalist *caïds,* and tribal leaders that France would emerge victorious. His conclusion was simple: foreign sedition could undermine French authority just as swift repression of seditionists could reinforce it.[27]

Several other factors complicated the task of regulating contacts between a subject Muslim population and disruptive external influences. One was the insecurity of Maghreb frontiers. Another was the movement of traders and Islamic pilgrims to foreign markets and the holy cities of the Hijaz. But the one that aroused most security service concern was the growing appeal of pan-Islamic ideology in the early twentieth century, particularly in Cairo and the major cities of the Ottoman Middle East. As Edmund Burke has demonstrated, before World War I began, pan-Islamic groups, most notably the Cairo-based *al-ittihad al-maghribi,* were active in French North Africa. And the reformist modernization espoused by the Young Turk movement was beginning to resonate among the urban elites of Morocco.[28] During the war itself, while the guiding associationist principles of Lyautey's administration were never entirely abandoned, the protectorate security services clamped down on dissidence and chased down foreign agents in a covert espionage war.

The rapid internment of those German civilians still in Morocco in late 1914 was a testament to the seriousness with which Lyautey's administration regarded the subversive activities of the Central Powers. At the apex of this intelligence war stood established Moroccan leaders, including the ex-sultan 'Abd al-Hafiz, who was interned by the French authorities at El Escorial, having been courted by German agents and the French intelligence service alike, and Amir 'Abd al-Malik, a son of the Algerian resistance hero Amir 'Abd al-Qadir, who, with German backing, maintained a rebel force of more than one thousand men in the eastern Rif throughout 1914–18. In northern, central, and southern Morocco, separate resistance forces contested French control throughout the First World War thanks in large part to the German material support they received.[29] French success in containing and ultimately quelling these diffuse movements amounted to a victory for the counterintelligence services of the French Army. Close tracking of German agents, interception of arms consignments, and effective counterpropaganda condemned German-Turkish efforts to undermine the protectorate to failure. The victory was, at best, partial. Only dimly understood during the war years, the longstanding cultural and educational ties between Morocco's educated elite and the 'ulamā of Cairo's influential al-Azhar University were more significant than German or Ottoman propaganda in sustaining an Islamic cultural purism that spurned European imperial control.[30]

In Algeria, too, colonial surveillance increased owing to official fears of the adverse consequences of European war, the withdrawal of military units from the colony, and, above all, the introduction of extended conscription to adult males. The North African imperial administrations tightened censorship regulations, imposing bans on Arabic newspapers, Islamic pamphlets, and Muslim soldiers' accounts of life in the trenches.[31] Local authorities in French North Africa and the predominantly Muslim colonies of Afrique Occidentale Francaise (AOF) were also instructed to restrict the dissemination of information about casualty rates on the Western Front.[32] Wounded colonial troops were increasingly transferred to secure compounds behind the lines in southern France to recuperate rather than being immediately repatriated for fear that their recollections and mere appearance might provoke disorder. Echoes of earlier intelligence panics persisted, it being assumed by the interministerial commission of Muslim affairs that uncontrolled rumor among colonial communities about the sacrifice of African soldiers in the trenches could unleash a revolt.[33]

Army censors were especially anxious to discover any indications of dissent arising from the heavy manpower demands of French conscription in Morocco and Algeria, the eastern department of Constantine and the Berber highlands of Kabylia above all. Between 1914 and 1918 at least 173,000 Algerian troops were recruited for service on the Western Front (some 3.6 percent of the Muslim population). Casualty rates were high—14.5 percent—but broadly in line with the rates for settler recruits. Government anxiety about popular resistance to conscription in Algeria intensified as the numbers killed grew inexorably and the demand for new recruits increased.[34] Serious but isolated disorders did occur, most notably in the Aurès Mountains in November 1916. Across the colony as a whole, crime rates were generally read as the most reliable indicator of Muslim hostility to military service. The Algiers government scrutinized infractions of the Muslim legal code to see whether conviction rates and the number of fines imposed showed any marked variation from the prewar position. In fact, in both cases, the relevant figures showed a marked decline for 1914–15.[35]

The Arab affairs specialists who read soldiers' mail struggled to persuade military superiors, determined to snuff out the first whiffs of rebellion, that Muslim opinion in French Africa remained as diffuse and complex as ever. The Algiers military intelligence office, for example, set little store by the formal professions of loyalty to France made by Muslim politicians, community leaders, and urban notables in August 1914. Service de Renseignements (SR) analysts preferred instead to gauge opinion in city mosques, Koranic schools, and Arab cafés. Soldiers' songs, the jokes doing the rounds among Muslim workers, and the Arab poetry sometimes recited in *cafés maures* offered a more reliable guide to popular attitudes to the war. Such cultural diversity was all very well, but the urgency of the war effort demanded instant analysis of opinion, not the academic surveys of social interaction to which Arabist intelligence officers were accustomed. On the one hand, the increased surveillance of Muslim populations in wartime conditions added to the bank of information on local politics available to colonial authorities in North and West Africa. On the other hand, the pressures of war stimulated a more reductive reading of indigenous society. The rituals and customs of Islamic observance took on a more threatening aspect to colonial officials nervous that their incessant demands for military and economic sacrifice might breed a violent counterreaction. Protests among Muslim colonial troops at the military authorities' occasional failure to observe Islamic burial rites for fallen comrades were taken as evidence of a deeper racial malaise among predominantly North African units suffering appalling losses.[36]

France, Intelligence, and Islam

In the context of religious opposition to the colonial presence, the war marked a watershed between what Fanny Colonna characterized as primarily tribal resistance and the shift toward urban-based religious opposition to French colonialism. In simple terms, across French North Africa, Sufism gave way to the puritanical Islam of the 'ulamā as the focal point for religious resistance to French rule.[37] Immediately after World War I, the Islamic reformism—or *salafiyya* movement—that linked the doctrinal renewal of Islam to socioeconomic modernization of Muslim states made a dramatic impact across the Maghreb. By the 1930s, Algeria's reformist 'ulamā, the foremost proponents of *Salafī* teaching in North Africa, called for Muslims to rediscover the purity of early Islam. From its inception in 1931, the Association of Reformist 'Ulamā pursued a vigorous educational campaign that identified French colonialism as the original cause of the debasement both of Algeria's "true religion" and of its authentic Muslim identity.[38] Prior to this, 'Abd el-Krim's Rif rebels were enthusiastic *Salafīs*. And Tunisia's Destour ("Constitution") movement, established in 1920, drew on the *Salafī* teachings of its founder, Sheikh 'Abd al-Aziz al-Thalaabi. Al-Thalaabi regarded the restoration of Tunisia's 1859 constitution as essential to reversing the deleterious impact of French rule on Tunisia's Muslim national identity.[39] His ideas were not pan-Islamic in inspiration, but indicative of an emergent nationalism capable of straddling the political-religious divide in Tunisia. Yet the fact that al-Thalaabi's influence stemmed from his religious authority immediately placed him within a spectrum of intelligence assessment inclined to view Islamic leaders differently from "ordinary" politicians. This was itself a product of the intelligence community's understanding of pan-Islamism.

French hostility to pan-Islamist and nationalist organizations in North Africa stemmed from these groups' capacity to mobilize Muslim opinion against the colonial state. This was especially galling because the colonial authorities maintained that France was a colonial power uniquely sensitive to the centrality of Islam in subject societies of the *dar al-Islam* (world of

Islam).[40] During the 1890s, French officials in the Maghreb even mooted the idea of a Franco-Muslim alliance to defend Islam against other imperial powers and meanwhile assist French penetration of western Sudan, Mauritania, Niger, and Chad.[41] By 1914, such ambitions seemed woefully overoptimistic.

The proliferation of imperial intelligence networks devoted to Islamism during World War I built on the foundations of colonial surveillance laid before the conflict began. Fear of pan-Islamism became more prevalent among Western colonial officials after the accession of Abdül Hamid II as the Ottoman sultan in 1876. The pan-Islamic ideal of transnational Muslim unity, rendered in Turkish as *Ittihad-i Islam,* or in Arabic as *wahdat al-Islam* or *al-Wahda al-Islamiyya,* was widely understood throughout the Muslim world. But the various constructions that intelligence analysts placed on such concepts had a decidedly European flavor. Indeed, the representation of pan-Islamism owed more to the fertile imaginations of specialist officials and sensationalist journalism than to any significant evidence of organized pan-Islamist opposition to Western imperialism among the Muslim community, or *umma.*[42]

Security service fears of a fanatical, populist, and potentially global movement capable of engulfing colonial territories from Morocco, through the Near East, to the Indian subcontinent and the Dutch East Indies were certainly overcooked. In fact, the broad appeal to Muslim unity inherent in pan-Islamism was often at variance with the particular socioeconomic circumstances that drove local communities to resist colonial rule. As so often in such matters, however, there was a kernel of truth to what were otherwise wildly exaggerated threat assessments. As a distinctive anti-Western philosophy that transcended ethnic, linguistic, and class boundaries, pan-Islamism had a unique capacity to mobilize Muslim opinion against European imperialism.

It was this transnational dimension that drove French and British colonial authorities to construct pan-Islamism as a uniquely menacing oppositional force. In this sense, pan-Islamism shared much in common with other forms of "primary resistance" among African peoples south of the Sahara, driven by the colonial presence to organize along lines of race and nation rather than tribe and locality.[43] Pan-Islam seemed capable of uniting town and countryside and even distinct tribes whose fierce territoriality and collective traditions, whether genealogical or political, had previously been regarded as barriers to national consciousness and state formation in Arab lands.[44]

Furthermore, Ottoman support for pan-Islam as a means to undermine— or at least retard—European encroachment in Muslim lands was altogether more tangible. In the first decade of the twentieth century, German financial backing and covert military aid for Ottoman projects to weaken both the

French grip on Morocco and British dominance in Egypt lent greater urgency to French and British security service surveillance of pan-Islamist supporters among the indigenous ruling elite of the sultan's *makhzen* administration and the Egyptian *khedive.*[45] Hence, another outcome of these anxieties was the creation of new networks of intercolonial intelligence contacts.

It was against this background that state surveillance of foreign-sponsored sedition developed rapidly in France's Muslim territories in the first two decades of the twentieth century, and extended southward to the French West African federation in the early 1920s. A government decree of 15 March 1923 established a federal military intelligence service in Dakar and thus completed the network of centralized intelligence bureaus throughout France's predominantly Muslim dependencies.[46] In October of the following year, Edouard Daladier, then the minister of colonies in Edouard Herriot's Cartel des Gauches government, reformed the Ministry's Muslim affairs service to ensure that its intelligence on the political activities of Muslim subjects was transmitted more rapidly to the political affairs directorate, and thence to the minister. Daladier justified these changes by reference to the growing support for pan-Islam in North and West Africa.[47]

French imperial authorities produced better-informed policy appreciations when local informers and district administrators were used to gather the raw intelligence on which these were based. By the 1920s there was a weight of experience to prove this. Members of the Algerian immigrant community in Greater Syria had supplied information to French consular staff throughout the late nineteenth century. By 1908, the Damascus consulate relied on its network of local Algerian agents to provide its most valuable humint on regional disorder.[48] The network of French Catholic and secular Mission Laïque educational establishments in the Fertile Crescent became a recruiting ground for local informants on events in Greater Syria during World War I. Missionaries fed information to the French authorities throughout the war. The risks involved were considerable and Turkish punishment severe. Once the conflict began, Ahmet Cemal Pasha's Fourth Army administration in Damascus singled out missionaries, and the Christian population of Greater Syria more generally, as potentially disloyal. Many were expelled, sent into internal exile, or imprisoned. But some still provided valuable intelligence on local political conditions. Antonin Jaussen, a Catholic priest and respected archaeologist, was assigned to French naval intelligence in 1915 and used his new posting to monitor events in wartime Transjordan until the Hashemite takeover. As Eugene Rogan puts it, "Jaussen effected a seamless transformation from the scholar priest moving through the stations of the Latin missionary network in pursuit of knowledge, to the dynamite priest providing accurate intelligence and running a team of informers through the same missionary network."[49]

Elsewhere, local networks of information about Arab opinion did little to correct exaggerated estimates of the strength of pan-Islamism. In the years immediately preceding the formal establishment of France's Moroccan protectorate in 1912, military intelligence analysts in Paris and their counterparts in General Lyautey's occupation forces saw the specter of widespread support for the ideal of a self-governing *umma* lurking behind Muslim opposition to French colonial penetration. This was especially worrisome because any movement that cut across tribal boundaries and social hierarchies threatened to undermine the incipient French policy of divide and rule. Yet the identification of pan-Islamism as a threat to the Western presence in the Maghreb also revealed just how much the French authorities had still to learn about the political ties and cultural practices of their Muslim subjects. Ironically, intelligence gathering often promoted misconceptions about a Muslim population rather than a deeper understanding of Maghrebi society. In this instance, intelligence reports of pan-Islamist activity led Lyautey's subordinates to conflate local Muslim grievances over French intrusion with implacable organized resistance to the French presence.

Seven years elapsed between the first Moroccan crisis in 1905 and Colonel Charles Mangin's decisive defeat of Moroccan tribal levies in the Sous Valley at Sidi Bou Outhman in September 1912. Mangin's victory assured French occupation of Marrakech and, thus, the survival of the fledgling protectorate. As Edmund Burke has shown, it also represented the defeat of a pan-Islamist secret society, Maghreb Unity (*al-ittihad a-maghribi*). Maghreb Unity was shaped by a multiplicity of foreign influences. Ottoman diplomatic pressure on the Moroccan sultanate and the presence of Turkish military advisers in Morocco were perhaps the most obvious. During World War I, German and Spanish efforts to subvert French control through provision of funds, arms, and supply routes to Maghreb Unity activists, Ottoman military advisers, and dissident Moroccan tribes also played their part.[50] But the long-standing cultural and educational ties between Morocco's educated elite and the 'ulamā of Cairo's influential al-Azhar University held the more lasting significance.[51]

Governmental concerns about a pan-Islamist rebellion inevitably intensified once the Western Allies went to war against Ottoman Turkey in October 1914. The campaign against the world's preeminent Muslim state stimulated fears among colonial officials from as far afield as Senegal, southern Libya, and the Anglo-Egyptian Sudan of a recrudescence in anticolonial millenarianism among Muslim tribes hostile to the presence of European infidels in their midst. The stereotypical image of fanatical pan-Islamist sedition survived.[52]

The French reacted most strongly, seeking out intelligence about how Muslim colonial subjects were reacting to the Allied campaign against Ottoman Turkey, support for the caliphate movement, and any signs of unrest at the casualties suffered by Muslim colonial units in Flanders.[53] Their consular staff, spies, and Sûreté officers tracked the meetings and statements of pan-Islamist activists in neutral Switzerland.[54] The War Ministry Muslim affairs division sifted through the Arabic press, enemy propaganda, and censored mail sent to and from Muslim units on the Western Front, trying to pinpoint evidence of sedition as well as more general indications of Muslim sentiment. Meanwhile, the Africa division of the French general staff continued to monitor links between German diplomats, couriers and agents, and dissident tribes in northern Morocco. Lyautey's occupation corps, depleted by the war's incessant manpower demands, exploited the intelligence gathered to concentrate its remaining forces in potential trouble spots such as the northern Rif, the Anti-Atlas, and the Saharan approaches of Tilifalet. Payments of preemptive subsidies to wavering tribal leaders were made on the basis of humint received about tribal loyalties. But it was the image intelligence provided by aerial reconnaissance that led to most punitive operations against dissident tribes. At the time of the armistice in November 1918, tribal *harka* massing for attacks on loyalist Berber clans faced repeated aerial bombardment.[55] Further south in Mauritania, colonial pacification was interrupted by the war. Here, too, the skeletal staff of the military garrison and governor's office relied on humint gathered among remote tribal populations to forestall rebellion. In August 1919, the Ministry of Colonies applauded France's administrator-in-chief in Mauritania for his success in thwarting Germany's wartime attempts to foment disorder among dissentient Touareg clans.[56]

In the immediate postwar years, in Algeria especially, military intelligence officers were never confident that Muslim loyalty to France was deeply rooted. A little-noticed article published in the *Revue Africaine* in 1932 discussed one of the wartime SR's favorite sources: the most popular Arabic and Berber folk songs to emerge in Algeria during 1914–18. It concluded that most were highly politicized and profoundly Francophobe. Several pilloried France as a nation in decline next to German power. Others lamented the predations of French recruiters. Still others questioned Muslim involvement in an essentially European conflict. Stimulated, in part, by the murderous Muslim pogrom against the Jewish population in Constantine in August 1934, in November of the following year the Algiers deuxième bureau reviewed the development of Muslim opinion in the colony during the final two years of World War I. Here again, the conclusions conflicted with the official rhetoric of unity and common sacrifice. France, it seemed, had got off lightly. Between 1915 and 1917 the Algiers authorities contained sporadic rebellions in Kabylia and the Aurès mountains that could easily have engulfed Algeria's three departments.[57] In May 1923, four and a half years after the armistice, the Algiers native affairs service still warned of a profound, emotive "turkophilia" among Algeria's

Muslims, whose respect for Turkey as the one Muslim state independent of European control increased even as Atatürk's avowedly secular regime took shape.[58]

It was a similar story in neighboring Morocco. The sultanate's leading Islamic scholars, *makhzen* officials, and urban notables paid close attention to the politics and religious pronouncements of al-Azhar staff after World War I, as did the leadership of the Syrian-Palestine Congress, itself based in Cairo from 1921.[59] The Egyptian capital thus remained a focal point for pan-Islamic propaganda, helping to sustain interest in the caliphate question throughout the early 1920s among the Muslims of French North Africa, Syria, and Lebanon. SR analysts in Beirut and Damascus were particularly exercised by Cairo's eclectic anti-imperialist groups. Both the SR and the Levant Sûreté explored the international connections between Cairo's political émigrés, convinced that the Syrian-Palestine Congress acted as a sort of pan-Arabist Comintern, issuing directives and policy guidelines to nationalist parties across the Arab world. In pan-Arabism and Islamic anti-Westernism, SR staff in Beirut perceived a more sinister threat, fueled by German, Turkish, and British intrigue, which nourished the francophobia among Syria's Muslims. In a lengthy report on "The Present Dangers of Islam" sent to the War Ministry on 25 September 1921, the Beirut SR tied the threads of Syrian nationalism, Sharifian monarchism, economic protest, and tribal disorder to an overarching rejection of Western values inherent in Islamic observance. Their nightmarish prognosis was that in stirring popular hostility to French rule, the German, Kemalist, or British sponsors of Arabism might unleash a jihad against European imperialism. There was scant evidence to support this conclusion. But the fact remained that the Levant SR considered the threat of an Islamic uprising very real.[60]

The unifying potential of either pan-Islam or the restoration of a caliph independent of external control should not, however, be exaggerated, even if numerous intelligence appreciations suggested otherwise. This was a point forcefully made by the French legation in Cairo in a memorandum dripping with exasperation and sent in February 1929, after a decade of relentless diplomatic reportage of popular support for pan-Islamic idealism across North Africa. The Cairo diplomatic team stressed that particularist nationalism, modeled on Atatürk's secular Turkish republic, exerted a stronger influence on opponents of European imperial control than any abstract allegiance to a global Muslim community.[61] The decline of pan-Islam accelerated in the early 1930s, by which time secularist pan-Arabism, a more clearly articulated Arab nationalism, and Muslim anger at British policy in Palestine eclipsed pan-Islamism and the appointment of a new caliph as triggers to international contacts between Muslim politicians and community leaders.[62]

The Cairo legation was correct in its analysis of the declining power of pan-Islam, but wide of the mark in its implied criticism of Quai d'Orsay interpretation of it. By 1925, the Foreign Ministry's Muslim affairs service, for one, spoke of pan-Islamism with a pronounced historical tone, treating it as an inchoate movement whose appeal was fast diminishing. The Ministry of Colonies, too, was increasingly sanguine in its assessment of the internationalist potential of popular Islamic devotion in the sub-Saharan territories under its control. Strongly influenced by Maurice Delafosse's anthropological approach to religious observance in West Africa, colonial officials and SR officers in AOF tended to stress the local particularities of West African Islam over and above any politicized loyalty to the *umma*. The persistence of popular Sufism based on worship of revered saints and holy men was frequently cited in official reports as affirmation that the cultural barriers separating Arab Islam from its southerly African cousin were as broad as the physical expanses of desert between them.[63] This is not to suggest that pan-Islamism was not taken very seriously indeed by colonial security services. Nonetheless, its long-term importance seemed to reside in the international networks of inter-Muslim contacts to which it gave rise during and after World War I. These networks were singled out as the precedent for similar internationalist links between pan-Arabists and Communist supporters in the Maghreb and the Levant mandates from the early 1920s onward.[64]

Abdelkadir Ben Ghabrit and the Paris Mosque

Security service anxiety over pan-Islam shook official confidence about France's imperial skills as a governor of Muslim peoples, but did not destroy it. Indeed, the high point of French assertiveness as a successful Muslim power was probably 1922. The crowning achievement of France's Muslim policy was the highly publicized ceremony that attended the laying of the foundations of the Paris Mosque on 19 October of that year. In his opening address, Abdelkadir Ben Ghabrit, head of the mosque's committee of patrons, looked forward to a new era of Franco-Muslim cooperation in fulfillment of France's imperial mission as "protector of Islam."[65]

Abdelkadir Ben Ghabrit personified the ideal Muslim auxiliary to France's North African colonialism. Vilified by Messali Hadj's Algerian nationalist followers in the Étoile Nord-Africaine (ENA) as a *Beni Oui-Oui*, or supplicant "yes man," Ben Ghabrit was an invaluable intermediary to the imperial authorities. He was born in the market town of Tlemcen, Algeria, ironically also the birthplace of Messali Hadj, who remained his most vociferous critic. In the 1890s, Ben Ghabrit entered French administrative service as a translator at the French legation in Tangiers. A series of high-profile appointments followed. In 1901 he served on the Franco-Moroccan commission appointed to delimit the Algeria-Morocco frontier. Five years later he assisted the French delegation at the Algeciras Conference. In

1907, Ben Ghabrit was assigned to the French expeditionary force in Morocco to help organize the sultanate's police forces. As liaison to Sultan Abdul Aziz, Ben Ghabrit then helped secure the sultanate's acceptance of the 30 March 1912 Treaty of Fez confirming France's protectorate over Morocco. General Lyautey, by then a personal friend, rewarded him with the post of chief of protocol to the sultan. During World War I, Ben Ghabrit secured another prestigious posting, as head of the French diplomatic mission to Mecca, whose objective was to persuade the malik of the Hijaz to break with the Turks and embrace the Allied cause.

Ben Ghabrit's wartime experience in the Hijaz helped assure his elevation in August 1919 to the presidency of the Société des habous des villes saintes, a Muslim cultural association based in Algiers and dedicated to the promotion of pilgrimage to the holy cities by the Maghrebi faithful.[66] Ben Ghabrit soon added further prestigious titles to his portfolio. It was thanks to one of these—the directorship of the Paris Muslim Institute, founded in 1920—that Ben Ghabrit achieved greater prominence in his native Algeria. As director, Ben Ghabrit spearheaded efforts to complete the Paris Mosque, which finally opened in May 1926.[67] His tireless lobbying for the Paris Mosque marked the culmination of an illustrious career as diplomat, envoy, and patron of Muslim culture. But what concerns us here is another facet of that career. Intelligence provision was a common thread linking each stage of Ben Ghabrit's professional work.

Throughout his public life, Ben Ghabrit furnished the French authorities with sensitive information about Muslim opinion. In the 1920s, the Quai d'Orsay's Africa-Levant division rated him one of their most trusted Arab informants.[68] From his early assignment in Tangiers, through his years in Rabat, to the wartime mission to Mecca and his postwar support for the Maghrebi immigrant community in Paris, Ben Ghabrit was always called on to provide intelligence about what his Arab clients thought of French supervision. In April 1920, for instance, he drew on his additional connections to elite Muslim opinion across North Africa acquired through the Société des habous des villes saintes, to provide the French premier and foreign minister Alexandre Millerand with a twenty-three-page report on Muslim attitudes to France across North Africa and the Levant. Not surprisingly, Ben Ghabrit's analysis was heavily tinged with special pleading for the conservative Arab notables and Islamic scholars then vying for a greater stake in the local administration of empire. His counsel was pragmatic. It would be prudent for French imperial authorities to concede increased administrative autonomy, more widespread use of Arabic in rudimentary education, and greater educational opportunities for the sons of the elite, both to consolidate French control and set France's Muslim policy apart from that of its British rival. As Ben Ghabrit put it, a wise industrialist did not wait for a strike to occur before granting improved conditions to his workforce. But his principal conclusion was that the Foreign Ministry should lend its support to the creation of the Paris Muslim Institute because it would bring an invaluable intelligence dividend. A central pillar of the cultural networks linking Muslim elite opinion throughout the empire, the Institute would serve equally well as a clearinghouse for all manner of political intelligence about France's Muslim subjects.[69] Abdelkadir Ben Ghabrit was the ultimate elite auxiliary of the intelligence state system.

Construction of Ben Ghabrit's beloved mosque and the nearby Islamic Institute was funded in large part by contributions from Muslim territories. Staff costs and educational programs for illiterate Muslim immigrants, as well as for French-speakers eager to learn vernacular Arabic, were also funded by foreign donation.[70] This was no protection against the hardship of the Depression. By 1931, the mosque and the Islamic Institute were in serious financial trouble. Mosque officials pleaded with colonial governments to increase their annual subvention to both institutions to prevent them from going under.[71] Only the Bibliothéque France-Orient, a Paris academic library assured of Foreign Ministry funding, entered the 1930s certain of its survival.[72]

Financially insecure it may have been, but by 1930 the Paris Mosque was part of the fabric of French security intelligence. The speed with which this occurred owed much to Ben Ghabrit, but it also tells us something deeper. By the 1930s, the French security services rarely suffered from a lack of information about their Muslim subjects; quite the reverse. A more fundamental problem for the imperial authorities was to synthesize the mass of incoming intelligence about Muslim populations quickly enough to generate useful policy advice. In Tunisia, one of France's smaller Muslim territories, Resident General Marcel Peyrouton conceded in February 1935 that his general secretariat was swamped with native affairs reports. The central administration simply could not process the mass of information about local politics provided by Tunisia's *contrôleurs civils*, still the cornerstone of the protectorate's Muslim affairs system.[73] The root problem, however, was political, not bureaucratic. Whatever the difficulties in sifting information, there was no shortage of incoming intelligence about Muslim politics, just a refusal by colonial governments to act on it.

Could the same be said regarding Communism, another long-term preoccupation of the security services?

Intelligence and Communism

Fear of Communism was integral to the huge expansion in colonial intelligence reportage in the interwar years. By the mid-1920s the plethora of analysts' appreciations of pan-Islamism and oppositional Muslim groups was matched by a constant stream of surveillance reports and predictive threat assessments about the dangers of Communist subversion in the Arab world. The limited numerical strength of Communist parties in Arab territories bore no correlation to the degree of security service interest in their activities in the French and British empires. Anxiety about potential growth of grassroots Communism was bound up with wider uncertainty about the consequences of industrialization, urbanization, and proletarianization for colonial societies.[74]

Before we focus on the French experience, a sideways glance at British territories will tell us something about imperial threat assessments regarding the spread of Communism. British strategic planners were unnerved by the sheer geographical scope of Soviet interests, a fear compounded by the Soviet Union's ideological rejection of the postwar international system.[75] As for the Middle East, Colonial Office officials were well aware that the Soviet regime recognized Turkish sovereignty over the Mosul *vilayet,* denied the legitimacy of the Middle East mandates, and claimed a share in administrative rights over the Shatt al-Arab waterway to the Persian Gulf.[76] For their part, security analysts in Egypt and Palestine worried about Soviet capacity to mobilize radical Islamist groups on the one hand, and the growing numbers of Jewish and, to a lesser extent, Palestinian, urban workers drawn to leftist radicalism on the other. The Egyptian police kept a weather eye on minority communities—Greeks and Jews above all—among whom support for left-wing causes was strong.[77] Postal censors repeatedly intercepted Comintern propaganda material in Arabic, allowing the police to gather evidence about its intended recipients, most of whom were non-Muslims. In one notable police swoop, twenty-two Russian Jews, five Italian émigrés, a Pole, a Romanian, and a single Syrian were arrested and deported from Egypt in February 1926.[78]

The security services in Cairo and Khartoum also conjured up Communist demons where none existed. After the Egyptian revolution of 1919 (discussed in the next chapter), false allegations of links between the Comintern and the Egyptian Wafd, the country's most powerful political party, were made. These served as a pretext for repression of local Wafdist and trade union activity and as a means to discredit Egypt's role as an administrative partner in the Sudan condominium.[79] Meanwhile, in Palestine, support among Jewish labor groups for the British general strike in 1926 made a singularly bad impression on security chiefs in Jerusalem.[80] Bristling with righteous indignation, the heads of the Criminal Investigation Departments in Palestine and Egypt were galvanized into closer cooperation with their counterparts in the Levant Sûreté in order to track the movements of known Communist agitators between Middle East territories.[81] During early 1928, the Palestine police also shut down a number of workers' clubs suspected of organizing Communist propaganda in Jerusalem

and Jaffa. Palestinians known to have traveled to Moscow, ostensibly for educational purposes, were also kept under surveillance.[82]

Only in Iraq were British administrators more sanguine. Faysal's regime
and the army officer corps that increasingly dominated national politics
were consistently hostile to what little Communist activity took place in the
country.[83] The Baghdad penal code was twice amended, in April 1936 and
September 1937, to facilitate the arrest of the few Communist activists
known to operate in the capital.[84] Iraq notwithstanding, Colonial Office
commentators were clearly perplexed by Soviet actions in the Arab world.
Palestine caused them most concern. As one unnamed official put it in
January 1932: "Soviet policy is always tortuous and difficult to interpret in
detail, but so far as we know their general policy in Palestine is to unite the
Jewish and Arab 'proletariat' against Arab landlords, Zionists and the British
government, which are all represented as working together for 'Imperialist'
ends."[85] Staunchly anti-Communist, in the late 1920s Stanley Baldwin's government showed no inclination to normalize relations with the USSR in the
Middle East or any other region of British imperial power. The Colonial
Office, too, preferred to dodge the sticky question of whether Soviet diplomatic and commercial missions in Arab capitals would ever be permissible.[86]

The Communist presence in the French Empire was of a different order
altogether. Local Communist parties were established in Algeria, Syria, and
Lebanon during the interwar period, each one independent of its counterpart in France. By contrast, Communists in Morocco and Tunisia adhered to
local sections of the French Communist Party (Parti Communiste
Français—PCF). Arab workers in Tunisia drawn to leftist radicalism were
less likely to sign up with the PCF than with the country's well-organized
trade union confederation, the Confédération Générale des Travailleurs
Tunisiens (CGTT), established in November 1924.[87] The differing affiliations among Communist groups in French Muslim territories was always of
secondary importance in determining the level of public support achieved
than the more fundamental issue of ethnicity. Communist supporters in
French North Africa—Algeria especially—were overwhelmingly drawn
from the settler community.[88] Membership of the Syrian and Lebanese
Communist Parties were more ethnically diverse, but was nonetheless predominantly composed of non-Arab minorities. This was both a reflection of
the relatively small numbers of French settlers in the French mandates and
of the commensurately larger influence of other minority communities,
Greeks and Armenian exiles in particular. Another feature common to colonial Communism in the Arab world before 1939 was its overwhelmingly
urban concentration. Unlike emergent Communist organizations in South
and Southeast Asia, Communist groups in North Africa and the Middle East
enjoyed relatively little success in winning adherents among either established nationalist organizations or the peasantry.[89]

The supreme irony for security services obsessed by the possibility of Communist sedition was that in the three North African territories and the Levant mandates nationalist groups were instrumental in limiting the mass appeal of Communism. Far from advancing the Communist cause, integral nationalists marginalized it. Whether, as in the case of the ENA and Néo-Destour, they cooperated with Communist groups or, as in the case of the Syrian People's Party and the Moroccan Action Bloc, they stole their radical thunder, anticolonial nationalists drowned out the calls to worker internationalism and peasant revolt. There was no fusion of Communism and anticolonial nationalism comparable to that achieved in Vietnam by the Indochinese Communist Party after 1931.[90] Few early Arab nationalists were Marxists; most were actively hostile to Communist doctrine.

Still, intelligence analysts were not persuaded that the Communist menace was minimal. Instead, colonial security services in French North Africa and the French Levant measured the alleged threat posed by local Communist groups in terms of their capacity to subvert the far larger nationalist parties that confined them to the political margins. Only then would Communism constitute a significant danger to colonial order. Put simply, to the colonial intelligence state, Communist numbers mattered less than Communist tactics of propaganda, manipulation, and control.[91] It was this assumption that justified an allocation of security service resources out of all proportion to the actual levels of popular support for Communist groups in France's Muslim territories. Counterespionage experts therefore invested enormous effort in tracking the movements of individual Comintern agents. Colonial state surveillance of known Comintern operatives in France's Muslim territories was predicated on these agents' potential to infiltrate popularly based nationalist organizations. Indeed, any foreign Communists who made contact with local political parties were typically referred to as "instructors."[92]

Section de Centralisation du Renseignement (SCR) staff in the Paris War Ministry also gathered a mass of humint on barrack-room politics, watching for any indications that Comintern agents or, as was always more likely, homegrown Communist activists, were distributing propaganda or recruiting sympathizers among metropolitan army units. The rhythm of intelligence gathering quickened in response to obvious external triggers such as the PCF's antimilitarist campaigns in 1923 (the Ruhr occupation) and 1925 (the Rif War) and the election of the Popular Front in May 1936.[93] But, in general terms, SCR scrutiny of potential Communist subversion intensified during Colonel Henri Roux's stewardship of French military intelligence between 1930 and the Popular Front election victory in mid-1936.[94]

The problem with such surveillance was that it contained a dynamic of its own. The more the security services searched for evidence of Communist

influence over anticolonial nationalism or army recruits, the less the intelligence analysts that read these reports felt able to dismiss the previous evidence of limited Communist success in either endeavor. The fear that colonial conscripts might be seduced by Communist propaganda was held to
justify official surveillance of barracks despite the minimal indications of any
groundswell in soldier sympathy for Communism. Troops' correspondence,
their reading matter, their barrack-room discussions, and their recreational
activity were therefore closely monitored by their senior officers working in
conjunction with soldier informants and local Sûreté officials.[95]

During the late 1920s, another factor, extraneous to the workings of local
Communist groups in French imperial territory, had driven the security services in French North Africa to regard Communist infiltration as a major
threat. This was the confluence of antimilitarism with anticolonialism
among leftist opponents of the French campaign to suppress the Rif
Republic in northern Morocco during 1925–26. Throughout 1925, the
Rabat Sûreté claimed to have identified Comintern agents, German banking consortia, and Turkish Islamists as elements in an international network
of support for 'Abd el-Krim's rebellion in the Moroccan Rif. Money, arms,
medical supplies, and military advisers allegedly were channeled to
Morocco via a Berlin-based Muslim committee, while Comintern agents
reportedly provided 'Abd el-Krim with up-to-date intelligence on Spanish
and French military deployments.[96]

In fact, French Communist mobilization against a supposedly clear-cut
instance of imperialist aggression was less formidable than the security services assumed. The weight of evidence of direct Communist involvement in
Moroccan events was hardly overwhelming. Indeed, the expulsions of
Communist agitators referred to earlier, related to only three settlers, Victor
Meyer, Antoinette Brebant and Antoine Galvano, each of whom was sentenced to twelve months' imprisonment by a Casablanca military tribunal
on 25 November 1925 for seditious propaganda and incitement of soldier
fraternization. In subsequent months, the Casablanca Sûreté tried but failed
to find any evidence of a Communist cell reputedly operating in the city as
a fund-raiser for the Rif rebellion. Nor did customs patrols or police surveillance lead to the discovery of any arms caches supposedly being
trafficked to Morocco's Atlantic coast en route to the Rif.[97]

Levels of verifiable Communist sedition in Tangiers were much the same.
At first glance, this was more surprising. The coastal city had a well-deserved
reputation for cosmopolitanism, political intrigue, and illicit trade. Foreign
Communist agitators had greater opportunity to conceal themselves among
a large, transient European population. Trade unionism was also well established among the port's European industrial workers. And Tangiers stood
on the fringe of Spanish Morocco and was thus directly engaged by the
longer-standing conflict between Riffian and Spanish forces that preceded

the southward spread of the war into the French protectorate. Although a handful of European enthusiasts inspired by the resistance of the Riffian Republic came and went, Communist supporters made few inroads in Tangiers. An international treaty port, Tangiers was a mini intelligence state all of its own. The regulatory arrangements established under the Treaty of Algeciras facilitated cooperation between consular authorities and European police agencies in their efforts to track the movements of known Communist sympathizers. Rapid expulsion usually followed.[98] Police targeting of people trafficking and the narcotics trade added to their expertise in covert surveillance of undesirables.[99]

The pattern of security service obsession with chimerical Communism was repeated in the Levant. During the Syrian revolt of 1925–26, the Cairo-based Syrian-Palestinian Congress coordinated international fund-raising for the rebellion, and used its contacts in Geneva to elicit further support among League of Nations delegates hostile to France. Agent surveillance of Congress members' comings and goings in Cairo, Beirut, Berlin, and Geneva, Sûreté monitoring of bank accounts and fund movements, plus regular interception of Congress members' correspondence seemed to confirm intelligence service estimates that pan-Arabism was inextricably tied to Germany and the USSR.[100] Reports from the French embassy in Berlin of German press depictions of a crisis of imperial control in French Muslim territories during 1925 lent weight to these suspicions.[101]

Between 1924 and 1925, unified Communist parties emerged from previously fragmented groups in Lebanon, Syria, and Palestine. And the Comintern itself increasingly shifted its organizational focus in the Middle East from left-wing Zionist groups in Palestine to Arab Communist groups in the Fertile Crescent. Arab labor militancy also increased markedly after 1925, nowhere more so than in Syria, where tax increases and inflationary pressure, exacerbated by the Druze revolt in the south of the country, generated mass protest by public-sector employees, women workers, and artisans.[102] Police seizures of Comintern documents in Syria and Palestine between 1924 and 1926 added fuel to the fire, indicating that Moscow agents directed the work of Arab Communist groups.[103]

At the height of the Syrian revolt in early 1926, the Beirut SR singled out the security services as "the principal obstacle to Syrian revolutionary agitation."[104] Hardly an objective evaluation, nor, as it transpired, an accurate one: neither Communists nor industrial workers played a central role in either the outbreak or the strategic direction of the Syrian revolt.[105] Politicians and other notables in Damascus and tribal sheikhs across the country were far more prominent, harnessing what began as a communal uprising among tribal leaders in the Jabal Druze to advance their sectarian interests as well as the cause of self-rule.[106] It was this more nationalist message that drew widespread public support.[107] Intelligence agencies found it hard, if not impossible, to come to terms with a populist nationalism that responded to the overwhelming desire among Syria's heterogeneous population for a rapid French exit from the mandate.

Throughout the Rif War and the Syrian revolt, members of the PCF political bureau were torn between Comintern instructions to attack French imperial militarism, a fear of hemorrhaging rank-and-file support to less stridently antiwar parties, the Socialist Section Française de l'Internationale Ouvrière especially, and the probability of renewed police repression if protest activity went too far. The Rif commanded greater public attention in France than events in the Jabal Druze. Even so, Jacques Doriot, the PCF's acknowledged expert in colonial matters, was the sole figure among the French Communist leadership eager to seize on the Rif War as the pretext for a campaign uniting anticolonialism and antimilitarism. At Doriot's insistence, on 10 September 1924, the PCF secretary-general and former railway union militant Pierre Sémard sent a highly publicized telegram of congratulation to 'Abd el-Krim following his recent victories over Spanish forces. But the PCF executive became more reticent once French forces entered the conflict the following April.[108]

An alternative strategy was soon found, designed in large part to placate Comintern insistence that action be taken. The Paris Prefecture of Police ensured that ministers were kept abreast of this. Within months of the PCF's creation at the Tours Congress in December 1920, Sûreté chiefs across France also began compiling summary reports of PCF involvement in anticolonial agitation for the minister of interior and the minister of colonies.[109] Doriot's activities in 1925 did not, therefore, come as a surprise. Nor did they please Doriot's Party bosses. Having kept him at arm's length for months, the PCF executive delegated Jacques Doriot to lead a highly personalized campaign against the Rif War.[110] In part, this marked an abdication of responsibility by Sémard, Maurice Thorez, Marcel Cachin, and other senior Party figures. Why, then, choose Doriot? The short answer is that he was ideally qualified both as a firebrand speaker and as a leader willing to risk a jail term, something likely to win additional sympathy for the Communist cause. His rhetorical skills had secured his appointment as political secretary of the National Federation of Communist Youth in May 1923. Moreover, he had served his first sentence for sedition in the fearsome La Santé prison from 8 December 1923 to 18 May 1924, an experience from which he emerged as an elected deputy for the 4° Secteur de la Seine, having won the local ballot in the Cartel des Gauches elections held in the week prior to his release. Over subsequent months, Doriot established his reputation as undisputed king of the Paris "red belt."[111] Once freed from prison, police inspectors and their network of informants among the PCF rank and file and the Communist-affiliated trade union confederation, the Confédération Générale du Travail Unitaire (CGTU), monitored his every move. Their interest seemed vindicated when Doriot was elevated to the Comintern executive committee at the Fifth Comintern Congress on 17 June 1924. By December, he was spokesman for the PCF's recently established colonial commission.[112]

Doriot's personal standing among colonial immigrant communities in France lent him additional influence. Over the preceding year he canvassed support for the PCF among Maghrebi and Vietnamese immigrant workers, and helped convene a congress of North African laborers in Paris on 7 December 1924.[113] Newspapers and tracts in French, Arabic, and Vietnamese were published in an effort to woo immigrant workers to the cause of revolutionary syndicalism. And Doriot encouraged the journalistic endeavors of pro-Communist colonial students, notably through the committee of intercolonial union, an internationalist organization that brought together aspiring colonial nationalists among the North African, Vietnamese, and Malagasy immigrant and student communities in France under PCF direction.[114]

Acting on Comintern advice, between May 1925 and March 1926 Doriot hijacked successive Chamber of Deputies debates on foreign affairs, defense spending, and colonial policy. He used the pages of the Party newspaper *L'Humanité* to issue appeals to French and colonial immigrant workers to wage class struggle (although not to fight for colonial independence) side by side.[115] And Doriot also coordinated CGTU plans for work stoppages in protest at operations in the Rif, as well as attempts to persuade armaments workers, transport staff, and Marseilles dock workers to disrupt the resupply of French forces in Morocco. It proved harder to replicate the Ruhr campaign for soldier fraternization with the local population, largely because there was no functioning Communist Party in Morocco to spread propaganda among the French garrison.[116]

More successful were antiwar meetings across France, many of which Doriot addressed in person. These were well publicized by Young Communist action committees. Nine such gatherings took place in Paris, the largest of them held at the Luna Park fairground on 16 May 1925. Here, Doriot recalled Jean Jaurès's principled opposition to the original annexation of Morocco and condemned the Socialists for voting military credits for an unjustifiable war of oppression.[117] The Young Communist campaign against the Rif War was by no means confined to the French capital. Seventy-three provincial antiwar meetings took place under PCF auspices. The most successful were in Périgueux, Rivesaltes, Bourges, Strasbourg, and Douai, at each of which attendance of more than two thousand was registered.[118]

Within his own party, however, the fiery Doriot remained isolated. From top to bottom the PCF membership displayed a distinct absence of fellow feeling with colonial comrades.[119] The Party's occasional statements about colonialism married the class analysis of Marxist-Leninism with ideas of scientific racism and hierarchies of ethnicity.[120] Far from setting themselves apart from the colonial officialdom they claimed to despise, the PCF leadership shared many of its underlying assumptions. Differing levels of "societal evolution" across the empire and crude calculations of numbers of waged workers in colonial cities became the yardstick by which the PCF Colonial Section gauged the revolutionary potential of individual colonies.[121] Opponents they may have been, but the Communist executive in France and the country's imperial security services shared many of the same ideas about colonial peoples. What worried the Sûreté and its ministerial chiefs at the Interior Ministry was less the PCF's commitment to anticolonialism, equivocal at it was, and more Doriot's personal capacity to inspire revolutionary agitators within the empire to follow his example.[122]

Wider international developments in the years immediately following the Rif War appeared to justify rising security service concerns about revolutionary ferment in colonial territories. In the early summer months of 1927, police spéciale offices in the North African protectorates intensified their search for indications of Communist subversion in Tunisia and Morocco.[123] The timing was significant. Intensified security service surveillance of Communist sedition across the empire was spurred by events in Asia. Vietnamese anticolonialism in French Indochina gathered momentum in 1927, culminating, at the end of the year, in the establishment of the Vietnamese Nationalist Party (Viet Nam Quoc Dan Dang), a group that mimicked Communist organizational methods.[124] A Communist-led uprising in the Dutch East Indies was bloodily suppressed over the winter of 1926–27 after coup plans were discovered by the Dutch colonial counterespionage service in Bandung.[125] Soviet advisers to the Chinese Kuomintang's northern expedition appeared critical to its advance on Shanghai, an event that prompted the British decision on 17 January to dispatch a division of troops to protect its port concession. Western imperialism, it seemed, faced more coordinated Communist opposition.[126] Further intelligence reached London over subsequent weeks about the extent of Moscow's influence in China. In March, Britain's most senior soldier, the chief of imperial general staff, Field Marshal Sir George Milne, noted that Soviet activities in Asia constituted "the gravest military menace which faces the British empire today."[127] Spurred on by renewed evidence of Soviet sedition in India, the British government severed diplomatic relations with the Soviet Union in May 1927.[128] Subsequent events in north China suggested that the Soviet Union would seize any opportunity to exploit colonial disorder or nationalist protest in the Indian subcontinent and the Middle East.[129]

A similar scare gripped the Foreign Ministry in Paris. Within a matter of weeks, the Quai d'Orsay's Asian division laid its hands on a secret memo written by the Russian military attaché in Beijing explaining how Soviet handlers could obtain privileged intelligence from foreign consulates by recruiting cleaners and local security staff to steal documents and sift through office rubbish in the search for discarded carbon copies. Recruits were advised not to steal any documents, which might expose their activities. Instead, they were to search for wax-copies and other duplicates of typed paper that were usually discarded. Embassy security procedures were tightened in response.[130]

Closer to home, in March 1927 Sûreté officers in the Tunisian port of Bizerta scored the most notable success against Communist organizers anywhere in French North Africa since the end of the war. Late that month the police detained one Louis Lemarchand, a known Communist agitator, for an alleged assault on a Sûreté agent named Olivieri. During the preceding year, Lemarchand had tried to set up a local Communist newspaper, *Le travailleur tunisien,* printed in the port of Ferryville (now Menzel Bourguiba) on the same presses formerly used to produce another Communist publication, *L'avenir social.* Lemarchand's new venture was intended to replace a previous Communist newssheet, *Prolétaire,* produced by another European settler, Jean Sebille, a worker in the Tunis arsenal. It was while Lemarchand was seeking funds to get *Le travailleur tunisien* into print that he was arrested.[131]

At his committal for trial, Lemarchand made a series of revelations about the extent of Communist organization in Tunisia and the key individuals involved.[132] He explained the cellular structure of the Tunisian Communist Party in Tunis, and even provided an address—50 rue Souk bel Khir—at which network meetings took place. Lemarchand went on to pinpoint the Party's five-man executive, identifying its key figures as Temime Hassouna, and two clerks, Maurice Zana and Maurice Abitbol. He named all the recipients in Bizerta of Communist tracts posted from Tunis, and identified those who also received Party funds in Bizerta and nearby Ferryville. In doing so, Lemarchand implicated several employees of the Postes et Télégraphes in Tunisia's main sorting offices. All these locations were immediately placed under surveillance. Lemarchand further explained how Tunisian Communists maintained contact with their senior PCF contacts through courier correspondence delivered by sympathetic merchant seamen plying the route between Tunis and Marseilles. Finally, he clarified the links between local Communists and the Tunisian Destour, the major political force in the country's Muslim politics. According to him, both groups supported an organization, L'amis de l'Ikdam, funded by the Communists and dedicated to widening popular support for Tunisian nationalism.[133] Following the Sûreté success in "turning" Lemarchand and arresting his Party colleagues, on 23 June 1927 the Tunis resident general Lucien Saint concluded on the basis of his most recent security intelligence that the Communist Party could be considered "virtually nonexistent in Tunisia."[134]

As if this was not pressure enough on the Moroccan security services to match their numerically smaller Tunisian counterparts, Lemarchand's arrest took place in the same week as the second of two high-profile international gatherings of the League against Imperialism and Colonial Oppression. The first of these was held at the Palais d'Egmont in Brussels in February. The second convened in Amsterdam on 30 March. These congresses brought together colonial nationalist representatives from as far afield as Vietnam, India, and Algeria with Western opponents of European imperial rule that included Comintern representatives, German KPD envoys, and other Communist front organizations.[135] In common with their colleagues in the Maghreb, French consular staff monitoring League of Nations lobby groups in Geneva and Sûreté officers at the Interior Ministry tended to treat anticolonialism and Communist internationalism as indistinguishable. Throughout the interwar period, anticolonialist groups were typically characterized as a front for Comintern activity. One of the first such French organizations, the Bureau international pour la défense des indigènes, originally established in 1913, was by 1921 identified by the Foreign Ministry as a Communist front because of the diversity of its contacts with other anticolonial groups, including the British Anti-Slavery Society, the Aboriginal Protection Society, and the German Geselleschaft für Eingeberenenschuts.[136] The Bureau's links with the PCF's colonial study committee emerged only three years later.[137]

The League against Imperialism and Colonial Oppression fit this internationalist mold, but it was not entirely under Communist control. Its most famous supporter in France was probably the author Henri Barbusse, a left-wing militant certainly, but more widely renowned as a committed pacifist.[138] Following an agreement among delegates at its 1928 Congress in Amsterdam, the League shifted its base of operations from Berlin to Paris and London. The London section was chaired by the Labor Party politician George Lansbury, a dedicated opponent of Bolshevism.[139] But the French security services were understandably more interested in what took place at the League's offices at 3 rue Parmentier in the Paris suburb of Neuilly-sur-Seine. Hitherto, the League's activities at the 48 Wilhelmstrasse address in Berlin had been monitored from a distance by Sûreté officers based in Luxembourg as well as by deuxième bureau staff attached to the French army of occupation in the Rhineland. The League's relocation to Paris made surveillance that much easier. The SCR counterespionage service took on the task.[140]

The increased flow of information about the League's operations did not make the French authorities, metropolitan or imperial, any more sanguine about its malign influence and its sinister international connections. As before, the League's main French organizers, G. Barty and Jacques Ventadour, received Comintern instructions in special mail deliveries. These were typically dispatched via Liège, Brussels, or Amsterdam, and then delivered by courier. Most appear to have been intercepted and read before delivery. But, if the Comintern link was well monitored, Jacques Doriot's PCF colonial section was by then just as well placed to offer advice and relay instructions.[141] The French intelligence community's absolute conviction that the League was merely a Communist front became clear when the Senegalese negrophile writer and future president, Léopold Sédar Senghor, was detained on charges of treason filed after his speech to the Brussels Congress in February.[142]

It makes sense to view heightened security service surveillance of Communist activity in French North Africa in 1927 against the backdrop of the Rif War and the League against Imperialism and Colonial Oppression's 1927 conferences. Both indicated that the French Communists and their Comintern advisers were eager to exploit anticolonial nationalism. The spate of arrests of alleged Communist sympathizers appeared to vindicate those intelligence analysts who had long stressed the capacity of Communist activists to mobilize both international and local opposition to imperial control. Far from gloating over the Sûreté's triumphs in Tunis and Bizerta, Lucien Saint advised the Foreign Ministry to redouble its commitment to Sûreté intelligence gathering "because of the continuing collusion with indigenous nationalist parties which, as the Brussels Congress has shown once more, the Communists rely on if need arises."[143] When League branches were subsequently established in Algiers and Tunis, the SCR also took a closer interest in the organization's links with North African nationalist groups.[144]

The fact remained that the League was marginal to politics in French North Africa: none of the locally organized political parties had yet signed on with it and few among the wider public knew of its existence. Why then were the security services so anxious about it? As always, the explanation has little to do with the real strength of Communist groups or other front organizations. Even intelligence that confirmed the eradication of a local Communist network could be interpreted as proof that Communism could just as easily reestablish itself, so long as any indigenous opposition to imperial rule persisted. In other words, the security services in French North Africa were almost programmed to see a Communist threat, whatever the indications to the contrary. On 2 May 1927, the Rabat protectorate security service filed a summary report on Moroccan Communism that emphasized the point. It is worth quoting at length as an indicator of the threat perceptions of intelligence personnel in a colonial state where fear of Communism outstripped practical experience of it:

Various Communist organizations have long sought to foment agitation in North Africa. This has been central to all [Soviet] Communist Party instructions to their propagandists. In accord with the Third International leadership, Morocco was singled out for Communist activity, first through the establishment of cells, next through propaganda organized by the members of these groups aimed at the tribes of the French zone with a view to their rebellion, and finally through aid to those tribes that have still to submit.

The establishment of cells could not be achieved. Alone, a few isolated individuals have tried discretely to attract a few "sympathizers," but their initiatives, soon discovered, have enabled the protectorate government to expel these propagandists. . . . To sum up, the protectorate police services, which receive regular intelligence on anything relating to Communism, notably lists of suspects and agitators, have not made any discovery up to now confirming the existence of Communist groups or the spread among the European or indigenous populations of the ideas the Third International tries to disseminate, whether to foment a revolutionary movement among the settlers or a tribal uprising in order to create a Soviet-style regime on the back of such troubles.[145]

Determined to prevent sedition of this sort, over the next twelve months the Moroccan Sûreté focused on the interception of Communist propaganda and the detention of those who tried to distribute it. Cooperation with city police chiefs and postal censors in Casablanca and Marseilles led to a series of Sûreté raids on the homes of suspected Communist organizers across northern Morocco in late February 1928. Two months later, police spéciale agents notified the Bouches-du-Rhône Prefecture of the activities of one Jean-Baptiste Valery, born in Paretto, Corsica, in 1898. An employee of the Messageries Maritimes shipping line, Valery was also secretary of the Marseilles branch of the International Merchant Seamen's Club. There, he sought to identify Communist sympathizers among the crewmen sailing regularly to North Africa, hoping to persuade them to smuggle Communist literature to his ideological confrères in the Maghreb.[146] At much the same time, intercepted mail posted from Paris to various addresses in Oujda, Fez, Meknès, and Rabat suggested that Communist and pan-Islamic literature was often sent together. This merely confirmed long-held security service opinion that the two were inextricably linked.[147]

The Rabat Residency was by then persuaded that a Moscow-based "Communist Moroccan action committee" stood at the apex of pan-Islamic networks in the protectorate. The committee was divided into two sections, one devoted to Communist propaganda targeted at settlers, the other to spreading the message of pan-Islam as a rallying cry for Arab independence. This latter section allegedly received instructions from the "Imperial pan-Islamic society," a shadowy organization based in Constantinople but funded by the Comintern. Two further groups, the Union Maghrébine and El Mountadda el Abaddi, both operating from Egypt, also lent support. The Union Maghrébine leaders Mohamed Pasha Cherai and Youssef Cheikhnali were well known to Sûreté personnel in French North Africa, having created country sections to liaise with nationalists, including Destour and ENA supporters in Tunisia and Algeria. On 27 December 1927, the Moroccan resident general Théodore Steeg advised the Foreign Ministry that the Union Maghrébine could count on some 1,500 supporters in Fez, Casablanca, and Tangiers alone.[148] As for those who organized the mailing of Communist and pan-Islamic literature from France, Maghrebi university students in Paris headed the list of police suspects. The Sûreté opened files on known members of the Association des étudiants musulmans nord-africains (North African Muslim Students Association), a group founded by a Tunisian student, Chadly ben Mustafa Khaïrallah, in December 1927.[149]

Taken together, these arrests and interceptions were unremarkable—part of the constant cycle of antiseditionist policing. The materials recovered did not amount to much: a few banned publications and Comintern statements sent through the post, as well as copies of amateurish Communist literature meant for distribution among Armée d'Afrique troops. Yet, according to Urbain Blanc, the long-serving chief delegate to the Rabat Residency and effectively the most senior French civil servant in Morocco, they confirmed an important intelligence lesson. Commenting on the February 1928 police raids, he wrote, "It is now possible to deduce that the Communist and revolutionary syndicalist effort in Morocco is currently at the preplanning (*pré-organisation*) stage, [and is] organized in part by French Communists and in part by the executive bureau of International Red Aid, whose agents also see Wahhabism as a means to build support among North African *indigènes*." According to France's senior professional bureaucrat in Rabat, it was a case of plus ça change. . . . "Wahhabism"—French shorthand for Islamic fundamentalism—and Communism remained potential, if not actual, bedfellows.

Blanc was not a man inclined to hyperbole. It is nevertheless hard to avoid the conclusion that he and his Sûreté advisers had got things wrong. The European settlers and non-Arab minorities that dominated Communist leaderships in North Africa and the Levant were less of a menace to colonial rule than their security service opponents realized. Time and again, the intelligence community in French North Africa and Syria exaggerated Communist capacity to manipulate indigenous nationalism and popular attachment to Islam. In doing so, they overlooked the organizational strides made by the Tunisian trade union movement, the CGTT, after its impressive coordination of dock strikes in Tunis and Bizerta in September 1924. After this founding event, the CGTT began to accrue much wider support, becoming the most effective force in left-wing politics in 1920s French North Africa. But the fact that it grew organically in Tunisia's industrial heartland, that it was Arab-controlled, and that it clearly targeted Muslim industrial workers all diminished its importance in the eyes of intelligence analysts obsessed with external agency in the politics of anticolonial protest.[150]

The assumption that the Muslim masses were putty in the hands of shrewd foreign ideologues was not confined to the security services. In common with their French colleagues, Communist leadership in the Maghreb and the Levant displayed the same patronizing attitude toward the Muslim masses they hoped to attract to Communism. The Parti Communiste Algérien (PCA), the strongest of the Communist groups in France's Muslim empire, first took root among the working-class European populations of Algiers and Oran and garnered further support among the more intellectual circles of urban professionals. Muslim support for Communist ideas, though not insignificant, was more closely tied to the development of workers' groups in general.[151] The Party newspaper, *Lutte Social* (*Social Struggle*), perpetually opposed government policy, mounting venomous campaigns against the Ruhr occupation and the Rif War. In the run-up to French parliamentary elections in 1924, the Algiers Sûreté estimated that a PCA candidate in the capital could count on between five and six thousand votes, an estimate based on the fact that the Party won 2,519 votes in earlier local elections to the colony's financial delegation. The city's rail and tramway workers as well as its dock laborers already provided a hard-core of support among the European worker population. Algerian Communists had a similar toehold in Oran, Sidi-bel-Abbès, Blida, Constantine, Philippeville, Menerville, and El-Affroun, towns with large railway workshops, docks, or warehousing facilities. But the PCA's core constituency of settler support interested the Sûreté less than its persistent attempts to win the allegiance of Muslims. The PCA pursued two strategies to this end: sometimes trying to work with the ENA and its successor parties, sometimes targeting specific communities of Muslim opinion. Intelligence analysts were anxious that such efforts should not succeed. The stock criticism in *Lutte Social* of Prime Minister Raymond Poincaré as a Ruhr warmonger in 1923 was of little concern, but the paper's subsequent incitement of Muslim revolt provoked immediate government sanction.[152]

Hence, the Algiers Sûreté focused its intelligence effort on two areas of PCA activity. First was the Party's effort to woo supporters of Messalism from 1925 to 1940.[153] Second was its appeal to Muslim troops in the Armée d'Afrique. Both intensified after the election of the Popular Front. The rancorous split between the PCA and the Parti Populaire Algérien during the winter of 1936–37 eased the Algiers government's worries about a Communist-nationalist alliance in the colony. By contrast, anxiety about Communist propaganda among colonial troops intensified after the outbreak of the Spanish Civil War. On 19 August 1936, the Algiers Corps Command requested local prefectures to appoint dedicated Sûreté staff to monitor any signs of PCA infiltration of army garrisons. A fortnight later, Armée d'Afrique barracks across Algeria were placed under heightened surveillance. This followed a conference of senior commanders and Sûreté officers at the Algiers command, who discussed how best to prevent

Communist sedition among Maghrebi units.[154] As we shall see in chapter 9, intensive surveillance of left-wing subversion in France's Muslim territories remained more or less constant until the crackdown against Communist organizations that followed the signature of the Nazi-Soviet pact in August 1939.

Conclusion

Having for decades prided themselves on their sensitivity to the currents of Muslim opinion, the French North African administrations in particular tended to downplay evidence of popular anticolonialism among their dependent populations. Racial prejudice played its part. Uneducated Muslim subjects were often dismissed as incapable of sustained political engagement. Ironically, however, the accumulated French knowledge of Islamic custom was equally misleading. Time after time, the intelligence communities in North Africa concluded that religion was the sole issue around which Muslims could unite. Hence their suspicion that emergent nationalist groups such as the Néo-Destour and Algeria's ENA, both of which were strongly socialistic, feigned an interest in Islam in order to attract greater support. The assumption was that, as long as French authority respected Islamic values, mass protest was unlikely.[155] This was to ignore the fact that nationalist politicians and Islamic clerics equated national consciousness with the assertion of a distinctly Muslim cultural identity.

Examples from early 1930s Tunisia prove the point. Destourian politicians and officials of the Tunis Grand Mosque criticized those members of the Arab elite who renounced their personal status as Muslims in order to acquire French citizenship, vilifying them as unpatriotic apostates. Tunisia's most senior cleric, the *Sheikh el Islam,* Si Tahar Ben Achour, soon found himself isolated, having agreed to a *fatwa* conceding that naturalized Tunisians could still be considered practicing Muslims. Students at the Grand Mosque refused to attend classes in protest at Ben Achour's action. Explicit rejection of the idea that one could be a French citizen and a Tunisian Muslim at the same time struck a chord with Tunisian subjects alienated by the injustices of the protectorate system. During 1933, protestors even denied naturalized Tunisians Islamic funeral rights, and prevented their burial in Muslim cemeteries. In some cases, the corpses of naturalized French Tunisians were even disinterred.[156] After well-publicized clashes at funeral ceremonies in Bizerta, Tunis, and Ferryville, Néo-Destour used the Arab language press to announce its support for the campaign to deny burial rights to naturalized citizens. Nationalism and religion seemed more entwined than ever. Residency officials even warned of "a sort of holy war" if the police attempted to oversee cemetery funerals.[157]

Because administrative reports repeatedly belittled the subject population's capacity for independent thought, it was perhaps inevitable that contrary evidence of systematic opposition—proof positive of the natives' "political maturity"—would prove hard to swallow. Colonial administration was, after all, intensely patriarchal. Moreover, the underlying belief that indigenous peasant laborers and industrial workers were only driven to protest because of chronic economic hardship added to the conviction that they lacked any deeply held political convictions. But defense of religious autonomy was inherently political, and lent itself to greater politicization owing to official efforts to divide the Muslim community. On 16 December 1931, Pierre Laval's government established a ministerial commission on Islamic affairs in recognition of the growing hostility to French rule among Muslim imperial subjects. The commission was a failure. It lacked any decision-making powers and had no point of contact with the French Cabinet.[158] But it also marked an important admission, brought home to French ministers and officials by the growing volume of intelligence reportage on the subject: France was no longer credible as a "Muslim power" ruling in conformity with the religious interests of its North African and Middle Eastern subjects. By then, the recurrent instances of armed opposition to European imperial control in the Arab world only underlined the fact that conflict was endemic to the colonial condition, and its containment the major priority of the intelligence state. It is to these confrontations that we now turn.

4

INTELLIGENCE AND REVOLT I

British Security Services and Communal Unrest
in Egypt, Iraq, and Sudan

The idea of the intelligence state presupposes that the intelligence gathered
by colonial security agencies was critical to the maintenance of order. It follows that disorder in such states was indicative of intelligence failure, or, at
least, of the inability of security agencies to preempt violent unrest through
the exploitation of information about potential rebellion. This chapter
tests this proposition, focusing on some of the better-known revolts against
British imperial rule across the Middle East in the years immediately after
World War I. It suggests that lapses, gaps, and distortions in the effective collection and analysis of information led consistently to a loss of political control. Sometimes this was temporary, sometimes longer-lasting, but it was
always directly related to what was or was not done with the security information collected by the colonial authorities.

Background

The British mandates of Iraq, Palestine, and Transjordan, formally established during 1920–21, were fragile creations. Between 1915 and 1919, the
leader of the Arab revolt, Amir al-Husayn, carefully avoided a binding territorial agreement with his British patrons. His aspirations for a self-governing
Arab state stood more chance of acceptance in the new international system
that emerged from the Paris Peace Conference. To a degree his caution was
rewarded. The new mandates were awarded conditionally and under the
supervision of an outside authority—the League of Nations.[1] The war precipitated major constitutional changes in other Arab territories in Britain's
informal empire. Foremost among these was Egypt, which, in December
1914, Britain had declared a protectorate in response to the outbreak of
hostilities with the Ottoman Empire.[2] Confronted with revolutionary

upheaval in the country—discussed later in this chapter—the British authorities first accorded Egypt "independence" in 1919, and then circumvented this decision by suspending the country's new constitutional settlement.[3] The struggle for influence between the British imperial state and Egypt's political elite soon spilled south into the Sudan, a territory largely controlled by Britain despite its constitutional status as an Anglo-Egyptian "condominium."[4]

In the decade after World War I, the populations of the mandated territories were arbitrarily and artificially divided. Britain and France used their status as mandatory powers to delineate new desert frontiers and communal boundaries. In Syria, the French went further, creating semiautonomous local states within a national polity. In theory, these new states were constitutionally organized to suit French and British strategic, economic, and political requirements. In practice, political reconstruction took place either in opposition to mass protest and communal rebellion, as in Syria and Iraq, or with only superficial consultation of a narrow Arab elite, as in Transjordan. Popular resistance to European control was strongest in Amir Faysal's short-lived Damascus regime, both among the Arab political societies dominated by Iraqi and Syrian officers of the Arab Army and among the wider population of Damascus and Aleppo, enraged by Faysal's capitulation to the French.[5] Factionalism and disputes over political tactics sapped the power of these groups, however.[6] In July 1920, French forces ousted Faysal from Syria after routing Arab Army forces at the battle of Maysalun. Failure also awaited the efforts of Iraq's leading Arab Army society, the al-'Ahd al-'Iraqi, to foment tribal unrest against British military administration in a bid to secure the *sanjak* of Dayr al-Zur on the upper Euphrates for an independent Iraq.[7]

These Arab officers were far from being the only organized threat to Britain's imperial control in the Middle East. Indeed, it was nearby southern Kurdistan that became the first British-administered region to erupt into rebellion after the final collapse of the Ottoman Empire in October 1918. It was not, however, the only site of British intelligence failure in the Middle East at the time. Nor were the roots of the intelligence problems in Kurdish areas as deep as those in Egypt, where British security procedures had been thoroughly disrupted during World War I. Rather, the intelligence apparatus in Kurdish areas of the Mosul *vilayet* became a pawn in the policy disagreements between the Baghdad civil commission and the Colonial Office, with disastrous results. By contrast, in Egypt the security services failed at a more basic level. The Residency's three main sources of political intelligence—the residue of wartime intelligence agencies in Cairo, the Egyptian police service, and the network of political officers (POs) posted throughout the Egyptian provinces—did not anticipate the wave of nationalist protests that engulfed the country in March 1919. The consequences of this failure, to which we now turn, were severe.

Intelligence Failure and the 1919 Disorders in Egypt

Immediately after World War I, a three-way contest between British imperial power, nationalist supporters of the Cairo lawyer Sa'd Zaghlul, a former vice-president of the Egyptian legislative assembly, and his opponents in the established Egyptian political elite dominated Egypt's national politics. This power struggle was, in turn, eclipsed in the mid-1920s as more radical nationalist groups emerged. Their more "Easternist" orientation mirrored a decline in Egyptian particularism, born of the increased influence of pan-Arab thinking and Islamist doctrine.[8] British imperial policy contributed to these shifts in opinion but never controlled them. Instead, the Cairo Residency became caught up in competing Egyptian visions of the country's future as liberal capitalist modernizers clashed with the traditionalist 'ulamā of al-Azhar University, student radicals, and the more populist Salafī movements that stressed Egypt's place as leader of the Arab Muslim world.[9] As Israel Gershoni and James Jankowski have demonstrated, during the 1930s, Egyptians in far greater numbers were drawn to a supranationalism grounded in concepts of shared Arab identity and Muslim culture rather than the territorially defined Egyptian nationalism of the Wafd, the "delegation" party that came to prominence as a consequence of the 1919 revolution.[10]

The origins of the 1919 intelligence failure stemmed from the coincidence of four factors. The first was entirely political. Abiding resentment among Cairo's political elite at Britain's imposition of a protectorate over Egypt in 1914 intensified in the latter stages of World War I as speculation increased about possible British annexation of the country.[11] Wartime disruption of Egypt's export trade and fears that the Cairo Residency would renege on General Sir John Maxwell's November 1914 proclamation pledging not to conscript Egyptians for the war effort stoked anti-British sentiment among the country's merchant classes and among the wider population, whose commitment to serve British imperial war aims was, understandably, limited.[12] The end of the war brought matters to a head, raising Egyptian expectations of greater autonomy, a voice at the Paris Peace Conference, and a clearer timetable for eventual British withdrawal.[13]

Sir Reginald Wingate, the British Resident, did not immediately quash this speculation. He conceded that Zaghlul's supporters considered President Woodrow Wilson, the apostle of self-determination, "a sort of political 'fairy godmother,' who will bring Egyptians to their own and put an end to further alien interference and tutelage." In this fevered atmosphere, rumors of imminent British evacuation gained credence among the Egyptian public.[14] But nationalist hopes were dashed by Britain's refusal in February 1919 to allow Wafdist delegates to attend the Versailles negotiations. Once news of this rejection spread, mass protests quickly followed. Egyptian workers now took a leading role, the lifting of wartime restrictions on labor activism enabling them to give vent to deep-seated political and economic grievances against the authorities.[15]

The other three factors behind Britain's intelligence failings in Egypt were more directly related to the security services. One was structural. Intelligence-gathering networks in Cairo, from the Arab Bureau to the city police, that had been built up during the war were quickly scaled back after the armistice. As a result, the volume of political intelligence collected and the speed with which it was analyzed both declined. The Residency was left poorly informed of the depth of public anger as protests developed. A linked factor stemmed from changed policing priorities. The shift in police work after 1914 away from internal security matters to war-related activities such as the supervision of conscription diminished the quality of police intelligence on Egyptian political opinion. The final factor was part methodological, part cultural. It turned on intelligence-gathering methods and the cultural assumptions made about the loyalty of identifiable social groups among the Egyptian population.

British POs depended on human intelligence, predominantly gathered by informants and local police. Before 1914, Egyptian police cadres did not represent a cross section of the population as a whole. City police forces, mounted units in particular, were drawn from the conservative landowning class. Vigorous police repression of the Mutual Brotherhood Society, the leading secret society in Cairo before 1914, further alienated Egypt's urban population from the security forces.[16] Reliance on the police as a primary source of political intelligence was therefore inherently problematic. The information collected was difficult to verify and often unreliable. Serious flaws in British intelligence assessment inevitably followed. Policing in the countryside fell in large part to a force of village policemen, or *ghaffirs*, with closer ties to the community they supervised. But a year before the outbreak of World War I, the *ghaffir* force completed a thorough reorganization initiated by Consul General Lord Kitchener. More than thirty thousand *ghaffirs* retrained as paramilitary police, their pay increased to reflect their increased professionalism. The militarization of police units accountable to British officers compounded public resentment of a police force increasingly seen as an adjunct of the army of occupation. Despite greater patrolling by uniformed *ghaffirs*, recorded crime increased sharply on the eve of war.[17]

It seemed that by 1914 neither city nor rural police were well placed to obtain reliable intelligence from the surrounding population other than by arbitrary, coercive means. Certainly, by 1919 British POs lacked high-quality humint from the police forces with whom they liased. No alternative intelligence sources were found, however. POs' surveys of public opinion still drew on informants' reports and local hearsay, leaving them prone to manipulation by the information providers. The consequent intelligence problems are analyzed later.

The rioting and political violence of March 1919 caught the various Cairo intelligence-gathering agencies off balance. Much expanded during the preceding four years, the British security services in Egypt were in the throes of a peacetime reorganization. At the start of the war in 1914, the Residency had two main sources of political intelligence. Foremost was the Department of Public Security, attached to the Egyptian Interior Ministry. The Department collated political intelligence from the city police forces of Cairo and Alexandria. It then fed this information to the Residency. But it struggled to cope with the volume of police reports it received, and, as we have seen, was too dependent on the police as sole providers of intelligence material. The Department of Public Security perspective mirrored that of the city police forces rather than distilling a broader range of opinion. The second source of political intelligence was the director of Sudan intelligence, a Cairo-based official principally concerned with external threats to British supremacy in Egypt and the Sudan. The director did not generally advise on internal security, except insofar as it was affected by foreign agitation. Furthermore, as his title implied, the director of Sudan intelligence was substantially preoccupied by the political relationship between Egypt and the Sudan.[18]

During the war years the military intelligence staff of the Egyptian general staff assumed primary responsibility for analysis of political intelligence from urban police forces and civil government officials. As the Egyptian Expeditionary Force (EEF) advanced northward into Palestine, Cairo military intelligence personnel also collated incoming political intelligence from behind the front line. The reduction in military intelligence staff that accompanied the withdrawal of the expeditionary force after the war left a gaping hole in intelligence assessment in early 1919. An Eastern Mediterranean Special Intelligence Bureau assumed the director of Sudan intelligence's role as principal watchdog of foreign espionage and frontier surveillance. But internal security was another matter. Only after the 1919 disorders were plans hastily introduced to expand the Department of Public Security with British personnel paid for by the Egyptian Treasury. The Department's work focused more clearly on nationalist groups, protest movements, and other sources of subversion. Wingate's successor in Cairo, the former EEF commander Field Marshal Viscount Allenby, acknowledged that in March 1919 the intelligence bureaucracy had "no adequate central control organization" capable of providing early warning of disorder.[19]

The outbreak of war brought with it a raft of legislative controls in Egypt. The primary duty of enforcement fell to the city police forces of Cairo, Alexandria, and the Suez Canal zone. Commodity prices, commerce, and the transport of goods were subject to additional regulation. Press controls and postal censorship were extended. Enemy aliens were required to register with the authorities, and their movements were restricted. The influx of servicemen to Egypt brought with it the accompanying social problems of public disorder, more widespread prostitution, and higher incidence of venereal disease. Additional responsibilities stretched police resources but were not intrinsically damaging to intelligence gathering. Police surveillance of political activity, as well as censorship of the vernacular press and private correspondence, gave a window onto social conditions and public opinion among literate society.[20] Nor did the war years herald any significant rise in the number of criminal offences committed. Egypt's prison population in December 1918 stood at 13,310, compared with 14,385 four years earlier.[21] By contrast, reported serious crime with violence almost doubled in Cairo, Alexandria, and Giza between February 1918 and February 1920. But these figures are somewhat misleading. For one thing, reported crime and police capacity to deal with it increased only after the 1919 disorders, not before. For another, capital crime remained rare. Four murders were recorded in Cairo in 1919, seven in 1920. In Alexandria, one murder was recorded in each year. Even violent thefts in both cities were counted at less than ten until 1920. Rises in reported crimes in the provinces were smaller still, and in some cases, Aswan, Minia, and Dakahlia for example, net declines took place. The most significant additional burdens on police time in 1919 lay elsewhere. Political violence aside, property crime, vagabondage, and juvenile homelessness in the major towns all showed the highest increases over the winter of 1919–20.[22]

The extra workload brought about by wartime economic controls, censorship, and criminal detection was not solely responsible for declining police efficiency as an intelligence-gathering body in Egyptian urban centers. More significant was the fact that Egyptian government efforts to meet British military demand for additional manpower to serve in the EEF Labor and Transport Corps deepened the rift between police and population. Introduction of full-blown conscription was incompatible with Britain's rights as a protecting power. It also raised fears of social unrest and of public refusal to fight fellow Muslims. The compromise reached between the British and Egyptian authorities delegated enlistment into labor battalions to native officials, assisted by British inspectors. POs monitored recruitment from district to district. Theoretically voluntary, the recruitment system was actually coercive; each area was required to fill a designated manpower quota. The enlistment process also invited widespread corruption as those able to buy exemptions by bribing sympathetic officials did so. The recruitment burden inevitably hit those least able to escape it, above all the peasantry, or *fellahin*. Terms of service were short, typically three months, but they disrupted the agricultural cycle as labor battalions operated far from the Nile Delta. By November 1918, almost a half-million Egyptians had served in the Labor and Transport Corps. Seen as enforcers of an unpopular, corrupt, and arbitrary system, the police became even more estranged from the Egyptian peasantry. By 1919, the volume of information passed from public to police in rural areas had tailed off, leaving police commanders shocked by the scale of rural violence and by the breadth of *fellahin* support for Zaghlul.[23]

That deficiencies in the intelligence bureaucracy and city police agencies in March 1919 reflected an incomplete adjustment from wartime activity to different peacetime roles is hardly surprising. A more profound cause of intelligence failure, however, lay in the prevalent cultural assumptions on which officers and officials judged the political information they received. The strength of Wadfist nationalism compelled British observers to revise their views about the composition and cohesion of the Egyptian political community. Intelligence assessments written immediately before the 1919 disturbances were dominated by discussion of high politics at the centers of political and commercial power in Cairo and Alexandria. Again, there is nothing remarkable in this. Leading aristocratic pasha families, the urban intelligentsia of professionals and journalists, and the burgeoning effendi class of literate junior officials achieved greater political prominence in the decade before 1919. British observers wrote copious reports about these groups in response. But quantity was no guide to quality. High commission reports to the Foreign Office Eastern Department were riddled with stereotypical generalizations about characteristically "Oriental" behavior, dubious typologies of Egyptian class and ethnicity, and assertions about Arab incapacity to unite around a national ideal. In these circumstances, the spurious intelligence service claims about Wafdist sympathy for Communist internationalism, mentioned in the previous chapter, become easier to understand. The suggestion that Zaghlul and his party lieutenants communicated with Comintern envoys in Paris, Geneva, and Cairo had no factual basis, but it was consistent with the profusion of exaggerated intelligence claims about Wafdist intentions.[24] Meanwhile, the mass of the working population in town and countryside—always a more likely source of leftist radicalism—were either overlooked as autonomous political actors or dismissed as even more factional and self-interested than their social superiors.[25] This, too, is unremarkable when placed in the quasi-colonial context of British rule in Egypt. It is not difficult to find traces of equivalent stereotyping in numerous other colonial settings of the time.

More revealing is the evidence adduced to substantiate these cultural assumptions. Egyptian political intelligence assessments were overwhelmingly based on humint supplied by Egyptians themselves. This begs the question of agency. Who was using whom in the process of intelligence collection and analysis in postwar Egypt? Control over old and new forms of social communication was critical to both sides. To the Residency's enduring interest in 'ulamā teachings, party political proclamations, and political gossip in the cafés and meeting rooms of Cairo and Alexandria were added

newer concerns about nationwide circulation of Wafd pamphlets and public petitions demanding autonomy. The arrest and subsequent deportation
to Malta of Zaghlul and three of his Wafd colleagues in early March 1919
further raised the stakes, triggering a wave of anti-British demonstrations
across the country. The heterogeneous composition of the protest movement, much of which was coordinated by Egyptian women with personal
contacts with senior Wafd figures, indicated its genuine revolutionary potential. The Wafdist cause, it seemed, had the power to unite Egyptians across
customary boundaries of gender, social class, religion, and locality.[26]

For years afterward, awareness that the Wafd could make or break sitting
governments was a starting point for political intelligence assessment in
Cairo.[27] So, too, was the knowledge of simmering tensions between differing
ethnic communities in the urban centers, exposed during the violence of
1919. In Alexandria especially, a powerful undercurrent of intercommunal
hatred was laid bare by the looting of commercial premises and street battles between gangs of young Arabs, Greeks, and Italians that left fifty-eight
dead and more than two hundred wounded.[28]

Zaghlul's nationalist clients and his Egyptian political opponents both
saw advantage in highlighting the power of popular nationalism, British
reliance on Egyptian auxiliaries to maintain order, and the urgent need for
fundamental reform. Yet, for all their contacts with the Egyptian political
elite, British observers clung to a view of Egyptian responses to British rule
at odds with the societal upheaval of 1919. Take, for example, two Residency analyses, one compiled before the 1919 revolution, the other immediately after it. The first of these was a survey of public opinion sent by
Wingate to Foreign Secretary Arthur Balfour on 28 November 1918. The
second was a detailed evaluation of the 1919 unrest submitted to the
Foreign Office by a Mr. Patterson, the director-general of state accounts in
Cairo.[29]

Wingate saw the dangers inherent in the Residency's diminishing capacity to limit public expressions of opposition. The central authorities found
themselves unable to regulate the degree of contact between town and
countryside or to prevent the resultant connection between urban political
activism and rural economic distress among the *fellahin*. Wingate understood the threat, but his reading of intelligence appreciations about
Egyptian dissent was loaded with a dismissive characterization of peasant
politics that underestimated the scale of the problem faced:

> Native opinion outside the capital and one or two of the larger towns is as yet
> scarcely affected. The "fellahin" dilute their dull sentimental prejudice against
> alien Christians with a sound appreciation of the fact that their interests will
> be best served by British supervision and control. Nothing but a campaign of
> misrepresentation and appeals to religious fanaticism, synchronizing with
> economic distress, would be likely to alter their present attitude towards us.

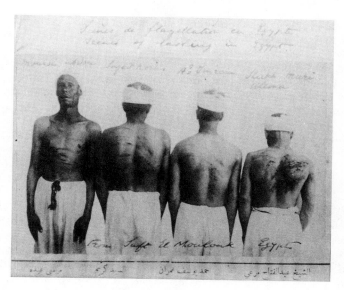

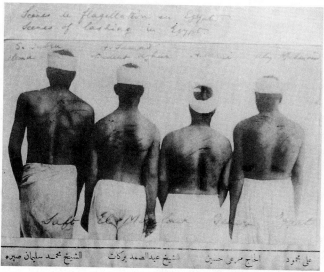

Figure 4. Egyptians beaten by British troops during the
spring 1919 disorders. These photographs formed part
of a dossier on British military abuses forwarded by Wafdist
representatives to the Paris Peace Conference on 18 April
1919. Note that the victims are variously identified as notable,
fellah, 'ulamā, and student at al-Azhar University. TNA,
FO 608/214. Crown copyright, reproduced courtesy of
the National Archives, London.

Nevertheless, in view of information that echoes of the political oratory at the capital had reached the provinces and were attracting a number of provincial notables "to hear this new thing," I prevented the circulation of papers for signature by members of the Legislative Assembly and others appointing Saad Pasha Zaghlul and his associates their representatives "to seek through peaceful and lawful means, whatever opportunities offer, to obtain the absolute independence of Egypt, etc." I also took occasion to remark to several of my native visitors—the Prime Minister [Rushdy Pasha] among them—that, while I saw no objection to private discussion of political subjects, agitation under the specious form of canvassing public opinion could not be allowed, and that advocacy of change in the present order of Government, a British protectorate, was technically sedition and, if necessary, punishable as such.[30]

Patterson provided a different, though equally comforting, narrative of events. In his description, Egyptians had not anticipated total Allied victory in 1918. The urban elite hoped to force constitutional concessions from a position of strength. Meanwhile, the wider population adjusted to the outcome of the war and was broadly reconciled to a continued British presence. Only then were Egyptian governmental demands to attend the Peace Conference hijacked by Zaghlul and his followers, making confrontation with the British authorities unavoidable.[31]

Typical of the reports sent to the Foreign Office by senior Cairo officials, the more striking feature of Patterson's analysis was its evidential basis. Reported conversations with Egyptian politicians and officials were mixed with hearsay to reinforce the stereotype of a loyalist population manipulated by a coterie of unrepresentative extremists in the pay of Germany and Turkey. Patterson cited the example of his house cook, accosted by nationalist activists and induced to sign an anti-British petition without understanding its contents. He referred to *fellahins'* field work songs in which labor service was recalled affectionately. And he highlighted the grievances of Egyptian politicians and a young clerical assistant. The former attacked British constitutional proposals, including the impending abolition of the capitulations system, as a prelude to direct rule. The latter condemned the two-tier structure of Anglo-Egyptian administration and the racial discrimination in education and government service that underpinned it. In Patterson's reading, however, it was the generosity of British reform that gave rise to these complaints: constitutional modernization would benefit Egyptian society, and educational development had generated a culture of expectation among young effendis that could be satisfied only in the longer term.[32]

Quite apart from its conclusions, the resultant political appreciation illustrated a key point. In early 1919, British policymakers in Cairo formed opinions about Egyptian nationalism on the basis of civilian officials' random conversations and anecdotal evidence. Such a composite picture might be revealing, but only if intelligence analysts could piece the incoming information together. As Allenby noted on 24 May when reviewing the raw intelligence available at the height of the disorders:

> Political officers are volunteers chosen from among British non-official civilians or British officials in Egyptian Government service who, for one reason or another, can be spared from their ordinary work. Their duty is, by virtue of their knowledge of the language and the country, to assist the military commanders to whom they are attached, particularly by acting as liaison officers between them and the Egyptian civil authorities; they are also expected to make any enquiries for which opportunity offers, and to forward information and expressions of opinion.[33]

There was the rub. Humint could be gathered only "as opportunity offers," a euphemistic understatement that nonetheless indicated that POs could only be as good as the contacts they managed to develop among indigenous civil society. And once their information was compiled, it still had to be refined into assessed intelligence. In early 1919 the Cairo authorities failed to keep abreast of the PO intelligence reaching them. The information order was not working.

Like their peers in Cairo, British POs in the Egyptian provinces used firsthand observation and reported conversations as the basis for their assessments. As Allenby's comments make plain, unlike the service personnel that filled the ranks of PO and assistant political officer (APO) in the Middle East mandates, most POs in Egypt were civilians on temporary detachment from the Egyptian civil service, or volunteers from the commercial sector with years of career experience in the locality. Conversational Arabic was the chief prerequisite for appointment because POs were expected to provide the link between Egyptian local government authorities and British Army commanders.[34] After the events of March 1919, provincial POs increasingly took on the preliminary task of intelligence assessment. Their reports distilled into a composite picture of public opinion the information they gathered during regional tours, meetings with Egyptian officials, landowners, and *omdas,* and discussions with local police officers and military personnel.[35] Anxious to avert any recurrence of peasant unrest, Allenby's high commission attached more importance to such information from outlying provinces and towns. But while POs' reports were more frequent and widely read in the months following the 1919 disorders, the process of rebuilding an effective information order took time. As the senior British Army commander later conceded, most of the individuals involved in attacks on the security forces escaped detection owing to the lack of public cooperation in their apprehension. With little prospect of a return to more consensual policing, martial law was not lifted in Egypt until 5 July 1923.[36]

The most valuable informational network for a colonial state drew on all constituencies of opinion, rather than relying exclusively on the advice of Europeans and locals connected in some way to the colonial order. Here, the British struggled to make progress. POs in Egypt rarely broke free of their dependence on regional officials, landowners, and literate professionals. Few POs developed contacts with 'ulamā and other leaders of Muslim opinion. Fewer still found the time to canvas *fellahin* opinion about anything other than agricultural market conditions. In mid-April 1919, the chief PO for the Western Delta area put this problem into context.

> The motorcar enables the English official to get about so fast that he never speaks to a *fellah*. A few years ago the English inspectors rode horses, and would overtake or be overtaken by omdas, sheikhs, or others on their donkeys, and they would ride a mile or two together, and each would get to know the other's point of view, whereas now the car flies past, covering the native with dust, scaring his family and animals, and, even if the official does shout a greeting, he is gone before it can be returned, which is hardly mannerly.[37]

The distances, physical, political, and cultural, that separated British intelligence gatherers from those at the lowest end of the social hierarchy were hard to bridge. POs' evaluations of elite opinion were often highly astute. But their comments regarding Islamic movements, peasant opinion, and worker attitudes were sometimes little more than caricature. Thus the assumption persisted that political change would inevitably be driven from above and not from below.[38] An important lesson of the events of 1919— that popular nationalism could galvanize Egyptian opposition to British rule throughout the country—was soon forgotten. By contrast, Egyptian politicians increasingly appreciated the importance of the provincial tour as an investigative tool and an unwelcome symbol of imperial oversight. In 1931, the Egyptian premier Ismail Sidky Pasha pressed the Cairo Residency to limit the number of inspection visits by members of the Residency's Oriental Secretariat. In the face of sustained Egyptian government pressure, in 1932 such tours were abandoned altogether.[39]

Intelligence gathered from provincial tours in 1919 certainly colored the Foreign Office summary assessment of the March outbreaks. Distributed to Cabinet ministers, interested Whitehall departments, and British colonial governments, this Foreign Office analysis roundly criticized Wingate's Cairo administration for its ineffective response to Zaghlul's call for national independence. It also painted a very different picture of Egyptian nationalism. Far from dismissing Egyptian politics as urban, sectarian, and elitist, the report's author, Sir Ronald Graham, conceded that public support for Egyptian independence was more widespread than previously thought: "If once the idea of independence received recognition and was fairly started, it must inevitably be so far more popular than any more moderate program, that no native, statesman or politician could hope to resist it. Further, we must lose all our [Egyptian] friends who would not dare stand by us for fear of the future consequences if independence came about."[40]

Graham relied on eyewitness testimony to reconstruct the sequence of mass demonstrations in Cairo, concluding that al-Azhar University students and Zaghlulist activists directed crowd disturbances. Yet cultural assumptions inevitably permeated the Foreign Office reading of its humint. The Eastern Department could not accept that Egyptians could orchestrate matters alone.[41] Long-standing British neglect of Egypt's educational system compounded the tendency to view student groups as recidivist and inherently anti-Western.[42] Nor would Graham concede that the extent of popular involvement in the disorders signified a profound opposition to the British presence that transcended the class boundaries previously considered the principal barrier to popular nationalism in Egypt. Outside the capital, the sabotage of communications lines and railroad tracks, plus attacks on provincial railroad stations and government buildings, drove the Foreign Office to conclude that Zaghlul's supporters had reactivated a German-Turkish scheme to overthrow British rule originally uncovered after the capture of a German spy at Alexandria in late 1914. Graham also stressed the power of rumor in a climate where the state's information order had broken down: "We do not know, and shall probably never learn, what wild tales as to our misdeeds and nefarious intentions have been circulated in the bazaars and villages. The result has been a systematically organized outbreak of extreme violence, and on an extended scale, which appears to have taken the local authorities completely by surprise."[43] Ultimately, it made sense to blame the unrest on two prime causes: a seditious plot, itself a hangover from the war, and a temporary breakdown in the Cairo authorities' intelligence system. British imperial policy was thereby absolved.[44]

Stung by this Whitehall criticism, the Department of Public Security provided more comprehensive and frequent intelligence reports in the wake of the 1919 disorders and the subsequent restructuring of the Egyptian government's intelligence bureaucracy. Political coverage of events in Cairo, Alexandria, and the provinces was much fuller than before. Informants' reports on nationalist meetings were cross-referenced against leaders' speeches and party tracts, some of which were reproduced in full.[45] C. F. Ryder, the director-general of public security, supervised two innovations. The department's weekly intelligence reports were subdivided into sections on economic conditions, the political situation, and a forecast of likely developments in the days ahead. And each report included a brief summary for distribution among British officials.[46]

Intelligence and the Kurdistan Revolt, 1919–1920

In 1919 and 1920, rebellions took hold across the northern and southern reaches of Mesopotamia as the predominantly Kurdish population of the Mosul *vilayet* and the Shi'ite majority community of the south asserted claims to self-government. Let us turn first to the Kurds. The British struggled to impose imperial authority over southern Kurdistan, the arc of territory to the south and west of Iraq's Turkish and Persian frontiers. This was partly the result of persistent disagreement over the alleged strategic and economic benefits of doing so. From 1918 to 1923, policymakers in London and the civil commission in Baghdad remained divided over the merits of integrating Kurdish areas into an Iraqi state. Until the British government resolved its attitude one way or the other, investment in Iraq's administration and defensive infrastructure was unlikely.

As matters stood in 1919–20, the lack of railway communications to Kurdish regions impeded the rapid deployment of troops north of the Shuraimiyah railhead. On 1 July 1919, the general officer commanding and his chief PO warned that "Kurdistan cannot be held and pacified" without construction of a railway line to Kirkuk.[47] Although the War Office and the Baghdad civil commission took up the strategic railway cause, British governmental uncertainty about future Iraqi government, combined with mounting Treasury pressure for cuts to imperial expenditure, meant that nothing was done.[48] Poor communications were not the only problem facing the new administration. As we shall see, the vicissitudes in British policy also reflected the politicization of intelligence personnel in southern Kurdistan and the blatant manipulation of incoming information by the Baghdad civil commission.

There was much at stake on the northern margins of what would soon become the Iraq mandate. The Franco-British dispute over long-term possession of the Mosul *vilayet* shaped British attitudes toward southern Kurdistan as a whole. But a far more pressing external threat lay across the frontier to the north. Turkish political influence in Kurdish regions remained strong from the Mudros armistice of October 1918 until the Lausanne Conference four years later. Kemalist leaders were quite prepared to intervene militarily to prevent the consolidation of an independent Kurdish state. Even after Lausanne, the relative thaw in Anglo-Turkish relations was easily reversed by tensions over Kurdistan. A major incursion of Kemalist forces over the Turkey-Iraq border in September 1924, to which British forces responded with aerial bombardment, was a reminder that the Ankara government would never acquiesce in Kurdish self-determination.[49] Ironically, the Kurds proved equally adept at self-government and united in opposition to foreign rule. There was little reason to suppose that Kurdish community leaders, who were bitterly hostile to any resumption of Turkish

control, would be any more welcoming to a British-backed Arab administration.[50] After years of Ottoman repression, the Kurdish population was
never likely to accept incorporation into an Arab-ruled state. As expected,
Kurdish electors overwhelmingly rejected Faysal as their ruler in the 1921
referendum on a unified Iraq.

Into this volatile mix the British injected a communally based imperial
policing system that was bound to make things worse. The high policy context is critical here. The future of Iraq and Palestine dominated the agenda
of the Cairo Conference convened under the then colonial secretary
Winston Churchill's chairmanship from 12 to 30 March 1921. The conference, which brought together representatives of British imperial administration throughout the Arab world, is better remembered for its decisions
about the reassignment of Whitehall responsibilities for policy formulation
in the Middle East, a process from which the Colonial Office Middle East
Department emerged the clear winner. While Churchill took charge of
these jurisdictional matters, a series of more pressing questions was handled
by a Military and Financial Committee chaired by Lieutenant-General Sir
Walter Congreve, who was Allenby's successor as commander-in-chief in
Egypt and Palestine. Determined to make savings of five and a half million
pounds in the Palestine and Iraq security budget, this committee made key
recommendations about the future of Kurdistan.[51]

Recognizing that the Kurds would resist Arab rule, the Baghdad high
commission was to bypass Faysal's government and deal direct with Kurdish
representatives until the status of southern Kurdistan, autonomous or otherwise, was resolved. In the interim, the British garrison at Kirkuk and the
irregular levies in the front line of repressive measures across southern
Kurdistan were to be withdrawn. It was hoped that a locally recruited, multi-
ethnic security force would eventually take their place. But for the foresee-
able future a levy force almost exclusively composed of displaced Assyrian
Christian refugees was designated to keep order among the predominantly
Muslim population of Kurds, Arabs, and Turks.[52] Security policy was therefore likely to inflame communal antagonisms, compounding the Kurds'
sense of injustice at Britain's denial of Kurdish autonomy.[53]

Only two years earlier, Kurdish self-government had seemed a real possibility, but by the time the Colonial Office assumed jurisdictional control
over British imperial policy in the Middle East at the Cairo Conference,
British attitudes to Kurdish autonomy reflected wider perceptions of the
Kemalist threat to northern Iraq and the requirements of a stable Sherifian
regime in Baghdad.[54] All the while, a fundamental split remained. Churchill's
Colonial Office favored Kurdish autonomy, whereas the Baghdad civil government was determined to thwart it.[55]

Intelligence gathering in southern Kurdistan thus acquired unprecedented importance. The British POs and their assistants, mainly army

officers, in the region's principal towns—Sulaimaniyah, Kirkuk, Arbil, and Mosul—became caught up in these arguments between Whitehall and Baghdad. Their intelligence reports on local politics, interethnic disputes, and tribal rivalries were used to justify policy choices that had little to do with dispassionate assessment of PO information. The outbreak of Kurdish revolts in 1919 and 1922 was inextricably linked to this misuse of intelligence. Baghdad civil commissioners Colonel Arnold Wilson and Sir Percy Cox, and their chief political advisor, Gertrude Bell, insisted that southern Kurdistan, stretching from Amadia in the north to Kifri and Khanaqin in the south, should be incorporated into the Iraqi state.[56] They each discerned a potentially disastrous domino effect. If Kurdistan secured meaningful autonomy, the resultant boost to communalism elsewhere in Iraq might undermine Britain's "veiled protectorate" over an Arab-ruled Iraq mandate.[57]

As if these problems were not enough, the British POs in Kurdish territory were underresourced and overstretched. They were ill equipped to gather information either about clan affiliation or the political sentiments of Kurdish peasant farmers. Social organization in the towns of Kurdistan was also poorly understood. The role of religious communities and craft corporations in the politics of urban quarters rarely emerged in POs' reports.[58] These shortcomings were compounded by uncertainty about the movements of Kemalist forces across the frontier, an intelligence shortfall that worsened in April 1919 when Captain C. Pearson, hitherto the principal supplier of humint about the neighboring Turkish zone, was murdered. Meanwhile, POs from Arbil to Sulaimaniyah had little idea how the worsening intercommunal violence among Kurds, Turkomens, Arabs, and Armenians would affect Sheikh Mahmud Khan Dizli's project for an independent Kurdistan.[59] Mahmud, whom the British had previously appointed *hukmdar* (governor) of southern Kurdistan, made no secret of his ambitions for Kurdish independence. During early 1919, he packed his administration with blood relatives and other political allies. Even so, it was months before the Baghdad civil commission and the responsible ministries in Whitehall woke up to Mahmud's iron grip over the region's municipal councils and tribal federations.[60]

The flow of intelligence from Kurdish regions to Baghdad, London, and Delhi was too slow to enable the civil administration in Mesopotamia or the British and Indian governments to preempt Mahmud's revolt. Furthermore, what information did reach more senior British officials was often contradictory because the few POs in situ in the Mosul *vilayet* had split into two distinct groups. Encouraged by British officials in Baghdad, one group overestimated their ability to manipulate Kurdish leaders and thereby control events. Such complacency reflected an underlying assumption common among British officials in Iraq throughout the interwar period, namely, that the Kurdish community was not intrinsically Anglophobic, but was, if any-thing, well disposed to Britain as a former enemy of Turkey and protector against untrammeled Arab rule.[61] Civil commission reliance on the POs deployed in Kurdistan calls to mind the relationship between Arab Bureau chiefs in Cairo and T. E. Lawrence, who supplied the most influential field intelligence about the Arab revolt.[62] But whereas Lawrence and the Arab Bureau broadly supported the Hashemite cause, the POs in this first group in Kurdistan lost political leverage because they aligned themselves against Mahmud. Thus antagonized, local community leaders denied them access to the councils, guilds, and other meetings that were the main forums of social communication in Kurdish towns.[63]

Other political officers, such as Captain Stephen Longrigg, an APO in Kirkuk, favored subtler methods. It was this second group that produced the more sophisticated intelligence. Yet their message was deceptively simple. Stability was impossible unless the British authorities took greater account of Kurdistan's interethnic composition and the strength of its clan-based civil society. Such advice was unwelcome to the Baghdad civil commission, which simply ignored their reports. Longrigg, for instance, highlighted the fallacy of reinstituting tribal administration in essentially nontribal areas, pointing out that it tended to facilitate Mahmud's efforts to impose per-sonal control at the expense of more representative institutions.[64] No one was listening.

Instead, Arnold Wilson in Baghdad hired and fired POs in Kurdish regions without hesitation when incoming intelligence challenged his pref-erence for the incorporation of Kurdistan into Iraq. Those who acknowl-edged the strength of Kurdish claims to self-rule, such as Major Edward Noel, were ousted and replaced by POs hostile to Kurdish autonomy. Depiction of the Kurdish leadership and of factionalism among Kurdish tribes and urban elites, even the assessments of Kurdish ethnicity, changed in response to this pressure from Baghdad, as the information supplied by POs became a weapon in the civil commission's campaign to dissuade Whitehall or the gov-ernment of India from endorsing Kurdish self-government. During 1919, Noel's successor, Major E. B. Soane, denigrated the Kurdish administration in Sulaimaniyah that Noel had done so much to consolidate.[65] Once Sheikh Mahmud, who had formerly worked closely with Noel, championed Kurdish autonomy, he was demonized in POs' assessments as a tyrant intent on estab-lishing a personal fiefdom and cleansing Kurdish regions of their non-Muslim population, including the ill-fated Assyrian refugee community.[66]

The Assyrians were strongly identified by the Kurds as collaborators in Britain's illegal occupation owing to the extensive recruitment of Assyrian levies to assist British imperial troops.[67] Animosity between the two commu-nities increased thereafter. Disregarding the Kurds' grievances about dis-criminatory treatment, British diplomats in the Middle East presumed that support for a self-governing Kurdistan was confined to an unrepresentative Kurdish minority. A dismissive March 1920 report from Admiral John de Robeck, attached to the British mission in Constantinople, revealed how far observers' perceptions were affected by PO reportage hostile to Kurdish autonomy:

> There exists much doubt whether independence or autonomy of Kurdistan is a proposition at all and in any case no such thing as "Kurdish opinion" in the sense of coherent public opinion can be said to exist. [The] great majority of Kurds in the country expect to be ruled from above, few looking higher than tribal Aghas or religious Sheikhs amongst whom there is little common ground but whose opposition it is desirable to avoid challenging if we wish to evolve a system ensuring reasonably good government for [the] mass of people including non-Kurdish minorities. The few educated Kurds outside Kurdistan holding separatist ideas are very apt to exaggerate their own influence and importance.[68]

British intelligence manipulation did not immediately affect the course of events in southern Kurdistan. During 1919, most of the Kurdish regions of the former Mosul *vilayet* fell under Sheikh Mahmud's control as governor of southern Kurdistan. He boasted an impressive lineage as head of the influential Barzanji family and leader of Sulaimaniyah's Qadiri Sufi order. Mahmud drew support from a wide spectrum of urban notables, leading commercial families, and Kurdish tribal groups, notably the Hamawand, based in and around Chemchemal. This was not how the POs reported matters. According to their appreciations, outlying Kurdish tribes and town dwellers were ambivalent about Mahmud, but saw no other option than to acquiesce in his project for an autonomous Kurdistan under his authoritarian rule.[69]

Armed with PO intelligence, in February 1919 Wilson insisted that the towns of Kifri and Kirkuk should not come under the jurisdiction of Mahmud's emergent South Kurdistan state. Major Soane, then PO for the Sulaimaniyah division, was instructed to coax wavering Kurdish tribal leaders into submission to British authority in an effort to diminish Mahmud's constituency of support. Faced with this challenge to his regional power base, Mahmud took stock of opinion among Kurdish groups across the Persian frontier and then, on 22 May 1919, rebelled. This initial attempt to construct a South Kurdistan state by seizing control in Kirkuk failed. Mahmud was captured, tried, and exiled to India.[70]

Over the next two years, Wilson and his successor, Percy Cox, laid the groundwork for direct rule from Baghdad, reincorporating Kurdish districts into the Mosul administrative division under British authority. By Christmas 1919, Cox persuaded the secretary of state for India, Lord Edmund Montagu, to reject Kurdish self-government as incompatible with Britain's strategic interest in a defensible Iraqi state incorporating the Mosul *vilayet*.[71]

The Colonial Office was less easily persuaded. Ultimately, Cox simply defied the recommendations of the Cairo Conference for a separate South Kurdistan state. He had wide latitude to make policy decisions in light of local circumstances, and justified his refusal to comply with the conference stipulations by highlighting the economic interdependence of Kurdish and Arab areas of northern Iraq. Political intelligence from the POs and APOs on the ground lent weight to Cox's assertions, preventing the Colonial Office from pushing the case for Kurdish autonomy.[72]

Meanwhile, Cox, like Wilson before him, removed those POs judged unduly sympathetic to Kurdish demands. These personnel changes were facilitated by the resumption of violence in Kurdish areas in which POs were targeted for assassination.[73] As intelligence gathering had failed to prevent disorder, Assyrian levies, Royal Air Force (RAF) squadrons, and Arab Iraqi troops took its place, conducting protracted operations and aerial bombardments that deepened Kurdish antagonism to British rule and sharpened the communal rivalries that would dog the region in the years ahead.[74] As David Omissi notes, after 1920 "Assyrian troops were employed almost exclusively in the suppression of Kurdish independence. . . . Kurdish separatists therefore detested the Assyrians as the apparently willing agents of centralizing state power, whether Arab or Imperial."[75]

Ironically, the initial success of the Assyrian levies' counterinsurgency made the British government more sanguine about resurrecting a scheme for limited Kurdish autonomy. In May 1922 Mahmud held secret talks over peace terms with the APO in Halabja.[76] As a result, at Colonial Office insistence he was allowed to return from exile in October to resume the experiment in Kurdish self-government. His return suggested a fundamental reversal in British policy. In the event, it was only a temporary one. Within weeks of Mahmud's installation as governor of Kurdistan, the collapse of the Lloyd George coalition, and conclusion of the Anglo-Turkish settlement at the Lausanne Conference in November revitalized Baghdad's policy of direct rule. Mahmud's supporters were driven to rebel once more.[77]

Intensive air attacks on rebel villages resumed. Some were preceded by airdrops of proclamations warning of the consequences of dissension; others were not.[78] Aircraft were also used to transport troops to Kirkuk hours after intelligence was received warning of an uprising in the town.[79] This time around, the network of intelligence providers across Kurdistan spoke with one voice. The earlier dismissals of POs, combined with the insertion of RAF special service officers (SSOs) to provide military intelligence, led to the production of net assessments more to the taste of the Baghdad high commission. In September 1924, British administrative inspectors and SSOs in southern Kurdistan urged more widespread use of air power and levy forces to crush pockets of resistance in the Sharbazhar region, the heartland of Mahmud's support.[80] This combination of punitive aerial bombardment and sweep operations by levy forces would be repeated in later efforts to suppress Kurdish insurgency, culminating in a renewed uprising led by the sheikh of Barzan as Iraq neared formal independence in 1932.[81] Then, as before, Kurdish autonomy fell victim to British strategic requirements and the high commission's unbending support for a unitary Iraqi state. The region's political intelligence system was, by then, completely arrogated to this objective.

Intelligence Used and Abused: Rebellion in Shi'ite Iraq

Nowhere were the limitations of mandate government more apparent than in the spheres of intelligence gathering and tribal policing. These tasks were inseparable and typically involved the same personnel. As we have seen in the case of Kurdistan, in the formative stages of the Iraq mandate, it fell to POs and their assistants to assess the potential for local unrest and to use their powers of persuasion to prevent it. During 1919–20, the forty or so POs and APOs across Iraq remained the sole agents of the imperial power operating nationwide. Most were on short-term assignment of no more than three years. These were the men supposed to keep the civil commission and the Colonial Office advised of the local intelligence picture, all the while preventing simmering political resentments about the British presence from boiling over. Their symbolic importance as the vanguard of imperial administration was apparent to all sides, something made more apparent by the assassination of Captain W. M. Marshall, the PO in Najaf, at the hands of the League of the Islamic Awakening (*Jim'yat al-Nahda al-Islamiya*), a Shi'ite secret society based in the city.[82]

Aside from the personal dangers they faced, political officers could not fulfill their designated role as district officials, judicial authorities, and intelligence gatherers pending the settlement of Iraq's national status and the creation of functioning police agencies. Most sought to fill the political vacuum by developing personal contacts with community leaders in their district. APOs' conversations—or confrontations—with sheikhs, *mukhtars,* former Ottoman officials, and communal leaders were transcribed and condensed into periodic intelligence assessments of local political conditions.[83] The Whitehall committee charged with reorganizing Middle East administration was understandably worried by this state of affairs.[84] By 1920, the prospects for a swift transition to mandatory control were undermined by the inability of the PO network either to conciliate or to coerce.

Community leaders in the major Shi'ite centers of southern Iraq from Basra to Nasariyah, Karbala, and Najaf were immune to British blandishments. Reports of the San Remo resolutions reached Iraq in the midst of Ramadan, which in 1920 fell in May. News of the terms of Britain's mandate over Iraq added venom to the *fatwas* issued against the British occupiers by

Shi'ite and Sunni religious leaders later that month. In this charged atmosphere, the decision of the PO in Diwaniya province to jail a sheikh of the Zawalim tribe for nonpayment of taxes on 30 June was sufficient to trigger the outbreak of violence. The sheikh's fellow tribesmen stormed his mud prison later the same day, declared a rebellion, and sabotaged the nearby railway. Within days, individual tribal confederations took up arms against British garrison forces, forcing the surrender of numerous isolated outposts.[85]

In late July 1920, Captain B. S. Thomas, the PO in Nasariyah, summarized the difficulties facing his APOs in Shi'ite Iraq in these terms:

Hostilities broke out a month ago and our well-wishers as well as our enemies are beginning to realize how weak we are militarily. Arms and ammunition are being bought and sold freely, tribesmen and travelers are carrying rifles, in the districts arms are being dug up from their holes, land grabbers are beginning to man their towers, old time enemies are watching one another and waiting. These are signs of the times and will tax the ingenuity of APOs to the very utmost in keeping the peace and tiding over the present troubles.[86]

Few succeeded. With up to 423 distinct sections organized into 36 large groups, the major Shi'ite tribal confederations south of Baghdad represented a complex but diffuse civil society determined to resist subjugation to alien rule. British POs had a mountain to climb if they were to build any kind of rapport with these tribal communities. Inspired by events in Egypt and Syria, Shi'ite 'ulamā and Euphrates tribal leaders urged their followers to rebel against British imperialism in defense of Arab independence and religious autonomy.[87] There was no functioning civilian authority to oppose them. Nor were British imperial forces well placed to reimpose control. Most were deployed in urban garrisons that could be easily cut off from one another. In the five months of the Shi'ite rebellion between July and November 1920, some were overrun and others were besieged. Imperial authority all but disappeared from southern Iraq. Shi'ite community leaders in Najaf established an independent municipal government with discrete ministries and tax raising powers. Only with the deployment of Indian Army reinforcements, systematic burning of Shi'ite villages and settlements, and the widespread use of aerial bombardment did the tide turn against the rebellion.[88]

Let us return briefly to Nasariyah in the summer of 1920. In early August, Captain Thomas concluded from the initial evidence relayed by his district APOs in areas in and around the Shi'ite holy cities of Najaf and Karbala that economic hardship and anxiety over future levels of taxation dominated public debate and communal politics.[89] The association of a heavier tax burden with foreign domination deepened hostility to the British presence among the Shi'ite population along the Euphrates.[90] The requirements of economic survival explained the functional coalitions among tribes, attitudes to the installation of Faysal as Iraqi ruler, and broader responses to British rule. Pan-Islamism was a secondary concern.[91] In other words, Shi'ite rebelliousness was rooted in poverty and maladministration, not religious fervor.

It was a thoughtful analysis, but it did not tally with the emerging British policy toward Hashemite Iraq, then in its formative stages after Faysal's expulsion from Damascus in July. To Faysal's Foreign Office supporters, the key "lesson" drawn from the field intelligence gathered in Shi'ite regions during 1919–20 was that a more powerful central authority was essential to impose administrative unity on an Iraq mandate whose resentful, heterogeneous population was clearly prone to extremism and violence. To War Office staff anxious to avoid the long-term costs of large imperial garrisons in the Middle East, reports of rising tension across Iraq fueled their hostility to Britain's deepening commitment to a Hashemite policy. To government of India officials aggrieved by their loss of jurisdictional control over Mesopotamia, evidence of intercommunal tension proved the fallacy of Whitehall-directed nation building in Iraq.[92] The same intelligence was used to justify diametrically opposed conclusions.

Conflicting interpretations of local intelligence mirrored doubts among the British political elite over the value and purpose of imperial control in the Arab world. Weeks before the outbreak of the Shi'ite revolt, during April and May 1920 Major-General William Thwaites toured British administrative centers across the Middle East. Thwaites knew the area well. He had been the director of military intelligence in Cairo during the 1919 uprising; indeed, it was his clear-sighted advice then that secured his elevation to the War Office general staff. It was on their behalf that he now drew up proposals for the creation of a central Middle East Intelligence Bureau in Whitehall to analyze all incoming military, political, and economic information from the region.[93] Thwaites saw an unprecedented opportunity to gather intelligence, capitalizing on the wider British civil-military presence throughout Arab territories. But poor coordination of this diverse information made a centralized intelligence agency with regional offices in Cairo, Baghdad, Constantinople, Jerusalem, and Geneva essential. Only then could assessments be relayed swiftly to local security forces to help maintain order. Thwaites suggested that this agency, which he rechristened "ARBUR," the former acronym for the Arab Bureau, should focus primarily on pan-Islamism and the development of Muslim opinion within the British Empire. Crucially, Thwaites was confident that better intelligence provision could ensure that clashes between British colonial states and their Muslim subjects would be averted.

A month after Thwaites reported his findings to the War Office, a very different intelligence survey crossed the desks of the India Office Political Department. This came from Major Norman Bray, a former officer of the

Bengal Lancers and now a member of the Secret Intelligence Service (SIS). As an SIS officer, Bray worked on assignment to Lord Montagu's India Office, which deputized him to report on pan-Islamist sedition in Arab territories. On 14 September 1920, he submitted a lengthy report on the causes of unrest in Iraq. Bray was widely acknowledged as an expert on pan-Islamist networks, particularly those with connections in Muslim India. He was also no stranger to the black arts of interdepartmental infighting between Whitehall ministries with a stake in the Middle East.[94] He had been sent to Jeddah by the Delhi government in late 1916, ostensibly to monitor the safe passage of hajj pilgrim traffic from India to Arabia, but actually to undercut the growing influence of the Cairo-based Arab Bureau over Britain's policy in the Hijaz.[95] Not surprisingly, his October 1920 report was politically loaded, and tailored to suit India Office arguments.[96]

Bray found abundant evidence of covert ties between the Kemalist government and three pan-Islamist groups—the Nadi-al-Arabi and the Elahd in Syria, and the Mouvahiddin Society in Ankara. He cited sigint intercepts of Turkish military dispatches to tribal sheikhs in Iraq, Syria, and southern Arabia that indicated plans were afoot for a concerted Arab uprising to evict the European imperial powers from the Middle East. Even more sinister was evidence of German financial support and Bolshevik assistance to pan-Arab and pan-Islamist sympathizers based in Berlin and Switzerland. The Hashemite authorities were condemned by implication. Bray insisted that it was inconceivable that such a sophisticated pan-Islamist network could develop without their active collusion.[97] His standing as a dispassionate analyst was reinforced by the array of intelligence he cited. Yet the nub of his argument owed more to prevailing government of India attitudes about Arab political consciousness than to intimate local knowledge.[98] Bray's analysis was also colored by racial and religious stereotypes. Political upheaval in the Middle East was imminent, but only outside forces— German money, Bolshevik organizers, Kemalist military expertise, and the foreign-educated Arab intelligentsia—could bring it about by organizing an Arab Muslim community otherwise incapable of unified political action. As Bray put it, "The pan-Arabs, the Nationalists, the disgruntled effendi, the tribesman impatient of his enforced inaction, and the fanatical priest taken separately are innocuous, taken collectively [they] form a very dangerous combination."[99]

It was an apocalyptic message, but it was deeply flawed. Aside from its racist and one-dimensional image of Arab irrationalism, Bray's account took no account of local economic conditions and made no reference to any shortcomings in the administration of Iraq, until recently under government of India control. Not surprisingly, former Arab Bureau staff attached to the Foreign Office leapt at the chance to discredit his conclusions. Contacts between pan-Islamist groups were circumstantial, not deeply rooted. Grievances over past British or, more precisely, India Office errors were explanation enough. Reorganization of British governmental responsibilities in Iraq was all that was required to dissipate the alleged pan-Islamist threat.[100] Once again, raw intelligence data were used to fight Whitehall battles over Middle East administrative control.

The tragedy was that in these disputes over interpretation of intelligence about pan-Islamism, the severity of the Shi'ite rebellion was obscured. Yet the Shi'ites of the Euphrates valley had been driven to mount the largest single uprising against British imperialism in the Middle East since World War I. Their resistance to central government oppression, the expropriation of tribal lands, and conscription would continue intermittently for the next generation.[101] In this turbulent and dynamic political environment, it was perhaps unsurprising that from 1922 onward, RAF SSOs were hard pressed to maintain an effective information supply. These SSOs assumed the former responsibilities of POs and APOs once the RAF assumed primary responsibility for imperial policing in Iraq following the 1921 Cairo Conference. It was they who henceforth supplied the bulk of raw intelligence about Iraq's religious and tribal politics. Few SSOs had the experience or connections necessary to comprehend the complexities of Shi'ite opinion. Fewer still could gain much sense of public opinion in the key urban centers of Karbala and Najaf, other than during the annual hajj, when both cities opened their gates to thousands of fellow Shi'ite pilgrims from Persia.

During 1924, the SSO in Ramadi relied on his Shi'ite manservant (who also served as a spy for King Faysal) for indications of the public mood in Najaf and evidence of insurrectionist plotting between the city's leading 'ulamā and sheikhs of the Shamiyah desert tribes to the south.[102] His SSO colleague in Basra toured southern Iraq in early 1925 in an effort to identify the network of contacts linking the 'ulamā with the Shi'ite Jaffari Party and their coreligionists in Persia.[103] Baghdad Air headquarters intelligence summaries, widely distributed among Whitehall ministries and other Middle East administrations, reduced Iraqi national politics to the interplay between the high commission, the Faysali government, and the Baghdad effendiyya on the one hand, and the paramount tribal sheikhs and their lesser chiefly rivals on the other.[104] High commission political intelligence surveys similarly devoted far more attention to the proceedings of the Baghdad Council of Ministers, the capital's press, and political gossip among the ruling elite than to events and opinion in the provinces.[105]

Yet SSOs and Hashemite officials deployed across southern Iraq were well aware that Shi'ite 'ulamā were central to political affiliations and public attitudes among the Shi'ite faithful. Agents' reports of Friday prayers, 'ulamā teachings, and the rivalries among Shi'ite clerics were integral to the imperial surveillance network throughout the south.[106] Over the summer of 1923, Faysal ordered the deportation to Persia of leading 'ulamā from Iraq's

Holy Cities. Residents and travelers were forbidden to enter or leave Kerbala and Najaf without a government pass. Evidence that local sheikhs approved this measure eclipsed the more astute agents' reports from inside the cities indicating public fury at the insensitive treatment of the Shi'ite community.[107] Continued SSO monitoring of rival Shi'ite clerics and contacts between Iraqi Shi'ites and their Persian religious brethren were gradually subsumed within broader intelligence summaries that attached greater weight to foreign direction of religious dissent. Put simply, official anxieties about pan-Islamism masked the local origins of popular grievance against British rule. The socioeconomic factors and systematic political marginalization that fed Shi'ite hostility to mandatory government in Iraq were underestimated as a result.[108]

Signature of the first Anglo-Iraqi treaty on 13 January 1926 added to high commission complacency toward intelligence of Shi'ites' dissent.[109] As plans for the end of formal mandatory control took more concrete form in the late 1920s, large-scale counterinsurgency operations were largely confined to southern Kurdistan.[110] Meanwhile, tribal policing, rather than surveillance of Shi'ite opinion, assumed greater importance across much of southern Iraq.[111] SSOs were nonetheless insistent that communal tension between Shi'ites and Sunnis dominated urban politics in the south.[112] Only the factionalism among Shi'ite clerics, fueled by memories of the 'ulamā expulsions of 1923, prevented the emergence of a coherent anti-Hashemite movement among the Shi'ite community. Mounting tribal grievances at increased tax exactions suggested that the rural population might be receptive to such a movement.[113] Once reports reached Air HQ of coordinated opposition among the Shi'ite tribes of the Middle Euphrates and the clerics of Kerbala and Najaf led by Hassan al-Isfahani and Mirza Hussein Naiyini, the Baghdad air staff identified priority targets for aerial bombardment in the Shi'ite Holy Cities and among Shi'ite tribal groups in case disorders broke out.[114] Until the final implementation of an Anglo-Iraqi treaty ending the mandate in 1932, intelligence of Shi'ite unrest throughout the south formed part of the background noise of political debate in Baghdad, rarely intruding on high policymaking, but never entirely absent from government concerns.[115]

Take, for example, the departing high commissioner Sir Henry Dobbs's warning of incipient conflict between central government in Baghdad and the Iraqi provinces in his final report to the Colonial Office on 4 December 1928:

> There is little affection or awe of the [Hashemite] Crown, no national consciousness outside the schools of Baghdad and Mosul and no respect for the courtiers or for the politicians. The strength of the Administration rests almost solely on the knowledge of British support and control and on the fear inspired by British aeroplanes and armored cars in the plains and by the

Assyrian Levies helped by British aeroplanes in the Kurdish hills. . . . Thus, although the existing state of security is complete and unprecedented, it rests on a precarious base and quite as much on British reputation and British reserve power outside the country as on the British forces actually present. If the already suspicious Shi'ite or Kurdish tribesmen were to feel that British policy towards them was being dragged at the heels of the anti-tribal Baghdad politicians and that there was no power in the land inclined to notice their complaints, scattered and spasmodic risings would soon begin which, unless quickly suppressed, would result in general disorder. . . . In the end, British public opinion would be shocked by the sight of British aeroplanes bombing the tribesmen of the Euphrates or Kurdistan to enforce tyrannical or mistaken decrees hatched amid the intrigues of the Baghdad coffee-shops or conceived by citizen pedants.[116]

The final, brutal suppression of Shi'ite tribal resistance among the Hatim, the Bani Rikab, and the Khafajah by General Bakr Sidqi's Iraqi Army forces in the spring of 1936 cleared the path for the army coup d'état of 29 October that same year, which placed Sidqi's nominee, Hikmat Sulayman, at the head of government.[117] The army's vicious repression of tribal dissent from the massacres of Assyrians in 1933 to the reduction of Shi'ite resistance three years later pointed to the increasing politicization of the military.[118] Again, intelligence played its part. Iraqi Army violence against the Assyrians and Shi'ites reflected the mounting influence of its intelligence department in determining the coercive measures employed to crush dissent.[119]

Intelligence and Unrest in the Sudan

If Iraqi anticolonialism was rooted in the communal politics practiced by the British mandatory, in the Sudan condominium another external power was pivotal to the growth of elite nationalist sentiment in the 1920s. Sudan's uneasy relationship with Egypt veered between the poles of fellow feeling toward British imperial intrusion and acute resentment at Egypt's own hegemonic, quasi-colonial claims over the Nile valley.[120] The British authorities in Khartoum exploited these tensions, all the while claiming decentralization as their mantra of administrative practice.[121] The country may have been governed under martial law, with all regulations issued by the governor-general in council, but Sudan's colonial government was hardly omnipresent in the lives of Sudanese outside the capital. Sudan was neatly segmented into fifteen provinces, each under a governor and district governmental staff, until an administrative overhaul in 1936 reduced the number of provinces to nine.[122] After World War I the territory was actually run by a shifting coalition of British administrators, Egyptian bureaucrats and military auxiliaries, and Sudanese intermediaries gradually introduced to the junior ranks of state bureaucracy as *ma'murs* and sub-*ma'murs* (district subofficers).

Training courses for Sudanese sub-*ma'murs* were instituted in 1919, and by December 1922 sixty-four had been appointed.[123] This "Sudanization" of the administrative service gathered renewed momentum in the late 1930s, with 414 Sudanese appointed to technical or clerical posts in 1937 alone. By this point, Sudanese held 73.4 percent of the total classified appointments in government service.[124] Those indigenous district officials appointed in the interwar years remained accountable to the British-staffed Sudan Political Service (SPS), created in 1900. A small, elite bureaucracy, loosely modeled on its far larger Indian forebear, the SPS retained the principal role in civil affairs.[125]

Aside from working with their sub-*ma'murs*, SPS officers, in turn, relied on distinct constituencies of indigenous Sudanese to maintain imperial control in what remained a sharply segmented society, profoundly cleaved between Arab north and black African south. Among the more significant reforms introduced soon after World War I were the creation of native advisory councils in the municipalities of Khartoum, Khartoum North, Omdurman, and Port Sudan between April and June 1921. Half of the contested seats in each council were reserved for local notables and merchants. A Sudanese magistracy was also expanded in the early 1920s, with some 133 Sudanese notables appointed as members of criminal courts by the end of 1921.[126] Advisory councils and a local magistracy sound impressive but represented little more than the institutionalization of traditional modes of governing and administering justice under customary law. Their creation pointed, not to the power of the British colonial state in the Sudan, but to its limits. This was a fact readily acknowledged by the Khartoum authorities whose annual administrative report for 1921 made the following point:

> Our object, in brief, is to leave administration, as far as possible, in the hands of the native authorities, wherever they exist, under the supervision of the Government, starting from things as it finds them, putting its veto on what is dangerous and unjust and supporting what is fair and equitable in the usage of the natives. Much obviously depends on the existence and efficacy of any local or tribal organization. When such does exist the aim of the Government is to foster and guide it along right channels. Where it has ceased to exist it may still be possible to re-create it. In pursuance of this policy the Government encourages native chiefs to administer their own tribes in accordance with native customs in so far as those customs are not entirely repugnant to ideas of justice and humanity and aims at non-interference except where necessary.[127]

The administrative and judicial reforms introduced in Sudan after 1919 marked the culmination of policies developed under the country's long-serving governor Sir Reginald Wingate before he moved north to take up the reins at the Cairo Residency. The governor also drew on the indirect rule schemes pioneered by Lord Lugard in Nigeria, a colony similarly divided between a Muslim north and a non-Muslim south.[128] But it is Wingate's intelligence background that concerns us here. Sudan's pioneering governor made his name as head of intelligence in the Egyptian Army during the Mahdist revolt and the subsequent imposition of British rule in the 1890s. His writings on the *Mahdiyya* remained required reading for all SPS inductees for years afterward.[129] During World War I, Wingate's Khartoum administration redoubled its efforts to coopt members of the capital's educated urban elite and tribal leaders of the major nomadic confederations of the north—Sheikhs, Omdas, and Nazirs—into the condominium system as tax collectors and judges of customary law.[130]

Wingate's strategy of divide and rule also embraced accommodation with northern Muslim religious leaders, none more so than 'Abd al-Rahman al-Mahdi, son of the Mahdi whom Wingate had done so much to denigrate. Even Sufi orders and *tariqas* previously viewed with suspicion as vestigial centers of Mahdist fanaticism were conciliated once it became clear that their cooperation would enhance Muslim loyalty during the war. Before 1914, Wingate aligned the administration with the institutions of orthodox Islam and used the Khartoum board of 'ulamā created in 1901 to attack Sufi heresy.[131] But once the war began, nonorthodox religious leaders were coopted into the government's intelligence-gathering apparatus, supplying information on their followers' opinions. In 1915, Wingate legalized Mahdist worship and set about rallying the Ansar, Sudan's largest Muslim sect, to the British war effort.[132] Idrisiya sheikhs formerly placed under government surveillance were even recruited by the Khartoum Intelligence Department as intermediaries to the Sanussi. Sudanese particularism, the Sufism of Sudan's northern *tariqas,* and regional hierarchies of chiefs were all conciliated, both to limit Egyptian influence and to consolidate elite cooperation with SPS officers on the ground.[133] Such arrangements amounted to a "tactical alliance": the British drove a wedge between Egyptian and Arab Sudanese nationalism; the Mahdists used Britain's requirement for a conservative auxiliary elite to undermine Egyptian pretensions to govern Sudan.[134]

Southern Sudan's largely black population was excluded from these patron-client relationships. SPS staff, many of whom articulated their ideas in the administration's scholarly journal, *Sudan Notes and Records,* promoted provincial integration and concepts of Sudanese national identity but never emulated the clientage system pursued in the north.[135] The vast southern provinces of Darfur, Kordofan, Bahr al-Ghazal, and Equatoria were instead ruled in a more rigid, unforgiving colonial style in which black lives were held appallingly cheap.[136] Punitive military operations, typically instigated on the basis of provincial governors' recommendations to the Khartoum intelligence directorate, were a constant feature of colonial control across southern Sudan.[137]

Humint supplied to the provincial governors by SPS district officers was the key evidential basis on which such operations were launched. Accounts of tribal resentment over the burden of colonial taxes and rumors of religious fanaticism, whether Mahdist or Christian, were enough to trigger the dispatch of mounted columns equipped with heavy machine guns to ensure that order was kept. Given the vast distances to be traversed, it was almost inevitable that imperial policing in the south was often a matter of retrospective punishment rather than preemptive crowd control. Even rapid intelligence provision that might in other locations have been used to prevent disorder was frequently stultified by the overwhelming problem of poor internal communications.

On 22 September 1921, for example, intelligence from the district inspector in Nyala district, southern Darfur, indicated that a certain Fiki Abdullah el-Siheini had declared himself "the prophet Jesus" and proclaimed jihad, and was marching on Nyala with up to five thousand followers. Four days later, the British administrative post and garrison were overrun. The two Britons present, the district inspector Captain Tennant McNeill and the British veterinary officer Captain H. Chown, were both killed, along with four civilian clerks. Official estimates put deaths among the attacking Sudanese force at six hundred. Worse was to follow. During October and November, troops of the West Yorkshire regiment "harried" rebel forces across south Darfur until no organized resistance remained. The death toll was never recorded.[138] Aside from these killings, livestock confiscations, weapons seizures, and village burnings represented the sharp end of Britain's collective punishment system in southern Sudan.[139]

By contrast to the harsher colonial conditions prevailing in the south, the system of clientage applied across northern Sudan rested on a series of delicate checks and balances. The central administration sought to accommodate Khartoum's growing urban intelligentsia by offering junior clerical and judicial posts to Arab Sudanese graduates. But the potential coalescence of organized nationalism around this educated urban elite encouraged the retention of a strongly martial flavor to Sudan's imperial government, the better to limit the opportunities for nationalist opposition to emerge.[140] Meanwhile, cooperation continued with notables of the principal tribal groups in northern Sudan: the Barabra and the Dongolowi. The British looked favorably on the Arab tribal elite loyal to the "three Sayyids," 'Abd al-Rahman al-Mahdi, 'Ali al-Mirghani, and al-Sharif Yusuf al-Hindi, as their allegiance to these conservative figures counteracted the centripetal pull of Khartoum in national politics.[141]

That said, the introduction of educated Sudanese to state bureaucracy, the police, and the Sudan Defense Force came under closer British scrutiny in 1919 as a result of the Egyptian uprising. The national identity and future status of Sudan remained a bone of contention between the Wafd and the British authorities after Zaghlul's return from exile and his ensuing negotiations with Lord Milner's investigative mission. The restoration of Egyptian parliamentary government was quickly followed by a reassertion of Egypt's claims to supremacy over the entire Nile Valley, something Milner had been at pains to rule out.[142] And the example of the 1919 uprising inspired a younger generation of Sudanese—many of them junior clerks, skilled urban workers, or students and cadets at Khartoum's Gordon College and the Sudan Military School—to articulate a Sudanese nationalism that embraced partnership, if not fusion, with Egypt.[143]

The upsurge in pro-Egyptian sentiment among younger, more politically active city-dwelling Sudanese provoked a strong reaction from the colonial government. The official reading of these early indicators of a new-style Sudanese nationalism was based on an amalgam of Khartoum Intelligence Department reports and Cairo political intelligence on Egyptian party political contacts with the handful of educated Sudanese soon to achieve notoriety as leaders of two groups: the League of Sudanese Union and the White Flag League. Intelligence agents in the Sudanese capital monitored suspicious gatherings of known activists, and the Khartoum Intelligence Department built up a substantial dossier on White Flag League activities from the organization's tentative beginnings among junior officers of the Egyptian Army garrison in July 1920.[144] Their security service colleagues in Cairo kept a close watch on senior Wafdist and nationalist (Watani) party figures.[145]

As so often before, the resultant intelligence analyses were a peculiarly colonial mixture, at once well informed and riddled with racial prejudice and flawed cultural assumptions. But the essence of their message was simple: the political ferment among young Sudanese in Khartoum was Egyptian inspired, the product of Wafdist and Watani intrigue.[146] Plainly put, their reading of events suggested that experienced political operators in Cairo were manipulating the political innocents of Khartoum.[147] It seemed inconceivable that the Sudanese military officers and junior clerical staff—many of them "detribalized" black southerners—who formed the White Flag League in early 1924 were autonomous political actors.[148]

In fact, the White Flag League's founder, 'Ali 'abd al-Latif, a southern ex-army officer of mixed Dinka and Nuba origin, gave voice to the protonationalist views of Khartoum's rising generation of indigenous auxiliaries. These were young men drawn to Egyptian patronage, certainly, but who still carved out a distinct vision of a Sudanese national identity that transcended the old tribal and interethnic divisions of north and south.[149] In doing so they cut across the ethnic enmities so critical to British capacity to retain administrative control. Little wonder that the Khartoum government demonized Egyptian external influence and 'Ali 'abd al-Latif from 1922 to 1924.[150]

There was another dimension to Britain's harsh reaction. Egyptian claims to hegemony in Sudan gained extra impetus from Zaghlul's election as prime minister in January 1924. Intense cross-party concern in Egypt over water and irrigation rights to the Nile heightened the pressure to stake Egyptian claims. Seen from Viscount Allenby's perspective in Cairo, the resulting Egyptian pressure for reserved rights in the Sudan threatened to derail negotiations for an Anglo-Egyptian treaty designed to entrench Britain's strategic and commercial dominance.[151] Security services and imperial government thus arrived at the same conclusion, albeit for different reasons: the sooner a clinical administrative separation was achieved between Sudan and Egypt the better.

The British decision to remove Egyptians from the ranks of the Sudanese administration and to withdraw the Egyptian garrison from Khartoum was not, however, entirely conditioned by the White Flag League's campaign for closer partnership with Egypt. The conviction that the presence of so many Egyptians in Sudan's government and military was a profoundly corruptive force went back much further. At the height of the 1919 disorders in Cairo, the Khartoum administration, fashioned by Wingate as governor-general and *sirdar* (commander-in-chief) over the previous seventeen years, resolved that Sudanese personnel should eventually replace the Egyptian clerical staff and army officer class that were pillars of British rule in the Sudan. The two British government inquiries into the Anglo-Egyptian relationship instigated after the 1919 unrest were of the same mind. The Keown-Boyd Report of 1920 and the more famous Milner Report of 1921 that led to Britain's unilateral declaration of Egyptian "independence" in the following year each suggested that Egyptian personnel be withdrawn from the civil service and standing military forces in Sudan be replaced by British-trained Sudanese.[152] The Khartoum Intelligence Department added its weight to these political assessments, convinced that diminution of Egyptian influence was essential to undermine nationalist pressure on both sides for closer union.[153] Exclusively British training for young Sudanese bureaucrats and security force officers might allow the Khartoum government to mold a concept of Sudanese national identity among the educated elite in conformity with Britain's requirement for sustained colonial control.[154]

Two Khartoum institutions were at the cutting edge of this process: Gordon College and the Sudan Military School. The former prepared its pupils for junior clerical and technical posts in civil government.[155] The latter trained recruits for the black and Arab battalions of the Egyptian Army. The cadres of both were kept under close surveillance, partly because British expectations of them were so high. According to Heather Sharkey, by 1922 some 1,800 Gordon College graduates held administrative positions, many as sub-*ma'murs* with responsibility for local policing.[156] Khartoum government sensitivity to the College curriculum and decisions about whether or not to appoint its graduates were shaped by intelligence appreciations of the extent to which indirect rule could be safely implemented across the Sudan. Similar evaluation of the replacement of Egyptian Army officers with former students of the Sudan Military School reflected threat assessments of the balance of risks involved. Retention of large numbers of Egyptian military personnel in Sudan as Egyptian nationalism gathered strength was clearly undesirable, but the military capacity and political loyalty of the Sudanese elite that would replace them was also under constant intelligence review.[157]

These conflicting pressures came to a head over the summer of 1924. The emergence of the White Flag League as a political force and the discovery of contacts between its senior members and leaders of the Egyptian nationalist opposition, the Watani party, suggested that intelligence assumptions about the malleability of educated Sudanese minds were unduly optimistic. White Flag League efforts to stimulate urban protests through pamphleteering and a propaganda campaign backed by the Egyptian press came together in June. It was then that British troops arrested Muhammad al'Mahdi, a League supporter, en route to the Cairo Parliament. His detention triggered demonstrations that spread from Khartoum to Omdurman, Port Sudan, and other northern towns. Urban workers' grievances over rising inflation and low wages, shared by Sudanese administrative and military personnel, became caught up in a protest movement originally sparked by the White Flag League's autonomist program. An undercurrent of intergenerational rivalry between older, socially conservative supporters of the Mahdi and the predominantly young, male followers of 'Ali 'abd al-Latif, some of them linked to the former group by family ties, was also manifest in the 1924 protests.[158] Once the unrest spread to Sudanese military units, including Khartoum Military School cadets and a railway battalion, which mutinied at Atbara on 11 August, the full force of the colonial state came down on the White Flag League.[159] 'Abd al-Latif received a three-year jail term (subsequently extended); other activists were tried, imprisoned, or exiled.[160]

What looked like swift, surgical repression was nothing of the sort. Hasty reenrollments of special police units in response to rumors of additional protests gave some clue to just how close the British had come to losing control.[161] Much worse was to follow. The assassination of Sudan's governor-general, Sir Lee Stack, in Cairo on 19 November and reports of jubilation at his killing among Egyptian troops stationed across northern Sudan provoked a furious British response. At 4.45 P.M. on the 22nd, Allenby issued an ultimatum to Zaghlul calling for the withdrawal of all Egyptian units from Sudan within twenty-four hours. Although not made clear at the time, Egyptian administrative personnel were also required to leave. The high commissioner set off for this meeting at the head of a regimental column of cavalry (the Sixteenth Lancers) for maximum coercive effect. Zaghlul nonetheless refused to comply. With a military confrontation between

British and Egyptian forces apparently imminent, strict censorship of all British government communications between Cairo and Khartoum was instituted immediately prior to the high commission order issued on the evening of the 23rd for British troops to surround the two battalions of Egyptian soldiers then garrisoned in the Sudanese capital.[162]

In Khartoum itself, the acting British military commander, Major-General H. J. Huddleston, took charge of the situation. After a tense standoff, one of the Egyptian battalions was disarmed and put aboard a train to Cairo on the evening of the 24th, machine guns trained on them all the while. The other battalion and a small Egyptian artillery unit refused to move unless expressly authorized to do so by the Cairo government. Huddleston ordered the immediate reinforcement of key garrison centers with the few remaining all-white units at his disposal.[163] While these redeployments were going on, he received news of violent disturbances in Khartoum Central Prison initiated by the Sudanese military cadets previously sentenced for involvement in the August demonstrations. Further intelligence reports of collusion among mixed Egyptian-Sudanese units, and a forty-eight-hour mutiny among troops of the Tenth and Eleventh Sudanese Battalions in which two British officers were killed, indicated that the coercive power of the British colonial state in Sudan was collapsing.[164]

Until British troop reinforcements arrived, during 27 and 28 November Huddleston's military command in Khartoum could do little to regain control over those barracks where Egyptian and Sudanese battalion troops refused to obey their British officers and claimed loyalty instead to the artillery officer, Ahmed Bey Rifaat. The capital's streets also became contested ground. Cadets of the musketry school and two platoons of Sudanese soldiers marched through the capital intending to link up with the Egyptian Fourth Battalion confined to barracks in the north of the city. Again, only the machine guns of the Argyll and Sutherland Highlanders stood between colonial order and a Sudanese military uprising.[165]

At this stage, the intelligence department could do nothing to help matters, but it had failed to appreciate either the depth of resentment over the earlier repression of the White Flag League or the extent of common interest between Egyptian and Sudanese military personnel. What saved the situation for the British in November 1924 was the fact that the military confrontations and army mutinies found no echo among Sudan's predominantly rural population. Had the unrest spread to the countryside, making the concentration of British forces in the key urban centers impossible, then the shortcomings of the information order in Sudan could have brought down the colonial state, even if only temporarily. The new governor-general, Sir Francis Archer, the former governor of Uganda appointed on 4 December, faced a difficult task. Only with the execution of several of the November mutineers and the constitution of a locally recruited and British-officered Sudan Defense Force in January 1925 did the colonial authorities begin to reassert their military supremacy.[166]

Meanwhile, the district commissioners and their assistants who had closest contact with Sudanese civil society in the rural interior redoubled their efforts to coopt conservative tribal leaders. The Nomad Sheikhs Ordinance of 1927 placed this arrangement on a more formal basis, widening the chiefly powers delineated in an earlier ordinance of February 1922. The object of the 1922 legislation was to regularize the immemorial system by which the chiefs of nomadic and seminomadic tribes exercised punitive power over their tribesmen and arbitral authority in intertribal disputes.[167] The 1927 ordinance went further, creating tribal magistrates with authority to uphold customary law and prosecute minor misdemeanors. It was presented as an exemplar of indirect rule that met British requirements for civil order and regular tax collection. But it was also a pragmatic response to the limitations of British authority revealed by SPS humint reports to the Khartoum Intelligence Department.[168] Just as significant, the Sudan government vested greater trust in selected chiefs rather than the Sudanese *ma'murs* and sub-*ma'murs* previously assigned limited powers. Under Archer's successor, Sir John Maffey, governor from 1926 to 1934, *ma'mur* numbers still grew, but this Sudanization was not matched by increased delegation of authority to them.[169]

Policing in the Sudan followed a similar pattern. There were general principles, certainly, but the development of security service operations reflected scanty resources, limited trust of educated Sudanese junior officials, and the consequent pressure on British officers. In 1935, the organization of intelligence services in the Sudan was reformed to cope with the regional instability generated by Italy's war in neighboring Abyssinia. Until then, the methods of intelligence collection and dissemination had remained essentially unchanged since the disorders of 1924. There was no military intelligence system dedicated to monitoring external threats until November 1935. Instead, the Sudan Defense Force maintained a staff of RAF intelligence officers that monitored internal security throughout the colony. These air force officers relied on personal contact with district administrators to provide them with raw intelligence on local conditions. The RAF personnel confined themselves to intelligence analysis rather than intelligence collection. The air staff in Sudan justified this demarcation of responsibility on the grounds that the SPS was well placed to acquire information about the local population, while military analysts were better suited to identifying potential threats from the mass of intelligence gathered.[170]

Before the Abyssinian conflict began in 1935, regional intelligence officers submitted either monthly diaries or quarterly reports to the Sudan Defense Force headquarters in Khartoum as part of their general administrative responsibilities. Most were dominated by environmental intelligence on the condition of roads and rivers, plus what little information on tribal affairs could be gleaned from occasional discussions with SPS personnel. Ostensibly military intelligence therefore bore the imprint of the civilian district officers that provided most of the useful details it contained. Provincial governors were expected to keep the Khartoum civil secretary informed of tribal politics in their localities, including any outbreaks of dissent requiring military intervention.[171] The deficiencies of this intelligence system became more apparent as organized opposition to the British presence grew. The senior RAF officer in Sudan put matters baldly in March 1936: "Civil administrators in semi-civilized countries have a habit of permitting the cauldron to bubble over before they notify Headquarters of potential trouble. In these circumstances the military are ultimately faced with an unnecessarily difficult problem, often a problem that could have been solved before it arose *if only information had been received in time.*"[172]

A year later matters seemed little changed. The *kaid,* or commander, of the Sudan Defense Force criticized the excessive bureaucratization of intelligence analysis in Sudan, noting ruefully,

> Monthly Diaries reached him too late to be of much value. The information first went from the D[istrict] C[ommissioner] to Province H.Q. where it was edited. That took time. The Diary was then transmitted to Khartoum where it started its rounds. When it reached him it was usually six weeks to two months old. These Diaries also contained a mass of statistics and data only of indirect interest to him and very little tribal information, which was of direct interest. He would like to receive information about a deteriorating situation but additionally information about a satisfactory situation. The latter was always reassuring.[173]

Concern about the rapidity of intelligence transmission is common among security services, it being generally acknowledged that the value of information as exploitable intelligence often declines over time. But in the context of imperial policing in the British Middle East, RAF officers had a particular vested interest in the quick relay of information. The very survival of the RAF as an independent service arm in the 1920s rested in large part on its capacity to prove itself as an economical means to uphold colonial control in the Arab world. Much has been written about the use of punitive aerial bombardment as a cost-effective method of force projection, bombing being cheaper than a punitive expedition by soldiers or police.[174] In the chilling jargon of the time, its "moral effect" was also greater, as its capacity to wreak targeted destruction was judged more intimidating.[175] Stray bombs were also dismissed as less murderous than unruly irregular troops. Losses of airmen and their aircraft were also relatively slight when compared with probable fatalities among military units. Casualties among airmen were more often the result of equipment failure than enemy retaliation. Aircraft could cover distances at more than ten times the speed of army patrols and could reach targets that were otherwise inaccessible by land. Aerial reconnaissance and photography, collectively known as image intelligence (imint), revolutionized the scale and quality of topographical and demographic information available to colonial authorities.[176] In short, "air substitution" was appealing to imperial governments on the grounds of cost (material and human), strategy, and geography.[177]

For all its deadly effectiveness, the use of air power in colonial policy had two Achilles' heels. In the first place, aircraft were generally ineffective in the prevention of cross-border raiding in situations such as Kurdistan where raiders could not be pursued across frontiers, in this case into Turkey or Persia. In other words, the "moral effect" of air power was greatest where the capacity to deliver punishment to a rebel force was unconstrained by the political necessities of international diplomacy.[178] In the second place, air policing was by definition conducted at one remove from the population being coerced. Aerial attacks did not produce the tangible results of land operations: occupation of hostile territory, the capture of rebels, and a permanent physical presence on the ground.[179] As a result, air policing could not generate a supply of conversational humint. Reconnaissance could provide some evidence of the success of aerial operations, but their longer-term impact on the local population had to be judged after the event by colonial officials in situ. This left the advocates of air policing feeling peculiarly insecure. They were reliant on district administrators and police personnel to advise them of the effectiveness of aerial operations, and they depended on these same authorities to tell them when to launch a punitive attack in the first place.[180]

If part of the answer to this slow filtration of regional intelligence was to equip district commissioners with telegraph facilities and wireless transmission equipment, the underlying problem was the hybridized nature of the colonial intelligence system in the Sudan.[181] Civilian administrators did the hard work of intelligence gathering but had precious little say in strategic analysis of the information they acquired.[182] Yet these civilian officials had a deeper knowledge of Sudanese society and were better trained linguistically to discuss it with indigenous informants. The reluctance of military personnel to surrender jurisdictional control over intelligence meshed with the similarly convoluted nature of Sudan's colonial policing more generally. As Douglas H. Johnson puts it, "The history of policing in the Sudan is the history of an incomplete transformation from an auxiliary military body to a civil force. It is a complex mixture of paramilitary, civil and tribal organizations; of civil and tribal courts administering different law; and of urban, rural and frontier duties, ranging from criminal investigation to the armed pursuit of nomad tax defaulters and frontier raiders."[183] The persistence of disorder in interwar Sudan suggests that the colonial state's intelligence system struggled to cope with the scale of the tasks it faced.

Conclusion

This chapter has discussed the ways in which intelligence failings were followed by the rapid escalation of unrest. At its heart is a paradox: intelligence failure only confirms the importance of effective information gathering to the colonial state. As we have seen, the political consequences of inadequate intelligence, as in postwar Egypt and Iraq's Shi'ite south, were severe. So, too, the political misuse of intelligence, as took place in southern Kurdistan, was directly linked to the incidence of rebellion. As for Sudan, the entire British administrative system rested on the quality (rather than the speed) of information fed to the Khartoum and Cairo administrations by SPS officers and military commanders in the field.

The Egyptian disorders in 1919 exposed the limitations of British intelligence gathering and provoked several changes to it. From 1920 onward, a reconstituted Egyptian intelligence staff tried to improve the quality of net assessment regarding internal threats to British imperial control. Cairo intelligence analysts exploited a more diverse range of information on which to base their political appreciations. Intercepted telegraph correspondence from key nationalist leaders, Zaghlul included, became a regular feature of summary reports. Gatherings in city mosques and the content of Friday prayers were closely monitored, as were student activists and clerics at al-Azhar University in Cairo. The Egyptian press was also studied more carefully as a barometer of urban opinion. Provincial intelligence reports from POs and other district officials were collated more systematically. Taken together, this raw information became the basis for the concluding sections in regular Cairo intelligence staff reports summarizing key developments and likely political trends. In temporal terms, the focus of such intelligence assessments changed from pinpointing the key aspects of recent events to adducing any potential threats from them.[184]

Violent protests in Egypt during 1919 had greater impact in London, but were more short-lived than the communal unrest that destabilized Mesopotamia in the three years that followed the British entry into Baghdad in 1917. From northern Kurdistan to the Basra hinterland, APOs were assigned to uphold British imperial authority in administrative subdistricts of Iraq's *vilayets*. Touring their administrative fiefdoms, a practice familiar to colonial administrators in Africa and Asia, was essentially a protracted exercise in gathering humint. The results were often at variance with the assumptions on which "high policy" in Baghdad, Cairo, or London was built. Interdepartmental competition over British Middle Eastern policy complicated matters. Intelligence assessments compiled by officials on the spot were often manipulated, exaggerated, or ignored by more senior administrators, military planners, and politicians eager to advance the regional interests of their particular departments or services. Intelligence reports from the POs responsible for supervising local administration in northern Iraq were instrumental in British actions toward the Kurds throughout the mandate period. Far from submitting politically neutral reports about developments in northern Iraq, the PO network was arrogated to two competing policy centers—the Baghdad civil commission and the Colonial Office Middle East Department. Intelligence information as a guide to policy was unremarkable. But the manipulation of intelligence and the insertion and extraction of intelligence providers to suit the requirements of high commission staff in Baghdad indicated the centrality of the information order to those colonial policymakers at the heart of the state-building project in Iraq.

From start to finish, mandatory Iraq was a failed intelligence state scarred by rebellion. This was not the fault of outside agitators or imported ideologies. Rather, the misuse of intelligence and the repressive application of coercive colonial power to benefit the Sunni elite at the center of the Hashemite government condemned the country to lasting instability.

Good long-term political intelligence was equally critical to the preservation of imperial control in the Anglo-Egyptian Sudan. The limitations of this system were laid bare by the emergence of the White Flag League and the subsequent disturbances across the towns of northern Sudan in 1924. It was hardly surprising that these events drove the SPS to place still greater emphasis on the conciliation of conservative tribal leaders in rural Sudan. In Sudan, it seems, the colonial state's information providers were expected to fill the administrative gaps that resulted from the effort to govern such a vast and heterogeneous country with few resources. Required to provide early intelligence of the development of urban opposition, SPS staff were also in the vanguard of government efforts to coopt of the leadership of rural society. Greater recourse to air power and air reconnaissance in the late 1930s was no substitute for local intelligence gathering. Here, as elsewhere in Britain's Arab territories, the intelligence apparatus was used to contain unrest, the original outbreak of which it could not prevent.

INTELLIGENCE AND REVOLT II

French Security Services and Communal Unrest in Morocco and Syria

Intelligence providers were in the forefront of British efforts to contain the widespread disorder in Arab territories after World War I. Rebellion in the French Empire gestated longer, but was even more severe. This chapter examines the French security services' response to postwar popular revolts in the two most volatile territories of France's Arab empire: the Moroccan protectorate and the Syria mandate. To be precise, it considers the activities of military intelligence bureaus—the Service de Renseignements (SR) and its subbranch, the native affairs service—in the origins, escalation, and suppression of the Rif War and the Syrian revolt.

The first of these conflicts, a war of independence fought by Berber clan groups in northern Morocco, began as a struggle to end Spanish occupation of the narrow coastal strip of territory designated a protectorate of Spain under the Act of Algeciras in 1906. On 10 June 1920, a government of the Rif Republic was reconstituted at its capital, Ajdir, a town just inland from Alhucemas Bay, which was the heartland of the principal Rif tribal confederation, the Beni Uriaghel. Their domains spanned the central territory of what was then the Spanish Moroccan Zone. A year later, the Ajdir administration issued an international Declaration of State notifying all powers of its intention to conserve Riffian independence:

> Before 1906, the Riff was bounded on the North by the Mediterranean Sea, on the West by the Atlantic Ocean, on the South and East by the French Moroccan Zone, with a territory of about 50,000 square kilometers and with a population of two million inhabitants forming a gathering of tribes retaining amongst them, thanks to their linguistic and ethnical affinity, good neighborly relations. These tribes led an independent life and joined hands strongly against the invader from wherever he came. . . . The Riff notifies solemnly to all Powers that it intends to preserve its political independence

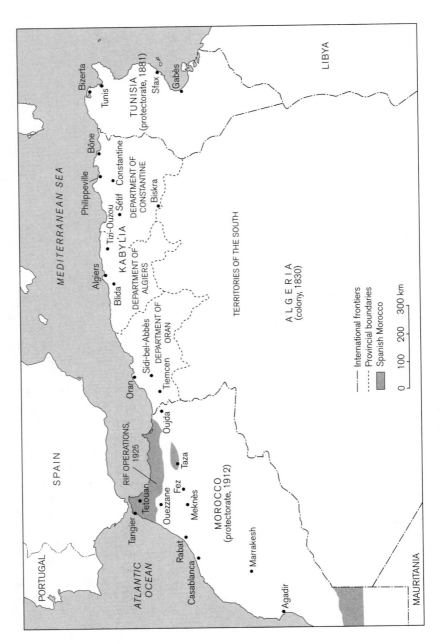

Map 2. The French North African territories.

absolutely and that she will continue to fight for official recognition as per-severingly as necessity demands.[1]

From the outset then, the Rif Republic defined its resistance to Spanish occupation as a war of national liberation. The conflict raged for four years before spilling across the highland frontier separating Spanish Morocco from its far larger French cousin to the south. From April 1925 onward, what had been a Spanish-Riffian war became a predominantly French-Riffian one: in Marshal Philippe Pétain's words, a war fought against "the most powerful and best armed enemy we have ever encountered in colonial operations."[2] Fighting in uneasy partnership with Spanish forces, ultimately it was French military might that crushed Berber resistance, bringing Mohammed Ben 'Abd el-Krim el-Khattabi's five-year experiment in Riffian republican government to an end.[3]

Intelligence provision and the French protectorate's security services played a central role in this, just as they did in a contemporaneous rebellion at the other end of the Mediterranean as the Syrian mandate erupted into violence over the summer of 1925. From the mandate's inception in 1920, French reconstruction costs and political divisions in Paris over the terri-tory's worth precluded any major investment of government funds in Syria's administration. Just as in Morocco, the combination of onerous pacification tasks and severe budgetary curbs ensured that French imperial administra-tion in Syria could not function without security service information net-works. Both Morocco and Syria were intelligence states, reliant on their security apparatus to forestall or contain major challenges to the colonial order. As we saw in chapter 2, many of the army officers appointed to the newly established Levant SR arrived direct from Moroccan postings, bring-ing with them the ideas and strategies of control developed under Lyautey's administration. In another parallel with French Morocco, after 1920 a dis-tinct intelligence elite quickly established itself as the bridge between regional government in Syria and the country's subject populations. And, in the final echo of Moroccan events, in Syria, too, what began as a localized struggle by a distinct ethnic group—in this case the heterodox Muslim Druze of southern Syria—escalated into a nationwide revolt fueled by pop-ular Syrian nationalism defined in opposition to the French presence in Damascus.[4]

The Rif War: Military Intelligence and Tribal Insurgency

Morocco remained the most challenging training ground for security ser-vice personnel in France's Arab territories. Military intelligence officers had been central to the pacification of Morocco since Lyautey first set about con-solidating the French protectorate in 1912. Once the French protectorate was formally established, Lyautey's main intelligence adviser, Colonel Henri Berriau, set up a Muslim affairs bureau loosely modeled on its Algerian equivalent. Like his mentor, Berriau was a veteran of frontier campaigns along the Algerian-Moroccan frontier.[5] When World War I ended, the pacification of Morocco's mountain populations was far from complete. Tribal control specialists in 1920s Morocco faced indigenous resistance to colonial penetration analogous to that of the conquest period in Algeria. As a result, Berriau's staff refined the use of locally raised irregulars to police tribal populations in the Rif, the Anti-Atlas, and southeastern Morocco. SR officers fomented interclan violence to undermine rural dissidence and even took charge of punitive *razzias,* or livestock raids, against dissentient tribes.[6] French district administrators supplied irregular units with intelligence on the location of flocks and herds and optimum routes for an attack. This ensured that a punitive raid inflicted the maximum loss at minimum cost to these auxiliary forces.[7]

Pacification of the more prosperous and fertile regions of northern Morocco, what Lyautey dubbed "useful Morocco," was not always violent, but the threat of force was integral to its progress. Here, too, the native affairs service held the key role, pursuing a complex amalgam of negotiation, material reward, intimidation, and outright coercion of tribal leaders and urban notables. Whether coaxing or cajoling, intelligence staff were in the vanguard of this double-edged strategy of political dialogue, gift giving, and occasional punitive operations. The police were equally active. Sûreté officers oversaw tighter controls over internal migration. They monitored the movement of traders and economic migrants between Moroccan districts and across the frontier between northern Morocco and Algeria from the commercial center of Oujda.[8] As tensions over the Rif escalated during 1924, Sûreté prominence in the policing of internal migration was matched by their closer surveillance of Moroccan worker immigration to France, a process that acquired a sharper political edge as the Interior and Foreign Ministries began to identify the Maghrebi immigrant community as the kernel of anticolonial nationalism in the mid-1920s.[9]

Outside the confines of "useful Morocco," the security service presence was smaller but even more important. Along the protectorate's northern and southern fringes, it fell to native affairs personnel to construct viable power-sharing arrangements with the established indigenous authorities. In the Berber-dominated Middle Atlas region centered on the town of Sefrou, SR officers of the protectorate's native affairs division compiled an archive of ethnographic data and geographical information on local tribal populations. From January 1915 onward, this material was analyzed and further disseminated by a Berber studies committee (*Comité d'études berbères*) based in Rabat.[10] As Colonel Henri Simon, then the director of the native affairs service, put it, it was the responsibility of SR officers in the Middle Atlas "to study Berber populations in depth; their particularities must be carefully examined and recorded in order to build up a documentary record thanks to which the rules of practices of political and administrative control may be worked out."[11] Native affairs policy in the Middle Atlas was therefore predicated on the quality of information gathered by SR specialists about the distribution, customs, and attitudes of a population about which the Rabat Residency knew virtually nothing.[12]

Meanwhile, in the southern Atlas region radiating south and east from the hinterland of Marrakech, the balance of political power between the sultanate, the French Residency, and the local Arab overlords, the *grands caïds,* was altogether different and more delicate than that pertaining in the more populous areas to the north. As Colin Newbury puts it, "Concentration of investment and colonization in the coastal region left much of the mountainous interior patrolled, rather than administered, preserving the division between the *makhzen* and regions outside government tax controls—a division equated loosely with 'Arab' and 'Berber' in French perceptions. Inexorably, a long period of 'pacification,' 1912–30, absorbed the tribes of the interior."[13]

The essence of French techniques of control in the south lay in building up the regional influence of El Hadj Thami Glaoui, the pasha of Marrakech and an early supporter of the protectorate, above that of his three main rivals, Abdesselem M'Tougui, El Hadj Taïeb Ben Mohamed el-Goundafi, and Layadi-bil-Hashmi.[14] All four were *grands caïds,* and the first three were pivotal to the initial French conquest of Morocco's southwest between 1912 and 1914.[15]

The *politique des grands caïds* was intelligence-led. That is to say, a handful of SR appointees held primary responsibility for ensuring that cooperation with the local overlords did not collapse. All the while, they worked to accrue power to the protectorate authorities. For his part, Lyautey recognized that the population dispersion and stronger clan loyalties to quasi-feudal overlords evident in the pre-Saharan territories of southern Morocco precluded the kind of tribal control policies pursued elsewhere.[16] He therefore delegated extensive police powers to the pasha of Marrakech. French advisers were assigned to work with him to ensure that known opponents of the protectorate were kept under close surveillance or house arrest.[17] After touring the Marrakech district in early 1923, the British consul in Casablanca summarized his observations thus:

In North and West Morocco the protectorate is that of the French protecting the Moors; in the south, in point of present fact, it is that of the *grands caïds* protecting a handful of French civilians and soldiers. In some districts, where the *caïds'* writ does not run, the French have gradually established military posts and [SR] intelligence officers, and aim at eventually wielding a permanent influence.

Again, in some areas directly under one of the *caïds,* intelligence officers have been established; these are quietly working away to sap away the *caïds'* exclusive authority; thus, an officer was sent some two years ago to Amizmiz, in the Goundafa region, and another is now to be established at Telouat, the kasbah of the Glaouï district. Notwithstanding this, nearly all the regions owing allegiance to one of the *Grand Caïds* would, in time of emergency, respond to his call rather than to that of the French.[18]

Seen from Rabat, this form of clientage—in practice little more than an awkward modus vivendi between the so-called lords of the Atlas and the protectorate authorities—brought recurrent problems. The *grands caïds* retained sufficient feudal power to govern at variance with the declared objectives of both the *makhzen* authorities and the Residency. Their local struggles for influence threatened to destabilize the entire southwest of the protectorate. And, whatever Lyautey's claims to the contrary, the supposed partnership at the heart of this arrangement belied French claims to undisputed ultimate control over Morocco. The senior SR officer in the region, Colonel Léopold Justinard, captured the resultant dilemma with the memorable phrase, "Who will guard the guardians?" A much-decorated war veteran and Lyautey's senior representative in Marrakech since joining the SR in 1916, Justinard was under no illusion that the *grands caïds'* loyalty to France was anything other than strictly conditional.[19]

Immediate War Origins

To connect military intelligence activities with the Rif War, we need first to examine how and why the conflict spread southward into French-controlled territory. This process takes us back to a cold Paris morning on 17 November 1923. It was then that the interministerial commission on Muslim affairs met to consider the deteriorating security position along the Rif frontier of the French Moroccan protectorate. Although it was not at the heart of government, the commission did meet regularly in the early 1920s, providing ministers and government departments with much-needed specialist appreciations of detailed political intelligence. At its November 1923 meeting, the commission discussed a lengthy report by one of its most experienced members, André Bonamy. He had observed French military operations in the Middle Atlas the previous June and had acquired a better appreciation of the strength of tribal insurgency during a subsequent incognito tour of Spanish Morocco. His views confirmed Rabat Resident General Lyautey's belief that Spanish efforts to crush Rif resistance were counterproductive.[20]

As matters stood in late 1923, Lyautey's administration had yet to face the disastrous breakdown of imperial control evident further north in the Spanish Rif. Furthermore, the pressure on Armée d'Afrique resources had recently diminished. French military withdrawal from the Turko-Syrian province of Cilicia the year before facilitated the administrative consolidation of a compact Syrian state.[21] Much to Lyautey's relief, the end of operations in Cilicia also eased the pressure for troop reinforcement from North Africa.[22] French officials recorded with satisfaction that disorder in North Africa and the French Levant had not yet reached the level of political violence in Egypt or the intercommunal bloodletting in Iraqi Kurdistan.[23]

All this was soon to change. In 1925, Lyautey's long-standing tribal control policies and the SR's operating assumptions about the protectorate's northern Berber populations collapsed as the Rif War spilled into French-ruled territory. More than forty French military outposts along the northern Moroccan frontier were overrun within days of the initial Rif assault on 12 April.[24] At the height of the Rif War, on 2 July 1925, Prime Minister Paul Painlevé addressed the French Senate. He described the French military engagements then under way in what would become the stock French official language regarding dirty colonial wars as "*une vaste opération de police.*" Painlevé dismissed anxious talk of a crisis of imperial authority as gross exaggeration. He pointed out that the four hundred or so French military losses to the start of July (mainly colonial troops) were not significantly greater than in earlier years of Moroccan pacification, and that the overall forces deployed in Morocco were only 25 percent higher than in former years. The prime minister did concede that 'Abd el-Krim's rebel tribesmen had launched an unprovoked attack on the French zone. But he insisted that it would soon be repulsed to safeguard "the civilizing work of France." Suitably reassured, the senators rewarded Painlevé's impressive performance with a vote of confidence passed by 290 votes to zero.[25]

A more heated debate on the situation in the Rif had opened in the Chamber of Deputies a week earlier, on 27 May. Diplomatic and press coverage of the ensuing parliamentary exchanges focused on three issues: the cross-party criticism of Lyautey's Rabat administration, the continuing acrimony between the Cartel des Gauches coalition and its right-wing opponents, and the formal censure of Jacques Doriot. The leading colonial spokesman of the PCF (the French Communist Party) drew government wrath for his advocacy of soldier fraternization with the Riffian rebels, a policy loudly endorsed by the PCF's Young Communist section in its newspapers *L'Avant Garde* and *La Caserne.*[26]

With tempers running high, the Chamber's discussion of the Rif War generated more heat than light, but, amid the insults, the Socialist deputy Pierre Rénaudel made a little-noticed but telling observation. He argued that the Residency's decision in 1924 to authorize military occupation of the fertile grain-producing basin of the Ouergha River valley, an area covering some forty kilometers from east to west and ten kilometers north of the disputed river, made 'Abd el-Krim's "invasion" inevitable. Berber clans throughout the Rif depended on free access to the Ouergha valley's wheat supplies. Their food supply was therefore threatened by French construction of a network of blockhouses and frontier posts along this more northerly line. Spain's concurrent imposition of a coastal blockade of the Rif Republic further impelled 'Abd el-Krim toward confrontation with France.[27] This theme of an inexorable descent into war resurfaced eighteen months later in the War Ministry's in camera autopsy on the origins of the Rif attack. Here, too, the army's installation along the commanding heights above the Ouergha River's northern bank was seen as critical, raising the stakes in the French-Berber contest for the loyalty of tribal populations in the surrounding area.[28]

Informed by SR advice, the primary military objective of the Morocco occupation corps in 1923–25 had been to eradicate tribal insurgency in the Middle Atlas region, thus ensuring greater protection of the towns of Taza and Fez and arterial communications between the two.[29] It was little wonder, therefore, that Lyautey's army intelligence staff attached such value to the consolidation of an outlying defensive perimeter.[30] Had this new system of fortifications not been established, both towns would have fallen in the opening phase of the Riffian attack.[31] There was, however, another side to this story. French occupation forces first laid claim to the northern flatlands of the Ouergha valley in July 1914. Ever since, frontier posts had been constructed, crisscrossing the area and introducing a stronger military presence to this tribal region. It was also generally known that Riffian tribes farther north relied on wheat purchases from the Ouergha district to supplement their homegrown grain supplies. Cast in this light, French action along the Ouergha fit into a broader strategy to sow dissension among Berber clans by exerting tighter control over the local economy and thus proving the physical extent of French dominion.[32]

The hidden hand of intelligence was very much at work here. The Ouergha valley occupation was the product of on-the-spot policy advice from the SR's native affairs officers working among the Berber clans. Their underlying objective was to break down the clan affiliations that held together the main tribal confederations along the Rif frontier. Here, as elsewhere in French North African tribal districts, the native affairs service strove to recruit supplementary forces, typically mounted irregulars, to serve alongside regular army units in the conduct of raids (*razzias*) on tribal communities that refused to submit to French authority. Once these partisan formations were established, SR officers would provide field commanders with the necessary intelligence about where and against whom they should strike.[33] Little by little, the "oil stain"—the famous analogy that General Gallieni had used to describe the process of pacification—would thus creep forward.[34] Native affairs service reports indicated the steady progression of pacification and the erosion of Berber unity in the face of this military pressure. Their cumulative effect was to suggest that the French

Moroccan zone could avert the disasters that had befallen the Spanish farther to the north.[35]

Lyautey's senior native affairs service officers convinced him that clan leaders in the frontier zone only joined the Riffian revolt because of intimidation and fear of reprisal. The native affairs service had learned from bitter experience that containment of rebellion in one area was pivotal to order and economic stability in regions far from the original sites of unrest. In the year before the Rif War spilled southward into French-ruled territory, the mounting tension along the northern frontier impeded the planting and harvesting of crops. This, and the gathering perception of a fundamental crisis in protectorate administration, eroded financial confidence in Morocco during 1924. Foodstuff prices rose, commerce declined, and peasant producers grew restive as living costs escalated. In Fez, Casablanca, and Marrakech, the SR reported that nationalist agitators had made significant inroads among Moroccan workers and students. In sum, the ripple effect of disorder in the Rif raised official fears of popular unrest throughout the towns of northern Morocco.[36]

Intelligence warnings of potential conflict escalation and eventual urban disorder formed part of a policy formulation process at the Residency in which the opinions of the civil and military authorities in Fez occupied a central place. The city itself was soon to become part of the Rif War front line and it was the most important strategic factor in Residency planning. Not surprisingly, the clamor for remedial action from the powerful voices inside its walls grew louder as Riffian successes multiplied. Lyautey's chef de Cabinet, Commandant Georges Lascroux, later complained that the demands of politicians, civil leaders, military chiefs, and settlers in Fez made it much harder to digest intelligence from the Northern Front itself. In consequence, the Residency struggled to keep pace with events as they unfolded in the first, decisive phase of the Rif assault.[37]

One thing remained constant. Lyautey clung to the belief of his SR advisers that Berber allegiance to the protectorate could be salvaged if tribal populations received stronger French Army protection. Subsequent intelligence reports revealed that Riffian rebel forces had laid waste to Amjot, home to the Beni Zeroual, the most important Berber clan in the area, taking large numbers of rival clansmen hostage in the process. Such predations only added weight to native affairs service advice.[38] The solution seemed to lie in the deployment of a stronger occupation force. Yet this seemed a heavy-handed military response, out of kilter with Lyautey's more measured style of tribal control. In deference to this, the Rabat authorities initially claimed that the military operations along the Northern Front took place first and foremost to protect pacified, loyal tribes from the predations of 'Abd el-Krim's forces.[39] Only later did it become clear that the intelligence itself was faulty and that the local population detested those who gathered it. The principal Berber clans throughout the Ouergha valley had, in fact, rallied to the Rif Republic. On the eve of the Rif attack in early April 1925, Beni Zeroual leaders even expelled the Residency's native agent, Shereef Derkaoui, who had tried and failed to prevent their defection. Derkaoui's eviction personified the collapse of the native affairs service policy of divide and rule among the Berber clan groups.[40]

Between 13 and 18 April 1925, an estimated three thousand Rif tribesmen organized into three *harkas* traversed the northern perimeter of the French protectorate. They advanced toward Ouezzan and Amjot in the west and down the Ouergha River valley toward Taza in the east. Over the next month, the size and composition of this force changed beyond recognition. The reason was simple: the two main Berber tribal confederations north of Fez—the Beni Zeroual and 'Abd el-Krim's own Beni Uriaghel—mobilized their forces in support of the rebellion. What had been characterized as the dissidence of a Berber minority against inept Spanish administration clearly amounted to a genuine popular rejection of any European presence in Rif lands.[41] The ferocity of tribal resistance also confirmed that the change in allegiance among Berber clans stemmed more from political conviction than rebel intimidation or the prospect of material gain.[42] Several of the clan groups involved had formerly been listed in SR reports as "pacified." The presumptions of the native affairs intelligence system were evidently at odds with the unfolding situation on the ground.[43]

To add insult to injury, at the height of the first Rif assault in May, intelligence came in of military secrets revealed to the enemy by tribal auxiliaries that had killed their French commanders and gone over to the rebels.[44] By this point, up to twenty thousand additional tribesmen and women had joined the Rif cause. Many came armed with guns previously supplied by the French Army at the SR's behest in recognition of earlier submission to protectorate authority.[45] Reviewing the military situation on 4 June, General Bernard Serrigny, the head of the general staff secretariat, summarized matters thus: "We are no longer battling against the Riffians properly called, but against tribes that were formerly submissive and are today dissidents that the Riffians can hurl against us."[46] This was a fine distinction, typical of the SR's reluctance to concede that native affairs pacification policy was substantially to blame for the rebellion's escalation among the Rif clan groups.

Fighting in familiar terrain and with great cohesion, by early July these tribal forces confronted some twenty French battalions, half of which were already reduced to half their normal combat strength.[47] Not surprisingly, the losses that Painlevé made light of in early July soon mounted. With the inclusion of colonial troops—something government statistics usually concealed—they made stark reading. By 15 October 1925, 2,176 soldiers had been killed and 8,297 wounded. It was the highest death toll sustained by the French armed forces since World War I, far outstripping the casualties incurred during French intervention in the Russian Civil War or in any other French colonial counterinsurgency of the 1920s. Rif War costs, already the subject of a supplementary credits bill, had climbed to nearly one billion francs. And, according to Philippe Pétain, who had been sent to Morocco to devise a rapid solution to the crisis, only a huge increase in French expenditure of blood and treasure would ensure the defeat of the rebellion. To that end, two further army corps were assembled from troops in Algeria and France. These reinforcements brought the total French military deployment along the Rif frontier to 158,000 men by late September 1925.[48] The Residency's operating assumptions about Berber loyalty and the success of divide and rule tactics were left in tatters. The Lyautey era, it seemed, was truly over.

What of the native affairs service and the intelligence it provided? The French decision to use overwhelming firepower and the tactics of European warfare to crush Rif resistance belies the fact that intelligence specialists remained integral to counterinsurgency strategy in Morocco. Neither War Ministry funds nor the Residency budget could withstand the long-term costs of an augmented occupation corps. Nor were Painlevé's Cabinet or the Army Staff prepared to tolerate such a significant diversion of military resources. An oppressive army occupation of the Rif highlands was also sure to breed local resentment.[49] It was therefore essential to withdraw the punitive columns that led the counteroffensive against 'Abd el-Krim's forces if political "normality" was to be restored. The war, after all, remained a contest for tribal submission and control over the natural resources on which these predominantly agricultural communities relied.[50] In these circumstances, the native affairs division retained its dual role as point of contact with Berber community leaders and provider of field intelligence about clan loyalties, economic resources, and military options.[51]

SR native affairs officers also provided more raw information than ever before, quickly reasserting their influence as the indispensable providers of field intelligence. Weekly intelligence summaries compiled in Rabat on the basis of native affairs service assessments of tribal politics were remarkably detailed. Village-by-village accounts of local grievances explored the inter-clan and even interfamilial links that sustained dissidence along the Northern Front.[52] Some villages changed hands repeatedly over the final months of the "mopping up" campaign along the Northern Front in 1926–27. In this febrile atmosphere, news that a village community had gone over to the rebels, the arrival of consignments of smuggled firearms, or noted successes against roving army units could be enough to persuade other villages to rejoin the insurgency. Quick dissemination of native affairs intelligence was essential to prevent such occurrences, or, at the very least, to minimize their consequences.[53] One such case was the Oued Dessaia valley, a dissident area from which French irregular forces were unable to dislodge a large rebel group led by the Beni Mastera clan. SR officers based in the valley were instrumental in the army command's eventual decision to deploy heavy artillery and additional levy forces to crush the remaining pockets of resistance in late May 1927. These native affairs specialists also provided local scouts to accompany the two roving army columns that then swept through the valley looking for rebel hideouts.[54]

Alongside these Muslim affairs operatives, the occupation corps' SR personnel held a unique strategic role in the army's campaign to pacify the Rif and Morocco's mountainous interior more generally. The arduous terrain and harsh winter climate of the Rif highlands and the Atlas range made winter campaigning by large columns of infantry difficult, if not impossible. West African colonial troops suffered most. They had not been provided with winter gear and boots, causing hundreds to be evacuated from the front line for amputation of frostbitten toes and feet.[55] During the months from October to March, it fell to military intelligence officers to keep the Residency and the War Ministry's African affairs planners informed about rebel dispositions and their capacity for renewed resistance in the spring. More significant, during the winter months, SR staff tried to sway those clan leaders still determined to fight on. Clan chiefs and village headmen were warned anew of the might of French forces and the consequences of rebellion.[56] Doubters were wooed with subsidies and the assurance of better military protection.[57] Part propaganda, part statement of fact, part informal dialogue, these exchanges acquired additional importance during the de facto winter truce that held over the winter of 1925–26. By the time operations resumed in the spring of 1926, 'Abd el-Krim's following was much diminished. Material hardship and fears of long-term loss of land among the dissident clans help account for this. But so, too, did the largely unseen work of the SR.

By this point in early 1926, the core difference between security service strategy in the more southerly hinterland of the *grands caïds* and in the northern Rif belt was that the war precluded any return to southern-style power sharing with the leadership of the Rif's foremost tribal confederations, the Beni Uriaghel and the Beni Zeroual. Instead, the SR was tasked with the consolidation of new working relationships with smaller, less intransigent Berber clan groups as a prelude to the eventual submission of all the Riffian Berbers in the French zone. Conversely, once the main Rif Berber confederations submitted to French authority and 'Abd el-Krim was shipped off to exile on the Indian Ocean island of Réunion in 1926, the focal point of army pacification operations shifted southward once more.[58] By the end of the decade, occupation troops were largely assigned to the pacification of the Atlas highlands and the Talifalet hinterland to curb tribal raiding against French outposts, commercial interests, and loyalist populations.[59]

SR field officers again determined these counterinsurgency priorities.

Their advice informed the army command's preference for a concentric advance from the Sous Valley in the west, the French fort at El Abid to the north, and the Talifalet oases to the east in order to encircle the dissident zone and eliminate tribal insurgency in a multipronged attack. But the long-term commitment of troops and funds required for such an ambitious undertaking found little support in Paris. Neither the army commission nor the finance commission of the Chamber of Deputies would back it. French parliamentarians insisted on the continuation of lower-level counterinsurgency based on gradual penetration of rebel areas by SR personnel backed by local levies and mobile columns of Armée d'Afrique professionals.

After the hiatus of the Rif War, French military intelligence in late 1920s Morocco became a victim of its own success. Parliamentary insistence on small-scale operations drew on the SR's accumulated political intelligence about clan strengths and affiliations as well as environmental intelligence about local topography, material resources, and the quality of interior communications.[60] There would be no major conflagration in southern Morocco to compare with the earlier operations in the Rif. Intractable and often bloody "pacification" of Morocco's rural populations was, however, set to continue for another decade.[61]

Intelligence and Revolt in Syria

When we turn to intelligence and governance in the Syrian mandate in the same period as the events in the Rif, a similar picture of intelligence provision at the heart of government policymaking emerges. A source of division among the Parisian political elite and often ignored by the wider public, France's Middle Eastern acquisitions never generated widespread imperialist fervor.[62] Initially, at least, interventionist schemes in the Levant mandates were conceived elsewhere. The financiers, commercial investors, professional diplomats, and strategic analysts—collectively, the so-called *Asiatiques* that belonged to various proempire lobby groups—entrenched French involvement in the Levant region before, during, and immediately after World War I.[63]

The limited engagement of the wider French political community with affairs in Syria and Lebanon was mirrored by the limitations of imperial rule in both states. Mandatory government was more a matter of surreptitious influence than rigid colonial control. The initial appointment of French "counselors" to each administrative department in the government of Lebanon provoked public fury once it became apparent that these advisers actually wielded veto power over local government decision making.[64] Modeled on the protectorate system in French North Africa, this practice would also be introduced to Damascus, where numerous Syrian administrative posts, including that of interior minister, were summarily abolished

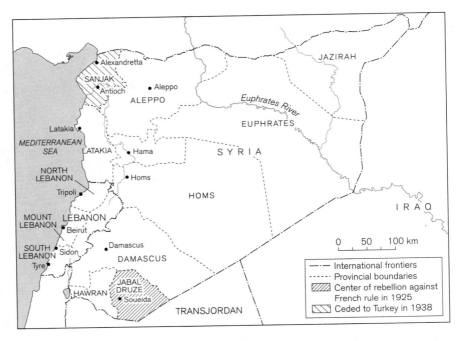

Map 3. The French mandates of Syria and Lebanon.

in May 1922.[65] It was difficult for the French officials installed across the Levant states to address the criticisms leveled at them when they lacked the funds or administrative wherewithal to restore basic services, such as urban street lighting, food and water supplies, and rural transportation systems disrupted by years of war and famine.[66]

Lacking the material or human resources to consolidate political control on their own terms, and fearful of a resurgent Kemalist Turkey to Syria's north, French mandatory rule turned on the relationships established with local intermediaries. As Philip Khoury has so convincingly demonstrated, Syria's so-called men of influence, whether politicians, community leaders, sheikhs, or members of elite urban families, were just as integral to the history of the French mandates as the successive high commissioners assigned to the central administration in Beirut's Grand Sérail.[67] Such individuals expected concessions, whether political or personal, in return for their cooperation in the day-to-day work of local government. Eager to escape dependence on these elites, French administrators sought other means to reserve ultimate power to the Beirut high commission. The outcome was what Khoury identifies as the "Moroccan formula" of government, a system adapted from Lyautey's method of rule in Rabat that was applied in the early stages of French administration in Syria.[68]

The Moroccan formula had three core components. First and foremost was a strategy that prevented the Sunni Arab majority from turning their numerical strength into real political power. Under General Henri Gouraud and his successor, General Maxime Weygand, the Levant high commission set about creating the administrative superstructure to make this achievable. In July 1922, Gouraud announced the creation of a Syrian federation made up of states nominally established on communal lines. What the historian Jean-David Mizrahi terms this "complex architecture" of Syrian administration was transparently designed to frustrate Sunni ambitions for a more unitary state by fostering political autonomy among two of Syria's ethnoreligious minorities—the Alawites and the Druze. It was a policy almost wholly executed by the officers of the Levant SR under their first chief, Colonel Henri Catroux.[69]

By the end of 1924, autonomous Alawite and Druze states were in place, respectively based on their "compact minority" populations of predominantly Shi'ite Alawites and heterodox Druze clans. As a result, the Alawite region centered on Latakia, and the Jabal Druze to the southeast, as well as the northwesterly *sanjak* of Alexandretta with its substantial Turkish minority population and the remote Jazirah region in the northeast, were all bureaucratically isolated from a Syrian state centered on the Damascus hinterland. After the humiliation of Syrian-Lebanese partition in 1920, the Damascene Sunni elite now faced another disaster: the apparent triumph of the policy championed since 1918 by the arch-*Asiatique* Robert de Caix and the Comité de l'Asie Française, which treated the Levant as an agglomeration of religious groups rather than the heart of the Arab "nation."[70]

The second element of the Moroccan formula was the effort made to drive a wedge between the interests of rural communities and those of Syria's towns in which established urban notables predominated. Third was the close attention paid to the composition and factionalism of this notable elite as French administrators sought to prevent the emergence of a united political class in opposition to the mandate.[71] Each component of this strategy was strongly intelligence-led. Whatever the shortcomings of the administrative apparatus erected in Syria during the 1920s, its intelligence priorities were at least easy to discern. The Levant SR and plainclothes Sûreté officers monitored and manipulated relations between Syria's differing communities. The quality of information received about ethnic minority politics, the rural economy, the loyalties of tribal sheikhs, and the personal and political connections among Syria's urban notables was pivotal to the mandatory authorities' chosen survival strategy of divide and rule.

As in Morocco, the raw data on which regional governors, high commission staff, and interested ministries relied to formulate policy in Syria derived in large part from the security services deployed in a hierarchical network of regional offices and rural outposts across the country.[72] SR native affairs specialists and SCR counterespionage officers reported to a military intelligence assessment center in Beirut: the Section d'études du Levant (SEL). The SEL transmitted intelligence to the high commission's civil cabinet in Beirut's Grand Sérail, the administrative nerve center of mandate government. Sûreté Générale offices in Syria's principal towns constituted a second, and complementary, intelligence network. Like their SR colleagues, police officers supplied the high commission with political and criminal intelligence as well as evaluations of local public opinion.

The Sûreté was never as close to the upper echelons of power as was the SR, whose development mirrored that of the high commission itself. The Levant SR was formally created on 8 June 1921. Some its officers had served in the French occupation administration set up prior to the deposition of Amir Faysal's Damascus regime in July 1920. Others transferred in from the Moroccan native affairs service, the organization after which the Levant SR styled itself. The overwhelming majority (93.6 percent) had seen war service, and most had volunteered for transfer to the Levant. Of those with previous colonial experience, most had served in the Maghreb, Morocco in particular.[73] Their overall numbers were remarkably small. From an initial peak of eighty-seven officers in 1921, SR numbers fell to only fifty-three in February 1925, gradually recovering to a figure of seventy-four in January 1928.[74] The ablest among them were typically posted to the autonomous Alawite and Druze states, where SR intervention in local government was most direct.[75]

The pivotal role of security agencies in times of unrest became still more apparent in Syria during the Great Revolt of 1925 to 1927.[76] In December 1925, a fortnight after his arrival in Beirut as Levant high commissioner, Henry de Jouvenel reorganized his civil cabinet in order to coordinate the government's response to the Syrian rebellion. By this point, the original uprising in the Jabal Druze had spread northward to the towns of Homs, Hama, and Aleppo, and northwest to the margins of Damascus itself. The intelligence war was also going the rebels' way. Colonel Charles Andréa, a much-respected Contrôle bédouin officer who would lead the decisive Levant Army offensive against the Jabal Druze heartland the following spring, confided to a British liaison officer in late December 1925 that the rebels' humint network of informers and sympathizers outstripped the French in anticipating the movement of hostile forces.[77]

De Jouvenel received a number of intelligence assessments that confirmed Andréa's views. One of the first SR situation reports to cross the new high commissioner's desk admitted that the rebellion enjoyed nationwide support, concluding that "our troops are powerless to ensure control or security across the whole of southern Syria." There was a real danger that the revolt would spill over into Lebanon as well.[78] The joint head of de Jouvenel's personal staff, Guy Perier de Féral, was directed to liaise with SR posts across Syria in a bid to match the rebels' knowledge of every locale. SR personnel were to submit fortnightly intelligence reports about rebel movements, public opinion, and the prospects for peace. The civil cabinet was, in turn, to ensure that military intelligence officers were kept abreast of government policy initiatives.[79]

SR and Sûreté informants also provided the most thorough intelligence on the leaders of the revolt. The quality of this material varied sharply after the spate of French military reverses that ignited the rebellion in the summer of 1925. Civil and military security agencies relied on an array of informants whose anonymity concealed their distinct political, ethnic, or career interests. Although impossible to verify, it seems that the information they supplied was often unreliable or partisan.[80] The requirement to evaluate the quality of the source information at the head of such reports was therefore critical to the process of intelligence analysis. Negative source evaluations by SR handlers alerted SEL analysts to their skepticism about the reliability of the intelligence sent. By the same token, positive source evaluations were a stamp of approval confirming that the SR personnel rated the material highly. The line between dispassionate evaluation of sources and the political sympathies of the officers and their informants, however, was sometimes impossible to see.[81] This was, in turn, part of a deeper problem: the politicization of the Levant SR.

The partiality of the military intelligence service apparent during the Syrian revolt reflected a longer-term trend. In the preceding administration of General Maurice Sarrail, the SR had become deeply factionalized, not to say disloyal. In differing regions of Syria, local administrators had pursued divergent policies.[82] The personnel concerned were typically either Levant Army officers or career bureaucrats who relied on SR staff to implement their decisions. Hence, for example, during the early months of 1925, the SR establishment in Aleppo went some way to conciliate local leaders, having witnessed a major local revolt in the Aleppo district six years earlier, whereas in Hama the SR command was primarily responsible for the outbreak of rebellion in the town in October.[83]

Such contrasting responses to local threat assessments indicated that mandatory rule in Syria lacked national coherence. The local particularities of SR-dominated administration in provincial Syria were fundamental to the transformation of the original Druze uprising into something more akin to a national rebellion.[84] The speed of the administrative breakdown during Sarrail's brief tenure as high commissioner in 1925 exposed the fragility of a system reliant on SR staff as intelligence providers, local governors, and enforcers of state directives. Military intelligence officers schooled in native affairs administration found it difficult to separate their duties as intelligence analysts from their role as intermediary between central government and the local communities they served.

In Paris, it suited Paul Painlevé's government and Sarrail's many parliamentary opponents to portray the disastrous escalation of the Druze revolt as entirely the high commissioner's responsibility. Yet Sarrail's de facto reliance on a narrow elite of military intelligence personnel to conduct much of the day-to-day administration in Syria was neither externally regulated nor centrally monitored. The brutal pacification operations subsequently conducted by General Maurice Gamelin in and around Damascus from October 1925 were in large part driven by the recognition that the shaky foundations of imperial authority had collapsed. In Gamelin's analysis, the local population had lost respect for French-imposed order.[85] Putting aside Lyautey's minimum force maxims, Gamelin insisted that more than a show of strength was required. He planned to amass some fifteen thousand troops to retake the Jabal Druze.[86] Meanwhile, unrestricted bombardments, greater recourse to ill-disciplined irregular forces, and hostage taking in villages suspected of rebel sympathies were intended to coerce the indigenous population into obedience. As a result of the earlier intelligence failures, colonial order in Syria came to rest more squarely on fear of the French military.[87]

Intelligence and Tribal Control during the Syrian Revolt

Much has been written about the course of the Syrian revolt, its contribution to the development of oppositional nationalism, and its impact on Syria's towns and national economy.[88] With the exception of Jean-David Mizrahi's indispensable 2003 study, rather less has been said about the role of intelligence gathering in French efforts to regain control of the Syrian interior.[89] Yet, as in the Moroccan Rif, army intelligence officers' efforts to sway the loyalties of Syria's tribal populations were critical to the nature and scale of eventual resistance the colonial state encountered.

During 1925–27, *méhariste* units of mounted troops led by an army native affairs officer assisted regular army operations against insurgent bands in rural areas outside the Jabal Druze heartland of the rebellion. Highly mobile and only lightly armed, the *méharistes'* principal task was to dissuade Bedouin tribes from joining the uprising. These mounted columns were the sharp end of the Contrôle bédouin section, a distinct desert subbranch of rural administration in mandatory Syria. (The work of the Contrôle bédouin is discussed in more detail in chapter 6.) Contrôle bédouin commanders recognized that tribal *razzias*—raids conducted for material gain, for restitution, or for punishment—were endemic to Bedouin life. The one consolation to the French authorities was their conviction that Bedouin tribal leaders were uninterested in emergent Syrian nationalism. On the other hand, in 1925 the combination of climate (an exceptionally harsh winter followed by severe drought and a widespread crop blight), the resultant delays to crop sowing and harvest, and an acute refugee crisis in southern Syria caused major social dislocation. These problems disrupted the migratory patterns of several Bedouin tribes normally concentrated in Syria's southern desert and the frontier region north of Aleppo. The influx of refugees caused unprecedented pressure on Bedouin grazing grounds. Foodstuffs were in short supply and nomadic tribes were driven into the cultivated areas outlying Damascus, Homs, and Hama.[90] Sedentary peasant farmers were also suffering. Late frosts in April 1925 damaged the Syrian fruit crop and an insect pest destroyed much of the cereal harvest.[91] Worried by Syria's deepening agricultural crisis, the Damascus delegation was also pessimistic about the immediate future. Incoming reports from rural districts indicated a sharp fall in crop sowing during the 1925 planting season.[92]

On 15 July 1925, the Contrôle bédouin filed its annual analysis of tribal migration. The report acknowledged that Bedouin loyalty had been tested by the tough winter and the inaccessibility of traditional pastures at the height of the revolt. Chronic water shortages in Iraq's western desert had also compelled certain nomadic groups to cross the frontier to Syrian grazing grounds for the first time since 1922. Of these, the Sbaa and the Fedaan created the greatest logistical difficulties. The former entered Syria with their entire herd of some hundred thousand goats and set up an itinerant encampment reckoned at 3,500 tents.[93] Such movements of population and livestock were exceptional, but not unique. More serious was the worsening feud between the country's two principal Bedouin confederations: the Syrian Fedaan loyal to Moujhen Ibn M'heid, and the Ruwala (also rendered as Rwala/Roualla/Ruwallah) led by Amir Nuri Sha'lan. The Fedaan tribes were congregated between Dayr al-Zur and Aleppo. The Ruwala generally camped in Syria's southern desert, the eastern Jabal, and northwest Transjordan. The feuding between the two groups threatened to spill over into the Syrian revolt as Druze and nationalist envoys promised material support to those tribal factions prepared to take up arms against French forces.

Three months earlier, in April 1925, Contrôle bédouin units set up three new posts in northern Syria at Saan es-Saan, el Hamra, and Sala miyah. Detachments from these blockhouses kept the hostile nomad bands apart and monitored tribal contacts with rebel leaders. The additional units also offered some protection to the sedentary tribes caught in the crossfire as raiding for livestock and weapons increased by establishing a neutral buffer zone between Abu Douhour and Hama. Meanwhile, the Contrôle bédouin commander, Captain Charles Terrier, instructed his staff to meet with individual tribal sheikhs in an effort to reverse the upsurge in Bedouin violence.

These exchanges paved the way for a plenary conference of tribal leaders in Hama, following which a "general peace" was announced on 11 June. Clashes diminished in subsequent months but the underlying causes of friction persisted. Disputed access to tribal land, contested water rights, and unresolved blood feuds threatened to become embroiled with Druze insurgency further south as the Ruwala in particular migrated toward grazing land in the Ghuta and Hauran, both areas of intense rebel activity.[94]

On 28 November 1925, the Damascus delegate Paul de Reffye predicted troubled times ahead in a crucial report to the Foreign Ministry secretary-general Philippe Berthelot. The Levant Army's workmanlike approach to counterinsurgency promised results. But the fact remained that General Gamelin's forces were widely dispersed. His troops were by then engaged in three separate offensives from the Homs-Hama region to the Damascus hinterland and the Jabal Druze. Meanwhile, the ranks of the army's rebel opponents had been augmented with Bedouin fighters, whose increasing involvement in dissent was potentially disastrous. Army units equipped to track down an insurgent force of five hundred could suddenly face up to fifteen hundred well-armed tribesmen. De Reffye predicted a collapse of military control if the revolt spilled over into Lebanon. His remedy was simple: a budgetary injection of eight hundred thousand francs. These funds would be spent in two ways. First, overdue wage payments would be made to the Circassian and Kurdish irregulars spearheading army operations. Second, the monies would replenish the secret service funds used to shore up the loyalty of Bedouin tribal sheikhs.[95]

De Reffye's remedies suggest that the stock-in-trade of tribal control was unchanged by the Great Revolt. Before the rebellion and after it, Contrôle bédouin policing combined persuasion and regular subsidies with exemplary punitive measures. In one instance of such punishment, in March 1926 the first *Compagnie méhariste,* acting on the orders of the regional military commander, seized 796 sheep and goats from the tribal populations grouped around the grazing lands of the Nasrani mountains in southern Syria, at the time a rebellion hotspot. The livestock was taken in response to alleged collusion between local herders and rebel groups. Sale of the animals served both practical needs and wider political purposes. The eighty thousand francs received for the confiscated animals paid for the *méhariste* operations. Local resale of the livestock fomented exploitable division among the agriculturalists themselves. To loser and purchaser alike, the message was the same: loyalty to France made economic sense.[96]

In a similar vein, the high commission delegates posted across Syria maximized the political capital gained from professions of support by Bedouin tribal leaders. In their contacts with tribal headmen, SR officers stressed the benefits accruing to those tribal confederations whose leaders spurned the revolt and kept their subordinate clansmen in check. In May 1927, for instance, the then head of the SR in Syria, Colonel Édouard Arnaud, traveled to Azrak in Transjordan, a border settlement that had become the principal refuge for Druze fighters. The presence of Druze gunmen masquerading as refugees caused bitter squabbles between French and British intelligence chiefs in Syria and Transjordan, but Arnaud's visit was motivated by another purpose entirely. En route to Amman, he held talks with Ismail Hariri, the paramount sheikh of the southern Syrian region of Hauran. Hariri had resisted French and rebel pressure to take sides in the revolt, and had chosen instead to lead his tribal followers to sanctuary across the border in Transjordan. Arnaud persuaded him to return, proof once again of the SR's pivotal importance to tribal control.[97] The foremost subject of SR attention, however, was not Hariri, but Amir Nuri Sha'lan, leader of the Ruwala.

Of Syria's nomadic Bedouin groups, the Ruwala's customary grazing grounds in southern Syria and western Transjordan were closest to the geographical centers of Druze unrest in the Jabal and in the Ghuta. During World War I and after it, Nuri Sha'lan and his son, Nawwaf al-Sha'lan, proved themselves accomplished political operators, determinedly independent, well-informed, and skilled calculators of risk. Sha'lan was one of many tribal leaders courted by the Turkish government and the Hashemite leadership during the Arab revolt. The Ruwala leader was showered with honorary titles, gifts, and promises of future concessions from the Turkish Fourth Army command in Damascus as the Arab revolt edged northward along the Hijaz coast. His refusal to join the Arab revolt was nonetheless based on careful assessment of the military capabilities of the Hashemite forces and the British expeditionary force in Palestine rather than any venality toward the Turks.[98] He measured his loyalty to the French mandate on the basis of tribal advantage and personal prestige. By the time the Syrian revolt broke out, Sha'lan was just as concerned by events to the south in Saudi Arabia, where Ibn Saud had recently established control. Angered by the Ruwala's refusal to acknowledge Wahhabi supremacy along the Hijaz frontier, over the summer of 1925 Ibn Saud's envoy in Damascus strove to convince the French authorities that Sha'lan colluded with Druze leaders.[99] As usual, Sha'lan remained one step ahead of his opponents. In September 1925, he offered to send Ruwala tribesmen to serve alongside French forces.[100] The gesture was enough to assure him a favored voice in the subsequent formulation of tribal control policy.

Amir Sha'lan was no stranger to French military intelligence. General Gouraud's intelligence staff, headed by Colonel Georges Catroux, had monitored the amir's contacts with Faysal's Syrian regime since October 1918, when Sha'lan supported Faysal's entry to Damascus. The Ruwala were severely menaced at the time by Wahhabi Ikhwan (Muslim brethren) raids launched from Central Arabia. According to Catroux's informants, these attacks encouraged Sha'lan to conclude a "secret treaty" with Faysal. The compact pledged Ruwala allegiance in return for monthly subsidies for Sha'lan's family and tribe from the Damascus administration. But the arrangement did not secure Ruwala loyalty to the Hashemite cause. Faysal reportedly expelled the sheikh from Damascus in response, and insisted that the Ruwala should depart Syria for the Hijaz. It was an empty threat and the tribe remained in southern Syria. It was there that Catroux's SR envoys made contact with Sha'lan in 1920. An agreement over French subventions soon followed, making the Ruwala the first major tribal group to submit formally to French rule prior to Gouraud's eviction of Faysal in July.[101] Over subsequent years, SR staff built a closer relationship with Sha'lan. In 1923, a senior Contrôle bédouin officer even managed the amir's family affairs while he performed the hajj to Mecca. When two of Sha'lan's granddaughters took advantage of his absence to go on a spending spree in Damascus, SR staff intervened, ordering them to return immediately to their tribe.[102]

In 1926, Sha'lan renewed his offer of a Ruwala contingent to work alongside the irregulars then engaged in "mopping up" operations in the Damascus hinterland. He was politely refused, the amir having made it a precondition that his fighters should be allowed to pillage freely. Furthermore, relations between the Ruwala and the Contrôle bédouin had become strained after the SR authorized aerial bombardment of tribesmen known to be heading into the Ghuta in June 1926. Ultimately, Sha'lan agreed with Terrier's staff that Ruwala nomads should move out of insurgent strongholds in central and southern Syria. The Contrôle bédouin duly provided Sha'lan with intelligence of anticipated rebel activity to enable the Ruwala to steer clear of trouble.[103]

Farther north, the Mawali Bedouin were the major tribal federation to support the insurrection in the Aleppo *vilayet* and the later uprising in Hama in October 1925. Again, the SR specialists of Contrôle bédouin tried to rectify matters. Mawali sheikhs agreed to submit to French authority in an elaborate ceremony timed to coincide with High Commissioner de Jouvenel's tour of northern districts in December 1925. This form of public recantation was consistent with Bedouin custom, but it was also a gambit to assure the loyalty of subordinate Mawali clansmen who had thus far ignored less formal statements of a change in tribal allegiance.[104] A decorous public display was no substitute for the redress of Mawali grievances, however. Famine conditions pervaded their traditional pasture grounds, and clan leaders complained of undue Contrôle bédouin interference in the intertribal dispute between the Mawali and the Hadidiyin, another Bedouin tribal group. Dissidence persisted among Mawali tribesmen two months after the December 1925 recantation, prompting SR officers attached to the Damascus delegation to recommend punitive operations against them.[105]

SR endorsement of attacks against the Mawali was consistent with general instructions issued by the Levant Army command on 1 December 1925 for the conduct of operations in areas of rebel activity. These were not specifically tailored to Bedouin populations, but they revealed the precepts of French mandatory control within heterogeneous communities. Attacks on rebel-held villages were to avoid firing on religious sites. Destruction of property was to be kept to a minimum—a precept the army conspicuously ignored in Syria, not least in Damascus itself. Collective fines on villages and settlements that had harbored rebels were to be restricted, a belated recognition that they alienated rural populations from French rule. Instead, where possible, hostage taking from families known to have aided the revolt was the preferred means to reimpose community obedience.[106] Again, the quality of local intelligence about who was implicated in the rebellion and who was not was bound to affect the level of public resentment at such punishments.

The December instructions stipulated that in disturbed areas of southern Lebanon, SR intelligence officers attached to the Lebanese gendarmerie should assist local commanders in ensuring that recalcitrant village leaders surrendered all rebels and weapons within their communities. Exemplary executions of hostages were sanctioned if villagers refused to cooperate. But units were told not to enter villages known to have remained loyal. Clearly, good intelligence was also vital here. The line between "loyal" villages and "rebel" ones was rarely clear-cut. Equipping trigger-happy irregulars with sweeping punitive powers was unlikely to improve matters. The steps taken to dampen intercommunal friction were no less explosive. Where the local population requested arms to defend themselves against rebel exactions, commanders were advised not to distribute weapons to members of a single religious group. This precaution against communal violence was undermined, however, by the stipulation that Sunni Muslims were not to be armed in this manner.[107]

The relevance of these instructions here lies in their derivation. SR officers trained in policing the Bedouin drew up the plans. Bedouin control techniques were evident in the use of hostages, the exploitation of communal division, and the management of collective punishment. But lessons from the harsh world of tribal control were inappropriate to sedentary peasant communities caught in the crossfire between government forces and the rebels. Most important, in Lebanon as in the Syrian desert, the crude assumption that all but Sunni Muslim town-dwellers were at least potentially loyal to French authority informed most policing decisions. Within weeks, the limitations of coercive policing of Syria's rural population were becoming apparent to intelligence analysts attached to Gamelin's headquarters staff. Local police and army commanders reported that the dispersal of rebel bands was only an essential first step toward pacification. Hatred of the French presence was deeply entrenched, making it easier for insurrectionists to obtain modern weapons. The army command estimated that in 1918 the retreating Ottoman Army had left at least one hundred thousand rifles behind in Syria. Only a small proportion of that number was seized during the revolt. More important, French penetration of the Syrian interior was superficial; the countryside was "intellectually closed" to Western influence. The newly subdued Druze remained hostile. Contrary to French efforts to encourage the sedentarization of the nomad population, Bedouin tribal confederations followed their customary migration routes and regulated their own civil and criminal disputes.[108] Perhaps tribal control was a misnomer after all.

Whatever the second thoughts among Gamelin's army advisers, the lessons of tribal control permeated beyond the confines of military intelligence. As the Syrian revolt dragged on into 1926, the Damascus delegate de Reffye still insisted that the Bedouin population held the key to victory. Provided tribal confederations stayed loyal, the geographical scope of rebel operations could be progressively narrowed. If, however, nomadic tribes such as the Mawali changed allegiance before migrating to their usual summer pastures in northern Syria, uprisings might follow in previously pacified areas of the Aleppo *vilayet*. With de Jouvenel's approval, de Reffye reiterated his earlier request for additional secret service funds to be disbursed among tribal sheikhs before their tribes' seasonal transhumance began.[109]

Money flows were always an important component of intelligence work in Syria. The SEL and the Beirut Sûreté monitored the source and scale of external subsidies to the Druze rebel leadership throughout the revolt. Financial support from the Syrian-Palestine Congress in Cairo was tracked, but never entirely blocked. The same went for funds distributed by the numerous voluntary agencies that collected donations in other Arab states. As for individual suppliers, the Transjordan premier Rida Pasha Rikabi, a Damascene who had headed the Council of State in Faysal's short-lived Syrian regime, became the Sûreté's primary surveillance target. Rikabi was alternately wooed and demonized by the French security services. SR staff monitored the movements of his envoy, Ramadan Chellache, described as "an adventurer" from Dayr al-Zor. Surveillance of Rikabi and his contacts led to Foreign Ministry allegations that Rikabi provided £30,000 to Sultan al-Atrash on the condition that the rebellion was confined to Syrian territory.[110] Rikabi's anxiety to prevent the Druze uprising from spilling into Transjordan was tangentially linked to the Amman regime's worsening problems with Ikhwan raiding (discussed in chapter 6). The inability of Abdullah's government to prevent pro-Saudi raiders from consolidating their grip on the desert area around Kaf, east of Amman, reflected a broader shift in Bedouin allegiance toward the Saudi government's Wahhabism at the expense of the Hashemite regimes in Transjordan and Iraq.[111]

The Amman government's problems with tribal control cut no ice with

French military intelligence, however. Rikabi's activities led Colonel Henri Fernand Dentz, a future Levant high commissioner, then working in the SEL headquarters in Beirut, to conclude in early September 1925 that what had started as an exclusively Druze revolt triggered by purely local grievances against French administration in the Jabal Druze, was being hijacked by Syrian nationalists and foreign pan-Arabists. Their objective was to make the Druze clan leader, Sultan al-Atrash, a figurehead for Islam in the Fertile Crescent comparable to 'Abd el-Krim in Northwest Africa.[112]

Ironically, al-Atrash himself added credibility to the SR's interpretation of events. On 21 August, the Druze leader gave a press interview to the *Gazette de Voss* in which he confirmed the purely local origins of the rebellion. The Druze had taken up arms because of the maladministration of Captain Gabriel Carbillet, a native affairs officer appointed in 1923 in contravention of a high commission pledge that the Druze would be allowed to select their own governor.[113] Severely wounded in September 1914, Carbillet's military career resumed its upward trajectory after he transferred to Syria in 1920. Brusque and self-assured, he lacked the negotiating skills essential to regional administration.[114]

Carbillet's insensitivity to Druze grievances was exemplified by his determination to pursue a modernization program in defiance of local clan leaders. His mistakes were compounded by High Commissioner Sarrail's refusal to listen to al-Atrash's complaints against the local administration. Seen from the perspective of SR intelligence analysts notoriously hostile to the outspoken and brash Sarrail, the Syrian revolt originated in the high commissioner's failure to act on sound intelligence about the misdeeds of a native affairs maverick.[115] This did not imply that the SR or its adjunct, the native affairs service, were inherently deficient. After Carbillet's disastrous spell as governor, the appointment of the Damascus SR station chief, Commandant Tommy-Martin, as his replacement underlined the indispensability of experienced military intelligence officers to mandate administration. Furthermore, it was Tommy-Martin's successor in Damascus, Major Auguste Mortier, who conducted talks with the remaining rebel groups after Colonel Andréa led the recapture of the Druze capital of Soueida in April 1926.[116]

The Levant SR also remained in the vanguard of French efforts to curb the activities of pro-Syrian Arab nationalists abroad. On 1 April 1926, the Beirut SR produced a fulsome list of Arab parties and associations conspiring against French interests from Cairo, Jerusalem, and various European capitals. Monitoring of the contacts between Dr. 'Abd al-Rahman Shahbandar's recently founded Syrian People's Party and the Syrian-Palestine Congress in Cairo ensured that it took pride of place. The inclusion of other organizations based in Egypt and Palestine, such as the Arab Club, the Muslim Charity Society, and the Islamic-Christian Committee, as well as numerous aid committees that raised funds for Arab victims of French violence in Syria, fueled the SR's simmering hostility to their British imperial neighbors.[117]

By the time the much-reinforced Levant Army moved in to crush the remaining pockets of Syrian resistance in the Jabal Druze and elsewhere in August 1926, both sides in the conflict used intelligence of one another's movements and political intentions to determine their options. In June 1926, the three Syrian People's Party ministers in Ahmad Nami's Damascus government were arrested for channeling official information to rebel leaders and the Syrian-Palestine Congress executive.[118] For their part, on 28 August the Beirut SR advised the War Ministry deuxième bureau that nationalist factionalism was deepening as splits emerged over whether to sue for peace or endorse continued Druze resistance. Supporters of the former policy, including senior members of the Congress executive and Lebanon's Druze leader, Amin Arslan, reportedly hoped that the high commission would negotiate a definitive settlement modeled on the Anglo-Iraqi treaty. But their hard-line opponents, 'Abd al-Rahman Shahbandar and Sultan al-Atrash among them, monitored French troop movements to gauge whether it made sense to fight on. Meanwhile, the SR drew on the Sûreté's surveillance network in Switzerland for confirmation of the divisions among the rebellion's principal Arab backers.[119] For both sides, intelligence was as critical to ending the Great Revolt as it had been to starting it.

Security Agencies after the Druze Revolt

It was no surprise that after the breakdown in relations between Sarrail's high commission and the mandate security services in 1925, the Levant SR was overhauled the next year. Counterespionage operations in Syria and Lebanon were also reorganized into a clearer hierarchical structure of five regional offices subordinate to the Beirut Sûreté Générale.[120] These administrative changes elicited little political comment at the time, but they soon acquired real significance. In 1928 and 1929, the mandate administration suspended the Syrian Constituent Assembly, bringing a temporary halt to the country's first experiment with multiparty government, modeled on the earlier creation of a parliamentary system in Lebanon. As a result, opposition groups were driven underground.[121]

By then, the new SR chief in Damascus, Colonel Philibert Collet, a former commander of Syria's ruthless Circassian irregular forces, advocated an uncompromising approach to nationalist politicians. He favored bribery of their opponents and vigorous counterpropaganda to limit their popular appeal. Collet was soon at odds with Henri Ponsot, de Jouvenel's successor as high commissioner, who approved an amnesty for former leaders of the Great Revolt in 1928 and worked methodically, if slowly, toward the restoration of parliamentary institutions and a treaty settlement paving the way for Syrian self-rule.[122] By contrast, Collet and his fellow intelligence officers shed few tears over the Constituent Assembly's passing.[123] Their influence was soon felt. As Ponsot edged toward treaty talks, the Sûreté drew up career profiles of the Syrian negotiators proposed. These analyses determined Foreign Ministry selection of suitable nominees from a list that excluded most of the leaders of Syria's most powerful nationalist group, the National Bloc.[124]

In the 1930s, the security agencies responded to additional challenges to mandatory rule. Pan-Arabist opposition coordinated by the Syrian-Palestinian Congress, rumbling dissent among the Druze, and the growth of local Arab nationalist parties remained perennial concerns. A greater sensitivity to wider societal pressures, social deprivation above all, also intruded more frequently into intelligence assessments. The Depression hit Syria's urban workforce hard. Labor militancy, commercial stoppages and industrial strikes, and a panoply of worker groups, women's associations, and Islamic organizations were added to the more established political parties monitored by the French security agencies.[125] The maintenance of imperial authority in the postrevolt period was also complicated by mounting evidence of Italian espionage, separatist violence in the northeastern Jazirah region, signs of Comintern activity in Beirut and Damascus, and, above all, Turkish irredentism in the Alexandretta *sanjak*.[126]

As a consequence, intelligence gathering became at once more diffuse and harder to integrate into the high commission's policymaking process. As the number of perceived threats increased, so the pursuit of policies founded on discrimination between differing Syrian communities became more dangerous. Evidence of worsening disaffection among Syria's minority populations imposed a greater burden of work on security agencies, police forces, and military units. This was at a time when the primary challenge to French authority remained the more organized Arab nationalist protest in Damascus, Homs, and Hama.[127] Syria under French rule still fit the model of an intelligence state, but by January 1936 and the beginning of a two-month general strike coordinated by the Syrian National Bloc in Damascus, it was a severely overstretched one.[128]

Conclusion

In the Morocco protectorate and the Syria mandate, distinct intelligence communities coalesced in the 1920s. As we saw in chapter 2, the political outlook, shared assumptions, and threat perceptions of these small, elite groups of military intelligence personnel informed state policymaking. This explains why the two territories investigated here exemplify the intelligence state model. Security service responsibility for—and control over—the critical information flows about indigenous society, local political rivalries, and sources of popular dissent determined policy responses in Rabat, Beirut, and Paris. Separated by distance but united by common problems, shared practice, and a growing opposition to European settlement, capitalist enterprise, and the sectarian interests of indigenous urban elites, the security services in French Morocco and the Syria mandate were remarkably homogeneous. They were also supremely confident in their own abilities to make imperial government work.

The growing sense of assurance apparent in French policymaking in these Muslim territories in the early 1920s was shattered in 1925. Here again, the intelligence services were central to events. In Morocco, it was the SR native affairs service that issued the critical policy advice about total military occupation of the Ouergha valley. And it was the SR's reading of Berber clan loyalties that shaped Lyautey's entire outlook toward the Rif War. Stung by their earlier miscalculations, once Pétain's deployment of overwhelming firepower turned the course of the conflict, SR intelligence provision became more systematic, thus quickly reestablishing native affairs service influence over counterinsurgency strategy.

Similarly, SR personnel in Syria, always few in number, were key conduits between local and central government in what was not merely a strongly military administration, but a military intelligence administration. The politicization of the Levant SR therefore assumed added importance because its officers were uniquely placed to use intelligence assessment as a means to portray mandate politics in whatever light they chose. SR officers and Contrôle bédouin specialists determined counterinsurgency strategy and relations with key tribes, and were equally critical both to the original outbreak and the eventual suppression of the rebellion in the Jabal Druze. During the later 1920s and into the 1930s, the containment of disorder in northern Morocco and southern Syria confirmed the centrality of the security agencies to imperial authority. The policing of rebellion had catalyzed the development of intelligence states in both countries.

6

POLICING THE DESERT FRONTIER

Intelligence, Environment, and
Bedouin Communities

Policing desert frontiers and the communities that inhabited them was never easy. Vast areas had to be covered, the territories mapped and new boundaries imposed, the challenges of terrain and climate overcome. Most important, desert-dwelling tribal groups, some of them nomadic, others sedentary and pastoral, had to be incorporated within the political, economic, and administrative structures of European rule. British and French efforts to control the Bedouin populations of the Middle East mandates fell in large part to specialist intelligence officers, many of which became regional administrators.[1] Their role as agents of the colonial state was crucial to the consolidation—or the rejection—of Western authority among the Bedouin. This chapter surveys tribal control policy in the southern deserts of the Middle East mandates. It suggests that the intelligence state was weakest among nomadic communities that the imperial authorities struggled to understand and to subjugate. Analyzing the role of native affairs specialists within the security apparatus of desert policing points to the limits of colonial control and compels us to reconsider the distribution of political power in large swathes of the Middle Eastern mandates.

Policing the nomad populations of Syria, Transjordan, and Iraq, and safeguarding them from the predations of their near neighbors within the Nejd and the Hijaz, confronted the mandatory powers with intractable problems, few of which were resolved. Tribal control defied easy categorization or force majeure solutions. It was quite unlike the authorities' concurrent struggles with nationalist protest and intercommunal violence among the sedentary populations of the new Middle Eastern states. Yet tribal organization was as multifaceted as the civil society of Arab towns. Nomadic herders may not have joined the clubs, voluntary associations, or political groups that are often taken as evidence of civil society in an urban context. But tribes' procedures to regulate their own affairs were no less sophisticated. Before and after the imposition of mandate rule, tribal clans followed well-defined processes to resolve personal, family, and intertribal disputes.[2]

For the mandatory power, the prevention of Bedouin dissent was less a matter of repressive policing than of penetrating nomad society to secure the cooperation of clan leaders. Success rested on tribal control officers' ability to forge working relationships with the communities to which they were assigned, and on their capacity to keep central government informed of their progress. In this context, environmental intelligence about the agricultural economy, climactic conditions, and planned migrations was every bit as significant as more obviously political reports about feuding, cross-border raiding, and the escalation of interclan violence. Intelligence priorities in the desert were therefore shaped by the seasonal practices and distinctive cultures of its population.

Historical Background

Historians of the period of mandate government in the Middle East have written extensively about the intensification of ethnic, communal, religious, and monarchical rivalries between Arab and non-Arab, Muslim and non-Muslim, Sunni and Shi'ites, Hashemites and Wahhabis, town and countryside.[3] Another constituency adversely affected by the new frontiers and centralized imperial systems imposed across the region were the confederacies of nomadic Bedouin,[4] and nowhere more so than in Transjordan, 46 percent of whose registered population of 225,350 in 1922 was composed of tribal peoples.[5] Bedouin society was structured into distinct clan groups linked by a shared genealogy and a recognized internal hierarchy of families, elders, and leaders. Typically organized into tribal chieftaincies, their nomadic practices conflicted with membership of—and confinement in— a single state.[6]

In the Syrian mandate especially, the French authorities attempted to transform nomadic Bedouin from migratory herders into sedentary farmers. The policy fit wider high commission schemes to reshape the fabric of land tenure, thus breaking the grip of powerful absentee landlords on peasant sharecroppers.[7] British tribal policy was less radical, but not dissimilar. It also attempted to confine the Bedouin to prescribed migration routes and grazing grounds. Both powers sought to reconcile their interpretations of Bedouin customary law with the overarching requirements of mandatory security and revenue generation. Payment of taxes and recognition of central government supremacy was ultimately expected.[8] As matters stood in the early 1920s, however, Bedouin tribes were far from the compliant herders envisaged by imperial planners. A brief detour into the recent past is instructive.

After the Tanzimat reforms of the mid-nineteenth century, the Ottoman authorities began codifying the unwritten customary laws that governed tribal society and land distribution in their Arab lands. After the Russo-Turkish war of 1878, the settlement of Muslim refugee communities from the Czarist Empire in Arab territories such as the 'Ajlun district of Jordan added impetus to state intervention in matters of land, taxation, and communications development.[9]

The Ottomans' efforts to extend the frontier of agricultural cultivation farther into the Syrian interior brought them into conflict with Bedouin herders whose traditional livestock grazing came under threat. Improvements in the internal communications system of the Ottoman Empire opened up Syria's southern desert, making census recording, systematic taxation, and even conscription of Arab tribal groups more viable propositions. After 1909, the unitary impulses of the Young Turk regime accelerated this process still further. In the quest for greater uniformity in imperial government, administrators clawed back the regional powers, local concessions, and loyalty payments that had previously contained tribal opposition to Turkish rule. Less tolerant of heterogeneity in the empire than their Ottoman forebears, the Young Turk regime refused to allow Arabs, Druze, and other dependent peoples to evade the full rigors of central government demands.[10]

More than anything else, the obligation to serve the state as taxpayers and conscripts provoked uprisings in Greater Syria in the early twentieth century. Rebellions in the Jabal Druze in 1909 and in the Karak district of Transjordan in 1910 were triggered by opposition to heightened central government impositions that marked an end to the regional accommodations that had guided Turkish relations with the local populations over the previous half-century. In each case, once the uprisings were put down, severe repression was swiftly followed by bureaucratic registration, as the local populations were disarmed and made liable for regular taxation and conscription. It was no coincidence that those caught up in the Karak revolt destroyed public buildings housing census documentation and other government records in an effort to wipe away the administrative presence of the Young Turk government.[11]

It was also in Karak that the British imperial authorities encountered the sternest resistance to the imposition of central government control and fiscal regulation after the establishment of the Transjordan mandate in 1921.[12] Acting on behalf of the Palestine high commission, Sir Ernest Dowson's scheme of land registration was not meant to disadvantage particular regions, communities, or established landholders. Dowson's plans, conceived in 1923 and implemented from December 1927 alongside a more ambitious fiscal survey of all cultivable land in Transjordan, nonetheless placed the requirements of Western written record and legal title to private property above the customary forms of social control over land that had previously facilitated its more collective use.[13] As Michael Fischbach points out, land policies represented the most significant state intervention in the lives of Transjordan's agricultural population in the mandate period, determining local reactions to central government control and shaping a shared sense of national identity based on clearly delimited geographical boundaries and common fiscal obligations.[14]

Another facet of the Ottoman regulatory system in Greater Syria that persisted into the mandate period was state interest in the sedentarization of Bedouin herdsmen. Turning nomadic herders into sedentary farmers was inevitably regarded as detribalization thinly disguised. This process was never completed under Turkish rule, and in numerous cases local arrangements were made that guaranteed an economic lifeline to Bedouin tribes threatened by the development of a modern agricultural economy in which farm produce could be transported by road and rail rather than carried by camel along Bedouin-run supply routes.[15] Yet, in spite of known opposition to it, the French mandate authorities, determined to rationalize Syria's agricultural economy, resumed the effort to sedentarize the country's Bedouin. This was bound to arouse stiff opposition. Hostility intensified because the inequities of land ownership, absentee landlordism, and peasant sharecropping were particularly severe in the economic conditions of the immediate postwar period. French collaboration with favored sheikhs and village leaders left prime agricultural land and the local instruments of administrative power in the hands of a privileged few.[16]

Initially, at least, in British Iraq and Transjordan, Bedouin control policies were more laissez-faire. Until 1927, state intervention in Bedouin affairs was essentially the by-product of two predominant concerns: government efforts to build networks of support for King Faysal and Amir Abdullah, and British attempts to stabilize the turbulent frontiers of the two Hashemite states.[17] But tribal control policy in the two British mandates also differed sharply. In Iraq, the Baghdad high commission attempted to coopt tribal sheikhs into rural administration, seeing the Bedouin as a useful counterweight to the power of urban notables.[18] The assumed dichotomy between town and countryside, between urban society and Bedouin tribal custom, led British officials to underestimate the complexity of the social and commercial interactions between the two. British tribal policy in Transjordan was simpler: the Amman authorities strove, above all, to enforce Bedouin compliance, both to consolidate state power and to contain the problems arising from cross-border raiding.[19]

Pioneering work on the Bedouin has brought together historians, anthropologists, and social scientists.[20] Recent anthropological studies of Jordan's tribes in particular have stressed the interaction of centralized authority and tribal groups in the process of state formation. The clan loyalties, genealogical bonds, and customs that characterized tribal society were especially significant in Transjordan. Arab tribal identity was crucial to a state that had little basis in previous history, and few ethnic or economic particularities by which to define its frontiers.[21] Prior to 1914, Bedouin clans in Transjordan had collected taxes and controlled regional trade in foodstuffs northward to Syria and southward to the Hijaz. The disruption occasioned by World War I transformed Bedouin relations with central authority, whether Ottoman, Hashemite, or British.[22] These were the unpropitious circumstances in which British and French tribal affairs specialists first intervened.

Policing and Competition for Desert Resources

To attempt a preliminary survey of these issues, we confine ourselves here to the 1920s, the decade in which the frontiers between the three mandated territories under consideration were delimited. As the French Levant Army commander General Maurice Gamelin acknowledged at the end of his Syrian pacification campaign in April 1927, tribal policing and rural tax collection were complicated by the artificiality of mandate frontiers. Rebellion and consequent social dislocation added another dimension to what was a long-standing problem throughout desert territories: communal usage of scarce resources.[23] At the international level, between 1924 and 1926, 'Abd al-'Aziz ibn Saud decisively defeated Sharif Husayn, capturing Mecca and Jeddah and assuming the joint titles of Amir of Nejd and King of the Hijaz. Ibn Saud's triumph marked the consolidation of a forceful, independent Wahhabi kingdom at the margins of European-controlled territory. The House of Saud's crushing victory over its Hashemite rival brought tribal loyalties into question in the more northerly British-ruled states. The years 1926–29 witnessed an upsurge in raiding and cross-border conflict between tribes loyal to Ibn Saud and those in the southern reaches of Transjordan and Iraq.[24]

The fallout from the Druze uprising in Syria between 1925 and 1927 created further problems. Much like Ibn Saud's victories, the Syrian revolt provoked shifts in tribal allegiance and caused a severe refugee problem in neighboring Transjordan.[25] Traditional migration routes were frequently closed off. Antagonistic populations of Bedouin herders and Druze refugees crisscrossed mandate frontiers nonetheless, attempting to escape the violence, to avoid French retribution, or simply to find livestock grazing. Faced with French complaints about inadequate frontier surveillance, the British Residency in Amman imposed additional restrictions on internal migration and movement of tribal encampments. Sheikhs in Transjordan's Ajlun district were instructed to prevent their clansmen from joining the Syrian revolt and were held to account in weekly meetings with political officers. Vagrancy laws were used to detain any suspects found without identity papers.[26] In late 1926, tribal control officers attached to the Transjordan Frontier Force introduced a system of armlets for the adult males in the refugee center of Azrak in an effort to differentiate those permitted to carry weapons from any Druze rebels hiding among their refugee compatriots.[27] A formal extradition agreement between the Syrian and Transjordan mandates followed in October 1927.[28]

Major rebellions, refugee crises, and stricter frontier policing caused greater disruption to desert-dwelling communities, but also signified the breakdown of tribal control. In more placid times, those intelligence officers responsible devoted greater effort to a more preventive policing based on the management of intercommunal rivalries and the accommodation of clan leaders. Tribal sheikhs expected political subsidies from their nominal political rulers. These funds were disbursed partly to assure tribal loyalty and partly to guarantee safe passage for officials and tax collectors through Bedouin lands.[29] Faysal's Damascus regime made similar payments for equivalent purposes. Arab Army commanders, anxious to ensure that powerful tribes backed national projects for independent Syrian and Iraqi states, had also offered subsidies to key sheikhs. Results were mixed. To take one example, during the course of 1919–20, nomad disdain for the Arabist message of town-based nationalist societies was evident in the shifting political alignments of tribal groups within the contested upper Euphrates region.[30]

If fellow Arabs offering money, arms, and a greater political role within self-governing states enjoyed little success in rallying Bedouin communities to their cause, surely the British and French authorities were unlikely to fare much better? This was no mere local problem. In 1919–20, Bedouin tribal unrest was a common occurrence across northern Syria and the Iraqi *vilayets* of Baghdad and Basra. In the short term, however, this dissent was eclipsed by other, larger conflicts: the French overthrow of Faysal's government, the revolt against British control in southern Kurdistan, the Shi'ite uprising in southern Iraq, and the uncertain outcome of the Greco-Turkish war.[31]

Once the violence abated, French and British administrators proved less willing to part with their money in order to accommodate Bedouin leaders. After the upheavals of 1920, subsidies were not entirely abandoned. But the mandatory authorities relied more heavily on a system of security intelligence spanning their desert territories to achieve Bedouin compliance. Swiftly delivered reports of livestock raiding between tribes, and information on the course of blood feuds among tribal confederations, became pivotal to the imposition of meaningful imperial control. Accumulating knowledge about customary migration routes, desert water supplies, and available grazing land was essential to the effective "management" of nomad populations in more peaceful times.[32] There was much to be learned. Evidence of limited Western understanding of Arab tribalism was most apparent in the British and French tendency to demarcate "tribes" by their geographical distribution rather than by the kinship ties and shared genealogical histories that actually defined tribal affiliation.[33]

As in other realms of information gathering, European techniques of tribal control drew on past precedent. In Iraq and Palestine, the Ottoman land code was gradually modified but not completely discarded. Its codification of state lands, albeit incomplete, remained useful in mandatory Palestine as Arab-Jewish competition for land intensified.[34] Its centralized regulation of land distribution in Syria was adapted to serve the interests of Faysal's government and those sheikhs loyal to it.[35]

In Transjordan, Ottoman practices of tribal administration were initially left intact. The few British officials in the area and the Arab elites vying for power in Amman lacked the means to impose unilateral control on the southern desert. During 1917–18, the Palestine campaign disrupted Bedouin food supply and livestock movement. This disruption proved a more important determinant of tribal allegiance than any popular attachment to the Hashemite cause.[36] In December 1920, the Transjordan Residency submitted a preliminary report on a huge tract of desert territory: the *mutessariflik* of Belka. The report noted that the region's major Bedouin tribes, the Bani Sakhr and the Bani Hamaideh, dominated Belka's administrative council. These groups had suffered badly from the food shortages and commercial collapse of World War I. Their continued involvement in local government was essential. The first task of British liaison officers was therefore to conciliate them. In this case, the authorities in Amman acknowledged that the security agencies could enforce law and order in tribal areas only with the assent of the nomadic populations themselves.[37]

In economies dominated by peasant agriculture, in which massive oil revenues remained a distant prospect, efficient control of land, water, and market communications was fundamental to imperial rule.[38] Before and after World War I, incidents of violence in the northern Sudanese desert were often sparked by disputed access to limited water supplies.[39] The Sudan Political Service (SPS) identified oases, wells, and wadis as flash points for intertribal clashes, livestock theft, and even killings of salt merchants and other travelers.[40] Sudan was by no means unique in this respect. Competition for livestock, water, and grazing between differing communities determined societal interaction between clan groups and between rural populations and the colonial state. In the Saharan territories and the southern deserts of Syria, Transjordan, and Iraq, reliable, up-to-date information about accessible water sources, available grazing, and nomadic migratory routes was just as pivotal to tribal control policy as political intelligence about clan loyalties and communal rivalries. And in French Africa, Service de Renseignements (SR) policy advice in August 1919 noted that arguments over water rights provoked most violence in France's Saharan possessions.[41] Peasant smallholders, sedentary tribes, and nomadic Bedouin in the Middle East mandates clashed more frequently as competition for water and grazing rights on desert margins increased during the early 1920s.[42]

From 1921, military intelligence officers in the Syrian interior worked with French agronomists in compiling data on soil, water resources, and planned irrigation schemes. A key goal was to ascertain where untapped cultivatable land existed. This was vital work. In Syria's Jabal Druze, for example, the installation of water fountains in the regional capital Soueida in December 1924 was an event of immense practical and political significance. An unprecedented show of public gratitude greeted the French completion of motorized pumping stations to provide permanent water supplies to Soueida and Dera'a in the neighboring Hauran. Both towns had previously relied on remote, stagnant water sources in the summer months. The Soueida water fountains alone were designed to provide up to forty liters per day for each of the town's inhabitants. During 1924, French Army engineers and Druze volunteer workers completed the eighteen-kilometer pipeline that transported the water from its source on the margins of the Jabal to Soueida's nine-hundred-meter altitude. An elaborately orchestrated ceremony followed in December of that year to celebrate what the Damascus authorities characterized as an exemplary display of cooperative imperial development. An estimated ten to twelve thousand Druze, out of a total population of only fifty-five thousand, gathered in Soueida to celebrate the first streams of safe drinking water to course through the new fountains. Among those joining the festivities were representatives from all the 155 Druze villages thus far registered by the French regional authorities.[43] Yet the fact that within a matter of months Druze chiefs would rise up against Governor Gabriel Carbillet's modernizing administration illustrated the fragility of French control.[44]

The weak French grip on the sedentary Druze was mirrored among Syria's nomadic peoples. Specialist intelligence officers struggled to penetrate the complex culture of the Bedouin. Tribes cherished their unique oral histories and were singularly reluctant to reveal them to outsiders. Common ancestry was fundamental to the self-perception of tribal clans. Submission to European control would compromise the integrity of this shared lineage.[45]

Nor were Arabic writings of much assistance to French and British officials. The rich print culture of the Islamic world paid little attention to the nonliterate histories of the migratory tribes. Prejudice against the supposed "backwardness" of the Bedouin remained strong among bourgeois, self-consciously modern Arabs in the administrative capitals of the Middle East. Western bureaucrats were compelled to rely on the romanticized writings of earlier European travelers for an insight into Bedouin customs. These works idealized Bedouin life. Agricultural migration was read as a love of freedom. The apparent absence of strong hierarchical control seemed proof of a resilient individualism and an underlying tribal egalitarianism.[46] Sometimes superficial, these works were nonetheless influential. T. E. Lawrence and Gertrude Bell, the chief political adviser to the Iraq high commissioner Sir Percy Cox, were perhaps the most famous officials seduced by this vision of Arab tribalism.[47] In short, Western officials accustomed to dealing with the printed page found "historical data" on the Bedouin almost impossible to find.

Understandably, field officers generally preferred to accumulate their own fund of knowledge by lived experience among the tribes. The English-language *History of Transjordan and Its Tribes,* produced by the Arab Legion commander Colonel Frederick Peake in 1935, typified this more anthropological approach. Peake made use of Bedouin oral tradition and poetry alongside documentary sources. His writings came loaded with a purpose, however. A former commander of the Egyptian Army's Camel Corps, Peake's initial assignment in Transjordan in 1920 placed him in charge of the creation of a gendarmerie—which he subsequently refashioned into the Arab Legion in October 1923. Its fundamental goal was to curb Bedouin capacity to defy state authority. The force was often deployed against local Bedouin as well as raiders from the Hijaz and was integrated into Peake's strategy to erode tribal autonomy in favor of stronger central control from Amman.[48] Peake's description of Bedouin culture fit Britain's wider objective of giving national cohesion to the administrative artifice that was Transjordan, an "imagined nation-state." Whatever his ulterior motives, Peake's work illustrated that the most effective rural administrators gathered intelligence among their subject populations directly by word of mouth.[49]

Sophisticated understanding of family relationships, moral codes, and tribal customs—from marriage rites to trade transactions and the settlement of property disputes—was vital if nomad populations were to acquiesce in European rule. In most cases, tribal intelligence officers relied on indigenous intermediaries from sheikhs to shepherds to secure their entrée to clan groups. Officials' dependence on local *interlocuteurs* suggests that the reality of tribal control was of grudging Bedouin toleration and minimal imperial authority. The remote Jazirah (Haute-Djezireh) region of northeastern Syria provides useful evidence of the limitations of tribal control. In early 1922, the local SR commander described the situation as anarchic. Even the Kemalist government in Ankara was willing to recognize French administration in the upper Euphrates valley if it meant the curtailment of tribal independence. In practice, the reverse applied. The willingness of local sheikhs to acknowledge French authority was strictly contingent. SR officers found it all but impossible to reconcile the French requirement for order with a high degree of tribal autonomy.[50]

The Jazirah was not untypical. In the absence of tangible state power across much of the desert interior, French and British representatives played more subtle games of compromise, bribery, and conciliation with their supposed Bedouin "subjects." Assessing the role of security intelligence to tribal control in Middle Eastern mandates thus raises deeper questions about the nature and extent of imperial rule and the fabric of the colonial state.

Tribal Control Personnel

After World War I, newly qualified native affairs personnel in Syria's desert interior were typically assigned as advisers to individual clan chiefs. They were supported, in some cases, by the *gendarmerie mobile*, but more often by French-officered camel companies (*méharistes*), usually 250 to 300 men strong. *Méhariste* columns provided Contrôle bédouin officers with intelligence on nomad movements, livestock and grazing rights, clan factionalism, and tribal grievances. The head of the Contrôle bédouin, Captain Charles Terrier, himself a *méhariste* commander, was the eyes and ears of the French administration in the Syrian desert. Terrier was at once policeman, politician, judge, and confidante to senior Bedouin sheikhs.[51]

As we saw in chapter 2, the high proportion of SR personnel trained in the native affairs bureaus of French North Africa ensured that most assigned to Contrôle bédouin units in the Syrian interior at least had some idea of what they would encounter. By contrast, in the British case, reliance on military intelligence officers to serve as local government officials was less a reflection of a distinct colonial philosophy than a short-term expedient. Immediately after the Mudros armistice in October 1918, the British administrations in the Middle East lacked sufficient civilian personnel to staff outlying districts. In the longer term, Egypt and Palestine swallowed greater bureaucratic resources than Iraq and Transjordan. The closest British equivalents to the SR and Contrôle bédouin were the special service officers (SSOs, mainly Royal Air Force personnel), and the tribal levies organized under British Army political officers in the deserts of Iraq and Transjordan.[52]

The service background of the British intelligence officers selected for tribal control work was critical. As we saw in chapter 4, after the Cairo conference in March 1921, the Royal Air Force (RAF) assumed primary responsibility for imperial policing in Iraq. Anxious to secure its future as an independent service arm, the air staff had much to prove in the face of widespread War Office and Admiralty hostility.[53] Hence the Air Ministry's preference for RAF appointees as SSOs, even though few of the air force personnel selected had prior knowledge of colonial government. Air Ministry favoritism soon abated. The army had a far larger pool of experienced officers to draw on, from both the Indian Army and Allenby's Egyptian Expeditionary Force. Army intelligence officers were typically the only available candidates with sufficient linguistic ability to parley with local leaders.

Most French and British intelligence personnel admired the Bedouin lifestyle and tried hard to learn its rules. The fact remained that their prime responsibility was to provide covert information to facilitate the subjugation of such tribal groups. Their security role was at variance with the common inclination among tribal control personnel to become immersed in Bedouin culture. By early 1924, SSOs assigned to tribal control tasks in Transjordan were required to submit fortnightly reports on intertribal relations and frontier raids to the chief political officer at the Amman Residency. These reached a wide audience. SSO memoranda were forwarded to the British high commission for Palestine and Transjordan in Jerusalem, the air officer commanding in Iraq, as well as the Colonial Office and Air Ministry in London.[54]

The tribal control officers producing these reports had little time to acclimatize. Unlike their French SR equivalents, British SSOs were ordered to run before they could crawl, a problem whose consequences soon became obvious. Their initial intelligence assessments often suggested political action inherently damaging to the very tribes to which they were assigned. After his appointment in June 1925 as SSO for northern Iraq's Kirkuk region, the flying officer H. A. Anson was instructed by Air headquarters intelligence in Baghdad to submit political and military intelligence covering an enormous area, much of it the scene of Kurdish unrest and Kemalist agitation.[55] This was not untypical. Many of the intelligence reports from desert outposts in Iraq and Transjordan were superficial summaries of recent local events. Connections within and between tribal groups were frequently missed or misunderstood.[56] The more assured reportage provided by the SPS in Sudan indicates that effective imperial policing required an experienced cohort of specialist intelligence officers.[57]

Even Captain John ("Pasha") Glubb, the archetypal British tribal control administrator, conceded that policy decisions were made with little appreciation of their social consequences for the Bedouin. Prior to his famous assignment in 1930 as organizer of Transjordan's Arab Legion, Glubb spent four years from 1926 as an administrative inspector in the southwestern desert of Iraq. Anxious to curb frontier incursions by Wahhabi attackers, Glubb and his fellow tribal control officers submitted intelligence reports urging stern measures against raiding parties. These included the mobilization of loyalist Bedouin to fight off Ikhwan assaults.[58]

The concentration on the interstate aspect of tribal raiding was revealing. On the one hand, it highlighted Britain's primary concern with the conciliation of relations with Ibn Saud's regime, often at the expense of tribes theoretically living under British protection in Transjordan. On the other, it obscured the fact that, on occasion, Bedouin groups within a single mandate territory attacked one another, largely because of their desperation to recover lost livestock and thus avoid starvation.[59] As raiding was gradually curbed, its vital role in the economic life of tribes came to be appreciated. Violent it undoubtedly was, but tribal raiding also redistributed wealth between the richest and poorest sections of Bedouin society.[60] In times of drought, locust infestation, or loss of livestock, Bedouin groups could not fall back on subsistence agriculture.[61] In these circumstances, the distribution of looted livestock among nomad raiders without animals or other tradable goods of their own helped prevent famine among clan groups. Only when Glubb's desert patrols began using subsidies with client sheikhs and employment of hard-pressed Bedouin as levies or workers on infrastructure and pipeline projects in the 1930s did the state provide some relief to Bedouin hardship in the wake of the Ikhwan rebellion.[62]

Understanding the Tribes

The historians Samira Haj and Toby Dodge both suggest that the British in Iraq misunderstood the nature of tribal society.[63] Western intelligence officers and a later generation of Iraqi historians discerned three supposedly distinctive characteristics of interwar Bedouin tribes. These were a separate system of social organization, cultural habits at variance with those of other Muslims, and clan adherence to the blood feud and livestock raiding. According to Haj, the migratory habits of the Bedouin reflected basic agronomics rather than unique cultural traditions. The single most important factor was the animals reared. Camel herding demanded more frequent movements to new pastures than did raising sheep, which required less seasonal migration but a greater local abundance of water and feedstuffs. The number and type of livestock kept therefore set the pattern of Bedouin migration to a greater extent than supposedly unique Bedouin social customs. Similarly, those sedentary tribes engaged in labor-intensive arable farming, notably the production of cereals and rice, relied on extended family groups and close clan affiliations to ensure that cultivation and harvesting could be completed. Again, practical economics dictated tribal custom.[64] These were lessons still to be learned by intelligence officers among the Iraqi Bedouin in the 1920s.

For these intelligence personnel in Iraq, Transjordan, and Syria the first objective of tribal control policy was to reduce the incidence of livestock raiding. The principal victims of these raids were semisedentarized Bedouin farmers, whose animals were stolen with greatest frequency. These agriculturalists received little useful protection from their new political masters in Baghdad, Amman, and Damascus. In the deserts of the Fertile Crescent, the colonial state meant little.

In the absence of effective state regulation, intertribal conflicts were settled on Bedouin terms. Disputes between individuals, communities, and tribes were still governed by the complex rules of Bedouin custom, of which the blood feud and retribution by raiding were the most striking manifestation to the outside observer.[65] The less spectacular pillars of tribal law— collective responsibility among a clan group, codes of mediation between disputants, and recognized scales of compensation—were a more effective means to restore local peace. Most tribal control officers warmed to these concepts of collective responsibility, mediation, and reconciliation. Their main point of contact with individual tribes remained the skeikhs who played a leading part in the resolution of clan quarrels, thus minimizing the costs of imperial policing.[66] Furthermore, where colonial police attempted to impose Western-style laws based on the concept of individual responsibility in punishment for tribal disputes, they ran into practical and conceptual difficulties. Detaining the individual perpetrator of a violent act was unlikely to resolve a long-standing feud between tribes. Individual detention also ran counter to the concept of a tribal group as a clan-based affiliation sharing collective responsibility for its members' actions.[67]

In July 1918, the British military authorities in Iraq issued instructions for the settlement of civil and criminal disputes involving tribal populations. These were essentially a Western interpretation of existing customary law. The political officers (POs) appointed as district administrators across the Iraqi interior relied in practice on sheikhs and, above all, local headmen to settle alleged breaches of tribal custom. The Baghdad high commission and individual POs theoretically retained discretionary powers to refer serious infractions to a criminal tribunal. In most instances, however, they accepted the recommendations of individual local assemblies, or *majlis*. What did this signify? In the early years of the British mandate in Iraq, Bedouin tribes were encouraged to resolve minor disputes among themselves. Even in instances of major livestock raiding involving substantial loss of life, British regulation was superimposed on the existing procedures governing the conduct of—and compensation for—raids, thefts, and blood feuds.[68] At its apex the system may have appeared British, but the corpus of law applied remained uniquely Arab.[69]

Just as intertribal conflict transgressed Western-imposed frontiers and flouted centralized state authority, so, too, did adherence to customary law in preference to the legal codes devised by British and French officialdom. In Transjordan, for example, the Tribal Courts Law of 1924 was superseded five years later by Bedouin control regulations that acknowledged British failure hitherto to impose an alien justice system. In 1936, further revisions were made to the 1929 Bedouin Control Law to correct numerous errors regarding tribal structure, clan affiliations, and customary practices.[70] British resort to traditional means of conflict resolution was consistent with the precepts of mandate government that precluded societal transformation to suit the interest of the governing power. But the perceived need to act in conformity with Bedouin custom begs the question of where real power lay. In matters of legal dispute, Britain's supremacy lacked substance.

French practice in Syria was remarkably similar, and SR staff studied the work of the POs in Iraq. Furthermore, French and British tribal control officers sometimes came together in an effort to reconcile tribal disputes involving confederations on either side of the frontiers between Syria, Iraq, and Transjordan.[71] The Contrôle bédouin commander Captain Charles Terrier thought it imperative to respect the unwritten Bedouin customs governing individual, communal, and intertribal conduct. Terrier estimated that a rigidly feudal system based on the authority of the sheikh could not be integrated into the fabric of common law practice, taxation policy, and limited political suffrage then being applied in the rest of the Syrian state. The patriarchal hierarchy of Bedouin society regulated the status of its members. Bedouin oral tradition amounted to a distinct "legislative system" embracing marriage and inheritance rights, clan disputes, and a penal code with complex scales of appropriate compensation. These procedures had worked for generations. To tamper with them was to court disaster. Terrier even discerned a nomad "patriotism" based on attachment to family and tribal custom rather than to geographical region. Any attempt to impose French or even Syrian legal regulation on the Bedouin would fail because they found the concept of nation-state meaningless.[72]

The Contrôle bédouin tried to regulate population movement as well as to integrate the Bedouin into the Syrian national polity. With the assent of tribal leaders, Terrier's staff introduced a system of nomad identity cards to help monitor Bedouin migration, any weapons held, births, marriages, and deaths. Contrôle bédouin staff took responsibility for the completion of these Bedouin "passports." A photograph of the holder was attached to the card and a duplicate kept for SR records. The passport ascribed a particular ethnic identity to its holder, defining the individual as both a member of a tribal confederation and a Syrian subject.[73] Its photographic record reinforced the connection between the passport-holder and a particular ethnic group from a particular location within Syrian territory.[74] These internal passports became integral to the rudimentary technology of surveillance available to the Contrôle bédouin. But their underlying assumption of an individual's attachment to a specific national entity was utterly alien to the Bedouin themselves.

Internal passports could be viewed as part of the wider French effort to encourage Bedouin sedentarization. They were also consistent with long-standing tribal control techniques in the Maghreb, where restrictions on internal migration were well established. In the mountainous Aurès region of eastern Algeria, for instance, decree legislation was in place from 1890 onward to restrict the movement of economic migrants and traders from the poor southern Aurès highlands to the local market center of Biskra or across the frontier to Tunisia. Customs agents based in Biskra issued "circulation permits" to any nonresidents wishing to trade in the town, their intention being to prevent the growth of a black market in staples such as cotton, coffee, and sugar between eastern Algeria and western Tunisia. Economic migration was similarly controlled by a system of regional passports that restricted movement between Algerian communes and departments. Travelers moving outside their communal boundary were liable to police spot checks.[75]

In Syria, however, Terrier's restrictions were rarely used to prevent internal or transnational migration among the country's nomadic population. Instead, passports and special passes were issued freely, permitting Bedouin from Syria and Iraq to travel to market centers on either side of the Syria-Iraq frontier.[76] Among Syria's Bedouin at least, the mandate authorities relied on sufferance more than force. Terrier insisted that respect for Bedouin legal custom fostered a symbiotic relationship between the French authorities and loyal sheikhs. From the outset of the French occupation in 1920, SR tribal control officers therefore deferred to customary law to settle feuds between tribes and capital crimes resulting from livestock raids. There was a Machiavellian aspect to this. Increasingly, Contrôle bédouin officers sat alongside sheikhs as arbiters in civil and criminal disputes. Once French personnel assumed a greater role in adjudicating customary law, they planned to prove the superiority of written common law to the tribes themselves. Here was the long-term strategic objective. In parallel with the effort to sedentarize nomad populations, tribal custom would be gradually supplanted by French legal regulation.[77] This scheme paralleled high commission plans after the Great Revolt to accord greater juridical protection to Syria's religious minorities. Muslim Shari'a law accorded formal legal recognition to associated Judaic religions, but did not recognize heterodox Muslim minority sects, including the Druze, the Isma'ilis, and the Ansaris. The encroachment of French law into Bedouin custom was thus presented as part of a wider strategy equalizing the individual legal status of Syria's minority populations.[78]

In April 1925, the French high commissioner, General Sarrail, approved Contrôle bédouin procedures for the punishment of tribal raiding and the settlement of Bedouin disputes in Syria. The regulations distinguished between crimes committed among nomadic Bedouin and those that affected sedentary tribes. Cases involving only nomads would be settled according to customary law under the supervision of SR officers and the tribal sheikhs involved. Where attacks on sedentary populations occurred, common law tribunals would issue punishment. This was a virtual duplicate of the system adopted by the British in Iraq in 1918. To ensure the fulfillment of sentences or the payment of compensation, tribal notables faced arrest if their community failed to meet any collective fines or sanctions imposed. If they fled, other hostages could be taken. Persistent criminal offenders faced permanent expulsion from Syria. Here again customary tribal practice was adapted to the requirements of mandate policing. The entire system rested on cooperation between Contrôle bédouin staff and the Bedouin sheikhs. In this relationship, the military resources of the former were intended to buttress the customary authority of the latter.[79]

French deference to Bedouin custom went furthest in the upper Euphrates region of northern Syria. By 1926, local Contrôle bédouin officers were convinced that the area should be separately administered in consultation with tribal leaders and in accordance with customary law. They advised French delegation staff in Damascus that a "Bedouin state," judicially autonomous and politically distinct from the rest of Syria, would facilitate tribal control. Prominent local Bedouin backed the proposal. Foremost among them were the leaders of the Oueldès, a seminomadic tribal group whose encampments were traditionally established along the banks of the Euphrates northwest of Dayr al-Zur. Their core demand was that the central government in Damascus should not govern Bedouin affairs. Instead, tribal disputes, tax payments, civil property cases, and criminal offences were to be judged by Contrôle bédouin personnel according to tribal custom. The high commissioner Henry de Jouvenel saw the plan's wisdom, but still felt compelled to reject it in March 1926 for fear of adverse reaction among urban nationalists hostile to the devolved state structure that had been imposed across Syria between 1920 and 1923.[80]

As Alice Conklin has shown, in French West Africa after World War I, district administrators buttressed the power of conservative chiefs to support the colonial state.[81] The abortive Bedouin autonomy scheme reveals echoes of this in Syria. Its failure suggests that indulgence toward tribal authorities was mitigated by abiding French hostility toward nomadic migration and the high commission's reliance on an urbanized Arab political class as auxiliaries in the governance of Syria. One reason that tribal sheikhs were valued so much as intermediaries was because the greater their engagement with Syrian national politics, the less their inclination to maintain the traditional migratory Bedouin lifestyle.[82] British courtship of Shi'ite tribal leaders followed much the same pattern after the shock of the 1920 uprising. Here, too, the offer of parliamentary seats and tax exemptions to favored sheikhs loosened their ties to their coreligionists.[83]

Revenue Collection

In addition to their role as policemen and prosecutors, tribal control officers in the Arab mandates were above all intelligence providers. Local government required accurate intelligence about the material assets of its dependent rural population in order to estimate how much revenue could be raised and at what political price. Intelligence therefore had an important part to play in the collection of crop and livestock taxes. Indirect taxes aside, within Iraq and Transjordan, taxation of agricultural produce provided the bulk of government income. Collection of these monies was tied to the cycle of crop harvesting and the movement and sale of livestock herds in differing seasonal pastures. In 1926, for example, 88 percent of the *koda,* a poll tax based on head counts of livestock, derived from the assessment of sheep flocks. The largest flocks either belonged to or were tended by Bedouin confederations, often in conjunction with Arab traders in market towns.[84] Since the nineteenth century, Bedouin in the Mosul region, for example, often "managed" their flocks in agreement with town merchants who settled a price for fleeces months in advance of delivery.[85]

French officials in Damascus were less impressed than their British neighbors by the revenue that could be generated from tax collection among the Bedouin. Nevertheless, the overhaul of land and livestock taxes throughout the Syrian and Lebanese countryside was central to French plans to build up a loyal class of peasant smallholders released from their former dependence on absentee landowners or the unproductive systems of crop rotation traditionally practiced on communally run village plots.[86] Between 1920 and 1923, General Gouraud's administration recognized that the uneven collection of livestock taxes across regions and between tribes was prejudicial to French prestige. The problem was complicated by Syria's administrative division into autonomous states, first as components of the Syrian federation proclaimed by Gouraud in 1922, and then as elements of the reorganized Syrian state put in place by Gouraud's successor, General Maxime Weygand, by 1924. The *gendarmerie mobile* was delegated to enforce the payment of taxes among peasant cultivators and sedentary tribes. Gendarmerie jurisdiction applied only at the state, not the federal, level, however. Police units could not pursue nomadic Bedouin across Syria's administrative boundaries. In November 1922, one *méhariste* officer, Lieutenant Delouze, led Contrôle bédouin calls for the introduction of a single tax collection system throughout Syria. SR chief Catroux rejected the idea. The net increase in policing costs required to implement a unified tax collection scheme among Bedouin tribes was likely to exceed the anticipated revenue of 1.5 million francs.[87]

Bedouin leaders were well aware of these jurisdictional limits. The Sbaa tribes of northern Syria, for example, frequently avoided French tax collection by moving across the Aleppo, Euphrates, and Damascus state boundaries. Their intelligence of the imminent arrival of mandate tax collectors surpassed that of the officials sent to track them. French authority over the Sbaa remained fragmentary until the Syrian revolt prompted a more systematic effort to police them. From 1922 to 1924, the Sbaa sheikhs, Bechir Ibn Merchid and Berges Ibn H'Deib, evaded tax collectors in Aleppo, defying Contrôle bédouin orders to surrender their weapons on entry to reserved grazing in the Mamoura region. Their dissent caused other problems. Tribes that paid their taxes resented French inability to ensure that the Sbaa did the same. Moreover, intertribal raiding was expected to increase once the disparity in weapons between proximate Bedouin groups became known.[88]

The officials who collected taxes among the Bedouin in Syria, Iraq, and Transjordan relied on military intelligence officers for reports of Bedouin migrations across frontiers to fresh grazing. From June 1923, for instance, the Contrôle bédouin managed the arrival, distribution, and encampment of three separate nomadic tribes that had moved into the upper Euphrates valley for winter pasturage. The SR even organized a gendarmerie to police the nomad camps and collect a forfeiture tax (*ouedi*) intended to discourage intertribal disputes.[89] The bitterest Bedouin protests stemmed from double taxation. Shepherds migrating among Syria, Iraq, and Turkey risked having their sheep counted by tax collectors in each country. During 1925, for example, Sbaa tribesmen, increasingly excluded from pastures in southern Anatolia, moved to grazing grounds between Aleppo and Hama. There they resisted French attempts to collect the *aghnam* tax imposed on sheepherders. Payments were made only after a *méhariste* unit resorted to what was euphemistically described as "energetic means of coercion."[90]

Accurate reports of Bedouin migration were essential to prevent violence over unfair taxation. In May 1926, for instance, the Baghdad high commission collated intelligence from RAF reconnaissance flights and outlying SSOs. As a result, Iraqi officials in Qaim were instructed to communicate with their Syrian neighbors across the frontier before assessing *koda* contributions in their region. The intention was to ensure that any Syrian Bedouin could withdraw back across the Syria-Iraq border prior to the livestock count. They would thus avoid unnecessary payment of *koda* in Iraq. The authorities in Qaim failed to do as ordered. Instead, when faced with complaints from Syrian Bedouin about the collection of *koda* for two hundred sheep, a fifteen-man camel corps unit was called out to enforce payment. Mishrif al Dandal, chief of the 'Aqaidat, the Bedouin tribe involved, immediately organized a reprisal attack on an Iraqi police detachment. In this instance, ignored intelligence caused an immediate breakdown in tribal control. The incident also provoked French complaints that the British authorities stirred tribal unrest on the frontier as a pretext for annexation of Abu Kemal, the local market center on the Euphrates just inside Syrian territory. A spy was even sent into Iraq by an overzealous SR officer based in Abu Kemal to find evidence of British incitement of tribal violence. Thus, an apparently minor dispute revealed the brittle quality of mandatory rule, the underlying friction between the imperial powers, and the vital need to disseminate rural intelligence swiftly.[91]

Controlling Nomad Populations

The imperial authorities were often found wanting when called on to live up to their self-image as lawgiver. The Bedouin populations of northern Syria and the tribes that migrated across the southern desert of Transjordan and Iraq suffered acutely in this respect. In the desert interior of the Middle East, the writ of the central government frequently counted for little to indigenous populations for whom banditry, livestock raiding, and intertribal dispute remained facts of life. The Bedouin of the Aleppo *vilayet* found their migration routes and customary grazing rights disrupted, first by the conflict between French and Kemalist forces over control of Cilicia in 1920–22, and then by French inability to persuade the Ankara government to abide by the terms agreed on regarding nomadic pasture rights in the frontier region between Killis and Aleppo.

The disputed territorial partition between Syria and Turkey was a regional disaster for the Arab populations involved. The outcome of the Alexandretta dispute in the late 1930s only confirmed the point. This was as much the case for the principal Bedouin tribal groups of the region, the Gayars, the El-Beglis, and the Bani Zeid, as it was for the Arab, Alawite, Kurdish, and Armenian residents of Alexandretta, Antioch, and their hinterland. For much of the interwar period, the Ankara government denied grazing rights to Syrian Bedouin, who traditionally migrated to summer encampments in southern Anatolia. Closing frontiers to Bedouin herders was part of Turkey's wider pressure on the French high commission for concessions over the Alexandretta *sanjak*.[92] Acting on intelligence from Kemalist officers in Killis, the Turks targeted those Bedouin sheikhs who had remained loyal to France during the earlier conflict over Cilicia. Tribal control was thus internationalized.[93] Always a yardstick of colonial state power, management of nomadic populations was also a bone of contention between the governments of the Middle East.

Tension was still more pronounced along the southern desert margins of Transjordan and Iraq where raiding by Ikhwan levies fiercely loyal to Saudi Wahhabism escalated during the late 1920s. As Ibn Saud extended Wahhabi control in the Hijaz, Bedouin in Transjordan and southern Iraq faced concerted pressure to acknowledge the House of Saud and submit to the Ikhwan's puritanical Islam. The four principal Bedouin confederations affected by Ikhwan raiding were the Syrian Ruwala, the Amarat Anizah of Iraq, and, above all, the Huwaytat and Bani Sakhr of Transjordan.[94]

On 11 January 1925, the SSOs based in Transjordan's southern desert warned that the repeated Ikhwan attacks suffered by these groups had persuaded them that British imperial protection was worthless.[95] Days later, a tribal envoy advised King Faysal in Baghdad that Ibn Saud had ordered the Ruwala sheikh Amir Nuri Sha'lan to declare allegiance to the Wahhabi regime. The Iraq high commissioner Sir Henry Dobbs now joined the chorus begun by the SSOs. Dobbs saw far-reaching consequences if British authority over the Bedouin were not quickly reaffirmed. If the Ruwala, the Huwaytat, and the Anizah became feudatories of Ibn Saud, British control over the air routes, pipelines, and railways across the southern desert would be lost. Communications between Faysal's Iraq and the Mediterranean would be ruptured.[96] Angered by Colonial Office reluctance to intervene in Jeddah, on 26 January Dobbs spelled out the threat of any extension of Wahhabi religious and political control over the southern desert Bedouin: "The result of this would be that Iraq's hold on the whole of the Euphrates would be precarious and [this would] cause panic in Kerbala and Najaf—the holy Shia cities. Actual attack on Ruwala and afterward on Amarat Anizah is not so much feared as their being completely won over to Bin Saud by [a] mixture of threats and cajolery, which would give no open cause for war."[97]

Ultimately, the Wahhabi threat to the Ruwala proved exaggerated. Not so for the Huwaytat and the Bani Sakhr. These tribal confederations suffered most at the hands of Wahhabi raiders. By 1931, sections of the Huwaytat faced starvation, having lost so much livestock to Ikhwan raids. The tribe's crop yields had also collapsed. Huwaytat clansmen reportedly abandoned the Bedouin lifestyle to seek work as laborers in the Gulf of Aqaba.[98] Their own counterraids into the northern Hijaz, sometimes undertaken in conjunction with other Bedouin tribes of Transjordan, did little to improve matters and were increasingly liable to punishment by the government in Amman.[99]

In September 1928, "Pasha" Glubb, then serving as a desert control officer in the Euphrates valley, expressed his frustration at the British authorities' failure to recognize the significance of the Ikhwan threat. British administrators tended to dismiss, even to romanticize, tribal raids as part of the eternal cycle of desert life. Evidently, intelligence of the imminent collapse of imperial authority made little impression in Whitehall. As Glubb warned, "The fallacy lies in the fact that there is little more similarity between the old-fashioned Bedouin raid and modern Ikhwan methods of warfare, than between international rugby football and a European war."[100]

But Glubb also blamed British efforts to sedentarize the Bedouin of southwestern Iraq for the worsening anarchy near the Hijaz frontier. For several years, Faysal's government had made little sustained effort to govern Iraq's Bedouin population. The political consequences of unwelcome state intervention were potentially severe, and the costs and problems of overland communication prohibitive. In 1925, Faysal's administration made known that raiding among Bedouin tribes within Iraq would be tolerated. As Glubb put it, "a Bedouin had only to camp twenty miles from the river, and he was independent of the government." The abrupt reversal of this policy in 1927 caused confusion and resentment.[101] Reversing his position again, in September 1928 Faysal proposed to enlist key tribes—the Shammar, the Amarat, and the Dhafir—as auxiliaries to launch counterraids into Saudi territory. High Commissioner Dobbs and the air force command in Baghdad immediately vetoed the scheme.[102] After Glubb's transfer from Iraq's southern desert, the appointment in May 1930 of Abdul Jaffar as *Qaimmaqam Sulman* responsible for Bedouin control was also poorly received, this time among the Bedouin themselves. SSOs noted that leading sheikhs considered Jaffar a classic urban effendi, unfamiliar with Bedouin life and contemptuous of it.[103]

The extension of central government authority to tribal areas inevitably challenged the traditional supremacy of Bedouin sheikhs. Those who declared their loyalty to the Wahhabi regime stood to recoup lost prestige, customary authority, and valuable revenue from local taxation and raiding activity.[104] Cross-border raids were never reducible to questions of material gain, however, nor could they be entirely explained as products of intertribal feuds and broader Wahhabi-Hashemite rivalry. Raids also stemmed from the conflict between the puritanical Islamic values upheld by the Ikhwan levies and the creeping Westernization of mandatory rule.[105]

The creation of settled Ikhwan communities composed of Nejd tribesmen devoted to Wahhabi unitarianism brought greater stability to Central Arabia and fostered popular loyalty to the Saudi authorities.[106] Further development of these Ikhwan agricultural settlements reduced nomadism and intertribal conflict among the major clans and tribal confederations loyal to the House of Saud.[107] The Ikhwan, in short, offered an organizational model proving that Bedouin practices could be reconciled with loyalty to a central authority, albeit only a Muslim one. Hence the anxiety of the Amman Residency and the Baghdad high commission to reduce crossfrontier raiding in conformity with Bedouin practices of retaliation, arbitration, and material compensation.[108]

Belatedly, then, the Ikhwan challenge precipitated the most systematic tribal control measures yet attempted by the British authorities: the creation of the Arab Legion to police the southern desert, and the organization of a Bedouin Control Board to arbitrate over raiding disputes.[109] In operation from 1929 onward, the new mobile force to patrol the southern desert, combined with a formal mechanism for high-level arbitration of Bedouin disputes, curtailed tribal conflict in the decade ahead. In the third quarter of 1929 alone, the Bedouin Control Board held seventeen meetings at which punishment was dispensed for thirty-eight recorded tribal raids.[110] But this image of an industrious and judicious organization is misleading. It belies the fact that the Board's sanctions largely applied to Bedouin tribes living within the confines of Britain's mandate frontiers, and then only to those that Amir Abdullah was willing to see punished. Punishing Saudi raiders was a different proposition altogether. Headed by Abdullah's kinsman, Shakir ibn Zayd, assisted by a former Egyptian government official M. S. McDonnel, the Board failed to ensure the restitution of livestock to the worst affected Bedouin tribes in Transjordan.[111] Far from representing the confluence of interests between the emirate and the British mandate, the Board signified the further diminution of Ibn Zayd's influence over Bedouin affairs.

This process was further accelerated by the acute economic conditions facing the country's tribal populations.[112] By the time a locust infestation decimated key desert pastures in the Wadi Sirhan during 1932, the Huwaytat and the Bani 'Attiyah faced famine. Arab Legion posts provided limited relief supplies.[113] In such extreme conditions, it is easy to see why the Legion's intelligence agents—the intermediaries responsible for gathering the evidence of alleged transgressions—became caught up in the intertribal disputes on which they reported.[114] As a result, the affected sheikhs accused the Board of biased treatment and ineffectiveness in the punishment of the Ikhwan.[115] Other sheikhs were coaxed into cooperation with the Bedouin Control Board only through the provision of secret service funds released for the purpose by the Palestine high commissioner Sir John Chancellor in June 1930.[116] Only with the institution of new appeal procedures and the establishment of local tribal courts in each *liwa* during 1936 was tribal control placed on a more equitable footing.[117] Meanwhile, in May 1932, the discovery of plans, covertly sponsored by Hashemite supporters in Cairo and Amman, to foment a tribal uprising against the Saudi regime highlighted the continuing need for effective policing of the southern desert frontier.[118]

While the fallout from tribal raiding dominated intelligence gathering and policing operations in Transjordan, tribal control in Iraq was, as ever, bound up with the country's communal and religious divisions. The introduction of conscription in Iraq, ardently supported by leading Sherifian officers since 1922, repeatedly debated between 1926 and 1933, and finally legislated into practice in 1934, had less of an effect on the Bedouin than on the country's sedentary Shi'ite tribes. They had long opposed it as a thinly veiled attempt by the Sunni officer elite to impose their hegemony.[119] Retention of the so-called *Nisbi* system, whereby, in the absence of reliable census data, Bedouin sheikhs were allowed to select recruits in a fixed ratio to the estimated tribal population, was less a concession to tribal particularity than a recognition that the most recent and much resented census, conducted in the immediate aftermath of the 1934 conscription law, was utterly unreliable.[120] In Iraq, as in Transjordan, tribal control was bound up with local resistance to creeping centralization.

Air Power and Tribal Control

The terms *imperial policing* and *counterinsurgency* conjure up images of one-sided encounters between heavily armed European forces and easily cowed Arab populations. British inability to curb Ikhwan raiding reminds us how misleading these terms can be. Despite the growing effectiveness of air power as "a swift agent of government," for much of the 1920s Bedouin raiding parties, often several hundred strong, held the initiative in the deserts of the Middle East mandates.[121] Raiders flouted imperial authority, aware that the major barriers they faced in raiding across frontiers were more environmental than military or political. At the height of a renewed wave of Ikhwan raiding into Iraq's Shamiyah desert over the winter of 1925–26, those most intimately involved in policing the area advocated a reversion to the use of armored car patrols, camel corps tours, and the construction of fixed frontier posts rather than exclusive reliance on retaliatory air strikes against raiding parties. In short, there was no substitute for a permanent police presence on the ground.[122] Only units in regular contact with affected tribes could gather intelligence and relay it quickly enough for punitive operations against raiding parties to succeed as an effective deterrent.[123]

Seen in this light, the widely accepted image of tribal populations overawed by air power seems wrong. In spite of greater reliance on air policing as the principal weapon of imperial control, internal security remained tenuous in British-controlled mandates. Bombers and aircraft machine guns could wreak havoc on dissentient tribesmen or rebel-held villages and even the flimsiest biplane could reconnoiter otherwise inaccessible frontiers, but aircraft were much less effective in assuring a long-term peace.[124]

In early 1926, Glubb, then responsible for policing Iraq's southwestern desert against raiding by the Ikhwan, urged a turn away from reliance on air power. Instead, he advocated a return to a more balanced combination of ground patrols, intelligence gathering among desert tribes, fixed frontier posts, and limited use of air attacks. Aware that rumors of British intentions to punish raiding parties spread quickly among itinerant tribes in the Shamiyah desert, Glubb was keen to put the desert rumor mill to good use as a deterrent. Targeted aerial bombardments and the more widespread use of armored car patrols for ordinary frontier policing tasks made more sense in this light than dependence on air policing alone.[125] Whichever policing techniques were adopted, the entire system was only as good as the intelligence that underpinned it.[126]

With the escalation in Ikhwan raiding in 1928, it soon became equally apparent in Transjordan that aerial reconnaissance was no substitute for old-style intelligence gathering by guards deployed along a line of frontier posts and mounted camel corps visiting tribal encampments and monitoring the comings and goings at wadis and other water sources.[127] In January 1930, the air staff advocated construction of a series of frontier posts east of the Hijaz railway, linked by telegraph to the RAF command in Amman. Aircraft could then respond immediately to intelligence of incursions by raiding parties.[128] On the other hand, military blockhouses implied the existence of frontier restrictions sure to antagonize Bedouin populations used

Figure 5. Air policing at work: aerial photographs of Chabaish village, on the Hammar Lake, Iraq. The village was bombed during air action against Aalim al-Khayun, the principal sheikh of the Muntafiq liwa. Villagers were warned to evacuate the village on 28 November 1924 and the sheikh was informed that his house would be bombed and destroyed. The sheikh's followers capitulated to the government a week later, immediately after the bombing took place. TNA, AIR 8/72. Crown copyright, reproduced courtesy of the National Archives, London.

to traversing the desert according to the seasonal demands of climate and pasturage. The sight of troops guarding essential water supplies was bound to arouse Bedouin fears of extortion and unwarranted restrictions on a natural birthright. The Amman Residency therefore preferred to invest more heavily in the Arab Legion and Transjordan Frontier Force, whose mobile columns would scout the region and maintain contact with the tribes in conjunction with the regional SSOs.[129]

In another clash between the advocates of air power and the devotees of itinerant land patrols, in March 1932, Glubb, by then in charge of policing Transjordan's southern frontier, clashed with the Foreign Office and Air Ministry over the economic plight of the Huwaytat, the tribal confederation pillaged most severely by Ikhwan raiders. Glubb's tours of Huwaytat encampments revealed a community in crisis, their livestock depleted and their traditional grazing sites inaccessible. But aerial reconnaissance suggested that the Huwaytat still possessed sufficient livestock to assure their survival, and that there was sufficient pasturage within reach of their encampments. It took the personal intervention of the assistant resident in Amman, A. S. Kirkbride, who toured the desert south to verify Glubb's increasingly alarmist reports, to convince Whitehall of the need for urgent relief measures.[130] The sufferings of the Huwaytat indicated the key role of intelligence swiftly relayed and acted on in improving desert conditions.[131]

During a tour of Palestine, Transjordan, and Iraq in February–March 1927, Sir John Shuckburgh, then a Colonial Office undersecretary and no stranger to the realities of policing in the Middle East, registered local improvements in law and order in the simplest terms. The Palestine situation he considered much ameliorated since his previous visit to the territory in 1925, basing his verdict on the observation that the major towns appeared safer to the casual visitor. Shuckburgh registered similarly basic improvements in Transjordan. He noted approvingly that "two years ago practically everybody in the country (shepherds, ploughmen etc.) went about with a rifle slung over their shoulders. Today it is quite exceptional to see anything of the kind." Significantly, however, Abdullah's government in Amman did not dare prohibit civilians from carrying weapons outright. As Shuckburgh continued his tour overland from Damascus to Baghdad, tribal unrest compelled his cortege to divert from the main trunk road. French forces still attempting to pacify the Syrian interior gave him an armored car escort to the Iraqi frontier. But lest the disorder in the aftermath of the Syrian revolt be contrasted too sharply with the greater calm in Iraq, Shuckburgh's final report noted that the RAF squadrons allocated to imperial policing duties in the Iraqi interior were all that prevented Faysal's administration from "falling to pieces."[132]

Shuckburgh's enthusiasm for air policing said as much about his perceptions of the Arab populations on the receiving end of aerial bombardment as about his support for a continuing Air Ministry role in the internal defense of the Middle East. As David Omissi and Priya Satia have pointed out, debates about the probable responses of indigenous peoples to air power illustrate how ideas become instruments with which social groups seek to advance their own interests. Opponents of air policing created an image of an insensitive and resilient "native" who would be immune to the terrors of sustained bombardment. The supporters of air power generated contrasting theories of "native" characteristics that furthered their rival objectives.[133] Shuckburgh and other British and French enthusiasts of air policing were predisposed to view indigenous populations as cowering before the irresistible power of the military airplane, whatever the evidence to the contrary.

In 1930, the Air Ministry's director of intelligence, Sir John Slessor, conceded that the RAF units responsible for imperial policing in Transjordan had little chance of preventing clashes between Bedouin raiders from Saudi Arabia and the seminomadic tribes of Transjordan's southern desert. "In point of fact," he admitted, "aircraft have not caught a raid in Transjordan for years." Only ground forces could chase down raiders effectively. But to admit this publicly would be to concede the RAF's shortcomings as Britain's primary imperial policing service in the Middle East. Far better, in Slessor's opinion, to create armored car companies under RAF control to relay intelligence about tribal movements to local air force commanders. That way, RAF bombardment could outperform soldiers' bullets in punishing raiding tribesmen.[134]

Slessor's report is revealing in two key respects. First was the acknowledgment that detailed security intelligence was the cornerstone of desert policing, a view shared by the air staff. Good, early intelligence of likely dissent allowed the air force to maximize its advantage of speed over conventional land forces, meting out punishment before or immediately after any rebellious activity. The salutary effect of such instantaneous retribution was only as effective as the original intelligence on which it was based. Faulty intelligence might result in disastrous attacks on the wrong target. Sluggishness in the intelligence relay system nullified the benefit of speed that air policing could confer.[135] The second, and more significant, revelation in Slessor's report was the admission that as late as 1930, much of southern Transjordan was not really "ruled" by Britain at all.

The position across the Syrian frontier was not much different. Budgetary cuts bit deeper into imperial defense expenditure from 1926 onward. Between 1927 and 1933, lack of funding limited the scope of French tribal control and frontier surveillance. The fortification system that Gamelin had proposed for Syria's most lawless regions remained incomplete five years after his departure. Alternative policing methods were not pursued. Instead, SR officers and Sûreté policemen bemoaned the cancellation of plans to build a string of strategic frontier posts along Syria's eastern rim intended to monitor movements of population.[136]

Figure 6. Relaying desert intelligence: one of the first mobile radio vans sent for use by Transjordan Frontier Force units in 1933. These radio vans were a vital asset to desert policing, relaying intelligence as Slessor recommended. TNA, AIR 5/1155. Crown copyright, reproduced courtesy of the National Archives, London.

Conclusion

Throughout the 1920s, French and British mandatory authorities pursued similar tribal control policies. Each relied on the cooperation of tribal sheikhs, sometimes at the expense of their subordinate clans.[137] And each followed established Ottoman precedent in encouraging the sedentarization of nomadic tribes. The attempt to "domesticate" migratory tribes amounted to an attack on the very fabric of their culture. It broke down clan relationships and it restricted the Bedouin's freedom of movement, thereby severing the links between nomads and traditional grazing grounds. Above all, it diminished the capacity of migratory Bedouin to manage large numbers of livestock. Once pushed into arable farming, the Bedouin could no longer maintain a nomadic lifestyle.

To secure tribal acquiescence in such fundamental change, the mandate authorities had to offer better protection against raiding and the assurance of a judicial system consistent with Bedouin customary law.[138] The personnel of the Contrôle bédouin were, on the whole, better qualified and more ambitious than their British counterparts. In practice, however, the greater self-assurance of French tribal control officers simply translated into a firmer resolve to sedentarize nomadic Bedouin.

In all mandate territory, land ownership and a sedentary lifestyle counted for nothing if the tribes concerned remained prey to attack. Political intelligence officers led the efforts made to protect these populations. The British and French authorities were quick to grasp that efficient policing of sedentary settlements demanded good intelligence gathering. Neither power maintained sufficient standing forces, local levies, or air force squadrons to deter all attacks on tribal settlements. Early detection of impending raids was therefore essential both to protect tribal settlements and to meet the wider objective of Bedouin sedentarization. Here, the French and British encountered persistent failure until the creation of larger frontier forces and closer regulation of intertribal disputes from 1927 onward. Quick transmission and exploitation of intelligence were key to the interception or pursuit of raiding parties. Regular frontier patrols and greater use of indigenous intelligence agents were essential to achieve this speed.[139] Even so, security in the southern deserts of Iraq and Transjordan remained tenuous until the incidence of Ikhwan raids diminished in the early 1930s, thanks in large part to Ibn Saud's cooperation.[140]

Another common facet of French and British tribal control policy was the prevailing assumption that Bedouin tribes constituted a distinct, autonomous culture within predominantly Arab states. In anticipation of elections to the Syrian National Assembly in January 1928, High Commissioner Henri Ponsot confidently predicted that the Damascus authorities could rely on the tribal sheikhs to deliver their clansmen's votes. In Ponsot's eyes, contested mass politics in the Syrian countryside did not exist. Sedentary agriculturalists and migratory Bedouin were merely pawns in the hands of the local powerbrokers whom tribal control officers were required to conciliate.[141]

The tendency to regard the tribes as quite unlike settled town and village populations underestimated the economic interactions and cultural symbiosis between the two. Instead, the distinctiveness of Bedouin culture became a means to divorce the problems of tribal control from the growth of Arab nationalism. The strict official demarcation between urban nationalism and rural politics was integral to pacification in the Middle East mandates. But it rested on specious assessments of the supposed insularity of tribal culture. In practice, the mechanisms of imperial control, from frontier delimitation to regular tax collection, undermined the culture of nomadism and the traditional cycles of Bedouin agriculture and commerce. Yet tribal populations were not entirely subjugated to imperial authority, nor could the imperial system function without the active cooperation of certain tribal groups. Ultimately, the adaptation of customary law to resolve intertribal disputes and the growing reliance on Bedouin levies to help police desert frontiers indicate that tribal recognition of mandatory authority was as much the product of compromise as of coercion.

INTELLIGENCE AND URBAN
OPPOSITION IN FRENCH TERRITORIES

This chapter moves us from a desert setting to an urban one, exploring the distinct political environment of Arab towns and cities under French rule. In the urban centers of North Africa and the Middle East, elite opposition coalesced with popular nationalism to present colonial states with greater security problems in the 1930s. Security agencies meanwhile acquired increasing importance in the ordering of colonial urban space over the course of the interwar period. City police forces became increasingly visible to town and city dwellers. They were better armed and self-consciously modern in style and substance as their policing priorities and bureaucratic procedures sought to impose the Europeanization of law and order. Yet urban policing was, as ever, reliant on the cooperation of indigenous intermediaries. Locally recruited police auxiliaries typically made up the rank and file, working under the supervision of white officers.[1] As a result, police services across the Arab world epitomized the contested sovereignty of Arab cities in the interwar period as colonial authorities and municipal leaders competed for political influence and economic power.[2] French colonial governments expected the Service de Renseignements (SR), the Sûreté Générale, their elite clients, and their informer networks to close the gap between nominal state authority and the actual fragility of the colonial order. Intelligence gathering about all facets of urban life, from political organization to city gangs and commercial activity, was fundamental to administrative decision making.

Intelligence and Urban Politics in Algeria

A little background information about the politics of colonial urbanism helps clarify the role of intelligence gathering in the municipal government of France's North African territories. Let us begin with the Algerian capital. Much of Algeria's precolonial urban infrastructure was destroyed in the decades following the 1830 conquest.[3] By 1850, the Arab heart of Algiers had been torn out, making way for the requirements of military government and urban policing. An enormous central square, the Place du Gouvernement, dominated the old port area, and broad streets were carved through the lower casbah to facilitate access to this new colonial administrative center.

By the end of the nineteenth century, these structural changes were matched by greater segregation of the city's Muslim and European populations. New settler quarters surrounded and contained the exclusively Muslim upper casbah of Algiers. The urban transformation of Algiers gave physical form to French domination and the economic marginalization of the Muslim population. By the 1860s, a new wave of European settlers had colonized the city's lower casbah, now redesignated the Marine Quarter. Colonial administrations in the last years of Napoleon III's Second Empire tolerated the remaining Muslim architectural facets of French African cities as curios in an otherwise French-controlled society. Mosques, medinas, hammams (bathhouses), and casbahs became living museums of a defunct Arab civilization that was now harnessed to French imperial power. But, after slowing down in the late 1860s, the wholesale destruction of precolonial Muslim housing, markets, and religious sites gathered fresh momentum after 1871.[4]

Faced with this continual cycle of urban renewal conducted on exclusively French terms, reformist officials faced a mammoth task in conciliating urban notables alienated by the systematic destruction of their cities, their culture, and their economic environment.[5] Jules Cambon, appointed as the Algiers governor general in January 1891, fostered closer relations with city dignitaries and leading Muslim clerics by promising to respect Islamic holy places in Algiers and elsewhere. Cambon secured state funding for a program of mosque construction in new colonial settlements. One of his successors, Charles Jonnart, followed a similar path. Between 1905 and 1911, Jonnart sponsored the creation of an Algerian Cultural Association, distinct from the colonial government, to supervise mosque administration and thereby comply with the 1905 legislation separating church and state in France. Jonnart released government funding for madrassas and sponsored a pro-French Arabic newspaper, *Kawkib Ifriqiya*. In 1911, Algiers' two largest mosques were designated as historic monuments to block settler developers eager to demolish them. These more sensitive policies yielded some rewards. George Joffé suggests that the 'ulamā, mosque officials, and madrassa staffs in North African towns, as well as the marabouts and Sufi congregations (the *tariqas*) in the countryside, "tended to accept colonial control to the extent that traditional Islamic political structures were retained, and to condemn it insofar as they were not."[6] World War I marked a watershed in this nascent religious opposition to the colonial assault on Algeria's Islamic culture. In the main, before 1914 religious notables and their followers tried to conserve their Islamic heritage and cultural integrity either by accommodation with the colonial power or by avoidance of it. The increasing intrusiveness of the colonial state thereafter heightened the appeal of Salafī teaching and the more assertive cultural nationalism of the reformist 'ulamā, a trend most apparent in the urban spaces of interwar Algeria.[7]

By 1914, the security services in Algerian cities operated in a physical environment substantially reconfigured to meet the colonial requirements of social control. This did not mean that policing became a more straightforward task. The major urban centers across French North Africa were now archetypal "dual cities"—if not formally segregated, then economically and politically divided between Muslims and Europeans.[8] Muslim resentment at the scale of French destruction of indigenous dwellings and Islamic sites fed the simmering anger over settlers' appropriation of prime land, property, and commercial wealth. Iniquitous distribution of municipal revenues and other fiscal income was another source of grievance. In these circumstances, Sûreté and SR analysts viewed the Maghreb's urban populations with suspicion, watching for the socioeconomic flash points or ideological sparks liable to ignite the powder keg of pent-up hostility to European privilege.

Urban policing in Algeria consumed more resources and security service attention during the early 1920s, as city populations increased, settler immigration picked up, and organized anticolonial protest intensified. The 1921 census recorded a total registered population of 4,923,186, an increase of more than 182,000 on the figure recorded a decade earlier. This relatively small increase in population—3.8 percent between 1911 and 1921—would soon be overtaken in the more peaceful conditions of the 1920s, a decade in which Muslim migration to Algeria's major cities would also rise dramatically.[9] Europeans and their local auxiliaries, however, were more exposed to violence in rural communities where the French security presence was correspondingly weaker. In July 1922, for instance, Algeria's Prefectures of Police recorded seven capital crimes. The victims were either settlers or Muslim officials such as caïds and rural policemen. Six of these attacks, including two murders and two shootings, were directed at commune administrators. There were no records of any capital cases involving victims unconnected to the colonial state during that month.[10] Even so, it was cities, not rural districts, that intelligence analysts considered the more politically explosive, because it was in urban milieus that organized nationalism first came to prominence.

Tracking the Organizers: Shakib Arslan and Amir Khaled

Before 1914, civilian municipal authorities generally authorized the deployment of troops to curb urban disorder in French North Africa.[11] This situation changed in anticipation of the demobilization of colonial troops and the influx of returning migrant war workers at the end of World War I. From 1919 onward, military commanders assumed wider powers to act in response to incoming intelligence about possible unrest in colonial cities.[12] The causes and perpetrators of such disorder were stereotyped in racialized, quasi-medical terms. The metropolitan contagions of Communist ideology, nationalist sentiment, and worker militancy threatened to "infect" North African territories. Maghrebi immigrants, university students, and political exiles were the principal carriers of such infection. But the virus of revolution was invariably traced back to the same sources: the Comintern in Moscow; the network of pan-Arabist groups and Islamist committees in Berlin and Switzerland; and Cairo, the hub of integral Arab nationalism in the Middle East.[13] British police repression of Wafdist student organizers and leaders of the Islamist Young Men's Muslim Association in the Egyptian capital after the 1919 revolution lent further credibility to this reading of events.[14] Again and again in the interwar period, police spéciale analysts in the Maghreb minimized the socioeconomic causes of urban unrest and exaggerated the role of professional "agitators" intent on stirring up revolutionary sedition.

Shakib Arslan stood out in this regard. As the chief propagandist for the Syrian-Palestine Congress and a supporter of numerous Arab nationalist groups across North Africa and the Fertile Crescent, Arslan was an obvious surveillance target.[15] He was subject to more intensive SR, Section de Centralisation du Renseignement (SCR), and Sûreté monitoring than any other Muslim politician active in the interwar French Empire.[16] The Beirut high commission attached highest priority to the interception of telegraphic correspondence between members of the Syrian-Palestine Congress executive in Cairo and Geneva, and leading nationalist figures inside Syria during and after the Great Revolt.[17] Meanwhile, the Algiers government and the Residencies in Rabat and Tunis tracked Arslan's contacts and correspondence with the emerging generation of integral nationalists in the Maghreb.[18]

By 1925, security service obsession with Arslan's alleged powers of political manipulation pervaded official thinking about Levantine politics. For instance, before taking up his post in Beirut, the Levant high commissioner Henry de Jouvenel made it his first priority to meet him face-to-face. Arslan was uniquely placed to stipulate how the Great Revolt might be ended through negotiation.[19] Yet, as de Jouvenel discovered, Arslan was not easily pigeonholed. Lebanese Druze by origin, he was a practicing Sunni and had distinguished himself before 1914 as a fervent pan-Islamist hostile to Arab separatism. He retained a profound respect for Turkey, strengthened by his political apprenticeship as a deputy to the Ottoman Parliament during World War I.[20] An accomplished linguist, in 1920 Arslan became the president of the Berlin Oriental Club, which directed a stream of pan-Islamic propaganda toward the Middle East in the immediate postwar years.[21] Once he openly adopted the Arab nationalist cause from 1921 onward, Arslan accumulated other offices, notably as a member of the Arab Academy and the League against Imperialism and Colonial Oppression (on which, see the discussion later in this chapter). It was his appointment as secretary of the Syrian-Palestine Congress, however, that ensured Arslan's place at the head of French intelligence assessments of the most dangerous figures in the international community of Arab political exiles.[22]

French security services were less engaged by the singularity of Shakib Arslan's views than by his unrivalled network of international clients. His contacts stretched from the North African immigrant community in the tenements of northern Paris to the royal palaces of Baghdad, where Arslan maintained a respectful, if argumentative, relationship with Faysal's political deputy, Nuri al-Said. Ahmed Balafrej and Habib Bourguiba, future leaders of Moroccan and Tunisian nationalist parties, also figured among his regular correspondents.[23] Sûreté analysts convinced the Quai d'Orsay's Levant division that Arslan was both an ideological guide and an organizational mentor to these young Maghrebi nationalists and student leaders.[24] In 1928, reports that Arslan had traveled to Moscow compounded police spéciale suspicions that he took Comintern instruction. This was an accusation repeatedly leveled against him since he first visited the Soviet Union in his capacity as president of the Berlin Oriental Club in 1921.[25] The renewed evidence of Arslan's Soviet links, combined with his attempt to curry favor with the Saudi ruler, 'Abd al-'Aziz ibn Saud, aroused the hostile interest of the British security services as well.[26]

Arslan's readiness to seek support from such diverse quarters highlighted his cosmopolitanism, tactical flexibility, and unrivaled powers of persuasion, but there was no ideological inconsistency here. Arslan was certainly no Communist. Rather, his enthusiasm for pan-Arabism shone through in *La Nation Arabe,* the monthly review he edited from his base in Cairo. His uncompromising defense of Arab culture against Western imperialist encroachment was what took him to Moscow and what endeared him to religious leaders such as Haj Amin al-Hussaini, the mufti of Jerusalem, and 'Abd al-Hamīd Ben Bādīs, the founder of Algeria's Association of Reformist 'Ulamā.[27]

The irony was that, for all his external influence, Shakib Arslan rarely set foot in French imperial territory. Sûreté and SR fixation with him tells us something about the way in which colonial intelligence agencies constructed an image of the indigenous opposition they faced. Take the Syrian case. Damascus, not Cairo, was the center of nationalist mobilization in Syria during and after the Great Revolt. The SR, so important in determining the military response to the 1925 rebellion, was poorly equipped to evaluate the urban politics on its doorstep, something that was considered more the Sûreté's terrain. SR officers were more interested in strategic assessment of Arslan's international pan-Arabist networks than in the changing inter-communal character of the lowest reaches of Damascene society. But the police, too, struggled to anticipate urban disorder. An influx of economic migrants and refugees almost doubled the population of the Syrian capital over the mandate period. The physical impenetrability of Damascus's older walled quarters made street-level policing and information gathering a tougher proposition.[28] At the height of the Syrian revolt, the French authorities abandoned the task. General Gamelin's Levant Army command justified indiscriminate bombardment of the city's al-Maydun quarter, thought to be a refuge for insurgents, by arguing that it was unsafe for police units and inaccessible to armored cars or infantry columns.[29]

Yet one should not exaggerate the differences between urban and rural intelligence gathering. Leading Damascene notables monitored by the SR and Sûreté were also absentee landlords, retaining close connections with the countryside, which remained their main income source.[30] In the city's older districts especially, the hierarchy of respected headmen, religious leaders, and local councils mirrored the traditional administrative structures of the Arab village.[31] Sûreté and SR reports rarely differentiated between distinct social groups within Syria's urban population, however, typically doing so only in reference to strike activity or economic protest by identifiable sections of the workforce. Nationalists and nationalism were thus treated monolithically in the intelligence assessments passed along the policymaking chain.

Acknowledgment of the political activities of Syrian women was rarer still, a chronic omission. As Ellen Fleischmann has shown, women's movements across the Middle East harnessed the power of nationalist discourse to advance their claims for enhanced women's rights through the press, public debate, and popular demonstrations.[32] Such mobilization was particularly well advanced in Syrian civil society.[33] In the late 1930s, the Arab revolt in Palestine further stimulated women's movements in Syria, Palestine, and Egypt to work in partnership. By the end of the interwar period, groups such as the Syrian Women's Committee for the Defense of Palestine and the Egyptian Women's Union had forged important links, both with one another and with pan-Arabist groups.[34] In the preceding twenty years, issues of gender, from dress codes to education and women's role in national politics, featured prominently in Levantine politics, often providing new focal points for opposition to French control.[35]

In Algeria, as in France's other Arab territories, the official impulse was to categorize "nationalists" not only as exclusively male, but also as populist revolutionaries in the Jacobin tradition—more products of the urban crowd than representatives of a notable elite. Such assessments were wide of the mark, but they reflected the conviction among local government officials and security analysts that deep cultural and political divides separated town and country. Urban politics in Algeria became more confrontational during 1919–20. This followed the limited extension of the Muslim male franchise under the so-called Jonnart Law, and the subsequent victory in the November 1919 Algiers municipal elections of Amir Khaled.[36] A decorated French Army officer, the amir was also the grandson of 'Abd al-Qadir, a connection that ensured his status as a powerful symbol of national resistance. Popular backing of his demands for greater Muslim representation in Parliament, the award of citizenship with retention of Muslim status, and use of Arabic in Algeria's educational system confirmed that newly enfranchised Muslim male voters would not be easily placated.[37]

While the municipal authorities contested the growth in Muslim support for Khaledism, politics across the Algiers *département* as a whole was bound up with conditions in the agricultural economy. The Algiers government's uncompromising attitude to Amir Khaled's demands for greater Muslim political rights and an extended Algerian franchise was nourished by open-source intelligence from the market towns and farming communes of the Algerian interior, which revealed minimal public interest in his campaign. According to the Algiers native affairs office, rural politics was dominated by harvest prospects, market prices, labor rates, and encroaching European settlement, to the virtual exclusion of "national" issues.[38] The Algiers native affairs bureau monthly survey for May 1923 concluded that the rural masses adhered to their "traditional materialism." Even though much of the Muslim population regarded Amir Khaled as a national figurehead, the rural population did not connect his electoral campaign with the agricultural and economic issues that mattered most to them. Evidence from native affairs bureaus, commune administrators, and police captains confirmed the slow emergence of nationalist politics in the civil society of rural Algeria, leading the government-general to devote greater attention to the surveillance of other targets: urban notables and workers in the major towns as well as the Algerian immigrant community in France.[39] The example of Khaled suggested that most early oppositional figures in North Africa would emerge from a privileged, well-educated Arab bourgeoisie, many of whose members sought closer assimilation with France rather than divorce from it.[40]

Intelligence and Integral Nationalism: The ENA and Messali Hadj

The one exception to this general rule of elite opposition was Messali Hadj's Étoile Nord-Africaine (ENA—literally, North African Star), an organization founded among the Algerian immigrant community in Paris in March 1926. The ENA was nominally a French political party.[41] It was therefore required to register formally with the Paris Prefecture of Police, something its founders were understandably reluctant to do. Their obstructionism was no barrier to a rigorous surveillance operation mounted from the prefecture headquarters in the Latin Quarter. Plainclothes police of the elite Renseignements Généraux (RG), the prefecture's political police, tailed members of the party executive, including Mohamed Marouf, Mohamed ben Luazid, and, above all, Messali Hadj. The RG kept a constant watch on his modest rental accommodation at number 6 rue du Repos, so much so that the police knew whether his monthly five-hundred-franc rent had been paid to his landlady, Emilie Buscot. The police also opened Messali's mail.[42] Partly, one suspects, because of her youth and non-Parisian origins (she was born in Meurthe-et-Moselle in 1901), Mme. Buscot was herself subjected to thorough investigation.[43] Police officers also tracked the comings and goings from the ENA's first office at 3 rue du Marché des Patriarches. The recording, photographing, and tailing of ENA activists continued when, in 1927, the party executive moved to larger premises at 71 rue Monge, ironically only a short hop from Paris police headquarters. Surveillance of party members convinced prefecture staff that the ENA had inherited the mantle of the Union Intercoloniale, a smaller but more cosmopolitan anticolonialist group whose members included several militant journalists, including its driving force, a young Ho Chi Minh.[44]

Over the next ten years the ENA cemented its reputation as Algeria's one truly nationalist party. By December 1927, the police estimated its membership among the Algerian immigrant community at thirty-five hundred, a remarkably high figure that represented only known activists who participated in the party's thirteen French sections, eight of which were in the capital. Meetings were held in local cooperative halls or trade union function rooms—easy to pack and easier still to monitor. Circulation levels of the party's Arabic and French publications gave further indications of the ENA's growing support. Print runs of the party's monthly newspaper, *L'Ikdam de Paris* (renamed *L'Ikdam Nord-Africain* after an Interior Ministry ban on the former title in February 1927), suggested that ENA's sympathizers far exceeded its paid-up membership.[45]

With its call for immediate abolition of the *indigénat*, the discriminatory legal code imposed on the lowest ranks of Muslim society, rather than for wider citizenship rights for the privileged Muslim elite, the ENA represented a new strain of Algerian nationalism.[46] Modernist and secular, the ENA was committed to national independence, not the limited concessions previously sought by the privileged minority of Algeria's educated Muslim elite.[47] At the inaugural Brussels Congress of the League against Imperialism and Colonial Oppression in 1927 the ENA became the first nationalist group to call for Algerian independence.[48]

Whether elitist or populist, early Arab nationalism was antithetical to the French right's integral nationalism. It was under the center-right coalitions that dominated French politics for most of the interwar period that state hostility toward the ENA intensified.[49] The interwar leaders of North African and Syrian nationalist protest were less militant than their post-1945 progeny, however.[50] The dubious official identification of organized nationalism in Muslim territories as a left-wing phenomenon suggests that the threat perceptions of colonial administrations were skewed by domestic French political concerns. Deepening sociopolitical divisions in metropolitan France added fuel to the interwar obsession with imperial policing and covert surveillance.[51] As we saw in chapter 3, overseas administrations equated secular pan-Arabism with Communist internationalism, just as, in the 1930s, they identified reactionary settler militancy with the metropolitan street violence of the ultrarightist Leagues.

The proscription of Arab trade unionism for much of the interwar period was also conditioned by increasing Confédération Générale du Travail (CGT) militancy in France rather than by the remarkable achievements of French North Africa's foremost union organization, Tunisia's Confédération Générale des Travailleurs Tunisiens (CGTT), a national trade union confederation dedicated to Muslim workers' rights and Tunisian self-government.[52] The tendency among French security agencies to read colonial dissent through the prism of metropolitan preoccupations continued into the mid-1930s. Official fears of sedition and mass protest gathered momentum in 1934, partly because of the wave of anti-Semitic violence that gripped eastern Algeria in the summer of that year, but also because of the consolidation of the Rassemblement Populaire, a forerunner to the Popular Front, in France itself. On the one hand, the intercommunal hatreds unleashed by the August 1934 pogrom in Constantine led the Rabat Residency's native affairs service to revise its estimates of the likelihood of violent clashes between Muslims and Jews in Morocco. As a result, police patrols of the urban boundaries between Muslim and Jewish districts in Morocco's major towns were increased.[53] On the other hand, the emergence of the Popular Front stimulated the SR to monitor the activities and organizational profile of Socialist and pro-Communist groups across the Maghreb more closely.[54]

Other factors led imperial authorities to draw parallels between perceived threats to the French Republic and the likelihood of urban colonial dissent. One was the prominent role played by French-based Arab students in newly founded nationalist organizations in Syria, Tunisia, and, above all, Morocco.[55] Another was the bedrock of support for the ENA among Algerian immigrant workers, which remained solid throughout the early Depression years despite repeated legal challenges to the party's activities.[56] The ENA's enduring appeal compounded security service fears that the contagion of nationalism (in this case interpreted as little more than a Communist front organization) might be transmitted from France to otherwise passive colonial territories.[57]

Indications that nationalist activity in the late 1920s was more pronounced among clusters of students, immigrant laborers, and political exiles living in French cities were hardly surprising, given the high concentrations of like-minded individuals able to exploit freedoms of speech and assembly denied to them at home. But security service anxiety about Maghrebi nationalists' Communist connections was misguided. The two most important groups involved—the ENA and the North African Muslim Students Association (Association des étudiants musulmans nord-africains—AEMNA), the latter founded in Paris in December 1927 by the Tunisian student leader Chadly ben Mustafa Khaïrallah—stressed concern for their members' national interests over any Communist loyalties.[58]

Security agencies in French North Africa, observing police operations against Maghrebi immigrants from the other side of the Mediterranean, did not see things this way. Reports of Arab nationalist organizations in France convinced police chiefs and SR officers that colonial urban populations could not be allowed any comparable freedom of association. Monitoring of contacts between immigrant workers, students, exiles, and their families and acquaintances in the major towns of the Maghreb and the Levant increased markedly after the emergence of anticolonial organizations and colonial student groups in the French capital during the early 1920s. Conversely, a complacent racism still underpinned intelligence assessments regarding the urban workforce in the cities of the Maghreb. Take, for example, this War Ministry deuxième bureau assessment from December 1923:

> The development of [French North Africa's] towns, its commerce, its industry, its culture, and, as a result, its internal communications, has principally affected Europeans, who have derived profit from it. With only a few exceptions, it has left the *indigène* indifferent. Those of a certain social rank and intellectual level have played virtually no part in the process, the bulk doing so only by furnishing the necessary manpower. This labor force is to be found in the ports as dockworkers and stokers, or in the countryside and mine works as laborers of all kinds, or in the towns as casual workers, cab drivers, street sweepers, all the dirty jobs in general. They are poor and relatively honest but, through their contact with Europeans, have acquired all their vices.
>
> So if the French think they have improved the lives of the *indigènes,* the *indigènes* themselves are less convinced. They note above all that they have to work to survive and that it requires an effort even to attain a standard of living that is poorer and more arduous than in times gone by. The fact is that throughout the [Maghreb] coastal region there exists a real Muslim rabble [*racaille*] that shuts out the hypocrites at the top of the social ladder who have abandoned them at the bottom.[59]

Such analyses reinforced two assumptions prevalent in the French security services, both civil and military: on the one hand, the urban poor could be manipulated by capable agitators, but, on the other, it took direct experience of life in France before Muslims typically acquired the political skills necessary to organize into effective oppositional groups. Once these politically acculturated migrants returned to North Africa, the consequences were bound to be severe. This more pessimistic threat assessment duly increased the army's involvement in covert surveillance and the policing of urban space in French North Africa and Syria. For example, thanks to the extensive employment of local agents, by 1933 the SR had joined the Sûreté in keeping detailed records on leading Muslim figures in the municipal politics of Casablanca, Rabat, and Marrakech who had been identified as potential nationalist troublemakers.[60]

French Surveillance of Colonial Immigrants

State surveillance of colonial immigrants in France meshed together French policies toward Muslim subjects with governmental obsession about the menace of Communism.[61] By the mid-1920s, the Interior Ministry, its Sûreté network in provincial France, and the Paris Prefecture of Police concurred that France's Muslim immigrants constituted a unique threat to colonial order, whether through the transmission of seditious ideas to their communities of origin or through their support for nationalist parties sure to be emulated or replicated in the Maghreb. These estimates had wartime roots. Organized nationalist movements, some with links to Communist groups but most without, presented the major challenge to colonial control after 1914. In March 1916, the Commissariat of Information established a Muslim section to provide early warning of any events in the Muslim world liable to affect France's imperial security or its colonial immigrant population. The Commissariat's Muslim section reviewed the Arab, Turkish, and Persian press and analyzed key publications by Islamic scholars that were deemed likely to affect the loyalties of Muslim subjects. It relayed this information to the interministerial commission on Muslim affairs and to another wartime creation, the parliamentary committee on foreign action (Comité parlémentaire d'action à l'étranger).[62]

For those on the receiving end, government information gathering was manifest in the rigorous legislative controls and police checks that colonial immigrants faced after the war began. Regulation of internal migration, intracolonial migration, and colonial immigration to France provided imperial authorities with a wealth of data on subject populations. Much of this was explicitly used as security information—identity card checks, fingerprinting, and checks of migrants' criminal records being obvious examples. Much of it was used to assist colonial economic planning, notably with regard to the allocation of skilled labor, and attempts to control the inflow and outflow of seasonal agricultural workers. But, lest one imagine an all-embracing net of customs checkpoints, border patrols, and immigration services, it should be stressed that none of this data was comprehensive.

The colonial immigrant population in mainland France was certainly subject to the most intensive surveillance. The requirement to carry detailed nationality certificates, police stop and search procedures, and restrictions on freedom of association among colonial workers were all well established by 1919, more than twenty years before their general introduction by the Vichy authorities in 1942. Between 1924 and 1930, even stricter legislative controls were introduced, built around more stringent identity card requirements for colonial immigrant workers. Police raids of immigrant lodgings, arbitrary arrests, and deportations all increased markedly. Aside from the police immigration service, the cornerstone of this rigorous monitoring system was the North African manpower commission, attached to the Interior Ministry's Algerian division. The commission was established by decree on 24 March 1924, midway through the brief life of the first Cartel des Gauches coalition headed by the prime minister and Radical Party leader Edouard Herriot. Ostensibly, the manpower commission's charge was to advise ministers on the regulation of immigration flows from North Africa and more efficient allocation of immigrant workers to French industry.[63] The Foreign Ministry's African division, the Paris offices of the Maghreb protectorates, and the Ministry of Hygiene were all represented at its meetings. Parliamentary deputies with an interest in North African policy also attended commission sessions. Foremost among these was the Socialist Marius Moutet. Later to become famous as the minister of colonies under the Popular Front, Moutet's colonial expertise in the 1920s stemmed from his wartime membership on the parliamentary foreign and colonial affairs commission and his role in devising 1919 legislation to extend the Muslim franchise in Algeria.[64]

But the driving force on the North African manpower division was an altogether less renowned politician: Pierre Godin, a caustic reactionary with experience of Algerian local government. He served as commission vice-president and was the Paris municipal councilor chiefly responsible for the establishment of the capital's North African police brigade (discussed in the next section). As Clifford Rosenberg notes, "Nowhere was the alliance between moderate national politicians and right-wing Parisian municipal councilors more striking than in the surveillance of colonial subjects."[65] Surveillance of colonial immigrants dominated Godin's professional career. He and his fellow commission members began their work from the proposition that 75 to 80 percent of new immigrant arrivals from North Africa had neither sufficient funds nor specific job offers to ensure that they avoided destitution. Their investigations confirmed this initial assessment, revealing high rates of destitution, widespread criminality, and a prevalence of epidemic illness, especially tuberculosis, and psychological disorders.

Their remedy was equally predictable: a much tougher regulatory system anchored to ports of entry and enforced by more systematic police stops and searches of immigrant workers.[66] As we have seen, this was hardly a new departure, marking a refinement of procedures established during and after World War I.

The experience of Moroccan immigrants was fairly typical in this respect.[67] From 1918 onward, municipal police authorities throughout northern Morocco issued nationality certificates to emigrants intending to seek work in France. This was in response to complaints from their colleagues in the Seine region about the rising number of unemployed Maghrebi workers left destitute and, more important from the police perspective, *sans papiers,* after their dismissal from war industries in and around the capital.[68] Provincial prefectures voiced similar concerns about North African field laborers formerly employed on hundreds of farms across northwestern France and the Midi.[69] In the immediate postwar years, the Rabat Residency worked with the five principal French Ministries most directly involved—Interior, Foreign Affairs, Labor, Agriculture, and Hygiene—to ensure the prompt repatriation of these immigrant workers. Monitoring of the Maghrebi immigrant population was inherent in this process, but, at least until 1920, incidental to it. A system of regulated repatriation from designated French ports (principally Bordeaux and Marseilles), funded by the North African governments, was finalized in early 1921. From then on, the focal point of state interest in colonial migrant labor shifted from repatriation to improved surveillance.[70]

Whether employed as industrial workers or farmhands, virtually no Moroccan immigrant workers held French citizenship. Few came equipped with comprehensive travel documents, as the sultanate had yet to adopt a French-style identity card system. As a result, nationality certificates and labor contracts (*contrats de travail*), essential to pass border checkpoints and gain entry to the French employment market, became highly tradable commodities. These work contracts were introduced by decree on 17 November 1920 in one of the first attempts by the right-wing Bloc National government to regulate peacetime immigration from Morocco.[71]

Nationality certificates were always surveillance tools. French Morocco's police appreciated this, and appended additional criteria to the certificates considered useful from an intelligence point of view. Holders were required to state their tribal affiliation, dialect spoken, and the identities of their local *caïd* and *chef de région.* These details counted for nothing, however, if immigrant workers exchanged the certificates among themselves.[72] In a bid to counteract this, Urbain Blanc, the chief delegate in the Rabat Residency, advised civil and military administrators across Morocco that intending migrant laborers could enter France only after obtaining written permission from their local authority. Approval was contingent on evidence that a specific job awaited them in France.[73]

The French Interior Ministry evidently doubted that this system, which was stringent in theory, worked in practice. It was here that the North African manpower commission came into play. Acting on commission advice, in May 1924 the Interior Ministry stipulated that police forces across French North Africa had to ensure that all immigrant workers, whether traveling to France for the first time or resident there for some years, held valid identity cards complete with photo identification and an authentication stamp from the district commissioner's office in their home region. Prior to departure, all Maghrebi immigrants were henceforth obliged to produce two additional items of paperwork. One was an employment certificate issued by the relevant regional office of the Ministry of Labor, confirming that the immigrant held a current job offer. The other was a medical certificate, to be issued only by state-registered doctors in the North African territories, indicating that the person in question was free of contagious illness (in reality, a tuberculosis examination) and physically capable of the labor he or she was to perform in France.[74]

Most administrators considered the need for these new bureaucratic procedures self-evident. The Moroccan case again illustrates the wider Maghreb situation. The Residency estimated that four to five thousand Moroccans were by then working in France without authentic work permits or the more temporary *cartes de séjour*. A single identity card authenticated by local government officers in Morocco would help resolve matters. Failure to produce this document when required by French police meant expulsion.[75]

By this point in the mid-1920s, the language used by French governmental agencies to describe Muslim immigrants had a harder edge, more evocative of nineteenth-century characterizations of vagabondage than the voguish terminology of associationism. Maghrebi workers were a monolithic, troublesome labor force that required rigid organization.[76] Their collective behavior and individual habits posed a threat to civic order, common decency, and public health.[77] Just as it may be rewarding to look forward from policing methods in the interwar period to the later racial repression of the Vichy state, so too there are obvious comparisons to be made by looking backward. Coercive interwar policing of colonial populations continued metropolitan practices developed over the preceding century. As we saw in chapter 2, police repression in nineteenth-century France was occasioned by food riots, popular demand for greater civil liberties, and worker protest in industrial disputes.[78] Colonial policing and the restrictions imposed on immigrants after what Clifford Rosenberg tellingly describes as "the watershed of World War I" applied these earlier metropolitan precedents to dependent peoples. Both in its preoccupation with crowd control and social stability, and in its strongly martial flavor, urban policing in the interwar empire was redolent of the containment of popular protest in pre-1914 France.[79]

New Bureaucracies of Immigrant Surveillance

In 1924, the Paris Prefecture of Police established a specialist North African Brigade to monitor North African workers throughout the city and its outer suburbs. It did so at the request of the capital's municipal council, on which, as we saw, Pierre Godin played a critical role. The Brigade's creation fulfilled a proposal floated on 12 January by Godin and his fellow municipal councilor Emile Massard for a dedicated police unit to monitor the growing population of Maghrebi workers in Paris. The Seine prefecture endorsed the idea, as did the capital's prefect of police, Alfred Morain, and his colleague, Jean Chiappe, then head of the Sûreté Générale.[80] The North African governors' conference in Rabat later that year took up the councilors' suggestion. Approval was, by then, a formality, the brigade idea having been endorsed by General Charles Huot, head of the SR in Morocco.[81]

It fell to Marshal Lyautey to codify the Brigade's role as a monitoring agency:

> It is necessary to create a special Paris police team adapted to its surveillance tasks and made up of French and *indigènes* seconded from Algeria, Tunisia, and Morocco, all of whom must speak Arabic and Kabyle dialect. This organization, acting in close liaison with representatives from our North African protectorates and colonies as well as certain existing private associations, should also handle issues of [industrial] insurance, unemployment, illness, housing, and repatriation. Furthermore, the need for such a body is particularly evident in Paris where the police have struggled to come to terms with the presence of around 50,000 North African *indigènes* spread across working-class neighborhoods, lacking the social discipline that they require, and incapable, unless guided, of adapting to our own.[82]

From its inception, this police brigade, supposedly established to monitor the welfare of Maghrebi immigrants and to administer immigrant shelters and health dispensaries in the French capital, undertook political surveillance as well. Based at rue Lecomte in the seventeenth arrondissement, home to the largest concentration of Algerian immigrant workers, the North African Brigade was, by 1937, composed of thirty-seven officers and agents. These were not elite, professional officers comparable to the RG, but rather "an irregular unit made up of colonial misfits with little hope of promotion."[83] Their primary task was to detect any signs of dissidence, strike action, or criminality among the Algerian immigrant community. Other prefecture police forces adopted similar methods, setting up dedicated covert units to monitor colonial immigrants in France's main provincial cities from Lille to Marseilles. Contacts between North African trade unionists, supporters of nationalist groups, and French Communist activists were carefully recorded, summarized in police reports to the local prefect, and thence relayed to the Sûreté's central offices attached to the Ministry of Interior.[84]

Some background information on interwar Algerian economic migration to Paris may be useful at this point. As Stéphane Sirot has established, apart from an estimated seven thousand Algerians living in France illegally, the great majority of North African laborers in the Seine Prefecture arrived after 1921. In that year, official figures registered 36,300 Algerians employed across France. Of these, 97 percent were male and the great majority were less than forty years old. Most of the war workers from the colonies were quickly repatriated in the months immediately following the armistice in anticipation of a reflux of French workers to their former industries upon demobilization.[85] Those who came to Paris in search of work typically took unskilled jobs in the metallurgical and car industries, warehousing, packing, sugar refineries, and the chemical industry. Algerians also cornered the market as so-called *laveurs de voitures,* their job being to clean Parisian taxis by night in preparation for the next day's work. Poorly paid, rarely unionized, and often assigned the dirtiest and most physically demanding factory jobs, which French workers were reluctant to perform, Algerian laborers were the proletariat's very own underclass.[86]

The North African Brigade was the vanguard of more stringent policing of Algerian, Moroccan, and Tunisian workers in the Paris region. The creation of a dedicated Muslim hospital in the working-class district of Bobigny in 1930, quickly followed by the establishment of two isolation wards in Colombes and Gennevilliers for North Africans suffering from contagious illnesses, provided additional opportunities to monitor the Maghrebi workforce while segregating them from the healthcare system already in place in northern Paris.[87] The North African Brigade used the cover of such welfare services to build up files about immigrants' political and trade union activities as well as their health. In the words of Clifford Rosenberg, "The hospital, dispensaries, job placement service, subsidized housing, and even language classes all collected information to nourish extensive police dossiers."[88] This was not an academic exercise. On the rare occasions that Algerian workers took strike action, the North African Brigade intervened, making arrests, cajoling laborers back to work under threat of expulsion from France, and helping employers find other immigrant workers prepared to act as strikebreakers. Extraneous factors increased the North African Brigade's appetite for repressive measures. One was limited evidence of left-wing support for immigrant workers, the Communist-controlled union confederation, the Confédération Générale du Travail Unitaire, having organized solidarity protests and relief funds for immigrant strikers.[89] Another was the residual strength of ENA membership after the party became subject to legal sanction in 1927.[90]

This was only the beginning of the Brigade's discriminatory activities.

The year 1934 was pivotal, remembered for bloody ultrarightist riots on 6 February, the subsequent emergence of Popular Frontism in France, an intensification in Franco-German animosity linked to the final collapse of the Geneva Disarmament Conference, and the fatal shooting of the French foreign minister, Louis Barthou, caught in the firing line of Croatian assassins who also murdered the Yugoslav monarch, King Alexander, during his state visit to Marseilles on 9 October.[91] In these changed circumstances, police surveillance of immigrants in France increasingly reflected government preoccupation with national security rather than with the confinement of immigrant activities within particular urban locales.

Yet, as Mary Dewhurst Lewis suggests in her treatment of interwar Marseilles, the legal distinctions now made between settled, long-term immigrants and more recent, rootless foreigners reinforced long-standing racial stereotypes regarding those immigrant groups that could be trusted and those that could not. Colonial immigrants suffered in both respects— faced with discrimination as rootless, casual laborers in the 1920s and early 1930s, and then subject to more frequent identity checks and expulsion orders after the introduction of additional identity card and residency requirements by Pierre-Etienne Flandin's government in 1935.[92] The growing support for the ENA lent a sharper political edge to this more intrusive security policing, the more so after the counterespionage specialists of the Paris SCR singled out Messali Hadj in October 1935 as "the principal revolutionary agitator" in French North Africa.[93]

French officials' residual attachment to the so-called Berber myth that distinguished the Berber population of Algeria's Kabylia region—and North Africa's Berbers more generally—from their Arab neighbors is relevant here.[94] Kabyle Berbers, always the largest Maghrebi immigrant group in interwar France, were considered less Islamic and more amenable to Western influence than "pure Arabs." So, too, Kabyles were thought to be more receptive to educational advancement and, in turn, to political activism.[95] Sûreté officers in Algeria and the North African Brigade in Paris concurred that economic migrants returning to Kabylia posed a singular threat to social stability in Algeria because so many were seduced by the ENA's leftist nationalism during their working lives in France. The Algiers government was equally ambivalent. It applauded Kabyle workers' willingness to emigrate, thereby easing skilled labor shortages in France and population pressure in Kabylia. Furthermore, worker remittances sent to families back home were known to be integral to Algeria's rural economy. Immigrants' exposure to French society might also accelerate the process of Berber acculturation to Western colonialism. But one overriding problem weighed against these various advantages: too many Kabyle migrants were returning to Algeria radicalized by their experiences of labor discrimination and political organization in France.[96]

The Algiers authorities therefore treated Kabyle workers in pseudo-medical terms as a disease-bearing minority requiring careful treatment and strict isolation. The source of their infection was political, not biological. Communism, as it appeared in Sûreté and SR reports, resembled a fearful epidemic of high infectivity. Ironically, in spite of the security services' wish to isolate the carriers, the remedy to infection by leftist ideas lay in the Kabyles' reimmersion in their traditional community. In April 1935, the Algiers Sûreté summarized the problem of Kabyle returnees thus: "The workers who return from metropolitan France more or less contaminated by Communist propaganda abandon their subversive ideas little by little through renewed contact with their coreligionists and their families; nevertheless, their stay in France leaves them with a more highly developed critical attitude, which must be kept under close surveillance."[97]

For its part, the Ministry of Colonies did not simply rely on the Ministry of Interior, the police, and army intelligence officers to provide information on anticolonial activists among the colonial immigrant population. Selected Ministry of Colonies bureaucrats took on the task themselves. Colonial subjects studying or working in France's major cities were monitored by specialist units of the Service de contrôle et d'assistance en France des indigènes des colonies (French regulatory and welfare service for colonial subjects). Members of these teams liased with local Sûreté branches and reported directly to the director of political affairs at the rue Oudinot. Much like their police colleagues, these Ministry of Colonies personnel tracked colonial student organizations, infiltrated anticolonialist organizations, and kept tabs on colonial subjects arriving at France's major port and rail terminals. In 1931, the Service de contrôle led the crackdown against Vietnamese students in Paris and Marseilles accused of organizing protests against the Colonial Exhibition that opened in the bois de Vincennes in eastern Paris on 6 May. By this point, the Sûreté Générale estimated the total number of Vietnamese students in France's nine largest cities at a little more than fifteen hundred, out of a total Vietnamese immigrant population of approximately twice that number.[98]

A Comité de lutte contre l'exposition (Antiexhibition Fighting Committee) was uncovered. Its supporters planned to distribute stickers denouncing the exhibition to visitors passing through the turnstiles. And Nguyen Van Tao, a member of the Indochinese Communist Party executive committee, was expelled from France for having led an anticolonial demonstration outside the Elysée Palace on 22 May. Underlying this heightened state surveillance was a simple premise: colonial student agitators posed a visible threat to colonial authority that belied their limited numbers and prankish actions. As repression of nationalist groups intensified in individual colonies, the remaining politically engaged students in France assumed leadership roles in newer, more extremist anticolonial movements.[99] In this sense, the security agencies were both prescient and curiously shortsighted. They correctly foresaw the major part that colonial students—from Ho Chi Minh to Habib Bourguiba—would play in nationalist mobilization, but they failed to grasp that, by outlawing more moderate nationalist groups and arresting nationalist leaders of an older generation, colonial police forces created a political void soon filled by the younger extremists they most feared.[100]

Internal Security in French North Africa during the Early 1930s

As the Muslim territories, along with the rest of the empire, slid into economic crisis in the early 1930s, signs of popular alienation proliferated.[101] In Syria, the National Bloc, other smaller nationalist parties, and the more factional Arab elites of the major towns recognized that ready cooperation with the high commission authorities played badly with their core supporters.[102] In Algeria, the older generation of Arab political leaders and Muslim clerics would see their local primacy successfully challenged by more radical nationalist and 'ulamā leaders over the course of the 1930s.[103] According to the SR's informants in the colony's major urban centers, 'ulamā opinions and teachings, and their mounting control over Algeria's Koranic schools in particular, were turning the new generation of Muslim youth against France. By connecting disciplined religious education to Islamic enlightenment and the revitalization of Arabic culture, the reformist 'ulamā spurned the French colonial project as corruptive and alien. Ironically, this turning inward terrified security analysts because it threatened to close off Muslim society, insulating the younger generation from effective surveillance and control.[104] Some Salafī-influenced schools were even accused of indoctrinating young minds into "a blind hatred" of the West in general. By 1935, the Algiers SR had concluded that the 'ulamā's Islamic revivalism—which they dubbed "neo-Wahhabism"—posed as great a menace to social stability in Algeria's cities as the mobilization of popular support for Algerian nationalism.[105] The latter might be steered toward accommodation with colonial authority, but the former, in its uncompromising rejection of Western cultural imperialism, could not.[106]

Even in Tunisia, always considered by the Quai d'Orsay the most Westernized of France's Muslim territories, the prewar decade was marked by greater nationalist militancy, Arab trade union protest, and clerical disputes over the legitimacy of a beylical administration tarnished by its subordination to the French Residency. Few in Tunisia's political elite envisaged a total rupture with France, but the boundaries of French authority were increasingly disputed as issues of religious observance, citizenship, worker rights, and Muslim cultural autonomy became more bitterly contested. In December 1931, the Tunis Residency hosted a cultural congress to celebrate Arab language, literature, and art. Far from demonstrating the authorities' sensitivity to their Arab subjects, the congress catalyzed public opposition to French hegemony. The Arab language press complained that a Frenchman had been called in to organize the congress's Arabic events. Tunisia's leading nationalist party, the Néo-Destour, organized student demonstrations against French control of the congress agenda. The event also divided Tunisia's senior 'ulamā. Some were willing to participate; others boycotted the congress in protest at French direction of a uniquely Muslim cultural event.[107]

The outcry over the Tunis cultural congress fit a wider pattern. As the Depression began to hit the Maghreb, SR analysts, Muslim affairs officers, and Sûreté personnel detected a widening gap between rulers and ruled. In December 1931, the army staff's Muslim affairs section characterized Tunisia's political climate thus: "latent opposition between 'France in Tunisia,' [denoting] officials and settlers, and the elite minority of indigenous nationalists who try hard to win the backing of the Muslim proletariat in the major Europeanized towns, of the beylical court whose loyalty remains dubious, and of Tunisian students whose education is conducted under their patronage."[108] In May 1933, the Residency secured wider decree powers to intern individuals suspected of subversion for up to two years without trial. A decree proscribing Néo-Destour came into force at the end of that month.[109] Security service fears of imminent disorder did not, however, subside.

During 1934, reports of arms trafficking, illicit overseas funding of Néo-Destour, and contacts between members of the party's executive and Shakib Arslan's Syrian-Palestinian Congress were easily verified after a series of police arrests backed up by SCR frontier surveillance and interception of mail. But the supposed connections between these seditious activities were more the product of fertile SCR imagination than of hard evidence.[110] One informant in particular, a water engineer identified as one G. Regnaudin, filed a stream of unsubstantiated reports in 1934–35. Regnaudin was convinced that Néo-Destour planned to launch an insurrection, coordinated by foreign agents, in conjunction with Algerian and Moroccan nationalist groups. The key point to note is that, although SR personnel rightly dismissed Regnaudin as unreliable, his accusations were nonetheless transmitted to the Ministry of Interior and the War Ministry deuxième bureau in Paris, in addition to Sûreté offices across the Maghreb. Thus did wild rumor mold official perceptions.[111]

To cite but one instance of this, on 10 July 1934, the Algiers SR sent the army's deuxième bureau a four-page intelligence assessment of likely developments in Néo-Destour operations. The report drew on various unidentified agents' reports classified as of "very good" reliability. The resultant analysis, a hodgepodge of unverified humint, was contradictory.

It attributed increasing nationalist militancy in Tunisia's cities to agitators who stirred up "the religious fanaticism of the Muslim masses." Yet it also made more astute observations about Néo-Destour's plans for economic modernization and social reform. SR officers in Paris and Algiers were well aware that the party's well-to-do leaders exaggerated their religiosity to garner popular support, none more so than Habib Bourguiba. So the idea that Néo-Destour would ride to power on the crest of an Islamist wave left them unconvinced. The problem was that the compilation of agents' reports with minimal prior evaluation of their content inevitably produced a much darker intelligence picture.[112]

Cooler heads in the Tunis intelligence community also recognized that Néo-Destour was not convincing as a party of jihad. But pessimism took hold as more humint came in reporting mass meetings and firebrand speeches. By the end of 1934, even long-serving SR and Sûreté personnel predisposed to doubt sensationalist intelligence concluded that only the heightened security force presence in the country's major towns prevented urban revolt in Tunisia. According to the Tunis SR, French authority rested entirely on legal sanction and the military force deployed to impose it. Order was upheld by the instinct for self-preservation among the Néo-Destour leadership rather than by any acceptance of the protectorate.[113]

So concerned was the military intelligence community in French North Africa about the Tunisian situation that in December 1934, the central SR headquarters in Algiers sent an investigative mission to Tunis to report on the likelihood of rebellion and its probable scale. The SR officers involved interviewed fellow intelligence analysts and Residency officials to compile what they admitted was more "an impression than an intelligence report."[114] Yet their conclusions were unequivocal. The investigative mission reaffirmed the views of their colleagues in the Tunisian capital—perhaps not surprising, because the Tunis SR provided the core information on which the new report was based. The key findings were these: Tunisian Muslims regarded French security forces as a hostile occupation force and were probing for signs of weakness in the army and police; increased taxation was bitterly resented in the difficult economic climate of the day because it accorded no tangible benefits to the Muslim majority; and the urban population avidly consumed Arabic press reports of colonial unrest and nationalist advances elsewhere in the Arab world. If there was no immediate danger of an uprising, it was simply because the protectorate's Muslim leaders knew that they lacked the weapons needed to stage one.[115]

The Rabat military intelligence bureau reached similar conclusions about nationalist opinion in Morocco. After the promulgation of the Berber *dahir* in May 1930, the SR, the Sûreté, and municipal police forces began more systematic political surveillance of street politics in Moroccan cities. The *dahir* was a decree that limited the applicability of customary Shari'a law in relation to French civil and criminal law in Morocco's Berber regions. It thereby denied the juridical supremacy of the sultanate by restricting the use of Koranic law among Morocco's majority Berber population. As such, it was fiercely resisted. Arab nationalists, 'ulamā clerics, and the urban bourgeoisie all interpreted the Berber *dahir* as an indirect attack on the administrative autonomy of the sultan's *makhzen* government and an underhanded French attempt to institutionalize communal divisions between Arab town-dwellers and Berber agriculturalists.[116]

The French authorities were taken aback by the intractability of urban protests against what it insisted was a purely administrative measure. The Residency secretariat knew that there was no clear line separating Maghrebi nationalist groups from the *makhzen* authorities. Senior members of the Moroccan bureaucratic elite, including Muslim judges and the pasha of Rabat's senior staff, were known to be in correspondence with ENA supporters in Paris. This had been revealed by RG surveillance of the ENA newspaper office in Paris initiated at the height of the Interior Ministry's red scare over anticolonialist links with Communist organizations in late 1927.[117] But the fact that city mosques became focal points for dissent in 1930 caused deeper unease among Residency officials. It fell to General Charles Noguès, then director of the Residency's native affairs bureau, to gather intelligence on the sources and perpetrators of urban protest. William Hoisington has contrasted the imprecision of the first native affairs bureau reports in the early stages of the *dahir* crisis with the sophisticated security intelligence system put in place by the time protests abated in October 1930. Henceforth, detailed files on young nationalist leaders such as Mohammed al-Ouezzani and Abdellatif Sbihi were carefully maintained and regularly updated. Junior Moroccan officials employed by overseas diplomatic missions and trading companies were also placed under regular police surveillance. The cross-referencing of all the files amassed by Noguès's staff facilitated more thorough social and economic profiling of the demonstrators. Over the next decade, security intelligence informed the Residency's efforts to contain urban dissent and isolate town-based Arab nationalism from Morocco's peasant majority.[118]

In November 1933, the Rabat SR warned that popular nationalism in Morocco's principal cities could not be suppressed. SR analysts linked the Jeunes Marocaines movement to the resurgence in Islamic observance, pan-Arabist propaganda, and illicit German and Italian funding of nationalist organizations. They concluded that the security agencies' first priority was to prevent the spread of nationalist ideas from the cities to the rural interior. Such intelligence analysis reinforced the associationist tenets of Residency policy. Tribal control in the Moroccan highlands was increasingly influenced by security service reports suggesting that the innate conservatism of tribal chieftaincy was the surest guarantee against the growth of nationalist militancy among the Moroccan peasantry.[119] Yet, perhaps the key point here is that the intelligence establishment in Morocco was convinced by the early 1930s that the French authorities could neither contain nor conciliate the emerging mass politics of integral Moroccan nationalism. In 1934—the very year when pacification operations in the Moroccan protectorate were declared over—the Comité d'Action Marocaine (Moroccan Action Committee, soon redesignated the National Action Bloc) published a detailed list of constitutional reforms that would set the agenda for nationalist protest for the next decade.[120]

Covert intelligence gathering in Algeria always had a sharper focal point than in the neighboring protectorates. Although ENA activities had been banned in the colony since 1927, the movement and its leader, Messali Hadj, dominated intelligence reports on Algerian internal security throughout the 1930s. The ENA's organizational foundation remained the Algerian immigrant communities of Paris, Lille, and Strasbourg, but party cells had been established in several Algerian towns by the early 1930s. Much as ENA supporters in Algeria drew on metropolitan example, so official repression of the ENA was modeled on the practices of the Paris police North African Brigade. The ENA's metropolitan origins, its working class constituency, and its links with the French left also distorted intelligence assessments of the movement's penetration in Algeria itself.

It is easy to see why. The ENA remained a party at one remove from its colonial homeland during its turbulent eleven-year existence. Its actions were widely reported in the Arabic press in Algeria. Yet the ENA was more closely woven into the fabric of French politics than into the more constricted political life of Algeria. Between the party's establishment in March 1926 and 26 January 1937, when the last and most comprehensive of the many proscriptions imposed on it over the preceding decade came into force, the ENA executive played a game of cat and mouse with the judiciary, as the party sought to circumvent the bans imposed on its French operations. As we saw earlier, ENA leaders in French cities were under constant police surveillance. Their mail was frequently intercepted, and they had to apply for permission to travel back to North Africa. In 1929, the party faced an outright ban in the biggest legal challenge yet mounted against it in France. Even so, the ENA still lobbied for support among Maghrebi immigrant workers in a semilegal twilight, sometimes changing its name, sometimes encouraging affiliation with other, authorized political groups in order to provide a cover for its condemnation of colonial rule. After a year of heightened propaganda activity by the renamed "Glorieuse ENA," the troika of senior ENA leaders—Messali Hadj, Amar Imache, and Belkacem Radjef—was imprisoned on 5 November 1934. All three were convicted of having reconstituted an illegal organization.

The ENA was by then well versed in sustained activity in the face of police harassment and hostile legal judgments. In spite of the arrest of its leaders, the party reformed once more in February 1935, this time as the Union Nationale des Musulmans Nord-Africains. It also mounted a successful court challenge of its own against the 1929 ban, which was declared invalid in April 1935 on the grounds of improper implementation. Messali and his two fellow ENA leaders were duly released on 1 May. Their taste of freedom was short-lived. Twenty-five days later, Messali, Imache, and Radjef were tried in absentia for inciting colonial soldiers to mutiny during meetings held in August and September of the previous year. The Paris *Tribune correctionnel* handed down sentences of one year, eight months, and six months, respectively. Amar Imache surrendered voluntarily and Belkacem Radjef was quickly detained, but Messali took refuge in Geneva, where he renewed his acquaintance with Shakib Arslan and the leadership of the Syrian-Palestine Congress.[121] Thanks to the combination of intensive security policing and relentless judicial hostility, any resumption of coordinated political activity by the ENA executive was now dependent on a change of government in Paris. This was not long in coming. As we shall see in chapter 9, the election in May 1936 of a center-left Popular Front coalition both transformed the very identity of the ENA and conditioned the security service response to it.

Conclusion

"The maintenance of law and order was a vital element in the political economy of all colonial territories, and the nature, level and intensity of policing said much about official perceptions of political security and stability." So argue David Anderson and David Killingray in their survey of policing and decolonization.[122] Perhaps their point should be taken further. Intensive policing in intelligence states not only reflected official perceptions of security, they shaped them. The information gathered by security agencies determined the manner in which policies were enacted by colonial authorities. This was particularly evident with regard to Arab nationalist movements, which presented the major challenge to colonial control in the interwar years. It was in the urban space where these groups mobilized mass opposition to imperial rule that intelligence gathering and police repression were most intense.

The strong cultural and political links between nationalist groups in French North Africa and the Maghrebi immigrant community in metropolitan France left a deep imprint on security service thinking. French police agencies had long monitored the entire colonial immigrant population, both to stem the flow of illegal entrants and to contain immigrant communities racially stereotyped as socially disruptive, sexually predatory, and inherently criminal. Identity cards, police stop and search policies, and restrictions on freedom of association among colonial workers were in place by the end of World War I, more than twenty years before their general introduction by the Vichy authorities in 1942. Throughout the interwar period, an underlying racism permeated police and security service surveillance, producing what Robert Paxton has dubbed an "interwar republican card-file mania." As Gérard Noiriel contends, the exclusionary and racially conceived monitoring of colonial immigrants between the wars provided a model for the racial authoritarianism of the Vichy state.[123] It also informed the expansion of the urban security apparatus in the intelligence states of North Africa and the French Levant. Whether in mainland France or in the empire, the imposition of racially ordered authority imposed an increasing burden on the network of state intelligence gathering. Alienation of the wider population only increased as a result.

DISORDER IN THE PALESTINE MANDATE

Intelligence and the Descent to War
in the British Middle East

The Palestine mandate was a profoundly unstable political environment that posed unique security challenges to the British imperial state. Palestinian society was scarred by worsening intercommunal tension between Arabs and Jews over immigration levels and over changes in socioeconomic opportunity in what has been variously described as either a single Palestinian economy gradually transformed by the growing Jewish presence, or a dual economy based on distinct, ethnically organized sectors of production and trade.[1] Within this economic system, communal tensions were sharpest over contested land claims and competition for housing. Repeated clashes also occurred over rights of access to—and control over—urban public space. Face-to-face talks between Palestinian and Zionist leaders were rare, despite increasing interaction between Arab and Jewish workers in key industries during the 1920s.[2] Driven by escalating Jewish immigration, land sales, and British support for more intensive agricultural production, the unique dynamics of intercommunal relations in Palestine were a special case.[3]

W. F. Abboushi, the son of the former mayor of Jenin, summarized the vicious circle characteristic of mandate politics before 1936 in the following terms:

> Diplomacy and violence alternated in certain basic patterns which are striking. Frequently, Zionist pressure on the government in Britain would establish a situation in Palestine favorable to the Zionists. The Palestinian Arabs would then attempt to use political or diplomatic means to obtain what they considered to be their rights and legitimate claims threatened by the Zionists. These efforts would be unsuccessful and rioting or other forms of violence would result. Commissions of inquiry investigated the disturbances and almost always produced reports sympathetic to the Arab side. A diplomatic battle then resulted in which Zionists used their superior political influence in Britain to

annul the influence of these reports and to re-establish a situation in Palestine favorable to them. And so the pattern went on.[4]

Albeit a reductive analysis with little concession to cultural factors or other local antagonisms, Abboushi's identification of the painful sense of déjà vu inherent in Palestine's civil disorders rings true. British intelligence gathering and security planning were predicated on the expectation of mounting Palestinian disenchantment, recurrent urban rioting, and attacks on the Yishuv, Palestine's Jewish community.[5] As a result, the security establishment in mandatory Palestine was central to British administration. The ultimate collapse of its information collection and analysis regime in the Arab revolt of 1936–39 heralded the end of Britain's intelligence state in Palestine.

Background

Interwar growth in Jewish settler immigration to Palestine was fueled by anti-Semitic repression in Central and Eastern Europe.[6] The declaration on 2 November 1917 by the British foreign secretary Arthur Balfour promising a Jewish national home in the Holy Land created a more or less permissive official environment for such settlement, but one that was immediately tempered by internal argument both among Whitehall departments and among officials on the spot.[7] Inevitably, the Arab clubs and Arab congresses that refined Palestinian national demands between the end of the Palestine campaign in 1918 and the formal implementation of the British mandate in September 1923 became alienated from an imperial administration that denied the Palestinian national movement a political voice and yet was willing to affirm its commitment to the creation of a Jewish national home.[8]

In the same period, arguments in Whitehall and the Houses of Parliament between fervent Zionists and Arab sympathizers were mirrored by the jurisdictional battle for control of Palestine policy between a largely pro-Zionist Colonial Office Middle East Department and a Foreign Office Eastern Department more tolerant of Arab grievances.[9] Ably promoted by Colonial Secretary Winston Churchill, the new Colonial Office department became the main destination for all incoming political intelligence from Britain's Arab territories.[10] Only in matters of Middle Eastern military intelligence did the War Office and Air Ministry retain primary Whitehall jurisdiction.[11]

In Palestine itself, Britain's first high commissioner, Sir Herbert Samuel, a key instigator of the Balfour Declaration, headed a civil administration sharply at odds with military intelligence officers who repeatedly stressed the weight of Arab grievances against the creation of a Jewish national home in Palestine.[12] After the confirmation of Britain's status as mandatory power in September 1923, Palestine's growing strategic importance as a junction between Britain's Arab territories, the home to the Haifa naval base, and the terminus for Britain's principal Middle East oil pipeline added spice to political and ethical quarrels between ministers and officials over the mandate's changing ethnic composition. These disputes were, in turn, eclipsed by local events.

Having failed to extract meaningful concessions from the British over either Arab representation in the mandatory system or permissible levels of Jewish immigration, the Arab national movement fractured in late 1923. Factionalism among the Arab elite undermined the cohesion of the twenty-four-member Arab Congress executive committee, more often referred to simply as the Arab Executive. Bitter personal enmities among Palestine's major Arab landowners and urban notables also sapped the authority of the Supreme Muslim Council, which held wide legal and financial responsibilities in the Muslim community. Intense rivalries among the leading notable families of Jerusalem were played out among a raft of new political parties that shared the same underlying national goals, but were nonetheless mutually antagonistic.[13] Although the Arab Executive was revived as an umbrella organization during 1928, it was the Palestine Arab Women's Congress, a movement founded in October 1929 by members of well-to-do urban families, that pointed the way to what could be achieved by a united national organization.[14] The recurrent divisions among the Arab elite helped radicalize a younger generation of Palestinians, many of whom served in junior administrative posts.[15] Others were organized into scouting groups, student bodies, and cultural associations, such as the Young Men's Muslim Association. Their frustration with the shortcomings of the Arab elite contributed to the more volatile political atmosphere on the streets of Palestine's major towns.[16]

Communal violence punctuated the entire history of the mandate. Two days of rioting in the old city of Jerusalem in April 1920, in which five Jews died and more than two hundred were injured,[17] were followed by still more serious disturbances in Jaffa and Ramleh from 1 to 7 May of the following year, which left forty-eight Arabs and forty-seven Jews dead.[18] Although there were no further communal killings on this scale until the end of the decade, the violence of 1920–21 was portentous. A renewed cycle of urban disorders began in earnest in 1929, and continued episodically thereafter until rebellion swept the country during the summer of 1936.[19] Arab protest against heightened Jewish immigration and British colonialism became more organized, more violent, and more nationalist in tone.[20] At issue was the very nature of Palestine itself, the ethno-religious character of a Palestinian state, and future control over its land and economy.[21]

It was no coincidence that one of the first acts of the mandate administration in Palestine was to carry out a land survey to underpin land registration procedures and new legal regulations for the sale and transfer of

Map 4. Map of Palestine showing the progress of British land surveys to 1936.

property, always a hotly contested issue in light of Jewish settlement.[22] A consistent refrain in district officers' reports from across rural Palestine was the inevitable tension between the overarching requirement for social stability in the Palestine countryside and high commission schemes for administrative development and agricultural modernization.[23] "Rationalization" of *fellahin* agriculture, attempts to establish greater security of tenure, improved provision of rural credit, and fiscal reform promised better rural living standards, but also amounted to profound, and potentially destabilizing, social change.[24] Mandatory rule altered the very complexion of the Palestinian landscape.[25] Reconfiguration of the socioeconomic structure of rural Palestine was pivotal to the outbreak of what began, in essence, as a peasant revolt in 1936.[26] Yet, as Warwick Tyler points out, the mandate government's primordial security requirements stunted rural development policy, producing half-measures that antagonized both the Arab and the Jewish communities.[27] Only after three years of Arab revolt did the British government finally concede that Arab majority rule held precedence over the creation of a Jewish national home. It was a decision whose consequences struck home in increasing violence after the end of World War II.[28]

Public Security and Policing

In light of the massive law and order tasks they faced, the numerical weakness of British security forces in Palestine is particularly striking. Article 17 of the Palestine mandate permitted the high commission to recruit volunteers for policing as long as these personnel were not used for any other purpose or in any other territory.[29] But cost, not international law, determined the overall complexion of the Palestine security forces. From the end of 1917 until a fundamental restructuring took place in 1925–26, total effectives in the Palestine police never much exceeded sixteen hundred, of which at least thirteen hundred were Palestinians. The British police officers in charge of them numbered only fifty or so.[30] The paramilitary Palestine gendarmerie was, by contrast, far stronger in the early 1920s at least. Its numbers swollen by an influx of former Royal Irish Constabulary policemen, the British section of the gendarmerie admitted more than seven hundred new recruits by mid-1922.[31]

Another oddity of security policy during the 1920s was that the fledgling Air Ministry in London and a Royal Air Force (RAF) officer commanding in Palestine determined overall strategic priorities. Although by no means unique in the wider context of Middle Eastern imperial policing after World War I, the air force's primary responsibility for Palestine's defense made little sense in a strategic environment in which the rapid escalation of intercommunal urban violence posed the main threat to internal order. The airplane was the sharpest weapon of instant colonial retribution in the Arab world. Its capacity for immediate, lethal, and often horrifically indiscriminate violence at minimal risk to the airmen involved enhanced its coercive power. Unless the Palestine high commission was willing to sanction a huge loss of life, however, aircraft could not bring a riotous city crowd under control. Nor could they play much useful part in urban intelligence gathering. These tasks would always fall to uniformed men, whether in the army, the police, or the paramilitary gendarmerie. Admittedly, RAF personnel acquired military and intelligence expertise as special service officers (SSOs), assistant political officers, armored car patrolmen, and security guards. It nonetheless became increasingly apparent to British government ministers, Treasury accountants, Colonial Office specialists, and the Air Ministry's long-standing detractors in the War Office that the air force was not as cost-effective or efficient as it claimed to be in safeguarding internal order in Palestine.[32]

There were also legal considerations. The mandate's judicial system was fiercely contested. Sir Herbert Samuel's administration initially adapted aspects of the Ottoman legal system to suit the purposes of mandatory rule, but ultimately introduced more than 150 new ordinances, primarily to regulate commerce, trade, and industrial activity in accordance with British wishes. The changes were matched by the gradual usurpation of the *Mejelle,* or Muslim civil code, with British statute law, a process overseen by Norman Bentwich, Britain's attorney general in Palestine until 1931.[33] Imposition of Western regulation of property rights, land purchase, and labor relations to fit British views of civil law shaped Arab and Jewish perceptions of mandatory rule.[34]

So, too, did the laws governing security force activity. As British imperial policing was theoretically based on the precepts of minimum force, military deployments were supposed to be kept to the lowest level consistent with public safety (whatever that meant), and replaced as soon as possible with a permanent police presence. In practice, troop deployment was widely understood by rulers and ruled alike to signify the inability of the police to maintain order. This was particularly so in rural areas, where the police presence was, in normal times, minimal and auxiliaries drawn from the Jewish and Arab communities were assigned prime responsibility for security in their settlements.[35]

Use of the armed forces to help the police retain or recover colonial control was governed by regulations colloquially known as "Duties in Aid of the Civil [Power]," most recently revised in 1929.[36] The regulations were invoked time and again during the Arab revolt in Palestine. During 1937, for instance, units of the Transjordan Frontier Force were deployed on seventy-seven occasions "in aid of the civil" to search for rebel bands, to conduct desert patrols, or to man roadblocks on the Palestine frontier.[37] Untrammeled use of military force required legislative authorization or a declaration of martial law, which, in effect, amounted to the abrogation of normal legal procedure.[38] The protracted agonizing in London and Jerusalem in late 1936 over a martial law declaration in response to the Arab rebellion stemmed from this inescapable fact.[39] Martial law actually signified a negation of due process.

State violence conducted while martial law was in force would require a special Act of Indemnity to protect its perpetrators from subsequent prosecution. However, the high commission's and Colonial Office's preferred alternative of exceptional legislation—in this case, a Defence Order-in-Council and Emergency Regulations, introduced on 19 April 1936—that conferred increased powers on the security forces in Palestine was an unsatisfactory compromise severely criticized by the War Office and military commanders on the ground.[40] The scope of these emergency measures nonetheless conferred numerous extraordinary powers on the security forces. Among the most notorious were the imposition of curfews; arbitrary powers of stop, search, and arrest; detention without trial; and media censorship.

Expanded on 22 May, the Emergency Regulations further restricted Arabs' freedom of movement and authorized civilian internment in designated camps for up to a year. Another raft of measures followed on 6 June, this time permitting collective punishments, forced labor to ensure roads were kept open, and the destruction of Palestinian homes "from which firearms had been discharged."[41] Curfews, collective fines, and demolition of Palestinian dwellings became commonplace. All major Arab towns were placed under curfew at some stage during the revolt. Nablus, Acre, Safad, and Lydda all faced collective fines in June 1936 alone. And on a single day in the same month, the security forces admitted to the destruction of 237 Arab houses in Jaffa.[42] Hardly distinguishable from martial law for those who experienced them, these regulations amounted to a recognition that the legal structures of the colonial state were insufficient to contend with public opposition to them.

At a meeting in Jerusalem on 16 April 1925, chaired by High Commissioner Samuel, Colonial Secretary Leo Amery and Air Minister Sir Samuel Hoare agreed on an outline plan for the reorganization of Palestine security forces. Their first principle was that a clear legal and operational separation should be made between police and military forces. As a result of their recommendations, the Palestine police force set up in 1922 absorbed the British component of the local gendarmerie.[43] A separate Palestine gendarmerie was to become fully militarized and was later renamed the Arab Legion. This force was, in turn, to provide the cadres for a Transjordan Frontier Force (TJFF).[44] This new military organization was created on 1 April 1926 on the recommendation of Lord Plumer, the new high commissioner. His instructions on arrival in Palestine were to reassess security requirements and make economies in British Grant-in-Aid.[45] By the end of that year it was

Figure 7. Transjordan Frontier Force motorized unit, 1934. TNA, AIR 5/1155. Crown copyright, reproduced courtesy of the National Archives, London.

agreed that the entire TJFF complement of 787 men should be deployed in Transjordan, with headquarters at Zerqa.[46]

With the British gendarmerie disbanded, the fate of the Arab Legion uncertain, and the TJFF reassigned to focus on border patrolling and tribal control, the upshot of the 1925–26 reorganization was to reinforce the primacy of the Palestine police in maintaining internal security. The recruitment of an additional twenty-two British police officers to join the Palestine police, the reequipment of police units with modern rifles, and the opening of a Palestine police training school in April 1926 underscored the shift toward the use of police rather than military forces for security tasks.[47]

Despite its title, the TJFF received its funding from the Palestine high commission. This remained a bone of contention between the authorities in Jerusalem and Amman, but illustrated that the former held sway in determining regional security policy.[48] Another consequence of the 1926 reforms, however, driven as they were by the Baldwin government's imperative requirement for defense cuts, was to cut back the reserves of military and paramilitary forces available to the police in the eventuality of major urban disorder.[49] These administrative changes were not just a matter of achieving economies, redesignating some security forces, and retiring others. Yishuv leaders regarded Plumer's defensive reorganization as evidence of remarkable complacency. By 1926, what the historian Martin Kolinsky rightly terms Palestine's "thin line of security" was stretched nearly to the breaking point.[50]

Security Force Restructuring and the Wailing Wall Riots

The army withdrawals and police reforms of the mid-1920s had tangible consequences that almost brought the colonial state to its knees during the spate of intercommunal clashes that began at Jerusalem's Wailing Wall in August 1929.[51]

Jerusalem's Western (Wailing) Wall was a focal point of disputed communal rights in the capital. The most sacred Jewish site in the city, the Wall also forms part of the south side of the Haram al-Sharif Temple Mount. It is literally integral to the foundations of the al-Aqsa Mosque. After his appointment as mufti of Jerusalem on 8 May 1921, Haj Amin al-Hussaini made the renovation of the al-Haram (Dome of the Rock) and al-Sharif (al-Aqsa Mosque) central to his bid for enhanced religious authority and political power.[52] A member of one of Jerusalem's leading Muslim families and a Palestinian political figurehead after his key role in the preceding year's anti-Jewish riots, the young mufti secured the presidency of the Supreme Muslim Council, a body established with high commission assent in January 1922 to manage Islamic religious endowments and supervise appointments to Muslim religious and judicial offices.[53] Al-Hussaini's battle for influence among Jerusalem's Arab population with other leading Jerusalem families, especially the Nashashibis and Khalidis, reduced the room for compromise over the Western Wall, seen by all these rivals as a yardstick of their commitment to uphold Arab rights in the capital.[54] But with the high commission broadly sympathetic to Arab complaints about Jewish infractions of their limited rights to place religious articles at the Wall (particularly screens to separate male and female worshippers), the mufti initially preferred legalism to violent protest in his bid to safeguard the Muslim holy sites.[55]

Arguments over access and forms of worship at the Wall assumed a more menacing character once they became bound up with a militant Zionist campaign coordinated by Vladimir Zabotinsky to expropriate the Wall entirely. Disputes over Jewish prayer services at the Wall, contested jurisdiction over its maintenance, and the emblematic power of a religious site central to Islam and Judaism confronted the mandate administration with an inescapable dilemma. Notionally committed to safeguard the interfaith status of the Wailing Wall under Article 13 of the mandate, the civil administration was nonetheless anxious to conciliate Chaim Weizmann's London-based Zionist Executive, which first took up the issue in May 1918. Throughout the 1920s, reports of restricted access to the Wall during major religious festivals scandalized Jews in Europe and the United States, and proved a potent weapon

Figure 8. Jewish worshippers at the Wailing Wall, circa 1911. This photograph was circulated to members of a British commission of inquiry into the August 1929 riots to highlight problems of access to and exit from the area. TNA, CO 733/163/7. Crown copyright, reproduced courtesy of the National Archives, London.

in radicalizing Zionist opinion.[56] Ultimately, the British municipal authorities in Jerusalem would have to decide which community held precedence at the Wall as it became increasingly obvious that peaceful coexistence and shared jurisdiction were not viable.[57]

Meanwhile, al-Hussaini's Supreme Muslim Council, the major Islamic religious authority in Jerusalem, struggled to devise an effective response to increasingly bullish Zionist demands. The Council disputed British and Jewish rights to exercise control over Arab property and civil rights, but still adhered to its legalistic approach to Jewish infringements of established religious custom at the Wall.[58] Seen from a Jewish perspective, the mufti deliberately exaggerated the Zionist threat to the Haram al-Sharif as part of a wider campaign to enhance Jerusalem's status as an Islamic holy place.[59] The result would be a substantial consolidation of his personal status as political leader of the Palestinian national movement.[60] At this stage, secular Arab nationalism aroused less interest among the Palestinian peasantry than a more visceral, apocalyptic message of Islam in peril.[61] Zionist agitation intensified in 1928 after a British police unit forcibly removed prohibited devotional items (fixed screens) from the Wall during the Yom Kippur festival. The Hagana and Zabotinsky's militant followers were increasingly defiant. They also outflanked the Supreme Muslim Council by courting Arab and British retaliation in their defense of uncontested Jewish rights to control the Wailing Wall.[62]

British efforts in the following year to find some definitive legal basis for a settlement based on enhanced Jewish access did nothing to dissipate the mounting tension.[63] With no resolution in sight, both communities mobilized their supporters in the struggle for control over the Wall. Zionist youth groups, prominent in the Jewish "defense squads" organized by Zabotinsky, brought matters to a head during a rowdy demonstration at the Wall on the holy day of Tisha b'Av in mid-August 1929. A week of bloody clashes followed. Even official estimates—almost certainly much underestimating the real death toll—conceded that 133 Jews and 116 Arabs had died, while a further 572 were seriously injured.[64] In some of the worst incidents, ten Jewish colonies were evacuated, some temporarily, others not.[65] A massacre of Jews in Safed and the murder of at least sixty members of the long-established Jewish community in Hebron were more shocking still.[66]

The overwhelming majority of the 110 Arabs killed died at the hands of British security forces during their efforts to restore order.[67] Muslim donations flooded in to a Central Relief Committee set up by the mufti to provide support for Arab victims of the violence, and to fund future political activity.[68] A frankly worded "situation report" from the British Residency in Amman confirmed that only Amir Abdullah's resolute refusal to condone the public clamor for intervention in support of their fellow Muslims in Palestine prevented the collapse of imperial control in Transjordan at a time when virtually all of the mandate's security forces had been hurriedly reassigned to help contain the violence inside Palestine.[69] Coming so soon after vocal protests by Arab Independence Party supporters in Amman against the signature of a 1928 Anglo-Transjordan treaty agreement, as well as the escalation in tribal raiding that undermined security throughout the desert interior, exposure of the weakness of the security forces in Transjordan in 1929 sapped the credibility of British imperial power.[70] Albeit briefly, the mandate authorities in Jerusalem and Amman had been made to appear powerless, if not irrelevant, hopelessly unable to arbitrate, to conciliate, or to coerce.

The killing of so many Arab civilians in such an obvious departure from minimum force–type policing reflected British reliance on special constables hurriedly called into service, Jewish volunteer auxiliaries, and, above all, RAF ground troops and regular army units from the Egypt garrison flown in to help restore order. The hiatus in the senior command of the Palestine police also helps explain the local security forces' inability to prevent the escalation in violence.[71] Key officers, among them the commandant of police, Arthur Mavrogordato, and Jerusalem's district superintendent, Major W. F. Wainwright, were absent when the riots broke out. Communication between districts and between town police commands often broke down, and municipal and national police commands had to be reorganized to cope with the disorders.[72] The arrival of RAF troops also led to the transfer of responsibility for public security to Group-Captain P. H. L. Playfair, the air force commander in Palestine and Transjordan, but an officer with little experience of intercommunal policing or riot control.[73]

In its analysis of the previous year's disorders, in June 1930 the British government's senior civil-military planning group, the Committee of Imperial Defence, focused rather more on the longer-term restructuring of security forces in Palestine. The long-term consequences of Plumer's reorganization had been disastrous:

> At the beginning of August 1925 there was considerable semi-military support for the Police by the presence of detachments (each composed of 4 officers and 80 men) of British Gendarmerie at the principal strategic centers of Palestine; and by the presence of detachments (each composed of 1 British officer, 1 British warrant officer and 50 Palestinians) of the Palestine Gendarmerie at the principal strategic points on the frontier between Palestine and Trans-Jordan. The responsibilities of the Palestine Police were also diminished by the fact that the Palestine Gendarmerie did all the Police work in the frontier zone.
>
> At the beginning of August 1929 on the other hand, there was no support for the Police in Palestine in the shape of organized military or semi-military land forces. The Police numbered about 1,300 as against 1,000 in 1928, but they were all engaged at the same time, so that no reserve force was available. It was therefore impossible to send reinforcements to places where disturbances arose or were threatened.[74]

Stretched to their limit in August 1929, before the arrival of troop reinforcements from outside the mandate, the Palestine police could only call on a local reserve of 170 special constables, hastily enlisted after the riots began.[75] It was nowhere near enough. The aircraft proved its worth once more, this time ferrying in army units from Egypt and Malta in a last-ditch effort to impose colonial control.

After the Wailing Wall riots, Air Ministry threat assessments of potential disorder in Palestine singled out further intercommunal clashes, whether in the form of urban riots or Arab attacks on Jewish colonists, as the chief menace to security. The danger inherent in such disturbances lay in their capacity to escalate rapidly into intercommunal violence throughout the mandate. Viewed from the standpoint of the RAF command in Palestine, it was but a short step from local disorder to general Arab rebellion. The air officer commanding concluded that a better early warning system and additional mobile forces were essential to avoid such conflict escalation. Rapid transmission of intelligence and military capacity to act on it were key to security.[76]

Chief of Air Staff Sir Hugh Trenchard thought differently. He agreed that the measure of effective security intelligence was its capacity to forewarn of—and thus prevent—disorder.[77] But he challenged those, including the high commissioner, Sir John Chancellor, who claimed that a permanent army garrison was urgently required in Palestine.[78] Writing in May 1930, amid Whitehall recriminations over the previous year's events in Jerusalem, Trenchard drew the opposite conclusion. Any semblance of a British military occupation could do untold political damage to Britain's authority as mandatory power. Trenchard's answer was to spread police resources more evenly, if thinly, by placing stronger detachments in rural areas and outlying towns. Trenchard's advice complemented Treasury worries over increased military expenditure as Britain's financial position went into steep decline in 1930–31.[79]

The views of Trenchard, the apostle of air policing, were less a reflection of any ethical qualms about a more visible military presence than a spirited defense of the air force's singular aptitude for colonial repression. His solution—a larger police force backed by air power—also ignored the available intelligence.[80] In his enthusiasm for a prominent RAF role, Trenchard took insufficient account of what the intelligence cycle of Air Headquarters weekly situation reports actually revealed, namely, that civil disorder was most likely to begin in Palestine's major towns, particularly those with a substantial mixed population of Arabs and Jews such as Jerusalem, Jaffa, Haifa, and Hebron.[81] Once intercommunal violence began, it would probably spread to densely populated residential areas on or near the urban front lines of communal settlement. Only foot patrols of armed police and troops quickly deployed could operate in the maze of streets and alleyways where most clashes were expected once initial flash points around public spaces, government buildings, mosques, and synagogues were secured.[82]

Trenchard's stubborn reluctance to admit that the security system in the Palestine mandate required fundamental reform suggested a limited grasp of the connections among intelligence gathering, threat assessment, and colonial state security. It certainly put him at odds with the Middle East Department and High Commissioner Chancellor.[83] On 5 December 1929, he reacted furiously to a damning Colonial Office review of the causes and consequences of the Wailing Wall riots. He attacked the Colonial Office's reading of events through the prism of police and local agent intelligence reports, press extracts, "or highly colored opinions of Arab extremists." Most were little more than rumor, and some were clearly prejudiced. Only the views of the high commissioner himself "can be considered at all serious."[84] This conveniently overlooked the fact that the high commission built up its security appreciations from raw police intelligence. Some of this material derived from agent humint, but most came from less covert sources: the periodic reports filed by the growing number of Arab district officers.[85] They, in turn, typically drew their information from village *mukhtars,* who were the backbone of rural administration.[86] Subsequent police headquarters' threat assessments, normally filed weekly, were submitted on a daily basis at the peak of the disorders.[87]

The interservice Palestine defense scheme devised in response to the 1929 disorders also placed intelligence assessment at the heart of security planning. Ironically, however, the net result of its declared intelligence assumptions was much the same as Trenchard's recommendation for a larger police presence but no significant expansion of the army garrison. The 1930 defense scheme posited an interval between early indications of dissent and the outbreak of rebellion sufficient to allow reinforcement of the military presence—what in planners' parlance was referred to as "defense climb." Past experience was adduced to justify this conclusion: "Actual disorders in the past have been preceded by a period of tension. It is likely that such will always be the case."[88]

The Palestine police were to try to maintain order in this "tension phase," and would continue to do so should disorders ensue. The army would be called out only if the police were clearly unable to restore control unaided. The entire scheme hinged on security force mobility, the quality of intelligence about imminent dissent, and the capacity to assess it quickly. Driven as much by cost as by strategic analysis, the plans were vulnerable in several respects. First, the mobile reserve of Palestine police would inevitably fall in time of tension, as large numbers of policemen would assume responsibility for the static defense of isolated Jewish colonies. Second, British troops from the Suez garrison were to enter Palestine on the Sinai military railway, a line that was particularly vulnerable to sabotage. Upon arrival, army units would then rely on motor transport for their final deployment, limiting their radius of operations to the rudimentary road system and making it easy for insurgents to monitor their movements. Third and most important, the entire scheme was only as good as the intelligence obtained about Palestinians' intentions. This alone would determine whether the security forces would indeed have time to respond to localized dissent before it escalated into rebellion.[89]

The emerging generation of more radical Palestinian nationalists were never passive objects of state repression, of course, but worked hard to remain a step ahead of the security forces. Even before the Wailing Wall disturbances, clandestine guerrilla groups were formed in Haifa, for example. Led by Sheikh Izz al-Din al-Qassam, a key figure in the city's Islamic establishment, five-member cells gathered intelligence about policing and military plans in preparation for attacks on British and Jewish targets.[90]

As Ylana Miller points out, the 1929 riots intensified British suspicions of Palestinian community leaders. These suspicions endured, despite the March 1930 findings of Sir Walter Shaw's commission of inquiry into the origins of the disturbances, which identified the socioeconomic disruption occasioned by Jewish immigration and land purchase as the root cause of Arab antagonism.[91] Ironically, the continual British security concern over the recrudescence of intercommunal violence in Palestine made Colonial Office Middle East Department analysts and high commission staff rather more sanguine about the influence of pan-Arabism as a primary source of unrest. As Shaw's commission pointed out, Palestine police intelligence had been too consumed with the search for Communist sedition and too little concerned with the growth of Arab militancy.[92] It was a harsh verdict. Police and military intelligence assessments recognized that Arab nationalism could mobilize mass opposition before the tragic events of August 1929, and they remained alert to the issue afterward. The deeper problems were twofold: first, accurate, exploitable information was not always obtained in time to help prevent outbreaks; and second, the instruments of state coercion had been poorly suited to meet the threats that such intelligence revealed. If police intelligence needed overhaul, so did the security forces in the field.

Heightened official sensitivity to the critical importance of accurate police intelligence resulted in large part from the restructuring of the Palestine Criminal Investigation Department (CID) undertaken by Sir Herbert Dowbiggin, the former inspector-general of police in Ceylon. Dowbiggin was appointed in response to a December 1929 call from High Commissioner Chancellor for an urgent and thorough inquiry into the role, size, and composition of the Palestine police in the face of diminishing public confidence in its effectiveness. Dowbiggin's investigation in early 1930 led to improved police protection of Jewish settlements and a radical overhaul of CID intelligence collection. A clearer command hierarchy was established, record-keeping procedures were improved, and new faces were brought in to lead the force.[93] Most important, Dowbiggin laid the basis for fuller and faster intelligence liaison among outlying police districts, divisional headquarters, district commissioners, and service personnel. But a crucial weakness remained: a revitalized intelligence-gathering network capable of processing incoming information of impending unrest was still only as good as the raw intelligence fed to it by local auxiliaries. While police agent numbers increased, Dowbiggin's reforms did little to build much-needed connections with Arab opinion as organized resistance to British rule again gathered momentum.[94] A functioning intelligence state in the Palestine mandate remained as elusive as ever.

In 1931, the Jerusalem Congress of Arab nationalist representatives and Muslim religious leaders opened a new phase of multinational contacts among groups at least nominally committed to pan-Arabism.[95] No Arab state was officially represented at the Congress, formally opened by the mufti of Jerusalem in the al-Aqsa Mosque on 6 December, but Palestinian, Syrian, and Iraqi delegates dominated the proceedings.[96] After years of security surveillance of diffuse pan-Arabist groups, here was clear evidence, duly condensed by the Palestine police CID, of the connections between them.[97] In another sense, however, the Jerusalem meeting, and other pan-Arab Congresses held in subsequent years in various Middle Eastern capitals, represented the normalization or, at least, the ritualization of pan-Arabism as a political instrument of Arab nationalism. This was certainly how the Colonial Office viewed pan-Arabism's development.[98] The Foreign Office Eastern Department was equally dismissive. Instructed by the Cabinet to revaluate the dangers presented by pan-Arabism prior to King Faysal's visit to London in June 1933, the Eastern Department took pains to avoid accusations of exaggerated threat assessment, which had been leveled at those officials who had foreseen imperial doom in the earlier rise of pan-Islamism. Its conclusions were therefore decidedly low-key:

> The phrase "Arab unity" is an extremely vague one, which has been used in many different senses. It is generally most in evidence on such occasions as Arab or Moslem congresses, and it was freely bandied about during the Moslem Congress at Jerusalem in the autumn of 1931. On such occasions it is generally used extremely loosely as a rallying cry against either "Western imperialism" or the Zionist movement; but in actual fact it seldom amounts to much more than a rather undigested idea of cooperation between Arabic-speaking people in matters of education and propaganda, and possibly also in such politico-religious questions as that of [control over] the Hijaz railway, the future of the Holy Places, etc. Arab unity in this sense is something rather akin to pan-Arabism, and appears to have no more practical significance than the rather shadowy pan-Islamic movement of which so much was heard some twenty years ago.[99]

The Jerusalem Congress and its successors triggered more heated reactions elsewhere. French resentment at Britain's reluctance to prohibit the Jerusalem Congress on the dubious grounds that it was a religious rather than a political gathering was outstripped by Kemalist annoyance with France for permitting the deposed Ottoman caliph, Abdülmecid, then living in comfortable exile in Nice, to apply for a visa from the Palestine high commission to attend the al-Aqsa gathering.[100] The Italian and Spanish governments were similarly offended by British failure to proscribe a meeting bound to criticize their repressive policies in Libya and Morocco.[101]

British security agencies in the Middle East remained deaf to these complaints, and were by this point less concerned than their European counterparts about pan-Arabism and far more animated by the repercussions of the growing influx into Palestine of Jewish refugees from Europe. They recognized that growing Muslim fear of Zionist projects and Jewish immigration to Palestine provided the subtext to the Jerusalem Congress proceedings. Persecution of Jewish populations in Central and Eastern Europe registered in heightened levels of immigration to Palestine in the mid-1920s, but immigrant numbers diminished in the Depression years immediately after the Wailing Wall riots. Immigration took off once more as the impact of Nazi anti-Semitism stimulated a greater Jewish exodus from 1933 onward.[102] At the local level, the high commission relied still more heavily on its district officers to provide reliable intelligence on rural opinion as land transfers gathered renewed momentum.[103] At the national and international levels, British intelligence analysts in Jerusalem and Whitehall accepted that the communal tensions generated by Jewish immigration to Palestine fueled pan-Arabist sentiment. But their French counterparts were quicker to link the two together. The greater French sensitivity to these links reflected the proliferation of Sûreté reportage on the network of international contacts between various pan-Arabist groups during the preceding decade. The centrality of the status of Palestine and the Muslim Holy Places in pan-Arabist propaganda was something with which the French security community in Geneva and the Levant were entirely familiar.[104]

From 1931 onward, French military intelligence analysts of the Beirut Service de Renseignements (SR) also monitored political developments in Palestine and Transjordan more closely. They foresaw that the Jewish influx to Palestine was bound to provide a rallying point for otherwise disparate Arab nationalist groups, replacing the restoration of a Muslim caliphate as a ready means to stir popular opposition to Western imperialism.[105] The War Ministry deuxième bureau took this thinking one step further, concluding that antagonism to British policy in Palestine throughout the Muslim world would rekindle popular support for pan-Arabism.[106]

It was only much later, faced with the prospect of general Arab revolt in early 1936, that British intelligence analysts and diplomatic observers arrived at a similar conclusion.[107] A spate of reports on pan-Arabism followed over the spring and summer of 1936. Some linked the earlier civil disturbances and general strike in Syria with the spread of similar disorders to Palestine.[108] In this reading of events, pan-Arabism expressed Muslim hostility to foreign rule rather than a deep-seated commitment to an Arab superstate.[109] Others detected a deeper socioeconomic malaise, propelled by population growth, underemployment, and the alienation of an emergent cosmopolitan intelligentsia educated in Middle Eastern—and especially Egyptian and Lebanese—universities and drawn to nationalist anti-colonialism.[110] All concurred that clear-cut distinctions between the religiously inspired pan-Islamism of old and the modernist undercurrent of pan-Arabism were impossible to make, and all agreed that the status of Palestine and the persecution of Palestinians united the Arab world far more than any other Middle Eastern crisis since 1918.[111] The Bludan Congress, convened in September 1937 to promote support for the Palestinian Arab cause, lent substance to these more abstract threat assessments. Endorsed by the Syrian National Bloc and the paramilitary Steel Shirts, who served as security guards during the conference proceedings, the Congress established an Arab National Bureau in Damascus that coordinated the Arabic propaganda effort against British actions in Palestine.[112]

The Bureau found a receptive audience. It opened subbranches in Egypt and Iraq, and liaised with an Arab Bureau in London that circulated allegations of British atrocities against Arab detainees.[113] Arab opinion hardened in opposition to British imperialism as repression of the Arab revolt in Palestine gathered momentum during 1937–38.[114] Stung by Foreign Office criticism of army methods in Palestine, on 9 February 1938 the War Office directorate of intelligence produced its most comprehensive assessment of the repercussions of the Palestine revolt throughout the Arab world. Britain's military intelligence planners had no truck with the concept of pan-Arabism as a tool for Arab nationalists to organize resistance against European imperialism in the Middle East.[115] Arab governments were too prone to being overthrown, their military resources too limited, and their local interests too pronounced to permit any serious pan-Arabist threat.[116]

The Foreign Office Eastern Department was unimpressed with such sangfroid. By linking pan-Arabism to governmental action, the directorate of intelligence had failed to grasp that the danger stemmed from the bottom of society, not the top. Disparate civil unrest and urban disorders sparked by popular hostility to British policy in Palestine, and fomented by foreign—especially Italian—propaganda and covert weapons supply, could destabilize imperial control.[117] Privy to an increasing volume of long-term intelligence analysis, principally built up from Middle Eastern consular reportage and Secret Intelligence Service agents' reports, the military establishment came round to Foreign Office thinking in subsequent months. The chiefs of staff Joint Intelligence Committee (JIC) warned in February 1939 that the wider ramifications of the Palestine revolt for Muslim opinion could undermine British rule in the Middle East.[118] If intelligence assessments in London were subject to such fundamental change, what about the nature and quality of the information gathered by the security services in Palestine itself?

The Collapse of an Information Order: The Palestine Revolt, 1936–1939

The Arab rebellion in Palestine of 1936–39 was the last major test of British security services in the Middle East before World War II.[119] The revolt also confirmed what grave consequences might follow when a community—in this case the Palestinian Arabs—tried to shut out the state's intelligence-gathering networks, impairing their ability to provide early warning of inter-communal disorder. Arab motivations for supporting revolt were not simply reducible to opposition to heightened Jewish immigration and ownership. The rebellion also meshed together a predominantly urban Arab national-ism with peasant economic grievances arising from rural poverty, landless-ness, and land sales to Jewish immigrants, for which British misrule was held responsible.[120] Whereas the violence of August 1929 was essentially inter-communal, the Palestine revolt targeted the political and economic appa-ratus of the British colonial state. Favored targets included the communi-cations network, pipelines, police stations (several of which were built by Jewish-owned construction companies in the aftermath of the 1929 distur-bances), and army outposts and those who manned them.[121] It was this, rather than rebel attacks on the Jewish community and Arab "collabora-tors," that most unnerved the high commission. The adoption of intelligence-led counterinsurgency strategies was integral to the partial restoration of imperial control.[122] The role of intelligence in stemming the rebellion thus provides some measure by which to assess the evolution of the British intel-ligence state model during the interwar years.

Three years of Arab unrest in Palestine began with a general strike in April 1936, triggered in part by the collapse of high commission plans to establish a Palestine Legislative Council with a majority Arab membership, and modeled on the earlier Arab strike in Damascus. From the outset, the more radical voices in the Arab Higher Committee (AHC), the umbrella organization created on April 25 to coordinate strike committees across the country, viewed the stoppage in more revolutionary terms as a vehicle to mobilize popular opposition to the mandate. Foremost among them were the leading members of the Palestinian Istiqlal, a party whose rapid growth in the early 1930s soon eclipsed the now defunct Arab Executive.[123] Strongly identified with pan-Arabism, the Istiqlal adapted capably to the task of nationalist mobilization.[124]

The general strike endured for almost six months, a remarkable testa-ment to the initial unity of purpose among the Arab population, town dwellers and rural *fellahin* alike. The AHC must take some of the credit for this, not least in its delineation of a strategy of civil disobedience. Formed from Palestine's six Arab political parties, it coordinated the strike in con-junction with a series of national committees based in the country's major towns. But much of the day-to-day organization of strike activity took place at the local level, meaning that British efforts to silence the AHC were insufficient to bring an end to the protest campaign.[125] Haj Amin al-Hussaini, the mufti of Jerusalem, leader of the Arab Party, AHC president, and a member of the country's most prestigious Arab family, was the obvious choice as the revolt's political figurehead.[126] But neither he, nor the AHC, nor its later descendant, the Central Committee of the National Jihad in Palestine, formed by Palestinian political exiles in Damascus, could control the rebel bands that proliferated in the Palestinian countryside over the summer of 1936.[127] The diffusion of strike committees and rural resistance groups was not unforeseen by the mandate authorities, but still presented massive challenges to their intelligence apparatus.

The strike, and the gradual spread of violence associated with it, conformed exactly to the "tension phase" anticipated by British military planners six years earlier, enabling the security forces to improve their intelligence system before a nationwide rebellion broke out. By June, three distinct British intelligence gathering organizations were in place. Foremost among these was the intelligence section ("I" Branch) at general staff headquarters in Jerusalem, which assessed raw intelligence supplied from Palestine and Transjordan. Second in importance was the Palestine police CID, which ran the largest network of agents in Palestine. The Arab Legion also maintained its own intelligence office ("I" Section), which monitored reported activity along the Transjordan side of the frontier with Palestine. As disorders escalated, particularly around Mount Samaria and along the eastern frontier with Syria, the volume of assessed military intelligence grew. The army command ("I" Branch) and battalion headquarters across Palestine issued a daily intelligence bulletin every afternoon detailing the political and military situation in their area up to 8 A.M. that day. This was in addition to the general officer commanding's daily situation reports on casualties, engagements, and force movements.[128] The Jerusalem command center also issued a weekly summary of political intelligence and press extracts that made some assessment of likely developments in the rebellion.[129]

The army intelligence officers who supplied raw intelligence to their battalion commands and "I" Branch worked alongside RAF SSOs, most of whom had greater local knowledge and were more proficient Arabic speakers. At the start of the revolt, there were four SSO stations, two in Palestine (Jerusalem and Haifa), and two in Transjordan (Amman and Ma'an). Others were quickly added at rebellion hotspots: Jaffa, Nablus, Nazareth, and in the Jordan Valley. In addition to the provision of supplementary military reports and topographic data, SSOs were the only military intelligence staff to analyze provincial opinion, building up networks of local informants for the purpose.[130] SSOs were also the sole military personnel authorized to run agents on their own initiative, and used regular inspection tours to keep their information system in place. In this respect, the British command learned from the shortcomings of intelligence gathering in Egypt, where the decline of the provincial tour system debilitated headquarters staff in Cairo anxious to know more about politics in the Nile delta.[131] SSOs reported directly to their local command headquarters, and their cars were fitted with wireless transmitters, allowing them to report high-grade intelligence to "I" Branch staff without delay.[132]

If the military intelligence system with SSOs at its center facilitated the rapid transmission of information to strategic commands, Palestine police intelligence drew army criticism for its slowness and inadequate sifting of reliable from unreliable information. Furthermore, police reports were often formulaic: dry facts compiled without analysis. This was certainly the criticism made by Thomas Hodgkin, soon to retire as the private secretary to High Commissioner Wauchope, whose job it was to sort through the incoming intelligence day by day.[133] CID intelligence networks were traditionally reliant on Arab police personnel, and naturally faced disruption as the Arab rank-and-file wrestled with divided loyalties and rebel threats to themselves and their families. As internally generated intelligence began to dry up, the CID came into competition with SSOs for the services of reliable Arab agents. The army command's greater respect for SSOs as intelligence analysts meant that they received the lion's share of funding for agent networks.[134]

The Palestine revolt also marked the definitive end of the Air Ministry's imperial policing strategy that privileged air power over the use of ground forces. During the rebellion, RAF aircraft still bombarded villages suspected of harboring insurgents and strafed rebel columns on the few occasions that these were spotted by day, but most flying time was expended on reconnaissance flights. With uncontested control of the skies, imperial air forces were able to fly unopposed, often at lower altitude than in European conflicts. The quality of reconnaissance in general, and aerial photography in particular, was commensurately high. Low-flying RAF squadrons in Palestine provided detailed intelligence on the location of road blocks and sabotaged bridges, railways, and pipelines. Radio communication with army units enabled airmen to provide close reconnaissance support to army units tracking rebel movements in the Jordan Valley. In addition, RAF aerial photographs were used to construct an entirely new mosaic of Arab settlement and population distribution.[135]

At the start of the rebellion in April 1936, the map in general use among military and police forces was the War Office 1:250,000 Lambert Grid series. Thanks to the efforts of the Palestine Government Survey Department, this was soon replaced with updated 1:100,000 topographical maps, variants of which remained in circulation until the end of the mandate and beyond.[136] Aside from the improvement in scale and relief, these maps were simply more accurate. They also contained phonetically correct spellings of place names and the locations of Jewish colonies (unlike the War Office version). Since attacks on Jewish colonies were identified as a major concern after the Wailing Wall riots, the poverty of information in army maps in early 1936 seemed inexcusable, the more so as numerous Jewish settlements were situated close to the Syrian and Transjordan frontiers, increasing the likelihood of Arab raids against them. With few tarmac roads to these settlements, police and army units also needed reliable topographical information about paths and tracks in order to pursue attackers into the surrounding hills and villages.[137] From April 1936 onward, the Survey Department raced through new additions to its more detailed map series, producing them at an average rate of one per month, so that half of the country was covered in this way by February 1938. Between April and November 1936 alone, the Survey Department issued some twenty-three thousand maps to the security forces.[138]

Aside from their outdated cartographic information, the security services faced a number of intractable problems in counteracting the spread of rural violence. What historians generally acknowledge to be the principal weaknesses of the rebel bands—namely, their factionalism, equipment shortages, and lack of a single, overarching politico-military authority—also presented intelligence gathering agencies with a formidable challenge: how to make sense of it all.[139] Isolated rebel bands around Haifa and northern Palestine had taken up arms against the mandate authorities at various points from 1931 to 1935.[140] The speed with which such groups emerged across the country over the summer of 1936 revealed the extent to which British imperial policing had been overwhelmingly urban in focus hitherto.[141] With so many insurgent groups to contend with, few of which fielded their full manpower strength at any one time, the task of predictive threat assessment became immensely complicated. Individual bands could easily be identified with a single leader based in a specific town or locality, but this was of little use unless the commander and his followers could be tracked down. Rebel organizers in northern Palestine such as 'Abd al'Rahim Hajj Muhammad, Arif 'Abd al'Raziq, and Yusuf Sa'id Abu Durra moved from place to place with a small permanent force, raising volunteer platoons (*fasa'il*) controlled by their subordinates in individual villages to carry out specific attacks, usually at night. Only Fakhri 'Abd al'Hadi, the rebel leader in an area bounded by Tulkarem, Jenin, and Afula, chose to maintain a force several hundred strong. But the ease with which its movements could be detected soon persuaded him to adopt the *fasa'il* system.[142]

From day to day, British military patrols simply could not find an enemy to engage. During daylight hours, in town and country, "active rebel" and "peaceful citizen" were indistinguishable. Urban *effendiyya* concealed their administrative and financial support for the rebels. So, too, did the gang members who collected funds and exacted retribution against those who collaborated with the mandate administration in the major towns. Most important, their supporters and their victims also recognized the personal dangers inherent in revealing anything to the army or police.[143] Meanwhile, the constant stream of funds, weapons, and other rebel supplies across Palestine's land frontiers added to the number of strategic points that had to be monitored. Writing in December 1938, Lieutenant-General R. H. Haining, the officer commanding in Palestine, acknowledged that security force efforts to detain *fasa'il* members and break the rebel grip on town populations depended on those local Arabs prepared to assist the army and police in picking out insurgents. This, in turn, would allow the security forces to make better use of intelligence previously gathered:

> The problem is . . . to identify and remove the active rebel element, both permanent and temporary, from the towns and villages where they are circulating unarmed and inextricably mixed with the civilian inhabitants. As a result of the information collected over the past two years and the increasing number of Arab informants now coming forward, the names of a very large proportion of the active rebels in the country are known. The real difficulty is identification. In almost all cases wanted men give false names and owing to terrorism are supported by the rest of the population. The only successful method is therefore for wanted men to be picked out by persons who can actually recognize them. The number of "identifiers" is limited. The Police can assist to a certain extent and there are now in most districts a number of Arabs who are volunteering to assist the Government Forces in this way, provided adequate steps are taken to protect them by concealing their identity. . . .
>
> It must be realized that when the innocent and the guilty are completely mixed together and quite indistinguishable at sight, there is no alternative to the collection of all males, irrespective of any excuse, if wanted men are to be prevented from slipping through the net by giving false accounts of themselves. Inevitably this process involves a certain amount of hardship which falls equally on the innocent and the guilty, and the spectacle of weeping women watching their men-folk marched off for identification, or reports of the temporary detention of honest Government servants, naturally offer opportunities for propaganda, but in the present conditions no other course is possible.[144]

Haining was loath to admit that these army cordon-and-search operations exposed Arab civilians to greater risk of security force violence or eventual rebel retribution and were therefore counterproductive.[145]

Less arbitrary methods of identification and intelligence collection were adopted only between May and November 1938. During this six-month period, Orde Wingate's special night squads (SNS) spearheaded the British counteroffensive against rebel formations with targeted attacks by troops, Jewish police auxiliaries, and Hagana volunteers. Operations were usually mounted on the basis of intelligence provided by a network of Arab informants. Meanwhile, the construction of the so-called Tegart Wire along the Palestine-Transjordan frontier, combined with heightened surveillance of favored border crossing points, restricted the ability of gangs either to evade British security forces or to ensure their resupply with additional men and equipment.[146] These frontier closures and the erection by Jewish subcontractors of a wire barrier across Arab farmers' fields and traditional grazing grounds provoked a furious local reaction, exemplified by repeated efforts during the summer of 1938 to tear down long sections of the offending fence. By its arbitrary nature, the Tegart Wire also symbolized the renewed security force commitment to stifle the rebellion with fewer qualms about local reaction, a physical equivalent to the irregular operations conducted by Wingate's specialist units.[147]

Prior to the ruthless but effective SNS campaign, Haining's predecessor as army commander, General John Dill, had vested more hope in the introduction of identity cards as a means to control the movement of people across frontiers and between districts. Dill's identity card plan was hampered by anticipated Jewish objections to a system that would also highlight the large numbers of illegal immigrants in the country.[148] In any event, it was only one component of the intelligence war. The army command was under no illusion that such a scheme would make it any easier to capture large numbers of insurgents. The absence of a clear chain of rebel command, and the propensity among bands to make exaggerated claims about their achievements, made it harder still to keep abreast of the power struggles between the AHC and military leaders increasingly at odds with one another. Long-standing clan feuds, entrenched cultural divisions between town and countryside, and bitter political rivalries between leading Palestinian notable families, such as the Hussainis and the Nashashibis in Jerusalem, and the Abboushis and the Abdul-Hadis in Jenin, added further layers of complexity to intelligence assessment.[149]

The key to success was less a matter of discovering what rebels were doing than of interpreting their actions, something that required an understanding of village society. As Yuval Arnon-Ohanna puts it:

> Composed primarily of rural men the bands quickly took on the mentality and way of life that was characteristic of the Arab village in Palestine in the second half of the 1930s. The absence of co-operation and mutual responsibility, the deep-seated divisiveness of a society based on patriarchal lines and *hamulas* (lineages), the ancient inter-village and inter-*hamula* wrangles over stretches of land and water sources, over blood feuds, family honor and marital problems—they were simply transferred to the bands movement.[150]

Perhaps too dismissive of any sense of Palestinian national identity, this assessment at least makes clear that rebel activity was more often the product of local circumstance than of executive command. Just as the AHC and its favored military commanders, Fawzi al-Din al-Qawuqji[151] and Muhammad al-Ashmar (both Syrians), could not establish a unified insurgency in 1936–

37, so their British opponents could not quash the revolt by striking at a single command center.[152] Unable to pinpoint its opponents, British counterinsurgency became more repressive. Army and police resorted to collective punishments, the destruction of villages and crops, and livestock killing to try to sever the ties between the rural population and rebel groups. Such actions only undermined Arab respect for mandate authority, making the process of information gathering harder still.[153]

Although the Palestine revolt took three years to suppress, it was marked by two distinct phases of intense rebel activity, the first from April to October 1936, the second from September 1937 until British troops shot down the rebellion's last commander, Ahmad Muhammad Hasan Abu Bakr, in May 1939.[154] The intervening lull was attributable not to decisive military victories, but rather to the arrival of the Peel Commission in November 1936 to investigate the rebellion's causes and make recommendations for the mandate's future organization. The descent back into violence was all but inevitable once the Commission's recommendation of Palestinian partition was published in July 1937.[155]

In each phase, the so-called triangle of terror between the West Bank towns of Nablus, Tulkarem, and Jenin witnessed the heaviest fighting between rebel bands on the one hand, and Palestinian police forces and British Army units on the other. Meanwhile, the collation of intelligence on incidents of rebel violence revealed consistently high levels of sniper attacks, firing on Jewish settlements, and sabotage of transport and communications in and around Palestine's principal urban centers.[156] The Royal Scots regiment, in particular, sustained heavy casualties and destroyed hundreds of Arab homes in reprisal. By the time Wingate's SNS set to work in May 1938, much of rural Palestine was in rebel hands. British authority was restricted to the major towns and the immediate hinterland of its garrison outposts.[157] The district commissioner in the Gaza-Bersheeba division, not an area of intensive rebel activity, conceded that by September the rebellion leaders controlled the dissemination of political information and operated a far more effective network of informers than their British rivals. Nor could the army protect those who previously had supplied intelligence about rebel movements. Government sympathizers and Arab policemen became a primary target for intimidation, reprisal, or assassination.[158]

British commanders in Jerusalem made the same admission. Army headquarters did not secure much useful intelligence from the civilian population. Captured insurgents rarely divulged information of strategic value. (The issue of how much information was extracted from detainees under torture did not feature in the official account of intelligence operations.) And Jews volunteered so much information that it proved impossible to evaluate it in time for it to be of much use. Moreover, the humint provided by the Jewish community was, it appears, often discounted because it was

Arabs Riot In Jerusalem: Mufti Arrives At Beirut In Disguise

PICTURE received in London last night, by air, of rioting in Jerusalem. Dust rises from the sun-parched street as Arabs clash with British troops. The trouble, which began after services in the mosques, was just an incident in the series of disturbances that have been organised all over Palestine.

★

HAJ AMIN EFFENDI EL HUSSEINI, Mufti of Jerusalem, President of the Supreme Moslem Council until the British authorities deposed him, is pictured below in the Bedouin disguise in which he fled from Jaffa. Motor-boat conveying him was topped by a French patrol, and the Mufti, accompanied by an officer of the Sûreté, was taken to Beirut, Syria, where he is under the surveillance of French officials.

Figure 9. British troops intervening against rioters at the Wailing Wall during the second phase of the Palestine revolt, October 1937. This photograph was widely published in the British national and provincial press. TNA, CO 733/333/8. Crown copyright, reproduced courtesy of the National Archives, London.

either too lurid to be credible or was transparently intended to ensure a stronger security force presence in a particular locality.[159] By contrast, throughout the rebellion the rebels gathered so much intelligence about army plans, police operations, and the day-to-day activities of the civil authorities that operations were repeatedly compromised.[160] Arab policemen and administration employees were prime suspects, but the elaborate network of camp watchers, telephone company employees, bar and café owners, and sympathetic workers contracted to provide services to army and police garrisons were the eyes and ears of this Arab intelligence system. Thanks to them, the majority of motorized troop movements were disclosed to rebel units in affected areas. Leaked intelligence facilitated the rebels' adoption of a strategy of targeted assassination of soldiers, policemen, and other alleged traitors, which sapped security force morale.[161] The information order was breaking down.

The struggle to salvage the information order, and so regain imperial control, was in large part an intelligence war. British security forces tried to secure reliable humint about rebel activities and dispositions; band leaders tried to deny it to them, cultivating support among the rural population and intimidating those considered disloyal to the Arab cause. Robin Martin, a junior Palestine police recruit in Hebron district, described the results:

> We were spending weeks at a time, out in the villages trying to locate and engage the local gang. We patrolled days and nights, picking up what information we could, but never a shot was fired at us. We often learned on doubling back that a gang had been following us. Prior information as to the gang's activities was hard to come by, but plenty of people would give a word or two after something had happened, so hoping to keep their villages in favor with the government. It was too much to expect that the villagers would readily give information about the rebels. In the first place they were all in sympathy because they didn't want to lose their homes to Jewish immigrants. In the second place, if they did give information to the government, the government could not give them the protection they wanted and the rebels took away informers and summarily executed them.[162]

As this quotation suggests, the root problem of a colonial intelligence system based on humint from local informants was whether these intelligence providers could be induced to believe that the state could and would protect them. Aside from those who provided occasional information about a specific event, most Arab informants were linked to the administrative apparatus of the colonial state as policemen, clerical staff, district officers, or village officials. Many faced intimidation and violent retribution if their activities became known in their communities, and few were insensitive to the plight of the Palestinian Arab community, the politics of Arab nationalism, and the rising tide of opposition to the British presence. In times of disorder, police and military officials, in turn, were torn between their de facto reliance on Arab auxiliaries to provide raw intelligence, their increasing disinclination to believe it, and their sense of responsibility for intelligence providers whose activities placed them in extreme danger. Arab agents' reports remained critical to security force deployments. They were treated with greater skepticism, however, as disorders worsened. By 1936, the acid test of the Palestine mandate as an intelligence state was whether its indigenous intelligence gathering system could survive in a period of rebellion, or what one contemporary commentator termed "sub-war."[163]

The answer was ambiguous. The indigenous intelligence network survived, but Arab employees of the British administration often leaked news of the information received to members of their own community. As long as the chain of intelligence relay from local provider, through British analyst, to security forces in the field remained in place, it was nearly impossible to exploit useful intelligence before it was compromised. Writing in 1937, the author H. J. Simson, a bitter critic of British policing in Palestine, passed acerbic judgment on the resultant failures of intelligence:

> Frequently the Palestine police asked for military help to surround some village and arrest armed men known to be harbored by its inhabitants. Frequently the help was given, but always the villagers knew all about it in plenty of time. Once notices were found on the house doors, "Please do not disturb the contents more than is absolutely necessary." . . . The trouble always was that the civil authorities and the police, and last of all the military, dealt with the absolutely reliable information received from some secret source. While all this dealing was going on, by telephone, by typewritten correspondence, or by conference, an Arab, employed in a district or police office, would slip away and inform the local scouts or a branch of the youth movement, and the sub-war machinery of warning would be set in motion.[164]

Meanwhile, British efforts to counteract intelligence leakages achieved limited success. Prior information about major troop deployments and police sweeps was withheld from all but senior officers, operations were increasingly planned and executed within the same twenty-four-hour period, and casual discussion of future activity, whether in the army canteen, the police station, or over the telephone, was discouraged. Punitive raids were generally conducted at night, and troops were often disguised in local dress, sometimes disembarking from slow-moving vehicles in an effort to mislead their targets. But army and police campaigns of misinformation and decoy operations rarely succeeded in concealing the genuine operational activity about to take place.[165]

Social communication lay at the heart of all this. Language was one of the few areas where the Arab population enjoyed a significant strategic advantage over their opponents. Palestinians were better placed to listen in on British conversations than vice versa. They could slip into local dialect when they wished to discuss sensitive information within earshot of occupying forces. With only one interpreter assigned to each army brigade, troop units were largely deaf to the dialogue going on around them. Headquarters' efforts to recruit non-Palestinian civilian volunteers as interpreters made little headway, even though there was an identifiable pool of skilled multilingual labor available among the employees of administrative departments, such as antiquities and public works, compelled to scale back their activities owing to the rebellion. Soldiers with "even a smattering of Arabic," usually picked up on long tours of duty in Egypt, were encouraged by their officers to take language instruction, for which the British Army introduced small incentive payments.[166] But compared to the police, professional army cadres had virtually no sense of Arab dialogue and opinion. And the police, too, became less rather than more efficient in this respect as Arab policemen— until 1936 the overwhelming majority of the rank and file—came under suspicion. To make matters worse, active-duty Arab police were always at risk of assassination, and understandably resented High Commissioner Wauchope's approval, on 26 January 1937, of proposals to recruit hundreds of Jewish auxiliary police and armed guards to perform the policing and static defense duties previously assigned to long-service Arab professionals.[167]

Security force reliance on Jewish auxiliary recruits was never officially admitted, but it was glaringly obvious. By the beginning of July 1938, more than 5,500 Jewish men had been given some military training, and 1,345 of them were employed as armed guards, largely to defend outlying Jewish settlements.[168] Three months later, on 11 September, the army command recommended another wave of recruitments. In the first instance, some two hundred Jewish auxiliaries were assigned to army units, mainly serving as security escorts for repair parties working on power lines, water pipes, and sections of railway sabotaged by the rebels.[169] More than thirteen hundred British ex-servicemen were also added to police numbers, an expedient reminiscent of the recruitment of Black and Tan units in the Anglo-Irish war.[170]

The obvious communal bias in security force recruitment of auxiliaries during the second and third years of the Palestine revolt was politically explosive and further damaged Britain's already battered prestige throughout the Muslim world. It was also an indictment of the failure of the intercommunalism supposedly central to mandatory government.[171] More pertinent to us here, the influx of Jewish irregulars and former British soldiers into the ranks of the security forces confirmed two lessons that were obvious to astute observers at the time. One was that the security of the colonial state in Palestine had rested on the services and loyalty of the Arab cadres that had previously filled the ranks of the Palestine police and the Arab Legion. The other was that once Arab cooperation was withheld, the intelligence structure of the colonial state collapsed. The intelligence state in Palestine relied on Arab intermediaries to unlock the door to influence, if not control, over indigenous Muslim opinion.

Faced with a resurgence in rebel attacks in late 1937, in January of the following year Sir Charles Tegart and his assistant, Sir David Petrie, sought an alternative means to stifle the rebellion, placing greater emphasis on foreign intelligence gathering and frontier closure. Both were convinced that the bulk of rebel attacks were organized in Syria.[172] During two days of talks on 11–12 January 1938 with Lieutenant-Colonel Gilbert MacKereth, the British consul in Damascus and a much-respected intelligence adviser, Tegart and Petrie lobbied for the assignment of a British intelligence officer to investigate the organization of Syrian support for the Palestine revolt. Acting under British consular protection, this intelligence officer would enjoy full diplomatic immunity. MacKereth blocked the plan. Levant Sûreté staff had frequently complained about the presence of Special Branch, RAF, and British Army intelligence officers operating covertly inside the French mandates. The presence of another—formally attached to the consulate— would undermine MacKereth's own efforts to cultivate ties with the Sûreté and the SR in order to secure information about the Syrian networks of support for the revolt.[173]

High Commissioner de Martel refused to lock up Palestinian exiles and their Syrian fund-raisers, actions sure to provoke a confrontation with Jamil Mardam's government and a resumption of urban protests in Damascus.[174] The Arab rank and file of the Syrian police and the Syrian Interior Ministry openly sympathized with the Palestinian cause to such an extent that they refused to assist French Sûreté agents in tracking down notorious Palestinian gang leaders known to have taken refuge in the Syrian capital.[175] The British had rejected de Martel's earlier offers to place a police cordon along the most sensitive points of the Syrian-Palestine frontier. Besides, he had agreed that his delegate in Damascus, Commandant Bonnot, would relay SR intelligence about pro-Palestinian sedition.[176]

On the one hand, MacKereth accepted that Syrian aid was critical to the rebellion and that more had to be done to stem it:

> Experience has shown that the mere collection of information in co-operation with the French Special Services [SR and Sûreté] concerning plots hatched in Damascus, the formation of terrorist bands, and the distribution of money is not in itself sufficiently dynamic to affect favorably the situation in Palestine. It has done no more than provide a fairly accurate shadow of coming events. The fact which emerges very strongly is that the Syrian authorities are by no means eager to proceed beyond assurances of sympathy and wordy nothings, and the mandatory [power] are unwilling to force their hands.[177]

On the other hand, bulldozing the French authorities into cooperation with British counterinsurgency was sure to be counterproductive. Reluctantly, Tegart gave way, promising instead to increase secret service funding for MacKereth's intelligence gathering in Damascus.[178] The search for information about how the rebels operated and how they were funded, supplied, and concealed was becoming desperate indeed.

MacKereth's abortive efforts to persuade the Beirut high commission and its Damascus delegation to clamp down on the rebellion's external backers in Syria revealed the extent to which the mandatory powers had already lost the initiative to the Arab administrations in Damascus and Beirut. Sûreté and SR officers in the Syrian capital had amassed detailed files on the local support networks for the Palestine rebellion.[179] But, with war on the horizon in early 1939, the Levant high commission was unwilling to jeopardize its fragile political truce with the National Bloc government.[180] In the event, the need for French support in combating the revolt diminished during the winter of 1938–39 as the arrival of additional reinforcements, extended curfews, and the reoccupation of the rebel strongholds in the Beersheba District gave General Haining's forces the upper hand. As Martin Kolinksy points out, a sure sign of the imminent collapse of the revolt was the resumption of a flow of intelligence from the Arab civilian population about rebel activities and arms caches.[181] By early February 1939, British efforts to bring the revolt to an end had shifted decisively once more from intelligence gathering, targeted counterinsurgency, and pressure on the Syrian support network to direct negotiations with Arab and Jewish leaders in London.[182] The role of the security services in Palestine changed commensurately, from the defeat of Arab insurgency, to the lockdown of all potential sources of political opposition, to mandatory control in the event of war.

British Territories and the Approach of War

The parallels between British and French imperial security concerns became more obvious as the risk of war in the Mediterranean loomed larger. The buildup of Italian forces in Libya and Ethiopia from 1936 onward endangered the security of Egypt and Sudan in much the same way as French Tunisia came under greater threat of invasion. The chiefs of staff, interested government departments, and Neville Chamberlain's Cabinet paid closer attention to Middle East intelligence of Italian troop movements and fleet dispositions.[183] Tortuous negotiations over the Anglo-Egyptian treaty of alliance, eventually concluded on 26 August 1936, had to take account of Wafdist demands for a clearer British commitment to the long-term defense of Egypt, and not just to the satisfaction of Britain's base requirements in the Suez Canal Zone and the port of Alexandria. The Egyptian premier Mustafa al-Nahhas and King Fuad made plain that future Egyptian military cooperation was also contingent on Britain's capacity to sustain its regional supremacy.[184] With the Royal Navy's Mediterranean fleet clearly overstretched by months of policing the League of Nations sanctions imposed on Italy for its October 1935 invasion of Abyssinia, and with the port defenses from Malta to Alexandria and Haifa still woefully inadequate to cope with a major air attack, British imperial prestige was rapidly declining.[185] The secrecy surrounding the service chiefs' 1935 Suez

Canal Defense Plan compounded Egyptians' suspicions of their imperial "protectors."[186]

In the twelve months intervening between the climax of the Czechoslovakian crisis and the outbreak of European war in September 1939, British intelligence assessment and Middle East strategic planning shifted into a higher gear. Within days of Prime Minister Chamberlain's return from the Munich conference, the Foreign Office began applying diplomatic pressure on client Arab governments from Saudi Arabia to Iraq to ensure that these states fell into line with Britain once war began.[187] During 1938–39, a standing Middle East subcommittee compiled updated regional threat assessments for the service chiefs and, through them, the Cabinet.[188]

But was the construction of a common Anglo-Arab front really viable? Intelligence assessments made since the beginning of the Palestine revolt suggested not. Abdullah's Transjordan, ostensibly the most loyal and placid of Britain's Arab client states, was also the scene of blatant vote rigging in prewar legislative council elections, and was simmering with anger over British treatment of the Palestinians.[189] From the start of the Palestine disorders in April 1936, rebel bands crossed back and forth across the Transjordan frontier, destabilizing the border regions of both countries.[190] Jordanians who were killed while fighting with rebel bands in Palestine were lauded as martyrs; those who died serving with the TJFF were often vilified as traitors and denied public funerals.[191] The loyalty of the country's leading Bedouin sheikhs depended more on the receipt of regular stipends from secret service funds than on any sense of imperial solidarity with Britain.[192]

Intelligence assessments confirmed that Arab tolerance of British imperial control was just as tenuous elsewhere. On 30 July 1936, the Foreign Office Eastern Department called for advice from British diplomatic envoys across the Arab world regarding probable local reactions to the appointment of Lord Peel's Royal Commission to investigate the causes of the Arab revolt.[193] Would the Peel Commission's endorsement of Britain's crackdown in Palestine provoke disorders in other British-controlled Muslim territories? Responses varied, but, with the exception of the Persian Gulf states, were generally pessimistic.[194] Political intelligence from Egypt's cities and provinces confirmed "that all educated and uneducated opinion . . . is convinced that Great Britain is committing a cruel injustice to a neighboring Moslem country."[195] Hashemite loyalists and Muslim communities across Iraq regarded British commitment to the creation of a Jewish national home as an act of betrayal.[196]

The contrast between Palestine's probable dismemberment under partition and the concession of national independence to the other Arab mandates, albeit still to be enacted in Syria and Lebanon, was bound to stimulate even deeper Muslim hostility to British imperialism. The Iraqi government registered its growing disdain for British policy by agreeing on an arms purchase deal with Nazi Germany in 1937, in flagrant violation of the Anglo-Iraqi treaty. The Chamberlain government responded, not with protests, but with a counteroffer to supply the Iraqi air force with additional aircraft, an indication of Britain's declining capacity to coerce its former imperial clients.[197] In November of that year, Foreign Secretary Anthony Eden connected this groundswell of Arab opposition to British policy to the pernicious influence of Italian propaganda in the Middle East. Fascist Italy and Nazi Germany had agreed on a demarcation of spheres of influence under the terms of the Rome-Berlin Axis in November 1936 that gave the Italians primary responsibility for subversion in the Arab world. As the Iraq arms agreement confirmed, this did not imply a complete German exclusion from the region, however.[198] More important, the Palestine problem had made the Arab world far more receptive to subversion than would otherwise have been the case.[199]

There was no improvement in the months ahead. On 17 December 1938, the Cairo ambassador, Sir Miles Lampson, reiterated Eden's earlier warnings. Lampson was well aware that the Egyptian political elite had been kept in the dark about the strategic implications of Britain's defense of Suez. Not only was the country bound to get sucked into the war from its beginning, it was also very likely to face attack by land and air.[200] In these circumstances, previous military intelligence, which questioned the loyalty of Egypt's fledgling national army, suggested that the British garrison would still be required to fulfill an internal policing role.[201] Analysis of public opinion in Egypt further convinced Lampson that it was crucial that the Palestinian situation be resolved "in such a way as to avoid [the] danger of its being a drain in wartime and our being faced with a hostile block of Arab countries."[202]

On 20 February 1939, the JIC, the principal Whitehall forum for the assessment of overt and covert strategic intelligence, amplified the unwelcome threat assessments received from British officials and diplomatic stations across the Middle East. The JIC concluded that the future complexion of a Palestinian state could trigger united Arab opposition to British imperial rule.[203] In light of this, how would Egyptians and Iraqis react to the news that His Majesty's government had decided unilaterally that they should enter the war as soon as it broke out, to help defend British imperial interests?[204] Did projected air attacks across the Yemen frontier, designed to deter any seizure of territory in the Aden protectorate, make sense, given the Yemeni government's indulgent attitude to Italian ambitions in the Red Sea?[205] How would Palestinian Arabs and Jews respond to the postponement of partition and the replacement of garrison forces with other imperial troops?[206] Would the Sudanese tolerate internal travel restrictions and the presence of roving columns of British forces as efforts were made to meet the threat from neighboring Italian East Africa? And what would be the reaction across the Arab world to state of siege regulations and the disruption of commerce and trade that were bound to follow the opening of hostilities?

Military intelligence analysts, diplomats in the field, and the British strategic planning staff who acted on their advice were much exercised by the probable consequences of these and other coercive measures expected to accompany any shift to wartime imperial rule. On 16 February 1939, the Committee of Imperial Defence, the senior civil-military strategic advisory committee to the Cabinet, proposed a number of "sweeteners" designed to ease this transition. The Iraqi government would be offered financial compensation for the loss of oil revenues in wartime. Payment would be assured for the use of the country's defensive facilities, particularly in the vicinity of the Abadan oilfields. The British Resident in Amman was to reactivate the old secret service funds, from which regular subsidies to key tribal sheikhs would be paid as necessary. Far larger subsidies—twenty times larger, to be precise—were authorized for payment to senior figures in the Saudi regime. Further special intelligence funds were also to be created for disbursement among the emirates in the Persian Gulf.[207] The newly established Ministry of Information was to coordinate a propaganda drive to highlight the shared interests of Britain and its Arab partners in fighting the Axis.[208] Limited initiatives such as these were unlikely to sway indigenous opinion. Diminished personal freedoms, the stifling of political activity, and the arbitrary detention of popular local politicians only deepened Arab hostility to British imperialism. Severe rationing restrictions and the very real prospect that Arab lands would once again become a battleground for competing imperialist powers made the political climate worse still.

Conclusion

The unique problems of imperial order in the fast-changing and unstable intercommunal environment of mandatory Palestine left the Jerusalem high commission struggling to cope with the social, political, and cultural consequences of increasing Jewish immigration. In periods of acute unrest, whether the episodic urban rioting of the 1920s or the more protracted rural rebellion of the late 1930s, British security services were constrained by high commission anxieties about the long-term political consequences of police intervention or unbridled military counterinsurgency.[209] But if the security forces felt constricted by the high commission's political concerns, a bigger challenge was to understand the indigenous society being policed. Here the security services fell short. Intelligence gathering in mandatory Palestine always meant, first and foremost, the acquisition of reliable, exploitable humint. Time and again, such information was either totally lacking or highly pessimistic.

On the morning that German tanks rolled across the border into Poland, the Foreign Office Eastern Department was assessing another series of responses from Middle Eastern capitals concerning likely local reaction to the planned arrests of the mufti of Jerusalem and his leading aides. Once again, British officials in Cairo, Baghdad, and, on this occasion, Damascus warned that all available intelligence indicated that such "drastic action" could compromise Britain and France's ability to carry their Arab client states with them into war.[210] In the event, on 3 September 1939 the Egyptian and Iraqi governments chose not to follow Britain into declaring war on Germany, although diplomatic and trade relations with Berlin were severed and German nationals were interned. Neither state showed any enthusiasm for direct military involvement.[211] Events took a similar course in Amman, although Abdullah and several leading sheikhs did offer to play a more active role in hostilities.[212]

The cracks in Britain's Middle East empire, hastily papered over in 1939, proved impossible to conceal. The British would adopt different strategies of looser political control with client states in the Middle East after 1945. Generally built around negotiated treaty rights and continued support for monarchical elites facing increased isolation and internal opposition, these efforts met with limited success. World War II had brought the intelligence state era of British colonial control to an end. Postwar imperial security policy and intelligence gathering were very different in circumstances of imminent decolonization, burgeoning Arab nationalism, and, in the last years of the Palestine mandate, undeclared civil war.[213]

DOMESTIC POLITICS, INTERNATIONAL THREATS, AND COLONIAL SECURITY IN FRENCH TERRITORIES, 1936–1939

As war approached, the job of the colonial security official became increasingly daunting as local challenges to order became more closely entwined with wider strategic threats to imperial stability. In the 1930s, French security services expanded in response to mounting official fears of nationalist opposition, labor unrest, Islamic radicalism, and Communist subversion. By 1936, even colonial governors loyal to Lyautey's principles of indirect rule, such as Charles Noguès in Morocco, Marcel Peyrouton in Tunisia, and Comte Damien de Martel in Beirut, were forced to concede that the associationist ideal of colonial policies devised to ensure harmonious Franco-Muslim coexistence was a figment of the imagination. Wishful thinking could not conceal the acute economic hardships and communal divisions apparent in French-ruled territories from Damascus to Rabat.

Summarizing a tour of inspection in early April 1937, Raoul Aubaud, the Interior Ministry undersecretary with special responsibility for Algerian affairs, made the following statement: "Algeria is an extremely sensitive echo chamber; the least word, the smallest [political] gesture has immediate repercussions, sometimes unforeseen, of which metropolitan France knows nothing. We are dealing with a very discerning, impressionable population, and we must avoid saying or doing things without due reflection."[1] Coming after days of talks with security service officers, Aubaud's warning mirrored their anxiety about Muslim dissent. The sensitivity of the Algerian situation was fairly typical. As we shall see in this chapter, the years 1936 to 1939 witnessed a sharp rise in security concerns throughout France's Muslim territories, a rise that paralleled Britain's deepening imperial problems in Palestine. Unlike the British case, however, the immediate spur to crisis in the French Empire was metropolitan in origin.

The Popular Front Comes to Power

In May 1936, an antifascist coalition was elected to power in France. The Popular Front government transformed nationalist politics in French North Africa and Syria, promoting a freer atmosphere, exemplified by amnesties of political prisoners, a surge in trade union activity, and widespread urban demonstrations. The sharp change of political direction following the election of the Popular Front was bound to release pent-up tensions among colonial immigrants and their communities of origin in North Africa. Socialist Party leader Léon Blum's accession to the premiership coincided with the recognition among France's imperial intelligence communities that internal opposition in North Africa and the Levant was increasing, not declining.

Blum's new ministry was dominated by the Socialist Party, which fared well in the spring 1936 national election, and by the Radical-Socialist Party, which did not. For the first time in its fifteen-year history, the French Communist Party (PCF) lent parliamentary support to the government, although leaders of the PCF still refused ministerial posts. As a result, Blum's government was the first interwar coalition since the short-lived Cartel des Gauches ministry of 1924 that was ideologically situated on the left of the French political spectrum. The point should not be overstressed. Very quickly, the Radicals became unnerved by the surge in worker protests across French cities, although these were more carnival than revolution. Radical Party grandees, key architects of the centrism traditionally dominant in the late Third Republic, therefore exerted a moderating influence, both within Blum's Cabinet and from the benches of the Senate. The upper house remained unashamedly hostile to the Popular Front's social spending, industrial reforms, and financial management. In June 1937, barely a year after Blum took office, his ministry collapsed after a Senate vote denied the government special powers to cope with a mounting debt crisis and severe downward pressure on the franc.[2]

So densely packed are the domestic crises and achievements of the Popular Front—from industrial strife to improved worker rights, enforced currency devaluation to systematic long-term rearmament, bourgeois fear of revolution to cultural renaissance—that its colonial policies have, until recently, been confined to the historical shadows. There is now a greater awareness of the government's limited scope for colonial reform, tempered by recognition that none of the governing parties were strongly committed to it.[3] Whatever its liberal inclinations, the Popular Front was, at root, as imperialist as its predecessors. Colonial reforms were devised in order to revitalize the colonial relationship, not to overturn it. Changes to colonial franchises, wider access to citizenship, investigative welfare missions, and social policy think tanks shared this fundamental goal. Ultimately, few reforms reached the statute book.[4]

The fact remains that the Popular Front is central to the interwar history of France's intelligence states in North Africa and Syria. The hopes it aroused in nationalist circles and the fear and loathing it inspired among imperial administrations go a long way to explaining this. So, too, do the specific policy pledges made. These included an extended Muslim male franchise in Algeria and a continuation of negotiations for treaties of independence in Lebanon and Syria. But less spectacular Popular Front reforms in two other policy areas made a more immediate impact on colonial order. These were the release of Muslim political prisoners and the gradual transfer to French North Africa and the Levant mandates of the industrial reforms enacted in France under the Matignon Accords of June 1936.[5] The former reinvigorated nationalist organizations across the region; the latter precipitated an explosion in worker militancy and trade union activism. As the measures enacted by the Popular Front were steadily rolled back from 1937 onward, more repressive intelligence state structures were put in place. The rest of this chapter investigates how this process occurred.

Nationalist Protest and the Security Response in French North Africa

Algeria

In what had become a familiar pattern, once the Popular Front took office, security analysts in Paris and the Maghreb superimposed the political polarization of metropolitan France and the specter of Communist infiltration onto the entirely different political map of North Africa. Within weeks of the May 1936 election, the War Ministry deuxième bureau was reassessing the influence of the PCF in the Maghreb and updating its files on known Communist organizers in North Africa's cities. The PCF maintained a regional bureau in Algiers, as did International Red Aid, commonly reckoned to be a Comintern front organization.[6] But neither aroused as much suspicion as Messali Hadj's Étoile Nord-Africaine (ENA). By December, the army staff's colonial intelligence section had persuaded itself that the ENA was the core element of a Communist-nationalist coalition controlled by the Comintern and coordinated by Spanish republicans determined to spread Spain's civil strife across the Maghreb.[7] To judge by their silence on this topic, Sûreté officers were more skeptical. It was thus the Service de Renseignements (SR) analysis center in Algiers that produced most threat assessments evaluating sources of sedition in North Africa.[8] In the Popular Front years, as before, it reported contacts among ENA activists, other Maghrebi nationalist groups, and the Association of Reformist 'Ulamā to the War and Interior Ministries and the government's new specialist advisory panel, the Mediterranean high committee.

Army analysts' preoccupation with the ENA's external links, and disagreement among civil and military security services over the ideological wellsprings and social constituencies of Algerian nationalism, were workaday features of the office politics of the Algiers intelligence agencies. Continuities were apparent in the intelligence assumptions of those involved, for whom surveillance and repression of the ENA were driven by several overlapping concerns. First was the mounting evidence of the party's inroads among young immigrant workers, whose militancy and organizational prowess shocked the security services. The ENA's membership was reckoned at four thousand at the time of the 1929 ban, a figure high enough to stir fears that a praetorian guard of radical nationalists existed that could spread havoc once they returned to Algeria. This linked to a second anxiety: the ENA's red tinge. Party rhetoric drew on the language of class antagonism and leftist anticolonialism, both of which acquired a sharper edge in the harsh economic conditions of the 1930s.[9] The ENA's organizational methods aped those of the PCF and the Communist trade union movement, the Confédération Générale du Travail Unitaire.

The development of the Popular Front between 1934 and 1936 added credibility to this estimation of a surreptitious Communist connection. Messali's enthusiastic endorsement of the Rassemblement Populaire, the broad antifascist coalition that took shape in 1934–35 to campaign for a Popular Front government, seemed to vindicate those in the French intelligence community who insisted that he and his followers were Communist wolves dressed in nationalist sheep's clothing. Most worrying, to the War Ministry deuxième bureau especially, were reports of ENA supporters establishing Communist-style party cells among the Algerian regiments of the Armée d'Afrique.[10]

The election of Blum's government in May 1936 enabled Messali to resume political activity in France and, to an unprecedented degree, Algeria. By October 1936, the ENA claimed eleven thousand paid-up members, grouped into thirty sections. The rapidity of the ENA's growth skewed security service analysis still further. SR, the Paris Renseignements Généraux, and the Algiers Sûreté focused on the party's expanded sphere of political activity rather than the Messalists' acrimonious split with the Communist parties in France and Algeria. By the summer of 1936, the ENA program was far more nationalist than Communist.[11] Yet a spate of Algiers SR reports led the then minister of national defense, Edouard Daladier, to advise his Interior Ministry colleague Jules Moch on Christmas Eve 1936 that "in Algeria the combined action of the 'ulamā, the ENA and the Communist Party become more menacing as each day passes."[12]

As Daladier's alarmist comment suggests, SR assessments compiled in Algiers and Paris predicted that Messali Hadj would play the religious card, exploiting his relationship with the 'ulamā leader 'Abd al-Hamīd Ben Bādīs to encourage Muslim resistance to French rule.[13] Both men had successfully mobilized Muslim opinion, making eastern Algeria in particular an epicenter of an integral nationalism that championed Muslim cultural identity.[14] On this, military intelligence was certainly right, as it was in its conclusion that both Messali and Ben Bādīs were strongly influenced by Shakib Arslan, still the bête noire of the Maghreb security agencies. SR based this deduction on analysis of Arslan's travel itinerary and intercepted correspondence, in addition to the writings, statements, and teachings of the leadership of the ENA and the Association of Reformist 'Ulamā.[15]

Other security service conclusions had less evidential support. As popular antagonism to the security forces deepened, SR reliance on informants' reports, often of dubious authenticity, compounded the tendency to exaggerate the threat of sedition. A notable instance of this occurred in Constantine following the outbreak of the anti-Semitic violence in and around the town in August 1934.[16] Before and after the August outbreak, intelligence from informants about local Arab militancy meshed with native affairs service reports of settler farmers selling everything and leaving as a consequence of the Depression to produce an image of a *département* on the brink of rebellion.[17]

It was largely because of this continuing dependency on humint from local informants that SR and Sûreté personnel in Algeria frequently sent contradictory messages to Paris about the probability of colonial revolt. Most SR and Sûreté officers recognized the tensions between secular nationalism, settler-based Communism, and the Islamic revivalism of Ben Bādīs's followers. Indeed, the largest party political gatherings in Algeria during the Popular Front period had little to do with the ENA or the 'ulamā. Dr. Mohamed-Salah Bendjelloul's Fédération des Elus Musulmans, an elite group founded in 1927 and committed to closer Franco-Algerian integration, drew crowds of up to nine thousand supporters in the Constantine department, Bendjelloul's regional stronghold. And Colonel de la Rocque's July 1937 tour of ultrarightist Parti Social Français (PSF) strongholds in Algiers, Bône, Constantine, and Orléansville attracted similar numbers of settler supporters.[18] Accustomed to viewing local political developments through the prism of French politics, SR and Sûreté assessments of indigenous opinion were distorted by a mixture of racial and class stereotyping. Only Algeria's educated Arab and Berber minorities were judged capable of sustained political engagement. Because it originated in the settler community, the racist violence of the PSF seemed less dangerous than the ENA's nonviolent integral nationalism.

Although dismissive of ordinary Algerians' capacity for autonomous political endeavor, the local police and military intelligence services did concur that Islamic revivalism could mobilize mass opposition to French rule.[19] Islamic teaching in madrassas, or "free schools," was, as always, closely monitored.[20] The Sûreté, individual mayoral offices, and the interministerial commission on Muslim affairs in Paris took an especially close interest in the schools' development.[21] By the time the Association of Reformist 'Ulamā convened for its annual congress in Algiers in October 1935, the teachings of Ben Bādīs's followers were linked to a more militant cultural exclusivity propagated through the growing number of religious schools offering free tuition to young Muslims.[22] During the 1934–35 school year, the Association of Reformist 'Ulamā controlled at least seventy such "free schools," with a total enrollment of between three and five thousand students. Additional Koranic schools were opening all the time, which, as noted earlier, caused alarm in security service circles because of the reformists' claim to exclusive and sacred cultural authority.[23] These madrassas were accused of inculcating a Wahhabite-style fundamentalism alien to Algerian Muslim tradition.

Anxious to find a pretext for the repression of Muslim teaching in a colony where the separation of church and state theoretically remained in force, the Algiers military intelligence bureau began to distinguish between "good" and "bad" Islamic observance. The upsurge in Islamic fundamentalism was thought to be a purely urban phenomenon. This association of radical Islam with the politics of the Arab street in Maghreb cities was soon strengthened by an unexpected turn of events. On 2 August 1936, Bendali Mahmoud, the mufti of the Algiers Grand Mosque, was fatally stabbed by a hired killer allegedly paid by Mahmoud's rival, Sheikh Tayeb el-Okbi, Biskra's leading 'ulamā and a longtime contact of Messali Hadj. Factional feuding, long a feature of Algerian urban Islam, had reached its violent apogee. The security services seized the moment, using the murder to justify a ban on the Association of Reformist 'Ulamā and tighter restrictions on the contents of Friday prayers in the mosques of Algeria's principal towns and cities.[24]

Beyond the urban environment, the security services calculated that Algeria's peasantry was wedded to a more tolerant and malleable Islamic tradition.[25] An SR intelligence summary from Kabylia for April 1935 was typical in this regard. Local politics, it claimed, were dominated by the consequences of a poor fruit crop, the repatriation from France of unemployed immigrant workers, and three years of tax increases. Organized nationalism and Islamic radicalism were dismissed as peripheral, and even immigrant returnees lost their interest in political activism once they settled back into their local community.[26] SR reports relayed from Algiers to Paris echoed these findings. Any short-term crisis of French authority in Algeria was primarily economic in origin. In the countryside at least, the long-term "evolution" of indigenous politics consequent on rising living standards and more widespread basic education posed the greater security challenge. Hence the importance of cultivating a loyal, educated elite to steer Muslims toward constructive political engagement.[27]

Informed by this crude economic determinism, SR intelligence predicted that as the Maghreb emerged from the worst of the Depression after 1935, the potential for rebellion should diminish. There was genuine surprise in the Algiers SR when supporters of the Parti Populaire Algérien (PPA)—the new incarnation of the recently dissolved ENA—clashed with police sent to break up a PPA meeting prohibited by the prefecture on 29 September 1937. What caused alarm was not the intensity of the violence, but the fact that several hundred Algerian workers were willing to risk injury and imprisonment to defend their right of assembly.[28]

In a similar vein, the Algiers SR reacted with astonishment in late January 1937 when leaders of the Algerian Muslim ex-servicemen's association petitioned the colony's deputies and mayors to demand changes to French citizenship requirements and attendant voting rights.[29] Wider Muslim access to citizenship was the central pillar of the Popular Front's so-called Blum-Viollette project. The project as originally conceived by Minister of State Maurice Viollette, a former Algiers governor, was intended to enfranchise a maximum of twenty-five thousand Algerian Muslim citizens.[30] As matters stood, however, those Algerian males eligible for citizenship of the secular French Republic thanks to educational qualification or public service had first to renounce their personal status as Muslims, a prerequisite that was anathema to the faithful. Furthermore, if, as threatened, the entire membership of the ex-servicemen's association claimed full citizenship rights, the Algiers government would be swamped with sixty thousand applications for naturalization. This it was determined to prevent. Security service officers reacted rather differently. What shocked them was not the matter at hand, but the strength of Muslim political conviction, this time among a constituency—former soldiers—usually depicted as socially responsible and politically conservative.[31]

Tunisia

Similar characterizations of nationalist organization and Arab unrest were apparent among the intelligence community in neighboring Tunisia. Here, too, the SR discerned international conspiracies variously involving local nationalists, pan-Arab militants, German and Italian propagandists, Comintern agents, and European arms traffickers.[32] It was no coincidence that these reports began to appear after the establishment of the counterespionage section attached to the Tunis Sûreté Générale in May 1930 (discussed later in this chapter). This section drew its intelligence from local agents who served the country's five regional police headquarters.[33] It was only a matter of time before an agency assigned to monitor illegal immigration, the loyalties of Tunisia's large Italian community, and the politics of Destourian nationalism should conflate all three into a single threat to French rule.

In September 1934, the Tunis *Tribune correctionnel* sent eight members of the Néo-Destour executive into internal exile for seditious activity. The eight were accused of fomenting urban protest and violent attacks on protectorate institutions.[34] The executive members were reinterned within days of their release twelve months later, this time for alleged collaboration with three local Communists accused of distributing seditious pamphlets to workers in and around the capital.[35]

Only the arrival of a new, more liberal resident general to replace the hard-line Marcel Peyrouton signaled a brief end to this legal merry-go-round of Sûreté evidence gathering, arrest, and detention of the Néo-Destour leadership. A Popular Front enthusiast, Armand Guillon was a former prefect in northern France who came to Tunis with a distinguished background in public health administration. He was quicker than his fellow North African governors to apply the Blum Cabinet's directive to grant amnesty to political prisoners. Differing rates of prisoner releases stemmed from the minister of colonies Marius Moutet's willingness to allow local administrations substantial leeway to apply the amnesty in light of prevailing political conditions. Moutet did, however, make plain that he expected the rhythm of such amnesties to pick up, indicating that he would personally review the dossiers of those political detainees still incarcerated in Vietnam, Madagascar, and elsewhere.[36] Foreign Minister Yvon Delbos, a Radical Party veteran renowned as a legal specialist, does not appear to have exerted similar pressure in the North African protectorates or the Levant mandates. The Tunisian nationalist internees released en bloc from their internal exile in the southern military district during May 1936 had Guillon to thank for their freedom.[37]

The upsurge in political violence in Tunisia mirrored the Popular Front's fortunes closely, a pattern discerned and exploited by Guillon's security service opponents. The introduction in France of industrial legislation over the summer of 1936, including the legalization of collective bargaining, labor contracts, and a forty-hour week, had immediate impact in Tunisia's cities, boosting Muslim support for the Confédération Générale du Travailleurs Tunisiens (CGTT), a trade union confederation already linked to its Communist-controlled French equivalent. Guillon's liberality toward political prisoners also allowed the Néo-Destour executive committee, led by Bourguiba, to reorganize after the preceding three years of severe repression at the hands of Peyrouton and his Sûreté allies. The effects of this release program became apparent only in August, when Guillon enacted further Popular Front reforms, this time lifting legal restrictions on political meetings, Muslims' right of assembly, trade union activity, and censorship of the Arabic press. He also curbed police powers to impose fines and short jail terms for minor criminal misdemeanors by Muslim subjects.[38] Demonstrators were now less likely to face arbitrary arrest by Garde républicaine mobile riot police at the first sign of a protest march.

A month later, Bourguiba set out Néo-Destour priorities at the first rally authorized under Guillon's more permissive regime. Almost certainly exaggerating, the settler press claimed that up to fifteen thousand party supporters gathered in Gambetta Park, a derelict amusement park in the capital.[39] The central tenets of the Néo-Destour program—an extended Muslim franchise in local and national elections, an equitable income tax structure, free and comprehensive primary education, and equal pay for European and Muslim employees—were hardly incendiary demands.[40] Indeed, Bourguiba's fellow executive members, Dr. Mahmoud Materi, Dr. Sliman Ben Sliman, Tahar Sfar, Bahri Guiga, and even the radical Salah Ben Youssef, were at pains to stress their loyalty to the beylical state and their belief in Franco-Tunisian partnership. In calling for an end to all settler privilege, from electoral rights to fiscal policy, however, their political platform fundamentally challenged the colonial order.[41]

Guillon's term as resident general marked a brief respite in police repression rather than an unalterable commitment to reform: the crackdown on nationalist activity resumed in March 1937, with violent clashes between police and shipyard workers at Métline near Bizerta in which six protesters were killed.[42] There was worse carnage in the iron ore and phosphate mines of southern Tunisia, where Senegalese troops and local gendarmerie shot dead sixteen strikers.[43] The cycle of wildcat strikes and demonstrations cut short by security force violence continued throughout the summer. Intercommunal tensions had become caught up in the ideological polarization symptomatic of the Popular Front era.

Events in Tunis on Bastille Day 1937 brought matters particularly close to home for the close-knit community of professional administrators and senior Armée d'Afrique personnel in the capital. The annual July 14th military parade always conveyed an overtly colonialist message. The march-past of white-officered colonial troops and *spahi* cavalry was meant to remove any doubt about where real power lay. This year, however, events took a different course. As the rhythmic clatter of boots and hooves receded, hundreds of Communist supporters poured onto the streets. They jammed the capital's central avenues in a rowdy protest punctuated by clenched fist salutes and verses of *L'Internationale*. The demonstrators were soon trading insults with a group of smartly dressed French women, who had watched the earlier review from a café terrace. Mainly officers' wives, they were not easily intimidated; indeed, the women responded in kind, allegedly with fascist salutes and cries of "*A bas les Juifs*," "*Vive la France*," and, in a few cases, "*Vive le Roi*." The café was later vandalized.[44]

Lest this be dismissed as an isolated incident, as the summer of 1937 turned to autumn, French North Africa's political violence went from bad to worse. In Tunis, the combination of unrelenting settler criticism and warnings from regional *contrôleurs civils* that the security forces were severely overstretched sent Residency policy into headlong retreat.[45] This led, in turn, to a radicalization of Néo-Destour demands, played out in the pages of the party newspaper, *El Amel* (*Action*) and monitored by the SR.[46] The eclipse of Guillon's reformist initiatives produced a rift among the party leadership, which left Bourguiba in sole charge of party strategy by November 1937.[47] He was determined to exploit worker grievances, his CGTT connections, the demonstrative power of nationalist youth groups and women's movements, and Néo-Destour's grassroots support among Tunisia's peasantry to mobilize mass opposition. With the security services anxious to reaffirm their place at the heart of policy formulation after Guillon's departure, a decisive showdown looked inevitable.[48]

General Charles Hanote, the commander of land forces in Tunisia, warned on 1 December that evidence of increased arms smuggling in Tunisia indicated that disorders could break out as soon as the protectorate moved to a war footing.[49] As if to confirm his suspicions, police raids in late December 1937 on the homes of Néo-Destour supporters in Tunis, Monastir, and Zaghouan yielded numerous caches of explosives, guns, and ammunition.[50] In fact, it was the Algiers SR that set in train this spate of arms seizures after their undercover agents purchased the first in a consignment of fifteen hundred Italian revolvers that had been offered for sale to Maghrebi nationalists by an arms dealer in Marseilles.[51] Reports from the Algiers Section de Centralisation du Renseignement (SCR) of additional arms finds in January 1938—variously seized from sources as diverse as Italian steamers docked in Maghreb ports to camel trains traversing the southern reaches of Morocco, Algeria, and Tunisia—lent weight to SR concern that North African nationalist movements not only received support from the Axis powers, but might launch an uprising to coincide with an Italian land invasion from Libya.[52]

Morocco

The cycle of greater state violence in response to increasing nationalist militancy, so apparent in Tunisia, was also repeated in Morocco. Here, too, the pattern of worsening security force confrontations with urban nationalists left Popular Front supporters unable to contest security service accusations that premature announcements of reform had unlocked a Pandora's box of pent-up Muslim hostility to protectorate rule. Between 14 and 17 November 1936, mass meetings were convened in Casablanca, Salé, and Fez in support of the National Action Bloc's 1934 demands for franchise reform. The police broke up these demonstrations and arrested more than 150 alleged ringleaders.[53] Over the winter of 1937–38, the Residency cracked down on Muslim political dissent and industrial unrest across northern Morocco. The first to feel the effects were Action Bloc supporters, by then reorganized into the Moroccan Action Party.[54]

The attitude of General Noguès's Residency toward the Action Bloc was determined by intelligence analysis of the movement's capacity to mobilize mass opposition in Morocco's urban centers.[55] Over the course of 1937, a series of alarming SR and Sûreté assessments, most of them based on agents' surveillance of secret political meetings, indicated that the Action Bloc/Party coordinated protests in much the same way as the Néo-Destour. Native affairs reports from rural districts confirmed this, revealing mounting peasant support for the Action Party program.[56] Indications that the rural population was neither as conservative nor as deferential to chiefly authority as previously assumed unsettled Residency officials, who knew that police resources were stretched to the limit maintaining order in the towns.[57] Noguès therefore reacted swiftly: on 18 March 1937 he signed a decree outlawing the Moroccan Action Party.

The March decree provided the legal pretext for a series of additional restrictions implemented by the security forces in the year ahead. It was not until the summer of 1937, however, that the rhythm of state repression really quickened. During July and August, the resident general and his deputy, Jean Morize, used Sûreté and SR intelligence to make the case for the complete proscription of nationalist activity. Their most damning evidence came from an unexpected source. Correspondence supplied by *makhzen* officials acting on the sultan's behalf confirmed Sûreté intelligence that the Action Party had remained active after the March ban and was rebuilding its support network in the towns of northern Morocco.[58] Armed with this information, the security forces went on high alert.

Matters came to a head in the northern city of Meknès on 2 September 1937. Meknès had not been considered a particularly difficult city to police. Yet the mood among the city's Muslims was particularly volatile at the time, following a decision by the municipal authorities to divert the nearby Boufekrane River to irrigate European farms, allegedly depriving Meknès of precious water resources. Action Party activists began a campaign in the local press claiming that the irrigation scheme was part of a Residency plan to enrich settler farmers at the expense of Muslim town dwellers and outlying smallholders. The allegations resonated among Meknès traders, who had yet to experience much sign of economic recovery after long years of Depression.[59] Official denials of any underhanded scheme made no impact. The appointment of a mixed commission to investigate the claims, chaired by the pasha of Meknès and the head of the city's municipal services, also backfired. Demonstrators gathered outside the commission offices, chanting, "They've taken our water—not a drop of it to the settlers!" The pasha

tried, but failed, to appease the crowd. Police snatch squads then intervened, arresting the protest organizers. Four of those detained were colleagues of the Action Party leader, Allal al-Fassi, and another, Si Mohamed
Berrada, was linked to el Fassi's main party rival, Mohammed Hassan al-
Ouezzani, a longtime associate of Shakib Arslan.[60]

It was the appearance of these individuals before a city court on 2
September that provoked a day of bloody clashes. News that the pasha's tribunal had handed down three-month jail sentences spread quickly through
the medina. Demonstrators persuaded some shopkeepers and business
owners—and cajoled others—into shutting down. A meeting hastily convened in the city's main mosque urged people to gather outside the pasha's
residence, where the prisoners were being held. Stones rained down on the
building and on the police lines outside it, and several revolver shots were
fired. When protesters tried to storm the gates, the army intervened. Mounted
spahis drove the crowd off the main thoroughfares during repeated charges
between ten and eleven-thirty in the morning. Foreign Legion reinforcements pursued the protesters into the back alleys. Thirteen Muslims were
killed and at least fifty injured. The cycle of intelligence collection, arrests,
and repression had turned especially vicious.

Several Jewish-owned businesses across Meknès were looted in the subsequent street battles, orchestrated, according to the SR, "by an enormous
mob of fanatical natives." Three pronationalist newspapers, *L'Action populaire*, *L'Action*, and *El Atlas*, were shut down days later.[61] Less violent demonstrations continued in other Moroccan cities during September and
October 1937, until most senior nationalist leaders were either arrested or
exiled.[62] Suppression of the Action Party's protest campaign completed the
reversal of the reforms promised by the Popular Front and kept the security
services at the center of government in Rabat as French Morocco geared up
for war in 1939.

In Algeria, by 1937 the colonial authorities were determined to clamp
down on dissent, convinced by SR and Sûreté intelligence that political violence would only escalate unless stricter security measures were enacted.
Careful analysis of the Arabic press, coordinated by Commandant Le
Forestier de Quillen, the head of the Algiers SR analysis center, revealed the
depth of Muslim antagonism toward the colonial government as Popular
Front reforms were jettisoned.[63] A recent article by Ben Bādīs in a leading
Arabic review was taken as proof that the 'ulamā leadership was moving
inexorably closer to militant rejection of the colonial regime. Even Bend-
jelloul's more moderate Federation of Elected Muslims threatened to resign
en masse from their local and national seats in protest at the collapse of the
Blum-Viollette project.[64] But it was the rearrest in August 1937 of Messali
Hadj and senior members of the PPA executive that heralded the end of the
freer atmosphere created during the Popular Front interlude. These arrests

were soon followed by ugly clashes at the Ouenza iron ore mines between Muslim miners and paramilitary Garde républicaine mobile units.[65]

Deuxième bureau analysts at the Algiers army command interpreted these events as the long-anticipated confluence of integral nationalism, Islamic revivalism, and industrial strife. The only element still left out of this volatile mixture was sedition among Muslim colonial troops. Armée d'Afrique officers were duly placed on heightened alert to watch for any signs of unrest among the Muslim rank-and-file.[66] The reformist 'ulamās' subsequent endorsement of Messalist candidates in cantonal elections held across Algeria on 17 October 1937 added weight to these security concerns. PPA activists focused their efforts on Algiers, Tizi-Ouzou, Blida, Médéa, and Tlemcen: all seats previously held by the party executive members arrested three months earlier. The October local elections were thus transformed into a plebiscite on the security crackdown of the late summer. The PPA registered strong electoral gains in the department of Algiers as more affluent voters and 'ulamā supporters deserted moderate parties to register their solidarity with the PPA "martyrs" in detention.[67]

Unable to operate freely, those PPA organizers who had escaped arrest changed tactics after the October 1937 elections. Street demonstrations, public meetings, and the drive to increase party membership gave way to more clandestine techniques designed to frustrate security service surveillance. The volume of party correspondence decreased dramatically and local PPA sections were restructured into smaller, clandestine cells, whose members were kept informed only about political activity in their immediate area.[68] By 1938, years of repression by the Algerian intelligence state had turned the PPA into a revolutionary organization.[69]

French North Africa and the Approach of War

By the time Edouard Daladier's Radical-dominated coalition took office on 10 April 1938, the Algiers SR complained that the extensive security crackdown left it with little reliable information about nationalist activity that had been driven underground.[70] SR personnel were reduced to scrutinizing weekly Arabic press bulletins for insights into nationalist preoccupations.[71] Their lack of sources aside, military intelligence analysts seemed satisfied with the restoration of "calm" across Algeria.[72]

It was a different story in Tunisia, where the security forces had been called out more frequently than in any other of France's Muslim territories during the Popular Front interlude of 1936–38. This pattern was set to continue until the outbreak of war. In late March 1938, Tunis students at Sadiki College and the university attached to Zitaouna Mosque, the principal centers of advanced learning for Tunisian Muslims, took to the streets in protest at the arrest of a lecturer for seditionist preaching. Student protests chimed with Néo-Destour plans for a general strike. In early April 1938, the daily clashes between students and police in Tunis meshed with the nationalists' call-out of Muslim workers. On 9 April, protesters fought a running battle with Garde républicaine mobile units that had been ordered to prevent students' efforts to storm the Palais de Justice, where the Sadiki lecturer was in custody.[73] Troops were called out to help restore order. Once again, the disorders ended tragically, if predictably, with security forces firing on the crowd. At least twenty-two died, probably many more. But Daladier's government was in no mood to apologize. Instead, the Cabinet reacted vigorously to what was its first serious colonial challenge. General Hanote assumed plenary powers under state of siege restrictions enacted in Tunis, Sousse, and Grombalia, the districts most affected by the violence. Néo-Destour found itself outlawed once more.[74]

The lifting of martial law restrictions five months later, on 17 August 1938, did not signal a change of heart toward the nationalist opposition. Political associations and processions were authorized, but only within the confines of decree legislation that forbade any expression of dissent. The Arabic press was also muzzled more tightly. Newspapers faced unlimited suspension rather than the temporary shutdowns that had been the standard punishment for pronationalist editorial policy. Hanote and the new resident, Eiric Labonne, who had been appointed to succeed Guillon in October 1938, were determined to choke off any Néo-Destour recovery, keeping the senior leadership, regional organizers, and hundreds of grassroots activists in detention. In a bid to stem nationalist penetration of the countryside, where the agricultural economy remained in deep recession, the Residency raised the minimum wage for farm workers and instituted a scheme to create rural councils (*associations communales*) to draw more politically active Muslims into the lower echelons of local government.[75]

The state's central concern with Tunisian nationalism continued throughout 1939. In the weeks preceding the German occupation of Prague on 15 March, the Tunis Residency was, as ever, preoccupied by what should be done with Habib Bourguiba. The Néo-Destour leader had been imprisoned awaiting a court appearance since the fatal rioting of 9 April 1938. Decisions had to be made about his future. The protectorate authorities were reluctant to stage a high-profile political trial in an atmosphere of high international tension.[76] Allegations about Bourguiba's relationship with the Rome government added to security service concerns. Large sums of Italian-supplied cash were reportedly found during a Sûreté search of Bourguiba's house, lending credibility to claims that he was in the pay of fascist envoys.[77] In the event, the Residency steered a middle course. Around six hundred of the less important political prisoners were amnestied by beylical decree in April 1939, but the leaders of Néo-Destour arrested after the disturbances a year earlier remained in detention.[78]

As the probability of war increased in 1938–39, perennial military worries about the loyalty of colonial troops also intensified. Ever since the countdown to the Rif War in 1924–25, the army corps commands in Morocco and Algeria had anticipated some degree of public disorder once a general mobilization was decreed.[79] But only after 1936 did they express serious anxiety about the loyalty of professional units. Two concerns stood out. The first was the worrying increase in nationalist and Communist pamphleteering among garrisons of North African soldiers in France, the Maghreb, and Syria. The second was the realization that many Maghrebi junior officers were intensely frustrated at their lack of promotion prospects within the racially codified hierarchy of the officer corps. In response, the War Ministry authorized a stricter segregation of Armée d'Afrique garrisons from the surrounding civilian population.[80] The North African counterespionage bureaus set up in early 1938 also submitted regular intelligence assessments of army morale.[81] At the close of the interwar period, much as at the beginning, the foundations of imperial order remained decidedly shaky. Not only was popular protest, labor militancy, and organized nationalism more pressing, but the linchpin of colonial order—the security forces themselves—were coming under suspicion.

State surveillance in France's Arab territories further expanded over the summer of 1939. Three PPA leaders, Messali Hadj among them, were released from prison in Algiers on 27 August. This show of clemency, however, was not what it first appeared. The police spéciale immediately tracked the movements of the former detainees, taking particular note of any conversations or meetings held. All visitors to Messali's Algiers home at 15 rue François Villar were meticulously recorded, providing Sûreté officers with a long, up-to-the-minute list of potential suspects. The visitor roll included four government-general employees among the thousand or so who visited the house in the first twenty-four hours after the PPA leader's release.[82]

As soon as it became public knowledge that Messali and his colleagues were to be freed, PPA supporters came onto the streets of Algeria's towns and cities, holding impromptu gatherings—more street celebration than organized campaigning—in defiance of the government ban on nationalist meetings. Much to police annoyance, portrait cards of Messali Hadj with the Algerian nationalist hymn on the reverse seemed to appear everywhere. Additional police informants were deployed in nationalist organizers' favored meeting places in anticipation of larger, more orchestrated protests. For example, local police agents kept the Algiers Maison-Carrée, the site of a large weekly market, under constant surveillance. They watched out for the arrival of known PPA activists and were instructed to inform the capital's Sûreté chief in the event of any political gatherings, spontaneous or otherwise.[83] This and other comparable surveillance operations continued throughout September and October 1939, by which point the implementation of military mobilization, rationing, and other economic restrictions had added another dimension entirely to government concern about public order.

Political and Economic Conditions in the Levant Mandates, 1936–1939

In many ways, events in the Levant mandates echoed those in North Africa in the three years following the Popular Front election, and the volume and intensity of intelligence collection also increased correspondingly. But there were also key differences. The mandatory state was less securely rooted than the Maghreb administrations, and Syrian and Lebanese opposition groups were, on the whole, stronger and more diverse. More important, from 1936 on, official threat perceptions and, consequently, intelligence-gathering priorities in the Levant states were shaped by two distinct sources of public anger: the dispute over France's mandate obligation to negotiate treaties of independence, and British repression of the Arab rebellion in neighboring Palestine.

The political ferment in Syria and Lebanon during 1936–39 added to the economic dislocation caused by extraneous events. Syrians' antagonism to mandatory rule was already deeply embedded in the Depression years. In common with other imperial territories with a local currency tied to franc values, foreign demand for Levant primary products augmented as the Syrian pound tracked the three devaluations of the franc in 1936–38. The money supply in the Levant states almost doubled in the eighteen months following the first devaluation in September 1936. The greater quantity of cash in circulation more than cancelled out the decrease in the value of the Syrian pound. What promised to be a strong export-led recovery in late 1936–37 was hampered in 1938–39 by mounting political instability within and adjacent to the Levant states.[84] The Palestine revolt, the threat of fascist expansionism, and Turkish irredentism along Syria's northern reaches all affected commercial traffic and financial confidence in the Fertile Crescent. The region's economic dislocation fed Arab political resentment. British and Zionist treatment of Palestine's Arab population stirred more controversy in Syria than any other international issue.[85] By August 1936, British diplomats in Syria were convinced that disorder in Palestine and the upsurge of political violence in Syria were intimately linked, even interdependent.[86] Yet the Palestine revolt did less damage to the Levant state economies than this might suggest. Palestine remained Syria's foremost export customer, and by 1937 Britain had supplanted France as principal supplier of Syrian and Lebanese imports.[87]

A more worrying economic change than the transient disruptions provoked by the Palestine revolt was the more permanent blow to commercial activity in northern Syria caused by Turkish annexation of the *sanjak* of

Alexandretta in July 1938. Turkey's long-standing claim on the *sanjak* was boosted by French reluctance to alienate the Kemalist regime, seen as a vital potential ally. The Section d'études du Levant estimated that for demographic, economic, and, above all, strategic reasons, Atatürk's regime would never renounce its claim to the territory. By implication, opposing Turkish demands was pointless.[88] Even SR intelligence of Turkish complicity in weapons smuggling into northern Syria and to separatist groups in the Jazirah was not allowed to interfere with the quest for support in Ankara.[89]

By March 1938, the French authorities acquiesced in a manifestly biased voting system devised by the League of Nations to ensure the victory of the minority ethnic Turkish community in a plebiscite on the *sanjak*'s future. The Turkish population of the *sanjak* was permitted to register for the plebiscite on the basis of ethnicity. But non-Turks were subdivided into confessional groups—Alawites, Arabs, Armenians, Greek Orthodox, and others. This cleavage between Alawite and Arab continued the long-standing French policy of setting differing confessional groups against one another across the *sanjak*, and throughout Syria more generally. But it also guaranteed Turkish victory in the plebiscite, particularly as checks were not made on those claiming to be Turkish voters resident in the *sanjak*, a decision that encouraged fraudulent registration by Turks introduced from neighboring Adana. Not surprisingly, this ill-disguised gerrymandering helped radicalize nationalist sentiment among those Arabs anxious to avoid the surrender of Alexandretta and Antioch to Turkish control.[90]

French acquiescence in the transformation of the former Syrian *sanjak* of Alexandretta into the Turkish autonomous region of Hatay was hardly unexpected. But this did not diminish the sense of betrayal felt by the region's Arab and Armenian populations.[91] Resentment also ran high among the commercial producers in and around Aleppo, for whom trade with the Alexandretta hinterland had been a critical lifeline during the Depression years.[92] The economy of northwestern Syria suffered badly from the commercial barriers erected between the Syrian mandate and Kemalist Turkey in the early 1920s. This was echoed a generation later when, on 13 April 1939, the Ankara government introduced new clearing arrangements for all trade transactions with the Hatay Republic. These regulations were a blow to the Syrian authorities, who had hoped to reverse the net decline in industrial production across the Aleppo district registered in 1938.[93]

Britain's partial withdrawal from neighboring Iraq under the terms of the Anglo-Iraqi treaty of independence between 1930 and 1932 sharpened popular disaffection in Syria in response to declining living standards, the political impasse over negotiated independence, and the linkage of the Syrian pound to the overvalued franc.[94] Hostility to French domination peaked in a thirty-six-day general strike called by the Syrian National Bloc, but organized by student radicals in Damascus on 27 January 1936. The suspension of parliamentary institutions, the manipulation of successive governments, and French efforts to marginalize nationalist groups fueled urban support for street protests and a more radical nationalist alternative.[95]

The more widespread popular political engagement characteristic of Faysal's regime resumed with a vengeance.[96] The Syrian People's Party made the transition from a cliquish group of urban notables to a modern secular party with a mass membership. Students' organizations, women's groups, and paramilitary columns of uniformed scouts proliferated. Their supporters across the frontier in Transjordan even tried to organize a copycat strike in Amman to coincide with the 27 January stoppage in Syria.[97] Ironically, it was the National Bloc, cornered into supporting the general strike, that profited most. It exploited the crisis to coax first Albert Sarraut's caretaker government and then Léon Blum's Popular Front coalition into preliminary talks over a treaty of independence.[98]

Popular opposition to mandatory rule grew more intense as it became apparent that the French National Assembly would not ratify the Franco-Syrian and Franco-Lebanese treaties of independence negotiated in late 1936. Local political leaders, fêted on their return home from the treaty talks in Paris, were vilified once it became apparent that France had no intention of implementing the agreements any time soon. Meanwhile, Syria's minority populations, notably the Alawites, the Druze, and even the Circassians, so prominent in the mandate's levy forces, were expected to oppose the unitary impulse of a predominantly Sunni nationalism.[99] What of the Bedouin? Reports of more widespread tax revolts among sedentary tribes suggested that they too were increasingly prepared to defy French rule, if for different reasons.[100] When Syria's prime minister, Jamil Mardam, returned to Syria on 20 December 1938 from his latest unsuccessful attempt to unblock the path to ratification, the only spectators who welcomed his return were paid to do so from the party funds of the governing National Bloc coalition in Damascus.[101]

Three weeks later, Gabriel Puaux, France's newly appointed Levant high commissioner, faced a more frosty reception. Within hours of Puaux's arrival at Beirut on 8 January 1939, a complete economic shutdown began in Aleppo, in a powerful demonstration of nationalist resolve. The Aleppo strike was especially poignant in light of the region's recent economic plight. Any commercial premises that dared to remain open over the next two days faced having their windows broken by groups of young nationalists as the local police stood by.[102] In the remaining nine months before war broke out in Europe, the disjuncture between the political crisis in the French Levant and its improving economic position grew sharper. Trade volumes for January–September 1939 were higher than in the previous year. There were even commercial milestones to celebrate. Beirut international airport was formally opened amid suitable pomp on 6 June, and

Lebanon's cool summer hill stations enjoyed a boom year, with more than fourteen thousand visitors, including King Ghazi of Iraq.[103]

Intelligence Assessment and the Mediterranean High Committee

In January 1937, Léon Blum's first Popular Front ministry transformed the Mediterranean high committee (MHC), the senior civil-military advisory group on North African affairs, into a forum for intelligence assessment. Albert Sarraut, the minister of state for North African affairs, took charge of the overhaul. He turned the committee from an ineffectual talking shop into the primary administrative instrument for the scrutiny of Maghreb security policy through all-source analysis of incoming diplomatic, economic, military, and Sûreté intelligence. One key change was to equip the committee with a permanent secretariat. Another was to ensure that the incoming intelligence the committee received about political conditions in the three North African territories and the Levant mandates was quickly circulated to all interested ministries. Finally, Sarraut proposed the creation of a standing commission, linked to the MHC, to study any issues affecting France's Muslim colonial subjects that might affect imperial security.[104]

Thus revitalized, during its March 1937 sessions the MHC reviewed its study commission reports on four related matters. First priority was given to reform of the native affairs bureaucracy. North African native affairs bureaus were widely considered to be outdated, overly complex, and unable to provide the volume of local information required by central government. This was confirmed by the commission's second report, a survey of political and religious affiliation in the Maghreb. Where native affairs officers had tended to downplay the influence of secular nationalism in rural communities, the MHC identified Maghrebi nationalist parties as the dominant groupings among Muslims in town and countryside.[105] The study commission pointed to the shared interests of party political activists, 'ulamā and Sufi marabouts, and representatives of the évolué elite in all three territories. The informal contacts and clientage networks among these constituencies of opinion facilitated the interpenetration of overlapping ideas. Anticolonial nationalism meshed with pan-Arabism, which mingled, in turn, with the reassertion of Muslim cultural identity. Thus the leaders of the PPA, the Moroccan Action Committee, and Néo-Destour found common cause with Islamic revivalists in Koranic schools and Sufi cults. All sympathized with the pan-Arabist cause articulated by Shakib Arslan's Syrian-Palestine Congress. As a result, Muslim opinion was presented as a more multifaceted, yet more cohesive, political force.[106]

The message was amplified in the study commission's third subject of inquiry—the Maghrebi immigrant community in France. As we have seen, North African workers in French cities came under increasing state surveillance during the interwar period. By 1937, the MHC could draw on fifteen years of municipal police reports, employment records, public health surveys, and customs data to build a detailed profile of the Muslim immigrant population. The study commission's key finding in this respect was deeply ironic. Years of intensive police checks, immigration restrictions, and entrenched employment discrimination had transformed the political profile of the Maghrebi community in France. Insular, self-reliant, and intensely suspicious of French authority, it was no surprise that North African workers had become increasingly militant. Their support for integral nationalism was not likely to change.[107] Although heightened surveillance gave the authorities privileged access to Muslim radicalism in France, the surveillance was also a prime cause of the radicalism. The study commission's fourth and final intelligence report, submitted to the MHC in March 1937, was more upbeat, reviewing the success of elective assemblies in accommodating the Europeanized Maghrebi elite to French rule.[108]

Apprised of these findings and a regular flow of incoming intelligence, the MHC needed to face up to some harsh truths revealed by the explosion of urban dissent in France's Arab territories in 1936–37. In March 1937, the committee secretary, Charles-André Julien, urged his colleagues to acknowledge that France was not proficient as a Muslim power. It did not even pursue a coherent policy toward the Muslim populations of the three Maghreb territories.[109] Such frankness was characteristic of the early days of Popular Front government. It was equally symptomatic of that period, however, that the admission of past errors was never translated into action.[110]

Because the MHC was created to bring greater coherence to imperial policy in France's North African and Levant territories, it was almost bound to make its mark through harsh criticism. But the circumstances of its creation tell us a good deal about the incoherence of colonial policy formulation in the late 1930s. The committee was established by Pierre Laval's right-wing government in February 1935 in response to parliamentary pressure for a more unitary and economical administrative system in French North Africa. Although it had a strictly advisory role, the committee was unusually independent. It was not attached to a particular ministry but rather to the prime minister's office at the Hôtel Matignon. Its organizing secretary, Charles-André Julien, was a liberal-minded academic and a noted authority on Arab societies, willing to confront the harsh realities of colonial authoritarianism. And the committee enjoyed the patronage of Albert Sarraut, who, after Marshal Lyautey's death, was the most widely respected voice of imperialism in interwar France.

Sarraut's support proved vital. Within days of its creation, the MHC was under attack from ministers in Laval's government nervous at a loss of jurisdictional autonomy to a potentially disruptive and peculiarly scholarly group of outsiders. The war minister, General Louis Maurin, refused to allow the new committee any power of oversight over the treatment or deployment of Muslim troops. The minister of colonies, Louis Rollin, pointed out that the committee had no responsibility for colonial policy, properly defined, because its purview did not extend to territories under rue Oudinot control. Crucially, Laval's cost-cutting Cabinet refused to provide the administrative support essential to enable the new committee to compile evidence and submit detailed reports.[111] Only with the advent of Sarraut's administration in January 1936 did the MHC obtain a permanent secretariat.[112] At last equipped to assess large volumes of intelligence from all of France's Muslim territories, between 1936 and 1939 the MHC found its voice in security policy. Monitoring the unfolding events in the Maghreb and the Levant, by 1939 the highest level of security analysis of these Muslim territories had shifted from the machinations of the notable elite and the inner workings of nationalist groups to the activities of the poorest in urban and rural society, what in modern journalistic parlance might be dubbed the politics of the Arab street.

Reorganization of Counterespionage

Concurrent with the reorganization of the MHC, in March 1937 the French army staff instructed SR bureaus throughout the Maghreb to devote more resources to counterespionage.[113] The principal foreign intelligence targets were German and Italian agents and Comintern propagandists.[114] As a result, the SCR compiled additional intelligence about Arab nationalist groups patronized by the Nazi government in Berlin. Its first objective was to discover where connections existed between the Nazi Propaganda Ministry, German intelligence agencies, and support for anticolonialist groups in the Maghreb.[115] In doing so, the counterespionage administration in French North Africa was brought more closely into line with the War Ministry's military intelligence service, which had been analyzing ever-increasing volumes of intelligence from the army staff's colonial section on German sedition in the French Empire since Hitler's accession to power in 1933.[116]

By the late 1930s, the French authorities were relatively successful in detecting foreign espionage on metropolitan soil.[117] State surveillance of potential spies intensified as the likelihood of war increased. In a single month in 1937, counterespionage services in France detained eleven times as many individuals for spying as in the years 1903–14. Total arrests for 1937 were four times higher than in 1933.[118] Detection rates in imperial territory were consistently lower, a reflection of shortages of trained specialists and the limited resources of dedicated police spéciale and SCR staffs.

The apparatus of counterespionage in the French Empire was inadequate to meet the scale of the tasks before it.[119] In September 1936, Captain

Paul Paillole, the outstanding organizer of SCR operations before and during the war, lamented the absence of counterespionage sections attached to individual army commands in France and overseas.[120] As mentioned earlier, working counterespionage services were put in place in French North Africa and the Levant mandates only from 1937 to 1939. In Algeria, for instance, Governor-General Georges Le Beau signed off plans to establish a *Service de surveillance du territoire* on 12 January 1938, only then implementing a counterespionage scheme for the colony first mooted four years earlier, in January 1934. With a central analysis section in Algiers, three subordinate branches in each of Algeria's departments, and two further "brigades" monitoring the territory's eastern and western frontiers, the administrative structure of Algerian counterespionage was logical, but thinly spread.[121] The belatedness of these changes and the limited allocation of resources over huge geographical areas compared unfavorably with the complex bureaucracy of state surveillance of foreign subversion in mainland France.[122]

At first glance, such laxity seems at odds with the extensive intelligence gathering regarding internal sources of sedition. This, however, reveals the fundamental difference between metropolitan and colonial territory. Whereas spying in France was looked on as an activity conducted by foreigners to undermine the security of a loyal population, in the colonies it was more difficult to distinguish between foreign subversion and indigenous resistance to European rule. Since the loyalty of colonial populations was never assured, it made more sense to focus the intelligence effort on domestic intelligence gathering. Colonial counterespionage was therefore secondary to domestic security surveillance and had become moribund. For several years before 1937, the authorities across French North Africa made no arrests at all for spying.[123]

Nowhere were these deficiencies more apparent than in Tunisia, France's most sensitive African frontier.[124] The territory occupied a key political and strategic position as the eastern buttress of French North Africa. Evidence of increasing Italian espionage added to official anxieties about the loyalty of Tunisia's Italian settler community. In July 1932, military intelligence planners concluded that the frontier between Tunisia and Italian Libya was dangerously porous.[125] A number of embarrassing incidents soon bore this out. Italian aircraft made frequent reconnaissance flights over sensitive French military installations in and around Tunis. On 12 July 1932, an Italian cargo vessel unloading crates of tomatoes in Tunis was found to be shipping weapons when one of the packing cases split apart to reveal a box of revolvers. Less than a month later, on 9 August, an Italian seaplane flew over the city of Tunis and its el-Aouina airbase. Its engine spluttering, the aircraft, thought to be a Savoia 55, was forced to make an emergency landing on the nearby Goulette canal. The crew hurriedly completed some makeshift repairs and took off before the French authorities could arrest them.[126]

It is not hard to find other examples of similar bizarre revelations and near misses in the SR files sent to the Tunis Residency. Evidently, they had a cumulative slow-burn effect, because it seems that a mixture of irritation, embarrassment, and alarm drove the restructuring of counterespionage in Tunisia. Discoveries of Italian misdemeanors chimed with reports that Tunisia was the focal point of fascist intelligence activity conducted from Tripoli and Palermo. The presence of a special police center attached to the Italian consulate in Tunis also aroused suspicion. Improved French counterespionage organization was essential to prevent Italy from amassing intelligence likely to facilitate an attack against French overseas interests either in fulfillment of Mussolini's dreams of imperial aggrandizement or as a result of more general conflict.[127]

As matters stood in 1932, Tunisia's existing counterespionage bureaucracy, though still in its infancy, was already overwhelmed by its workload. In May 1930, a general intelligence section had been created in the offices of the Tunis Sûreté. A divisional commissioner was brought in from France to get the new section running. His staff comprised a deputy plus four French inspectors, two local agents, and one secretary. Chronically shorthanded, the new section's area of responsibility was vast. It was expected to monitor Communist propaganda and Tunisian nationalist activity, in addition to its counterespionage and frontier surveillance tasks. Moreover, the general intelligence section's organizational structure was modeled on the Sûreté system in metropolitan France and took no account of the peculiar conditions of a colonial environment.

Counterespionage in France was conducted under the aegis of the Sûreté Générale. It was subdivided between 136 special commissioners, principally assigned to frontier regions. Until the 1932 reforms, Tunisia's counterespionage personnel were simply attached to regional offices of the national police. In an effort to improve efficiency, in July 1932 the Tunis Residency acted on War Ministry recommendations to create a *police spéciale* to work in closer liaison with the French and Algerian Sûreté. Recruits were to be drawn by preference from other Sûreté and SR establishments rather than from the ordinary rank and file of the Tunisian police. In other respects the new bureaucracy was not dissimilar to its predecessor except insofar as it was more clearly focused on frontier surveillance. In addition to the central SCR coordinatory office in Tunis, six regional surveillance posts were established at Tunisia's most sensitive strategic points: Bizerta, La Goulette, Ghardimaou, Ben Gardane, Sfax, and Sousse.[128] The SCR's operational priorities were clarified, with most resources devoted to surveillance of frontiers, ports and shipping, military installations, foreign missions, international travelers, and telegraphic and postal correspondence.[129]

Italy's invasion of Ethiopia in October 1935 added new complexities to security service concerns. The bulk of Tunisian crude oil was sold on the

Italian market and the majority of Tunisia's Italian settlers loudly endorsed Mussolini's imperial ambitions in East Africa. With even the major French-language newspaper, the notoriously reactionary *Dépêche Tunisienne,* supporting Italy's claim to rule in Addis Ababa, there was little appetite among Residency staff for the adoption of a stridently anti-Italian line, spearheaded by oil sanctions. If growing support among the settler community for ultra-rightist French political groups caused the police some concern, the SR feared that Tunisia's ethnic Italians might be open to foreign subversion.[130] Incoming intelligence indicated the Rome regime's deepening involvement in anti-French activity in Tunis.[131] The SCR spotlight therefore focused more intensely on the Italian settler community. Counterespionage agents reported on settler politics, infiltrated Italian sporting and cultural associations, and traced the movements of influential community members, including priests, doctors, and known political activists. The Residency received notification of any evidence of Italian governmental efforts to contact settler leaders.[132]

The restructuring of counterespionage in Tunisia highlighted the SCR's reliance on its network of frontier posts for information on foreign agents and hostile intelligence activity. Among the seven such SCR posts in existence by 1937, two were in French North Africa—at Algiers and Tunis. Following the model of its SR cousin, the SCR's central staff was subdivided into specialist geographical sections, each handling the surveillance of intelligence activity by the major European powers, Germany, Italy, and the Soviet Union most prominent among them. Faced with the rise of Nazism, French counterespionage services expanded steadily during the late 1930s. The way to expansion was opened by an April 1934 decree establishing a Direction centrale de la Sûreté Nationale, headed by a controller-general of counterespionage. In June of the same year, frontier surveillance, in addition to passport control and identity card checks, was delegated to eleven regional SCR centers across metropolitan France and North Africa. General Noguès, by then the commander-of-chief in French North Africa, also maintained discrete intelligence sections in the Maghreb territories—the Services d'informations du Sud—to monitor cross-border infiltration by Axis agents and propagandists. Staffed by SCR officers, these units reported directly to Noguès, advising him of Italian military movements along the Tunisia-Libya frontier and the activity of German agents, military advisers, and commercial representatives in Spanish Morocco.[133]

In practice, the boundaries between SCR and Sûreté responsibilities for the control of foreign espionage proved harder to discern than their clearly stated obligations on paper might suggest. Generally short of funding and specialized personnel, civil-military liaison in counterespionage matters was sometimes chaotic.[134] As the volume of work increased hugely during the 1930s, SCR officers complained they had neither the men nor the means to protect France against foreign-inspired sedition.[135] Three separate ministerial instructions, issued on 12 March 1937, 30 September 1939, and 16 November 1939, authorized the appointment of counterespionage officers within each army corps, indicating the procedures by which these specialist personnel were to exploit incoming unit intelligence. But these appointments were slow to take effect, especially among those forces stationed in imperial territory. On 6 May 1940, almost the eve of the battle of France, the Levant Army command warned that its counterespionage personnel had neither the specialist training nor the bureaucratic support to perform their task effectively. It was only at this late stage that the Levant Army commander, General Henri Caillault, instituted a system of monthly counterespionage reports to be filed by military district in Damascus, Aleppo, and Beirut, and then forwarded to the War Ministry's counterespionage office, the Bureau de Centralisation de Renseignements.[136]

Technically, it fell to the minister of war and the interior minister to ensure that SCR and Sûreté staff worked hand-in-glove. Each ministry was to keep the other notified of its active intelligence personnel and provide for points of contact between the two. In particular, the deuxième bureau was to set the parameters of SR and SCR intelligence operations, defining priorities regarding the states to be monitored and the locations, materials, agents, and informers that required most attention. A clear distinction was also drawn between the Sûreté's ultimate responsibility for counterespionage work within French territory and the SR-SCR's greater competence in intelligence operations conducted on foreign soil. Again, imperial territory proved to be the environment in which these notionally precise spheres of responsibility were most frequently confused. Although the tricolor flew throughout dependent territory, the individuals with whom French intelligence personnel were most concerned were overwhelmingly either foreign nationals or imperial subjects.[137]

From 1937, increasing numbers of SR personnel and Sûreté police officers were also reassigned to surveillance of Communist sedition locally and overseas. In Tunisia, for example, in March 1938, three Sûreté "counterespionage brigades" were set up in Bizerta, Gabès, and Sfax to report directly to the Tunis Residency.[138] In the same month, counterespionage services were reorganized in Morocco with Sûreté *brigades de surveillance du territoire* established in Rabat, Casablanca, Marrakech, Agadir, Fez, Arabaoua, Meknès, and Oujda. Targeted at foreign agent activity, these Sûreté units worked in close cooperation with the army's SCR.[139] Irrespective of this heightened surveillance of agents provocateurs, perennial concerns about the loyalty of the subject population remained. The SR officer sent to the Maghreb to supervise the joint Sûreté and SCR counterespionage effort drew an arbitrary, and wildly optimistic, distinction between public loyalty in France and North Africa:

When mobilization is decreed in metropolitan France . . . former political differences will be extinguished by the unanimity of the nation confronted by a
pressing threat. In North Africa the sources of discord, strengthened by foreign powers, threaten to provoke a general uprising if France is attacked. It is
impossible to maintain internal security in French North Africa without taking
into account the external threats to its borders, foreign subversion and, at the
same time, their likely effects on internal unrest.[140]

This SR prediction of political calm in France, compared with increased
colonial sedition at the outbreak of war, suggested that the empire was
becoming a greater source of concern to the French intelligence community. As war loomed larger, anti-French political protest naturally acquired a
more seditious aspect in the eyes of its proponents and among those security agencies detailed to suppress it. Within France, the PCF attracted
heightened police attention after the final remnants of Popular Frontism
collapsed in the spring of 1938. The Daladier government released police
figures indicating that between May 1938 and March 1940 the police conducted 10,550 house-to-house searches and made 3,400 arrests in the crackdown on French Communists.[141]

The shocking announcement of the Nazi-Soviet pact on 23 August 1939
triggered a wave of "anticommunist hysteria" in France. European refugee
communities were one focal point of suspicion, both popular and official. In
the first two weeks of September, resident foreigners of German origin,
many of them committed antifascists quite willing to serve in the French
armed forces, were interned. Earlier plans to utilize the influx of Spanish
republican, German, Jewish, and Eastern European refugees in the French
military were abandoned in favor of indiscriminate confinement.[142] The
intensification of anticommunism and suspicion of foreign "fifth column"
activity in 1939 also rebounded on colonial immigrants and nationalist
politicians within French overseas territory, paving the way for more repressive security measures in the empire.

French Territories and the Outbreak of War

Martial law was enforced throughout French North Africa from 3 September 1939, including the death penalty for any person found tampering with
telegraph wires, a form of nationalist agitation recently much in favor.
Suspect individuals on the Maghreb administrations' Carnet B lists were
soon rounded up. In Tunis, for example, Italian settlers inscribed on the
local Carnet B were arrested on the night of 1 September, within hours of
the announcement of general mobilization.[143] State regulation of French
North Africa's war economy was presaged by a series of mobilization decrees
brought into effect in the final month of the Czech crisis between 23 August
and 28 September 1938. The nervous countdown to the Munich confer-

ence had also given the security services a good idea of the likely response to war with Germany among the Maghreb's settler population.[144]

Twelve months later, in the first three days of the war, Sultan Mohammed V of Morocco and Ahmed Pasha Bey of Tunisia formally endorsed the application of these earlier state of siege provisions.[145] The bey of Tunis renewed his declaration of unalterable attachment to France, and Tunisia's population was reportedly "calm and disciplined."[146] The Algiers government also reported that the colony's Europeans and Muslims were rallying to the defense of France. Long skeptical about Muslim community leaders' public professions of loyalty to the empire, the Algiers Sûreté was gratified by the public's reaction to the declaration of hostilities in September 1939.[147] The Algiers commissioner of police detected no signs of dissent in the capital, only anxiety, particularly among Muslim women, over the likely impact of mobilization.[148] Postal censorship revealed that wild rumors about the war's initial engagements and the extent of French requisitioning were commonplace, but criticism was scarce, as were arrests for seditionist activity.[149] In Kabylia, always the major center for the recruitment of Algerian Berber troops, the SR reported a "disciplined" and "enthusiastic" call-up, endorsed by the region's community leaders. But the disruption to the year's autumn grain harvest suggested that grave food shortages might be just around the corner.[150]

Among Algeria's European population, to the delight of the Algiers Sûreté, news of the Nazi-Soviet pact provoked splits in the Algerian Communist Party and the local section of the Confédération Général du Travail that echoed those among Communists in France. Even the powerful Algiers and Oran sections of Jacques Doriot's ultrarightist Parti Populaire Français declared their opposition to "pan-Germanism." Early indicators of Muslim opinion seemed equally encouraging. The few 'ulamā and dissenting imams who questioned Algeria's automatic engagement in the war were, apparently, shouted down for doing so. The nationalists were quieter still: much of the senior leadership of Messali Hadj's Parti Populaire Algérien, including Messali himself, had been placed in detention months before the war began.[151]

The picture was more varied by the time Poland fell three weeks later. Police raided the homes of Communist organizers in Algeria's cities immediately after the government outlawed the French Communist Party on 26 September. And, in an effort to improve the security services' detection and arrest rates, on 6 October Paul Paillole arrived in Algiers to begin a five-day inspection of the counterespionage services in French North Africa. His findings resulted in a major shake-up of the chain of command, from individual SCR and Sûreté stations to Nogués's headquarters staff.[152] The security service's early wartime focus on detention of Communists and foreign spies should not conceal the fact that popular nationalism, not seditious extremism, posed the greater long-term threat to the colonial state in Algeria. Neither the detention of Algerian Communist activists nor the discovery of "revolutionary propaganda" had much impact on the colony's Muslim population, for whom the earlier incarceration of the PPA executive was understandably more important.[153] The show of Muslim support for the war did not imply any diminution in underlying public support for Messalism, but it did allow the Sûreté and SR to concentrate their activities elsewhere. Particular cause for concern was the steep rise in anti-Semitic attacks in Algiers and Oran, fomented mainly by settlers, not Muslims. This suggested that the façade of intercommunal unity in the first days of the war was cracking.[154]

In Tunisia, Ahmed Zaouche, a senior official in the Arab municipality of Tunis, advised British consular staff that Muslim resentment at their exclusion from local government simmered on. This was hardly a revelation. More significant was Zaouche's reference to popular grievances that had arisen in the first weeks of the war. The monthly disbursement of poor relief in Tunis had been reduced by half, at a stroke cutting the number of destitute people being fed from fifty thousand to twenty-five thousand. There was also growing anxiety about the inadequacy of measures to protect the capital's Arab quarters from air attack. Because most Arab dwellings could not withstand bombardment, an evacuation scheme seemed essential, but the Residency ruled this out on the grounds of cost. Shortage of funds also explained why no gas masks had been distributed to the Arab population.[155]

Urban disquiet was soon eclipsed by unrest among Tunisian troops conscripted over the preceding months. On the evening of 26 September 1939, Tunisian infantry, joined by a number of sympathetic Arab civilians, mutinied at Kairaoun. Press restrictions prevented any reportage of the mutiny, but American and British consular officials in Tunis and Sousse sent word of the events to their home governments. At first glance, the soldiers' grievances seemed material rather than political. Some complained about the quality of clothing and bedding provided, others about the quantity or quality of the food, lack of footwear, and, above all, the fact that their pay was in arrears. But a closer examination of events indicates how practical hardships became intertwined with deeper political convictions. Destourian activists from the Sousse region had instigated events, although only an estimated one hundred of the ten thousand or so native *tirailleurs* billeted at Kairaoun refused to obey orders. Once the mutiny began, these troops tried to force open the town prison's gate in an effort to release political detainees. White troops restored order, but only after shots were fired. The racial dimension of the mutiny was evident in the casualties on both sides. A French officer and Kairaoun's police commissioner were injured, and a French noncommissioned officer's house was ransacked. Three Arabs were killed and ten wounded.[156]

The Kairaoun outbreak was singularly violent, but it reflected wider Muslim anger at the severity of the wartime controls enacted in Tunisia. A week after the mutiny, the naval officer commanding the Tunis harbor defenses near Sidi-bou-Said informed the British vice-consul that local residents strewed broken glass on the road to puncture the tires of military vehicles, and used handcarts to block the approach to one of the coastal defense batteries. The inhabitants were officially warned that they would face a curfew if their protests were repeated.[157] Reports from garrisons in the Tunisian interior were no more encouraging. Dysentery and mange reportedly were rife among troops billeted in the south. Illness and enforced inaction also sapped the morale of troops manning the Mareth Line of fortifications along the Tunisia-Libya frontier. According to their French officers, the risk of epidemic posed a greater threat than Italy's entry to the war. In one regiment, 60 percent of troops reportedly were sick, and infection rates were aggravated by the unsanitary conditions and slowness of the troop trains that carried recruits southward from the railhead at Gabès.[158]

Again, these material hardships were compounded by a deeper grievance, this time less political than economic. The speed and breadth of the call-up in August–September 1939 brought Tunisia's predominantly agricultural economy to a virtual standstill. General Blanc, the general officer commanding in Tunisia, acknowledged as much in his preliminary inquiry into the Kairaoun mutiny. Excessive mobilization in September caused commercial and administrative chaos. The strategic justification for mobilization on such a scale seemed tenuous, as the conscripts were to be sent immediately neither to France nor to fight the still nonbelligerent Italians in North Africa. Instead, the huge numbers put into uniform demanded wholesale requisitioning of transport and food supplies, with untold damage to the agricultural sector. Food prices soared as the military authorities withdrew available stocks from the commercial market. The poorest were simply unable to buy goods on the open market, a situation that threatened widespread winter famine.[159]

In a sense, the military authorities across the Maghreb were victims of their own success. Commander in Chief Noguès, still Morocco's resident minister, had moved swiftly to enact full mobilization. In the light of Mussolini's recent actions, he could hardly be blamed for deploying forces in the expectation of Italy's entry to the war. Furthermore, Noguès moved quickly to ameliorate the economic situation. On 1 October 1939, he discharged Tunisian reservists belonging to the 1909 class, and indicated that reservists of the 1910 and 1911 classes, though subject to military recall, would be allowed to return home over the subsequent fortnight. Fathers with large families were accorded priority in all discharge requests.[160] It proved a more difficult task to improve material conditions for the younger conscripts that remained in uniform. By December, the problems of ill health and low morale among Muslim troops stationed in southern Tunisia were exacerbated by shortages of clean drinking water. According to a priest of the White Fathers missionary order attached to the Arab units, conscripts felt that the French government should decide whether war with Italy was in sight. If not, they believed that demobilization should follow.[161] In the early months of 1940, reports of Muslim anger over iniquitous foodstuff rationing caused the security services greater pause than the continued surveillance of Néo-Destour militants that had escaped the earlier round of Sûreté arrests. Muslim poverty had supplanted nationalist ideology as the principal source of intelligence analysts' concern.[162]

The Levant high commission followed the French North African authorities in applying the lessons of mobilization learned at the height of the Czech crisis in September 1938. In August 1939, as war loomed, the Beirut high commission introduced drastic restrictions on credit operations in a race to safeguard the banking sector before the anticipated rush by savers to withdraw their deposits. Decrees issued between 25 and 31 August banned the export of foodstuffs and petroleum derivatives, thus diminishing the public impulse to hoard vital commodities. These measures were largely successful. Food shortages were averted; price controls and draconian penalties for illicit stockpiling prevented foodstuff inflation from spiraling out of control. The removal of customs duties on imported wheat on 20 September and the arrival of fresh consignments of sugar and rice even caused a fall in the prices of these staples by the end of the month. In other respects, however, the first weeks of the war were chaotic. Postal communications with Europe all but ceased throughout September. And the Levant Army command set about military requisitioning and gasoline rationing with such enthusiasm that Syria's internal transportation system collapsed, leaving isolated rural areas without supplies.[163]

The economic controls introduced in the Levant states immediately before and after the outbreak of war in Europe were comparable in cause and effect to those in the Maghreb. French policies to maintain order in Syria and Lebanon were more distinctive. Gabriel Puaux's staff in Beirut and, more especially, Damascus reacted to the unending political deadlock over the long-term future of the mandates with a series of legislative restrictions introduced months before the conflict in Europe began. This accretion of power by the mandatory authorities began in earnest in February 1939. On 18 February, Jamil Mardam's Syrian government resigned. The immediate pretext was its refusal to implement a high commission decree regulating the status of religious communities in Syria. Resignation over an issue of such material and symbolic importance allowed the National Bloc to reassert its independence and so prevent a hemorrhage of support to its rival, the People's Party. The ensuing constitutional crisis culminated in the appointment of an ineffectual ministry led by Mardam's former minister of finance, Lutfi al-Haffar.[164]

The conflict between the high commission and Syria's leading national-ist parties soon found its echo on the street, where daily clashes between demonstrators and the security forces assumed an almost ritualistic quality. By 20 March, High Commissioner Puaux was facing the prospect of a renewed general strike in Damascus. As soon as gendarmerie commanders advised him that protestors were erecting barricades to bar entry to police units, he authorized the military to reimpose order in the Syrian capital. Cavalry squadrons, armored cars, and the much-feared *tirailleurs sénégalais* were deployed throughout the city in measures reminiscent of the street battles at the height of the Syrian revolt in 1925.[165] Within weeks, the Da-mascus government was stripped of key powers as the 1936 treaty settlement unraveled. The mandate authorities resumed control of the Syrian police, and French officials took over as governors in the Jabal Druze and the Alawite region, home to Syria's two principal ethnic minorities. This de facto arrangement continued until the war in Europe enabled the high commission to consolidate the martial law regime by announcing a state of siege on 9 September 1939. Three weeks later, on 23 September, the Lebanese constitution was suspended as martial law was extended to cover the entire French Levant.[166]

Conclusion

It was a sad irony that Popular Front reforms intended to reconcile depen-dent populations to French rule ultimately had the opposite effect. As the promise of reform receded in 1936–37, the security services accrued greater influence over policy formulation, urban policing, and social con-trol. Parallel changes were taking place in Paris as well. Brought to the cen-ter of security analysis in 1936, over the next three years the MHC concen-trated on mass opinion to the virtual exclusion of the educated elite that had once dominated municipal politics in French North Africa. By the time war was declared in September 1939, the security services that supplied the MHC's raw data held unprecedented authority within the administrative fabric of the French Empire, paving the way for the rigorous authoritarian-ism of the war years.

Aside from the fallout from a brief spell of left-wing government in France, the deteriorating international situation broadened the security agencies' threat horizons in the late 1930s. The greater likelihood of Italian aggression in Tunisia following the Abyssinian war, and the increased dan-ger of Spanish irredentism in Morocco once Franco's nationalists secured victory in Spain's civil war, left French North Africa dangerously exposed to land and air attack on its eastern and western flanks. Extensive Italian and German intervention in the Spanish conflict prompted the Supreme Council of National Defense to prepare contingency plans predicated on the fascist powers using Spanish territory as an assembly point for attacks on the Maghreb.[167] In a worst-case scenario, Spanish forces might traverse the Rif highlands to sever the arterial rail and road connections between Rabat and Tunis, thus impeding any reinforcement of Tunisia's eastern frontier and leaving it prone to attack from neighboring Italian Libya.[168]

The possibility of unrestricted Italian submarine warfare and large-scale aerial bombardments in the western Mediterranean basin also raised the specter of severed communications among France's southern ports, North Africa, and Lebanon. This was alarming. Essential colonial troop reinforcement to France in the first stages of war would be disrupted. Colonial supremacy in the Maghreb might be undermined. With more than 90 percent of its fuel oil and petroleum stores located in the two ports of Toulon and Bizerta, the French Mediterranean fleet might find its operational capacity diminished.[169] It fell to the French Navy's string of sigint monitoring stations from Bizerta to Oran to counteract this danger of Italian attack by alerting the Ministry of Marine's intelligence section to any hostile shipping movements.[170] In December 1937, Admiral Jean-François Darlan's naval staff and its air force counterpart warned the government's national defense committee that the army's concentration on protection of the Rhine frontier should not be permitted to leave France's Arab territories ill-prepared for any attack.[171]

Improved transmission, assessment, and exploitation of incoming intelligence were certainly needed in the changing strategic circumstances of the Mediterranean theater. An effective intelligence cycle was critical to French colonial security, minimizing any possibility of surprise attack and consequent internal unrest. If external menaces to French imperial control in the Maghreb increased in the two years before war broke out, public expressions of internal opposition to colonial control were much diminished. By the summer of 1938, most of the prominent nationalist leaders, trade union organizers, Muslim 'ulamā, and Communist activists across France's three North African territories were targets of an imperial crackdown that continued unabated until the fall of France two years later. Other more compliant political figures, such as the Federation of Elected Muslims, abandoned their earlier dalliance with more militant protest and mass resignation, preferring to work within the confines of the colonial system rather than face proscription or arrest.[172] By the time the war began, the security services in France's Muslim territories defined how the colonial state would respond to the challenge of organized nationalism. If the outbreak of World War II signaled the end of the intelligence state in Britain's Arab territories, in the neighboring French territories 1939–40 marked the transition to the more intensive surveillance and expanded police powers characteristic of the Vichy years.

CONCLUSION

Intelligence, Security, and the Colonial State

The fundamental dilemma confronting the victor powers after World War I was how to sustain order in the new international system. The fundamental dilemma of empire in the same period was how to achieve order in colonial systems where the scope to use local institutions packed with "reliable" local clients as mechanisms of political control was constrained by the countervailing reluctance to concede meaningful political authority to indigenous populations.[1] The two problems were interlinked. The extension of British and French imperial hegemony throughout most of the Arab world after 1919 was a direct consequence of the outcome of the war.[2] And the intensification of international crises over the course of the next twenty years bore directly on the capacity of these imperial powers to keep their empires intact in the face of mounting internal opposition.[3]

Fear of dissent therefore preoccupied European officials in the Muslim states stretching from the southern littoral of the Mediterranean to the Middle Eastern mandates forged in the deal making of the First World War. European authority over indigenous populations was variously disputed: by traditional elites displaced from positions of influence; by educated *évolués* denied opportunities for economic advancement within the colonial order; by tribal confederations that spurned the physical and cultural boundaries of European rule; by urban workers increasingly drawn to organized unionism; and by a rural peasantry struggling to maintain customary forms of land tenure in the face of foreign settlement and harsh interwar economic conditions. Moreover, fear of dissent was constructed in new ways. As Ann Stoler has shown in the context of the interwar Dutch East Indies, instances of indigenous violence against Europeans were increasingly read as indicators of impending social breakdown and malevolent external influence.[4] In these circumstances, some means had to be found to close or at least narrow the gaps between the ruling power and all strata of indigenous society. The result was the "information order"—a combination of intelligence provision, threat assessment, and state efforts to control social communication in colonial society. Seen in this light, the French and British imperial administrations were a vast security apparatus. Central government depended on incoming information to maintain order in the towns, cities, and rural interior of overseas territories.

As the web of European imperial rule spread further after the First World War, security agencies acquired additional importance. Theoretically, pulses of intelligence information relayed from the periphery of this web to its administrative center enabled colonial governments, garrison commanders, and police inspectors to deploy limited resources to maximum effect at minimum cost. In practice, the imperial security system was woefully overstretched and often outflanked, as evidenced by the proliferation of parties, associations, unions, and religious foundations variously opposed to European rule. As a result, the information order repeatedly broke down, with serious consequences. Troops taking to the streets or the hills "in aid of the civil power" generally indicated that the mechanisms of the intelligence state had failed. Such intelligence failure was usually the product of one of two causes: either the intelligence-gathering system proved inadequate and therefore unable to anticipate the probable scale of unrest, as in Egypt and Iraq in 1919–20 and Palestine in 1936, or the intelligence gatherers had overreached, overconfident of their power to control events, as in southern Kurdistan in 1919–21, in Syria's Jabal Druze in 1923–25, and in the Moroccan Rif prior to the outbreak of war with 'Abd el-Krim. In these last three cases, native affairs officers had tried to manipulate tribal loyalties only to find their efforts thwarted as the subjects of their attention—Kurdish clans, Druze chiefs, and Rif Berbers—reacted violently against such presumptuous intrusion.

What do these examples tell us? Above all, they suggest that political policing and intelligence gathering were driven by a recognition of the limits of colonial state power in societies governed through systems of uneasy clientage and elite cooption.[5] This point may also be put rather differently: the colonial environment in which the British and French security services operated was, in and of itself, the principal barrier to their success. Consider for a moment the primary determinants of intelligence activity. For one thing, until at least 1936, within the imperial territories studied here, the greatest threats to state security were internally, not externally, generated. To argue that direct challenges to the colonial state determined interwar intelligence gathering and security force deployment in the Arab world is too reductive, however. Three additional considerations must also be borne in mind: the level of European settlement, the scale of local economic activity, and the anticipated likelihood of intercommunal clashes. One or more

of these factors typically weighed heavily in decisions about target identification and resource allocation.

The growth of settler power in interwar Algeria had profound economic,
cultural, and political consequences for the long-term stability of colonial
control. In mandate Palestine, Jewish immigration and British land law
wrought equally fundamental changes in the socioeconomic fabric of Arab
society.[6] In other territories, what were thought to be stable client-patron
relationships between peasant farmers and urban notables, many of them
absentee landlords, turned out to be volatile. The rise of Wahhabism in the
mid-1920s, the erosion of nomadic lifestyles, and discontent among tribesmen facing economic impoverishment at the margin of the capitalist cash
economy in Arab states all contributed to profound social change among
rural populations.

After World War I, conflicts over access to agricultural land, whether for
settlement, arable cultivation, or pasturage, occasioned more security force
intervention than anything else in the rural interior of Middle Eastern and
North African territories.[7] Police commanders were also well aware that
crime rates among the indigenous population, property theft especially,
were closely linked to levels of agricultural employment, scarcity of food,
and resentment at loss of land or traditional grazing grounds.[8] Explanations
of the dominant agricultural concerns among the local community featured
prominently in the politics of village councils and tribal assemblies as
reported by native affairs officers from Morocco to Iraq.[9] Imperial security
services were expected to know about such matters, to anticipate them, and
to police them. A further imperative was the control of urban public space.
This was understood in terms of regulating freedom of movement, enforcing varying degrees of racial segregation between areas of European and
indigenous settlement, and controlling housing policy and commercial
zoning in a period of unprecedented urban growth.[10] Such control had a
dynamic of its own—the more regulation imposed, the greater the obligation to enforce it.[11]

Another recurrent theme of this book has been that colonial states
relied on intelligence gathering to survive. This is not to suggest that intelligence analysis was synonymous with policymaking, an altogether too one-
dimensional approach.[12] Nor can colonial intelligence assessment be
regarded instrumentally as a form of power. But it is to suggest that a more
catholic vision of the parameters and purpose of state intelligence gathering may aid our understanding of how colonial states endured. State surveillance is a likely, if not inevitable, consequence of complex *societal* organization. As we have seen, it was an established feature of British and
French society in the interwar period. Cast in this light, state surveillance
may serve the people as well as controlling them. The relative importance
of these two functions varies between societies. At one extreme, recent

work on early Soviet surveillance techniques of population classification—by class, by ethnicity, by profession, or more generally as loyal or untrustworthy citizens—draws out the coercive potential of administrative technologies of surveillance such as passports, identity cards, and tax codes.[13] At the other end of the spectrum, more in tune with Max Weber's theories of state development, record keeping about a subject population tends not to be seen as threatening, but as pivotal to the efficient promotion of the collective good.[14]

It is useful here to consider what one discerning intelligence scholar has identified as the four primary obstacles to the effective exploitation of intelligence: "time and space, organization, politicization, and cognition."[15] Let us take these categories in turn.

Time and, more particularly, space—in other words, geographical distance—were critical in large colonial territories characterized by rudimentary infrastructure and minimal development of electronic communication. Comprehensive information collection and rapid, astute intelligence assessment were integral to the effective deployment of the coercive instruments of colonial power: police units, military formations, or aircraft squadrons. The acquisition, transmission, analysis, and dissemination of sensitive intelligence had to outstrip the speed with which the subject at hand could develop into a more severe threat to colonial security.[16] Put crudely, the troops had to be out on the streets before anticipated protests escalated into general disorder. When they were not—as in Palestine following the Wailing Wall riots of August 1929—imperial authority came perilously close to collapse.

Intelligence activities were not only designed to fill the gaps left by the limited strength of colonial armed forces. They were more multifaceted than this. Here we encounter the second potential obstacle to success: organization, or rather, organizational deficiency. The bureaucracy of colonial state security was expected to feed sensitive information to policymakers and the enforcers of colonial power. Its organizational structure needed to be sufficiently simple to prevent information getting lost in a bureaucratic tangle, but sufficiently sophisticated for intelligence analysts to filter out the critical intelligence from the background "noise" of workaday information. Colonial security services were therefore organized to furnish sufficient intelligence about local social organization to enable government to function. This sphere of intelligence activity ranged from police operations, threat assessments, criminal profiling, and infiltration of protonationalist groups to ostensibly innocuous data collection such as topographical surveys, taxation assessments, census returns, and anthropological studies of tribal and clan affiliations.

Intelligence gatherers and intelligence analysts were also intelligence disseminators. This brings us to the third obstacle to intelligence effectiveness:

politicization. Dissemination of information, and state action in response to it, completed an intelligence cycle that began with acquisition, reportage, and evaluation. The evaluation, dissemination, and action phases of this process were all points at which intelligence and policy intersected.[17]

At every stage of the intelligence cycle, threat assessment was inherently politicized by the dominant ideology of imperialism with its coded hierarchies of racial difference, gender discrimination, and European supremacy. The identification of whom or what constituted a danger to the colonial state stigmatized certain individuals, political parties, tribes, religious communities, and even entire ethnic groups. The lines separating evaluation of threats from cultural prejudice and racial stereotyping were blurred as deep-rooted assumptions about indigenous communities and their likely behavior informed intelligence analysis. Intelligence officers, senior officials, and colonial governors often shared similar attitudes, creating a further problem of mutual reinforcement of prevailing views. Here we encounter the question of cognition—the fourth and final obstacle to effective intelligence exploitation. Colonial states sought information about the entire dependent population. But those that provided it had to prioritize among groups to make their work manageable. Allocation of resources to intelligence targets reflected their underlying assumptions about where potential dangers lay. These assumptions, in turn, reflected their understanding—or cognition—of the society in which they operated.

At one level, this is merely to state the obvious. Social actors use their understanding of a local environment to decide on appropriate courses of action. At another level, however, cognition could present difficulties if it meant that intelligence collection and assessment were devoted to gathering information that merely reaffirmed the preexisting ideas of those in charge.[18] Put another way, cognition manifested itself as an obstacle to effective intelligence assessment when the colonial state's information-providers could not digest information that ran counter to their fundamental operating assumptions. Trapped by their cultural outlook, in such circumstances intelligence analysts simply told their political masters what they expected—or wanted—to hear. The point should not be overstressed. In most of the colonial settings studied here, intelligence communities tried to remain dispassionate and analytical. Their assessment of individuals, groups, and events nonetheless remained that of a colonial elite governing a racially ordered society.

Problems of cultural bias influenced source selection, threat rankings, and policy predictions. Intelligence warnings about dangers to colonial order were contingent; in other words, the problems foreseen were not considered inevitable.[19] Rather, the estimated likelihood of dissent reflected the received wisdom, the past experience, and the dominant attitudes of the intelligence communities that supplied information to colonial government. All this boiled down to cognition. Taken together, problems of politicization and cognition crept into colonial intelligence assessment less in the form of overt political direction from government intelligence "consumers" to the security service intelligence "producers" than in the mutual reinforcement of their attitudes as colonizers toward the dependent peoples under their charge.

All this reminds us that intelligence gathering was one thing, the formulation and implementation of effective security policy quite another. The bureaucratic structures, community affiliations, and cultural markings of colonial intelligence gathering reveal some things to the historian, but not others. Even high-quality intelligence made available quickly could not prevent the growth of indigenous opposition. This, however, was not its primary purpose. Security policy was more about containment than prevention. It was a compensatory strategy designed to overcome the inability of colonial states to impose their authority either by coercion or consent. Unable and unwilling to rule imperial territories as police states, the preferred alternative of French and British administrators across North Africa and the Middle East was what I have referred to here as the intelligence state.

From Morocco to Iraq, these intelligence states were not quite the domain of spies, uniformed officers, and huge secret police forces that the name may imply. Security service work was only rarely sensational. More often it was predictable, methodical, even tedious: more office work and record keeping than cloak and dagger. Committee meetings and laborious collation of personnel files and statistical data took up more time than face-to-face contacts between local informants and secret service operatives. Office-based analysis of long-term socioeconomic trends and short-term threats to the colonial order consumed far more resources than agent surveillance of dissidents.

There were, of course, important variations between territories, and between urban and rural intelligence gathering in individual states. Take Iraq as an example. Before and after the end of the Iraq mandate, government security forces devoted more resources to the suppression of tribal or separatist disorder than to the containment of nationalist opposition. But the frequency of disorder and the deployment of troops was not necessarily a reliable guide to the severity of the threat posed to government. Tribal rebellion might continue for years without endangering central administration. A few days of mass protest in the major towns and cities of Iraq might unseat the entire regime. It was therefore vital to balance intelligence gathering in the mainly outlying locations of tribal or separatist unrest against the far greater menace of organized urban political protest that might strike at the heart of the state apparatus.[20]

Iraq was not alone in this respect. The rise of organized nationalism in interwar empires was mirrored in intelligence reportage by the security services in North Africa and the Middle East. Yet it is striking that other issues entirely dominated the bulk of intelligence reports from both regions. Administrative intelligence and environmental intelligence consumed far more ink than political discussion of nationalist groups. Intelligence communities in the Middle East mandates and Sudan attached as much importance to tribal movements, cross-border incursions, and livestock raiding as to the predominantly urban phenomena of party politics and nationalist protest. Throughout the 1920s, field intelligence, mainly derived from humint, often focused on tribal politics, agricultural conditions, and economic resources. Such information collection sometimes contrasted with central government preoccupation with wider issues of geostrategy and economies of scale in imperial administration. As its designation implies, human intelligence told a story about politics from below, whereas ministers and senior departmental advisers in Paris and London tended to discuss political change from above.

This is not to suggest that security agencies had no role in high politics; quite the reverse. In each of the territories studied here, the military personnel and police officers that dominated security agency work made up a cohesive imperial "intelligence community." Its members were united in the belief that their jurisdictional and operational boundaries should be as wide as possible. Imperial governments tried to exert influence over indigenous political elites, usually by linking enfranchisement and access to subordinate office with naturalization, educational qualifications, and/or economic resources. Just as important as this political imperative was its economic equivalent: the regulation of the colonial economy by ordering metropolitan needs above the demands of local consumption. In each field, intelligence gathering, surveillance of dissent, and monitoring of local economic conditions were essential components of administrative decision making.

To play devil's advocate a moment, surely this characterization exaggerates the importance of intelligence to colonial government. Why should we regard essentially political reportage—governors' reports, district commissioners' correspondence, administrative surveys of prevailing conditions—as something more, as security intelligence pivotal to the survival of the colonial state? The reason is simple and fundamental: its predictive value. It was the nature of colonial rule (specifically, its denial of democratic inclusion) that made even low-level political appreciations a matter of colonial state security. Colonial power was grounded in racial dominance. The host of justifications advanced in defense of Western rule—from promises of economic modernization, to control of intercommunal conflict, to more efficient central administration—could never disguise this. After the unprecedented trials of World War I, imperial governments were acutely conscious that the alienation of dependent populations from a political system that systematically excluded them was, at best, a strong possibility, and at worst, only a matter of time. Political reportage followed this trend, seeking to anticipate the opposition inherent to a racially ordered system of government.

Colonial intelligence was thus set apart from metropolitan intelligence gathering about foreign opponents. Unlike strategic intelligence warnings of external threats to a country, which were predicated on foreseeing the unusual, the "surprise attack," colonial intelligence was based on the steady accumulation of information about an identified constituency—the internal population—whose underlying hostility to foreign rule was taken for granted.[21] Success in colonial governance was measured in popular acquiescence in European rule rather than willing acceptance of it. As the Algiers Sûreté concluded in May 1935, "It would be an undue expectation to 'be liked' by the *indigène,* and we do not believe that the authorities are liked. But, on the basis of numerous observations in very different locales, we do believe that the great majority does not harbor any systematic hostility to our presence and retains confidence in us."[22] Here was success neatly defined—as the absence of violent opposition.

This book has suggested that we should view political reportage as part of the intelligence apparatus of the colonial state for at least four other key reasons. One is that imperial authorities installed in Middle Eastern capitals between 1917 and 1920 were still in the early stages of amassing essential information about the territories and populations under their nominal control. Another is that colonial governments faced the urgent task of finding "reliable" local intermediaries to help administer justice, keep the peace, and collect taxes. Political reportage served both to identify collaborative personnel and to monitor their loyalty and performance. Political intelligence was also writ large in imperial security for a third reason, namely, the widely shared official assumption that disorder originated in changes to social conditions over which the imperial authorities exercised little or no control. In predominantly agricultural societies, climatic conditions, poor harvests, foodstuff shortages, economic migration, and other seasonal population movements were all potentially disruptive to the legal, fiscal, military, and social regulations that imperial governments sought to impose. Information about such events was therefore critical if chosen policies were not to be derailed. Swift government response to peasant hardship was also essential to limit the human misery involved, and thus contain the popular anger that might otherwise result.

The fourth reason that connects political reportage with security intelligence relates more specifically to organized political opposition to Western rule. As nationalist organizations proliferated across the Muslim world in the 1920s, colonial governments became more convinced that anticolonial nationalism was not merely the product of local circumstance but also a reflection of external manipulation. Hence the significance attached to evidence of Communist infiltration, pan-Arabist propaganda, and the growth in colonial student associations and other coordinating bodies eager to unite differing nationalist groups in opposition to European dominance. Surely this was proof that anticolonialism was as much the product of outside interference as it was of colonial misrule. How comforting it was to attribute mounting public hostility toward imperial policy to external subversion rather than to concede that imperial rule was locally detested!

Organized anticolonialism in Arab territories was thus conflated with external threats to empire. Hence the widespread tendency to exaggerate the role of the Comintern, of covert German funding for nationalist organization, and of pan-Arabist coordination of local nationalist protest. Here again we confront the underlying issue: lack of consensual authority in a colonial setting. Colonial authorities meshed local opposition with external dangers because state repression presented opportunities for foreign opponents to exploit the inevitable discontent of subject populations. Confronted with intractable opposition and a mass of colonial subjects denied meaningful political rights, imperial administration was hamstrung by another characteristic of colonial rule: shortage of state funds.

Colonial government on a shoestring was nothing new. Nor was it likely to change. It had long been a principle of British and French imperialism that dependent states should pay their own way—what in France was known for centuries as "the colonial compact."[23] Although this basic rule was frequently relaxed, colonial economies and the fiscal revenue generated from colonial taxpayers were expected to support the costs of imperial government, including expenditure on policing and internal security. Here, too, there were recurrent problems. After 1919, and still more so in the Depression years of the early 1930s, most colonial governments taxed their subject populations heavily. But the monetary resources of the taxable population in most colonial territories were too limited to fund extensive government spending. Taxes levied in kind, typically on agricultural produce and livestock, brought in additional monies once these goods were sold. Such sales did not alter the fact that few colonial governments were entirely self-supporting. Time after time in the interwar years colonial governors the length and breadth of Africa and the Middle East went cap in hand to their metropolitan Treasury for stopgap funding. The financial boundaries between colony and mother country became more nebulous as a consequence. This was particularly evident both in matters of internal policing, theoretically paid for locally, and external defense, whose costs were shared by colonial and metropolitan governments.

The salient point here is that the revenue base of colonial states was severely limited in the testing economic conditions that prevailed for a good portion of the interwar period. There was little capacity for internal spending to ameliorate social conditions, regardless of whether the political will to make such investment existed. Short of funds for internal economic development and increasingly open to popular challenge, colonial states were condemned to exist in a limbo between their articulation of policy objectives and the achievement of them. Financial stringency increased once the global Depression affected North Africa and the Middle East in 1929–30. Imperial authorities now found it harder still to reconcile their requirement for social control with the limited coercive means at their disposal. More than ever, the role of political intelligence in the colonial state was to reduce this deficit of repressive power.

Anxiety about external challenges to colonial rule was a constant feature of these interwar intelligence states. Even so, the increased threat of European war in the late 1930s caused a shift in priorities. The danger of another European conflagration reverberated through imperial policing and colonial intelligence assessment, and shaped security responses to the more widespread urban disorder and worker protest in Arab territories under British and French control after 1936.[24] But the menace of war was not the only factor affecting security policy in these prewar years. In the British case, Muslim outrage at the repression of the Palestine revolt and anger over Britain's ineffective response to Italian annexation of Ethiopia in 1935–36 gave a powerful fillip to public protests with other, more local causes.[25] These included the negotiation of an Anglo-Egyptian settlement over use of the Suez Canal, the uncertain future of the Sudan condominium, and the slide into worsening instability in posttreaty Iraq under King Ghazi.[26]

In the French case, the primary catalyst for worsening civil unrest in its overseas empire was the state repression attendant on the abandonment of Popular Front reforms in 1937–38. Just as nationalist parties, trade unions, and religious associations had tried to capitalize on the Popular Front's readiness to contemplate colonial reform, so they were first in line when Daladier's government, with strong support from the Senate and the colonial service, threw the reform process into reverse. The arrest of troublesome colonial leaders, the renewal of bans on union strike actions and collective bargaining, and the Sûreté sweeps against suspected Communist cells marked a reversion to "normal" interwar colonial conditions.[27] It was the freer political atmosphere that the Popular Front had tried to create that was extraordinary. In French North Africa and Indochina, the coercive containment of colonial nationalism in 1938–40 fit a longer-term pattern of state surveillance and legal restriction altered only fleetingly in 1936–37.

The French general staff's attempt to integrate the defense of empire into planning for war against Germany in Europe inevitably subordinated the colonies' strategic requirements to those of mainland France. In consequence, there were precious few resources that could be spared for overseas territories after the protection of France's borders was taken into account.[28] For Britain, the defense of its Asian possessions against Japanese attack posed a similar dilemma, and one typified by arguments within government and outside it over the feasibility of sending a battleship fleet to defend the Malay barrier and the Singapore naval base.[29] The prospect of simultaneous engagement against Germany, Italy, and Japan created insoluble strategic dilemmas for French and British imperial defense planners. By contrast, the preservation of colonial state control in the face of mounting internal opposition as war drew nearer presented challenges that seemed both more familiar and more manageable.

It would, therefore, be wrong to see the heightened interest in empire security after 1936 as a radical departure from the preceding fifteen years of colonial intelligence gathering. More widespread civil strife in Arab territories in the immediate prewar years caused an intensification of security service activity, rather than a major reconfiguration of its fundamental tenets. Obsession with German and, to a lesser extent, Italian support for anti-Western Muslim sedition had never entirely gone away after 1918. Contacts between pan-Islamist, pan-Arab, and nationalist groups and all manner of foreign governments were always obvious surveillance targets. By 1935, the primacy of local intelligence gathering focused on nationalist and other internal dissent was coming to an end. Britain's security agencies from Sudan to Iraq devoted much greater attention to monitoring contacts between their domestic opponents and foreign governments hostile to the Western powers.[30] Covert intelligence gathering also shifted toward discovery and containment of Axis activity in the Muslim world, a transition mirrored in the Levant SR.[31] These were not abrupt changes; they were prefigured years earlier.

It makes no sense to view the extent of intelligence gathering in colonial states as a corruption of their declared purpose to enhance the power of imperialist nations and introduce Western norms to the government of dependent societies. Rather, intelligence and empire were codependent. The central contention of this book has been that the North African and Middle Eastern territories studied here shared a fundamental characteristic: at root, they were intelligence states—shaped by the process of information gathering about the populations they claimed to control.

GLOSSARY

Armée d'Afrique:	the professional army of French North Africa, including French cavalry units (*chasseurs d'Afrique*), units of Moroccan irregulars (*goums*), North African cavalry units (*spahis*), North African infantry (*tirailleurs*), French infantry units (*zouaves*), and Foreign Legion regiments
bey:	reigning prince of the Husaynid dynasty in Tunisia, formerly subordinate to the Ottoman sultan
beylical:	relating to the administration of Tunisia's monarch, or *bey*
bureaux arabes:	the French Army's Algerian native affairs service
caïd:	tribal representative or administrator
caliph:	usually refers to the Moroccan or Ottoman sultan as successor to the Prophet Mohammed
cercle:	colonial administrative district, headed by a French district officer
La Coloniale:	the French colonial army after 1900, apart from forces raised in French North Africa. Largely made up of professional metropolitan regiments (Coloniale blanche) and colonial infantry regiments (*tirailleurs*).
commandant de cercle:	French colonial district officer
Contrôle bédouin:	French tribal control administration in the Levant mandates
dahir:	decree legislation passed by the Moroccan sultanate
dar al-Islam:	the Islamic world

Destour:	the Arabic term for *constitution,* and the title adopted by the Tunisian Constitutionalist Party
direction des affaires indigènes:	French colonial native affairs office
djemâa:	village assembly in colonial Algeria
effendiyya:	educated urban middle class in Arab cities, often junior officials
évolué:	a francophone colonial subject that had received a European-style education, often employed as a government clerk or junior official
fasa'il:	volunteer platoon
fellah:	peasant farmer
ghaffir:	village policeman
goum:	a small force of Moroccan irregular infantry, typically numbering 150–175 men
habous:	property or land bequeathed for a religious or charitable purpose
harka:	an organized military force
Hashemite:	direct descendant of Hashim, the great-grandfather of Muhammed
Hijaz:	the western region of the Arabian Peninsula
indigénat:	colonial legislative code that empowered French regional officials to punish colonial subjects with fines or a short prison sentence without recourse to trial
Istiqlal:	Arabic for *independence.* A title adopted by nationalist parties in Syria and Morocco.
khalifa:	a *caïd*'s representative
khedive:	Ottoman viceroy in Egypt
koda:	a poll tax based on head counts of livestock
Maghreb:	collective term for the countries and region of Northwest Africa; used here to denote Morocco, Algeria, and Tunisia
makhzen:	the collective term for the Moroccan government and its administrative services
ma'mur:	district subofficer, Sudan Condominium
marabout:	Muslim holy man, typically the local leader of a religious sanctuary, or *zawiya*
madrassa (*médersa*):	a religious school of advanced Muslim learning, often linked to a mosque
méharistes:	French-officered camel companies

métis(se):	offspring of mixed-race parents
métissage:	miscegenation, or the interbreeding of people classified as members of different racial groups
mukhtar:	Muslim village headman or head of a town quarter
pasha:	urban administrator of the Moroccan sultanate
qadi (cadi):	a magistrate or judge of Shari'a Law
razzia:	livestock raid
sanjak:	Ottoman administrative subdistrict of a *vilayet;* hence, "the *sanjak* of Alexandretta" in French Syria
Sharif:	a leader directly descended from the Prophet Mohammed
sheikh:	the leader of a tribal fraction, a recognized elder, or the head of a religious institution such as a *zawiya*
spahi:	French North African cavalry of the Armée d'Afrique
Sufism:	Islamic mysticism, often associated with a revered saint
tariqa:	a Muslim religious brotherhood
tirailleurs:	literally, riflemen. Usually applied to Coloniale infantry; hence, *tirailleurs sénégalais,* referring to West African infantry units.
'ulamā:	a recognized Koranic teacher
umma:	the Muslim community
vilayet (in Turkish, *wilayet*):	Ottoman province
Wahhabism:	a puritannical Muslim sect
zawiya:	a Sufi Muslim religious institution, based around the tomb of a saint and sometimes including a school and/or hospice

NOTES

SHAA	Service Historique de l'Armée de l'Air, Vincennes
SHM	Service Historique de la Marine, Vincennes
TNA	The National Archives, Kew, London
WO	War Office

INTRODUCTION

1. Regarding limited (or "negative") sovereignty and "quasi-states" in colonial and contemporary Africa, see Carolyn M. Warner, "The Political Economy of 'Quasi-Statehood' and the Demise of 19th Century African Politics," *Review of International Studies* 25, no. 2 (1999): 233–55; and Robert H. Jackson, *Quasi-States: Sovereignty, International Relations and the Third World* (Cambridge: Cambridge University Press, 1993), especially 21–31. For a challenge to the idea of the state as the main organizing element in contemporary Africa, see M. Bratton, "Beyond the State: Civil Society and Associational Life in Africa," *World Politics* 41, no. 3 (1989): 407–30.

2. John Ferris, "Intelligence," in *The Origins of World War Two: The Debate Continues*, ed. Robert Boyce and Joe Maiolo (London: Palgrave, 2003), 308; also cited in Peter Jackson, "Historical Reflections on the Uses and Limits of Intelligence," in *Intelligence and Statecraft: The Use and Limits of Intelligence in International Society*, ed. Peter Jackson and Jennifer Siegel (Westport, Conn.: Praeger, 2005), 12.

3. One of the first to explain this process was the sociologist Immanuel Wallerstein, in "Elites in French-Speaking West Africa: The Social Basis of Ideas," *Journal of Modern African Studies* 3, no. 1 (1965): 1–33.

4. Philip S. Khoury, *Syria and the French Mandate: The Politics of Arab Nationalism, 1920–1945* (Princeton, N.J.: Princeton University Press, 1987); Gérard D. Khoury, *La France et l'Orient arabe: Naissance du Liban moderne, 1914–1920* (Paris: Armand Colin, 1993); Hanna Batatu, *The Old Social Classes and the Revolutionary Movements of Iraq* (Princeton, N.J.: Princeton University Press, 1978); Eugene L. Rogan, *Frontiers of the State in the Late Ottoman Empire: Transjordan, 1850–1921* (Cambridge: Cambridge University Press, 1999), especially chapter 2. Regarding Palestine, see Bernard Wasserstein, *The British in Palestine: The Mandatory Government and the Arab-Jewish Conflict, 1917–1929* (Oxford: Basil Blackwell, 1991); Martin Kolinsky, *Law, Order and Riots in Mandatory Palestine, 1928–1935* (London: Macmillan, 1993); and Sahar Huneidi, *A Broken Trust: Herbert Samuel, Zionism and the Palestinians (1920–25)* (London: I. B. Tauris, 2001).

5. Colin Newbury, *Patrons, Clients, and Empire: Chieftaincy and Over-Rule in Asia, Africa, and the Pacific* (Oxford: Oxford University Press, 2003), 257–58. For a succinct explanation of the theoretical complexities behind the term *indirect rule*, see John W. Cell, "Colonial Rule," in *The Oxford History of the British Empire*, vol. 4, *The Twentieth Century*, ed. Judith Brown and William Roger Louis (Oxford: Oxford University Press, 1999), 237–43.

6. Newbury, *Patrons, Clients, and Empire*, 1–7.

7. For a relevant discussion of the role of endogenous rural society in shaping state formation in sub-Saharan Africa, see Catherine Boone, *Political Topographies of the African State: Territorial Authority and Institutional Choice* (Cambridge: Cambridge University Press, 2003).

8. Newbury, *Patrons, Clients, and Empire*, 257.

9. See, for example, Wallerstein, "Elites in French-Speaking West Africa," 4–7.

10. Newbury, *Patrons, Clients, and Empire*, 257–68.

11. Robert Gildea, *Barricades and Borders: Europe, 1800–1914*, 3rd edition (Oxford: Oxford University Press, 2003), chapters 9 and 13; Susan Bayly, "French Anthropology and the Durkheimians in Colonial Indochina," *Modern Asian Studies* 34, no. 3 (2000): 581–622.

12. Christopher Dandeker, *Surveillance, Power and Modernity: Bureaucracy and Discipline from 1700 to the Present Day* (London: Polity Press, 1990), 5.

13. Ann Laura Stoler, "Sexual Affronts and Racial Frontiers: European Identities and the Cultural Politics of Exclusion in Colonial Southeast Asia," *Comparative Studies in Society and History* 34, no. 3 (1992): 514–51; also in Stoler, *Carnal Knowledge and Imperial Power: Race and the Intimate in Colonial Rule* (Berkeley and Los Angeles: University of California Press, 2002), chapter 4.

14. D. George Boyce, "From Assaye to the *Assaye:* Reflections on British Government Force and Moral Authority in India," *Journal of Military History* 63, no. 3 (1999): 643–64.

15. William Eckhardt, "Civilizations, Empire and Wars," *Journal of Peace Research* 27, no. 1 (1990): 14.

16. Patrick Chabal, ed., *Political Domination in Africa: Reflection on the Limits of Power* (Cambridge: Cambridge University Press, 1986), 13; also cited in Crawford Young, *The African Colonial State in Comparative Perspective* (New Haven, Conn.: Yale University Press, 1994), 6.

17. Carolyn M. Warner, "The Rise of the State System in Africa," in *Empires, Systems and States: Great Transformations in International Politics*, ed. Michael Cox, Tim Dunne, and Ken Booth (Cambridge: Cambridge University Press, 2001), 86.

18. Roger Owen, *State, Power and Politics in the Making of the Modern Middle East* (London: Routledge, 1992), 3–7; Sami Zubaida, *Islam, the People and the State*, 2nd edition (London: I. B. Tauris, 1993), 121–26; also cited in Yoav Alon, "Tribal Shaykhs and the Limits of British Imperial Rule in Transjordan, 1920–46," *Journal of Imperial and Commonwealth History* 32, no. 1 (2004): 89n6.

19. Alon, "Tribal Shaykhs and the Limits of British Imperial Rule," 71.

20. A point made in Iraq's case in Toby Dodge, "International Obligation, Domestic Pressure and Colonial Nationalism: The Birth of the Iraqi State under the Mandate System," in *The British and French Mandates in Comparative Perspectives*, ed. Nadine Méouchy and Peter Sluglett (Leiden: Brill, 2004), 143–64.

21. The concept of "warning failure" is usually discussed in relation to a state's failure to anticipate or act on an imminent threat of external attack. The inherent difficulties in providing a comprehensive warning system are of relevance here, however; see Richard K. Betts, "Analysis, War, and Decision: Why Intelligence Failures Are Inevitable," *World Politics* 31, no. 1 (1978): 61–89.

22. Michael Herman, *Intelligence Power in Peace and War* (Cambridge: Cambridge University Press, 1996), 284–87.

23. The comments here follow Alice Hills's typology for African police forces; see her "Towards a Critique of Policing and National Development in Africa," *Journal of Modern African Studies* 34, no. 2 (1996): 273.

24. Hannah Arendt, *On Violence* (London: Harcourt, 1970).

25. Jock McCulloch, "Empire and Violence, 1900–1939," in *Gender and Empire,*

ed. Philippa Levine, Oxford History of the British Empire Companion Series (Oxford: Oxford University Press, 2004), 220–39.

26. Jim House and Neil MacMaster, *Paris 1961: Algerians, State Terror, and Memory* (Oxford: Oxford University Press, 2006), especially chapter 1.

27. For a discussion of political reaction to the killings, see Derek Sayer, "British Reaction to the Amritsar Massacre, 1919–1920," *Past and Present* 131 (1991): 130–64; Boyce, "From Assaye to the *Assaye*," 655–68.

28. Gil Merom, *How Democracies Lose Small Wars: State, Society, and the Failures of France in Algeria, Israel in Lebanon, and the United States in Vietnam* (Cambridge: Cambridge University Press, 2003), 48–49, 64–65.

29. Christopher Andrew, "The Nature of Military Intelligence," in *Go Spy the Land: Military Intelligence in History*, ed. Keith Neilson and B. J. C. McKercher (Westport, Conn.: Praeger, 1992), 1–16.

30. Richard Roberts and Kristan Mann, eds., *Law in Colonial Africa* (Portsmouth, N.H.: Heinemann, 1991), 3–5. As Roberts and Mann note in their opening remarks, "Laws and courts, police and prisons formed essential elements in European efforts to establish and maintain political domination. . . . Colonialism sought to impose a new moral as well as political and economic order, founded on loyalty to metropolitan and colonial states and on discipline, order, and regularity in work, leisure, and bodily habits."

31. Warner, "Rise of the State System in Africa," 65–66, 78–79.

32. Ibid., 67–69.

33. Crawford Young, "The Colonial State and Post-colonial Crisis," in *Decolonization and African Independence: The Transfers of Power, 1960–1980*, ed. Prosser Gifford and William Roger Louis (New Haven, Conn.: Yale University Press, 1988), 7.

34. On the moral economy of African states after decolonization, see William A. Munro, "Power, Peasants and Political Development: Reconsidering State Construction in Africa," *Comparative Studies in Society and History* 38, no. 1 (1996): 112–15.

35. G. John Ikenberry, *After Victory: Institutions, Strategic Restraint, and the Rebuilding of Order after Major Wars* (Princeton, N.J.: Princeton University Press, 2001).

36. Jackson, *Quasi-States*, 21–23, 69–71. Jackson's perceptive comments about the consequences of what he terms "negative sovereignty" in postcolonial black Africa draw on his reading of the effects of late colonialism on state structures in the developing world.

37. For discussion of the Egyptian and Sudan examples, see Roger Owen, *Lord Cromer: Victorian Imperialist, Edwardian Proconsul* (Oxford: Oxford University Press, 2004); and Peter Woodward, *Sudan, 1898–1989: The Unstable State* (London: I. B. Tauris, 1989).

38. On the British experience in India, see David Page, *Prelude to Partition: The Indian Muslims and the Imperial System of Control, 1920–1932* (Delhi: Oxford University Press, 1982); Gyanendra Pandey, *The Construction of Communalism in Colonial North India* (Delhi: Oxford University Press, 1990); C. A. Bayly, *Imperial Meridian: The British Empire and the World, 1730–1830* (London: Longman, 1989); and Thomas R. Metcalf, *Ideologies of the Raj* (Cambridge: Cambridge University Press, 1997). On Malaya, see William R. Roff, *The Origins of Malay Nationalism* (New Haven, Conn.: Yale University Press, 1967); Anthony Milner, *The Invention of Politics in Colonial Malaya: Contesting Nationalism and the Expansion of the Public Sphere* (Cambridge: Cam-

bridge University Press, 1995); and Simon C. Smith, *British Relations with the Malay Rulers from Decentralization to Malayan Independence, 1930–1957* (Kuala Lumpur: Oxford University Press, 1995). On Arabia, see Elie Kedourie, *In the Anglo-Arab Labyrinth: The McMahon-Husayn Correspondence and Its Interpretations, 1914–1939* (Cambridge: Cambridge University Press, 1976); Elizabeth Monroe, *Britain's Moment in the Middle East, 1914–1971*, new edition (London: Chatto and Windus, 1981); Timothy J. Paris, *Britain, the Hashemites and Arab Rule, 1920–1925: The Sharifian Solution* (London: Frank Cass, 2003); and, from the perspective of decolonization, Glen Balfour-Paul, *The End of Empire in the Middle East: Britain's Relinquishment of Power in Her Last Three Arab Dependencies* (Cambridge: Cambridge University Press, 1991).

39. Informative studies are Christopher Harrison, *France and Islam in West Africa, 1860–1960* (Cambridge: Cambridge University Press, 1988); and David Robinson, *Paths of Accommodation: Muslim Societies and French Colonial Authorities in Senegal and Mauritania, 1880–1920* (Athens: Ohio University Press, 2000). See also David Robinson, "French 'Islamic' Policy and Practice in Late Nineteenth-Century Senegal," *Journal of African History* 29 (1988): 415–35.

40. Such misinterpretation occurred in the Mauritanian western Sahara. See Timothy Cleaveland, "Islam and the Construction of Social Identity in the Nineteenth-Century Sahara," *Journal of African History* 39 (1998): 366–8.

41. George Joffé, "Maghribi Islam and Islam in the Maghrib: The Eternal Dichotomy," in *African Islam and Islam in Africa: Encounters between Sufis and Islamists,* ed. David Westerlund and Eva Evers Rosander (London: Hurst, 1997), 64.

42. For Algerian examples, see James McDougall, *History and the Culture of Nationalism in Algeria* (Cambridge: Cambridge University Press, 2006), chapters 2–3; Allen Christelow, "The Mosque at the Edge of the Plaza: Islam in the Algerian Colonial City," *Maghreb Review* 25, nos. 3–4 (2000): 296–98.

43. Three studies of French colonial urbanism have made explicit links with the state's security needs: Janet L. Abu-Lughod, *Rabat: Urban Apartheid in Morocco* (Princeton, N.J.: Princeton University Press, 1980); Gwendolyn Wright, *The Politics of Design in French Colonial Urbanism* (Chicago: University of Chicago Press, 1991); and Zeynep Çelik, *Urban Forms and Colonial Confrontations: Algiers under French Rule* (Berkeley and Los Angeles: University of California Press, 1997).

44. See Christopher Andrew and David Dilks, eds., *The Missing Dimension: Governments and Intelligence Communities in the Twentieth Century* (London: Macmillan, 1984).

CHAPTER 1

1. See, for example, MAE, série K: Afrique, sous-série Affaires musulmanes, vol. 1, no. 601, Algiers Governor to Foreign Ministry, "A/S de publications de propagande allemande," 7 July 1918.

2. For instance, Britain's internal security service, MI5, grew from fourteen staff members in 1914 to nearly 850 by 1919. By 1925, its permanent staff had been cut back to twenty-five. See Edward Higgs, *The Information State in England: The Central Collection of Information on Citizens since 1500* (London: Palgrave, 2004), 144–46.

3. Philip S. Khoury, *Syria and the French Mandate: The Politics of Arab Nationalism, 1920–1945* (Princeton, N.J.: Princeton University Press, 1987), 78.

4. In this context, Antonio Gramsci's ideas of hegemonic state control help explain the frictions between colonial states and subject peoples. An outstanding example of work on colonialism in the Middle East that incorporates Gramsci's theories is Joseph A. Massad, *Colonial Effects: The Making of National Identity in Jordan* (New York: Columbia University Press, 2001).

5. Rashid Khalidi, "The Formation of Palestinian Identity: The Critical Years, 1917–1923," in *Rethinking Nationalism in the Arab Middle East,* ed. James Jankowski and Israel Gershoni (New York: Columbia University Press, 1997), 171–90.

6. James L. Gelvin, *Divided Loyalties: Nationalism and Mass Politics in Syria at the Close of Empire* (Berkeley and Los Angeles: University of California Press, 1998); Gelvin, "The Social Origins of Popular Nationalism in Syria: Evidence for a New Framework," *International Journal of Middle East Studies* 26 (1994): 645–61.

7. Reeva S. Simon, "The Imposition of Nationalism on a Non-nation State: The Case of Iraq during the Interwar Period, 1921–1941," in *Rethinking Nationalism in the Arab Middle East,* ed. James Jankowski and Israel Gershoni (New York: Columbia University Press, 1997), 87–104.

8. Toby Dodge, *Inventing Iraq: The Failure of Nation Building and a History Denied* (New York: Columbia University Press, 2003).

9. For discussion of the parameters of military and security intelligence, see Michael Herman, *Intelligence Power in Peace and War* (Cambridge: Cambridge University Press, 1996), 16–21.

10. See the Ministry of Colonies political affairs directorate records in CAOM, 1affpol/907.

11. Serge Berstein and Jean-Jacques Becker, *Histoire de l'anti-communisme en France,* vol. 1, *1917–1940* (Paris: Olivier Orban, 1987), chapter 6; Sophie Coeuré, *La grande lueur à l'est: Les français et l'Union soviétique* (Paris: Éditions du Seuil, 1999); Frédéric Monier, *Le complot dans la République: Stratégies du secret de Boulanger à la Cagoule* (Paris: Éditions La Découverte, 1998); Michael B. Miller, *Shanghai on the Métro: Spies, Intrigue, and the French between the Wars* (Berkeley and Los Angeles: University of California Press, 1994).

12. As examples, see Jacques Marseille, *Empire colonial et capitalisme français: Histoire d'un divorce* (Paris: Albin Michel, 1984), 218–39. Some colonial governments had severe deficits by the early 1930s; see, for example, Daniel Lefeuvre, *Chère Algérie: Comptes et mécomptes de la tutelle coloniale, 1930–1962* (Paris: Société Française d'Histoire d'Outre-Mer, 1997), 48–49, 72–74.

13. John Willis, "Colonial Policing in Aden, 1937–1967," *Arab Studies Journal* 5, no. 1 (1997): 66–67.

14. Roger Davidson, "Treasury Control and Labour Intelligence in Late Victorian and Edwardian Britain," *Historical Journal* 28, no. 3 (1985): 719–26.

15. Higgs, *Information State in England,* 123.

16. Roger Price, "Techniques of Repression: The Control of Popular Protest in Mid-Nineteenth-Century France," *Historical Journal* 25, no. 4 (1982): 861–64.

17. Higgs, *Information State in England,* 123–41.

18. John Horne, "Remobilizing for 'Total War': France and Britain, 1917–1918," in *State, Society, and Mobilization in Europe during the First World War,* ed. John Horne (Cambridge: Cambridge University Press, 1997), 195–211.

19. Christopher Dandeker, *Surveillance, Power and Modernity: Bureaucracy and Discipline from 1700 to the Present Day* (London: Polity Press, 1990), 2–3, 101–3.

20. See, in particular, Anthony Giddens, *The Consequences of Modernity* (Stanford, Calif.: Stanford University Press, 1990).

21. For the Soviet case, see David Shearer, "Elements Near and Alien: Passportization, Policing, and Identity in the Stalinist State, 1932–1952," *Journal of Modern History* 76, no. 4 (2004): 835–37.

22. Anthony Giddens, *The Nation-State and Violence* (Cambridge: Cambridge University Press, 1985), 46–47; also cited in Shearer, "Elements Near and Alien," 836.

23. As Roger Price has shown, this was something the French learned during the food riots and agricultural protests of the mid-nineteenth century; see his *The Modernization of Rural France: Communications Networks and Agricultural Market Structures in Nineteenth-Century France* (London: Hutchinson, 1985).

24. Take the example of Ottoman Syria as described in Eugene L. Rogan, "Instant Communications: The Impact of the Telegraph in Ottoman Syria," in *The Syrian Land: Processes of Integration and Fragmentation, Bilad al-Sham from the 18th to the 20th Century,* ed. Thomas Philipp and Birgit Schaebler (Stuttgart: F. Steiner, 1998), 113–28.

25. See, for instance, C. W. Newbury, *British Policy towards West Africa: Select Documents, 1875–1914* (Oxford: Clarendon Press, 1971), section II, doc. 58, DMI to Colonial Office, 2 May 1898.

26. One such was Colonel F. S. Newcombe, who produced a detailed topographic map of Palestine for the British authorities in Cairo on the eve of World War I; see Dov Gavish, "Foreign Intelligence Maps: Offshoots of the 1:100,000 Topographic Map of Israel," *Imago Mundi* 48 (1996): 174.

27. This process is nicely illustrated by the prevalence of military intelligence and crown agents' advice in the development of communications and infrastructure in British West Africa before World War I. See Newbury, *British Policy towards West Africa,* section IV/B, docs. 4–11.

28. R. Rivet, "Ethnographie et conquête du Moyen Atlas (1912–1931)," in *Sciences de l'homme et conquête coloniale: Constitution et usages des sciences humaines en Afrique, XIXᵉ–XXᵉ siècles* (Paris: Rue de l'Ulm, 1980).

29. As an example: TNA, WO 106/232, Sudan Intelligence Report no. 178/B: Harold MacMichael, "Ethnological Notes on the Kababish Tribe," n.d. [May 1909]. MacMichael's work in the Sudan Political Service cemented his reputation as a social anthropologist; see Abdullah Ali Ibrahim, "Breaking the Pen of Harold MacMichael: The Ja'aliyyin Identity Revisited," *International Journal of African Historical Studies* 21, no. 2 (1988): 217–31.

30. TNA, CO 1047/60, parts 1–4, Survey of Egypt, 1935–36.

31. Eliezer Tauber, "The Struggle for Dayr al-Zur: The Determination of Borders between Syria and Iraq," *International Journal of Middle East Studies* 23 (1991): 361–85; J. C. Wilkinson, "Nomadic Territory as a Factor in Defining Arabia's Boundaries," in *The Transformation of Nomadic Society in the Arab East,* ed. Martha Mundy and Basim Musallam (Cambridge: Cambridge University Press, 2000), 51–53.

32. Lahsen Jennin, "Le Moyen Atlas et les français: Évolution des connaissances et du savoir sur l'espace et sur la société rurale," in *Présences et images franco-marocaines au temps du protectorat,* ed. Jean-Claude Allain (Paris: l'Harmattan, 2003), 58.

33. Peter Jackson, "Historical Reflections on the Uses and Limits of Intelligence," in *Intelligence and Statecraft: The Use and Limits of Intelligence in International Society,* ed. Peter Jackson and Jennifer Siegel (Westport, Conn.: Praeger, 2005), 17–28.

34. TNA, CO 323/990/5, Annual Colonial Reports: Minutes and Report by Committee, 1927–28. From 1928 on, all annual colonial reports were standardized to include distinct sections covering local geography and languages, general political events, finance, production, trade and economics, communications, justice and policing, public works, public health, lands and survey, and labor.

35. TNA, CO 730/115/1, Iraq High Commission report, "The Comparative Financial Importance of the Various Articles of Revenue Administered by the Revenue Department," n.d. [1926].

36. Algerian agricultural taxes included the *zekkat* payable on livestock, the *ushur* payable on crops, the *lezma* payable on dates, the *hikr* payable on land ownership in the eastern department of Constantine, and a distinct capitation tax in the more heavily populated area of Kabylia; see TNA, WO 106/232, Sudan Intelligence Report no. 177, April 1909: "Notes on a Journey in Tripoli, Tunisia, Algeria, Tangiers by El Kaimakan F. G. Poole Bey."

37. Kenneth W. Stein, *The Land Question in Palestine, 1917–1919* (Chapel Hill: University of North Carolina Press, 1984); Warwick P. N. Tyler, *State Lands and Rural Development in Mandatory Palestine, 1920–1948* (Brighton: Sussex Academic Press, 2001).

38. For incisive discussion of the links between colonialism, public health, and state secrecy, see Alison Bashford, *Imperial Hygiene: A Critical History of Colonialism, Nationalism and Public Health* (London: Palgrave-Macmillan, 2004); and her introduction to Alison Bashford, ed., *Medicine at the Border: Disease, Globalization, and Security, 1850 to the Present* (London: Palgrave-Macmillan, 2007).

39. Gwendolyn Wright, *The Politics of Design in French Colonial Urbanism* (Chicago: University of Chicago Press, 1991), 71–72, citing Georges Hardy, *Géographie et colonisation* (Paris: Gallimard, 1933), 203.

40. Anne Godlewska and Neil Smith, eds., *Geography and Empire* (Oxford: Blackwell, 1994); Emmanuelle Sibeud, *Une science impériale pour l'Afrique? La construction des savoirs africanistes en France, 1878–1930* (Paris: EHESS, 2003); Alice L. Conklin, "The New 'Ethnology' and 'la Situation Coloniale' in Interwar France," *French, Politics, Culture and Society* 20, no. 2 (2002): 29–46.

41. For background, see Maurice Pearton, *The Knowledgeable State: Diplomacy, War and Technology since 1830* (London: Burnett Books, 1982), 20–26.

42. Herman, *Intelligence Power in Peace and War,* 61–63. Herman's model of a pyramid of humint sources, from the broad array of casual informants and government contacts at the bottom to the most sensitive and specialist agents' reports at the top, makes sense in this context.

43. CADN, Fonds Beyrouth, Cabinet Politique, vol. 842/D8, Beirut Inspector-General of Police annual report for 1927; TNA, CO 732/28/13, Baghdad Council of Ministers secretariat to Iraq High Commission, 28 August 1927.

44. Paula Mohs, "British Intelligence and the Arab Revolt in the Hejaz, 1914–1917" (Ph.D. diss., Cambridge University, 2003), 2–4.

45. Jean-Baptiste Manchon, "Recherches archéologiques et l'aviation militaire du Levant," *Revue Historique des Armées* 4 (2000): 91–96.

46. Christopher Andrew, "The Nature of Military Intelligence," in *Go Spy the Land: Military Intelligence in History*, ed. Keith Neilson and B. J. C. McKercher (Westport, Conn.: Praeger, 1992), 4.

47. Nathan J. Brown, "Law and Imperialism: Egypt in Comparative Perspective," *Law and Society Review* 29, no. 1 (1995): 103–4.

48. C. A. Bayly, *Empire and Information: Intelligence Gathering and Social Communication in India, 1780–1870* (Cambridge: Cambridge University Press, 1996), 3–6, 365.

49. Roger Price notes that a key function of rural policing in mid-nineteenth-century France was to prevent the spread of rumors about social deprivation or local disorder; see his "Techniques of Repression," 865.

50. Regarding the tendency among intelligence providers in closed societies to succumb to paranoia about potential threats, see Andrew, "Nature of Military Intelligence," 11.

51. CAOM, affpol/859, Commission d'étude des questions coloniales posées par la Guerre, rapport II: "La politique indigène de la France," 31 May 1918; Anne Summers and R. W. Johnson, "World War I Conscription and Social Change in Guinea," *Journal of African History* 19, no. 1 (1978): 25–38. Regarding troops' experiences in France, see Joe Lunn, *Memoirs of the Maelstrom: A Senegalese Oral History of the First World War* (Portsmouth, N.H.: Heinemann, 1999); Tyler Stovall, "The Color Line behind the Lines: Racial Violence in France during the First World War," *American Historical Review* 103, no. 3 (1998): 739–69.

52. James E. Genova, *Colonial Ambivalence, Cultural Authenticity, and the Limitations of Mimicry in French-Ruled West Africa, 1914–1956* (New York: Peter Lang, 2004), 16–17.

53. Byron D. Cannon, "Irreconcilability of Reconciliation: Employment of Algerian Veterans under the *Plan Jonnart*, 1919–1926," *Maghreb Review* 24, nos. 1–2 (1999): 42–50. These schemes were not a success, and numerous reserved posts remained unfilled.

54. Conklin, "New 'Ethnology' and 'la Situation Coloniale' in Interwar France," 29–46.

55. Genova, *Colonial Ambivalence*, 94–95.

56. Antony Best, *British Intelligence and the Japanese Challenge in Asia, 1914–1941* (London: Palgrave Macmillan, 2002), 4, 17–18, 35–38. Work on British intelligence officials' racial stereotyping of the Japanese military is particularly revealing; see John Ferris, " 'Worthy of Some Better Enemy?': The British Estimate of the Imperial Japanese Army, 1919–41, and the Fall of Singapore," *Canadian Journal of History* 28 (1993): 223–56; Antony Best, "Constructing an Image: British Intelligence and Whitehall's Perception of Japan, 1931–39," *Intelligence and National Security* 11, no. 3 (1996): 403–23.

57. Bayly, *Empire and Information*, 6.

58. Ibid., 161–74, 315–37 passim.

59. David Arnold, *Police Power and Colonial Rule: Madras, 1859–1947* (Oxford: Oxford University Press, 1986), 118–19.

60. David M. Anderson and David Killingray, "Consent, Coercion and Colonial Control: Policing the Empire, 1830–1940," and Douglas H. Johnson, "From Military to Tribal Police: Policing the Upper Nile Province of the Sudan," both in *Polic-*

ing the Empire: Government, Authority and Control, 1830–1940, ed. David M. Anderson and David Killingray (Manchester: Manchester University Press, 1991), 6, 153–63.

61. See Charles R. Pennell, *A Country with a Government and a Flag: The Rif War in Morocco* (Wisbech: Middle East and North African Studies Press, 1986); Lenka Bokova, *La confrontation franco-syrienne à l'époque du Mandat, 1925–1927* (Paris: l'Harmattan, 1990); Heather Sharkey, *Living with Colonialism. Nationalism and Culture in the Anglo-Egyptian Sudan* (Berkeley and Los Angeles: University of California Press, 2003); and Willis, "Colonial Policing in Aden," 60–61, 77.

62. Tim Moreman, "'Watch and Ward': The Army in India and the North-West Frontier, 1920–1939," in *Guardians of Empire: The Armed Forces of the Colonial Powers, c. 1700–1964*, ed. David Killingray and David Omissi (Manchester: Manchester University Press, 1999), 137–56; Bayly, *Empire and Information*, 97–141 passim.

63. Provincial tours remained popular in British Middle Eastern territories during the 1920s: TNA, FO 371/13841, enclosures 1–4 in R. H. Hoare (Cairo) to Sir Austen Chamberlain, 1 March 1929.

64. See, for example, TNA, WO 33/999, Sudan monthly intelligence reports, 1922–1925; FO 371/4984, Egypt Intelligence Staff reports summarizing provincial intelligence, 1920; India Office Archive, Political and Secret Department files for Mesopotamia and Kurdistan, 1917–22: L/PS/10/621–2, L/PS/10/762, L/PS/10/781–2. Periodic intelligence summaries compiled by the native affairs sections in the French North African administrations were similarly structured; see CAOM, GGA, sous-série 11H: Service des affaires indigènes, "Rapports politiques périodiques."

65. TNA, WO 33/999, Sudan monthly intelligence reports, nos. 342–61 (January 1923–August 1924), covering the development of the White Flag League and the 1924 army mutinies. For a comparable French example, see the Algiers native affairs bureau reports on support for Amir Khaled and his program of limited democratization, or "Khalédisme": CAOM, GGA, 11H46, Direction des affaires indigènes, Rapports mensuels, 1919–21.

66. See, for instance, the varying content in the native affairs division reports submitted to Algeria's prefectures before the Second World War: SHA, Moscow, C223/D123, Prefecture d'Oran affaires indigènes, Centre d'informations et d'études, "Bulletins mensuels d'informations concernant la politique indigène dans le département d'Oran," monthly political reports, 1937–39.

67. In the context of the Iraq mandate, Toby Dodge refers to this tendency presciently as "the divided social imagination of late colonialism"; see his *Inventing Iraq*, 63–82.

68. As examples: CAOM, GGA, 11H46, Direction des affaires indigènes, "Rapport mensuel sur la situation politique des indigènes," reports for July 1918, March and November 1919.

69. See Indian Office Archive, L/PS/10/686, note by India Office Political Department, "Mesopotamia: Civil Administration," 12 April 1918, which summarizes Cox's first reports.

70. Dodge, *Inventing Iraq*, 17–18.

71. Eliezer Tauber, *The Formation of Modern Syria and Iraq* (London: Frank Cass, 1995), 179–97; Wamich Jo Nahdmi, "The Political, Intellectual and Social Roots of the Iraq Independence Movement 1920" (Ph.D. diss., University of Durham, 1974), 138–59.

72. Indian Office Archive, L/PS/10/686, B283, enclosure, note by Sir Percy Cox, "The Future of Mesopotamia," forwarded to Eastern Committee on 12 April 1918. Gertrude Bell's appreciation of Sir Percy Cox's administrative methods may be seen in her private paper correspondence, publicly available on the University of Newcastle Library special collections Web site: www.gerty.ncl.ac.uk.

73. Indian Office Archive, L/PS/10/686, tel. 1049, Sir Percy Cox to Secretary of State for India, 7 May 1917; note by Sir Arnold Wilson, 27 September 1918.

74. *Documents diplomatiques français* (hereafter *DDF*), 1920/II, docs. 30 and 107, both Millerand to Gouraud, 27 May and 13 June 1920.

75. CADN, Fonds Beyrouth, vol. 840/D1, SR summary review, n.d. [probably 1930].

76. *DDF*, 1920/I, doc. 133, Gouraud to Millerand, 18 February 1920.

77. SHA, Moscow, C623/D1419, CSTL, 2ᵉ Bureau, "Aperçu général sur l'activité des services de renseignements étrangers en Syrie et au Liban," n.d. [November 1935].

78. The best analysis of SR activities in Syria is Jean-David Mizrahi, *Genèse de l'État mandataire: Service de renseignements et bandes armées en Syrie et au Liban dans les années 1920* (Paris: Publications de la Sorbonne, 2003).

79. Robert J. Goldstein, *Political Repression in 19th-Century Europe* (London: Croom Helm, 1983), 69–72.

80. D. L. L. Parry, "Clemenceau, Caillaux and the Political Use of Intelligence," *Intelligence and National Security* 9, no. 3 (1994): 472–94.

81. This section draws heavily on Bertrand Warusfel, "Histoire de l'organisation du contre-espionnage français entre 1871 et 1945," in *Cahiers du Centre d'Etudes d'Histoire de la Défense*, vol. 1, *Renseignement* (Paris: CCEHD, 1996), 13–40; and SHA Fonds Privés archive guide: "Les Archives du deuxième bureau SR-SCR récupérées de Russie."

82. Clifford Rosenberg, *Policing Paris: The Origins of Modern Immigration Control between the Wars* (Ithaca, N.Y.: Cornell University Press, 2006), 42–44.

83. SHA, Fonds Privés, Moscow Archives (hereafter "Moscow"), Dossier relatif à l'organisation des services de contre-espionnage 1932–1936.

84. SHA, Moscow, Colonel Catroux (Levant SR), "Instruction sur l'organisation et le fonctionnement du service de contre-espionnage dans les territoires sous mandat français," 13 January 1937.

85. SHA, Fonds Privés, Moscow, Dossier rélatif à l'organisation des services de contre-espionnage 1932–1936: Note sur le fonctionnement des services de contre-espionnage.

86. SHA, Moscow, C286/D429, no. 169/TV, Commissaire divisionnaire de Police spéciale (Nice) note, "Propagande Nationaliste Révolutionnaire Musulmane," 6 January 1934. The Sûreté monitored North African construction workers building defensive works along France's eastern frontier, and surveyed contacts between workers and colonial troops garrisoned in the Midi. French provincial police adopted many of the practices of their counterparts in Paris, although the Paris Prefecture of Police was separately organized; see Rosenberg, *Policing Paris*, 9.

87. SHA, Moscow, C223/D122, SEA report, "La situation des indigènes en Kabylie," 16 April 1935.

88. CAOM, GGA, 9H32, Service des affaires indigènes (Algiers), "Note sur les emplois réservés aux anciens militaires indigènes," 5 July 1927.

89. John Ferris, "Before 'Room 40': The British Empire and Signals Intelligence, 1898–1914," *Journal of Strategic Studies* 12, no. 4 (1989): 431–57

90. Ibid.

91. John Ferris, "The British Army and Signals Intelligence in the Field during the First World War," *Intelligence and National Security* 3, no. 1 (1988): 23–48.

92. Yigal Sheffy, *British Military Intelligence in the Palestine Campaign, 1914–1918* (London: Frank Cass, 1998), 324–25.

93. Ferris, "Before 'Room 40,' " 444.

94. Sheffy, *British Military Intelligence in the Palestine Campaign,* 156–58.

95. Peter Morris, "Intelligence and Its Interpretation: Mesopotamia, 1914–1916," in *Intelligence and International Relations, 1900–1945,* ed. Christopher Andrew and Jeremy Noakes (Exeter: University of Exeter Press, 1987), 77–81.

96. Ferris, "Before 'Room 40,' " 438–42.

97. Richard J. Popplewell, *Intelligence and Imperial Defence: British Intelligence and the Defence of the Indian Empire, 1904–1924* (London: Frank Cass, 1995): for details of Curzon's reforms and unrest in Bengal, see chapters 2 and 4; regarding wartime India, see chapter 7.

98. G. H. Bennett, *British Foreign Policy during the Curzon Period, 1919–24* (London: Macmillan, 1995), 60–71.

99. Victor Madeira, " 'No Wishful Thinking Allowed': Secret Service Committee and Intelligence Reform in Great Britain, 1919–23," *Intelligence and National Security* 18, no. 1 (2003): 1–10.

100. Rhodes House Library, MSS BRIT EMP s.390, Clarence Buxton papers 1/5, Buxton letter to William D. Battershill, Palestine Chief Secretary, 16 March 1939.

101. This trend was manifest in public attitudes toward the police in Ireland: Charles Townshend, "Policing Insurgency in Ireland, 1914–23," in *Policing the Empire: Government, Authority and Control, 1830–1940,* ed. David M. Anderson and David Killingray (Manchester: Manchester University Press, 1991), 24–25.

102. Massad, *Colonial Effects,* chapter 3; Eugene L. Rogan, "Bringing the State Back: The Limits of Ottoman Rule in Jordan, 1840–1910," in *Village, Steppe and State: The Social Origins of Modern Jordan,* ed. Eugene L. Rogan and Tariq Tell (London: British Academic Press, 1994), 32–57.

103. TNA, FO 371/7765, Allenby (Cairo) to FO Eastern Department, "Egypt, Annual Report, 1921: Chapter VI, sub-section Public Security."

104. Ibid., "Chapter VI, sub-section Police."

105. David Arnold, "Police Power and the Demise of British Rule in India, 1930–47," in *Policing the Empire: Government, Authority and Control, 1830–1940,* ed. David M. Anderson and David Killingray (Manchester: Manchester University Press, 1991), 44.

106. Townshend, "Policing Insurgency in Ireland," 24–39.

107. TNA, FO 371/14503, E1555/41/93, Colonial Office to Sir Francis Humphrys, 20 March 1930.

108. TNA, PRO 30/69/338, Ramsay MacDonald Private Office papers, copy of Colonial Office Middle East Department memorandum, "Police in Iraq," 26 September 1929.

109. *British Documents on Foreign Affairs* (hereafter *BDFA*), ed. K. Bourne and D. Cameron Watt (Frederick, Md.: University Publications of America, 1985 et seq.),

part II, series B, vol. 8, ed. Robin Bidwell, doc. 206, Sir John Simon to Sir Francis Humphrys (Baghdad), 8 December 1932.

110. TNA, AIR 23/120, High Commissioner H. Dodds memorandum to Air HQ Baghdad, "Composition of the Iraq Army," 8 June 1925; Reeva Spector Simon, *Iraq between the Two World Wars: The Militarist Origins of Tyranny* (New York: Columbia University Press, 2004), 107–18.

111. British advisers at the Iraq Interior Ministry considered the threat of air attack decisive in preventing further escalation of widespread strikes and protests against taxation rates in Iraq over the summer of 1931; see TNA, FO 371/15342, E5732/3715/93, C. J. Edmonds, acting advisor, Ministry of Interior, secret dispatch, 10 October 1931. It is noteworthy, however, that the strikes achieved their declared purpose of securing across-the-board tax reductions.

112. For details, see Jafna L. Cox, "A Splendid Training Ground: The Importance to the Royal Air Force of Its Role in Iraq, 1919–32", *Journal of Imperial and Commonwealth History* 13, no. 2 (1985): 157–84.

113. TNA, FO 371/14502, Air Staff note, "Military Aspects of the Treaty with Iraq," 2 January 1930.

114. TNA, PRO 30/69/338, Ramsay MacDonald Private Office papers, Major-General Rowan Robinson memorandum, "Appreciation of the Situation in Iraq," 15 August 15 1933.

115. TNA, FO 406/71, E663/31/25, Enclosure: Sir P. Cunliffe-Lister to Sir A. Wauchope, summary of British policy in Arabian affairs, 1 February 1933.

116. TNA, WO 32/4138, Iraq: Army Council instructions to military mission, Baghdad, 16 June 1937.

117. Anderson and Killingray, *Policing and Decolonization,* 8–9; for examples, see Heather Streets, *Martial Races and Masculinity in the British Army, 1857–1914* (Manchester: Manchester University Press, 2004). For more detail on the Iraqi and Indian examples, see Mohammad Tarbush, *The Role of the Military in Politics: A Case Study of Iraq to 1941* (London: KPI, 1982); and A. Gupta, *The Police in British India, 1861–1947* (New Delhi: Concept, 1979).

118. Martin Kolinsky, "The Collapse and Restoration of Public Security," in *Britain and the Middle East in the 1930s: Security Problems, 1935–1939,* ed. Michael J. Cohen and Martin Kolinsky (London: Macmillan, 1992), 153–62; Tom Bowden, "The Politics of the Arab Rebellion in Palestine, 1936–39," *Middle Eastern Studies* 11, no. 2 (1975): 153–69; and Charles Smith, "Communal Conflict and Insurrection in Palestine, 1936–48," in *Policing the Empire: Government, Authority and Control, 1830–1940,* ed. David M. Anderson and David Killingray (Manchester: Manchester University Press, 1991), 66–67.

119. TNA, FO 406/71, E6229/7/93, enclosure to Sir Francis Humphrys telegram to Sir John Simon, 12 October 1933: "Historical Summary of the Development of the Assyrian Question in Iraq."

120. TNA, FO 406/71, E5685/7/93, enclosure 1: Brigadier Hugo Headlam (acting inspector-general, Iraqi Army), "Report on the Assyrian Rebellion in Northern Iraq in July and August 1933," 6 September 1933; FO 371/19985, E5370/1/93, FO Eastern Department, "Memorandum on the Assyrian Question," 25 August 1934; Simon, *Iraq between the Two World Wars,* 112. Arab units of the Iraq Army commanded by Colonel Bakr Sidqi-el-Askiri were accused of summarily exe-

cuting former Assyrian levies that had rebelled against the Iraqi state and crossed into Syria in July 1933. The Assyrian rebels were, in turn, accused of mutilating Arab Iraqi troops killed after the rebels crossed the Tigris back into Iraq, where they engaged the Iraqi force sent to disarm them. These events triggered attacks on Assyrian refugee settlements across northern Iraq in which large numbers of civilians, including the entire male population of the village of Sumayl, were massacred by Iraqi Army units. These killings compelled the League of Nations to take a more active role in the search for a safe haven for the Assyrian community. In 1935, the French authorities agreed to permit the resettlement of Assyrian refugees in the Orontes River valley in the Ghab district of Syria; TNA, FO 371/19985, E795/4/93, Eastern Department, "Plan for Settling the Assyrians," 11 February 1936.

121. TNA, CO 732/16, Colonial Office minutes relating to the recruitment of native police auxiliaries in mandated territories, February 1925.

122. Arnold, "Police Power and the Demise of British Rule," 44.

123. Anderson and Killingray, introduction to *Policing and Decolonization*, 4–17.

CHAPTER 2

1. Carolyn M. Warner, "The Rise of the State System in Africa," in *Empires, Systems and States: Great Transformations in International Politics*, ed. Michael Cox, Tim Dunne, and Ken Booth (Cambridge: Cambridge University Press, 2001), 70–71.

2. Timothy Cleaveland, "Islam and the Construction of Social Identity in the Nineteenth-Century Sahara," *Journal of African History* 39, no. 3 (1998): 365–88.

3. Warner, "Rise of the State System in Africa," 71–76. Disputes over Arab land transfers were bitterest in Palestine, where possession of, and title to, land was bound up with the issue of Jewish colonization; see Ylana N. Miller, *Government and Society in Rural Palestine, 1920–1948* (Austin: University of Texas Press, 1985), especially chapters 2 and 5.

4. H. V. Brasted, "Irish Models and the Indian National Congress, 1870–1922," *South Asia* 8, no. 1 (1985): 24–45; Peter Heehs, "Foreign Influences on Bengali Revolutionary Terrorism, 1902–1908," *Modern Asian Studies* 28, no. 3 (1994): 533–56; Michael Silvestri, "'The Sinn Féin of India': Irish Nationalism and the Policing of Revolutionary Terrorism in Bengal," *Journal of British Studies* 39 (October 2000): 455–59.

5. Peter Robb, "The Ordering of Rural India: The Policing of Nineteenth-Century Bengal and Bihar," in *Policing the Empire: Government, Authority and Control, 1830–1940*, ed. David M. Anderson and David Killingray (Manchester: Manchester University Press, 1991), 145.

6. David Arnold, *Police Power and Colonial Rule: Madras, 1859–1947* (Oxford: Oxford University Press, 1986), 122–28, 138–39. The introduction of fingerprinting by the Sudan Police Identification Bureau after World War I was, for example, hailed as a major success because it enabled provincial police forces to establish whether detainees had previous convictions; see TNA, FO 371/7765, E14447, Allenby to Curzon, 16 December 1922: "Annual Report for Sudan, 1921."

7. TNA, CO 733/131/5, Report on Palestine and Transjordan, 1926, 25 March 1927, includes "Comparative Table of Incidence of the Most Frequent Forms of Heinous Crimes."

8. Quotation cited in D. George Boyce, *Decolonisation and the British Empire, 1775–1997* (London: Macmillan, 1999), 19.

9. John Gallagher, "Nationalisms and the Crisis of Empire, 1919–1922," *Modern Asian Studies* 15, no. 3 (1981): 355–68.

10. See, for example, Silvestri, "'The Sinn Féin of India,'" 473–74, 476–78; and, more generally, Keith Jeffery, "The Irish Military Tradition and the British Empire," in *An Irish Empire? Aspects of Ireland and the British Empire,* ed. Keith Jeffery (Manchester: Manchester University Press, 1996), 94–122.

11. Charles Townshend, "The Irish Republican Army and the Development of Guerrilla Warfare, 1916–21," *English Historical Review* 94, no. 371 (1979): 318–45; Thomas Hennessey, *Dividing Ireland: World War One and Partition* (London: Routledge, 1998).

12. For details, see Charles Townshend, *The British Campaign in Ireland, 1919–1921* (Oxford: Oxford University Press, 1975); and Townshend, "Policing Insurgency in Ireland, 1914–23," in *Policing and Decolonisation: Politics, Nationalism and the Police, 1917–65,* ed. David M. Anderson and David Killingray (Manchester: Manchester University Press, 1992), 22–41.

13. Charles Townshend, "Martial Law: Legal and Administrative Problems of Civil Emergency in Britain and the Empire, 1800–1940," *Historical Journal* 25, no. 1 (1982): 185.

14. H. J. Simson, *British Rule, and Rebellion* (Edinburgh: William Blackwood, 1938), 14–19.

15. Kent Fedorowich, "The Problems of Disbandment: The Royal Irish Constabulary and Imperial Migration, 1919–1929," *Irish Historical Studies* 30, no. 117 (1996): 88–110.

16. Thomas Bartlett and Keith Jeffery, eds., *A Military History of Ireland* (Cambridge: Cambridge University Press, 1997).

17. T. R. Moreman, *The Army in India and the Development of Frontier Warfare, 1849–1947* (London: Macmillan, 1998), 35–137 passim.

18. Gyanesh Kudaisya, "'In Aid of Civil Power': The Colonial Army in Northern India, c. 1919–42," *Journal of Imperial and Commonwealth History* 32, no. 1 (2004): 41–68; Tim Moreman, "'Small Wars' and 'Imperial Policing': The British Army and the Theory and Practice of Colonial Warfare in the British Empire, 1919–1939," *Journal of Strategic Studies* 19, no. 4 (1996): 105–31.

19. Richard Popplewell, "The Surveillance of Indian Revolutionaries in Great Britain and on the Continent, 1905–14," *Intelligence and National Security* 3, no. 1 (1988): 56–58.

20. Colin Newbury, *Patrons, Clients, and Empire: Chieftaincy and Over-Rule in Asia, Africa, and the Pacific* (Oxford: Oxford University Press, 2003), 83–85. For the links between Evelyn Baring's administrative experience in India and Egypt from 1872 onward, see Roger Owen, *Lord Cromer: Victorian Imperialist, Edwardian Proconsul* (Oxford: Oxford University Press, 2004), part 2.

21. Michael R. Fischbach, "British Land Policy in Transjordan," in *Village, Steppe and State: The Social Origins of Modern Jordan,* ed. Eugene L. Rogan and Tariq Tell (London: British Academic Press, 1994), 80–107.

22. TNA, CO 730/13, Middle East Interdepartmental Committee Report, 31 January 1921, section IV: Civilian Services; David E. Omissi, *Air Power and Colonial*

Control: The Royal Air Force, 1919–1939 (Manchester: Manchester University Press, 1990), 76–80.

23. John Ferris, " 'Far Too Dangerous a Gamble'? British Intelligence and Policy during the Chanak Crisis, September–October 1922," *Diplomacy and Statecraft* 14, no. 2 (2003): 146–47.

24. A. J. Kingsley-Heath, "The Palestine Police Force under the Mandate," *Police Journal* 1 (1928): 78–88; Tom Bowden, *The Breakdown of Public Security: The Case of Ireland 1916–1921 and Palestine 1936–1939* (London: Frank Cass, 1977); Fedorowich, "Problems of Disbandment," 88–110.

25. Georgina Sinclair, *At the End of the Line: Colonial Policing and the Imperial Endgame, 1945–80* (Manchester: Manchester University Press, 2006), 115–17.

26. Townshend, "Policing Insurgency in Ireland," 35. Several RIC undercover intelligence officers were among the twelve men assassinated by the Irish Republican Army on 21 November 1920.

27. Richard Hawkins, "The 'Irish Model' and the Empire: A Case for Reassessment," in *Policing the Empire: Government, Authority and Control, 1830–1940*, ed. David M. Anderson and David Killingray (Manchester: Manchester University Press, 1991), 18–19. Hawkins warns against reading the prevalence of Irish constabulary-type policing backward into the nineteenth century but acknowledges the greater relevance of the "Irish model" in the early twentieth century.

28. See, for example, the references to colleagues with RIC experience in Colin Imray, *Policeman in Palestine: Memoirs of the Early Years* (Bideford, Devon: Edward Gaskell, 1995).

29. Keith Jeffery, *The British Army and the Crisis of Empire, 1918–1922* (Manchester: Manchester University Press, 1984), 73–74; Townshend, *British Campaign in Ireland*, 106–16.

30. Ronen Shamir, *The Colonies of Law: Colonialism, Zionism and Law in Early Mandate Palestine* (Cambridge: Cambridge University Press, 2000), 9.

31. The improvisation characteristic of EEF political intelligence emerges in Matthew Hughes, *Allenby and British Strategy in the Middle East, 1917–1919* (London: Frank Cass, 1999), part 2. Whitehall arguments over the Middle East situation after Ottoman Turkey's defeat are discussed in John Fisher, *Curzon and British Imperialism in the Middle East, 1916–19* (London: Frank Cass, 1999), 223–38; and Fisher, "Syria and Mesopotamia in British Middle Eastern Policy in 1919," *Middle Eastern Studies* 34, no. 2 (1998): 129–70. See also John Darwin, *Britain, Egypt and the Middle East: Imperial Policy in the Aftermath of War, 1918–1922* (London: Macmillan, 1981), chapters 6 and 7.

32. The North-West Frontier remained the dominant exemplar for British imperial policing throughout the interwar period; see Moreman, *Army in India and the Development of Frontier Warfare*. Regarding administrative lessons from the Sudan, see Heather J. Sharkey, *Living with Colonialism: Nationalism and Culture in the Anglo-Egyptian Sudan* (Berkeley and Los Angeles: University of California Press, 2003), 95–111 passim.

33. Bruce Westrate, *The Arab Bureau: British Policy in the Middle East, 1916–1920* (University Park: Pennsylvania State University Press, 1992), chapter 8.

34. Robert J. Blyth, *The Empire of the Raj: India, Eastern Africa and the Middle East, 1858–1947* (London: Palgrave-Macmillan, 2003), 94; Darwin, *Britain, Egypt and the*

Middle East, 228–30; Sahar Huneidi, "Was Balfour Policy Reversible? The Colonial Office and Palestine, 1921–23," *Journal of Palestine Studies* 27, no. 2 (1998): 24. After 1921, the Indian government's Political Residency at Bushire was its principal remaining outpost in the Arab world.

35. Westrate, *Arab Bureau,* 22–38; J. S. Galbraith, "No Man's Child: The Campaign in Mesopotamia, 1914–1916," *International History Review* 6, no. 3 (1984): 358–85; David French, "The Dardanelles, Mecca and Kut: Prestige as a Factor in British Eastern Strategy, 1914–1916," *War and Society* 5, no. 1 (1987): 45–61.

36. Paula Mohs, "British Intelligence and the Arab Revolt in the Hejaz, 1914–1917" (Ph.D. diss., Cambridge University, 2003), 52–56.

37. Ibid., 56–57.

38. Westrate, *Arab Bureau,* 22–31.

39. Ibid., 32–33.

40. John W. Frost, "Memories of the Sudan Civil Service," in *The British in the Sudan,* ed. Robert O. Collins and Francis M. Deng (London: Macmillan, 1984), 79.

41. Mohs, "British Intelligence and the Arab Revolt in the Hejaz," 57.

42. Westrate, *Arab Bureau,* 34–35, 40–43.

43. Fisher, *Curzon and British Imperialism in the Middle East,* 89–90.

44. Mohs, "British Intelligence and the Arab Revolt in the Hejaz," 58.

45. Westrate, *Arab Bureau,* 206.

46. See the review of historiography in Westrate, *Arab Bureau,* 4–11.

47. TNA, CO 877/11/2, CO minutes by R. D. Furse, 1 November 1934.

48. TNA, CO 877/11/2, Form CS/No. 51, SPS information for candidates, printed January 1933. The nine universities were Oxford, Cambridge, London, Trinity College Dublin, Edinburgh, Glasgow, St. Andrews, Durham, and the University of Wales, Cardiff.

49. Ibid. In 1933, probationers were paid a starting salary of just under £500 per year.

50. The Arab Legion commander Sir Frederick Peake published a lengthy anthropological study of Transjordan's peoples in 1935. On MacMichael and Sudan, see Eve M. Troutt Powell, *A Different Shade of Colonialism: Egypt, Great Britain, and the Mastery of the Sudan* (Berkeley and Los Angeles: University of California Press, 2003), 178.

51. Gabriel Warburg, "The Wingate Literature Revisited: The Sudan as Seen by Members of the Sudan Political Service during the Condominium, 1899–1956," *Middle Eastern Studies* 41, no. 3 (2005): 375.

52. TNA, CO 831/37/3, Major J. Glubb, "Monthly Report on the Administration of the Deserts of Transjordan, July 1936." Joseph Massad also points out Sandeman's powerful influence on the development of Glubb's views about the Jordanian Bedouin; see Massad, *Colonial Effects: The Making of National Identity in Jordan* (New York: Columbia University Press, 2001), 112.

53. Leland Barrows, "The Impact of Empire on the French Armed Forces, 1830–1920," in *Double Impact: France and Africa in the Age of Imperialism,* ed. G. Wesley Johnson (Westport, Conn.: Greenwood Press, 1985), 59; Jean-David Mizrahi, *Genèse de l'État mandataire: Service de renseignements et bandes armées en Syrie et au Liban dans les années 1920* (Paris: Publications de la Sorbonne, 2003), 16–17.

54. TNA, WO 106/232, Sudan Intelligence Report no. 177, April 1909: "Notes on a Journey in Tripoli, Tunisia, Algeria, Tangiers by El Kaimakan F. G. Poole Bey."

55. Mizrahi, *Genèse de l'État mandataire*, 20–22; Jim House and Neil MacMaster, *Paris 1961: Algerians, State Terror, and Memory* (Oxford: Oxford University Press, 2006), 45.

56. MAE, série M, vol. 91, Direction des affaires indigènes bulletin, "Situation politique et militaire du 7 au 13 mai 1929."

57. Newbury, *Patrons, Clients, and Empire*, 90–93.

58. Edmund Burke III, "A Comparative View of French Native Policy in Morocco and Syria, 1912–1925," *Middle Eastern Studies* 9 (1973): 175–86; Philip S. Khoury, *Syria and the French Mandate: The Politics of Arab Nationalism, 1920–1945* (Princeton, N.J.: Princeton University Press, 1987), 55–6, 155–6.

59. Elisabeth Mouilleau, *Fonctionnaires de la République et artisans de l'Empire: Le cas des contrôleurs civils en Tunisie (1881–1956)* (Paris: l'Harmattan, 2000), 37–42, 170–82.

60. MAE, série P, vol. 669: Police, personnel, no. 247, Foreign Ministry to Interior Ministry Direction de la Sûreté Générale, 22 March 1930. Fourteen Sûreté inspectors serving in mainland France were approached about placements in Tunisia in 1930. At the date of this correspondence, four had agreed, six had refused, and six more were undecided.

61. C. M. Andrew and A. S. Kanya-Forstner, "Centre and Periphery in the Making of the Second French Colonial Empire, 1815–1920," *Journal of Imperial and Commonwealth History* 16, no. 3 (1988): 9–34.

62. Renowned for his tenure at the Foreign Ministry between 1898 and 1905, Delcassé steered the creation of the Ministry of Colonies through the National Assembly in 1893–94, and served as the first minister of colonies from May 1894 to January 1895. Doumergue held the colonies post longer than any other politician before 1920, serving at the rue Oudinot in Emile Combes's government from June 1902 to January 1905, as well as in three wartime ministries from August 1914 to March 1917. Both men were instrumental in the French conquest of Morocco; see Christopher M. Andrew, *Théophile Delcassé and the Making of the Entente Cordiale: A Reappraisal of French Foreign Policy* (London: Macmillan, 1968).

63. SHA, 9H1: Inde française, *Annuaires du Ministère des Colonies* (Paris: Alphonse Dupin, 1918–21, and 1928–29).

64. Philip Curtin, *Disease and Empire: The Health of European Troops in the Conquest of Africa* (Cambridge: Cambridge University Press, 1998), 186–92; William B. Cohen, "Malaria and French Imperialism," *Journal of African History* 24, no. 1 (1983): 23–36.

65. Stephen Ellis, "The Political Elite of Imerina and the Revolt of the Menalamba: The Creation of a Colonial Myth in Madagascar, 1895–1898," *Journal of African History* 21 (1980): 220–21.

66. Ibid., 221–28.

67. Gallieni's political skills emerged once he returned from Madagascar to Paris to lobby for support for the conquest; see Pascal Venier, "A Campaign of Colonial Propaganda: Gallieni, Lyautey and the Defence of the Military Regime in Madagascar, May 1899 to July 1900," in *Promoting the Colonial Idea: Propaganda and Visions of Empire in France*, ed. Tony Chafer and Amanda Sackur (London: Palgrave, 2002), 29–39.

68. Douglas Porch, "Bugeaud, Gallieni, Lyautey: The Development of French

Colonial Warfare," in *Makers of Modern Strategy from Machiavelli to the Nuclear Age*, ed. Peter Paret (Oxford: Oxford University Press, 1986), 376–407.

69. Paul Rabinow, *French Modern: Norms and Forms of the Social Environment* (Chicago: University of Chicago Press, 1989), 129–62. Lamarck's 1809 text *Zoological Philosophy* remained influential among racial theorists in France throughout the nineteenth century.

70. Quoted in Rabinow, *French Modern*, 147.

71. Ibid., 149, 159–60.

72. John F. Laffey, "Imperialists Divided: The Views of Tonkin's Colons before 1914," *Histoire Sociale/Social History* 9 (May 1977): 94–95.

73. Roger Price, "Techniques of Repression: The Control of Popular Protest in Mid-Nineteenth-Century France," *Historical Journal* 25, no. 4 (1982): 862–63.

74. Rabinow, *French Modern*, 146–49, 162–64, quotation at 164.

75. Kim Munholland, "Rival Approaches to Morocco: Delcassé, Lyautey, and the Algerian-Moroccan Border, 1903–1905," *French Historical Studies* 5 (1968): 328–43, comment on Gallieni at 334–35.

76. Bushra Hamad, "*Sudan Notes and Records* and Sudanese Nationalism, 1918–1956," *History in Africa* 22 (1995): 243.

77. Troutt Powell, *Different Shade of Colonialism*, 178.

78. TNA, WO 106/232, Sudan Intelligence Report no. 178, section B: A. H. MacMichael report, "Ethnological Notes on the Kababish Tribe," n.d. [May 1909].

79. Ibid.

80. Robert Collins and Richard Herzog, "Early British Administration in the Southern Sudan," *Journal of African Studies* 2, no. 1 (1961): 126–27.

81. TNA, WO 106/232, Sudan Intelligence Report no. 176, March 1909: Cairo Intelligence News, Western Sudan, p. 5. On the value of tours for intelligence collection, see Gary Wilder, *The French Imperial Nation-State: Negritude and Colonial Humanism between the Two World Wars* (Chicago: University of Chicago Press, 2005), 69.

82. Algeria was the prime example of this process in action, the "lessons" of the classics reinforced by evidence of the former Roman civilization in North Africa; see Patricia M. E. Lorcin, "Rome and France in Africa: Recovering Colonial Algeria's Latin Past," *French Historical Studies* 25, no. 2 (2002): 295–329; and Michael Greenhalgh, "The New Centurions: French Reliance on the Roman Past during the Conquest of Algeria," *War and Society* 16, no. 1 (1998): 1–28.

83. MAE, série K Afrique, sous-série AOF, vol. 1, no. 1380, Lyautey note, "Coopération inter-Saharienne," 26 December 1919; Lieutenant-Colonel Lefebvre memo, "Affaires Sahariennes territoire militaire du Niger," 27 July 1920.

84. Raymond Gervais, "La plus riche des colonies pauvres: La politique monétaire et fiscale de la France au Tchad 1900–1920," *Canadian Journal of African Studies* 16, no. 1 (1982): 93–112.

85. Pierre Boilley, "Les sociétés nomades aux franges de l'AOF: Intégration ou marginalisation?" in *AOF: Réalités et héritages. Sociétés ouest-africaines et ordre colonial, 1895–1960*, ed. Charles Becker, Saliou Mbaye, and Ibrahim Thioub (Dakar: Archives Nationale, 1997), 1:900–901.

86. CAOM, GGA, 11H46, no. 2665, Administrateur de la Commune mixte du Djebel Nadir to Affaires indigènes (Oran), "A/S des nomads—opérations de police," 22 June 1920.

87. MAE, série K Afrique, sous-série AOF, vol. 1, no. 1380, Lyautey note, "Coopération inter-Saharienne," 26 December 1919; Lieutenant-Colonel Lefebvre memo, "Affaires Sahariennes territoire militaire du Niger," 27 July 1920.

88. MAE, série K Afrique, sous-série AOF, vol. 1, no. 9240, EMA Section d'Afrique, "Note du Général Laperrine sur les territoires Sahariens."

89. MAE, série K Afrique, sous-série AOF, vol. 1, no. 1380, Lyautey note, "Coopération inter-Saharienne," 26 December 1919.

90. MAE, série K Afrique, sous-série AOF, vol. 1, "Directives de police Saharienne du 1ᵉ Août 1919."

91. Susan Bayly, "French Anthropology and the Durkheimians in Colonial Indochina," *Modern Asian Studies* 34, no. 3 (2000): 590–96.

92. SR personnel in Morocco are profiled in Daniel Rivet, *Lyautey et l'institution du protectorat français au Maroc, 1912–1925* (Paris: l'Harmattan, 1988), 2:45–55. There were 194 SR officers in the Moroccan interior in 1913, and 273 by 1925. Regarding Moroccan-Syrian interchange, see Burke, "Comparative View of French Native Policy," 179–86.

93. The training and preparatory reading undertaken by Levant SR officers was also similar to that of the native affairs personnel in Morocco; see Mizrahi, *Genèse de l'État mandataire*, 225–31.

94. Elizabeth Thompson, *Colonial Citizens: Republican Rights, Paternal Privilege, and Gender in French Syria and Lebanon* (New York: Columbia University Press, 2000), 50–66 passim.

95. Christopher M. Andrew, "Déchiffrement et diplomatie: Le cabinet noir du Quai d'Orsay sous la Troisième République," *Relations Internationales* 3, no. 5 (1976): 3–64.

96. Mary Dewhurst Lewis, "The Strangeness of Foreigners: Policing Migration and Nation in Interwar Marseille," *French Politics, Culture, and Society* 20, no. 3 (2002): 66.

97. See E. K. Bramstedt, *Dictatorship and Political Police* (1945; reprint, New York: Oxford University Press, 1976); Higgs, *The Information State in England: The Central Collection of Information on Citizens since 1500* (London: Palgrave, 2004), 113–14. In the early twentieth century, British Criminal Investigation Departments turned away from Bertillon's preferred system of photographic identification and bodily measurement for criminal record keeping, relying instead on fingerprint records.

98. Robert Tombs, *The War against Paris, 1871* (Cambridge: Cambridge University Press, 1981), 168–93.

99. Robert Tombs, "Crime and the Security of the State: The 'Dangerous Classes' and Insurrection in Nineteenth-Century Paris," in *Crime and the Law: The Social History of Crime in Western Europe since 1500*, ed. V. A. C. Gatrell, Bruce Lenman, and Geoffrey Parker (London: Europa, 1980), 214–37.

100. Donald N. Baker, "The Surveillance of Subversion in Interwar France: The Carnet B in the Seine, 1922–1940," *French Historical Studies* 10, no. 3 (1978): 487–88.

101. Allan Mitchell, "The Xenophobic Style: French Counterespionage and the Emergence of the Dreyfus Affair," *Journal of Modern History* 52 (1980): 414–25.

102. MAE, série M, vol. 838: Police, no. 50, Foreign Ministry note to Sûreté Générale, "Carnet B," 4 February 1913.

103. MAE, série M, vol. 838: Police, copy tel., Interior Ministry to Foreign Ministry Direction des affaires politiques, "A/S de la tenue du Carnet B au Maroc," 16 May 1914. The Carnet system survived beyond 1918, although its focus narrowed toward an overwhelming concentration on Germans living in France. A Carnet B list from the Seine Prefecture of Police reveals that 85 percent (512 of a total of 601) of those listed were German; see Donald N. Baker, "The Surveillance of Subversion in Interwar France: An Addendum," *French Historical Studies* 11, no. 1 (1979): 132.

104. Price, "Techniques of Repression," 859–82.

105. Robert J. Goldstein, *Political Repression in 19th-Century Europe* (London: Croom Helm, 1983), 68, 249–50, 270–75.

106. Anja Johansen, *Soldiers as Police: The French and Prussian Armies and the Policing of Popular Protest, 1889–1914* (Aldershot: Ashgate, 2005), chapters 3 and 5.

107. Anja Johansen, "Violent Repression or Modern Strategies of Crowd Management: Soldiers as Riot Police in France and Germany, 1890–1914," *French History* 15, no. 4 (2001): 400–20.

108. MAE, série M, vol. 796, no. 8564, War Minister Paul Painlevé to Théodore Steeg, 12 October 1926; no. 2462, War Ministry to Foreign Ministry Direction des affaires politiques, 31 May 1927.

109. MAE, série M, vol. 796, no. 5706, Residency report to War Ministry Direction de la gendarmerie, bureau technique, 12 October 1927.

110. Ibid.

111. François Alègre de la Soujeole and Christian Chocquet, "La professionalisation du maintien de l'ordre," *Revue Historique des Armées* 4 (2001): 97–112.

112. Witness, for example, the wartime growth of the gendarmerie's counterespionage work as described in Louis N. Panel, *Gendarmerie et contre-espionnage (1914–1918)* (Paris: Service de la Gendarmerie Nationale, 2004).

113. The paragraphs that follow draw on Peter Holquist, "'Information Is the Alpha and Omega of Our Work': Bolshevik Surveillance in Its Pan-European Context," *Journal of Modern History* 69 (September 1997): 415–50.

114. The subtlest treatment of military postal censorship and what it revealed about the complex motivations of frontline French troops in 1917 is Leonard V. Smith, *Between Mutiny and Obedience: The Case of the French Fifth Infantry Division during World War I* (Princeton, N.J.: Princeton University Press, 1993).

115. Jean-Noël Jeanneney, "Les archives des commissions de contrôle postale aux armées (1916–1918)," *Revue d'Histoire Moderne et Contemporaine* 15 (1968): 209–33; Nicholas Hiley, "Counter-espionage and Security in Great Britain during the First World War," *English Historical Review* 101 (1986): 635–70; also cited in Holquist, "'Information Is the Alpha and Omega of Our Work,'" 440–41.

116. Stephen Ward, "Intelligence Surveillance of British Ex-servicemen, 1918–1920," *Historical Journal* 16, no. 1 (1973): 179–88.

117. Bodleian Library, Oxford, Viscount Alfred Milner papers, MS ENG HIST c.696, Supreme War Council, "Report on the Political Situation in France for the Month of May 1918"; Translation of Interior Ministry memo, "Report on the Present Morale of the Country," 28 May 1918.

118. Holquist, "'Information Is the Alpha and Omega of Our Work,'" 443.

119. As examples: MAE, série M, vol. 89, Direction des Affaires indigènes/SR, "Rapports Mensuels d'Ensemble du Protectorat," and 7N4093, EMA, 1ᵉ Bureau Sec-

tion d'Outre-Mer, "Bulletins de renseignements mensuels des questions musulmanes, 1937–1940."

120. AN, F⁶⁰202, Haut Comité Méditerranéen rapport no. 1, "Le Haut Comité Méditerranéen et les organismes d'information musulmane," 9 March 1937.

121. Mohs, "British Intelligence and the Arab Revolt in the Hejaz," 138–45.

122. See, for example, High Commission Secretariat intelligence reports in TNA, CO 730/105/1.

123. The emphasis on the inclusion of an indigenous elite in administrative apparatus was far less evident in the African mandates established after 1918; see Michael D. Callahan, *Mandates and Empire: The League of Nations and Africa, 1914–1931* (Brighton: Sussex Academic Press, 1999).

124. For discussion of the mandate concept as applied in Africa, see Callahan, *Mandates and Empire.*

125. See, for example, Eliezer Tauber, "The Struggle for Dayr al-Zur: The Determination of Borders between Syria and Iraq," *International Journal of Middle East Studies* 23 (1991): 361–85.

126. Transformation of the Palestinian landscape wrought by the mandate is explored in Roza El-Eini, *Mandated Landscape: British Imperial Rule in Palestine, 1929–1948* (London: Frank Cass, 2004).

127. Crawford Young, "The Colonial State and Post-colonial Crisis," in *Decolonization and African Independence: The Transfers of Power, 1960–1980,* ed. Prosser Gifford and William Roger Louis (New Haven, Conn.: Yale University Press, 1988), 3–4.

128. Mike Brogden, "The Emergence of the Police: The Colonial Dimension," *British Journal of Criminology* 27, no. 1 (1987): 4–14.

129. John Willis, "Colonial Policing in Aden, 1937–1967," *Arab Studies Journal* 5, no. 1 (1997): 60.

130. TNA, FO 624/1, Extracts from Iraq Police monthly abstracts of intelligence, 1933; Vice Consulate Kirkuk, confidential report no. 1, 16 April 1933.

131. TNA, FO 624/2, file 26, tel. 317, A. Clerk Kerr to Sir Samuel Hoare, 11 June 1935. By 1935, seventy-five British advisers were still employed in Iraqi government departments, not including Britons employed by Iraqi railways and the port of Basra. Significantly, the contracts for police advisory staff were allowed to expire. Regarding Yasin al-Hashimi's rise to power and his rivalry with Nuri al-Sa'id, see Reeva Spector Simon, *Iraq between the Two World Wars: The Militarist Origins of Tyranny,* new edition (New York: Columbia University Press, 2004), 54–59.

132. A. H. M. Kirk-Greene, "The Thin White Line: The Size of the British Colonial Service in Africa," *African Affairs* 79, no. 314 (1980): 25–44.

133. A. H. M. Kirk-Greene, "The Sudan Political Service: A Profile in the Sociology of Imperialism," *International Journal of African Historical Studies* 15, no. 1 (1982): 21.

134. Kirk-Greene, "Thin White Line," 33–38.

CHAPTER 3

1. David Stafford, "Spies and Gentlemen: The Birth of the British Spy Novel, 1893–1914," *Victorian Studies* 24 (Summer 1981): 489–509; David Trotter, "The Politics of Adventure in the Early British Spy Novel," *Intelligence and National Security* 5, no. 4 (1990): 30–31.

2. David French, "Spy Fever in Britain, 1900–1915," *Historical Journal* 21, no. 2 (1978): 355–70. David French reminds us that William Le Queux's popular novel *The Invasion of 1910*, serialized in the *Daily Mail* in March 1906, was written in collaboration with Lord Roberts, then Britain's most revered general. It sold millions of copies when published.

3. Nicholas Hiley, "Decoding German Spies: British Spy Fiction, 1908–1918," *Intelligence and National Security* 5, no. 4 (1990): 55–79.

4. Panikos Panaye, *German Immigrants in Britain during the 19th Century, 1815–1914* (Oxford: Berg, 1995).

5. Christopher M. Andrew, *Secret Service* (London: Hodder and Stoughton, 1986), 33–34; Hiley, "Decoding German Spies," 56, 61.

6. Michael Paris, "Air Power and Imperial Defence, 1880–1919," *Journal of Contemporary History* 24 (1989): 210–17.

7. A point central to C. A. Bayly, *Empire and Information: Intelligence Gathering and Social Communication in India, 1780–1870* (Cambridge: Cambridge University Press, 1996).

8. Selim Deringil, *The Well-Protected Domains: Ideology and the Legitimation of Power in the Ottoman Empire, 1876–1909* (London: I. B. Tauris, 1998), 48–49, 67–68.

9. David French, "The Dardanelles, Mecca and Kut: Prestige as a Factor in British Eastern Strategy, 1914–1916," *War and Society* 5, no. 1 (1987): 45–61.

10. TNA, KV 1/15–17—MI5 Records 1909–19: D Branch reports/Imperial Overseas Intelligence.

11. Richard Popplewell, "The Surveillance of Indian 'Seditionists' in North America, 1905–1915," in *Intelligence and International Relations, 1900–1945*, ed. Christopher Andrew and Jeremy Noakes (Exeter: University of Exeter Press, 1987), 49–76.

12. Richard Popplewell, *Intelligence and Imperial Defence: British Intelligence and the Defence of the Indian Empire, 1904–1924* (London: Frank Cass, 1995), 164–72.

13. Peter Morris, "Intelligence and Its Interpretation: Mesopotamia, 1914–1916," in *Intelligence and International Relations, 1900–1945*, ed. Christopher Andrew and Jeremy Noakes (Exeter: University of Exeter Press, 1987), 89.

14. TNA, CO 537/859, Major H. W. Young letter to Clayton, 14 September 1923.

15. Ibid. This was a flaw to which Young alluded, as he asked Clayton to verify whether Arab nationalism was merely the "unconscious tool" of pan-Islamist policy. Ministerial discussion of pan-Islamism is explored in John Fisher, "The Interdepartmental Committee on Eastern Unrest and British Responses to Bolshevik and Other Intrigues against the Empire during the 1920s", *Journal of Asian History* 34, no. 1 (2000): 1–34.

16. TNA, CO 537/859, Clayton reply to Young, 5 October 1923.

17. CAOM, GGA, 11H46, Direction des affaires indigènes, Rapport mensuel sur la situation politique des indigènes pendant le mois de novembre 1919; Ahmed Koulakssis and Gilbert Meynier, *L'Emir Khaled premier za'im? Identité algérienne et colonialisme français* (Paris: l'Harmattan, 1987), 263–64; Mahfoud Kaddache, *L'Emir Khaled: Documents et témoignages pour servir à l'étude du nationalisme algérien* (Algiers: Office des publications universitaires, 1987), 121–24.

18. TNA, WO 33/999, Sudan Monthly Intelligence Reports, nos. 345 and 346,

April and May 1923, submitted by Director of Intelligence C. Armine-Willis, Khartoum, 21 May and 20 June 1923.

19. Frederick Cooper and Ann Laura Stoler, eds., *Tensions of Empire: Colonial Cultures in a Bourgeois World* (Berkeley and Los Angeles: University of California Press, 1997), 21–22.

20. SHA, Moscow, C223/D122, EMA-2, SEA report, "État d'esprit des indigènes en Algérie pendant la guerre 1914–1918," 4 November 1935.

21. As examples: TNA, WO 106/259, memo by Captain J. E. Philipps (chief intelligence officer, East Africa), "'Africa for the African' and 'Pan-Islam': Recent Developments in Central and East Africa," 15 July 1917; CO 732/21/2: Persian political intelligence summaries, 1926.

22. See, for example, TNA, AIR 23/454: SSO Iraq, Intelligence reports on Shi'i 'ulamā, 1924.

23. Thomas G. Fraser, "Germany and Indian Revolution, 1914–18," *Journal of Contemporary History* 12, no. 2 (1977): 255–72.

24. Edmund Burke III, "Moroccan Resistance, Pan-Islam and German War Strategy, 1914–1918," *Francia* 3 (1975): 434–64; Fraser, "Germany and Indian Revolution"; Popplewell, *Intelligence and Imperial Defence;* Best, *British Intelligence and the Japanese Challenge in Asia, 1914–1941* (London: Palgrave Macmillan, 2002), 13–14, 23–28, 47–48.

25. Peter Dunwoodie, *Writing French Algeria* (Oxford: Clarendon Press, 1998), 27.

26. Burke, "Moroccan Resistance."

27. Barnett Singer, "Lyautey: An Interpretation of the Man and French Imperialism," *Journal of Contemporary History* 26 (1991): 141.

28. Burke, "Moroccan Resistance."

29. *DDF,* 1915, vol. 1, doc. 93, Foreign Minister Delcassé to General Lyautey, 24 January 1915; *DDF,* 1915, vol. 2, doc. 134, Delcassé to Madrid Ambassador Geoffray, 6 October 1915.

30. Edmund Burke III, "Pan-Islam and Moroccan Resistance to French Colonial Penetration, 1900–1912," *Journal of African History* 13, no. 1 (1972): 111–17.

31. MAE, série K: Afrique, sous-série Affaires musulmanes, vol. 1, no. 601, Algiers governor-general to Direction des affaires politiques, "A/S de publications de propagande allemande," 7 July 1918.

32. See, for example, government instruction to Lyautey's Rabat administration: *DDF,* 1914, doc. 521, Lyautey to Théophile Delcassé, 12 November 1914.

33. *DDF,* 1915/I, doc. 47, "Procès-verbal de la séance de la commission interministérielle des affaires musulmanes," fourth meeting, 12 January 1915.

34. *DDF,* 1914, no. 534, "Procès-verbal de la séance de la commission interministérielle des affaires musulmanes du 14 novembre 1914."

35. Vincent Confer, *France and Algeria: The Problem of Civil and Political Reform* (Syracuse, NY: Syracuse University Press, 1966), 96–97.

36. SHA, Moscow, C223/D122, no. 5535/G, SEA renseignement, "État d'esprit des indigènes en Algérie pendant la guerre 1914–1918."

37. Fanny Colonna, "Cultural Resistance and Religious Legitimacy in Colonial Algeria," in *Islam in Tribal Societies: From the Atlas to the Indus,* ed. Akbar S. Ahmed and David M. Hart (London: Routledge, 1984), 108–16.

38. James McDougall, *History and the Culture of Nationalism in Algeria* (Cambridge: Cambridge University Press, 2006), 12–15.

39. George Joffé, "Maghribi Islam and Islam in the Maghrib: The Eternal Dichotomy," in *African Islam and Islam in Africa: Encounters between Sufis and Islamists,* ed. David Westerlund and Eva Evers Rosander (London: Hurst, 1997), 66–67.

40. David Robinson, *Paths of Accommodation. Muslim Societies and French Colonial Authorities in Senegal and Mauritania, 1880–1920* (Athens: Ohio University Press, 2000). It is worth noting that al-Thalaabi was marginal to Tunisia's more powerful Néo-Destour, a movement largely impervious to 'ulamā teaching; see McDougall, *History and the Culture of Nationalism in Algeria,* 39.

41. Timothy Cleaveland, "Islam and the Construction of Social Identity in the Nineteenth-Century Sahara." *Journal of African History* 39, no. 3 (1998): 366–68.

42. Jacob M. Landau, *The Politics of Pan-Islam: Ideology and Organization* (Oxford: Clarendon Press, 1990), 1–5.

43. See the classic two-part article by T. O. Ranger, "Connexions between 'Primary Resistance' Movements and Modern Mass Nationalism in East and Central Africa," *Journal of African History* 9, no. 3 (1968): 437–53, and *Journal of African History* 9, no. 4 (1968): 631–41.

44. Patricia Crone, "The Tribe and the State," in *States in History,* ed. John A. Hall (Oxford: Blackwell, 1986), 48–55.

45. Nikki R. Keddie, "Pan-Islam as Proto-Nationalism," *Journal of Modern History* 41, no. 1 (1969): 17–28; Burke, "Pan-Islam and Moroccan Resistance," 97–118. On the primary resistance idea, see Ranger, "Connexions between 'Primary Resistance' Movements and Modern Mass Nationalism in East and Central Africa."

46. CAOM, 19G22, AOF government-general, Direction des affaires politiques et administratives, "Rapport no. 2 sur les directives générales du SR de l'AOF," 26 March 1923.

47. CAOM, 1affpol/907, Service des affaires musulmanes note to Foreign Ministry, 21 October 1924.

48. Eugene L. Rogan, *Frontiers of the State in the Late Ottoman Empire: Transjordan, 1850–1921* (Cambridge: Cambridge University Press, 1999), 200.

49. Ibid., 218–19, quotation at 219.

50. *DDF,* 1915, vol. 1, doc. 93, Foreign Minister Delcassé to General Lyautey, 24 January 1915; *DDF,* 1915, vol. 2, doc. 134, Delcassé to Madrid Ambassador Geoffray, 6 October 1915.

51. Burke, "Pan-Islam and Moroccan Resistance," 111–17.

52. SHA, Moscow, C223/D122, Section Musulmane, report no. 20, "Propagande chez les Musulmanes," 20 October 1916; Gabriel Warburg, *The Sudan under Wingate: Administration in the Anglo-Egyptian Sudan, 1899–1916* (London: Frank Cass, 1971), 106.

53. *DDF,* 1914, doc. 534, "Procès-verbal de la séance de la commission interministérielle des affaires musulmanes," first meeting, 14 November 1914.

54. *DDF,* 1915, vol. 2, doc. 211, Geneva Consul, Pascal d'Aix, to René Viviani, 19 October 1915.

55. MAE, série K: Afrique, sous-série Affaires musulmanes, vol. 1, no. 7933–9/11, EMA Section d'Afrique, bulletin de renseignements, 10 November 1918.

56. MAE, série K: Afrique, sous-série Afrique Occidentale Française, vol. 1, no. 167, Ministry of Colonies to Foreign Ministry Africa sub-division, 1 August 1919.

57. SHA, Moscow, C223/D122, EMA-2, SEA report, "État d'esprit des indigènes en Algérie pendant la guerre 1914–1918," 4 November 1935.

58. CAOM, Direction des affaires indigènes (Alger), "Rapport sur la situation politique et administrative des indigènes de l'Algérie au 1er mai 1923."

59. CAOM, 1affpol/907, no. 2016, Urbain Blanc to Section Afrique-Levant, 7 November 1924.

60. SHA, 7N4186/D4, SR Beirut report, "Les dangers présents de l'Islam," 25 September 1921.

61. MAE, série K Afrique 1918–1940, sous-série Affaires musulmanes, vol. 9, tel. 34, Cairo dispatch to sous-direction d'Afrique, 22 February 1929.

62. CAOM, 1affpol/907, no. 365, Section Afrique-Levant memo, "Congrès Islamique de Jerusalem et Khalifat," 3 December 1931. The shift in emphasis was confirmed by the 1931 Jerusalem Congress.

63. MAE, série K Afrique 1918–1940, sous-série Affaires musulmanes, vol. 9, K101–2, Unsigned Dakar government-general report, "Les populations musulmanes de l'Afrique Occidentale et Equatoriale Françaises et la politique islamique de la France," n.d.

64. CAOM, 1affpol/907, "Note du Service des affaires musulmanes demandée par M. le Rapporteur du budget des Colonies au Senat," n.d. [1925].

65. ADA, Sarraut Papers, 12J162/D2, "La France amie et protectrice de l'Islam." Article in Les Annales Coloniales by Emile Morinaud, Deputy-Mayor of Constantine, 22 March 1922.

66. MAE, série K: Afrique, sous-série Affaires musulmanes, vol. 1, Société des habous des villes saintes, procès-verbal, séance tenue Alger, 10 August 1919.

67. MAE, série K: Afrique, sous-série Affaires musulmanes, vol. 14, Foreign Ministry, "Note au sujet de Si Kaddour Ben Ghabrit," 18 May 1935.

68. MAE, série K: Afrique, sous-série Affaires musulmanes, vol. 1, Abdelkadir Ben Ghabrit report to Alexandre Millerand, "Rapport sur la politique française en pays musulmans," 8 April 1920.

69. Ibid.

70. AN, Papiers Lyautey, 475AP155/D7, Lyautey coded telegram to Rabat Residency, 2 October 1922.

71. CAOM, AOF fonds modernes, Série 21G: Police/Sûreté, 21G48, Abdelkadir Ben Ghabrit to Governor Brévié, 1 June 1931. The mosque and the Islamic Institute had amassed a deficit of 179,000 francs.

72. CAOM, 1affpol/907, Comité France-Orient letter to Directeur des affaires musulmanes (Colonies), 18 December 1930. The Parti colonial lobby group, the Comité France-Orient, established the library in 1913.

73. MAE, Série P: Tunisie 1917–1940, vol. 386, Residency note, 9 February 1935.

74. See, for example, surveillance reports in TNA, WO 32/5916; Martin Thomas, "Economic Conditions and the Limits to Mobilization in the French Empire, 1936–1939," Historical Journal 48, no. 2 (2005): 486–89.

75. TNA, WO 32/5916, CID memo 782B, "Soviet Activities in China," 3 October 1927.

76. TNA, CO 732/41/22, J. H. Hall (Colonial Office) to O. G. R. Williams, 24 October 1929.

77. TNA, CO 732/53/3, Palestine high commission, "Report on the Pan-Islamic Movement," n.d. [January 1932]; Zachary Lockman, *Comrades and Enemies: Arab and Jewish Workers in Palestine, 1906–1948* (Berkeley and Los Angeles: University of California Press, 1996), 66, 80–81, 130; Joel Beinin and Zachary Lockman, *Workers on the Nile: Nationalism, Communism, Islam and the Egyptian Working Class, 1882–1954* (Cairo: American University in Cairo Press, 1998), chapter 5; Ellis Goldberg, *Tinker, Tailor, and Textile Worker: Class and Politics in Egypt, 1930–1952* (Berkeley and Los Angeles: University of California Press, 1986), especially chapter 4. The appeal of atheistic Communism to Islamic groups such as the Young Men's Muslim Association in Egypt was understandably limited.

78. TNA, FO 407/202, J494/213/16, Lord Lloyd (Cairo) to FO, 28 February 1926.

79. This argument is made in Mohammed Nuri El-Amin, "International Communism, the Egyptian Wafd Party and the Sudan," *British Society for Middle East Studies Bulletin* 12, no. 2 (1985): 27–48.

80. TNA, AIR 23/408, Air Officer Commanding, Palestine, Summary of Intelligence, June 1926. Security service hostility was probably sharpened by the stronger identification between Jewish labor militancy and Zionist nationalism in key industrial disputes in Palestine during the 1920s; see David De Vries, "Drawing the Repertoire of Collective Action: Labour Zionism and Strikes in 1920s Palestine," *Middle Eastern Studies* 38, no. 3 (2002): 93–122.

81. TNA, CO 732/28/13: Criminal investigation liaison in Middle East territories, August–September 1927 correspondence between Foreign Office and Scotland Yard.

82. TNA, AIR 23/409, TJP/7/AIR 1, Air Staff intelligence, Amman, Monthly intelligence summary, May 1928, dispatched to Air Ministry, 8 June 1928.

83. TNA, FO 624/7, file 387/4/36, C. H. Bateman to Dr. Fritz Grobba (German Minister, Baghdad), 13 July 1936.

84. TNA, FO 624/9, file 516: Communism, Sir Archibald Clark Kerr (Baghdad) to Foreign Office, 27 November 1937. Eleven Iraqi air force technicians and two railway workers were arrested for alleged Communist sedition following the second of these legal changes.

85. TNA, CO 732/53/3, anonymous CO minutes, n.d. [January 1932].

86. TNA, CO 732/41/2, Minutes by J. H. Hall (Colonial Office), 24 October 1929. Expressing the Colonial Office Middle East Department view, Hall noted, "It is bad enough to put the United States in a position [through consular representation] where they have almost unlimited powers of interference and an effective veto on our action in Iraq and Palestine; it would, I submit, be little short of lunacy to place the Soviet Government in a similar position."

87. Ahmad Eqbal and Stuart Schaar, "M'hamed Ali: Tunisian Labor Organizer," in *Struggle and Survival in the Modern Middle East,* ed. Edmund Burke III (London: I. B. Tauris, 1993), 199–203.

88. Allison Drew, "Bolshevizing Communist Parties: The Algerian and South African Experiences," *International Review of Social History* 48 (2003): 167–87; François Alexandre, "Le P.C.A. de 1919 à 1939—données en vue d'éclaircir son

action et son rôle," *Revue Algérienne des Sciences Juridiques, Economiques et Politiques* 11, no. 4 (1974): 175–214.

89. Benjamin Stora, *Nationalistes algériens et révolutionnaires français au temps du Front Populaire* (Paris: l'Harmattan, 1987), 53–66.

90. Pierre Brocheux, "L'implantation du mouvement communiste en Indochine française: Le cas du Nghe-Tinh (1930–1931)," *Revue d'Histoire Moderne et Contemporaine* 24, no. 1 (1977): 49–74; R. B. Smith, "The Foundation of the Indochinese Communist Party, 1929–1930," *Modern Asian Studies* 32, no. 4 (1998): 769–805.

91. SHA, Moscow, C67/D2192, EMA-2, "Renseignement: Organization de la propagande communiste dans les colonies" ["Bonne source"], 5 June 1936.

92. SHA, Moscow, C67/D2192, EMA-2, SCR report, "A/S de l'activité du Komintern dans les colonies" ["Assez bonne source"], 18 June 1936.

93. SHA, Moscow, C67/D2192, EMA-2, "A/S de l'activité du Komintern dans l'armée" ["Assez bonne source"], 30 April 1936; SCR report, "L'activité communiste dans l'armée" ["Bonne source—mais sous réserves"], 23 June 1936.

94. SHA, Moscow, C67/D2192, SCR report, "A/S des instructions données par le Komintern au parti communiste français," 24 February 1936. For background to Roux's career, see Peter Jackson, *France and the Nazi Menace: Intelligence and Policy Making, 1933–1939* (Oxford: Oxford University Press, 2000), 18.

95. MAE, série K Afrique, sous-série Affaires musulmanes, vol. 23, Rabat secretariat, Service de la sécurité générale, "Note au sujet du Communisme au Maroc," 2 May 1927.

96. SHA, Moscow, C878/D997, EMA-2, no. 126, "La mouvement Riffain et l'aide intermusulmane," 16 September 1925.

97. Ibid.

98. MAE, série K Afrique, sous-série Affaires musulmanes, vol. 23, tel. 50, Consul Vitasse (Tangiers) to Sous-direction d'Afrique, report on Communist activity, 30 April 1927.

99. People trafficking and illegal narcotics were, however, less of a drain on police time in the 1920s than in another European treaty port, Shanghai. See Frederic Wakeman Jr., *Policing Shanghai, 1927–1937* (Berkeley and Los Angeles: University of California Press, 1995), 260–61.

100. AN, F7/13411, Syrie, no. 1446, Commissaire spécial (Annemasse), "Rapport: A/S/ du mouvement syrien," 14 May 1926.

101. MAE, série E: Levant, vol. 193, tel. 1068, Pierre de Margerie (Berlin) to Aristide Briand, 4 September 1925.

102. Lockman, *Comrades and Enemies*, 80–82; Elizabeth Thompson, *Colonial Citizens: Republican Rights, Paternal Privilege, and Gender in French Syria and Lebanon* (New York: Columbia University Press, 2000), 100–103.

103. AN, F7/13411, SCR-2, "Le mouvement communiste en Palestine et en Syrie," 25 March 1926.

104. SHA, Moscow, C623/D1419, EMA-2, "Le SR de Beyrouth et la S.D.N.," n.d. [April 1926].

105. Michael Provence, "An Investigation into the Local Origins of the Great Revolt," in *France, Syrie et Liban, 1918–1946: Les ambigüités et les dynamiques de la relation mandataire*, ed. Nadine Méouchy (Damascus: IFEAD, 2002), 378–93.

106. Michael Provence, *The Great Syrian Revolt and the Rise of Arab Nationalism* (Austin: University of Texas Press, 2005).

107. Philip S. Khoury, *Syria and the French Mandate: The Politics of Arab Nationalism, 1920–1945* (Princeton, N.J.: Princeton University Press, 1987), chapters 6–8.

108. Serge Berstein and Jean-Jacques Becker, *Histoire de l'anti-communisme en France*, vol. 1, *1917–1940* (Paris: Olivier Orban, 1987), 170–71.

109. See ADA, Sarraut papers,12J43, Dossier: Discours de Doriot, 1921–27.

110. Doriot's campaign is fully explained in David H. Slavin, "The French Left and the Rif War, 1924–25: Racism and the Limits of Internationalism," *Journal of Contemporary History* 26 (1991): 6–27.

111. Jean-Paul Brunet discusses Communist politics in Clichy–Saint-Denis in his *Saint-Denis, la ville rouge: Socialisme et communisme en banlieue ouvrière, 1890–1939* (Paris: Hachette, 1980). As Tyler Stovall notes, several of the Paris "red suburbs" retained strong allegiance to maverick Communist figures such as Doriot, rather than to more orthodox Party men like Jean-Marie Clamamus, the mayor of nearby Bobigny, the district studied by Stovall in *The Rise of the Paris Red Belt* (Berkeley and Los Angeles: University of California Press, 1990), 104–5. Stovall also explores Communism and Parisian race politics in "From Red Belt to Black Belt: Race, Class, and Urban Marginality in Twentieth-Century Paris," in *The Color of Liberty: Histories of Race in France*, ed. Sue Peabody and Tyler Stovall (Durham, N.C.: Duke University Press, 2003), 351–69.

112. ADA, Sarraut papers, 12J43, M.P.5, "A/S du Député Doriot," 20 June 1927.

113. Neil MacMaster, *Colonial Migrants and Racism: Algerians in France, 1900–62* (London: Macmillan, 1997), 125; Slavin, "French Left and the Rif War," 10.

114. Kamel Bouguessa, *Aux sources du nationalisme algérien: Les pioniers du populisme révolutionnaire en marche* (Algiers: Éditions Casbah, 2000), 221–48.

115. Nicole Le Guenac, "Le P.C.F. et la guerre du Rif," *Mouvement Social* 78, no. 1 (1972): 50; Bouguessa, *Aux sources du nationalisme algérien*, 206–7.

116. Le Guenac, "Le P.C.F. et la guerre du Rif," 56; Slavin, "French Left and the Rif War," 13–17. David Slavin identifies the large numbers of professional troops and Foreign Legionnaires as obstacles to the fraternization strategy.

117. ADA, Sarraut papers, 12J43, "Meeting organizé par le comité d'action de la région parisienne du Parti Communiste, Luna Park," 16 May 1925.

118. Georges Oved, *La gauche française et le nationalisme marocain, 1905–1954* (Paris: l'Harmattan, 1984), 1:231–37; M'Barka Hamed-Touati, *Immigration maghrébine et activités politiques en France de la première guerre mondiale à la veille du front populaire* (Tunis: Université de Tunis, 1994), 158–59. Attendance estimates for these meetings vary markedly. The Luna Park meeting drew between 3,500 and 15,000, many of whom were not active PCF supporters. *L'Humanité* supplied the higher figure.

119. MacMaster, *Colonial Migrants and Racism*, 125–26.

120. Kamel Bouguessa argues that such was the case as regards government policy toward Maghrebi immigrants; see *Aux sources du nationalisme algérien*, 163–65.

121. Gilbert Meynier, "Volonté de propagande ou inconscient affiche? Images et imaginaire coloniaux français dans l'entre-deux-guerres," in *Images et Colonies: Iconographie et Propagande Coloniale de 1880 à 1962*, ed. Pascal Blanchard and Armelle Chatelier (Paris: ACHAC, 1993), 47.

122. ADA, Sarraut papers, 12J44, Service de Contrôle et d'Assistance en France des Indigènes des Colonies Françaises, to Interior Ministry Direction de la Sûreté Générale, "État d'esprit des indigènes résidant en France," 30 April 1927.

123. SHA, Moscow, C552/D1427, no. 717, EMA-2 circular to overseas commands, "A/S des mesures de protection contre l'espionnage et la propagande révolutionnaire," 21 February 1927.

124. Hue-Tam Ho Tai, *Radicalism and the Origins of the Vietnamese Revolution* (Cambridge, Mass.: Harvard University Press, 1992), 217–23; Hunyh Kim Khánh, *Vietnamese Communism, 1925–1945* (Ithaca, N.Y.: Cornell University Press, 1982), 91–93.

125. MAE, série K Afrique, sous-série Affaires musulmanes, vol. 24, Batavia Consul memo, "La situation politique à Java," 5 August 1927. The Dutch Resident in Bandung told the French Consul that the most frightening aspect of the rebellion was the apparent ease with which local Communists enlisted the support of various Indonesian nationalist groups and Javanese chiefs.

126. Best, *British Intelligence and the Japanese Challenge in Asia*, 61–68; S. A. Smith, "The Comintern, the Chinese Communist Party and the Three Armed Uprisings in Shanghai, 1926–27," in *International Communism and the Communist International 1919–43*, ed. Tim Rees and Andrew Thorpe (Manchester: Manchester University Press, 1998), 254–70.

127. TNA, WO 32/5916, CIGS minutes, 5 March 1927.

128. Christopher Andrew, "British Intelligence and the Breach with Russia in 1927," *Historical Journal* 25, no. 4 (1982): 957–64.

129. TNA, WO 32/5916, CID memorandum 782B, "Soviet activities in China," 3 October 1927.

130. MAE, série K Afrique, sous-série Affaires musulmanes, vol. 24, Direction Asie-Océanie, Soviet Military Attaché intercept, "Instructions for the Enlistment of Secret Co-workers in Foreign Consulates," 4 April 1927.

131. MAE, série K Afrique, sous-série Affaires musulmanes, vol. 23, no. 724, "Rapport du Résident-général Lucien Saint sur la situation politique en Tunisie," 23 June 1927.

132. Ibid. Lemarchand was imprisoned for three months and fined fifty francs, a relatively light sentence when compared with that of his fellow Tunisian Communist, Robert Beck, who was sentenced in March 1926 for inciting mutiny among French troops. Beck received a one-year prison term.

133. MAE, série K Afrique, sous-série Affaires musulmanes, vol. 23, no. 1518, Direction de la Sûreté publique (Bizerta), report to Tunis Sûreté, "Parti Communiste en Tunisie," 31 March 1927.

134. MAE, série K Afrique, sous-série Affaires musulmanes, vol. 23, no. 724, "Rapport du Résident-général Lucien Saint sur la situation politique en Tunisie," 23 June 1927.

135. SHA, Moscow, C482/D1513, surveillance reports, Ligue contre l'impérialisme et l'oppression coloniale.

136. MAE, série K Afrique, sous-série Questions générales, vol. 125, no. 221, Geneva consulate memo, "A/S Bureau international pour la défense des indigènes," 19 October 1921.

137. MAE, série K Afrique, sous-série Questions générales, vol. 125, Service

français de la Société des Nations note for Sous-direction d'Afrique, 28 February 1924.

138. SHA, Moscow, C482/D1513, SCR renseignement, "La Ligue contre l'impérialisme et l'oppression coloniale" ["Bonne source"], 18 May 1936. Barbusse supported a further Congress against imperialist war in Amsterdam in August 1932; see Norman Ingram, *The Politics of Dissent: Pacifism in France, 1919–1939* (Oxford: Clarendon Press, 1991), 80–81, 153.

139. Partha Sarathi Gupta, *Imperialism and the British Labour Movement, 1914–1964* (London: Macmillan, 1975), 112–13.

140. SHA, Moscow, C482/D1513, no. 786, Armée française du Rhin, EMA-2, report compiled with the Service de Sûreté Luxembourg sector, "Ligue contre oppression coloniale," 10 December 1928.

141. SHA, Moscow, C482/D1513, no. 5363/SCR, "Renseignement: Ligue contre l'oppression coloniale et l'impérialisme," 26 November 1928. Intelligence analysts could not agree on the League's exact title.

142. MAE, série K Afrique, sous-série Affaires musulmanes, vol. 23, Sous-direction d'Afrique note, "Réunion à Amsterdam du Comité exécutif de la Ligue contre l'oppression coloniale," 4 April 1927.

143. MAE, série K Afrique, sous-série Affaires musulmanes, vol. 23, no. 724, "Rapport du Résident-général Lucien Saint sur la situation politique en Tunisie," 23 June 1927.

144. SHA, C67/D2192, SCR agent report ["Assez bon—Source communiste"], 22 February 1936.

145. MAE, série K Afrique, sous-série Affaires musulmanes, vol. 23, Rabat secretariat, Service de la sécurité générale, "Note au sujet du Communisme au Maroc," 2 May 1927.

146. MAE, série K Afrique, sous-série Affaires musulmanes, vol. 25, Urbain Blanc (Rabat) note, "Propagande antimilitariste et communiste," 29 February 1928; Bouches-du-Rhône Prefect to Interior Ministry/Sûreté-générale, "Propagande extrémiste au Maroc," 8 April 1928.

147. MAE, série K Afrique, sous-série Affaires musulmanes, vol. 25, no. 749, Théodore Steeg (Rabat) to Sous-direction d'Afrique, "A/S propagande anti-française et communiste," 3 May 1928.

148. MAE, série K Afrique, sous-série Affaires musulmanes, vol. 25, no. 2025, Théodore Steeg memo to Foreign Ministry, "Le Communisme et les Comités panislamiques au Maroc," 27 December 1927.

149. For nationalist politics among North African students in interwar France, see Guy Pervillé, *Les étudiants algériens de l'université française (1880–1962)* (Paris: CNRS, 1984); Pervillé, "Le sentiment national des étudiants algériens de culture français de 1912 à 1942," *Relations Internationales* 2 (1974): 233–59; and Charles-Robert Ageron, "L'association des étudiants musulmans nord-africains en France durant l'entre-deux-guerres: Contribution à l'étude des nationalismes maghrébins," *Revue Française d'Histoire d'Outre-Mer* 70, no. 258 (1983): 25–56.

150. The Tunis Residency still derived its intelligence on CGTT activities not from Muslims but from monitoring its settler members: MAE, série K Afrique, sous-série Affaires musulmanes, vol. 24, no. 1128, Tunis Residency for Foreign Ministry,

"Propagande communiste. Commémoration des incidents du 11 septembre 1924 à Bizerte," 18 September 1927.

151. Ahmed Koulakssis and Gilbert Meynier, "Sur le mouvement ouvrier et les communistes algériens d'Algérie au lendemain de la première guerre mondiale," *Le Mouvement Social* 1 (1985): 3–32.

152. SHA, Moscow, C223/D122, Compte-rendu de renseignements généraux no. 28, "Les parties politiques en Algérie et les elections de 1924," 31 October 1923.

153. CAOM, Algiers department files, F111/D1, Police spéciale reports: "Parti Communiste, 1939–40."

154. CAOM, Algiers department files, F111/D1, no. 21,314, Algiers prefecture, direction des affaires indigènes to GOC, Algiers, 25 August 1936.

155. MAE, série P: Tunisie 1930–1940, vol. 377, Direction Afrique-Levant note, 24 April 1933.

156. Bernard Marcel Peyrouton, *Du service public à la prison commune. Souvenirs: Tunis, Rabat, Buenos Aires, Vichy, Alger, Frèsnes* (Paris: Plon, 1950), 46.

157. MAE, série P: Tunisie 1930–1940 vol. 377, no. 504, Tunis Residency report, "Incidents au sujet de la question des naturalisés," 29 April 1933.

158. AN, F60202, Haut Comité Méditerranéen rapport no. 1, "Le Haut Comité Méditerranéen et les organismes d'information musulmane," 9 March 1937.

CHAPTER 4

1. C. Ernest Dawn, *From Ottomanism to Arabism: Essays on the Origins of Arab Nationalism* (Urbana: University of Illinois Press, 1973), 117.

2. Glen Balfour-Paul, "Britain's Informal Empire in the Middle East," in *The Oxford History of the British Empire*, vol. 4, *The Twentieth Century*, ed. Judith Brown and William Roger Louis (Oxford: Oxford University Press, 1999), 492–94.

3. Israel Gershoni and James P. Jankowski, *Egypt, Islam, and the Arabs: The Search for Egyptian Nationhood* (Oxford: Oxford University Press, 1986), 83–89.

4. Heather J. Sharkey, *Living with Colonialism: Nationalism and Culture in the Anglo-Egyptian Sudan* (Berkeley and Los Angeles: University of California Press, 2003), 76–80.

5. James C. Gelvin, "The Other Arab Nationalism: Syrian/Arab Populism in Its Historical and International Contexts," in *Rethinking Nationalism in the Arab Middle East*, ed. James P. Jankowski and Israel Gershoni (New York: Columbia University Press, 1997), 231–33, 239–41.

6. Eliezer Tauber, *The Formation of Modern Syria and Iraq* (London: Frank Cass, 1995), 11–39, 49–54; Reeva Spector Simon, *Iraq between the Two World Wars: The Militarist Origins of Tyranny*, new edition (New York: Columbia University Press, 2004), 45–53; Abdul-Karim Rafeq, "Arabism, Society and Economy in Syria, 1918–1919," in *State and Society in Syria and Lebanon*, ed. Y. Choueiri (Exeter: University of Exeter Press, 1993), 12–15.

7. Eliezer Tauber, "The Struggle for Dayr al-Zur: The Determination of Borders between Syria and Iraq," *International Journal of Middle East Studies* 23 (1991): 361–85; Tauber, *Formation of Modern Syria and Iraq*, especially chapter 7.

8. Gershoni and Jankowski, *Egypt, Islam, and the Arabs*, 40–52, 254–69.

9. Charles D. Smith, "The Crisis of Orientation: The Shift of Egyptian Intellectuals

to Islamic Subjects in the 1930s," *International Journal of Middle East Studies* 4 (1973): 382–410; Haggai Erlich, "British Internal Security and Egyptian Youth," in *Britain and the Middle East in the 1930s: Security Problems,* ed. Michael J. Cohen and Martin Kolinsky (London: Macmillan, 1992), 98–112. For discussion of how these competing visions affected Egyptian women, see Giora Eliraz, "Egyptian Intellectuals and Women's Emancipation, 1919–1939," *Asian and African Affairs* 16, no. 1 (1982): 95–120.

10. Israel Gershoni and James Jankowski, *Redefining the Egyptian Nation, 1930–1945* (Cambridge: Cambridge University Press, 1995), 22–28.

11. TNA, FO 407/103, doc. 102, Minutes by Sir Ronald Graham, 19 May 1917.

12. TNA, FO 407/183, doc. 104, Enclosures 1 and 2, General Sir A. Murray to Wingate, and reply, 22 and 23 May 1917.

13. Eve M. Troutt Powell, *A Different Shade of Colonialism: Egypt, Great Britain, and the Mastery of the Sudan* (Berkeley and Los Angeles: University of California Press, 2003), 173.

14. TNA, FO 407/183, doc. 147, Wingate to Arthur Balfour, 20 November 1918.

15. TNA, FO 407/184, doc. 152, "Memorandum by Sir Ronald Graham on the Unrest in Egypt," 9 April 1919; Joel Beinin and Zachary Lockman, *Workers on the Nile: Nationalism, Communism, Islam and the Egyptian Working Class, 1882–1954* (Cairo: American University in Cairo Press, 1998), 80–82.

16. Harold Tollefson, *Policing Islam: The British Occupation of Egypt and the Anglo-Egyptian Struggle over Control of the Police, 1882–1914* (Westport, Conn.: Greenwood Press, 1999), 150, 180–87.

17. Ibid., 171.

18. TNA, FO 407/186, E1488/1488/16, Allenby to Curzon, 26 February 1920.

19. Ibid.

20. TNA, FO 407/186, High Commission annual survey, 1919, item 41: City Police, p. 376.

21. Ibid., item 43: Prisons, p. 377.

22. TNA, FO 371/4984, E3588/93/16, State form 31A , Comparative table showing crimes reported to the police, February 1918–February 1920 (Cairo), 25 March 1920.

23. TNA, FO 407/184, doc. 152, "Memorandum by Sir Ronald Graham on the Unrest in Egypt," 9 April 1919, p. 120g.

24. Mohammed Nuri El-Amin, "International Communism, the Egyptian Wafd Party and the Sudan," *British Society for Middle East Studies Bulletin* 12, no. 2 (1985): 28–38. El-Amin suggests that the British intelligence effort singled out the Wafd because it was the only political group thought capable of mobilizing mass opposition. By contrast, the Egyptian Communist Party, founded in 1922, was not treated as a serious threat.

25. TNA, FO 407/183, doc. 156, Wingate to Balfour, 28 November 1918.

26. Troutt Powell, *Different Shade of Colonialism,* 173–74, 183–84.

27. See, for example, FO 407/209, J 2852/5/16, Sir Percy Loraine telegrams (Ramleh) to Arthur Henderson, 12 September and 4 October 1929.

28. TNA, WO 33/1085, GOC Egypt, "Military Report on Egypt, 1926."

29. TNA, FO 407/183, doc. 156, Wingate to Balfour, 28 November 1918; FO 407/184, doc. 339, "Memorandum by Mr Patterson, Director-General of State Accounts, 1919."

30. TNA, FO 407/183, doc. 156, Wingate to Balfour, 28 November 1918, quotation at p. 246.

31. TNA, FO 407/184, doc. 339, "Memorandum by Mr Patterson, Director-General of State Accounts, 1919."

32. Ibid.

33. Ibid., doc. 373, Allenby to Curzon, 24 May 1919.

34. Ibid.

35. TNA, FO 141/768, Cairo registry, "Oriental Secretariat: Provincial Tours," 20 December 1932.

36. TNA, WO 33/1085, GOC Egypt, "Military Report on Egypt, 1926."

37. TNA, FO 407/184, doc. 373, "Western Delta Area: Chief Officer's Report," 13–20 April 1919.

38. See, for example, TNA, FO 407/184, doc. 373, "Expressions of Opinion on Political Conditions in Provinces Extracted Mainly from the Reports of British Political Officers," 24 May 1919.

39. TNA, FO 141/768, Cairo registry, "Oriental Secretariat: Provincial Tours," 20 December 1932.

40. TNA, FO 407/184, doc. 152, "Memorandum by Sir Ronald Graham on the Unrest in Egypt," 9 April 1919, pp. 120b–c.

41. Ibid., p. 120f.

42. Erlich, "British Internal Security and Egyptian Youth," 99–101.

43. TNA, FO 407/184, doc. 152, "Memorandum by Sir Ronald Graham on the Unrest in Egypt," 9 April 1919, p. 120f.

44. Ibid., p. 120d. Graham singled out civil-military failure to anticipate disorder or to keep sufficient security forces on standby to cope with it.

45. TNA, FO 407/189, E5136/431/16, C. F. Ryder, Director-General of Public Security, "Report on General Situation in Egypt," 23 April 1921.

46. As examples: TNA, FO 407/189, doc. 30, C. F. Ryder, "Report on General Situation in Egypt, March 24 to 30, 1921"; E4667/431/16, Allenby report, 11 April 1921; E5769/431/16, Allenby report, 10 May 1921; E5981/431/16, Allenby report, 16 May 1921.

47. TNA, WO 32/5219, War Office note to FO Permanent Under-Secretary, 1 July 1919.

48. TNA, WO 32/5219, "General Staff Note on Railway Situation in Mesopotamia and Proposed Extension of Lines to Erbil and Hit," 14 July 1920. This inactivity was doubly ironic because railway construction was put forward as a means to reduce garrison forces in Iraq, those troops that remained being better placed to travel to danger spots by rail.

49. TNA 30/69/222, Colonial Secretary circular to Dominion governments, "Recent Events in Iraq," 30 September 1924.

50. Saad Eskander, "Britain's Policy in Southern Kurdistan: The Formation and the Termination of the First Kurdish Government, 1918–1919," *British Journal of Middle Eastern Studies* 27, no. 2 (2000): 139–63.

51. TNA, AIR 9/19, "Report on Middle East Conference Held in Cairo and Jerusalem, March 12 to 30, 1921," section 1: "Events Leading Up to the Conference and Procedure Adopted."

52. Ibid., section 2: Mesopotamia.

53. In May 1924, for instance, a dispute between traders and Assyrian levies in Kirkuk's main bazaar, orchestrated by Mahmud's supporters in the city, provoked bloody clashes that almost led to a temporary withdrawal of the occupying forces; see TNA, AIR 23/562, SSO, Kirkuk, "Special Report on the Recent Disturbances in Kirkuk," 8 May 1924.

54. TNA, CO 730/13, CO49727, Sir John Shuckburgh (CO Middle East Department) minutes on War Office memo, "Garrison of Mesopotamia," 14 October 1921.

55. Saad Eskander, "Southern Kurdistan under Britain's Mesopotamian Mandate: From Separation to Incorporation, 1920–23," *Middle Eastern Studies* 37, no. 2 (2001): 153–80.

56. See Eskander, "Britain's Policy in Southern Kurdistan"; and Eskander, "Southern Kurdistan under Britain's Mesopotamian Mandate."

57. Sir Percy Cox coined this phrase; see IOA, L/PS/10/686, "The Future of Mesopotamia," enclosure to Eastern Committee memo, B283, 12 April 1918.

58. On the importance of these units of Kurdish social organization, see Sami Zubaida, "Contested Nations: Iraq and the Assyrians," *Nations and Nationalism* 6, no. 3 (2000): 364–65.

59. IOA, L/PS/10/782, Report by G. L. Bell, "Northern Kurdistan," 8 March 1920.

60. TNA, CO 730/13, Major E. B. Soane, "Administration Report of Sulaimaniyah Division, 1919," 19 May 1920.

61. TNA, FO 406/72, E1422/1170/93, Sir Francis Humphrys to Sir John Simon, 22 February 1934.

62. See Paula Mohs, "British Intelligence and the Arab Revolt in the Hejaz, 1914–1917" (Ph.D. diss., Cambridge University, 2003), 35–36, 56–57, 90–98.

63. IOA, L/PS/10/782, Political Officer Sulaimaniyah to Civil Commissioner (Baghdad), 5 February 1920.

64. TNA, CO 730/13, Major E. B. Soane, "Administration Report of Sulaimaniyah Division, 1919," 19 May 1920.

65. Eskander, "Britain's Policy in Southern Kurdistan," 145–52.

66. IOA, L/PS/10/782, Report by G. L. Bell, "Northern Kurdistan," 8 March 1920; TNA, FO 371/7771, Iraq Intelligence Reports, nos. 10 and 11, 15 May and 15 June 1922.

67. TNA, FO 406/71, E6229/7/93, Enclosure to Sir. Francis Humphrys telegram to Sir John Simon, October 12 1933: "Historical Summary of the Development of the Assyrian Question in Iraq."

68. IOA, L/PS/10/782, tel. 302, Admiral de Robeck (Constantinople) to FO, 29 March 1920.

69. TNA, CO 730/13, "Administration Report of Sulaimaniyah Division, 1919," 19 May 1920.

70. Ibid.

71. IOA, L/PS/11/193, no. P7701, Sir Arthur Hirtzel, "Kurdistan—India Office Recommendations," 20 December 1919.

72. Eskander, "Southern Kurdistan under Britain's Mesopotamian Mandate," 154–59.

73. Ibid., 164–67.

74. Robert Olson, *The Emergence of Kurdish Nationalism and the Sheikh Said Rebellion, 1880–1925* (Austin: University of Texas Press, 1989), especially chapters 2 and 3.

344 NOTES TO PAGES 125–129

75. David Omissi, "Britain, the Assyrians and the Iraq Levies, 1919–1932," *Journal of Imperial and Commonwealth History* 17, no. 3 (1989): 304–11, quotation at 308.

76. TNA, FO 371/7771, Baghdad High Commission Intelligence Report no. 9, May 1 1922.

77. Eskander, "Southern Kurdistan under Britain's Mesopotamian Mandate," 171–75.

78. TNA, AIR 23/568, SSO Sulaimaniyah to Air HQ "I" Branch (Baghdad), 14 September 1924; CC1155, A. J. Chapman, Sulaimaniyah, to Administrative Inspector, Kirkuk, 16 September 1924.

79. TNA, AIR 23/562, AIR HQ Iraq, "Transport of Troops by Air," 11 September 1924. The aircraft, Vickers Vernons and Vickers Victoria, carried detachments of twelve and twenty men, respectively.

80. TNA, AIR 23/568, CC106, Chapman, Sulaimaniyah, to Administrative Inspector, Kirkuk, 14 September 1924; AV163, SSO Sulaimaniyah to AIR HQ "I" Branch (Baghdad), 6 October 1924. More intensive bombardments were also adopted to suppress the rebellion before the winter set in.

81. TNA, CO 730/163/5: Operations against Sheikh Mahmud, Baghdad Residency conference, 13 January 1931; FO 406/72, E1422/1170/93, Sir Francis Humphrys to FO, 22 February 1934.

82. Amal Vinogradov, "The 1920 Revolt in Iraq Reconsidered: The Role of the Tribes in National Politics," *International Journal of Middle East Studies* 3, no. 1 (1972): 133. Marshall's assassination was apparently part of a broader attempt by the League to trigger a Shi'ite uprising.

83. TNA, FO 371/5230, E12038/2719/44, Captain B. S. Thomas, PO, Muntafik division, Nasariyah, to Civil Commissioner, Baghdad, 31 July 1920.

84. TNA, CO 730/13, Middle East Interdepartmental Committee Report, 31 January 1921, para. 44: "Advisers and Political Officers—Mesopotamia."

85. Vinogradov, "1920 Revolt in Iraq Reconsidered," 136–37.

86. TNA, FO 371/5230, E12038/2719/44, Captain B. S. Thomas, PO, Muntafik division, Nasariyah, to Civil Commissioner, Baghdad, 31 July 1920.

87. Vinogradov, "1920 Revolt in Iraq Reconsidered," 126–27.

88. Ibid., 136–37.

89. TNA, FO 371/5230, E12038/2719/44, Muntafik division report on local unrest during Ramadan, 1 August 1920.

90. Vinogradov, "1920 Revolt in Iraq Reconsidered," 123–24.

91. TNA, FO 371/5230, E12038/2719/44, Muntafik division report on local unrest during Ramadan, 1 August 1920.

92. Robert J. Blyth, *The Empire of the Raj: India, Eastern Africa and the Middle East, 1858–1947* (London: Palgrave, 2003), 165–66.

93. Bodleian Library, Oxford, Viscount Alfred Milner papers, Major-General William Thwaites memo, "ARBUR: The Intelligence Service of the Near and Middle East," 6 August 1920.

94. Bray was heavily involved in the departmental infighting over the Arab revolt; see John Fisher, "The Rabegh Crisis, 1916–1917: 'A Comparatively Trivial Question' or 'A Self-Willed Disaster,'" *Middle Eastern Studies* 38, no. 3 (2002): 73–92.

95. Bruce Westrate, *The Arab Bureau: British Policy in the Middle East, 1916–1920* (University Park: Pennsylvania State University Press, 1992), 69.

96. TNA, FO 371/5230, E12339/2719/44, "Mesopotamia: Preliminary Report on Causes of Unrest," 14 September 1920.

97. Ibid.

98. John Fisher, *Curzon and British Imperialism in the Middle East, 1916–19* (London: Frank Cass, 1999), 128–29. Fisher makes plain the long-standing skepticism among Indian government officials about a Hashemite-ruled Iraq administration and their greater sympathy for the House of Saud. Iraq's Shi'ites had little to gain from either.

99. TNA, FO 371/5230, E12339/2719/44, "Mesopotamia: Preliminary Report on Causes of Unrest," 14 September 1920.

100. TNA, FO 371/5230, E12339/2719/44, C. Cornwallis and H. W. Young notes, 12 October 1920.

101. Regarding the high point of the Shi'ite uprising, see TNA, FO 406/74, E1575/1575/93, Sir Archibald Clark Kerr (Baghdad) to Sir Anthony Eden, 5 March 1936; regarding its suppression, see FO 406/74, E3062/1575/93, Clark Kerr to Eden, May 22, 1936; regarding Shi'ite grievances, see also TNA, FO 624/6, file 27, Baghdad Embassy tel. 133, "Conscription," 11 March 1936.

102. TNA, AIR 23/454, SSO Ramadi, weekly intelligence report, 21 November 1924; Office of SSO Baghdad to Air Staff Intelligence, 30 December 1924.

103. TNA, AIR 23/454, SSO Basra to Air Staff Intelligence, Baghdad, 21 March 1935.

104. TNA, AIR 23/2, Air Staff Intelligence summaries, "Situation in Iraq on 30 September 1922."

105. As examples, TNA, FO 371/7771, Baghdad High Commission Intelligence Reports nos. 9–14, 1 May–15 June 1922. These reports contained sections on Council of Ministers sessions, press editorials, and public opinion in Baghdad.

106. TNA, AIR 23/453: files on 'ulamā treatment and deportation, 1923.

107. TNA, AIR 23/453, SSO, Hillah, to Air HQ (Baghdad), 2 July 1923.

108. See, for example, TNA, AIR 23/379: intelligence reports on the 'ulamā, IB118, SSO, Nasariyah, to Air HQ (Baghdad), 19 December 1925.

109. TNA, CO 730/105/1, Baghdad High Commission Intelligence Report no. 2, 26 January 1926.

110. TNA, CO 730/115/1, Annual report on the administration of Iraq, 1926.

111. See, for example, the extensive tribal raiding files in record groups CO 730, CO 732, and AIR 23.

112. TNA, AIR 23/432, SSO, Diwaniyah, "Internal Intelligence Najaf and Karbalah," 24 April 1927.

113. Ibid., AIR HQ Baghdad summary of agents' reports on the Shi'ite leadership, 25 April 1927.

114. Ibid., SSO, Baghdad, to Air Staff Intelligence, 4 July 1927.

115. TNA, FO 406/63, doc. 108, Colonial Office, "Political Survey of Iraq," 7 February 1929.

116. Ibid., Enclosure to doc. 108, Sir H. Dobbs to Sir Leo Amery, 4 December 1928.

117. TNA, FO 406/74, E7145/1419/93, Sir Archibald Clark Kerr (Baghdad) to Sir Anthony Eden, 2 November 1936; Simon, *Iraq between the Two World Wars*, 118–19. Sidqi, a Kurd, was, in turn, assassinated by pan-Arabist army officers at Mosul air-

port in August 1937. For a full account, see *BDFA*, II: B, vol. 12, doc. 203, Oswald Scott (Baghdad) to Sir Anthony Eden, 18 August 1937.

118. Further military coups followed in August 1937 and December 1938. Nuri al-Sa'id's government put down another coup attempt in March 1939, allowing him to exact revenge on the original perpetrators of the October 1936 coup in which his brother-in-law Ja'far al-Askiri had been murdered; see TNA, FO 406/77, E72/72/93, Sir Maurice Peterson (Baghdad) to Viscount Halifax, 27 December 1938; FO 371/23201, tel. 130, Peterson to Halifax, 30 March 1939.

119. TNA, FO 371/21846, Baghdad Embassy note, "The Political Situation and the Army, June 1938"; regarding civil-military relations in the 1930s, see Simon, *Iraq between the Two World Wars*, 118–26.

120. The racial and cultural dimensions of Egypt's quasi-colonial attitude toward Sudan and the Sudanese are explored in Troutt Powell, *Different Shade of Colonialism.*

121. TNA, WO 33/997, Khartoum intelligence report no. 297, 18 May 1919.

122. E. N. Corbyn, "The Administration of the Sudan in 1937," *Journal of the Royal African Society* 38, no. 151 (1939): 283. An administrative reorganization, completed in 1936, left nine remaining provinces: Northern, Kassala, Khartoum, Blue Nile, White Nile, Kordofan, Darfur, Upper Nile, and Equatoria.

123. TNA, FO 371/7765, E14447, Allenby, "Annual Report for Sudan, 1921."

124. Corbyn, "Administration of the Sudan in 1937," 288.

125. J. A. Mangin, "The Education of an Elite Imperial Administration: The Sudan Political Service and the British Public School System," *International Journal of African Historical Studies* 15, no. 4 (1982): 671–99.

126. TNA, FO 371/7765, E14447, Allenby, "Annual Report for Sudan, 1921."

127. Ibid.

128. Bushra Hamad, "*Sudan Notes and Records* and Sudanese Nationalism, 1918–1956," *History in Africa* 22 (1995): 241–42, 247.

129. Gabriel Warburg, "The Wingate Literature Revisited: The Sudan as Seen by Members of the Sudan Political Service during the Condominium, 1899–1956," *Middle Eastern Studies* 41, no. 3 (2005): 373–75. Wingate depicted the Mahdist movement as oppressive and fanatical, thereby justifying British imperialism as a salvation from tyranny.

130. Peter Woodward, *Sudan, 1898–1989: The Unstable State* (London: I. B. Tauris, 1989), 29–39.

131. Gabriel Warburg, *The Sudan under Wingate: Administration in the Anglo-Egyptian Sudan, 1899–1916* (London: Frank Cass, 1971), 96–97.

132. Gabriel Warburg, "Mahdism and Islamism in Sudan," *International Journal of Middle East Studies* 27, no. 2 (1995): 220.

133. Warburg, *Sudan under Wingate*, 107–8.

134. Troutt Powell, *Different Shade of Colonialism*, 205.

135. Hamad, "*Sudan Notes and Records* and Sudanese Nationalism," 239–49.

136. Colin Newbury, *Patrons, Clients, and Empire: Chieftaincy and Over-Rule in Asia, Africa, and the Pacific* (Oxford: Oxford University Press, 2003), 88.

137. See, for example, the accounts of punitive operations in TNA, WO 33/999, Khartoum Intelligence Department, Annual Report, 1923: part III, Tribal Disturbances, filed 22 April 1924.

138. TNA, FO 371/7765, E14447, Allenby to Curzon, December 16 1922: "Annual Report for Sudan, 1921: Rising in the Nyala District—Southern Darfur."

139. TNA, WO 33/999, "Extract from Report on Patrol 113, by Governor, Nuba Mountains Province," Appendix to Khartoum Intelligence Department, Annual Report, 1923.

140. Newbury, *Patrons, Clients, and Empire,* 88–89.

141. Troutt Powell, *Different Shade of Colonialism,* 209.

142. Ibid., 206–8.

143. The military cadets of Gordon College are profiled in Sharkey, *Living with Colonialism.*

144. TNA, WO 33/999, Director of Intelligence C. Armine Willis, "The League of the White Flag," 20 July 1924; also reproduced in FO 371/10051. The League was not formally launched until 1923.

145. TNA, FO 371/10050, E6347/735/16, Allenby (Cairo) to Ramsay Mac-Donald, 13 July 1924.

146. TNA, FO 371/10050, Khartoum intelligence report, 16 June 1924, enclosure 3. Director of Intelligence C. Armine Willis singled out Watani leaders as organizers of White Flag League activity.

147. Sharkey, *Living with Colonialism,* 77.

148. Troutt Powell, *Different Shade of Colonialism,* 209; Sharkey, *Living with Colonialism,* 78. Both authors note the British propensity to blame the 1924 protests on the "detribalization" of the southern Sudanese who had migrated to work or study in Khartoum.

149. Troutt Powell, *Different Shade of Colonialism,* 208–10. Eve Troutt Powell quite rightly stresses the White Flag League's restriction of membership to Sudanese of both Arab and black African background, a stipulation designed to bar entry to Egyptians.

150. TNA, WO 33/997, Khartoum Intelligence Department, Annual Report, 1922, p. 4: "Egyptian Nationalist Propaganda," sent to War Office, 3 March 1923.

151. TNA, FO 371/10051, E6659/735/16, Allenby (Cairo) to MacDonald, 26 July 1924; Troutt Powell, *Different Shade of Colonialism,* 210.

152. Sharkey, *Living with Colonialism,* 76.

153. TNA, WO 33/999, Sudan monthly intelligence reports, nos. 345 and 346, April and May 1923.

154. TNA, FO 407/184, Enclosure to doc. 126, "Note on the Growth of National Aspirations in the Sudan," sent to FO, 26 March 1919.

155. Sharkey, *Living with Colonialism,* especially chapters 2 and 3.

156. Ibid., 77.

157. TNA, FO 407/184, Enclosure to doc. 126, "Note on the Growth of National Aspirations in the Sudan," sent to FO, 26 March 1919.

158. Sharkey, *Living with Colonialism,* 77; Troutt Powell, *Different Shade of Colonialism,* 210.

159. TNA, WO 33/999, Khartoum intelligence report, "Account of Events Connected with Pro-Egyptian Propaganda in the Sudan during August 1924"; Sudan monthly intelligence report no. 361, August 1924, submitted by A. W. Skrine, 22 September 1924; for another account of events, see TNA 30/69/222, Colonial Secretary telegram to Dominion governments, 21 August 1924.

160. Sharkey, *Living with Colonialism*, 78.

161. TNA, WO 33/999, Khartoum Intelligence Department report, "Account of Events Connected with Pro-Egyptian Propaganda in Various Parts of the Sudan during August 1924."

162. TNA, WO 33/999, "Diary of events Affecting the Sudan Subsequent to the Murder of Sir Lee Stack, 19th to 30th November 1924."

163. Ibid. The troops in question were from the Argyll and Sutherland Highlanders, mounted Camel Corps, and the Leicestershire and Dorsetshire regiments.

164. TNA, WO 33/999, Khartoum Intelligence Department, Annual Report, 1924.

165. Ibid.

166. TNA, WO 33/999, Khartoum intelligence report, "The Mutiny of 27th and 28th November 1924."

167. TNA, FO 371/7765, E14447, Allenby to Curzon, 16 December 1922: "Annual Report for Sudan, 1921." The February 1922 ordinance was drafted in Khartoum during 1921.

168. TNA, WO 33/2764, War Office general staff, "Military Report on the Sudan, 1927."

169. Sharkey, *Living with Colonialism*, 80–82.

170. TNA, AIR 20/678, Notes on a meeting in Civil Secretary's Office, 28 May 1937.

171. TNA, WO 32/4155, Brigadier commanding British troops in the Sudan, "General Report on the [Abyssinian] Emergency in the Sudan, 1936," 25 October 1936.

172. TNA, AIR 20/678, "Comments by Air Staff Officer on Palace Discussion," 31 March 1936. Emphasis added.

173. Ibid., Notes on a meeting in Civil Secretary's Office, 28 May 1937.

174. David Omissi, *Air Power and Colonial Control: The Royal Air Force, 1919–1939* (Manchester: Manchester University Press, 1990); David Killingray, "'A Swift Agent of Government': Air Power in British Colonial Africa, 1916–1939," *Journal of African History* 25, no. 4 (1984): 429–44.

175. TNA, AIR 20/674, "Note by the Air Staff on the Regulation of Air Control in Undeveloped Countries: Moral Effect of Air Power," 21 November 1928.

176. British experience in the Arab revolt and the Palestine campaign illustrated imint's importance; see Mohs, "British Intelligence and the Arab Revolt in the Hejaz," 3–4; Yigal Sheffy, *British Military Intelligence in the Palestine Campaign, 1914–1918* (London: Frank Cass, 1998), 48–53, 196–200.

177. Omissi, *Air Power and Colonial Control*, 60–76, 148.

178. TNA, AIR 9/41/4, Directorate of plans, "Note on the Use of Air Power," 6 July 1925.

179. Omissi, *Air Power and Colonial Control*, 82. Hence the need for ground support from Royal Air Force armored car battalions.

180. TNA, AIR 20/674, "Note by the Air Staff on the Regulation of Air Control in Undeveloped Countries," 21 November 1928.

181. TNA, AIR 20/678, Note by Wing Commander Breen, "Resumé of the Discussion of Tribal Intelligence on 28 May 1937."

182. TNA, AIR 20/173, Squadron Leader F. Woolley memo, "Intelligence Organization—Sudan," n.d. [1936].

183. Douglas H. Johnson, "From Military to Tribal Police: Policing the Upper Nile Province of the Sudan," in *Policing the Empire: Government, Authority and Control, 1830–1940,* ed. David M. Anderson and David Killingray (Manchester: Manchester University Press, 1991), 151.

184. See, for example, TNA, FO 407/186, doc. 326, Enclosure 1: "Report of Egyptian Intelligence Staff for the Period from June 1 to 7, 1920."

CHAPTER 5

1. TNA, FO 371/9474, Government of the Riff Republic, "Declaration of State and Proclamation to All Nations," reissued at Ajdir, 1 July 1923.

2. SHA, 3H602, Pétain Moroccan inspection mission report, 4 August 1925.

3. SR and Section de Centralisation du Renseignement (SCR) agents' reports kept the French high command well informed about Spain's poor military performance in Morocco and the likelihood of a negotiated peace between Primo de Rivera's regime and the Rif Republic. As an example: SHA, Moscow, C505/D183, SCR agent report, "La situation intérieur espagnole et sa répercussion sur la politique française," 15 December 1924.

4. The best study of the Syrian revolt is Michael Provence, *The Great Syrian Revolt and the Rise of Arab Nationalism* (Austin: University of Texas Press, 2005).

5. William A. Hoisington Jr., *Lyautey and the French Conquest of Morocco* (London: Macmillan, 1995), 21–23, 52.

6. Daniel Rivet, *Lyautey et l'institution du protectorat français au Maroc* (Paris: l'Harmattan, 1988), 2:62–65, 82–84.

7. SHA, 3H107, no. 6487/DR/I, Lyautey to EMA Section d'Afrique: "Emploi des partisans en Maroc," 18 November 1922.

8. MAE, série M, sous-série Police, vol. 839, tel. 464, Rabat Residency to Direction des affaires politiques et commerciales/Afrique, 12 March 1924.

9. Ibid., tel. 1527, Office du protectorat (Rabat) to Sous-direction d'Afrique, 8 May 1924.

10. Lahsen Jennin, "Le Moyen Atlas et les Français: Évolution des connaissances et du savoir sur l'espace et sur la société rurale," in *Présences et images franco-marocaines au temps du protectorat,* ed. Jean-Claude Allain (Paris: l'Harmattan, 2003), 58–59.

11. Henri Simon, "Les études berbères au Maroc et leurs applications en matière de politique et administration," *Archives Berbères* (1915–16): 9, cited in Jennin, "Le Moyen Atlas et les Français," 59.

12. Jennin, "Le Moyen Atlas et les Français," 60–61. Between 1915 and 1920, the SR direction générale in Rabat issued detailed questionnaires to its native affairs officers for use in compiling the requisite information about Berber tribal society in the Middle Atlas.

13. Colin Newbury, *Patrons, Clients, and Empire: Chieftaincy and Over-Rule in Asia, Africa, and the Pacific* (Oxford: Oxford University Press, 2003), 92.

14. TNA, FO 371/9494, W2076/2076/28, Consul C. E. Heathcote-Smith (Casablanca), "Memorandum on the Division of Power in Southern Morocco," 8 March 1923.

15. Hoisington, *Lyautey and the French Conquest of Morocco,* 94–104.

16. MAE, série K Afrique, sous-série AOF, vol. 1, no. 1380, Lyautey to Foreign Ministry, "Coopération inter-Saharienne," 26 December 1919.

17. MAE, série M, vol. 838: Police, no. 67/CMD, Note for M. Beaumarchais, Foreign Ministry Sous-directeur d'Afrique, 8 March 1921; no. 3765, SCR intelligence report, "A/S de Mohamed el Cheikh—Suspect," 16 April 1921.

18. TNA, FO 371/9494, W2076/2076/28, Consul C. E. Heathcote-Smith (Casablanca), "Memorandum on the Division of Power in Southern Morocco," 8 March 1923, p. 2.

19. Cited in Hoisington, *Lyautey and the French Conquest of Morocco*, 108, 230n33.

20. The commission convened 109 times between November 1918 and November 1923; see CAOM, AOF fonds modernes, 17G22, Commission interministérielle des affaires musulmanes, compte-rendu, 17 November 1923.

21. SHA, 7N4192/Dossier: "L'effort militaire français au Levant, 19 novembre 1919 au 18 août 1921"; 20N1089/D1, Levant SR to EMA-2, intelligence summaries, nos. 169 and 175, 4 and 12 May 1921.

22. Lyautey criticized the earlier diversion of North African and Foreign Legion units to the Levant; see AN, Lyautey Papers, 475AP107/D2, no. 5252/9/11, War Minister Flaminius Raiberti to Lyautey, 24 December 1920; no. 566/9/11, War Minister Louis Barthou to Lyautey, 8 February 1921. Franco-Turkish agreement over Cilicia in March 1921 was pivotal to French efforts to pacify the Alawite region and northern Syria; see Philip S. Khoury, *Syria and the French Mandate: The Politics of Arab Nationalism, 1920–1945* (Princeton, N.J.: Princeton University Press, 1987), 50, 100–101.

23. See, for example, the Foreign Ministry and Ministry of Marine reports on the 1919 Zaghlulist uprising and its aftermath in Egypt in SHA, 7N4183/D3.

24. C. R. Pennell, *A Country with a Government and a Flag: The Rif War in Morocco* (Wisbech: Middle East and North African Studies Press, 1986), 186–91.

25. TNA, FO 371/11078, W6433/39/28, Marquess of Crewe (Paris) to FO, 6 July 1925. The theme of unprovoked Riffian attack was reiterated in a Spanish government press communiqué issued the following week: W6734/39/28, Gurney (Madrid) to FO, 11 July 1925.

26. TNA, FO 413/69, W5092/186/28, Marquess of Crewe (Paris) to Chamberlain, 2 June 1925.; M'Barka Hamed-Touati, *Immigration maghrébine et activités politiques en France de la première guerre mondiale à la veille du front populaire* (Tunis: Université de Tunis, 1994), 155–56.

27. TNA, FO 413/69, W1288/39/28 and W5092/186/28, both Assistant Military Attaché Graham to Marquess of Crewe (Paris), 12 February and 29 May 1925.

28. SHA, 3H107/EMA, Ministère de Guerre, "Note au sujet des origines de l'agression Rifiane," n.d. [probably late 1926].

29. Ibid. For a penetrating account of the origins and outcome of the Rif War, see Moshe Gershovich, *French Military Rule in Morocco: Colonialism and Its Consequences* (London: Frank Cass, 2000), 128–41.

30. TNA, FO 371/11083, W4281/4281/28, R. H. Clive (Tangiers) to FO: "Annual Report on Morocco for 1924," p. 16.

31. TNA, FO 413/69, W5092/186/28, Graham to Marquess of Crewe, 29 May 1925.

32. TNA, FO 371/11081, W7798/186/28, Vice-Consul Were (Fez) to Rabat Consulate, 31 July 1925.

33. SHA, 3H107/Notes et travaux divers, no. 6487/DR/I, Direction des affaires indigènes et du SR memo to EMA Section d'Afrique, 18 November 1922.

34. Patrice Morlat, *Les affaires politiques de l'Indochine (1895–1923): Les grands commis du savoir au pouvoir* (Paris: l'Harmattan, 1995), 251–54. Regarding Gallieni's representation of his Madagascar achievements, see Pascal Venier, "A Campaign of Colonial Propaganda: Gallieni, Lyautey and the Defence of the Military Regime in Madagascar, May 1899 to July 1900," in *Promoting the Colonial Idea: Propaganda and Visions of Empire in France,* ed. Tony Chafer and Amanda Sackur (London: Palgrave, 2002), 29–39. An excellent biography is Marc Michel, *Gallieni* (Paris: Fayard, 1989).

35. This theme can be traced in native affairs service monthly intelligence reports. See SHAA, 2C35/D3, Direction des affaires indigènes "Rapport mensuel d'ensemble du protectorat," February 1921; SHA, 3H101/EMA Section d'Afrique, Direction des affaires indigènes situation reports, 1925.

36. MAE, série M: Maroc, 1917–1940, vol. 89, Direction des affaires indigènes/SR, "Rapport mensuel d'ensemble du protectorat: Situation politique et militaire, janvier 1924."

37. SHA, 3H602, "Éxtrait d'une lettre du 6 juin [1925] du Commandant Lascroux."

38. Ibid., General Serrigny, CSDN secretariat, to Ministry of War/Cabinet, 4 June 1925.

39. SHA, 3H101/EMA, Résidence générale (Rabat), Bulletin périodique, 29 April 1925.

40. TNA, FO 371/11081, W7798/186/28, Vice-Consul Were (Fez) to Rabat Consulate 31 July 1925.

41. MAE, série M: Maroc, 1917–1940, vol. 89, Direction des affaires indigènes/SR, "Rapport mensuel d'ensemble du protectorat: Situation politique et militaire, mars 1924"; see also "Rapport mensuel, mars 1925;" TNA, FO 371/11083, W9934/4011/28, Consul-General Ryan (Rabat) to Sir Austen Chamberlain, 13 October 1925.

42. TNA, FO 371/11081, W7798/186/28, Vice-Consul Were (Fez) to Rabat Consulate, 31 July 1925.

43. MAE, série M, vol. 89, Direction des affaires indigènes/SR, "Rapport mensuel sur la situation politique et militaire au Maroc, Mars 1925"; SHA, 3H101/EMA Section d'Afrique, Résidence générale (Rabat), Bulletin périodique, 29 April 1925.

44. SHA, 3H101/EMA Section d'Afrique, Direction des affaires indigènes report, "Situation politique et militaire du 19 au 25 mai 1925."

45. SHA, 3H602, General Serrigny, CSDN secretariat, to Ministry of War/Cabinet, 4 June 1925; Gershovich, *French Military Rule in Morocco,* 130–32.

46. SHA, 3H602, General Serrigny, CSDN secretariat, to Ministry of War/Cabinet, 4 June 1925.

47. Ibid., Commandement général du Front nord, 3ᵉ Bureau, General Daugan to Lyautey, 5 July 1925. According to Daugan, the Northern Front commander, the reinforcements initially sent from Algeria to assist these forces had little experience of this type of counterinsurgency.

48. TNA, FO 371/11081, W10017/186/28, Marquess of Crewe to FO, 23 October 1925.

49. SHA, 3H101/Périodiques M. Pétain, no. 319, Pétain report, "Bulletin périodique du 30 septembre au 4 octobre 1925." Pétain stated that the wave of tribal submissions then under way reflected gratitude for liberation from Riffian "terror," but he was also anxious to disarm the local population.

50. SHA, 3H602, EMA Section d'Afrique, "But et conditions des actions à entreprendre pour rétablir la situation sur le Front nord du Maroc," 14 August 1925.

51. MAE, série M, vol. 91, Direction des affaires indigènes weekly bulletin, "Situation politique et militaire du 16 au 22 novembre 1926." Native affairs officers tracked autumn migrations of Berber sheep herds, noting that the army's capacity to protect key pasturage was critical to pacification.

52. See, for example, MAE, série M, vol. 91, Direction des affaires indigènes weekly bulletin, "Situation politique et militaire du 9 au 16 novembre 1926." The report detailed the actions of the two dissident clans, the Beni Mestara and Ghezaoua, identifying the families that had assisted them.

53. MAE, série M, vol. 91, Direction des affaires indigènes weekly bulletin, "Situation politique et militaire du 8 au 14 mars 1927." This report noted that a successful attack on a troop column by Beni Mastera and Beni Faghloun Berbers allowed the rebels to retake the village of Zaouia, the third time the village had changed hands in six months. Four nearby villages went over to the rebels as a result, encouraged by the death of the local French military commander in the earlier engagement and the distribution of a consignment of rifles. This intelligence led to renewed aerial bombardment of the affected area; see the subsequent bulletin, "Situation politique et militaire du 15 au 21 mars 1927."

54. MAE, série M, vol. 91, Direction des affaires indigènes weekly bulletin, "Situation politique et militaire du 17 au 23 mai 1927." After artillery bombardment of rebel villages in the valley on 20 May, several village headmen made their submissions of loyalty to native affairs officers.

55. SHA, 9N269/D7: "Troupes coloniales au Maroc, 1921–27."

56. TNA, FO 371/11081, W10017/186/28, Enclosure: Report by Military Attaché Major-General G. S. Clive, 22 October 1925.

57. SHA, 3H602, "Observations faites par le Maréchal Pétain au cours de ses visites à Rabat et au Front nord," 22 July 1925.

58. MAE, série M, vol. 91, Direction des affaires indigènes weekly bulletin, "Situation politique et militaire du 15 au 21 mai 1928."

59. TNA, FO 371/14911, W341/341/17, Lord Tyrell, "Annual Report on France for 1929," p. 32.

60. Ibid., pp. 37–38.

61. Clashes with dissident clans could be severe; see Moshe Gershovich, "The Ait Ya'qub Incident and the Crisis of French Military Policy in Morocco," *Journal of Military History* 62, no. 1 (1998): 57–73.

62. Acquisition of the Middle East mandates was not commemorated or monumentalized in memorials, street names, or exhibitions to an extent comparable with earlier colonial conquests or the acquisition of the Moroccan protectorate; see Robert Aldrich, *Vestiges of the Colonial Empire in France: Monuments, Museums and Colonial Memories* (London: Palgrave-Macmillan, 2005).

63. Christopher M. Andrew and A. S. Kanya-Forstner, *France Overseas: The Great War and the Climax of French Imperial Expansion* (London: Thames and Hudson, 1981), 28, 171–208 passim. The term *Asiatiques* connoted Parti Colonial members with particular interest in the Levant and, to a lesser extent, Indochina. They were organized into several committees, the foremost of which were the Comité de l'Asie Française, the Comité de l'Orient, and the Comité France-Syrie. Membership of these groups overlapped.

64. Ibid.

65. TNA, FO 371/7847, E5514/274/89, Consul C. E. S. Palmer (Damascus) to FO, 16 May 1922.

66. Linda Schatkowski Schilcher, "The Famine of 1915–1918 in Greater Syria," in *Problems of the Modern Middle East in Historical Perspective: Essays in Honour of Albert Hourani*, ed. J. Spagnolo (Reading: Ithaca Press, 1992), 229–58; Hasan Kayali, *Arabs and Young Turks. Ottomanism, Arabism, and Islamism in the Ottoman Empire, 1908–1918* (Berkeley and Los Angeles: University of California Press, 1997), 192–99.

67. Khoury, *Syria and the French Mandate*, especially chapters 10 and 11. For a comparable treatment of the Lebanese political community, see Meir Zamir, *Lebanon's Quest: The Road to Statehood, 1926–1939* (London: I. B. Taurus, 1997), chapter 2.

68. Khoury, *Syria and the French Mandate*, 55–56.

69. Mizrahi, *Genèse de l'État mandataire: Service de renseignements et bandes armées en Syrie et au Liban dans les années 1920* (Paris: Publications de la Sorbonne, 2003), 76–77, 95–96.

70. Itamar Rabinovitch, "The Compact Minorities and the Syrian state, 1918–45," *Journal of Contemporary History* 14, no. 4 (1979): 693–97; Mizrahi, *Genèse de l'État mandataire*, 90–93.

71. Khoury, *Syria and the French Mandate*, 58–70.

72. Mizrahi, *Genèse de l'État mandataire*, 88–90.

73. Ibid., 186–98.

74. Ibid., 185.

75. CADN, Fonds Beyrouth, vol. 840/D1, SR summary review, n.d. [probably 1930]; Khoury, *Syria and the French Mandate*, 78n30.

76. Mizrahi, *Genèse de l'État mandataire*, 369–70.

77. TNA, AIR 23/89, BS/S/10, British Liaison Officer Major A. Salisbury-Jones, record of meeting with Colonel Andréa, 22 December 1925.

78. SHA, Moscow, C 581/D370, EMA-2, SR report, "Syrie et Palestine," 15 November 1925. The report also lashed out at the Jerusalem high commission and Shakib Arslan's Syrian-Palestine Congress, accusing the former of stirring pan-Arabism, and the latter of fomenting sedition in Syria.

79. SHA, 4H67/D1, Haut Commissariat, Cabinet Civil bulletin d'information 1, 21 December 1925.

80. SHA, Moscow, C581/D370, EMA-2, no. 4053, SCR report, "A/S du mouvement insurrectionnel en Syrie et en Liban," sent to War Ministry, 16 September 1925.

81. SHA, Moscow, C581/D370, SCR report, "Les événements en Syrie" ["Bonne source"], 16 March 1926.

82. Succinct accounts are Jan Karl Tanenbaum, *General Maurice Sarrail, 1856–1929: The French Army and Left-Wing Politics* (Chapel Hill: University of North Car-

olina Press, 1974); Lenka Bokova, *La confrontation franco-syrienne à l'époque du Mandat, 1925–1927* (Paris: l'Harmattan, 1990).

83. Ibrahim Hanunu's 1919 revolt in Aleppo is described in Khoury, *Syria and the French Mandate,* 102–14; regarding Hama, see N. E. Bou-Nacklie, "Tumult in Syria's Hama in 1925: The Failure of a Revolt," *Journal of Contemporary History* 33, no. 2 (1998): 273–90.

84. Regarding this change in the nature of the Great Revolt, see Michael Provence, "A Nationalist Rebellion without Nationalists? Popular Mobilizations in Mandatory Syria, 1925–1926," in *The British and French Mandates in Comparative Perspectives,* ed. Nadine Méouchy and Peter Sluglett (Leiden: Brill, 2004), 673–91.

85. TNA, AIR 23/91, British Liaison Officer Major J. Codrington to GHQ Amman, 8 November 1926.

86. TNA, AIR 23/89, British Liaison Officer Major A. Salisbury-Jones report, "The Capture of Soueida," 5 May 1926. There was a recent precedent for the application of overwhelming military force to crush rebellion in the Jabal Druze in Ottoman operations mounted against an earlier Druze revolt between August and November 1910; see Eugene L. Rogan, "Bringing the State Back: The Limits of Ottoman Rule in Jordan, 1840–1910," in *Village, Steppe and State: The Social Origins of Modern Jordan,* ed. Eugene L. Rogan and Tariq Tell (London: British Academic Press, 1994), 53–54.

87. SHA, 4H67/D2, no. 936/2, Gamelin, Commandant supérieur des troupes du Levant, to Cabinet du Ministre (Guerre), 1 July 1926.

88. Indispensable works include Khoury, *Syria and the French Mandate;* Bokova, *La confrontation franco-syrienne;* C. J. E. Andréa, *La révolte druze et l'insurrection de Damas* (Paris: Payot, 1937); Michael Provence, "An Investigation into the Local Origins of the Great Revolt," in *France, Syrie et Liban, 1918–1946: Les ambigüités et les dynamiques de la relation mandataire,* ed. Nadine Méouchy (Damascus: IFEAD, 2002), 378–93; and Provence, "Nationalist Rebellion without Nationalists?" 673–91. The key work is Provence, *Great Syrian Revolt.*

89. Mizrahi, *Genèse de l'État mandataire,* especially chapters 10 and 11.

90. Khoury, *Syria and the French Mandate,* 168–69.

91. *BDFA,* II: B, vol. 5, doc. 30, Smart (Damascus) enclosure, 17 August 1925.

92. MAE, série E, 1922–29, vol. 195, De Reffye report to Berthelot, 28 November 1925.

93. CADN, Fonds Beyrouth, Cabinet Politique, vol. 986, DR25, SR Contrôle bédouin, "État de la transhumance au 15 juillet 1925."

94. Ibid.

95. MAE, série E, 1922–29, vol. 195, De Reffye report to Berthelot, November 28 1925; report also cited in Khoury, *Syria and the French Mandate,* 206n3.

96. CADN, Fonds Beyrouth, Cabinet Politique, vol. 895, no. 4280/BS/4, Pierre Alypé to Henry de Jouvenel, 31 May 1926.

97. TNA, AIR 23/408, Royal Air Force Headquarters Transjordan, "Monthly Intelligence, May 1927," 13 June 1927.

98. Paula Mohs, "British Intelligence and the Arab Revolt in the Hejaz, 1914–1917" (Ph.D. diss., Cambridge University, 2003), 78–79; Eugene L. Rogan, *Frontiers of the State in the Late Ottoman Empire: Transjordan, 1850–1921* (Cambridge: Cambridge University Press, 1999), 227–29.

99. *BDFA,* II: B, vol. 5, doc. 29, Smart (Damascus) to Austen Chamberlain, 21 August 1925.

100. MAE, série E, 1922–29, vol. 193, no. 344, Sous-direction Asie to Sarrail, 9 September 1925.

101. CADN, Fonds Beyrouth, Services Spéciaux, vol. 2199: Renseignements d'informateurs, 1920–37, HC bureau politique, "Note au sujet de Noury Chaalan," 29 July 1920.

102. CADN, Fonds Beyrouth, Cabinet Politique, vol. 986, DR: Affaires bédouines, 1923–24, Commandant Tommy Martin report, "Action du Contrôle bédouin en 1923," 29 February 1924.

103. Ibid., DR24, no. 9520/ES/2, SR report by Terrier, "Mouvance de Damas," 23 November 1926.

104. MAE, série E, 1922–29, vol. 196, no. 648, Henry de Jouvenel to Foreign Ministry, 15 December 1925.

105. Khoury, *Syria and the French Mandate,* 173; MAE, série E, 1922–29, vol. 197, no. 131/6, de Reffye report to Foreign Ministry, 10 February 1926.

106. MAE, série E, 1922–29, vol. 196, "Note pour le chef d'état-major de l'armée française du Levant," 1 December 1925.

107. Ibid.

108. SHA, 7N4181/D1, no. 393/1G, Gamelin to War Ministry/EMA-1, 10 February 1926.

109. MAE, série E, 1922–29, vol. 197, no. 131/6, de Reffye to Foreign Ministry, 10 February 1926.

110. MAE, série E, 1922–29, vol. 195, Sous-direction Asie note for de Jouvenel, 17 November 1925; Khoury, *Syria and the French Mandate,* 130–31.

111. MAE, Henry de Jouvenel papers, PA-AP 092, vol. 2, de Jouvenel to Foreign Ministry, n.d. [1926].

112. MAE, série E, vol. 193, no. 3969/bis, "SR note au sujet de l'insurrection du Djebel Druze," signed by Dentz, 4 September 1925. Dentz became high commissioner under Vichy in December 1940, putting him at odds with his former SR mentor, Henri Catroux, later a leading Free French general.

113. MAE, série E, vol. 193, no. E412/1, Relations commerciales note, "A/S de déclarations du Sultan Atrach," 8 September 1925.

114. Mizrahi, *Genèse de l'État mandataire,* 367–68.

115. Tanenbaum, *General Maurice Sarrail,* 191–206 passim; TNA, FO 371/10851, E5576/357/89, Crewe to Chamberlain, 15 September 1925.

116. Bokova, *La confrontation franco-syrienne,* chapter 4; Khoury, *Syria and the French Mandate,* 137–38, 155–59; General Charles Andréa, the general who led the assault on the Jabal Druze, wrote a detailed account of the expedition, *La révolte druze et l'insurrection de Damas.*

117. SHA, 7N4171/D1, no. 1199/K2, SR Levant report, "Liste des associations, partis du comité de l'extérieur travaillant ou ayant travaillé contre le mandat de la France en Syrie," 1 April 1926. These suspicions intensified when rebel leaders including Sultan al-Atrash took refuge in Transjordan and eastern Palestine during 1926–27.

118. MAE, Henry de Jouvenel papers, tel. 403, de Reffye to Foreign Ministry, 15 June 1926; Khoury, *Syria and the French Mandate,* 198–200.

119. SHA, 7N4171/D1, EMA-2, no. 4099, SR report, "Le mouvement insurrectionnel en Syrie," 28 August 1926; no. 1038, "A/S des événements en Syrie," date unclear, 1926.

120. SHA, Moscow, C623/D1409, "Instruction sur l'organisation et fonctionnement du SCE," 13 January 1927.

121. SHA, Moscow, C581/D370, EMA-2, SR report, "L'attitude des nationalistes syriens" ["Source sérieuse"], 15 September 1931. Regarding Lebanon's earlier experiment with constitutional parliamentary government, see Zamir, *Lebanon's Quest*, 28–83.

122. Peter Shambrook, *French Imperialism in Syria, 1927–1936* (Reading: Ithaca Press, 1998), 27–35; Khoury, *Syria and the French Mandate*, 247–49.

123. CADN, Fonds Beyrouth, vol. 953/D1, no. 763/DV, Damascus SR note, "Activité des extrémistes de Damas," 20 March 1928; Khoury, *Syria and the French Mandate*, 341–42. Regarding Ponsot's constitutional reforms, see Shambrook, *French Imperialism in Syria*, chapters 2 and 3.

124. SHA, 7N4190/D2, Damascus Sûreté Générale, fiche individuelle no. 294/SGC, 5 May 1928; Khoury, *Syria and the French Mandate*, 268–69.

125. Elizabeth Thompson, *Colonial Citizens: Republican Rights, Paternal Privilege, and Gender in French Syria and Lebanon* (New York: Columbia University Press, 2000), 156–61; Khoury, *Syria and the French Mandate*, chapters 15–16.

126. SHA, Moscow, C873/D2006, SEL note, "Activité de la propagande italienne en Syrie," n.d. [1939]; C609/D374, SEL no. 3176, "Situation du Parti Communiste Syro-Libanais à la veille de la guerre," 12 April 1940; EMA-2, "TMSF—Activité Turque," 11 January 1937.

127. See, for example, surveillance of minority groups in SHA, Moscow, C609/D374 and D375.

128. MAE, série E: Levant, vol. 492, Comte de Martel report to Foreign Ministry, 3 January 1936; Subki Bey Barakat to de Martel, 22 January 1936. The strike began on 20 January 1936 in response to the closure of a National Bloc office in the capital and the arrest of Fakri al-Barudi, the National Bloc spokesman in Damascus, and the nationalist youth movement leader Sayf al-Din al-Ma'mun.

CHAPTER 6

1. Administrative reliance on tribal control specialists emerges strongly in an account by the British liaison officer in Beirut of his overland journey from Beirut to Amman in 1927: TNA, AIR 23/91, Major J. Codrington to Royal Air Force headquarters (RAF HQ) Amman, 4 June 1927.

2. Tribal "civil society" is explored in Richard T. Antoun, "Civil Society, Tribal Process, and Change in Jordan: An Anthropological View," *International Journal of Middle East Studies* 32 (2000): 441–51.

3. Much of the English-language historiography of the Syria and Iraq mandates focuses on the origins and nature of Arab nationalism in both states. A thoughtful introduction to the state of current debate is Israel Gershoni, "Rethinking the Formation of Arab Nationalism in the Middle East, 1920–1945: Old and New Narratives," in *Rethinking Nationalism in the Arab Middle East*, ed. James Jankowski and Israel Gershoni (New York: Columbia University Press, 1997), 3–25. Other key works

include C. Ernest Dawn, *From Ottomanism to Arabism: Essays on the Origins of Arab Nationalism* (Urbana: University of Illinois Press, 1973); Said Amir Arjomand, ed., *From Nationalism to Revolutionary Islam* (Albany: State University of New York Press, 1984); and Rashid Khalidi, ed., *The Origins of Arab Nationalism* (New York: Columbia University Press, 1991). Key studies of interwar Syria include Philip S. Khoury, *Syria and the French Mandate: The Politics of Arab Nationalism 1920–1945* (Princeton, N.J.: Princeton University Press, 1987); Peter A. Shambrook, *French Imperialism in Syria, 1927–1936* (Reading: Ithaca Press, 1998); James L. Gelvin, *Divided Loyalties: Nationalism and Mass Politics in Syria at the Close of Empire* (Berkeley and Los Angeles: University of California Press, 1998); and Elizabeth Thompson, *Colonial Citizens: Republican Rights, Paternal Privilege and Gender in French Syria and Lebanon* (New York: Columbia University Press, 2000). For discussion of interwar Iraq, see Peter Sluglett, *Britain in Iraq, 1914–1932* (London: Ithaca Press,1976); Hanna Batutu, *The Old Social Classes and the Revolutionary Movements of Iraq* (Princeton, N.J.: Princeton University Press, 1978); Mohammad Tarbush, *The Role of the Military in Politics: A Case Study of Iraq* (London: KPI, 1982); Eliezer Tauber, *The Formation of Modern Syria and Iraq* (London: Frank Cass, 1995); and Reeva Spector Simon, *Iraq between the Two World Wars: The Militarist Origins of Tyranny,* new edition (New York: Columbia University Press, 2004). The Iraqi elite is analyzed in Michael Eppel, "The Elite, the *Effendiyya,* and the Growth of Nationalism and Pan-Arabism in Hashemite Iraq, 1921–1958," *International Journal of Middle East Studies* 30 (1998): 227–50.

4. See, for example, the survey of a decade of frontier policing along the Transjordan-Nejd border delineated by the Hadda Agreement of 2 November 1925: TNA, CO 831/32/9, Transjordan Residency, draft annual report, 1934.

5. Joseph A. Massad, *Colonial Effects: The Making of National Identity in Jordan* (New York: Columbia University Press, 2001), figures at p. 56.

6. Yoav Alon, "The Tribal System in the Face of the State-Formation Process: Mandatory Transjordan, 1921–46," *International Journal of Middle East Studies* 37 (2005): 213–40; Riccardo Bocco and Tariq M. M. Tell, "*Pax Britannica* in the Steppe: British Policy and the Transjordan Bedouin," in *Village, Steppe and State: The Social Origins of Modern Jordan,* ed. Eugene L. Rogan and Tariq Tell (London: British Academic Press, 1994), 108–27.

7. Khoury, *Syria and the French Mandate,* 60–63.

8. Yoav Alon, "Tribal Shaykhs and the Limits of British Imperial Rule in Transjordan, 1920–46," *Journal of Imperial and Commonwealth History* 32, no. 1 (2004): 69–92.

9. Eugene L. Rogan, "Bringing the State Back: The Limits of Ottoman Rule in Jordan, 1840–1910," in *Village, Steppe and State: The Social Origins of Modern Jordan,* ed. Eugene L. Rogan and Tariq Tell (London: British Academic Press, 1994), 45–49.

10. Eugene L. Rogan, *Frontiers of the State in the Late Ottoman Empire: Transjordan, 1850–1921* (Cambridge: Cambridge University Press, 1999), 45–57.

11. Ibid., 191–204.

12. TNA, FO 684/1, Chief British representative H. S. B. Philby, "Appreciation of the Situation in Transjordan," 12 May 1922.

13. Michael R. Fischbach, "British Land Policy," in *Village, Steppe and State: The Social Origins of Modern Jordan,* ed. Eugene L. Rogan and Tariq Tell (London: British Academic Press, 1994), 81–90, 102–5. Similar land policies would be adopted in

Iraq from 1926; see Toby Dodge, *Inventing Iraq: The Failure of Nation Building and a History Denied* (New York: Columbia University Press, 2003), 106–15.

14. Michael R. Fischbach, "The British Land Program, State-Societal Cooperation, and Popular Imagination in Transjordan," in *The British and French Mandates in Comparative Perspectives,* ed. Nadine Méouchy and Peter Sluglett (Leiden: Brill, 2004), 480–95.

15. Rogan, *Frontiers of the State in the Late Ottoman Empire,* 114–15, 188.

16. Thompson, *Colonial Citizens,* 54.

17. Mary C. Wilson, *King Abdullah, Britain and the Making of Jordan* (Cambridge: Cambridge University Press, 1987), 72–73, 87–91.

18. Batutu, *Old Social Classes and the Revolutionary Movements of Iraq,* 63–152, also cited in Alon, "Tribal System in the Face of the State-Formation Process," 221–22; Dodge, *Inventing Iraq,* chapter 5.

19. Alon, "Tribal System in the Face of the State-Formation Process," 220–24.

20. See, for example, William Irons and Neville Dyson-Hudson, eds., *Perspectives on Nomadism* (Leiden: E. J. Brill, 1972); Cynthia Nelson, ed., *The Desert and the Sown: Nomads in the Wider Society* (Berkeley and Los Angeles: University of California Press, 1973); Norman Lewis, *Nomads and Settlers in Syria and Jordan, 1800–1980* (Cambridge: Cambridge University Press, 1987); and Richard Tapper, "Anthropologists, Historians, and Tribespeople on Tribe and State Formation in the Middle East," in *Tribes and State Formation in the Middle East,* ed. Philip Khoury and Joseph Kostiner (Berkeley and Los Angeles: University of California Press, 1991), 48–73.

21. See, for example, Schirin H. Fathi, *Jordan—An Invented Nation? Tribe-State Dymanics and the Formation of National Identity* (Hamburg: Deutsches-Orient Institut, 1994); and Andrew Shryock, *Nationalism and the Genealogical Imagination: Oral History and Textual Authority in Tribal Jordan* (Berkeley and Los Angeles: University of California Press, 1997). Two classic Western texts on Jordanian tribes are Alois Musil, *The Manners and Customs of the Rwala Bedouins* (New York: American Geographical Society, 1928); and Frederick Peake, *History of Transjordan and Its Tribes* (1935), reprinted as *A History of Jordan and Its Tribes* (Coral Gables, Fla.: University of Miami Press, 1958).

22. Tariq Tell, "Guns, Gold, and Grain: War and Food Supply in the Making of Transjordan," in *War, Institutions and Social Change,* ed. Stephen Heydemann (Berkeley and Los Angeles: University of California Press, 2000), 35–52.

23. SHA, 7N4181/Dossier 2, no. 942/1G, Gamelin to War Ministry/EMA-1, 20 April 1927.

24. TNA, CO 732/24/6, Reports on raiding between Nejd and Syrian tribes through Iraq or Transjordan, 1927; Joseph Kostiner, "Britain and the Challenge of the Axis Powers in Arabia: The Decline of British-Saudi Cooperation in the 1930s," in *Britain and the Middle East in the 1930s: Security Problems,* ed. Michael J. Cohen and Martin Kolinsky (London: Macmillan, 1992), 129.

25. TNA, CO 733/132/1, Amman Residency report, 5 August 1927.

26. TNA, CO 732/132/1, E. Stafford to Sir John Shuckburgh, January 11, 1927: "Activities in Transjordan Undertaken on Behalf of French Authorities in Syria during 1926."

27. TNA, CO 732/132/1, no. 878/27, Lord Plumer to Leo Amery, 31 January 1927.

28. TNA, CO 831/37/8, Lord Plumer to Levant High Commissioner Ponsot, 4 October 1927.

29. CADN, Fonds Beyrouth, Cabinet Politique, vol. 986, DR: Affaires bédouines, 1923–24, Commandant Tommy-Martin report, "Action du Contrôle bédouin en 1923," 29 February 1924.

30. Eliezer Tauber, "The Struggle for Dayr al-Zur: The Determination of Borders between Syria and Iraq," *International Journal of Middle East Studies* 23 (1991): 368–69, 373–75.

31. SHA, 7N4183/D2, no. 23A, Commandant Sciard, French Mission chief Baghdad, to Section d'Afrique, 7 Dec. 1918; 7N4192/Dossier: "L'effort militaire français au Levant, 19 novembre 1919—19 août 1921."

32. David E. Omissi, *Air Power and Colonial Control: The Royal Air Force, 1919–1939* (Manchester: Manchester University Press, 1990), 86, 157.

33. Fathi, *Jordan*, 52–54.

34. Warwick P. N. Tyler, *State Lands and Rural Development in Mandatory Palestine, 1920–1948* (Brighton: Sussex Academic Press, 2001), 21–48 passim.

35. Tarbush, *Role of the Military in Politics*, 24–30.

36. Tell, "Guns, Gold, and Grain," 47–48.

37. *BDFA*, II: B, vol. 2, doc. 131, Report on Mutessariflik of Belka, 21 December 1920.

38. Regarding industrial and agricultural modernization in Syria and Iraq, see Roger Owen, *The Middle East in the World Economy, 1800–1914* (London: Methuen, 1981), 253–64, 279–86; and Charles Issawi, *An Economic History of the Middle East and North Africa* (New York: Columbia, 1982), 122–31, 159–61.

39. Robert Collins and Richard Herzog, "Early British Administration in the Southern Sudan," *Journal of African Studies* 2, no. 1 (1961): 119–23. These authors also singled out cattle theft, access to women, and intergenerational feuds as triggers to intertribal violence among the non-Muslim populations of the south.

40. TNA, WO 106/232, Sudan Intelligence Report no. 196, March 1909.

41. MAE, série K, Afrique, sous-série AOF, vol. 1, "Directives de police Saharienne du 1e Août 1919."

42. CADN, Fonds Beyrouth, vol. 840/D1, SR rapport, n.d. [1930].

43. Ministère des Affaires Etrangères, Paris (hereafter MAE), série E: Levant, Syrie-Liban, 1922–29, vol. 270, tel. 882, Ministre plenipotentiare to Section Asie-Océanie, 24 December 1924. Governor Carbillet and Damascus delegate Schoeffler presided at the opening ceremony.

44. Regarding studies of the Syrian revolt, see note 88 to chapter 5.

45. A fascinating account of the accumulation of Bedouin oral history traditions is: Shryock, *Nationalism and the Genealogical Imagination*, especially chapters 1, 6, and 7.

46. Fathi, *Jordan*, 55.

47. The romanticism attached to desert settlement and tribal life figures large in Gertrude Bell's letters to her parents. See, for example, Bell's letters to her father, 11 July, 22 July, and 6 August 1918, in Gertrude Bell papers, Newcastle University Library, also available online at www.gerty.ncl.ac.uk/letters; Shryock, *Nationalism and the Genealogical Imagination*, 17–30.

48. Massad, *Colonial Effects*, 103–8.

49. See the descriptions of tribal custom in part 2 of Peake's *History of Jordan and*

Its Tribes. Andrew Shryock provides a critique of Peake's work on the Bedouin in *Nationalism and the Genealogical Imagination*, 221–25.

50. SHA, 20N1089/D3, SR bulletin périodique no. 43, 1–20 March 1922. The tenuous French position in Jazirah is vividly recalled by the former SR officer Louis Dillemann in his "Les français en Haute-Djezireh (1919–1939)," *Revue Française d'Histoire d'Outre-Mer* 66, no. 242 (1979): 33–58.

51. SHA, 7N4192, Comité Consultatif de Défense des Colonies, manuel colonial 1923–1925, chapter 4: "Organisation des unités auxiliaires spéciales au pays," 31 Jan. 1925; Philip S. Khoury, "The Tribal Shaykh, French Tribal Policy, and the Nationalist Movement in Syria between Two World Wars," *Middle Eastern Studies* 18, no. 2 (1982): 182–86.

52. SSO files are compiled by district in TNA, AIR 23: RAF Overseas Command files.

53. Omissi, *Air Power and Colonial Control*, 25–27; Maurice Pearton, *The Knowledgeable State: Diplomacy, War and Technology since 1830* (London: Burnett Books, 1982), 192–93; Darwin, *Britain, Egypt and the Middle East: Imperial Policy in the Aftermath of War, 1918–1922* (London: Macmillan, 1981), 228–30.

54. TNA, AIR 23/83, Transjordan SSO reports, 1924–1929.

55. TNA, AIR 23/337, Air Staff Intelligence to H. A. Anson, SSO Halabja, 22 June 1925.

56. See, for example, TNA, CO 730/13, Administration report of Sulaimaniyah division, 1919, 19 May 1920.

57. TNA, WO 33/997: Khartoum Intelligence Directorate reports, 1919–21.

58. TNA, CO 730/140/8, Glubb intelligence summary to Baghdad high commission, 12 June 1930; CO 730/158/21, Hubert Young comments on Glubb Report on Southern Desert, 1 August 1930.

59. Bocco and Tell, "*Pax Britannica* in the Steppe," 108–12.

60. Omissi, *Air Power and Colonial Control*, 92–93.

61. Bocco and Tell, "*Pax Britannica* in the Steppe," 109.

62. Ibid., 120–22.

63. Samira Haj, "The Problems of Tribalism: The Case of Nineteenth-Century Iraqi History," *Social History* 16, no. 1 (1991): 45–58; Dodge, *Inventing Iraq*, especially chapters 4 and 5.

64. Haj, "Problems of Tribalism," 45–58.

65. In the summer of 1939, the recrudescence of an eighteen-year-old blood feud between the Ubaid and Shammar tribes drew Iraqi press interest after the tit-for-tat killings of sheikhs from both tribes; see TNA, FO 371/23201, E4086/258/93, Basil Newton (Baghdad) to Viscount Halifax, 1 June 1939.

66. Fathi, *Jordan*, 57–58, 96.

67. John Willis, "Colonial Policing in Aden, 1937–1967," *Arab Studies Journal* 5, no. 1 (1997): 65.

68. SHA, 7N4183/D2, H. O. Fanshawe (Baghdad), French translation of GHQ memo, "Règlement des querelles entre tribus," 27 July 1918; TNA, CO 730/140/8, Glubb report, 12 June 1929.

69. Hanna Batutu, "Of the Diversity of Iraqis, the Incohesiveness of Their Society, and Their Progress in the Monarchic Period toward a Consolidated Political

Structure," in *The Modern Middle East: A Reader,* ed. A. Hourani, P. S. Khoury, and M. C. Wilson (Berkeley and Los Angeles: University of California Press, 1993), 512.

70. TNA, CO 831/37/7, Amman dispatch 49 to Colonial Office, 4 April 1936; Fathi, *Jordan,* 98.

71. TNA, AIR 23/91, 1/R/3, SSO Ramadi, report on the Anah conference, 16 April 1927.

72. CADN, Fonds Beyrouth, Cabinet Politique, vol. 986, Dossier bédouin, Terrier memo, "Essai de legislation bédouine," n.d. [Oct. 1924].

73. SHA, 7N4192 annex to Contrôle bédouin memo, 9 February 1927.

74. David Shearer makes the same point with regard to the internal passport system introduced in Soviet Russia in the 1930s; see his "Elements Near and Alien: Passportization, Policing, and Identity in the Stalinist State, 1932–1952," *Journal of Modern History* 76, no. 4 (2004): 838.

75. CAOM, GGA, 9H32, Constantine prefect to Algiers native affairs office, 21 November 1928.

76. TNA, AIR 23/90, SSO Mosul intelligence report no. 12, 18 October 1926. This document records the issue of travel passes for Shammar tribesmen intending to buy and sell goods in Dayr al-Zur.

77. CADN, Fonds Beyrouth, Cabinet Politique, vol. 986, Dossier bédouin, Terrier memo, "Essai de legislation bédouine," n.d. [Oct. 1924].

78. MAE, série E, vol. 274, Conseiller législatif Gennardi, "Contrôle général des Wakfs," n.d. [February 1928].

79. CADN, Fonds Beyrouth, Cabinet Politique, vol. 986, SR arrêté no. 100/S, 20 April 1925.

80. CADN, Fonds Beyrouth, Cabinet politique, vol. 986: tribus 1923–26/DR24, no. 1079, Pierre Alype to de Jouvenel, 12 February 1926; no. 877/K111, Henry de Jouvenel note, 11 March 1926.

81. Alice L. Conklin, *A Mission to Civilize: The Republican Idea of Empire in France and West Africa, 1895–1930* (Stanford, Calif.: Stanford University Press, 1997), 175–76, 191–94.

82. Khoury, "Tribal Shaykh, French Tribal Policy, and the Nationalist Movement in Syria between Two World Wars," 186–87.

83. Reeva S. Simon, "The Imposition of Nationalism on a Non-nation State: The Case of Iraq during the Interwar period, 1921–1941," in *Rethinking Nationalism in the Arab Middle East,* ed. James Jankowski and Israel Gershoni (New York: Columbia University Press, 1997), 91.

84. TNA, CO 730/115/1, Iraq high commission annual report, 1926; Haj, "Problems of Tribalism," 53–54.

85. Sarah D. Shields, "Sheep, Nomads and Merchants in Nineteenth-Century Mosul: Creating Transformations in an Ottoman Society," *Journal of Social History* 25, no. 4 (1992): 776–80.

86. Khoury, *Syria and the French Mandate,* 61–62.

87. CADN, Fonds Beyrouth, Cabinet Politique, vol. 986, DR: Affaires bédouines 1923–24, no. 1894/SP, Catroux comments on report by Lieutenant Delouze, 7 November 1922.

88. Ibid., no. 326/SP/3, Terrier report to Catroux (Damascus), 29 April 1924.

89. Ibid., Commandant Martin memo, "Action du Contrôle bédouin en 1923," 29 February 1924.

90. CADN, Fonds Beyrouth, Cabinet Politique, vol. 986, DR25, SR Contrôle bédouin, "État de la transhumance au 15 juillet 1925."

91. TNA, CO 730/105/1, High commission secretariat intelligence report no. 10, 13 May 1926.

92. MAE, série E, 1922–29, vol. 193, no. 1056/NS/2, Beulale Desloges to Sarrail/Cabinet civil, 8 July 1925, no. 7138/AP, Délégué adjoint, Alep, to Sarrail, 11 August 1925.

93. Ibid., vol. 193, no. 968/ES/2, Damascus delegation report to Sarrail, 2 June 1925. This was confirmed by intelligence from the SR station at Djérablous.

94. TNA, CO 831/1/2, tel. 8175/28, Amman Resident C. H. F. Cox, "Report on the Situation in Transjordan, January 1, 1928 to March 31, 1928." Druze tribesmen who crossed into Transjordan from Syria also raided the Bani Sakhr; see CO 831/4/8, Amman Residency tel. 11, 15 March 1929.

95. TNA, AIR 23/18, SSO Ikhwan defense report, 11 January 1925.

96. TNA, FO 684/2, tel. 31, Baghdad high commission to Leo Amery, 16 January 1925.

97. Ibid., tel. 50, Dobbs (Baghdad) to Colonial Office, 26 January 1925.

98. TNA, CO 831/11/1, CO minutes by K. W. Blaxter, 24 February 1931; CO 831/19/8, C. H. F. Cox (Amman) to Jerusalem high commission, 14 March 1932.

99. Ibid., C. H. F. Cox, Amman Residency quarterly reports on situation in Transjordan, 1928. The escalation in tribal raiding between Transjordan and Saudi Arabia in 1928–29 is also described in *BDFA*, II: B, vol. 6, docs. 93, 305, 355.

100. TNA, CO 730/137/9, Glubb memo, "Plans for Forthcoming Raiding Season," 6 September 1928.

101. TNA, CO 730/140/8, Glubb report to Iraqi government, sent to Colonial Office, 12 June 1929.

102. TNA, CO 730/137/9, High Commissioner Dodds to King Faysal, 5 September 1928.

103. TNA, CO 730/158/21, SSO Sulman, report no. I/SD/24, 24 May 1930.

104. Bocco and Tell, "*Pax Britannica* in the Steppe," 114–15.

105. TNA, CO 730/137/9, J. B. Glubb, "Plans for Forthcoming Raiding Season," 6 September 1928.

106. TNA, CO 732/34/9, F. G. Peake, "A Brief History of the Wahhabi Movement," 21 March 1928.

107. John Habib, *Ibn Saud's Warriors of Islam: The Ikhwan of Najd and Their Role in the Creation of the Saudi Kingdom, 1910–1930* (Leiden: Brill, 1978), chapters 5, 6, and 9.

108. TNA, 730/137/9, King Faysal to Sir Henry Dobbs, 11 September 1928.

109. TNA, CO 831/6/13, Amman Residency quarterly situation report, July–September 1929; CO 831/10/1, High Commissioner Sir John Chancellor to Lord Passfield, 26 June 1930.

110. TNA, FO 684/4, Amman Residency Situation Report, 1 July–30 Sept. 1929.

111. TNA, CO 831/7/8, Air Vice-Marshal Dowding, "Report on the Raiding Situation on the Transjordan-Nejd Frontier," enclosure to secret dispatch of 25 January 1930.

112. Alon, "Tribal System in the Face of the State-Formation Process," 220, 225–26.

113. Bocco and Tell, "*Pax Britannica* in the Steppe," 117, 120–21.

114. TNA, CO 831/10/1, Sir John Chancellor to Lord Passfield, 26 June 1930. Chancellor felt that the Arab Legion lacked enough secret service funds to gather information from other tribal sources.

115. Ibid.

116. TNA, CO 831/7/8, Colonel C. H. F. Cox (Amman) to Colonial Office, 28 August 1930.

117. TNA, CO 831/37/7, J. Halhorn-Hall to J. H. Thomas, 4 April 1936.

118. *BDFA,* II: B, vol. 8, docs. 58, 59, 63. The revolt was led by Ibn Rifada, a Hijazi exile, who had first rebelled against Ibn Saud in 1929. His incursion into the northern Hijaz with some four hundred armed levies on the night of 20–21 May 1932 was reportedly engineered by the Cairo-based Hizb-al-Hijazi.

119. Simon, *Iraq between the Two World Wars,* 108–13.

120. TNA, FO 371/21846, E2011/45/93, Captain A. Holt letter to H. L. Baggallay, summarizing RAF intelligence reports, 23 March 1938; FO 624/12/file 30: census, Press extract from *Al Zamin,* "General Census of Population," 28 March 1938.

121. David Killingray, "'A Swift Agent of Government': Air Power in British Colonial Africa, 1916–1939," *Journal of African History* 25, no. 4 (1984): 429–44; Omissi, *Air Power and Colonial Control,* chapters 2 and 9.

122. TNA, AIR 23/23, Captain John Glubb to RAF HQ, Baghdad, 28 December 1925; SSO Nasiriyah memo to Baghdad "I" Branch, "Patrols by Armed Cars from Basra to Abu Ghar," 18 January 1926.

123. TNA, AIR 23/624, RAF HQ Baghdad, "Historical Summary of the Situation in the [Iraqi] Southern Desert, 19 December 1929 to 10 February 1930."

124. British bombardments of Transjordan's Shuraydi clan at Tibna in 1921 or of rebellious 'Adwan tribesmen in September 1923 illustrate the point; see Wilson, *King Abdullah, Britain and the Making of Jordan,* 64, 78.

125. TNA, AIR 23/23, Glubb tel. to RAF HQ Baghdad, 28 December 1925; SSO Nasiriyah memo to Bagdad "I" Branch, "Patrols by Armed Cars from Basra to Abu Ghar," 18 January 1926.

126. TNA, AIR 23/624, Baghdad RAF HQ, "Historical Summary of the Situation in the [Iraqi] Southern Desert, 19 December 1929 to 10 February 1939."

127. Even the Air Council conceded that this was the case along Transjordan's frontier with Saudi Arabia; see TNA, CO 831/10/1, no. 29192/32, Air Council note to Amman Residency, 20 August 1928.

128. TNA, CO 831/7/8, Air Vice-Marshal Dowding, "Report on the Raiding Situation on the Transjordan-Nejd Frontier," enclosure to secret dispatch of 25 January 1930.

129. Ibid., no. 59493/28, Record of meeting between RAF commander, acting chief secretary to the Residency, and TJFF OC, n.d [August 1928].

130. TNA, CO 831/19/8, C. H. F. Cox to Jerusalem high commission, 14 March 1932: relays report on conditions in the southern desert by A. S. Kirkbride.

131. TNA, CO 730/11/1. T. G. Peake, AOC Arab Legion, to Amman Residency, 24 December 1930.

132. TNA, CO 732/25/8, Sir John Shuckburgh report on visit to Palestine and Iraq, 19 April 1927.

133. Omissi, *Air Power and Colonial Control,* 111; Priya Satia, "The Defense of Inhumanity: Air Control and the British Idea of Arabia," *American Historical Review* 111, no.1 (2006):16–51.

134. TNA, AIR 9/61, J. Slessor to DDOI, 16 February 1930; see Jafna L. Cox, "A Splendid Training Ground: The Importance to the Royal Air Force of Its Role in Iraq, 1919–32," *Journal of Imperial and Commonwealth History* 13, no. 2 (1985): 157–84.

135. TNA, AIR 20/674, Air Staff, "Regulation of Air Control in Undeveloped Countries," 21 November 1928.

136. CADN, Sûreté Générale, vol. 842, sous-dossier: budget: 1927–33.

137. Haj, "Problems of Tribalism," 55.

138. CADN, Fonds Beyrouth, Cabinet Politique, vol. 986, Captain Terrier memo to General Weygand, "Exemple d'une transhumance complète (année 1923) et ses enseignements," n.d.

139. TNA, CO 831/11/1, Captain J. B. Glubb, "Note on the Situation on the Southern Frontier of Transjordan," 1 January 1931; FO 406/72, E2764/546/25, "Notes by Captain Calvert, 20 February to 1 March 1934."

140. TNA, FO 371/20055, E6742/7/25, Enclosure: Major J. Glubb, "Monthly Report on the Administration of the Deserts of Transjordan, July 1936."

141. CADN, Fonds Beyrouth, Cabinet Politique, vol. 466, Ponsot to Foreign Ministry, 6 January 1928.

CHAPTER 7

1. See, for example, the case of the Palestine, Syria, and Lebanon police forces: TNA, CO 323/1113, CID 348-C, CID memo, "Palestine Garrison," 27 June 1930; CADN, Fonds Beyrouth, Cabinet politique, vols. 894 and 904: Armée, gendarmerie, police.

2. A comparable struggle for sovereign control over city policing took place in interwar Shanghai between the nationalist authorities and the international treaty powers; see Frederic Wakeman Jr., *Policing Shanghai, 1927–1937* (Berkeley and Los Angeles: University of California Press, 1995), chapters 4 and 5.

3. Djilali Sari, "The Role of the Medinas in the Reconstruction of Algerian Culture and Identity," in *The Walled Arab City in Literature, Architecture and History: The Living Medina in the Maghrib,* ed. Susan Slyomovics (London: Frank Cass, 2001), 69–70.

4. Shirine Hamadeh, "Creating the Traditional City," in *Forms of Dominance: On the Architecture and Urbanism of the Colonial Enterprise,* ed. Nezar Al Sayyad (Avebury: Ashgate, 1992), 244–46.

5. Zeynep Çelik, *Urban Forms and Colonial Confrontations: Algiers under French Rule* (Berkeley and Los Angeles: University of California Press, 1997), 28–38; Michele Lamprakos, "Le Corbusier and Algiers: The Plan Obus as Colonial Urbanism," in *Forms of Dominance: On the Architecture and Urbanism of the Colonial Enterprise,* ed. Nezar Al Sayyad (Avebury: Ashgate, 1992), 187.

6. George Joffé, "Maghribi Islam," in *African Islam and Islam in Africa: Encounters between Sufis and Islamists,* ed. David Westerlund and Eva Evers Rosander (London: Hurst, 1997), 64.

7. James McDougall, *History and the Culture of Nationalism in Algeria* (Cambridge: Cambridge University Press, 2006), 35, 93–94.

8. The dual city phenomenon in French North Africa is explored in Janet Abu-Lughod, *Rabat: Urban Apartheid in Morocco* (Princeton, N.J.: Princeton University Press, 1980). For a British imperial comparison, see her "Tale of Two Cities: The Origins of Modern Cairo," *Comparative Studies in Society and History* 7, no. 4 (1965): 429–57. For a vivid literary description of the colonial dual city, see Marguerite Duras, *A Sea of Troubles* (London: Methuen, 1953), pp. 121–24; this is an English translation of *Un Barrage contre le Pacifique* (Paris, 1950).

9. Mahfoud Kaddache, *Histoire du nationalisme algérien*, vol. 1, *1919–1939* (Algiers: EDIF, 2000), 19.

10. CAOM, GGA, 11H46, no. 10272, Direction de la sécurité générale (Algiers), "État des crimes et délits importants commis par les indigènes contre les européens ou de fonctionnaires indigènes pendant le mois de juillet 1922." The seventh capital crime recorded was the gang rape of a settler woman, who committed suicide before the case could be brought to trial.

11. SHA, Fonds Privés, Papiers du Général de Monsabert, 1K380/Carton 2, "Instruction rélative à la participation de l'armée au maintien de l'ordre public," 20 August 1907.

12. In black Africa and Indochina, the allocation of responsibility between civil, military, and police authorities was formalized by a series of seven decrees passed between 1886 and 1909. This legislation was supplemented by additional decrees passed in the interwar years to integrate intelligence services into the security apparatus. Regarding the pre–World War I decree legislation, see SHA, 7N4196/D1, Ministère des Colonies Services militaires 1er bureau circulaire, 19 July 1912.

13. SHA, Moscow, C1109/D667, no. 6620, EMA Section d'Outre-Mer renseignement, "A/S/ Préparatifs pour action musulmane en Afrique du Nord," 7 September 1935.

14. TNA, FO 407/207, J3071/4/16, Acting High Commissioner R. H. Hoare memo, enclosure: "Summary of Police Instructions"; Haggai Erlich, "British Internal Security and Egyptian Youth," in *Britain and the Middle East in the 1930s: Security Problems*, ed. Michael J. Cohen and Martin Kolinsky (London: Macmillan, 1992), 101–8.

15. For background to Shakib Arslan's varied career, see Juliette Bessis, "Chekib Arslan et les mouvements nationalistes au Maghreb," *Revue Historique* 259, no. 2 (1978): 467–89.

16. See, for instance, the Annemasse police spéciale files on Shakib Arslan in AN, F713468/D6.

17. See, for example, the evidence of Arslan's contacts with the nationalist leadership in Aleppo detailed in TNA, AIR 23/90, BL/S/10, 23 September 1926.

18. SHA, Moscow, C878/D997, "SCR note de renseignement: Emir Chekib Arslan," 17 August 1930.

19. SHA, Moscow, C581/D370, SCR "Renseignement d'Egypte," 16 February 1926 ["Bonne source"]; Philip S. Khoury, "Factionalism among Syrian Nationalists during the French Mandate," *International Journal of Middle East Studies* 13 (1981): 456–57; Safiuddin Joarder, "The Syrian Nationalist Uprising (1925–1927) and Henri de Jouvenel," *Muslim World* 68 (July 1977): 194.

20. William S. Cleveland, *Islam against the West: Shakib Arslan and the Campaign for Islamic Nationalism* (London: Al Saqi Books, 1985), 20–27. Arslan served as deputy for the Hauran region of southern Syria from 1914 to 1918.

21. Ibid., 41–42. Arslan was at this stage still closely associated with former Young Turk leaders, including Enver Pasha.

22. Ibid., 48–57.

23. SHA, Moscow, C878/D997, no. 1768, SCR report, "A/S de né BALAFREJ," March 22 1934; C878/D998, copy of *L'Action Tunisienne* [Néo-Destour newspaper], 3 June 1937; Jean-Pierre Biondi, *Les anticolonialistes (1881–1962)* (Paris: Éditions Robert Laffont, 1992), 177, 231.

24. Cleveland, *Islam against the West,* 103–13. The French Foreign Ministry even claimed that the Maghrebi student group, the Association des étudiants musulmans nord-africains (AEMNA), took its instructions direct from Arslan.

25. Ibid., 42.

26. TNA, CO 732/31/12, Lord Lloyd (Cairo) to Sir Austen Chamberlain, 14 January 1928. Britain's Conservative government was then concerned about Bolshevik penetration of Arabia, Yemen, and the Aden protectorate in particular; see CO 732/41/1: Bolshevik activities in Arabia, 1929.

27. SHA, Moscow, C878/D997 and D998: both dossiers contain extensive surveillance files on Arslan. Sale of *La Nation Arabe* was banned in the French Empire.

28. C. J. E. Andréa, *La révolte druze et l'insurrection de Damas* (Paris: Payot, 1937), 77–87.

29. MAE, série E, sous-série Syrie-Liban, vol. 194, no. 600/KD, Sarrail report to Direction Asie-Océanie, 25 October 1925.

30. For parallels with urban elites in mandate Palestine, see Joel S. Migdal, "Urbanization and Political Change: The Impact of Foreign Rule," *Comparative Studies in Society and History* 19 (1977): 337–39.

31. Philip S. Khoury, "Syrian Urban Politics in Transition: The Quarters of Damascus during the French Mandate," *International Journal of Middle East Studies* 16 (1984): 514–15; Gabriel Baer, "The Office and Functions of the Village Mukhtar," in *Palestinian Society and Politics,* by Joel S. Migdal (Princeton, N.J.: Princeton University Press, 1980), 109–17.

32. Ellen Fleischmann, "The Other 'Awakening': The Emergence of Women's Movements in the Modern Middle East, 1900–1940," in *A Social History of Women and Gender in the Modern Middle East,* ed. Margaret L. Meriwether and Judith Tucker (Boulder, Colo.: Westview Press, 1999), 96–97. The linkage of women's rights with nationalist demands also occurred in mandatory Iraq; for example, see Noga Efrati, "The Other 'Awakening' in Iraq: The Women's Movement in the First Half of the Twentieth Century," *British Journal of Middle Eastern Studies* 31, no. 2 (2004): 153–73.

33. Elizabeth Thompson, *Colonial Citizens: Republican Rights, Paternal Privilege, and Gender in French Syria and Lebanon* (New York: Columbia University Press, 2000), parts 3 and 4.

34. TNA, CO 733/368/1, E3591/10/31, Gilbert MacKereth (Damascus) to FO, 8 June 1938.

35. Women's political action in the Faysal period in Damascus is discussed in James L. Gelvin, *Divided Loyalties: Nationalism and Mass Politics in Syria at the Close of Empire* (Berkeley and Los Angeles: University of California Press, 1998), 148–49,

191–92, 213–14. Also instructive is the political storm over women's rights caused by the writings of Zayn al-Din, discussed in Thompson, *Colonial Citizens*, 127–35.

36. Regarding the Jonnart Law, see Vincent Confer, *France and Algeria: The Problem of Civil and Political Reform, 1870–1920* (Syracuse, N.Y.: Syracuse University Press, 1966), 99–110; regarding Khaled, see Ahmed Koulakssis and Gilbert Meynier, *L'Emir Khaled premier za'im? Identité algérienne et colonialisme français* (Paris: l'Harmattan, 1987).

37. CAOM, GGA, 11H46, Direction des affaires indigènes, "Rapport mensuel sur la situation politique des indigènes pendant le mois de novembre 1919."

38. CAOM, GGA, 11H46, Algiers Service des affaires indigènes, "Rapport sur la situation politique et administrative des indigènes pendant le mois de mars 1919," 29 April 1919.

39. CAOM, GGA, 11H46, Administrateur de la Commune mixte de Belezma (Constantine department), "La situation agricole," 3 November 1920; Direction des affairs indigènes (Algiers), "Rapport sur la situation politique et administrative des indigènes de l'Algérie au 1er Mai 1923."

40. For general introductions, see Rashid Khalidi, Lisa Anderson, Muhammad Muslih, and Reeva S. Simon, eds., *The Origins of Arab Nationalism* (New York: Columbia University Press, 1991); Israel Gershoni, "Rethinking the Formation of Arab Nationalism in the Middle East," in *Rethinking Nationalism in the Arab Middle East,* ed. James Jankowski and Israel Gershoni (New York: Columbia University Press, 1997), 3–25; C. Ernest Dawn, "The Formation of Pan-Arab Ideology in the Interwar years," *International Journal of Middle East Studies* 20 (1988): 67–91; and Mahmoud Haddad, "The Origins of Arab Nationalism Reconsidered," *International Journal of Middle East Studies* 26 (1994): 201–22. For early Algerian nationalists, see Claude Collot and Jean-Robert Henry, eds., *Le mouvement national algérien: Textes, 1912–1954* (Paris: l'Harmattan, 1978); Monique Gadant, *Le nationalisme algérien et les femmes* (Paris: l'Harmattan, 1995); Koulakssis and Meynier, *L'Emir Khaled premier za'im?;* and Kaddache, *Histoire du nationalisme algérien,* vol. 1. Regarding the Levant states, see Gérard D. Khoury, *La France et l'Orient arabe: Naissance du Liban moderne* (Paris: Armand Colin, 1993); Philip S. Khoury, *Syria and the French Mandate: The Politics of Arab Nationalism, 1920–1945* (Princeton, N.J.: Princeton University Press, 1987); Meir Zamir, *Lebanon's Quest: The Road to Statehood, 1926–1939* (London: I. B. Tauris, 1997).

41. Jacques Simon, *L'Étoile Nord-Africaine (1926–1937)* (Paris: l'Harmattan, 2003).

42. SHA, Moscow, C223/D123, ENA circular sent from the rue du Repos address, 12 April 1927.

43. MAE, série K Afrique, sous-série Affaires musulmanes, vol. 25, no. 9155, Sûreté Générale memo, "A/S de l'organisation communiste musulmane," 17 December 1927.

44. MAE, série K Afrique, vol. 25, no. 9155, Sûreté Générale memo, 17 December 1927; William J. Duiker, *Ho Chi Minh: A Life* (New York: Hyperion, 2000), 78–79.

45. MAE, série K Afrique, vol. 25, no. 9155, Sûreté Générale memo, 17 December 1927.

46. "Tract de l'Etoile Nord-Africaine: Lutte contre l'impérialisme français, 1928," in *Messali Hadj par les textes,* ed. Jacques Simon (Paris: Éditions Bouchène, 2000), doc. 2.

47. Rabah Aissaoui, "'Nous voulons déchirer le baillon et briser nos chaînes': Racism, Colonialism and Universalism in the Discourse of Algerian Nationalists in France between the Wars," *French History* 17, no. 2 (2003): 186–209.

48. "Revendications algériennes, présentées par Messali au Congrès de Bruxelles (10–14 février 1927)," in *Le mouvement national algérien: Textes,* ed. Claude Collot and Jean-Robert Henry (Paris: l'Harmattan, 1978), 39; "Discours de Messali Hadj au Congrès de Bruxelles," in *Messali Hadj par les texts,* doc. 1.

49. Martin Thomas, "Albert Sarraut, French Colonial Development, and the Communist Threat, 1919–30," *Journal of Modern History* 55, no. 4 (2005): 927–55.

50. For examples, see Georges Oved, *La gauche française et le nationalisme marocain, 1905–1954,* vol. 1 (Paris: l'Harmattan, 1984); Kamel Bouguessa, *Aux sources du nationalisme algérien: Les pionniers de populisme révolutionnaire en marche* (Algiers: Éditions Casbah, 2000); and Samya El Mechat, *Le nationalisme tunisien: Scission et conflits* (Paris: l'Harmattan, 2002).

51. Extensive security surveillance in the late Third Republic is highlighted in Michael Miller, *Shanghai on the Métro: Spies, Intrigue, and the French between the Wars* (Berkeley and Los Angeles: University of California Press, 1994); and Gérard Noiriel, *Les origines républicaines de Vichy* (Paris: Hachette, 1999).

52. Regarding the CGTT, see Juliette Bessis, "Le mouvement ouvrier tunisien: De ses origines à l'indépendance," *Le Mouvement Social* 89 (1974): 85–108; and Ahmad Eqbal and Stuart Schaar, "M'hamed Ali: Tunisian Labor Organizer," in *Struggle and Survival in the Modern Middle East,* ed. Edmund Burke III (London: I. B. Tauris, 1993), 199–203.

53. SHA, Moscow, Carton 286/D428, no. 1780, Direction des affaires indigènes (Rabat), "A/S des incidents de Constantine et de leur repercussion possible au Maroc," 23 August 1934; regarding the Constantine pogrom, see Michel Attal, *Les émeutes de Constantine: 5 août 1934* (Paris: Éditions Romillot, 2002); and Charles-Robert Ageron, "Une émeute anti-juive à Constantine (août 1934)," *Revue de l'Occident Musulman et de la Méditerranée* 3 (1973): 23–40.

54. SHA, Moscow, Carton 286/D428, EMA Section d'Outre-Mer, "La crise marocaine et le parti socialiste," 3 April 1936. For links between Maghrebi nationalists and the French left, see Benjamin Stora, *Nationalistes algériens et révolutionnaires français au temps du Front Populaire* (Paris: l'Harmattan, 1987).

55. Guy Pervillé, *Les étudiants algériens de l'université française (1880–1962)* (Paris: CNRS, 1984); Pervillé, "Le sentiment national des étudiants algériens de culture français de 1912 à 1942," *Relations Internationales* 2 (1974): 233–59; Charles-Robert Ageron, "L'association des étudiants musulmans nord-africains en France durant l'entre-deux-guerres: Contribution à l'étude des nationalismes maghrébins," *Revue Française d'Histoire d'Outre-Mer* 70, no. 258 (1983): 25–56; Mohammed Bekraoui, "Les étudiants marocains en France à l'époque du protectorat, 1927–1939," in *Présences et images franco-marocaines au temps du protectorat,* ed. Jean-Claude Allain (Paris: l'Harmattan, 2003), 89–111.

56. Kaddache, *Histoire du nationalisme algérien,* 1:317–23.

57. Archives de la Prefecture de Police (APP), Paris, Série BA, Carton BA2170, fo. 7, Service des renseignements généraux, 1er bureau, "A/S de l'organisation communiste musulmane—L'Etoile Nord-Africaine," 30 November 1927.

58. Bouguessa, *Aux sources du nationalisme algérien,* 337–41.

59. SHA, 7N4133, EMA-2, "Politique et le militaire dans l'Afrique du Nord," n.d. [December 1923].

60. SHA, Moscow, C286/D429, SR reports, "Nationalisme marocain à Rabat," 20 November 1933 ["Source: Bon informateur très bien placé"]; "Casablanca—principaux nationalistes marocains," 22 November 1933 ["Très bonne source"]; "Nationalisme à Marrakech," 28 November 1933 ["Bonne source"].

61. ADA, Sarraut Papers, 12J172, "Note pour le chef du Service du contrôle et de l'assistance des indigènes en France," 8 September 1924; Neil MacMaster, *Colonial Migrants and Racism: Algerians in France, 1900–62* (London: Macmillan, 1997), 127–30; see also Clifford Rosenberg, "The Colonial Politics of Healthcare Provision in Interwar Paris," *French Historical Studies* 27, no. 3 (2004): 637–68; and his *Policing Paris: The Origins of Modern Immigration Control between the Wars* (Ithaca, N.Y.: Cornell University Press, 2006), chapter 7.

62. MAE, série K Afrique, sous-série Affaires musulmanes, vol. 1, Commissariat général à l'Information et à la Propagande, "Note sur la Section Musulmane du 3 rue François I," 5 September 1919.

63. MAE, série K Afrique, sous-série Questions africaines, vol. 31, Direction des affaires algériennes, Commission interministérielle de la main d'oeuvre nord-africain, procès-verbal, 26 June 1924; Rosenberg, *Policing Paris*, 92–94, 160–64.

64. Confer, *France and Algeria*, 99–109.

65. Rosenberg, *Policing Paris*, 146–55, quotation at p. 148.

66. MAE, série K Afrique, sous-série Questions africaines, vol. 31, Direction des affaires algériennes, Commission interministérielle de la main d'oeuvre nord-africain, procès-verbal, 26 June 1924.

67. For details of interwar Moroccan immigration levels to France, see Tayeb Biad, "Les ouvriers marocains en France pendant l'entre-deux-guerres," in *Présences et images franco-marocaines au temps du protectorat*, ed. Jean-Claude Allain (Paris: l'Harmattan, 2003), 113–29, figures at p. 120. Biad suggests that Moroccan immigrant numbers peaked at 21,000 in 1929, falling back to only 13,000 by 1938.

68. MAE, série M, sous-série Police, vol. 839, Office du protectorat (Rabat) tel. 1527, 8 May 1924.

69. MAE, série K Afrique, sous-série Questions générales africaines, vol. 31, Note by Interior Ministry Direction du Contrôle, "Repatriement de travailleurs coloniaux," 23 June 1922.

70. Ibid., no. 3552, Office du Protectorat (Paris) to Foreign Ministry, 22 July 1922.

71. Ibid., no. 1479, Ministère du Travail, Service de la main d'oeuvre étrangère report, 17 June 1922.

72. MAE, série M, sous-série Police, vol. 839, Office du protectorat (Rabat) tel. 1527, 8 May 1924.

73. MAE, série K Afrique, sous-série Questions générales africaines, vol. 31, no. 1116, Urbain Blanc to Foreign Ministry, 25 July 1922.

74. Ibid., Direction des affaires algériennes, Commission interministérielle de la main d'oeuvre nord-africain, procès-verbal, 26 June 1924.

75. MAE, série M, sous-série Police, vol. 839, Office du protectorat (Rabat), tel. 1527, 8 May 1924.

76. MAE, série K Afrique, sous-série Questions générales africaines, vol. 31,

Edouiard Herriot correspondence, "Les Kabyles notables de Tizi Ouzou," 8 November 1924.

77. Ibid., Interior Ministry Direction des affaires algériennes note, "Exode des indigènes 'Nord Africains' dans la Métropole," 14 January 1924.

78. Robert J. Goldstein, *Political Repression in 19th-Century Europe* (London: Croom Helm, 1983), 336–39.

79. Rosenberg, *Policing Paris*, 44–58; Anja Johansen, *Soldiers as Police: The French and Prussian Armies and the Policing of Popular Protest, 1889–1914* (Aldershot: Ashgate, 2005), 85–86.

80. M'Barka Hamed-Touati, *Immigration maghrébine et activités politiques en France de la première guerre mondiale à la veille du front populaire* (Tunis: Université de Tunis, 1994), 94; Rosenberg, *Policing Paris*, 148. Morain published his memoirs in 1929, making his exploits as prefect of police well known. These were translated into English as *Underworld of Paris: Secrets of the Sûreté* (New York: Dutton, 1931).

81. MAE, série K Afrique, sous-série Questions générales, vol. 125, no. 593, Rabat Residency memo, "A/S Surveillance à Paris des indigènes de l'Afrique du Nord," 2 April 1924.

82. Ibid., "A/S Surveillance à Paris des indigènes de l'Afrique du Nord," 2 April 1924.

83. Rosenberg, *Policing Paris*, 157.

84. Hamed-Touati, *Immigration maghrébine*, 202–3.

85. Stéphane Sirot, "Les conditions de travail et les grèves des ouvriers colonaiux à Paris des lendemains de la Première Guerre Mondiale à la veille du Front Populaire," *Revue Française d'Histoire d'Outre-Mer* 83, no. 311 (1996): 65–92.

86. Ibid., 91.

87. Hamed-Touati, *Immigration maghrébine*, 95–97; Rosenberg, *Policing Paris*, 170, 185–87.

88. Rosenberg, *Policing Paris*, 198.

89. Sirot, "Les conditions de travail," 86–92.

90. APP, Paris, BA2170, "Note sur l'activité de l'Étoile Nord-Africaine depuis sa création jusqu'au 15 Novembre 1934"; on this subject more generally, see Clifford Rosenberg, "Republican Surveillance: Immigration, Citizenship, and the Police in Interwar Paris" (Ph.D. diss., Princeton University, 2000).

91. The idea of 1934 as a watershed year is a common one. See, for example, Nicholas Atkin, *The French at War, 1934–1944* (London: Longman, 2001).

92. Mary Dewhurst Lewis, "The Strangeness of Foreigners: Policing Migration and Nation in Interwar Marseille," *French Politics, Culture, and Society* 20, no. 3 (2002): 66–67, 77–83.

93. SHA, Moscow, C1109/D609, SCR report ["source—très sûre"], "Activité révolutionnaire en Afrique du Nord de l'agitateur Messali Hadj," 2 October 1935.

94. The most exhaustive treatments of the Berber myth are Patricia M. E. Lorcin, *Imperial Identities: Stereotyping, Prejudice and Race in Colonial Algeria* (London: I. B. Taurus, 1999); and Gilles Lafuente, *La politique berbère de la France et le nationalisme marocain* (Paris: l'Harmattan, 1999).

95. MacMaster, *Colonial Migrants and Racism*, 34–49.

96. SHA, Moscow, C223/D122, SEA report, "Note sur les conditions psychologiques d'une mobilisation générale en Algérie (Mai 1935)."

97. SHA, Moscow, SEA, "La situation des indigènes en Kabylie," 16 April 1935.

98. Herman Lebovics, *True France: The Wars over Cultural Identity, 1900–1945* (Ithaca, N.Y.: Cornell University Press, 1992), 102n12, 116n38. Lebovics gives the Sûreté figures compiled in March 1930 as 1,556 and 2,924, respectively. Regarding similar surveillance of West African immigrants, see Gary Wilder, *The French Imperial Nation-State: Negritude and Colonial Humanism between the Two World Wars* (Chicago: University of Chicago Press, 2005), 141–42, 157–58.

99. Lebovics, *True France*, 103–5.

100. See ibid., 105, 110n23. For the Vietnamese case, see Scott McConnell, *Leftward Journey: The Education of Vietnamese Students in France, 1919–1939* (New Brunswick, N.J.: Transaction, 1989).

101. Catherine Coquery-Vidrovitch, "L'Afrique coloniale française et la crise de 1930: Crise structurelle et genèse du sous-développement," *Revue Française d'Histoire d'Outre-Mer* 63, no. 232 (1976): 386–424; Pierre Brocheux, "Crise économique et société en Indochine française," *Revue Française d'Histoire d'Outre-Mer* 63, no. 232 (1976): 655–67; Martin Thomas, *The French Empire between the Wars: Imperialism, Politics and Society* (Manchester: Manchester University Press, 2005), chapter 3.

102. Khoury, *Syria and the French Mandate*, 276–78, 387–88.

103. Kaddache, *Histoire du nationalisme algérien*, 1:302–24, 466–70; Gilbert Meynier, *Histoire intérieure du F.L.N., 1954–1962* (Paris: Fayard, 2002), 52–59.

104. SHA, Moscow, C930/D680, SEA report, "Propagande et influence des ulémas à Tlemcen et en Oranie," 4 March 1936; McDougall, *History and the Culture of Nationalism in Algeria*, 110–12.

105. Ibid., SEA, "Renseignement Algérie: enseignement des oulémas," 4 July 1935.

106. SHA, Moscow, C223/D122, SEA report, "Note sur les conditions psychologiques d'une mobilisation générale en Algérie (Mai 1935)."

107. MAE, série P: Tunisie 1930–1940, vol. 377, no. 109, Residency report, "A/S du Congrès de langue, litterature et arts musulmans tenu à Tunis," 23 January 1932.

108. SHA, 7N4133/D6, no. 2947, EMA Section d'études, "La situation politique en Tunisie," 14 December 1931.

109. MAE, série P: Tunisie 1930–1940, vol. 377, Tunis Residency to Joseph Paul Boncour, 12 June 1933.

110. SHA, Moscow, C1109/D667, EMA Section d'Outre-Mer, "Note au sujet de la contrebande et de la préparation d'une insurrection en AFN," 15 November 1934.

111. Ibid., Commandant Delor, SEA, to Commandant Rivet, "Informations fournies par REGNAUDIN," 27 November 1934.

112. SHA, Moscow, C286/D429, no. 1039/G, SEA, "Renseignement—Tunisie: Agitation nationaliste," 10 July 1934.

113. SHA, Moscow, C1109/D667, no. 1970/G, SEA, "Note sur la question tunisienne," 29 December 1934.

114. SHA, Moscow, C1109/D669, SEA, "Note sur la question tunisienne, 16 décembre 1934."

115. Ibid., pp. 1–3.

116. William A. Hoisington Jr., "Cities in Revolt: The Berber Dahir (1930) and

France's Union Strategy in Morocco," *Journal of Contemporary History* 13 (1978): 433–48; Charles-André Julien, *L'Afrique du Nord en marche: Algérie-Tunisie-Maroc, 1880–1952* (reprint, Paris: Omnibus, 2002), 130–33. For comprehensive background to the dispute, see Lafuente, *La politique berbère de la France*.

117. MAE, série K Afrique, sous-série Affaires musulmanes, vol. 24, no. 1730, Urbain Blanc to Sous-direction d'Afrique, "A/S Étoile Nord-Africaine," 10 September 1927.

118. Hoisington, "Cities in Revolt," 433–48.

119. SHA, Moscow, C306/D426, no. 17,622, Officier de liaison (Rabat), "Le mouvement nationaliste marocaine," 5 November 1933. This was consistent with the resurgence of conservative associationist ideology in French West Africa discussed by Alice Conklin in her *A Mission to Civilize: The Republican Idea of Empire in France and West Africa, 1895–1930* (Stanford, Calif.: Stanford University Press, 1997), 174–211.

120. William A. Hoisington Jr., *The Casablanca Connection: French Colonial Policy, 1936–1943* (Chapel Hill: University of North Carolina Press, 1984), 40–51; E. Joffé, "The Moroccan Nationalist Movement: Istiqlal, the Sultan and the Country," *Journal of African History* 26 (1985): 290–94.

121. CAOM, 8H61/D1, HCM March 1937 session, report 2: "Les grands courants d'opinion dans l'Islam nord-africain," 5 March 1937.

122. David M. Anderson and David Killingray, eds., *Policing and Decolonisation: Politics, Nationalism and the Police, 1917–65* (Manchester: Manchester University Press, 1992), 2.

123. See Robert Paxton's review of Noiriel's *Les origines républicaines de Vichy* in *French Politics, Culture and Society* 18, no. 2 (2000): 99–103; and Noiriel, *Les origines,* 183–85.

CHAPTER 8

1. Jacob Metzer, *The Divided Economy of Mandatory Palestine* (Cambridge: Cambridge University Press, 1998), 1–27. Metzer provides the best analysis of these debates, and favors the dual—or divided—economy model.

2. Neil Caplan, "Arab-Jewish Contacts in Palestine after the First World War," *Journal of Contemporary History* 12, no. 4 (1977): 642–54. Regarding worker contacts and unionization, particularly in the railway industry, see Zachary Lochman, *Comrades and Enemies: Arab and Jewish Workers in Palestine, 1906–1948* (Berkeley and Los Angeles: University of California Press, 1996), 68–72, 116–45.

3. Ylana N. Miller, *Government and Society in Rural Palestine, 1920–1948* (Austin: University of Texas Press, 1985), 7–8, 23–24.

4. W. F. Abboushi, "The Road to Rebellion: Arab Palestine in the 1930s," *Journal of Palestine Studies* 6, no. 3 (1977): 23.

5. Gad Kroizer, "From Dowbiggin to Tegart: Revolutionary Change in the Colonial Police in Palestine during the 1930s," *Journal of Imperial and Commonwealth History* 32, no. 2 (2004): 115.

6. For detailed statistics on interwar immigration, population growth, and labor force structure in Palestine, see Metzer, *Divided Economy of Mandatory Palestine,* 213–20.

7. Sahar Huneidi, "Was Balfour Policy Reversible? The Colonial Office and Palestine, 1921–23," *Journal of Palestine Studies* 27, no. 2 (1998), 23–41; Bernard

Wasserstein, *The British in Palestine: The Mandatory Government and the Arab-Jewish Conflict, 1917–1929* (Oxford: Basil Blackwell, 1991), 75–76; Miller, *Government and Society in Rural Palestine*, 3–7.

8. Ann Mosely Lesch, *Arab Politics in Palestine, 1917–1939: The Frustration of a Nationalist Movement* (Ithaca, N.Y.: Cornell University Press, 1979), 17–19, 80–95.

9. Mutual suspicion between these two Whitehall departments persisted throughout the interwar period. The Middle East Department head, Sir John Shuckburgh, accused the Foreign Office of undermining Colonial Office support for the Jewish national home by pushing consular staff to exaggerate Arab hostility to it; see TNA, CO 733/368/1, Shuckburgh note on FO dispatch E3034/10/31, 21 June 1938.

10. TNA, AIR 9/19, "Report on Middle East Conference in Cairo and Jerusalem, March 12 to 30, 1921."

11. TNA, CO 730/13, Middle East Interdepartmental Committee Report, 31 January 1921: para. 28 "Relations between Civil and Military Authorities."

12. Huneidi, "Was Balfour Policy Reversible?" 24–27; Huneidi, *A Broken Trust: Herbert Samuel, Zionism and the Palestinians (1920–25)* (London: I. B. Tauris, 2001), chapter 3. Bernard Wasserstein suggests that Samuel's high commission staff recognized the weight of Arab grievances after the Jaffa riots of 1921; see his *British in Palestine*, 141–49. Army hostility to Zionist demands was one of the key reasons for Colonial Secretary Winston Churchill's support for the transition to Air Ministry control over imperial policing and military intelligence in Palestine in 1921.

13. Lesch, *Arab Politics in Palestine*, 96–97. The Palestine Arab National Party, created in November 1923 by leading members of the Nashashibi and al-Dajani families, was the first of these more sectarian groups.

14. Ibid., 95–103. By 1928, the Arab Executive was in secret talks with the high commission over the creation of a Palestine Legislative Council that would serve as the mouthpiece of the Arab elite.

15. Regarding Arab officials' conflicting loyalties, see Wasserstein, *British in Palestine*, 165–67, 177–78.

16. Lesch, *Arab Politics in Palestine*, 105–10. Regarding the achievements of the women's groups, see Ellen L. Fleischmann, *The Nation and Its "New" Women: The Palestinian Women's Movement, 1920–1948* (Berkeley and Los Angeles: University of California Press, 2003), chapters 4–6, especially 137–75 passim.

17. Muhammad Haj Amin al-Hussaini, the future mufti of Jerusalem, and 'Arif al'Arif, the editor of the newspaper *Suriyyah al-Janubiyyah* (*Southern Syria*), fled to Transjordan after being charged with incitement of the Jerusalem riots. See Taysir Jbara, *Palestinian Leader: Hajj Amin al-Husayni Mufti of Jerusalem* (Princeton: Kingston Press, 1985), 32–35; Zvi Elpeleg, *The Grand Mufti Haj Amin al-Hussaini, Founder of the Palestinian National Movement*, trans. David Harvey (London: Frank Cass, 1993), 6.

18. Martin Kolinsky, *Law, Order and Riots in Mandatory Palestine, 1928–35* (London: Macmillan, 1993), 32; Wasserstein, *British in Palestine*, 100–105. High Commissioner Samuel suspended Jewish immigration in response to the 1921 unrest.

19. Kolinsky, *Law, Order and Riots in Mandatory Palestine*, chapters 3, 4, and 9. Further rioting in protest against heightened Jewish immigration occurred in Jaffa in October 1933; see Colin Imray, *Policeman in Palestine: Memoirs of the Early Years* (Devon: Edward Gaskell, 1995), 93–95.

20. Joseph Nevo, "Palestinian-Arab Violent Activity during the 1930s," in *Britain and the Middle East in the 1930s: Security Problems,* ed. Michael J. Cohen and Martin Kolinsky (London: Macmillan, 1992), 169–89; Yehoshuah Porath, *The Palestinian Arab National Movement, 1929–1939: From Riots to Rebellion* (London: Frank Cass, 1977), chapters 1 to 4.

21. CAOM, GGA, 11H46, Algiers Service des affaires indigènes, "Rapports politiques périodiques," 1918–21.

22. Ronen Shamir, *The Colonies of Law: Colonialism, Zionism and Law in Early Mandate Palestine* (Cambridge: Cambridge University Press, 2000), 13.

23. Miller, *Government and Society in Rural Palestine,* 76–82.

24. Warwick P. N. Tyler, *State Lands and Rural Development in Mandatory Palestine, 1920–1948* (Brighton: Sussex Academic Press, 2001), 160–87. Similar problems arose in Transjordan; see Fischbach, "British Land Policy in Transjordan," in *Village, Steppe and State: The Social Origins of Modern Jordan,* ed. Eugene L. Rogan and Tariq Tell (London: British Academic Press, 1994), 102–7.

25. Roza El-Eini, *Mandated Landscape: British Imperial Rule in Palestine, 1929–1948* (London: Frank Cass, 2004).

26. Tom Bowden, "The Politics of the Arab Rebellion in Palestine, 1936–39," *Middle Eastern Studies* 11, no. 2 (1975): 147–48, 169.

27. Tyler, *State Lands and Rural Development in Mandatory Palestine,* 43, 209–10.

28. Michael J. Cohen, "Appeasement in the Middle East: The British White Paper on Palestine, May 1939," *Historical Journal* 16, no. 3 (1973): 571–96.

29. TNA, CO 732/16, CO 9531, "CO Minutes Relating the Recruitment of Natives in Mandated Territories," January–February 1925. The War Office was nonetheless eager to recruit Palestinian interpreters to serve with the British Army in Egypt.

30. TNA, CO 323/1113, CID 348-C, "Palestine Garrison," 27 June 1930: Enclosure 5, "Memorandum Enumerating the Decisions Taken in Regard to the Establishments of the Police and Defence Forces in Palestine and Trans-Jordan since 1925." In addition to the fifty British police officers, there were some two hundred other British policemen of other ranks at any one time in 1920s Palestine.

31. Georgina Sinclair highlights the discrepancies in official figures for the gendarmerie; see Sinclair, *At the End of the Line: Colonial Policing and the Imperial Endgame, 1945–80* (Manchester: Manchester University Press, 2006), 21–22, 32n56.

32. TNA, CO 323/1113, CID 348-C, "Palestine Garrison," 27 June 1930: Enclosure 5, "Memorandum Enumerating the Decisions Taken in Regard to the Establishments of the Police and Defence Forces in Palestine and Trans-Jordan since 1925."

33. Kolinsky, *Law, Order and Riots in Mandatory Palestine,* 7–8.

34. Ronen Shamir notes that the legacy of British legal regulation is rarely acknowledged in the historiography of the mandate or the creation of the Israeli state; see his *Colonies of Law,* 10–12. For the impact of administrative regulation on the Arab community before 1939, see Ylana N. Miller, "Administrative Policy in Rural Palestine: The Impact of British Norms on Arab Community Life, 1920–1948," in *Palestinian Society and Politics,* by Joel S. Migdal (Princeton, N.J.: Princeton University Press, 1980), 124–37.

35. H. J. Simson, *British Rule, and Rebellion* (Edinburgh: William Blackwood, 1938), 55–66.

36. Gyanesh Kudaisya, "'In Aid of Civil Power': The Colonial Army in Northern India, c. 1919–42," *Journal of Imperial and Commonwealth History* 32, no. 1 (2004): 41–68.

37. TNA, CO 831/45/5, TJFF, Zerqa HQ, annual report for 1937, 16 January 1938.

38. Simson, *British Rule, and Rebellion,* 99–100.

39. Charles Townshend, "Martial Law: Legal and Administrative Problems of Civil Emergency in Britain and the Empire, 1800–1940," *Historical Journal* 25, no. 1 (1982): 167–95.

40. TNA, WO 32/4176, Colonial Secretary William Ormsby-Gore to Palestine high commissioner, 3 June 1936.

41. Abboushi, "Road to Rebellion," 36.

42. Ibid., 37.

43. Wasserstein, *British in Palestine,* 168.

44. TNA, CO 323/1113, CO dispatch 11/705/S/26 to high commissioner, 16 July 1925. It is worth noting that in 1926–27, the French North African administrations also demarcated more clearly between police and military duties, causing confusion to the paramilitary gendarmerie; see MAE, série M, vol. 796, no. 5706, Residency report to Direction de la gendarmerie, 12 October 1927.

45. TNA, CO 733/131/5, Draft report on the administration of Palestine and Transjordan, 1926, submitted to Colonial Office on 25 March 1927, p. 69. Commanded by Lieutenant-Colonel F. W. Bewsher, in the 1926–27 financial year, set-up costs for the Transjordan Frontier Force amounted to £216,000, of which £108,000 was a grant-in-aid from the British Treasury.

46. The creation of the Transjordan Frontier Force supplanted the mixed gendarmerie and the "Reserve Force" established in 1921–22 to uphold security in the fledgling mandate; see TNA, FO 684/1, Chief British representative H. S. B. Philby, "Appreciation of the Situation in Transjordan," 12 May 1922.

47. TNA, CO 733/131/5, Draft report on the administration of Palestine and Transjordan, 1926, submitted to Colonial Office on 25 March 1927.

48. Mary C. Wilson, *King Abdullah, Britain and the Making of Jordan* (Cambridge: Cambridge University Press, 1987), 86–87.

49. TNA, CO 323/1113, CID 348-C, "Palestine Garrison," 27 June 1930: Enclosure 5.

50. Kolinsky, *Law, Order and Riots in Mandatory Palestine,* 24–30.

51. Kroizer, "From Dowbiggin to Tegart," 117. Ironically, Plumer was praised for his initial success in reducing intercommunal tensions in Palestine; see TNA, CO 732/25/8, Sir John Shuckburgh, "Report on Visit to Palestine and Iraq," 19 April 1927.

52. Jbara, *Palestinian Leader,* 61–65.

53. Elpeleg, *Grand Mufti Haj Amin al-Hussaini,* 8–15. Sir Herbert Samuel's willingness to appoint Haj Amin al-Hussaini reflected intelligence assessments, which indicated that the mufti could guarantee law and order. The factionalism characteristic of municipal politics in Jerusalem intensified when the mufti's main rival, Raghib al-Nashashibi, was appointed mayor of Jerusalem in the wake of the 1920 riots. Al-Nashashibi and his followers remained bitter opponents of the Supreme Muslim Council under al-Hussaini.

54. Jbara, *Palestinian Leader*, 46–55; Michael J. Cohen, *Palestine, Retreat from the Mandate: The Making of British Policy, 1936–1945* (London: Paul Elek, 1978), 10–12.

55. Philip Mattar, "The Role of the Mufti of Jerusalem in the Political Struggle over the Western Wall, 1928–1929," *Middle Eastern Studies* 19, no. 1 (1983): 104–18; Elpeleg, *Grand Mufti Haj Amin al-Hussaini*, 19. The Supreme Muslim Council was also anxious not to jeopardize high commission plans to create a Palestine Legislative Council.

56. Mary Ellen Lundsten, "Wall Politics: Zionist and Palestinian Strategies in Jerusalem, 1928," *Journal of Palestine Studies* 8, no. 1 (1978): 7–12.

57. Ibid., 9–11.

58. Ibid., 11–12.

59. Kroizer, "From Dowbiggin to Tegart," 115–16.

60. Jbara, *Palestinian Leader*, 80–81; Elpeleg, *Grand Mufti Haj Amin al-Hussaini*, 17–18.

61. Jbara, *Palestinian Leader*, 80.

62. Lundsten, "Wall Politics," 13–22.

63. Kolinsky, *Law, Order and Riots in Mandatory Palestine*, 40.

64. Lundsten, "Wall Politics," 3n2, 22–24.

65. A. Sela, "The 'Wailing Wall' Riots of 1929 as a Watershed in the Palestine Conflict," *Muslim World* 84 (1994): 82; also cited in Kroizer, "From Dowbiggin to Tegart," 116.

66. Elpeleg, *Grand Mufti Haj Amin al-Hussaini*, 22.

67. Kolinsky, *Law, Order and Riots in Mandatory Palestine*, 42. In addition to the deaths in both communities, the high commission recorded a further 339 Jews and 232 Arabs as wounded. Arab casualties were probably far higher. Many of those killed or injured by the security forces were never officially identified or did not go to a hospital.

68. The high commission was certain that relief funds were diverted to fund political activity; see Jbara, *Palestinian Leader*, 88.

69. TNA, FO 684/4, British Resident Amman, "Situation Report on Transjordan for the Period July 1, 1929 to September 30, 1929."

70. TNA, CO 831/2/6, High Commissioner Plumer dispatches to Leo Amery, 18 May and 19 September 1928; CO 831/20/12, High Commissioner Wauchope to Sir Philip Cunliffe-Lister recording conversation with Amir Abdullah about the Arab Independence Party, 24 September 1932.

71. Charles Townshend, "Going to the Wall: The Failure of British Rule in Palestine, 1928–31," *Journal of Imperial and Commonwealth History* 30, no. 2 (2002): 25–52.

72. Kolinsky, *Law, Order, and Riots in Mandatory Palestine*, 42–53, 97. Mavrogordato lost his job in the reorganization of the police conducted by Sir Herbert Dowbiggin after the 1929 disturbances.

73. Ibid., 48.

74. TNA, CO 323/1113, CID 348-C, "Palestine Garrison," 27 June 1930: enclosure 5, quotation at p. 29.

75. Ibid.

76. TNA, AIR 9/19, RAF HQ, Fighting Area, to Air Minister Lord Thomson, 10 January 1930. The air officer commanding suggested the deployment of a TJFF unit

Ethnic Population in Four Towns in Palestine, 1930

	Muslims	Jews	Christians
Jerusalem	13,400	41,000	14,700
Jaffa	20,000	5,085	40
Haifa	9,400	15,000	8,850
Hebron	16,074	430	73

in Jerusalem as a mobile reserve that could be deployed in response to intelligence warnings. See also Kolinsky, *Law, Order and Riots in Mandatory Palestine*, 91–93.

77. TNA, CO 733/175/4, copy of Trenchard memorandum to Secretary of State for Air, 5 December 1929, cited in Kolinsky, *Law, Order and Riots in Mandatory Palestine*, 79.

78. TNA, CO 323/1065/10, Affairs in the colonies, "Notes for the Information of the Prime Minister," 12 November 1929.

79. Ibid. Proposals to station a regular army battalion in Palestine or to transfer in an equivalent strength force of Assyrian levies from Iraq were ruled out on the grounds of cost.

80. TNA, CO 323/1113, Trenchard memo, "Defence and Internal Security in Palestine," 13 May 1930; Sinclair, *At the End of the Line*, 106. Almost three hundred additional British officers were added to Palestine police numbers in 1930 alone.

81. TNA, CO 323/1113, Palestine and Transjordan Defence Scheme, n.d. [January 1930], chapter 1: "The General Defence Problem." In January 1930, the population in these four towns was estimated as given in the table above.

82. Ibid.

83. Kolinsky, *Law, Order and Riots in Mandatory Palestine*, 60–63. Chancellor was another notable absentee from Palestine during the Wailing Wall disorders.

84. TNA, AIR 9/19, Chief of Air Staff memo in response to CP343(29), "The Situation in Palestine," 5 December 1929.

85. Miller, *Government and Society in Rural Palestine*, 49–50.

86. On the *mukhtar* system, see ibid., 54–62.

87. TNA, CO 323/1113, Palestine and Transjordan Defence Scheme, January 1930, chapter 4: "Army Measures to Be Taken in Peace during the Precautionary Stage and at the Outset of the Action Stage."

88. TNA, CO 323/1113, Palestine and Transjordan Defence Scheme, n.d. [January 1930], chapter 2: "Defence Plan," 13.

89. Ibid., 13–14.

90. Lesch, *Arab Politics in Palestine*, 212–13; Nevo, "Palestinian-Arab Violent Activity during the 1930s," 173–74.

91. Miller, *Government and Society in Rural Palestine*, 9–10; Kolinsky, *Law, Order and Riots in Mandatory Palestine*, 71–72. A 1930 Colonial Office inquiry under Sir John Hope Simpson into Jewish immigration and land settlement reached similar conclusions. Simpson's findings were, however, nullified by Prime Minister Ramsay

MacDonald's infamous "black letter" to Dr. Chaim Weizmann promising that Shaw's recommendations for stringent limits to immigration would not be implemented.

92. TNA, CO 733/177/4: Report of Commission of Inquiry into 1929 Disturbances [Shaw Commission report], March 1930, p. 148, also cited in Kolinsky, *Law, Order and Riots in Mandatory Palestine*, 76.

93. Kolinsky, *Law, Order and Riots in Mandatory Palestine*, 93–100. On Dowbiggin's advice, the long-serving Criminal Investigation Department chief Joseph Broadhurst was replaced, first by E. P. Quigley, a police commander in southern Palestine, and then by Deputy Superintendent A. J. Kingsley-Heath. Kingsley-Heath took over the Palestine Police Training School in July 1932, allowing Harry Rice, a former Kenya colonial police officer, to supervise the Criminal Investigation Department.

94. Ibid., 101–3.

95. Martin Kramer, *Islam Assembled: The Advent of the Muslim Congresses* (New York: Columbia University Press, 1986), chapter 11.

96. TNA, FO 141/768, "List of the Principal Members of the Istiqlal Party in the Middle East," n.d. [December 1932].

97. The CID sent the Colonial Office Middle East Department details of Congress proceedings; see TNA, CO 732/53/3, Undated high commission report on the pan-Islamic movement.

98. See, for example, the discussions surrounding King Faysal's support for a proposed pan-Arab Congress in Baghdad, scheduled for 1933: TNA, CO 732/58/3, E6888/4478/65, Sir F. Humphrys (Baghdad) to Sir John Simon, 21 December 1932.

99. TNA, FO 371/16855, E3119/347/65, Eastern Department memo (signed by G. W. Rendel), "Attitude of His Majesty's Government towards the Question of Arab Unity," 13 June 1933.

100. Kramer, *Islam Assembled*, 126–30. Much to the relief of Turkey, Palestine High Commissioner Sir Arthur Wauchope refused the visa application.

101. TNA, CO 732/51/6, OGRW18/11, Secretary of State for Colonies tel. to Officer Administering Government of Palestine, 18 November 1931.

102. Metzer, *Divided Economy of Mandatory Palestine*, 217, table A.3.

103. Miller, *Government and Society in Rural Palestine*, 51–52.

104. As examples: AN, F/7/13468/D6, Commissaire spécial d'Annemasse memos, "Rapport sur la situation en Palestine," 18 July 1924, and "Rapport sur le mouvement pan-Arabe," 1 August 1924.

105. SHA, 7N4171/D1, EMA-2, Agent's report from a "well-placed informant," "La situation en Palestine," 28 April 1931; Section d'études du Levant Beirut, "A/S Congrès Islamique de Jerusalem," 4 November 1931.

106. See, for example, SHA, 7N4171/D1, EMA-2, "Situation en Palestine et Transjordanie—le Sionisme," 7 August 1931.

107. TNA, FO 371/20065, E1326/381/65, Sudan Agency (Cairo), "Report on the Pan-Islamic Arab Movement," 14 February 1936.

108. *BDFA*, II: B, vol. 12, doc.12, doc. 55, Robert Parr (Aleppo Consul) to FO, "Memorandum on the Interdependence of the Outbreaks in Syria and Palestine during 1936," 20 August 1936.

109. TNA, FO 406/74, Gilbert MacKereth (Damascus), "Memorandum Respecting Pan-Arabism," 15 May 1936.

110. TNA, FO 371/20065, E1326/381/65, Sudan Agency (Cairo), "Report on the Pan-Islamic Arab Movement," 14 February 1936.

111. TNA, FO 684/9, Sir Archibald Clark Kerr to Anthony Eden, 28 May 1936.

112. Elie Kedourie, "The Bludan Congress on Palestine, September 1937," *Middle Eastern Studies* 17 (1981): 107–25; Philip S. Khoury, *Syria and the French Mandate: The Politics of Arab Nationalism, 1920–1945* (Princeton, N.J.: Princeton University Press, 1987), 554–55; TNA, CO 733/368/4, E1947/10/31, G. T. Havard (Beirut) to Foreign Office, 30 March 1938.

113. TNA, WO 32/4562, Lieutenant-General R. H. Haining (GOC, Palestine), "Hostile Propaganda in Palestine: Its Origin and Progress in 1938," 1 December 1938.

114. Egyptian and Syrian attitudes to the status of Palestine are discussed in James Jankowski, "Egyptian Responses to the Palestine Problem in the Interwar Period," *International Journal of Middle East Studies* 12 (1980): 1–38; and Philip S. Khoury, "Divided Loyalties? Syria and the Question of Palestine, 1919–39," *Middle Eastern Studies* 21, no. 3 (1985): 324–48.

115. TNA, CO 732/81/3, Major W. J. Cawthorn, MI2 report, "Notes on the Possibility of Concerted Military Action to H.M. Government's Policy in Palestine," 9 February 1938.

116. Ibid., "Local Problems Affecting Co-operation between the Governments of Arabic Speaking Countries."

117. TNA, CO 732/81/3, E. G. Etherington-Smith (Foreign Office) to W. J. Cawthorn, 1 April 1938.

118. TNA, WO 106/2018B, COS 847(JIC), "Attitude of the 'Arab World' to Great Britain with Particular Reference to the Palestine Conference," 20 February 1939.

119. For differing perspectives on the revolt, see Porath, *Palestinian Arab National Movement;* Cohen, *Palestine, Retreat from the Mandate;* Charles Townshend, "The Defence of Palestine: Insurrection and Public Security, 1936–1939," *English Historical Review* 103 (1988): 919–49; Miller, *Government and Society in Rural Palestine,* 121–38; and Bowden, "Politics of the Arab Rebellion in Palestine," 147–74.

120. Miller, *Government and Society in Rural Palestine,* 122; Bowden, "Politics of the Arab Rebellion in Palestine," 147–51.

121. Kroizer, "From Dowbiggin to Tegart," 116.

122. Townshend, "Defence of Palestine," 917–49.

123. Lesch, *Arab Politics in Palestine,* 114–18.

124. For a summary of Istiqlal members' involvement with pan-Arabism from 1918, see TNA, FO 141/768, Cairo Residency report, "Memorandum on the Proposed Arab Congress," 30 December 1932.

125. Lesch, *Arab Politics in Palestine,* 118.

126. Abboushi, "Road to Rebellion," 30–31, 37–38.

127. Yuval Arnon-Ohanna, "The Bands in the Palestinian Arab Revolt, 1936–1939: Structure and Organization," *Asian and African Studies* 15, no. 2 (1981): 229–47.

128. This requirement for GOC daily situation reports was laid down in the 1930 defense scheme; see TNA, CO 323/1113, Palestine and Transjordan Defense Scheme, n.d. [January 1930], chapter 4: "Army Measures to Be Taken in Peace during the Precautionary Stage and at the Outset of the Action Stage."

129. TNA, WO 191/170, GHQ Palestine and Transjordan, "Military Lessons of the Arab Rebellion," chapter 6: "Intelligence and Intercommunication," compiled in February 1938.

130. Ibid.

131. TNA, FO 141/768, Cairo registry, "Provincial Tours of the Oriental Secretariat," 20 December 1932.

132. TNA, WO 191/170, GHQ Palestine and Transjordan, "Military Lessons of the Arab Rebellion," chapter 6: "Intelligence and Intercommunication."

133. Writing to his brother on 19 April 1936, Hodgkin complained of "bare police accounts written in hackneyed terms [that] don't give me any idea of what is really happening"; E. C. Hodgkin, ed., *Thomas Hodgkin: Letters from Palestine, 1932–1936* (London: Quartet Books, 1986), 160.

134. Ibid.

135. TNA, WO 191/170, GHQ Palestine and Transjordan, "Military Lessons of the Arab Rebellion," chapter 6: "Intelligence and Intercommunication: Aircraft," n.d. [February 1938].

136. Dov Gavish, "Foreign Intelligence Maps: Offshoots of the 1:100,000 Topographic Map of Israel," *Imago Mundi* 48 (1996): 174–84.

137. TNA, CO 323/1113, Palestine and Transjordan Defense Scheme, n.d. [January 1930], chapter 1: "The General Defence Problem."

138. Ibid., chapter 6: "Intelligence and Intercommunication: Maps."

139. Arnon-Ohanna, "Bands in the Palestinian Arab Revolt," 229–30; Abboushi, "Road to Rebellion," 40–42; Bowden, "Politics of the Arab Rebellion in Palestine," 150–52. Bowden is especially critical of the insurgents' organizational failings and their lack of clear political direction. He does, however, acknowledge the rebels' intelligence-gathering capacity as one of their strengths.

140. Ted Swedenburg, "The Role of the Palestinian Peasantry in the Great Revolt (1936–1939)," in *Islam, Politics, and Social Movements*, ed. Edmund Burke III and Ira M. Lapidus (Berkeley and Los Angeles: University of California Press, 1988), 184–90.

141. Ibid., 229. One such group, led by Sheikh Izzedin al-Qassim, fought a gun battle with British troops in November 1935 in which al-Qassim was killed; see Abboushi, "Road to Rebellion," 33.

142. Arnon-Ohanna, "Bands in the Palestinian Arab Revolt," 231–32.

143. TNA, WO 32/4562, Lieutenant-General R. H. Haining (GOC, Palestine), "Hostile Propaganda in Palestine: Its Origin and Progress in 1938," 1 December 1938.

144. Ibid., quotation at pp. 6–7.

145. Charges of British brutality, arbitrary killings, and inhumane treatment of detainees rounded up during check-and-search operations persisted long after the end of the rebellion; see TNA, WO 32/4562, dispatch no. 607, MacMichael to Colonial Secretary MacDonald, 22 September 1939.

146. Bowden, "Politics of the Arab Rebellion in Palestine," 166–67.

147. Martin Kolinsky, "The Collapse and Restoration of Public Security," in *Britain and the Middle East in the 1930s: Security Problems,* ed. Michael J. Cohen and Martin Kolinsky (London: Macmillan, 1992), 158.

148. TNA, CO 733/368/4, Major T. O. Tulloch letter to Sir Cosmo Parkinson, 10 January 1938. Supporters of identity cards favored an amnesty for illegal immigrants to win Jewish support.

149. Abboushi, "Road to Rebellion," 27, 40–44.

150. Arnon-Ohanna, "Bands in the Palestinian Arab Revolt," 247.

151. According to W. F. Abboushi, al-Qawuqji had served French military intelligence before joining the Syrian revolt in 1925; Abboushi, "Road to Rebellion," 41.

152. Arnon-Ohanna, "Bands in the Palestinian Arab Revolt," 234–39. Fawzi al-Din al-Qawuqji commanded the first phase of the rebellion, between August and October 1936; Muhammad al-Ashmar led a company of Syrian volunteers in this phase, and was later asked by al-Hussaini to assume command of rebel forces in November 1937.

153. Miller, *Government and Society in Rural Palestine*, 126–28.

154. Arnon-Ohanna, "Bands in the Palestinian Arab Revolt," 232, 241; Nevo, "Palestinian-Arab Violent Activity during the 1930s," 175–83.

155. Kolinsky, "Collapse and Restoration of Public Security," 148–56; Cohen, *Palestine, Retreat from the Mandate*, 32–40; Aaron S. Klieman, "The Divisiveness of Palestine: Foreign Office vs. Colonial Office on the Issue of Partition, 1937," *Historical Journal* 22 (1979): 423–42.

156. TNA, CO 814/13/1938, Palestine high commission annual report, table detailing incidents of violence in 1938, also cited in Bowden, "Politics of the Arab Rebellion in Palestine," 153.

157. Rhodes House Library, MSS BRIT EMP s.514, Robin Martin, "Reminiscences of the Palestine Police Force," pp. 31–36.

158. Rhodes House Library, MSS BRIT EMP s.390, Clarence Buxton papers 1/5, Buxton letter to William D. Battershill, Palestine Chief Secretary, 16 February 1939.

159. TNA, WO 191/170, GHQ Palestine and Transjordan, "Military Lessons of the Arab Rebellion," chapter 6: "Intelligence and Intercommunication."

160. Prior to the outbreak of the rebellion, one of the five sections in Sheikh Izz al-Din al-Qassam's secret "Black Hand" organization was exclusively devoted to such intelligence gathering; see Nevo, "Palestinian-Arab Violent Activity during the 1930s," 174.

161. Ibid.

162. Rhodes House Library, MSS BRIT EMP s.514, Robin Martin, "Reminiscences of the Palestine Police Force," p. 37.

163. Simson, *British Rule, and Rebellion*, 36–37. Simson defined "sub-war" as "half-way between a political strike on a national scale and civil war. . . . In sub-war, every effort is made to use force under cover of the laws of the Government which is being attacked. Organization is secret. Military formations are avoided as much as possible. Control is maintained by intimidation."

164. Ibid., 63–64.

165. TNA, WO 191/170, GHQ Palestine and Transjordan, "Military Lessons of the Arab Rebellion," chapter 6: "Intelligence and Intercommunication."

166. Ibid.

167. TNA, WO 32/4176, SF/629/36, MacMichael to Colonial Office, 2 July 1938.

168. Ibid.

169. TNA, WO 32/4176, tel. 566, MacMichael to Colonial Office: GOC's advice, 11 September 1938.

170. Kolinsky, "Collapse and Restoration of Public Security," 157.

171. A point implicitly acknowledged by High Commissioner MacMichael: TNA, WO 32/4176, MacMichael letter to Malcolm MacDonald, 17 September 1938.

172. *BDFA*, II: B, vol. 13, doc. 13, Gilbert MacKereth (Damascus) to FO, 13 January 1938.

173. *BDFA*, II: B, vol. 13, doc. 14, "Memorandum Summarizing the Talks on January 11 and 12 in Jerusalem between Sir C. Tegart, Sir D. Petrie and Lieutenant-Colonel G. MacKereth on Terrorist Activities in Palestine Organized from Syria," 13 January 1938.

174. TNA, CO 733/368/4, Damascus dispatch no. 7, MacKereth to Jerusalem high commission, 5 February 1938. Regarding MacKereth's efforts to dissuade the National Bloc government from backing the rebellion, see Khoury, *Syria and the French Mandate*, 553–57.

175. TNA, CO 733/368/4, E1848/2207/2, Damascus dispatch no. 45, 5 September 1938: details the arrest, detention, and escape of Fawzi Rashid from police custody.

176. TNA, CO 733/368/4, E7601/22/31, Sir Eric Phipps (Paris) record of conversation with M. de Saint-Quentin, director of Foreign Ministry Levant division, 28 December 1937.

177. TNA, CO 733/368/4, E862/10/31, MacKereth, Damascus dispatch no. 5, 5 February 1938.

178. *BDFA*, II: B, vol. 13, doc. 14.

179. See, for example, SHA, Moscow, C609/D375, SEA summary report, "A/S d'une 'bande' en Syrie destinée à la Palestine," 25 August 1939.

180. TNA, CO 733/398/5, Damascus dispatch no. 4, MacKereth to Foreign Office, 6 January 1939.

181. Kolinsky, "Collapse and Restoration of Public Security," 160–61.

182. TNA, CO 732/84/15, GSI, HQ Jerusalem, "Summary of Intelligence," 24 February 1939.

183. TNA, CAB 4/26, COS sub-committee memoranda, 1346B and 1364B, "Situation in the Mediterranean and Middle East," 28 July and 26 October 1937; CAB 4/27, Foreign Office memorandum, "Concentration of Italian Troops in Libya," 15 December 1937.

184. TNA, ADM 116/3588, Sir Anthony Eden to Lampson (Cairo), 20 February 1936; Martin Kolinsky, *Britain's War in the Middle East: Strategy and Diplomacy, 1936–42* (London: Macmillan, 1995), 85–99.

185. TNA, ADM 116/3468, C-in-C. Med., "Recent Emergency in Eastern Mediterranean," 19 March 1936; FO 371/21136, JDC draft memo, "Counter-Bombardment Defences," n.d. [January 1937].

186. Steven Morewood, "Protecting the Jugular Vein of Empire: The Suez Canal in British Defence Strategy, 1919–1941," *War and Society* 10, no. 1 (1992): 86–88.

187. *BDFA*, II: B, vol. 13, doc. 114, W. E. Houstoun-Boswell (Baghdad) to Viscount Halifax, 5 October 1938, and doc. 115, Sir M. Peterson to Iraqi Acting Minister for Foreign Affairs, 10 October 1938.

188. TNA, FO 371/21838, E6998/692/65, K. W. Blaxter letter to C. W. Baxter, 13 October 1938.

189. TNA, CO 831/37/8, Colonial Office minutes, 20 June 1936, on the Transjordan Residency annual report for 1935. The presence of Palestinian rebels and

Syrian political exiles contributed to the volatile political atmosphere in prewar Transjordan; see TNA, FO 371/20055, E6742/7/25, Glubb, "Monthly Report on the Administration of the Deserts of Transjordan, July 1936"; see also the August 1936 report in the same file. Glubb's anxiety that resentment about British treatment of the Palestinian Arabs would spill over into violence in Transjordan intensified in 1937. In his March 1937 report on the local political situation, he noted, "The mental revolution which takes place in every Arab who lives for even a short period in Palestine is really remarkable. His character seems to be warped, and he becomes mean, hostile and suspicious while those who were present in Palestine last summer and return, have grown accustomed to the idea of disorder and violence." See TNA, CO 831/41/11.

190. TNA, CO 831/41/8, TC/18/37, C. H. F. Cox, Amman Residency, "Report on the Political Situation, November 1937"; CO 831/51/8, TC/10/39, "Secret Report on the Political Situation, April 1939." Palestinian rebel bands remained active around Ajlun through the early months of 1939.

191. TNA, CO 831/46/6, TC/8/38, C. H. F. Cox, Amman Residency situation report, August 1938.

192. TNA, CO 831/41/11, Sir Arthur Wauchope to David Ormsby-Gore, 9 January 1937. The Palestine high commissioner rejected Glubb's request for an increase in the secret service funds disbursed among Bedouin sheikhs, insisting that the Arab Legion could enforce desert security "in normal times."

193. BDFA, II: B, vol. 12, doc. 51, Sir Anthony Eden to Cairo, Baghdad, and Jedda, 30 July 1936.

194. BDFA, II: B, vol. 12, docs. 52, 54, 57, 80, 81, 82.

195. BDFA, II: B, vol. 12, doc. 53, Lampson memo, "The Attitude of Public Opinion in Egypt towards the Situation in Palestine," 12 August 1936.

196. BDFA, II: B, vol. 12, doc. 58, Captain V. Holt (Baghdad Oriental Secretary), "Repercussions in Iraq of the Creation of a National Home for the Jews in Palestine," sent to FO, 17 August 1936.

197. Liora Lukitz, "Axioms Reconsidered: The Rethinking of British Strategic Policy in Iraq during the 1930s," in Britain and the Middle East in the 1930s: Security Problems, ed. Michael J. Cohen and Martin Kolinsky (London: Macmillan, 1992), 121–22.

198. Renate Dieterich, "Germany's Relations with Iraq and Transjordan from the Weimar Republic to the End of the Second World War," Middle Eastern Studies 44, no. 4 (2005): 465.

199. TNA, CAB 24/273/CP 281 (37), Eden memorandum, "Palestine," 19 November 1937.

200. TNA, ADM 1/9864, "Cairo's Views of the Suez Canal Defence Plan," 17 December 1938; G. Sheffer, "Principles of Pragmatism: A Reevaluation of British Policies toward Palestine in the 1930s," in The Great Powers in the Middle East, 1919–1939, ed. Uriel Dann (New York: Holmes, 1988), 109–27.

201. TNA, CAB 16/140, Defence Policy and Requirements Committee analysis, 29 September 1936.

202. TNA, ADM 1/9864, "Cairo's Views of the Suez Canal Defence Plan," 17 December 1938.

203. TNA, WO 106/2018B, COS847(JIC), "Attitude of the 'Arab World' to G.B.," 20 February 1939.

204. TNA, CO 831/41/11, Minutes of CID, 340th meeting, 1 December 1938: "Treaty Obligations of Egypt and Iraq in the Event of HMG Being Engaged in War."

205. Ibid., CID paper 1490B: "Air Action against Yemen," and FO minutes, 5 and 13 December 1938.

206. TNA, FO 371/23193, CID 355th meeting, 2 May 1939: "Formation of Colonial Divisions."

207. TNA, FO 371/23193, CID, 347th meeting, 16 February 1939: "Measures to Influence Arab States and Minor Powers in the Middle East on the Outbreak of a European War involving the UK."

208. Ibid. This effort extended to Iran as well; TNA, FO 371/21838, Tehran tel. 305, 31 August 1938.

209. This is the argument developed by Tom Bowden in his "Politics of the Arab Rebellion in Palestine," 147–74.

210. BDFA, II: B, vol. 13, doc. 370, Halifax to Consul-General (Beirut), 1 September 1939.

211. TNA, FO 371/24559, E500/500/93, Sir Basil Newton to Halifax, 20 January 1940. Article 4 of the 1930 Anglo-Iraqi Treaty of Alliance obliged the Iraqi government to act as it did in September 1939.

212. TNA, CO 831/51/8, TC/10/39, Amman Residency, "Secret Political Report on Transjordan for the Month of September 1939," 11 October 1939.

213. David A. Charters, "British Intelligence in the Palestine Campaign, 1945–47," Intelligence and National Security 6, no. 1 (1991): 115–40.

CHAPTER 9

1. SHA, 7N4093, no. 1754, EMA-2, "Bulletin de renseignements, questions musulmanes," 10 May 1937.

2. The best treatment of the coalition's activities more generally remains Julian Jackson, The Popular Front in France: Defending Democracy, 1934–38 (Cambridge: Cambridge University Press, 1988); for insight into policing and public order concerns, see Simon Kitson, "Police and Politics in Marseille, 1936–8," European History Quarterly 37, no. 1 (2007): 81–108.

3. Renewed interest in the Popular Front's colonial policies began with two key works: William B. Cohen's article, "The Colonial Policy of the Popular Front," French Historical Studies 7, no. 3 (1972): 368–93; and a special issue of the journal Le Mouvement Social 107 (avril–juin 1979). An excellent edited collection addresses the coalition's colonial policies: Tony Chafer and Amanda Sackur, eds., French Colonial Empire and Popular Front: Hope and Disillusion (London: Macmillan, 1999).

4. Martin Thomas, The French Empire between the Wars: Imperialism, Politics and Society (Manchester: Manchester University Press, 2005), chapter 9.

5. Key provisions of the Matignon accords included an eight-hour working day, annual holiday entitlements, minimum working conditions, recognition of employer liability for industrial injury, and the right to collective bargaining.

6. SHA, Moscow, C67/D2192, EMA-2 renseignement, "Organisation de la propagande communiste dans les colonies," 5 June 1936.

7. SHA, 7N71333/D6, EMA Section d'Outre-Mer, "Synthèse de renseignements intéressant l'Afrique du Nord, mois de décembre 1936."

8. Reports from the Algiers SR office formed the basis for fortnightly North African political intelligence assessments compiled by the War Ministry deuxième bureau: SHA, Moscow, C388/D132: Renseignements Afrique du Nord, 1937–38.

9. "Manifeste de l'Etoile Nord-Africaine, 1928," in *Messali Hadj par les textes*, ed. Jacques Simon (Paris: Éditions Bouchène, 2000), doc. 3.

10. SHA, 7N4133/D4, EMA Section d'Outre-Mer, "Note au sujet de l'association 'L'Étoile Nord Africaine' et son président Massali Hadj," 22 June 1936.

11. SHA, 7N71333/D6, EMA Section d'Outre-Mer, "Synthèse de renseignements intéressant l'Afrique du Nord, mois de décembre 1936."

12. SHA, 7N4133/D4, no. 4177, Edouard Daladier letter to Direction du contrôle de la compatabilité et des affaires algériennes, 24 December 1936.

13. SHA, Moscow, C878/D998, SR (Algiers), "Les Ulémas d'Algérie, Chekib Arslan et l'Etoile Nord-Africaine," 7 Dec. 1936; SHA, 7N4093, no. 1754/EMA-2, "Bulletin de renseignements des questions musulmanes," 10 May 1937.

14. John Damis, "The Free-School Phenomenon: The Cases of Algeria and Tunisia," *International Journal of Middle East Studies* 5 (1974): 440–41. The three leading figures of the Association of Reformist 'Ulamā all came from eastern Algeria: Ben Bādīs from Constantine, Bashir al-Ibrahimi from Sétif, and Tayyib al-Uqbi from Biskra.

15. SHA, Moscow, C878/D998, SR (Algiers), "Les Ulémas d'Algérie, Chekib Arslan et l'Etoile Nord-Africaine," 7 Dec. 1936; Sûreté nationale report, "Activité de l'Emir Chekib Arslan," 14 May 1937.

16. Charles-Robert Ageron, "Une émeute anti-juive à Constantine (août 1934)," *Revue de l'Occident Musulman et de la Méditerranée* 3 (1973): 23–40.

17. As an example: SHA, Moscow, C1109/D667, no. 1978/G, SEA: Renseignement Algérie, "Bruits de révolte indigène dans le département de Constantine," 3 January 1934.

18. SHA, Moscow, C388/D132, 19e Corps d'Armée, EMA-2, bulletin de renseignements no. 20, 14 Aug. 1937; "Compte-rendu de quinzaine," 19 August 1937.

19. SHA, Moscow, C930/D680, SEA, "Propagande et influence des ulémas à Tlemcen et en Oranie," 4 March 1936.

20. SHA, Moscow, C930/D680, SEA, "Renseignement Algérie: enseignement des oulémas," 4 July 1935; SEA report, "Association pour la conservation du Coran," 13 September 1935.

21. Damis, "Free-School Phenomenon," 443–44.

22. SHA, Moscow, C223/D122, SCR, "A/S, réunion annuelle des ulémas," 11 October 1935.

23. James McDougall, *History and the Culture of Nationalism in Algeria* (Cambridge: Cambridge University Press, 2006), 97–98; Damis, "Free-School Phenomenon," 441–42. John Damis calculates that the total number of free schools in Algeria was closer to one hundred by the end of 1935, and by 1938 a further 150 cultural associations were affiliated with the Koranic schools in some way.

24. SHA, 7N4133, EMA Section d'Outre-Mer, "Synthèse de renseignements," 1 December 1936.

25. According to the Algiers SR, living standards were all that the peasantry cared about: SHA, Moscow, C1109/C667, SEA, "Note sur la situation indigène dans le département d'Oran," 14 January 1935.

26. SHA, Moscow, C223/D122, SEA report, "Situation des indigènes en Kabylie," 16 April 1935.

27. SHA, Moscow, C223/D122, Commandant Delor (SEA) to Colonel Rivet, 22 May 1935.

28. SHA, Moscow, C1109/C667, SEA note, "Collision entre la police et les partisans de Messali," n.d. [September 1937].

29. SHA, Moscow, C223/D122, no. 191/K, SEA, "Renseignement autour du projet Violette [sic]," 23 January 1937.

30. SHA, Moscow, C223/D122, no. 299/K, SEA, "A/S du projet de loi Viollette pour l'attribution des droits politiques aux indigènes," 5 February 1937.

31. SHA, Moscow, C223/D122, no. 191/K, SEA, "Renseignement autour du projet Violette [sic]," 23 January 1937.

32. SHA, Moscow, C1109/D669, SEA, "Note sur la question tunisienne, 16 décembre 1934."

33. Ibid., "SCR note sur le fonctionnement du contre-espionnage en Tunisie," 3 January 1935.

34. Marcel Peyrouton, Du service public à la prison commune. Souvenirs: Tunis, Rabat, Buenos Aires, Vichy, Alger, Frèsnes (Paris: Plon, 1950), 48.

35. TNA, FO 371/19872, C292/292/17, Sir H. Satow (Tunis) to FO, 9 January 1936. The ringleader of this Communist cell was a certain M. Dupont, an employee of the Sidi Abdullah arsenal in Tunis.

36. CAOM, Marius Moutet Papers, PA28/1/D1, sous-dossier C: "Notes sur les réalisations d'ordre politique du ministère, 1936–7"; Peter Zinoman, The Colonial Bastille: A History of Imprisonment in Vietnam, 1862–1940 (Berkeley and Los Angeles: University of California Press, 2001), 267–78.

37. TNA, FO 371/19872, C4299/292/17, Satow (Tunis) to FO, 5 June 1936.

38. TNA, FO 371/19872, C6045/292/17, Vibert (Tunis) to FO, 18 August 1936. These measures were introduced during the week of August 7–11.

39. TNA, FO 371/19872, C6362/292/17, Satow (Tunis) to FO, 4 September 1936, citing figures from La Dépêche tunisienne.

40. TNA, FO 371/19872, C6635/292/17, Satow to FO, 19 September 1936. Bourguiba publicly affirmed that there was no question of "throwing the French into the sea."

41. TNA, FO 371/19872, C7009/292/17, Satow to FO, 2 October 1936.

42. Charles-André Julien, L'Afrique du Nord en marche: Algérie-Tunisie-Maroc, 1880–1952 (Paris: Julliard, 1952; reprint, Paris: Omnibus, 2002), 81.

43. TNA, FO 371/20695, C2224/238/17, Satow (Tunis) to FO, 8 March 1937.

44. TNA, FO 371/20695, C5254/238/17, Consul Knight (Tunis) to FO, 16 July 1937.

45. MAE, série P: Tunisie 1917–1940, vol. 388, "Note sur les principaux incidents survenus en Tunisie depuis le mois de mars 1937."

46. SHA, Moscow, C223/D122, no. 1720/K, "Renseignement Tunisie: Nouveau journal en langue arabe" ["Source: Très bonne"], 10 August 1937.

47. "L'exposé de M. Albert Sarraut sur l'Afrique du Nord," Le Temps, 28 November 1937.

48. It seems reasonable to conclude from their previous and subsequent actions that Sûreté, SR, and SCR personnel sympathized with settler outrage at Guillon's

conciliatory policies; see TNA, FO 371/19872, C7009/292/17, Satow to FO, 2 October 1936.

49. SHA, Moscow, C133/D1526, General Hanote to Préfet maritime, 4ᵉ région, 1 December 1937.

50. SHA, Moscow, C133/D1526, SR (Algiers), "Renseignement—Tunisie," 27 December 1937.

51. SHA, Moscow, C133/D1526, no. 2497/K, SEA, "Alger—renseignement Tunisie," 26 November 1937. The SR also kept track of extensive arms smuggling from Italian Ethiopia and Somaliland across the Red Sea to Yemen; see SHA, Moscow, C133/D1524.

52. SHA, Moscow, C133/D1526, no. 1473, CSTT, EMA-2/SCR report to deuxième bureau, 27 December 1937; no. 530, Paul Paillole report to SR Direction des services militaires, 26 January 1938.

53. William A. Hoisington Jr., *The Casablanca Connection: French Colonial Policy, 1936–1943* (Chapel Hill: University of North Carolina Press, 1984), 44–51.

54. MAE, série M, vol. 92, no. 1610, Direction des affaires politiques report, "Situation politique et économique, (période du 17 au 23 juillet 1937)," sent to Foreign Ministry, 5 August 1937.

55. Regarding the shift in political protest from countryside to town in Morocco, see Gwendolyn Wright, *The Politics of Design in French Colonial Urbanism* (Chicago: University of Chicago Press, 1991), 301–3.

56. Hoisington, *Casablanca Connection*, 55–60.

57. Moroccan smallholders who bought cheap land in the depression years were widely seen as a bedrock of rural conservatism; see E. Joffé, "The Moroccan Nationalist Movement," *Journal of African History* 26 (1985): 296–99.

58. MAE, série M, vol. 92, no. 1787, Direction des affaires politiques report, "Situation politique et économique, (période du 7 au 13 août 1937)," sent to Foreign Ministry, 31 August 1937. Letters sent to the sultan's palace by "local sections of the nationalist party" were published in the Party newspaper, *L'Action Marocaine,* on 7 August 1937.

59. TNA, FO 371/21589, Rabat Consulate, "Morocco, Economic (B) Report," 22 September 1938.

60. MAE, série Maroc, vol. 92, no. 1977, Direction des affaires politiques report, "Situation politique et économique (période du 28 août au 10 septembre 1937)," sent to Foreign Ministry, 11 October 1937.

61. SHA, 7N4093, no. 3337, EMA-2, Bulletin de renseignements des questions musulmanes, 11 September 1937. Fifty-two members of the security forces were injured, two of them by gunfire.

62. Hoisington, *Casablanca Connection*, 61–73.

63. SHA, Moscow, C223/D123, "Bulletin mensuel de press indigène d'Algérie, Octobre 1937," sent by Commandant Le Forestier de Quillen to Colonet Rivet, 10 December 1937.

64. SHA, Moscow, C223/D123, Préfecture d'Oran, Centre d'informations et d'études, "Bulletin mensuel d'informations: la politique indigène dans le Département d'Oran," 1 October 1937.

65. SHA, Moscow, C223/D123, 19ᵉ Corps d'Armée, 2ᵉ Bureau, "Compte-rendu (2ᵉ quinzaine d'Août)."

66. Ibid.

67. SHA, Moscow, C223/D123, SEA memo, "Les elections indigènes au Conseil Général dans le Département d'Alger," 27 October 1937. There was less violence in the western department of Oran; see C223/D123, no. 258, Oran prefecture centre d'informations et d'études, "Bulletin mensuel d'informations concernant la politique indigène dans le Département d'Oran," 1 October 1937.

68. SHA, Moscow, C280/D140, no. 1802, Commandant Delor, SEA, to Colonel Rivet, "L'activité indigène dans le département d'Alger," 11 July 1938.

69. SHA, Moscow, C280/D140, no. 3136/B, Captain Clipet, SEA, to Colonel Rivet, "L'activité indigène dans le département d'Alger, mois d'octobre 1938," 18 November 1938.

70. SHA, Moscow, C223/D123, 19e Corps d'Armée, 2e Bureau, "Compte-rendu, 1e quinzaine d'Avril 1938."

71. SHA, Moscow, C194/D134, no. 59/C, SEA report to SCR (Paris), 30 August 1939.

72. SHA, Moscow, C223/D123, 19e Corps d'Armée, 2e Bureau, "Compte-rendu, 1e quinzaine d'Avril 1938."

73. TNA, FO 371/21590, Tunis Consulate dispatches 39 and 48 to FO, 30 March and 11 April 1938.

74. Julien, *L'Afrique du Nord en marche*, 83–84.

75. MAE, série Tunisie, 1944–1955, vol. 300, Section Afrique-Levant memo, "Habib Bourguiba," n.d. [1951]; TNA, FO 371/21590, Tunis consulate dispatch, 22 August 1938. Tunisian political groups were required to register as legal associations with a written commitment to abide by the protectorate treaty.

76. TNA, FO 371/22920, C5495/226/17, Knight (Tunis) to FO, 14 April 1939.

77. TNA, FO 371/22920, C2409/226/17, Consul-General W. Knight (Tunis) to FO, 21 February 1939.

78. TNA, FO 371/22920, C8390/226/17, Knight (Tunis) to FO, 6 June 1939. It had been widely expected among Tunisia's urban elite that Albert Lebrun's reelection to the French presidency might provide the opportunity for a more comprehensive amnesty of North African political prisoners.

79. SHA, 7N4133/D4, no. 3539, EMA, Section d'Afrique et d'Orient note, 10 December 1926.

80. SHA, 7N4133/D4, no. 43469/EMA, Section d'Outre-Mer, "Note sur l'état d'esprit des militaires indigènes nord africains en 1937," 26 September 1938.

81. SHA, Moscow, C464/D180, no. 15947–5, SCR report, "Vade mecum du chef des services spéciaux de l'armée," 9 June 1940.

82. CAOM, Algiers Department archives, F111/D1, no. 7863, Algiers police spéciale, divisional commissioner's report, 28 August 1939.

83. CAOM, Algiers Department archives, F111/D1, no. 8044, Police départementale, report by agents Keddar and Akli, 2 September 1939.

84. TNA, FO 371/23279, E4276/347/89, Beirut Consulate, "Annual report, Economic (A), on Syria and the Lebanon for 1938," sent to Foreign Office on 16 May 1939.

85. Regarding Palestine, see Philip S. Khoury, "Divided Loyalties? Syria and the Question of Palestine, 1919–39," *Middle Eastern Studies* 21, no. 3 (1985): 324–48. For a wider Middle East perspective, see Basheer M. Nafi, *Arabism, Nationalism and the*

Palestine Question, 1908–1941 (Reading: Ithaca Press, 1998); and James Jankowski, "Egyptian Responses to the Palestine Problem in the Interwar Period," *International Journal of Middle East Studies* 12, no. 1 (1980): 1–38.

86. *BDFA*, II: B, vol. 12, doc. 55, Robert Parr (Aleppo), "Memorandum on the Interdependence of the Outbreaks in Syria and Palestine during 1936," 20 August 1936; doc. 56, F. C. Ogden (Damascus), "Reactions in the Damascus District to the Palestine Disturbances," 21 August 1936.

87. TNA, FO 371/23279, E4276/347/89, enclosure, Beirut consulate, "Annual Report, Economic (A), on Syria and the Lebanon for 1938," sent to Foreign Office, 16 May 1939.

88. SHA, Moscow, C581/D371, SEL report, "Aspect politique de la question du Sandjak," 16 January 1937.

89. SHA, Moscow, C133/D1526, SEL reports, "Distribution de munitions par les autorités turques," 25 November 1937, and "Proche Orient—contrebande des armes," n.d. [November 1937].

90. Keith D. Watenpaugh, "'Creating Phantoms': Zaki al-Arsuzi, the Alexandretta Crisis and the Formation of Modern Arab Nationalism in Syria," *International Journal of Middle East Studies* 28 (1996): 366, 369–70. French figures from 1936 indicated that only 39 percent of the *sanjak*'s 220,000 inhabitants were "ethnic Turks," while Arabic speakers constituted 46 percent.

91. Philip S. Khoury, *Syria and the French Mandate: The Politics of Arab Nationalism, 1920–1945* (Princeton, N.J.: Princeton University Press, 1987); Jacques Thobie, "Le nouveau cours des relations franco-turques et l'affaire du sandjak d'Alexandrette, 1921–1939," *Relations Internationales* 19 (autumn 1979): 355–74; Martin Thomas, "Imperial Defence or Diversionary Attack? Anglo-French Strategic Planning in the Near East, 1936–40," in *Anglo-French Defence Relations between the Wars*, ed. Martin S. Alexander and William J. Philpott (London: Palgrave/Macmillan, 2003), 168–72. For a Turkish perspective, see Yücel Güçlü, *The Question of the Sanjak of Alexandretta: A Study of French-Turkish-Syrian Relations* (Ankara: Turkish Historical Society, 2001).

92. SHA, Moscow, C581/D371, SEL report ["Source bien placée"], "Situation dans le Nord-Syrie," 27 January 1937.

93. TNA, FO 371/23279, E4276/347/89, enclosure, Beirut consulate, "Annual Report, Economic (A), on Syria and the Lebanon for 1938," sent to Foreign Office, 16 May 1939.

94. CADN, Fonds Beyrouth, Cabinet politique, vol. 477/D1, Cabinet politique memo, "Comparaison entre les divers traits intervenus dans le Proche Orient," n.d. [1936].

95. *BDFA*, II: B, vol. 11, docs. 195 and 207, Sudan Agency (Cairo), "Memorandum Respecting the Pan-Arab Islamic Movement" (in two parts), 14 February 1936.

96. On popular nationalism in Faysal's Syria, see Gelvin, *Divided Loyalties: Nationalism and Mass Politics in Syria at the Close of Empire* (Berkeley and Los Angeles: University of California Press, 1998).

97. TNA, CO 831/37/1, TC/10/36, Amman Residency, "Report on the Political Situation for the Month of January 1936," 5 February 1936.

98. Khoury, *Syria and the French Mandate*, 458–67.

99. *BDFA*, II: B, vol. 12, doc. 34, MacKereth (Damascus) to FO, 27 October

1936; doc. 36, FO Eastern Department, "Main Provisions in the Franco-Syrian Treaty," 6 November 1936.

100. CADN, Fonds Beyrouth, Cabinet politique, vol. 481, no. 541/CP, Damas délégué report to Cabinet politique, Haut Commissariat, 1 April 1936.

101. TNA, FO 371/23276, Syria political report no. 6, 28 December 1938.

102. TNA, FO 371/23276, dispatch no. 4., A. W. Davis (Aleppo) to FO, 11 January 1939.

103. TNA, FO 371/23279, E7571/347/89, Consul-General Havard (Beirut) to FO, "Annual Report, Economic (B), for 1939," 8 November 1939.

104. CAOM, 8H61/D1, President Albert Lebrun letter to Albert Sarraut, 9 January 1937.

105. CAOM, 8H61/D1, HCM March 1937 session, report 1: "Organismes d'information musulmane"; see also report 5: "Le régime administrative en Afrique du Nord."

106. CAOM, 8H61/D1, HCM March 1937 session, report 2: "Les grands courants d'opinion dans l'Islam nord-africain."

107. CAOM, 8H61/D1, HCM March 1937 session, report 3: "Les nords-africains en France."

108. CAOM, 8H61/D1, HCM March 1937 session, report 4: "Les Assemblées élues en Afrique du Nord," n.d. [March 1937].

109. AN, F60202, HCM report no. 1, "Le Haut Comité Méditerranéen et les organismes d'information musulmane," 9 March 1937. The minutes of the Committee's March 1937 and March sessions indicate that Julien was the driving force behind the decisions made.

110. Marc Lagana, "L'échec de la commission d'enquête coloniale du Front Populaire," *Historical Reflections* 16, no. 1 (1989): 79–97.

111. For a good summary of the committee's troubled history, see William A. William A. Hoisington Jr., "The Mediterranean Committee and French North Africa, 1935–1940," *The Historian* 53, no. 2 (1991): 255–66.

112. AN, F60202, Haut Comité Méditerranéen rapport no. 1, "Le Haut Comité Méditerranéen et les organismes d'information musulmane," 9 March 1937.

113. SHA, Moscow, C464/D174, "Rapport du mission du Commandant Schlesser, Mars–Avril 1938."

114. It is worth noting that the Algiers SR was also concerned about the activities of Britain's Secret Intelligence Service station in Valletta, Malta, which was particularly active in the Maghreb: SHA, Moscow, C230/D107, SEA, "Renseignement: Malte, Services Spéciaux Britanniques," 12 March 1937.

115. SHA, Moscow, C223/D123. The file contains the largest number of SCR reports on German agent activity in the Maghreb and analyses of German press claims for colonial restitution. See, for example, SCR renseignement, "Agitation allemande en Afrique du Nord," 6 January 1938 ["Source: Bonne"].

116. See, for instance, SHA, Moscow, C223/D123, EMA Section d'Outre-Mer, "Note au sujet des agissements allemands en Afrique du Nord," 3 May 1935. Such reports tended to focus on German consular activity, anti-French articles in the German press, Nazi propaganda regarding Muslim populations living under colonial rule, and desertions among colonial and Foreign Legion troops.

117. For successes achieved, see Paul Paillole, *Services Spéciaux, 1935–1945* (Paris: Robert Lafont, 1975).

118. SHAA, 2B43, EMA-5, SCR memo, "Quelques procès d'espionnage en 1937," n.d.

119. MAE, Série K: Afrique 1918–1940, sous-série: Défense Nationale, vol. 31, Défense Nationale, "Note sur le contre-espionnage en Tunisie." 1 March 1933.

120. SHA, Moscow, C467/D132, Compte-rendu de mission de Capitaine Paillole, "Observations générales sur les manoeuvres du Sud-Est et du Sud-Ouest," 12 September 1936. Regarding Paillole's wartime career, see Simon Kitson, *Vichy et la chasse aux espions nazis, 1940–1942* (Paris: Éditions Autrement, 2005), 54, 77–97, 127–40 passim.

121. SHA, C463/D64, Algiers government-general, "Arrêté—CE Algérie," 12 January 1938.

122. SHA, Moscow, C623/D1419, EMA-2 note, "Création de brigades de contre-espionnage," 15 April 1938; General Caillault (Beirut) to EMA-2, "Organisation du contre-espionnage," 25 April 1939.

123. SHA, Moscow, C464/D174, "Rapport du mission du Commandant Schlesser: Le problème du contre-espionnage en Afrique du Nord," March–April 1938.

124. SHA, C464/D174, "Rapport du mission du Commandant Schlesser, Mars–Avril 1938: Note sur la situation politique générale en Tunisie," 1 March 1938.

125. MAE, Série K: Afrique, sous-série: Défense Nationale, vol. 31, EMA 2ᵉ Bureau to Sous-direction d'Afrique, "A/S Contre-espionnage en Tunisie," 5 July 1932.

126. MAE, Série K: Afrique, sous-série: Défense Nationale, vol. 31, no. 368, Navy Ministry 2ᵉ Bureau to Foreign Ministry Sous-direction d'Afrique, 31 August 1932.

127. Regarding the evolution of Mussolini's Mediterranean strategy and French responses to it, see Reynolds M. Salerno, *Vital Crossroads: Mediterranean Origins of the Second World War, 1935–1940* (Ithaca, N.Y.: Cornell University Press, 2002).

128. MAE, Série K: Afrique, sous-série: Défense Nationale, vol. 31, EMA 2ᵉ Bureau to Sous-direction d'Afrique, "A/S contre-espionnage en Tunisie," 5 July 1932.

129. MAE, Série K: Afrique, sous-série: Défense Nationale, vol. 31, "Instruction sur le contre-espionnage et la surveillance du territoire Tunisien en temps de paix," sent to Foreign Ministry, 24 May 1933.

130. Serge La Berbera, *Les Français de Tunisie (1930–1950)* (Paris: l'Harmattan, 2006), 114–16, 133–38.

131. TNA, FO 371/19872, C292/292/17, Sir H. Satow (Tunis) to FO, 9 January 1936.

132. MAE, Série K: Afrique, sous-série: Défense Nationale, vol. 31, Protectorat Français Régence de Tunis, "Instruction sur le contre-espionnage et la surveillance du territoire Tunisien en temps de paix," sent to Foreign Ministry, 24 May 1933.

133. SHA, Moscow, C194/D134, no. 59/C, SEA report to SCR, 30 August 1939; C306/D424, CLR (Rabat), "Renseignement, Maroc Espagnol: Activité Allemande" [Source: "Bien placée"], 4 July 1939.

134. SHA, Moscow, C552/D1426, no. 1542/BCR2, EMA-2 note, "Relations entre le 2ᵉ Bureau de l'État-Major des Troupes de Tunisie et le service de la Sûreté Tunisienne," 17 December 1937.

135. SHA, Moscow, Dossier relatif à l'organisation des services de contre-espionnage 1932-1936: Note sur le fonctionnement des services de contre-espionnage.

136. SHA, Moscow, C873/D2007, Général Caillault note de service no. 2143/BCR, 6 May 1940.

137. SHA, Moscow, Archives SCR, Ministry of Interior and War Ministry joint instruction, "Instruction sur le Service des Renseignements du Ministère de la Guerre et sur le concours prêté aux officiers de ce service par les fonctionnaires de la Sûreté Générale," 1 October 1924.

138. SHA, Moscow, CC464/D174, SCR note, "Création de brigades de contre-espionnage," 25 March 1938.

139. SHA, C464/D174, no. 1785, Direction de la sécurité publique (Rabat), "Réorganisation du service de surveillance du territoire et des étrangers," 1 March 1938.

140. SHA, Moscow, C464/D174, "Rapport du mission du Commandant Schlesser, Mars-Avril 1938: Note sur le problème du renseignement en Afrique du Nord."

141. Regina M. Delacor, "From Potential Friends to Potential Enemies: The Internment of 'Hostile Foreigners' in France at the Beginning of the Second World War," *Journal of Contemporary History* 35, no. 3 (2000): 366n30.

142. Ibid., 361-68.

143. SHA, Moscow, C194/D134, General A. Blanc to War Ministry, 9 September 1939.

144. SHA, Moscow, C280/D140, no. 509, DST, Algérie, "Rapport hebdomadaire de la répercussion de la situation internationale sur les populations algériennes," 4 October 1938.

145. "L'Afrique du Nord et la Guerre," 215-19.

146. TNA, FO 371/22920, C13153/226/17, Knight (Tunis) to FO, 7 September 1939.

147. SHA, Moscow, C223/D122, no. 5535/G, SEA renseignement, "État d'esprit des indigènes en Algérie pendant la guerre, 1914-1918."

148. CAOM, Algiers department files, F111/D1, no. 8045, Divisional commissioner (Algiers), "Rapport: mobilisation générale," 2 September 1939.

149. CAOM, Gouvernement Général d'Algérie (GGA), 9H32, Direction de la sécurité générale (Algiers), "Rapport hebdomadaire," 16 September 1939.

150. SHA, Moscow, C280/D140, no. 4365/B, SEA, "Renseignement—Algérie, mobilisation et état d'esprit des indigènes en Kabylie," 29 September 1939.

151. CAOM, Gouvernement Général d'Algérie (GGA), 9H32, Direction de la sécurité générale (Algiers), "Rapport hebdomadaire," 23 and 30 September 1939.

152. SHA, Moscow, C467/D135, "Compte-rendu: Mission effectuée par le Capitaine Paillole à Alger du 6 à 10 Octobre 1939." Paillole conducted another, longer inspection of counterespionage services in Algeria and Morocco in April 1940; see C467/D136, "Compte-rendu de la mission effectuée par le Capitaine Paillole en Algérie et au Maroc du 13 au 26 Avril 1940."

153. CAOM, Gouvernement Général d'Algérie (GGA), 9H32, Direction de la sécurité générale (Algiers), "Rapport hebdomadaire," 10 October 1939.

154. CAOM, Gouvernement Général d'Algérie (GGA), 9H32, Direction de la sécurité générale (Algiers), "Rapport hebdomadaire," 30 September 1939.

155. TNA, FO 371/22920, C15212/226/17, Knight (Tunis) to FO, 22 September 1939.

156. TNA, FO 371/22920, C15835/226/17, Knight (Tunis) to FO, 3 October 1939.

157. Ibid.

158. TNA, FO 371/22920, C17715/226/17, Knight (Tunis) to FO, 31 October 1939.

159. TNA, FO 371/22920, C16691/226/17, Knight (Tunis) to FO, 3 October 1939.

160. Ibid.

161. TNA, FO 371/22920, C20118/226/17, Knight (Tunis) to FO, 6 December 1939.

162. SHA, Moscow, C280/D142, nos. 3397 and 3830, SEA, Notes de renseignements—Tunisie, "État d'esprit de la population indigène," 7 February and 13 March 1940.

163. TNA, FO 371/23279, E7571/347/89, Consul-General Havard (Beirut) to FO, "Annual Report, Economic (B), for 1939," 8 November 1939.

164. TNA, FO 371/23276, Damascus Consulate, "Political Report—Syria, no. 12," 18 February 1939.

165. TNA, FO 371/23276, Damascus Consulate, "Political Report—Syria, no. 15," 22 March 1939.

166. TNA, FO 371/23279, E7571/347/89, Consul-General Havard (Beirut) to FO, "Annual Report, Economic (B), for 1939," 8 November 1939.

167. SHA, 7N4194/EMA-2, Afrique du Nord, synthèse de renseignements no. 6, "L'intervention étrangère dans la guerre civile espagnole," n.d. [December 1936]; N224/D2, CSDN "Note sur l'importance stratégique de l'Espagne," 24 April 1938.

168. SHA, 2N227/D3, EMA-2, General Noiret report, "Importance de l'ensemble Espagne, Maroc Espagnol, Baléares sur le théâtre d'opérations éventuels en Méditerranée," 25 April 1938. Regarding French intelligence assessments of the strategic importance of the Spanish civil war more generally, see Peter Jackson, "French Strategy and the Spanish Civil War," in *Spain in an International Context, 1936–1959,* ed. Christian Leitz and David J. Dunthorn (Oxford: Berg, 1999), 55–79.

169. TNA, ADM 116/3398, copy of French naval staff memo, "Situation des bâtiments français en Méditerranée," 22 November 1935.

170. Henri Navarre et al., *Le Service de Renseignements, 1871–1944* (Paris: Plon, 1978), 118.

171. SHA, 2N24/Comité Permanent de la Défense Nationale minutes, 8 December 1937; regarding French preparations for war in the Mediterranean, see Salerno, *Vital Crossroads,* chapters 1–4.

172. SHA, Moscow, C223/D123, 19ᵉ Corps d'Armée, 2ᵉ Bureau, "Compte-rendu, 1ᵉ quinzaine de Décembre 1937." Not all members of the Federation of elected Muslims were so compliant. In Tlemcen, for instance, elections were held in February 1938 to find replacements for twelve Federation councilors who resigned between August and October 1937 over the failure of suffrage reform; see C223/D123, no. 115, Préfecture d'Oran, Centre d'informations et d'études, "Bul-

letin mensuel d'informations concernant la politique indigène dans le Département d'Oran," 2 March 1938.

CONCLUSION

1. G. John Ikenberry, *After Victory: Institutions, Strategic Restraint, and the Rebuilding of Order after Major Wars* (Princeton, N.J.: Princeton University Press, 2001), 4–5, 118–19.

2. David Fromkin, *A Peace to End All Peace: Creating the Modern Middle East, 1914–1922* (New York: Henry Holt, 1989); John Darwin, *Britain, Egypt and the Middle East: Imperial Policy in the Aftermath of War, 1918–1922* (London: Macmillan, 1981); Eliezer Tauber, *The Formation of Modern Syria and Iraq* (London: Frank Cass, 1995).

3. Robert Gilpin, *War and Change in World Politics* (Cambridge: Cambridge University Press, 1981), 41–44; also cited in Ikenberry, *After Victory*, 5.

4. Ann Stoler, "Perceptions of Protest: Defining the Dangerous in Colonial Sumatra," *American Ethnologist* 12, no. 4 (1985): 642–58.

5. Colin Newbury, *Patrons, Clients, and Empire: Chieftaincy and Over-Rule in Asia, Africa, and the Pacific* (Oxford: Oxford University Press, 2003), 269–71.

6. Ted Swedenburg, "The Role of the Palestinian Peasantry in the Great Revolt (1936–1939)," in *Islam, Politics, and Social Movements*, ed. Edmund Burke III and Ira M. Lapidus (Berkeley and Los Angeles: University of California Press, 1988), 169–203.

7. CAOM, GGA, 11H46, Algiers Service des affaires indigènes: Rapports politiques périodiques, 1918–21.

8. See, for example, CAOM, GGA, 11H46, Algiers Direction des affaires indigènes, "Rapport mensuel sur la situation politique des indigènes, juillet 1918." The report noted that the success of the 1918 tax collection depended on the quality of that year's harvest.

9. SHA, 7N4192, Comité Consultatif de la Défense des Colonies, Manuel colonial 1923–1925, 31 January 1925.

10. The literature on French colonial urbanism is extensive. The regulation of urban space in interwar North Africa is discussed in Janet Abu-Lughod, *Rabat: Urban Apartheid in Morocco* (Princeton, N.J.: Princeton University Press, 1980); Paul Rabinow, *French Modern: Norms and Forms of the Social Environment* (Chicago: University of Chicago Press, 1989); David Prochaska, *Making Algeria French: Colonialism in Bône, 1870–1920* (Cambridge: Cambridge University Press, 1990); Gwendolyn Wright, *The Politics of Design in French Colonial Urbanism* (Chicago: University of Chicago Press, 1991); Zeynep Çelik, *Urban Forms and Colonial Confrontations: Algiers under French Rule* (Berkeley and Los Angeles: University of California Press, 1997); Allan Christelow, "The Mosque at the Edge of the Plaza: Islam in the Algerian Colonial City," *Maghreb Review* 25, nos. 3–4 (2000): 289–308; and Shirine Hamadeh, "Creating the Traditional City," in *Forms of Dominance: On the Architecture and Urbanism of the Colonial Enterprise*, ed. Nezar Al Sayyad (Avebury: Ashgate, 1992), 241–59.

11. Hence, in Lebanon and Syria, where cinemas provided a convenient meeting point for political groups and an obvious forum in which to subvert the supremacy of French culture generally portrayed on screen, the police spéciale kept a close watch on audience behavior. The censors determined what films and newsreel footage could be shown, but the secret police still found it necessary to monitor

audience reaction; see Elizabeth Thompson, *Colonial Citizens: Republican Rights, Paternal Privilege, and Gender in French Syria and Lebanon* (New York: Columbia University Press, 2000), 200–201.

12. A point made in Antony Best, *British Intelligence and the Japanese Challenge in Asia, 1914–1941* (London: Palgrave-Macmillan 2002), 2.

13. Shearer, "Elements Near and Alien: Passportization, Policing, and Identity in the Stalinist State, 1932–1952," *Journal of Modern History* 76, no. 4 (2004): 835–81; Sheila Fitzpatrick, "Ascribing Class: The Construction of Social Identity in Soviet Russia," *Journal of Modern History* 65, no. 4 (1993): 745–70; John Torpey, "An Analysis of Passport Controls in the French, Russian, and Chinese Revolutions," *Theory and Society* 26 (1997): 837–68. For insight into the scale of the Soviet Union's interwar repression of insurgency in its Muslim republics, see Bruce Grant, "An Average Azeri Village (1930): Remembering Rebellion in the Caucasus Mountains," *Slavic Review* 63, no. 4 (2004): 705–31.

14. Christopher Dandeker, *Surveillance, Power and Modernity: Bureaucracy and Discipline from 1700 to the Present Day* (London: Polity Press, 1990), 4–29.

15. Peter Jackson, "Historical Reflections on the Uses and Limits of Intelligence," in *Intelligence and Statecraft: The Use and Limits of Intelligence in International Society*, ed. Peter Jackson and Jennifer Siegel (Westport, Conn.: Praeger, 2005), 13.

16. Ibid., 14.

17. Ibid., 15.

18. Ibid., 17–18.

19. On contingency, cultural bias, and warning failures, see Steve Chan, "The Intelligence of Stupidity: Understanding Failures in Strategic Warning," *American Political Science Review* 73, no. 1 (1979): 172–73.

20. TNA, FO 406/72, E1422/1170/93, Sir Francis Humphrys to Sir John Simon, 22 February 1934.

21. Ibid.

22. SHA, Moscow, C223/D122, SEA report, "Note sur les conditions psychologiques d'une mobilisation générale en Algérie (Mai 1935)."

23. Pierre H. Boulle and D. Gillian Thompson, "France Overseas," in *Old Regime France*, ed. William Doyle (Oxford: Oxford University Press, 2001), 106–7, 121.

24. Killearn papers, *1936 Diary*, Cabinet conversations, 5 and 23 June 1936; Michael J. Cohen, *Palestine, Retreat from the Mandate: The Making of British Policy, 1936–1945* (London: Paul Elek, 1978), 1–4; David Omissi, "The Mediterranean and the Middle East in British Global Strategy, 1935–39," in *Britain and the Middle East in the 1930s: Security Problems*, ed. Michael J. Cohen and Martin Kolinsky (London: Macmillan, 1992), 3–20.

25. James Jankowski, "Egyptian Responses to the Palestine Problem in the Interwar Period," *International Journal of Middle East Studies* 12 (1980): 1–38; Haggai Erlich, "British Internal Security and Egyptian Youth," in *Britain and the Middle East in the 1930s: Security Problems*, ed. Michael J. Cohen and Martin Kolinsky (London: Macmillan, 1992), 104–7. See also Philip S. Khoury, "Divided Loyalties? Syria and the Question of Palestine, 1919–39," *Middle Eastern Studies* 21, no. 3 (1985): 324–48.

26. See, for example, the correspondence on Britain's strategic position in the Middle East in TNA, WO 106/2018A, Notes on tour of Egypt and Palestine by CIGS, January–February 1939; WO 201/262, Sudan: General defense questions, 1937–

39; FO 371/23201, E2628/72/93, Houstoun Boswell (Baghdad) to Foreign Office, 10 April 1939. For background, see James Jankowski, "Egyptian Regional Policy in the Wake of the Anglo-Egyptian Treaty of 1936: Arab Alliance or Islamic Caliphate?" and Liora Lukitz, "Axioms Reconsidered: The Rethinking of British Strategic Policy in Iraq during the 1930s," both in *Britain and the Middle East in the 1930s: Security Problems,* ed. Michael J. Cohen and Martin Kolinsky (London: Macmillan, 1992), 81–88, 119–21.

27. See, for example, SHA, Moscow, C609/D374, SCR summary report, "Activité communiste en territoires sous mandat français," 12 April 1940.

28. Martin Thomas, "At the Heart of Things? French Imperial Defense Planning in the Late 1930s," *French Historical Studies* 21, no. 2 (1998): 325–61.

29. Work on the "Singapore strategy" is immense. Good discussions of the strategic dilemma involved are W. David McIntyre, *The Rise and Fall of the Singapore Naval Base* (London: Macmillan, 1979); Wesley K. Wark, "In Search of a Suitable Japan: British Naval Intelligence in the Pacific before the Second World War," *Intelligence and National Security* 1, no. 2 (1986): 189–212; Malcolm Murfett, "Living in the Past: A Critical Re-examination of the Singapore Naval Strategy, 1918–1941," *War and Society* 11 (May 1993): 73–103; Ian Cowman, *Dominion or Decline: Anglo-American Naval Relations in the Pacific, 1937–1941* (Oxford: Berg, 1997); and Christopher M. Bell, "The 'Singapore Strategy' and the Deterrence of Japan: Winston Churchill, the Admiralty and the Dispatch of Force Z," *English Historical Review* 114, no. 662 (2001): 604–34.

30. See, for example, TNA, AIR 20/678, "Intelligence organization," 26 March 1936, and "Notes on the Intelligence Organization in the Sudan," n.d. [1936].

31. TNA, CO 926/1/1 and CO 926/1/4, Anti-British propaganda/Mediterranean: Colonial Office summaries of German and Italian Arabic broadcasts during 1938 and 1939. Regarding the Levant SR, see SHA, Moscow, C878/D998, SCR report, "Activité étrangère," 31 July 1937; C873/D2006, SEL report, "Activité de la propagande italienne en Syrie," 8 December 1939.

SELECTED BIBLIOGRAPHY

PRIMARY SOURCES

Great Britain: The National Archives (TNA), London

Admiralty Files

ADM 116 Admiralty and secretariat cases
ADM 223 Naval Intelligence Department memoranda

Air Ministry Files

AIR 9 Director of Plans files
AIR 19 Private Office papers
AIR 20 Air historical branch papers
AIR 23 Overseas command files

Cabinet Files

CAB 16 Committee of Imperial Defence subcommittees
CAB 56 Joint Intelligence Committee files
CAB 104 Supplementary registered files

Colonial Office Files

CO 323 General correspondence
CO 537 Colonial Office confidential original correspondence
CO 725 Aden original correspondence
CO 730 Iraq original correspondence
CO 732 Middle East original correspondence
CO 733 Palestine original correspondence
CO 820 Military branch original correspondence
CO 831 Transjordan original correspondence
CO 877 Correspondence with Sudan government office
CO 926 Mediterranean original correspondence

CO 967 Private Office papers
CO 1047 Maps and plans series

Foreign Office Files

FO 141 Cairo residency files
FO 371 Foreign Office general correspondence
FO 406 Eastern affairs confidential print
FO 407 Egypt/Sudan confidential print
FO 413 Morocco confidential print
FO 443 Embassy and consular archives: Rabat
FO 618 Embassy and consular archives: Turkey/Damascus
FO 624 Embassy and consular archives: Iraq
FO 684 Consulate papers: Damascus
FO 882 Arab Bureau papers

Intelligence Service Files

KV 1/15–17—MI5 Records 1909–19: D Branch reports/Imperial Overseas
    Intelligence
KV 3 Security Service subject files

Private Paper Collections

FO 1011 Sir Percy Loraine papers
PRO 30/69 Ramsey MacDonald papers
PRO 30/94 Frederick W. Foster-Turner papers

War Office Files

WO 32 Registered papers general series
WO 33 War Office reports/miscellaneous papers
WO 106 Directorate of Military Operations and Intelligence; Sudan Intelligence
    Reports
WO 190 Directorate of Military Intelligence appreciation files
WO 191 Headquarters records: Palestine
WO 193 Directorate of Military Operations collation files

India Office Archive, British Library, London

Political and Secret Department

L/PS/10 subject series: Mesopotamia files

Other Archives and Libraries, United Kingdom

First Baron Killearn (Sir Miles Lampson) papers, St. Antony's College Middle East
    Centre Archive, Oxford
Viscount Alfred Milner papers, Bodleian Library, Oxford
MSS BRIT EMP s.390, Clarence Buxton papers; MSS BRIT EMP s.514, Robin Martin,
    "Reminiscences of the Palestine Police Force," Rhodes House Library, Oxford
Gertrude Bell papers, Newcastle University Library

France: Centre des Archives d'Outre-Mer (CAOM), Aix-en-Provence

Afrique Occidentale Française Fonds Moderne

Série 17G Affaires politiques
Série 19G Affaires musulmanes
Série 21G Police et sûreté

Département d'Alger

Série F Police et maintien de l'ordre

Gouvernement Général d'Algérie (GGA)

Série H Affaires indigènes: sous-série 8H Organisation administrative
Sous-série 9H Surveillance des indigènes
Sous-série 11H Rapports politiques périodiques

Gouvernement Général de l'Indochine (GGI)

Série D Administration générale
Série F Affaires politiques
Nouveau fonds

Papiers d'Agents, série PA

Georges Mandel papers (PA18)
Marius Moutet papers (PA28)
Albert Sarraut papers (PA9)

Ministère des Affaires Etrangères (MAE), Paris

Série E Asie, 1918–1929
Série E Syrie-Liban, 1918–1929/1930–1940
Série M Maroc, 1917–1940
Série P Tunisie, 1917–1940

Papiers d'Agents

Henry de Jouvenel papers (PA 09)
Gabriel Puaux papers (PA S252)

Service Historique de l'Armée (SHA), Vincennes

Série H Outre-Mer: sous-série 4H Levant
Série 1N Conseil Supérieur de la Guerre (CSG)
Série 2N Comité Permanent de la Défense Nationale (CPDN)
Série 7N Etat-Major de l'Armée (EMA) deuxième bureau files
Série 9N Direction de l'infanterie—9N268—9N270: Direction des troupes coloniales

Fonds Privés

Fonds de Moscou (Moscow) Archives repatriées de Russie

General Fernand Gambiez papers (1K540)
General Maxime Weygand papers (1K130)

Service Historique de l'Armée de l'Air (SHAA), Vincennes

Série C: Présence aérienne française hors métropole
Sous-série 1C Forces aériennes françaises au Levant
Sous-série 2C Forces aériennes françaises au Maroc
Guy La Chambre papers

Centre des Archives Diplomatiques, Nantes (CADN)

Fonds Beyrouth
Série: Cabinet politique

Fonds Protectorat du Maroc
Sous-série: Direction des affaires chérifiennes, 1912–1956

Fonds Protectorat de Tunisie
Série: Cabinet politique

Archives Nationales (AN), Paris

Série F7: Interior Ministry, Police files
Série F60: Prime Minister's Office files

Fonds Privés
Louis-Hubert Lyautey papers
Paul Painlevé papers
Joseph Paul-Boncour papers

Services des Archives de la Préfecture de Police (APP), Paris

Série BA: Police surveillance files: colonial immigrants/colonial nationalist parties

Archives Départementales de l'Aude (ADA), Carcassonne

Albert Sarraut papers: Sous-série 12J

Published Documents, Official Publications

British Documents on Foreign Affairs, part 2, series B: *Turkey, Iran, and the Middle East, 1918–1939*, volumes 1–13. Frederick, Md.: University Publications of America, 1985–86.
British Documents on the End of Empire, series A, volume 1: *Imperial Policy and Colonial Practice, 1925–1945*, parts 1 and 2. London: HMSO, 1996.

Documents diplomatiques français, 1914, 3 août—31 décembre. Paris: Imprimerie Nationale, 1999; *1915,* volumes 1 and 2. Brussels: Peter Lang, 2002 et seq.; *1920,* volumes 1 and 2. Paris: Imprimerie Nationale, 1997 et seq.; *1921,* volumes 1 and 2. Brussels: Peter Lang, 2004 et seq.

SECONDARY SOURCES

Memoirs

Andréa, C. J. E. *La révolte druze et l'insurrection de Damas.* Paris: Payot, 1937.

Berque, Jacques. *Essai sur la méthode juridique maghrébine.* Rabat: Marcel Leforestier, 1944.

Bowman, Humphrey. *Middle East Window.* London: Longmans, 1942.

Hodgkin, E. C., ed. *Thomas Hodgkin: Letters from Palestine, 1932–36.* London: Quartet Books, 1986.

Imray, Colin. *Policeman in Palestine: Memoirs of the Early Years.* Bideford, Devon: Edward Gaskell, 1995.

Marty, Paul. *La Justice civile musulmane au Maroc.* Paris: Libraire Orientaliste Paul Geuthner, 1933.

Morain, Alfred. *Underworld of Paris: Secrets of the Sûreté.* New York: Dutton, 1931.

Morand, Marcel. *Études de droit musulman et le droit coutumier berbère.* Algiers: Jules Carbonel, 1931.

Peake, Frederick G. *History of Jordan and Its Tribes.* Reprint, Coral Gables, Fla.: University of Miami Press, 1958.

Peyrouton, Bernard Marcel. *Du service public à la prison commune. Souvenirs: Tunis, Rabat, Buenos Aires, Vichy, Alger, Frèsnes.* Paris: Plon, 1950.

Simon, Jacques, ed. *Messali Hadj par les textes.* Paris: Éditions Bouchène, 2000.

Wilson, Arnold T. *Mesopotamia, 1917–1920: A Clash of Loyalties.* London: Oxford University Press, 1931.

Selected Readings

Abu-Lughod, Janet. *Rabat: Urban Apartheid in Morocco.* Princeton, N.J.: Princeton University Press, 1980.

Ageron, Charles-Robert, ed. *Les chemins de la décolonisation de l'empire français 1936–1956.* Paris: CNRS, 1986.

Ahmed, Akbar S., and David M. Hart. *Islam in Tribal Societies: From the Atlas to the Indus.* London: Routledge, 1984.

Allain, Jean-Claude, ed. *Présences et images franco-marocaines au temps du protectorat.* Paris: l'Harmattan, 2003.

Anderson, David M., and David Killingray, eds. *Policing the Empire: Government, Authority and Control, 1830–1940.* Manchester: Manchester University Press, 1991.

———, eds. *Policing and Decolonisation: Politics, Nationalism and the Police, 1917–65.* Manchester: Manchester University Press, 1992.

Andrew, Christopher M. *Secret Service.* London: Hodder and Stoughton, 1986.

Andrew, Christopher M., and A. S. Kanya-Forstner. *France Overseas: The Great War and the Climax of French Imperial Expansion.* London: Thames and Hudson, 1981.

Arnold, David. *Police Power and Colonial Rule: Madras, 1859–1947*. Oxford: Oxford University Press, 1986.

Bakatti, Souad. *La femme tunisienne au temps de la colonisation, 1881–1956*. Paris: l'Harmattan, 1996.

Baron, Beth. *Egypt as a Woman: Nationalism, Gender, and Politics*. Berkeley and Los Angeles: University of California Press, 2005.

Bashford, Alison. *Imperial Hygiene: A Critical History of Colonialism, Nationalism and Public Health*. London: Palgrave-Macmillan, 2004.

———, ed. *Medicine at the Border: Disease, Globalization and Security, 1850 to the Present*. London: Palgrave-Macmillan, 2007.

Batatu, Hanna. *The Old Social Classes and the Revolutionary Movements of Iraq*. Princeton, N.J.: Princeton University Press, 1978.

———. *Syria's Peasantry, the Descendants of the Lesser Rural Notables, and Their Politics*. Princeton, N.J.: Princeton University Press, 1999.

Bayly, C. A. *Empire and Information: Intelligence Gathering and Social Communication in India, 1780–1870*. Cambridge: Cambridge University Press, 1996.

Beinen, Joel, and Zachary Lockman. *Workers on the Nile: Nationalism, Communism, Islam and the Egyptian Working Class, 1882–1954*. Cairo: American University in Cairo Press, 1998.

Berstein, Serge, and Jean-Jacques Becker. *Histoire de l'anti-communisme en France*, vol. 1, *1917–1940*. Paris: Olivier Orban, 1987.

Best, Antony. *British Intelligence and the Japanese Challenge in Asia, 1914–1941*. London: Palgrave Macmillan, 2002.

Betts, Raymond. *Assimilation and Association in French Colonial Theory, 1890–1914*. New York: Columbia University Press, 1961.

Blyth, Robert J. *The Empire of the Raj: India, Eastern Africa and the Middle East, 1858–1947*. London: Palgrave, 2003.

Bokova, Lenka. *La confrontation franco-syrienne à l'époque du Mandat, 1925–1927*. Paris: l'Harmattan, 1990.

Bouguessa, Kamel. *Aux sources du nationalisme algérien: Les pioniers du populisme révolutionnaire en marche*. Algiers: Éditions Casbah, 2000.

Bowden, Tom. *The Breakdown of Public Security: The Case of Ireland 1916–1921 and Palestine 1936–1939*. London: Frank Cass, 1977.

Brown, Judith, and William Roger Louis, eds. *The Oxford History of the British Empire*, vol. 4, *The Twentieth Century*. Oxford: Oxford University Press, 1999.

Brown, Nathan J. *Peasant Politics in Modern Egypt: The Struggle against the State*. New Haven, Conn.: Yale University Press, 1990.

Burke, Edmund, III, ed. *Struggle and Survival in the Modern Middle East*. London: I. B. Tauris, 1993.

Burke, Edmund, III, and Ira M. Lapidus, eds. *Islam, Politics, and Social Movements*. Berkeley and Los Angeles: University of California Press, 1988.

Çelik, Zeynep. *Urban Forms and Colonial Confrontations: Algiers under French Rule*. Berkeley and Los Angeles: University of California Press, 1997.

Chabal, Patrick, and Jean-Pascal Daloz. *Africa Works: Disorder as Political Instrument*. Oxford: James Currey, 1999.

Chafer, Tony, and Amanda Sackur, eds. *French Colonial Empire and Popular Front: Hope and Disillusion*. London: Macmillan, 1999.

Clancy-Smith, Julia, and Frances Gouda, eds. *Domesticating the Empire: Race, Gender, and Family Life in French and Dutch Colonialism.* Charlottesville: University Press of Virginia, 1998.

Cleveland, William S. *Islam against the West: Shakib Arslan and the Campaign for Islamic Nationalism.* London: Al Saqi Books, 1985.

Coeuré, Sophie. *La grande lueur à l'est: Les français et l'Union soviétique, 1917–1939.* Paris: Éditions du Seuil, 1999.

Cohen, Michael J., and Martin Kolinsky, eds. *Britain and the Middle East in the 1930s: Security Problems.* London: Macmillan, 1992.

Cohen, William B. *Rulers of Empire: The French Colonial Service in Africa.* Stanford, Calif.: Hoover Institution Press, 1971.

Conklin, Alice L. *A Mission to Civilize: The Republican Idea of Empire in France and West Africa, 1895–1930.* Stanford, Calif.: Stanford University Press, 1997.

Cooper, Frederick, and Ann Laura Stoler, eds. *Tensions of Empire: Colonial Cultures in a Bourgeois World.* Berkeley and Los Angeles: University of California Press, 1997.

Dandeker, Christopher. *Surveillance, Power and Modernity: Bureaucracy and Discipline from 1700 to the Present Day.* London: Polity Press, 1990.

Dann, Uriel. *Studies in the History of Transjordan, 1920–1949: The Making of a State.* Boulder, Colo.: Westview Press, 1984.

Darwin, John. *Britain, Egypt and the Middle East: Imperial Policy in the Aftermath of War, 1918–1922.* London: Macmillan, 1981.

Dodge, Toby. *Inventing Iraq: The Failure of Nation Building and a History Denied.* New York: Columbia University Press, 2003.

Driver, Felix, and David Gilbert, eds. *Imperial Cities: Landscape, Display and Identity.* Manchester: Manchester University Press, 1999.

El-Eini, Roza. *Mandated Landscape: British Imperial Rule in Palestine, 1929–1948.* London: Frank Cass, 2004.

Elpeleg, Zvi. *The Grand Mufti Haj Amin al-Hussaini, Founder of the Palestinian National Movement.* Trans. David Harvey. London: Frank Cass, 1993.

Fathi, Schirin. *Jordan—An Invented Nation? Tribe-State Dynamics and the Formation of National Identity.* Hamburg: Deutsches-Orient Institut, 1994.

Fischbach, Michael R. *State, Society, and Land in Jordan.* Leiden: Brill, 2000.

Fleischmann, Ellen L. *The Nation and Its "New" Women: The Palestinian Women's Movement 1920–1948.* Berkeley and Los Angeles: University of California Press, 2003.

Forcade, Olivier, and Sebastien Laurent. *Secrets d'État: Pouvoirs et renseignement dans le monde contemporain.* Paris: Armand Colin, 2005.

Gatrell, V. A. C., Bruce Lenman, and Geoffrey Parker, eds. *Crime and the Law: The Social History of Crime in Western Europe since 1500.* London: Europa, 1980.

Gellner, Ernest, and John Waterbury, eds. *Patrons and Clients in Mediterranean Societies.* London: Duckworth, 1977.

Gelvin, James L. *Divided Loyalties: Nationalism and Mass Politics in Syria at the Close of Empire.* Berkeley and Los Angeles: University of California Press, 1998.

Gershoni, Israel, and James P. Jankowski. *Egypt, Islam, and the Arabs: The Search for Egyptian Nationhood, 1900–1930.* Oxford: Oxford University Press, 1986.

———. *Redefining the Egyptian Nation, 1930–1945.* Cambridge: Cambridge University Press, 1995.

Gershovich, Moshe. *French Military Rule in Morocco: Colonialism and Its Consequences.* London: Frank Cass, 2000.

Goldberg, Ellis. *Tinker, Tailor, and Textile Worker: Class and Politics in Egypt, 1930–1952.* Berkeley and Los Angeles: University of California Press, 1986.

Grévoz, Daniel. *Les Méharistes français à la conquête du Sahara, 1900–1930.* Paris: l'Harmattan, 1994.

Gupta, A. *The Police in British India, 1861–1947.* New Delhi: Concept Publishing, 1979.

Hamed-Touati, M'Barka. *Immigration maghrébine et activités politiques en France de la première guerre mondiale à la veille du front populaire.* Tunis: Université de Tunis, 1994.

Hart, David M. *Tribe and Society in Rural Morocco.* London: Frank Cass, 2000.

Henry, Jean-Robert, and François Balique. *La doctrine coloniale du droit musulman algérien.* Paris: CNRS, 1979.

Heydemann, Stephen, ed. *War, Institutions, and Social Change in the Middle East.* Berkeley and Los Angeles: University of California Press, 2000.

Higgs, Edward. *The Information State in England: The Central Collection of Information on Citizens since 1500.* London: Palgrave, 2004.

House, Jim, and Neil MacMaster. *Paris 1961: Algerians, State Terror, and Memory.* Oxford: Oxford University Press, 2006.

Hughes, Matthew. *Allenby and British Strategy in the Middle East, 1917–1919.* London: Frank Cass, 1999.

Huneidi, Sahar. *A Broken Trust: Herbert Samuel, Zionism and the Palestinians (1920–25).* London: I. B. Tauris, 2001.

Ikenberry, G. John. *After Victory: Institutions, Strategic Restraint, and the Rebuilding of Order after Major Wars.* Princeton, N.J.: Princeton University Press, 2001.

Institut des hautes etudes de la sécurité intérieure. *Les cahiers de la sécurité intérieure.* Paris: Documentation Française, 1992.

El Iraki, Aziz El Maoula. *Des notables du makhzen à l'épreuve de la "gouvernance."* Paris: l'Harmattan, 2003.

Jackson, Julian. *The Popular Front in France: Defending Democracy, 1934–38.* Cambridge: Cambridge University Press, 1988.

Jackson, Peter. *France and the Nazi Menace: Intelligence and Policy Making, 1933–1939.* Oxford: Oxford University Press, 2000.

Jackson, Peter, and Jennifer Siegel, eds. *Intelligence and Statecraft: The Use and Limits of Intelligence in International Society.* Westport, Conn.: Praeger, 2005.

Jackson, Robert H. *Quasi-States: Sovereignty, International Relations and the Third World.* Cambridge: Cambridge University Press, 1993.

Jankowski, James, and Israel Gershoni, eds. *Rethinking Nationalism in the Arab Middle East.* New York: Columbia University Press, 1997.

Johansen, Anja. *Soldiers as Police: The French and Prussian Armies and the Policing of Popular Protest, 1889–1914.* Aldershot: Ashgate, 2005.

Julien, Charles-André. *L'Afrique du Nord en marche: Algérie-Tunisie-Maroc, 1880–1952.* Paris: Julliard, 1952; Reprint, Paris: Omnibus, 2002.

Kaddache, Mahfoud. *Histoire du nationalisme algérien, 1919–1951.* Algiers: EDIF, 2000.

Kayali, Hasan. *Arabs and Young Turks: Ottomanism, Arabism and Islamism in the Ottoman Empire, 1908–1918.* Berkeley and Los Angeles: University of California Press, 1997.

Khoury, Gérard. *La France et l'Orient arabe: Naissance du Liban moderne, 1914–1920.* Paris: Armand Colin, 1993.

Khoury, Philip S. *Syria and the French Mandate: The Politics of Arab Nationalism, 1920–1945.* Princeton, N.J.: Princeton University Press, 1987.

Khoury, Philip S., and Joseph Kostiner, eds. *Tribes and State Formation in the Middle East.* Berkeley and Los Angeles: University of California Press, 1991.

Killingray, David, and David Omissi, eds. *Guardians of Empire: The Armed Forces of the Colonial Powers, c. 1700–1964.* Manchester: Manchester University Press, 1999.

Kitson, Simon. *Vichy et la chasse aux espions nazis, 1940–1942.* Paris: Éditions Autrement, 2005.

Kolinsky, Martin. *Law, Order and Riots in Mandatory Palestine, 1928–35.* London: Macmillan, 1993.

Koulakssis, Ahmed, and Gilbert Meynier. *L'Emir Khaled premier za'im? Identité algérienne et colonialisme français.* Paris: l'Harmattan, 1987.

Kramer, Martin. *Islam Assembled: The Advent of the Muslim Congresses.* New York: Columbia University Press, 1986.

Lafuente, Gilles. *La politique berbère de la France et le nationalisme marocain.* Paris: l'Harmattan, 1999.

Landau, Jacob M. *The Politics of Pan-Islam: Ideology and Organization.* Oxford: Clarendon Press, 1990.

Lefeuvre, Daniel. *Chère Algérie: Comptes et mécomptes de la tutelle coloniale, 1930–1962.* Paris: Société Française d'Histoire d'Outre-Mer, 1997.

Lesch, Ann Mosely. *Arab Politics in Palestine, 1917–1939: The Frustration of a Nationalist Movement.* Ithaca, N.Y.: Cornell University Press, 1979.

Lockman, Zachary. *Comrades and Enemies: Arab and Jewish Workers in Palestine, 1906–1948.* Berkeley and Los Angeles: University of California Press, 1996.

Lorcin, Patricia M. E. *Imperial Identities: Stereotyping, Prejudice and Race in Colonial Algeria.* London: I. B. Taurus, 1999.

MacMaster, Neil. *Colonial Migrants and Racism: Algerians in France, 1900–62.* London: Macmillan, 1997.

Mahsas, A. *Le mouvement révolutionnaire en Algérie de la première guerre mondiale à 1954.* Paris: l'Harmattan, 1979.

Mamdani, Mahmood. *Citizen and Subject: Contemporary Africa and the Legacy of Late Colonialism.* Princeton, N.J.: Princeton University Press, 1996.

Marseille, Jacques. *Empire colonial et capitalisme français: Histoire d'un divorce.* Paris: Albin Michel, 1984.

Massad, Joseph A. *Colonial Effects: The Making of National Identity in Jordan.* New York: Columbia University Press, 2001.

McDougall, James. *History and the Culture of Nationalism in Algeria.* Cambridge: Cambridge University Press, 2006.

Mechat, Samya El. *Le nationalisme tunisien: Scission et conflits.* Paris: l'Harmattan, 2002.

Méouchy, Nadine, ed. *France, Syrie et Liban, 1918–1946: Les ambigüités et les dynamiques de la relation mandataire.* Damascus: IFEAD, 2002.

Méouchy, Nadine, and Peter Sluglett, eds. *The British and French Mandates in Comparative Perspectives.* Leiden: Brill, 2004.

Meriwether, Margaret L., and Judith Tucker, eds. *A Social History of Women and Gender in the Modern Middle East.* Boulder, Colo.: Westview Press, 1999.

Merom, Gil. *How Democracies Lose Small Wars: State, Society, and the Failures of France in Algeria, Israel in Lebanon, and the United States in Vietnam.* Cambridge: Cambridge University Press, 2003.

Metzer, Jacob. *The Divided Economy of Mandatory Palestine.* Cambridge: Cambridge University Press, 1998.

Meynier, Gilbert. *Histoire intérieure du F.L.N., 1954–1962.* Paris: Fayard, 2002.

Migdal, Joel S. *Palestinian Society and Politics.* Princeton, N.J.: Princeton University Press, 1980.

Miller, Michael B. *Shanghai on the Métro: Spies, Intrigue, and the French between the Wars.* Berkeley and Los Angeles: University of California Press, 1994.

Miller, Ylana M. *Government and Society in Rural Palestine, 1920–1948.* Austin: University of Texas Press, 1985.

Mitchell, Timothy. *Colonising Egypt.* Cambridge: Cambridge University Press, 1988.

Mizrahi, Jean-David. *Genèse de l'État mandataire: Service de renseignements et bandes armées en Syrie et au Liban dans les années 1920.* Paris: Publications de la Sorbonne, 2003.

Monier, Frédéric. *Le complot dans la République: Stratégies du secret de Boulanger à la Cagoule.* Paris: Éditions La Découverte, 1998.

Moreman, T. R. *The Army in India and the Development of Frontier Warfare, 1849–1947.* London: Macmillan, 1998.

Moulleau, Elisabeth. *Fonctionnaires de la République et artisans de l'Empire: Le cas des contrôleurs civils en Tunisie (1881–1956).* Paris: l'Harmattan, 2000.

Mundy, Martha, and Basim Musallam, eds. *The Transformation of Nomadic Society in the Arab East.* Cambridge: Cambridge University Press, 2000.

Nasser, Hoda Gamal Abdel. *Britain and the Egyptian Nationalist Movement, 1936–1952.* Reading: Ithaca Press, 1994.

Navarre, Henri, et al. *Le Service de Renseignements, 1871–1944.* Paris: Plon, 1978.

Neilson, Keith, and B. J. C. McKercher, eds. *Go Spy the Land: Military Intelligence in History.* Westport, Conn.: Praeger, 1992.

Newbury, Colin. *Patrons, Clients, and Empire: Chieftaincy and Over-Rule in Asia, Africa, and the Pacific.* Oxford: Oxford University Press, 2003.

Nowell-Smith, Geoffrey, ed. *Antonio Gramsci, Selections from the Prison Notebooks.* London: Laurence and Wishart, 1973.

Olson, Robert. *The Emergence of Kurdish Nationalism and the Sheikh Said Rebellion, 1880–1925.* Austin: University of Texas Press, 1989.

Omissi, David E. *Air Power and Colonial Control: The Royal Air Force, 1919–1939.* Manchester: Manchester University Press, 1990.

Oved, Georges. *La gauche française et le nationalisme marocain, 1905–1954,* vol. 1. Paris: l'Harmattan, 1984.

Owen, Roger. *The Middle East in the World Economy, 1800–1914.* London: Methuen, 1981.

———. *Lord Cromer: Victorian Imperialist, Edwardian Proconsul.* Oxford: Oxford University Press, 2004.

Paillole, Paul. *Services Spéciaux, 1935–1945.* Paris: Robert Lafont, 1975.

Panel, Louis N. *Gendarmerie et contre-espionnage (1914–1918).* Paris: Service de la Gendarmerie Nationale, 2004.

Paris, Timothy J. *Britain, the Hashemites and Arab Rule, 1920–1925: The Sherifian Solution.* London: Frank Cass, 2003.

Pearton, Maurice. *The Knowledgeable State: Diplomacy, War and Technology since 1830.* London: Burnett Books, 1982.

Pennell, Charles R. *A Country with a Government and a Flag: The Rif War in Morocco.* Wisbech: Middle East and North African Studies Press, 1986.

Popplewell, Richard J. *Intelligence and Imperial Defence: British Intelligence and the Defence of the Indian Empire, 1904–1924.* London: Frank Cass, 1995.

Porath, Yehoshuah. *The Emergence of the Palestinian-Arab National Movement, 1918–1929.* London: Frank Cass, 1974.

―――. *The Palestinian Arab National Movement: From Riots to Rebellion, 1929–1939.* London: Frank Cass, 1977.

Provence, Michael. *The Great Syrian Revolt and the Rise of Arab Nationalism.* Austin: University of Texas Press, 2005.

Qurёshi, M. Naeem. *Pan-Islam in British Indian Politics: A Study of the Khalifat Movement, 1918–1924.* Leiden: Brill, 1999.

Rabinow, Paul. *French Modern: Norms and Forms of the Social Environment.* Chicago: University of Chicago Press, 1989.

Rivet, Daniel. *Lyautey et l'institution du protectorat français au Maroc, 1912–1925.* Paris: l'Harmattan, 1988.

Roberts, Richard, and Kristan Mann, eds. *Law in Colonial Africa.* Portsmouth, N.H.: Heinemann, 1991.

Robinson, David. *Paths of Accommodation: Muslim Societies and French Colonial Authorities in Senegal and Mauritania, 1880–1920.* Athens: Ohio University Press, 2000.

Rogan, Eugene L. *Frontiers of the State in the Late Ottoman Empire: Transjordan, 1850–1921.* Cambridge: Cambridge University Press, 1999.

Rogan, Eugene L., and Tariq Tell, eds. *Village, Steppe and State: The Social Origins of Modern Jordan.* London: British Academic Press, 1994.

Rosenberg, Clifford. *Policing Paris: The Origins of Modern Immigration Control between the Wars.* Ithaca, N.Y.: Cornell University Press, 2006.

Ruedy, John. *Modern Algeria: The Origins and Development of a Nation.* Bloomington: Indiana University Press, 1992.

Savarese, Eric. *L'ordre colonial et sa légitimation en France métropolitaine.* Paris: l'Harmattan, 1998.

Shambrook, Peter. *French Imperialism in Syria, 1927–1936.* Reading: Ithaca Press, 1998.

Shamir, Ronen. *The Colonies of Law: Colonialism, Zionism and Law in Early Mandate Palestine.* Cambridge: Cambridge University Press, 2000.

Sharkey, Heather J. *Living with Colonialism: Nationalism and Culture in the Anglo-Egyptian Sudan.* Berkeley and Los Angeles: University of California Press, 2003.

Sheffy, Yigal. *British Military Intelligence in the Palestine Campaign, 1914–1918.* London: Frank Cass, 1998.

Shikari, Ahmad A. R. *Iraqi Politics, 1921–41: The Interaction between Domestic Politics and Foreign Policy.* London: LAAM, 1987.

Shryock, Andrew. *Nationalism and the Genealogical Imagination: Oral History and Textual Authority in Tribal Jordan.* Berkeley and Los Angeles: University of California Press, 1997.

Sibeud, Emmanuelle. *Une science impériale pour l'Afrique? La construction des savoirs africainistes en France, 1878–1930.* Paris: EHESS, 2003.

Silverman, Maxim. *Deconstructing the Nation: Immigration, Racism and Citizenship in Modern France.* London: Routledge, 1992.

Simon, Jacques. *L'Étoile Nord-Africaine (1926–1937).* Paris: l'Harmattan, 2003.

Simon, Reeva Spector. *Iraq between the Two World Wars: The Militarist Origins of Tyranny.* New edition. New York: Columbia University Press, 2004.

Sinclair, Georgina. *At the End of the Line: Colonial Policies and the Imperial Endgame, 1945–80.* Manchester: Manchester University Press, 2006.

Sivan, Emmanuel. *Communisme et nationalisme en Algérie, 1920–1960.* Paris: FNSP, 1976.

Soutou, Georges-Henri, Jacques Frémeaux, and Olivier Forcade, eds. *L'exploitation du renseignement en Europe et aux Etats-Unis des années 1930 aux années 1960.* Paris: Economica, 2001.

Stein, Kenneth W. *The Land Question in Palestine, 1917–1919.* Chapel Hill: University of North Carolina Press, 1984.

Stora, Benjamin. *Nationalistes algériens et révolutionnaires français au temps du Front Populaire.* Paris: l'Harmattan, 1987.

Stovall, Tyler, and Georges Van Den Abbeele, eds. *French Colonialism and Its Discontents: Nationalism, Colonialism, Race.* Oxford: Lexington Books 2004.

Streets, Heather. *Martial Races and Masculinity in the British Army, 1857–1914.* Manchester: Manchester University Press, 2004.

Swedenburg, Ted. *Memories of Revolt: The 1936–1939 Rebellion and the Palestinian National Past.* Little Rock: University of Arkansas Press, 2003.

Tanenbaum, Jan Karl. *General Maurice Sarrail, 1856–1929: The French Army and Left-Wing Politics.* Chapel Hill: University of North Carolina Press, 1974.

Tarbush, Mohammad. *The Role of the Military in Politics: A Case Study of Iraq to 1941.* London: KPI, 1982.

Tauber, Eliezer. *The Formation of Modern Syria and Iraq.* London: Frank Cass, 1995.

Thomas, Martin. *The French Empire between the Wars: Imperialism, Politics and Society.* Manchester: Manchester University Press, 2005.

Thompson, Elizabeth. *Colonial Citizens: Republican Rights, Paternal Privilege, and Gender in French Syria and Lebanon.* New York: Columbia University Press, 2000.

Tollefson, Harold. *Policing Islam: The British Occupation of Egypt and the Anglo-Egyptian Struggle over Control of the Police, 1882–1914.* Westport, Conn.: Greenwood Press, 1999.

Torpey, John. *The Invention of the Passport: Surveillance, Citizenship, and the State.* Cambridge: Cambridge University Press, 2000.

Townshend, Charles. *Britain's Civil Wars: Counterinsurgency in the Twentieth Century.* London: Faber, 1986.

Troutt Powell, Eve M. *A Different Shade of Colonialism: Egypt, Great Britain, and the Mastery of the Sudan.* Berkeley and Los Angeles: University of California Press, 2003.

Tyler, Warwick P. N. *State Lands and Rural Development in Mandatory Palestine, 1920–1948.* Brighton: Sussex Academic Press, 2001.

Ungar, Steven, and Tom Conley, eds. *Identity Papers: Contested Nationhood in Twentieth-Century France.* Minneapolis: University of Minnesota Press, 1996.

Wakeman, Frederic, Jr. *Policing Shanghai, 1927–1937.* Berkeley and Los Angeles: University of California Press, 1995.

Warburg, Gabriel. *The Sudan under Wingate: Administration in the Anglo-Egyptian Sudan, 1899–1916*. London: Frank Cass, 1971.

Wasserstein, Bernard. *The British in Palestine: The Mandatory Government and the Arab-Jewish Conflict, 1917–1929*. Oxford: Basil Blackwell, 1991.

Westerlund, David, and Eva Evers Rosander, eds. *African Islam and Islam in Africa: Encounters between Sufis and Islamists*. London: Hurst, 1997.

Wilson, Mary C. *King Abdullah, Britain and the Making of Jordan*. Cambridge: Cambridge University Press, 1987.

Woodward, Peter. *Sudan, 1898–1989: The Unstable State*. London: I. B. Tauris, 1989.

Wright, Gwendolyn. *The Politics of Design in French Colonial Urbanism*. Chicago: University of Chicago Press, 1991.

Young, Crawford. *The African Colonial State in Comparative Perspective*. New Haven, Conn.: Yale University Press, 1994.

Zamir, Meir. *Lebanon's Quest: The Road to Statehood 1926–1939*. London: I. B. Taurus, 1997.

Zubaida, Sami. *Islam, the People and the State*. 2nd edition. London: I. B. Tauris, 1993.

ARTICLES AND CHAPTERS IN EDITED COLLECTIONS

Abboushi, W. F. "The Road to Rebellion: Arab Palestine in the 1930s." *Journal of Palestine Studies* 6, no. 3 (1977): 23–46.

Ageron, Charles-Robert. "L'association des étudiants musulmans nord-africains en France durant l'entre-deux-guerres: Contribution à l'étude des nationalismes maghrébins." *Revue Française d'Histoire d'Outre-Mer* 70, no. 258 (1983): 25–56.

Aissaoui, Rabah. " 'Nous voulons déchirer le baillon et briser nos chaînes': Racism, Colonialism and Universalism in the Discourse of Algerian Nationalists in France between the Wars." *French History* 17, no. 2 (2003): 186–209.

Alègre de la Soujeole, François, and Christian Chocquet. "La professionalisation du maintien de l'ordre." *Revue Historique des Armées* 4 (2001): 97–112.

Alexandre, François. "Le P.C.A. de 1919 à 1939—données en vue d'éclaircir son action et son rôle." *Revue Algérienne des Sciences Juridiques, Economiques et Politiques* 11, no. 4 (1974): 175–214.

Alon, Yoav. "Tribal Shaykhs and the Limits of British Imperial Rule in Transjordan, 1920–46." *Journal of Imperial and Commonwealth History* 32, no. 1 (2004): 69–92.

———. "The Tribal System in the Face of the State-Formation Process: Mandatory Transjordan, 1921–46." *International Journal of Middle East Studies* 37 (2005): 213–40.

Andrew, Christopher. "Déchiffrement et diplomatie: Le cabinet noir du Quai d'Orsay sous la Troisième République." *Relations Internationales* 3, no. 5 (1976): 3–64.

Antouin, Richard T. "Civil Society, Tribal Process, and Change in Jordan: An Anthropological View." *International Journal of Middle East Studies* 32, no. 4 (2000): 441–63.

Aouimeur, Mouloud. "Contribution à l'étude de la propagande socialiste en Algérie dans les années 20 et 30." *Revue Française d'Histoire d'Outre-Mer* 89, no. 324 (1999): 65–78.

Arnold, D. "The Armed Police and Colonial Rule in South India, 1914–1947." *Modern Asian Studies* 11 (1977): 101–25.

Arnon-Ohanna, Yuval. "The Bands in the Palestinian Arab Revolt, 1936–1939: Structure and Organization." *Asian and African Studies* 15 (1981): 229–47.

Baker, Donald N. "The Surveillance of Subversion in Interwar France: The Carnet B in the Seine, 1922–1940." *French Historical Studies* 10, no. 3 (1978): 486–512.

Bar-Yosef, Eitan. "The Last Crusade? British Propaganda and the Palestine Campaign, 1917–18." *Journal of Contemporary History* 36, no. 1 (2001): 87–109.

Beinen, Joel. "The Palestine Communist Party, 1919–1948." *MERIP Reports* 55 (1977): 3–17.

Benton, Lauren. "Colonial Law and Cultural Difference: Jurisdictional Politics and the Formation of the Colonial State." *Comparative Studies in Society and History* 41, no. 3 (1999): 563–88.

Bessis, Juliette. "Chekib Arslan et les mouvements nationalists au Maghreb." *Revue Historique* 259, no. 2 (1978): 467–89.

Best, Antony. "Intelligence, Diplomacy and the Japanese Threat to British Interests, 1914–41." *Intelligence and National Security* 17, no. 1 (2002): 87–102.

Betts, Richard K. "Analysis, War, and Decision: Why Intelligence Failures Are Inevitable." *World Politics* 31, no. 1 (1978): 61–89.

Betts, Richard K., and Samuel P. Huntington. "Dead Dictators and Rioting Mobs: Does the Demise of Authoritarian Rulers Lead to Political Instability?" *International Security* 10, no. 3 (1985): 112–46.

Bou-Nacklie, N. E. "Les Troupes Spéciales: Religious and Ethnic Recruitment, 1916–46." *International Journal of Middle East Studies* 25 (1993): 645–60.

———. "Tumult in Syria's Hama in 1925: The Failure of a Revolt." *Journal of Contemporary History* 33, no. 2 (1998): 273–90.

Bowden, Tom. "The Politics of the Arab Rebellion in Palestine, 1936–39." *Middle Eastern Studies* 11, no. 2 (1975): 147–74.

Boyce, D. George. "From Assaye to the *Assaye:* Reflections on British Government Force and Moral Authority in India." *Journal of Military History* 63, no. 3 (1999): 643–64.

Bratton, M. "Beyond the State: Civil Society and Associational Life in Africa." *World Politics* 41, no. 3 (1989): 407–30.

Brogden, Mike. "The Emergence of the Police: The Colonial Dimension." *British Journal of Criminology* 27, no. 1 (1987): 4–14.

Brown, Nathan J. "Law and Imperialism: Egypt in Comparative Perspective." *Law and Society Review* 29, no. 1 (1995): 103–26.

Bunton, Martin. "Inventing the Status Quo: Ottoman Land Law during the Palestine Mandate, 1917–1936." *International History Review* 21, no. 1 (1999): 29–56.

Burke, Edmund, III. "Pan-Islam and Moroccan Resistance to French Colonial Penetration, 1900–1912." *Journal of African History* 13, no. 1 (1972): 97–118.

———. "A Comparative View of French Native Policy in Morocco and Syria, 1912–1925." *Middle Eastern Studies* 9 (1973): 175–86.

———. "Moroccan Resistance, Pan-Islam and German War Strategy, 1914–1918." *Francia* 3 (1975): 434–64.

Campion, David A. "Authority, Accountability and Representation: The United Provinces Police and the Dilemmas of the Colonial Policeman in British India, 1902–39." *Historical Research* 76, no. 192 (2003): 217–37.

Cannon, Byron D. "Irreconciliability of Reconciliation: Employment of Algerian Veterans under the *Plan Jonnart,* 1919–1926." *Maghreb Review* 24, nos. 1–2 (1999): 42–50.

Cantier, Jacques. "Les gouverneurs Viollette et Bordes et la politique algérienne de la France à la fin des années vingt." *Revue Française d'Histoire d'Outre-Mer* 84, no. 314 (1997): 25–49.

Caplan, Neil. "Zionist Visions of Palestine, 1917–1936." *Muslim World* 84, nos. 1–2 (1994): 19–35.

Chaker, Salem. "L'affirmation identitaire berbère à partir de 1900: Constantes et mutations (Kabylie)." *Revue de l'Occident musulman et de la Méditerranée* 44 (1987): 14–33.

Chan, Steve. "The Intelligence of Stupidity: Understanding Failures in Strategic Warning." *American Political Science Review* 73, no. 1 (1979): 171–80.

Christelow, Allan. "The Muslim Judge and Municipal Politics in Colonial Algeria and Senegal." *Comparative Studies in Society and History* 24, no. 1 (1982): 3–24.

———. "The Mosque at the Edge of the Plaza: Islam in the Algerian Colonial City." *Maghreb Review* 25, nos. 3–4 (2000): 289–308.

Cleaveland, Timothy. "Islam and the Construction of Social Identity in the Nineteenth-Century Sahara." *Journal of African History* 39, no. 3 (1998): 365–88.

Cohen, Michael J. "Sir Arthur Wauchope, the Army, and Rebellion in Palestine, 1926." *Middle Eastern Studies* 9, no. 1 (1973): 19–32.

———. "Secret Diplomacy and Rebellion in Palestine, 1936–1939." *International Journal of Middle East Studies* 8 (1977): 379–404.

Cole, Juan R. I. "Of Crowds and Empires: Afro-Asian Riots and European Expansion, 1857–1882." *Comparative Studies in Society and History* 31, no. 1 (1989): 106–33.

Conklin, Alice L. "The New 'Ethnology' and 'la Situation Coloniale' in Interwar France." *French Politics, Culture and Society* 20, no. 2 (2002): 29–46.

Coquery-Vidrovitch, Catherine. "L'Afrique coloniale française et la crise de 1930: Crise structurelle et genèse du sous-développement." *Revue Française d'Histoire d'Outre-Mer* 63, no. 232 (1976): 386–424.

Coury, Ralph M. "Who 'Invented' Egyptian Arab Nationalism?" parts I and II. *International Journal of Middle East Studies* 14 (1982): 249–81 and 459–79.

Cox, Jafna L. "A Splendid Training Ground: The Importance to the Royal Air Force of Its Role in Iraq, 1919–32." *Journal of Imperial and Commonwealth History* 13, no. 2 (1985): 157–84.

Damis, John. "The Free-School Phenomenon: The Cases of Algeria and Tunisia." *International Journal of Middle East Studies* 5 (1974): 434–49.

Darwin, John. "An Undeclared Empire: The British in the Middle East, 1918–1939." *Journal of Imperial and Commonwealth History* (1999): 159–76.

Dawn, C. Ernest. "The Formation of Pan-Arab Ideology in the Interwar Years." *International Journal of Middle East Studies* 20 (1988): 67–91.

Delacor, Regina M. "From Potential Friends to Potential Enemies: The Internment of 'Hostile Foreigners' in France at the Beginning of the Second World War." *Journal of Contemporary History* 35, no. 3 (2000): 339–59.

De Vries, David. "Drawing the Repertoire of Collective Action: Labour Zionism and Strikes in 1920s Palestine." *Middle Eastern Studies* 38, no. 3 (2002): 93–122.

Dillemann, Louis. "Les Druzes et la révolte syrienne de 1925." *Revue Française d'Histoire d'Outre-Mer* 69, no. 254 (1982): 49–54.

Eckhardt, William. "Civilizations, Empire and Wars." *Journal of Peace Research* 27, no. 1 (1990): 9–24.

Efrati, Noga. "The Other 'Awakening' in Iraq: The Women's Movement in the First Half of the Twentieth Century." *British Journal of Middle Eastern Studies* 31, no. 2 (2004): 153–73.

Eisenstadt, S. N., and Louis Roniger. "Patron-Client Relations as a Model of Structuring Social Exchange." *Comparative Studies in Society and History* 22, no. 1 (1980): 42–78.

El-Amin, Mohammed Nuri. "International Communism, the Egyptian Wafd Party and the Sudan." *British Society for Middle East Studies Bulletin* 12, no. 2 (1985): 27–48.

Eldar, Dan. "France in Syria: The Abolition of Sharifian Government, April–July 1920." *Middle Eastern Studies* 29, no. 3 (1993): 487–504.

Eliraz, Giora. "Egyptian Intellectuals and Women's Emancipation, 1919–1939." *Asian and African Affairs* 16, no. 1 (1982): 95–120.

Eppel, Michael. "The Elite, the *Effendiyya,* and the Growth of Nationalism and Pan-Arabism in Hashemite Iraq, 1921–1958." *International Journal of Middle East Studies* 30 (1998): 227–50.

Ergut, Ferdan. "Policing the Poor in the Late Ottoman Empire." *Middle Eastern Studies* 38, no. 2 (2002): 149–64.

Escander, Saad. "Britain's Policy in Southern Kurdistan: The Formation and the Termination of the First Kurdish Government, 1918–1919." *British Journal of Middle Eastern Studies* 27, no. 2 (2000): 139–63.

———. "Southern Kurdistan under Britain's Mesopotamian Mandate: From Separation to Incorporation, 1920–23." *Middle Eastern Studies* 37, no. 2 (2001): 153–80.

Ferris, John. "Before 'Room 40': The British Empire and Signals Intelligence, 1898–1914." *Journal of Strategic Studies* 12, no. 4 (1989): 431–57.

———. "The British Army and Signals Intelligence in the Field during the First World War." *Intelligence and National Security* 3, no. 1 (1988): 23–48.

———. "'Far Too Dangerous a Gamble'? British Intelligence and Policy during the Chanak Crisis, September–October 1922." *Diplomacy and Statecraft* 14, no. 2 (2003): 139–84.

Fisher, John. "The Interdepartmental Committee on Eastern Unrest and British Responses to Bolshevik and Other Intrigues against the Empire during the 1920s." *Journal of Asian History* 34, no. 1 (2000): 1–34.

Fitzgerald, Edward Peter. "France's Middle Eastern Ambitions, the Sykes-Picot Negotiations and the Oil Fields of Mosul, 1915–1918." *Journal of Modern History* 66 (1994): 697–725.

French, David. "Spy Fever in Britain, 1900–1915." *Historical Journal* 21, no. 2 (1978): 355–70.

———. "The Dardanelles, Mecca and Kut: Prestige as a Factor in British Eastern Strategy, 1914–1916." *War and Society* 5, no. 1 (1987): 45–61.

Galbraith, J. S. "No Man's Child: The Campaign in Mesopotamia, 1914–1916." *International History Review* 6, no. 3 (1984): 358–85.

Gallagher, John. "Nationalisms and the Crisis of Empire, 1919–1922." *Modern Asian Studies* 15, no. 3 (1981): 355–68.

Gavish, Dov. "Foreign Intelligence Maps: Offshoots of the 1:100,000 Topographic Map of Israel." *Imago Mundi* 48 (1996): 174–84.

Gelvin, James L. "The Social Origins of Popular Nationalism in Syria: Evidence for a New Framework." *International Journal of Middle East Studies* 26 (1994): 645–61.

Gershoni, Israel. "The Emergence of Pan-nationalism in Egypt: Pan-Islamism and Pan-Arabism in the 1930s." *Asian and African Affairs* 16, no. 1 (1982): 59–94.

Gershovich, Moshe. "The Ait Ya'qub Incident and the Crisis of French Military Policy in Morocco." *Journal of Military History* 62, no. 1 (1998): 57–73.

Goldberg, Ellis. "Peasants in Revolt—Egypt 1919." *International Journal of Middle East Studies* 24 (1992): 261–80.

Le Guenac, Nicole. "Le P.C.F. et la guerre du Rif." *Mouvement Social* 78, no. 1 (1972): 48–59.

Haddad, Mahmoud. "The Origins of Arab Nationalism Reconsidered." *International Journal of Middle East Studies* 26 (1994): 201–22.

Haj, Samira. "The Problems of Tribalism: The Case of Nineteenth-Century Iraqi History." *Social History* 16, no. 1 (1991): 45–58.

Hall, Hines H. "The Turkish Conundrum: French Diplomacy and the Occupation of Cilicia, 1919–1921." *Proceedings of the Western Society for French History* 24 (1997): 198–210.

Hamad, Bushra. "*Sudan Notes and Records* and Sudanese Nationalism, 1918–1956." *History in Africa* 22 (1995): 239–70.

Hannant, Larry. "Inter-war Security Screening in Britain, the United States and Canada." *Intelligence and National Security* 6, no. 4 (1991): 711–35.

Henni, Ahmed. "La naissance d'une classe moyenne paysanne musulmane après la Première Guerre Mondiale." *Revue Française d'Histoire d'Outre-Mer* 83, no. 311 (1996): 47–64.

Hiley, Nicholas. "Counter-espionage and Security in Great Britain during the First World War." *English Historical Review* 101 (1986): 635–70.

———. "Decoding German Spies: British Spy Fiction, 1908–1918." *Intelligence and National Security* 5, no. 4 (1990): 55–79.

Hills, Alice. "Towards a Critique of Policing and National Development in Africa." *Journal of Modern African Studies* 34, no. 2 (1996): 271–91.

Hoisington, William A., Jr. "Cities in Revolt: The Berber Dahir (1930) and France's Union Strategy in Morocco." *Journal of Contemporary History* 13 (1978): 433–48.

———. "The Mediterranean Committee and French North Africa, 1935–1940." *The Historian* 53, no. 2 (1991): 255–66.

Holquist, Peter. "'Information Is the Alpha and Omega of Our Work': Bolshevik Surveillance in Its Pan-European Context." *Journal of Modern History* 69 (September 1997): 415–50.

Huneidi, Sahar. "Was Balfour Policy Reversible? The Colonial Office and Palestine, 1921–23." *Journal of Palestine Studies* 27, no. 2 (1998): 23–41.

Ibrahim, Abdullah Ali. "Breaking the Pen of Harold MacMichael: The Ja'aliyyin Identity Revisited." *International Journal of African Historical Studies* 21, no. 2 (1988): 217–31.

Ibrahim, Hasan Ahmed. "Mahdist Risings against the Condominium Government in the Sudan, 1900–1927." *International Journal of African Historical Studies* 12, no. 3 (1979): 440–70.

Ihrai-Aouchar, Amina. "La presse nationaliste et le régime de protectorat au Maroc dans l'entre-deux-guerres." *Revue de l'Occident Musulman et de la Méditerranée* 34 (1983): 91–104.

Jankowski, James. "The Egyptian Blue Shirts and the Egyptian Wafd, 1935–1938." *Middle Eastern Studies* 6 (1970): 77–95.

———. "Egyptian Responses to the Palestine Problem in the Interwar Period." *International Journal of Middle East Studies* 12 (1980): 1–38.

Jeanneney, Jean-Noël. "Les archives des commissions de contrôle postale aux armées (1916–1918)." *Revue d'Histoire Moderne et Contemporaine* 15 (1968): 209–33.

Jeffery, Keith. "Sir Henry Wilson and the Defence of the British Empire, 1918–22." *Journal of Imperial and Commonwealth History* 5, no. 3 (1977): 270–93.

———. "Intelligence and Counter-insurgency Operations: Some Reflections on the British Experience." *Intelligence and National Security* 2, no. 1 (1987): 118–45.

Joarder, Safiuddin. "The Syrian Nationalist Uprising (1925–1927) and Henri de Jouvenel." *Muslim World* 68 (July 1977): 185–204.

Joffé, E. "The Moroccan Nationalist Movement: Istiqlal, the Sultan and the Country." *Journal of African History* 26 (1985): 289–307.

Johansen, Anja. "Violent Repression or Modern Strategies of Crowd Management: Soldiers as Riot Police in France and Germany, 1890–1914." *French History* 15, no. 4 (2001): 400–20.

Karsh, Efraim. "Reactive Imperialism: Britain, the Hashemites, and the Creation of Modern Iraq." *Journal of Imperial and Commonwealth History* 30, no. 3 (2002): 55–70.

Kedourie, Elie. "The Bludan Congress on Palestine, September 1937." *Middle Eastern Studies* 17 (1980): 107–25.

Khoury, Philip S. "The Tribal Shaykh, French Tribal Policy, and the Nationalist Movement in Syria between Two World Wars." *Middle Eastern Studies* 18, no. 2 (1982): 180–93.

———. "Syrian Urban Politics in Transition: The Quarters of Damascus during the French Mandate." *International Journal of Middle East Studies* 16 (1984): 507–40.

———. "Divided Loyalties? Syria and the Question of Palestine, 1919–39." *Middle Eastern Studies* 21, no. 3 (1985): 324–48.

Killingray, David. "'A Swift Agent of Government': Air Power in British Colonial Africa, 1916–1939." *Journal of African History* 25, no. 4 (1984): 429–44.

———. "The Maintenance of Law and Order in British Colonial Africa." *African Affairs* 85 (1986): 41–37.

Kingsley-Heath, A. J. "The Palestine Police Force under the Mandate." *Police Journal* 1 (1928): 78–88.

Kirk-Greene, A. H. M. "The Thin White Line: The Size of the British Colonial Service in Africa." *African Affairs* 79, no. 314 (1980): 25–44.

———. "The Sudan Political Service: A Profile in the Sociology of Imperialism." *International Journal of African Historical Studies* 15, no. 1 (1982): 21–48.

Kitson, Simon. "Police and Politics in Marseille, 1936–8." *European History Quarterly* 37, no. 1 (2007): 81–108.

Klieman, Aaron S. "The Divisiveness of Palestine: Foreign Office vs. Colonial Office on the Issue of Partition, 1937." *Historical Journal* 22 (1979): 423–42.

———. "The Resolution of Conflicts through Territorial Partition: The Palestine Experience." *Comparative Studies in Society and History* 22, no. 2 (1980): 281–300.

Kolinsky, Martin. "Reorganization of Palestinian Police after the Riots of 1929." *Studies in Zionism* 10, no. 2 (1989): 155–73.

Koulakssis, Ahmed, and Gilbert Meynier. "Sur le mouvement ouvrier et les communistes algériens d'Algérie au lendemain de la première guerre mondiale." *Le Mouvement Social* 1 (1985): 3–32.

Kroizer, Gad. "From Dowbiggin to Tegart: Revolutionary Change in the Colonial Police in Palestine during the 1930s." *Journal of Imperial and Commonwealth History* 32, no. 2 (2004): 115–33.

Kudaisya, Gyanesh. "'In Aid of Civil Power': The Colonial Army in Northern India, c. 1919–42." *Journal of Imperial and Commonwealth History* 32, no. 1 (2004): 41–68.

Lafuente, Gilles. "Dossier marocain sur le dahir berbère de 1930." *Revue de l'Occident Musulman et de la Méditerranée* 38 (1985): 83–116.

Lawrence, Paul. "'Un flot d'agitateurs politiques, de fauteurs de désordre et de criminels': Adverse Perceptions of Immigrants in France between the Wars." *French History* 14, no. 2 (2000): 201–21.

Lewis, Mary Dewhurst. "The Strangeness of Foreigners: Policing Migration and Nation in Interwar Marseille." *French Politics, Culture and Society* 20, no. 3 (2002): 65–96.

Likhovski, Assaf. "In Our Image: Colonial Discourse and the Anglicization of the Law in Mandatory Palestine." *Israel Law Review* 29, no. 3 (1995): 291–359.

Lockman, Zachary. "British Policy towards Egyptian Labour Activism, 1882–1936." *International Journal of Middle East Studies* 20 (1988): 265–85.

Lundsten, Mary Ellen. "Wall Politics: Zionist and Palestinian Strategies in Jerusalem, 1928." *Journal of Palestine Studies* 8, no. 1 (1978): 3–27.

Macfie, A. L. "British Intelligence and the Causes of Unrest in Mesopotamia, 1919–1921." *Middle Eastern Studies* 35, no. 1 (1999): 165–77.

Madeira, Victor. "'No Wishful Thinking Allowed': Secret Service Committee and Intelligence Reform in Great Britain, 1919–23." *Intelligence and National Security* 18, no. 1 (2003): 1–20.

Major, Andrew J. "States and Criminal Tribes in Colonial Punjab: Surveillance, Control and Reclamation of the 'Dangerous Classes.'" *Modern Asian Studies* 33, no. 3 (1999): 657–88.

Maktabi, Rania. "The Lebanese Census of 1932 Revisited: Who Are the Lebanese?" *British Journal of Middle Eastern Studies* 26, no. 2 (1999): 219–41.

Mangan, J. A. "The Education of an Elite Imperial Administration: The Sudan Political Service and the British Public School System." *International Journal of African Historical Studies* 15, no. 4 (1982): 671–99.

Manigand, Christine. "Henry de Jouvenel, haut-commissaire de la République française en Syrie et au Liban (1925–1926)." *Guerres Mondiales et Conflits Contemporains* 192 (1998): 101–12.

Mattar, Philip. "The Role of the Mufti of Jerusalem in the Political Struggle over the Western Wall, 1928–1929." *Middle Eastern Studies* 19, no. 1 (1983): 104–18.

McTague, John. "The British Military Administration in Palestine, 1917–1920." *Journal of Palestine Studies* 7, no. 3 (1978): 55–78.

Migdal, Joel S. "Urbanization and Political Change: The Impact of Foreign Rule." *Comparative Studies in Society and History* 19 (1977): 328–49.

Mitchell, Allan. "The Xenophobic Style: French Counterespionage and the Emergence of the Dreyfus Affair." *Journal of Modern History* 52 (1980): 414–25.

Moreman, Tim. "'Small Wars' and 'Imperial Policing': The British Army and the Theory and Practice of Colonial Warfare in the British Empire, 1919–1939." *Journal of Strategic Studies* 19, no. 4 (1996): 105–31.

Munholland, Kim. "Rival Approaches to Morocco: Delcassé, Lyautey, and the Algerian-Moroccan Border, 1903–1905." *French Historical Studies* 5 (1968): 328–43.

Munro, William A. "Power, Peasants and Political Development: Reconsidering State Construction in Africa." *Comparative Studies in Society and History* 38, no. 1 (1996): 112–48.

Newbury, Colin. "Patrons, Clients, and Empire: The Subordination of Indigenous Hierarchies in Asia and Africa." *Journal of World History* 11 (2000): 227–63.

Newell, Jonathan Q. C. "Learning the Hard Way: Allenby in Egypt and Palestine, 1917–19." *Journal of Strategic Studies* 14, no. 3 (1991): 363–87.

Nicault, Catherine. "Diplomatie et violence politique: Autour des troubles palestiniens de 1929." *Revue d'Histoire Moderne et Contemporaine* 47, no. 1 (2000): 159–76.

Nicosia, Francis. "Arab Nationalism and National Socialist Germany, 1933–1939: Ideological and Strategic Incompatibility." *International Journal of Middle East Studies* 12 (1980): 351–72.

Ofer, Pinhas. "The Commission on the Palestine Disturbances of August 1929: Appointment, Terms of Reference, Procedure and Report." *Middle Eastern Studies* 21, no. 3 (1985): 349–61.

Omissi, David. "Britain, the Assyrians and the Iraq Levies, 1919–1932." *Journal of Imperial and Commonwealth History* 17, no. 3 (1989): 301–22.

———. "Technology and Repression: Air Control in Palestine, 1922–36." *Journal of Strategic Studies* (1990): 41–63.

Parry, D. L. L. "Clemenceau, Caillaux and the Political Use of Intelligence." *Intelligence and National Security* 9, no. 3 (1994): 472–94.

Pateman, Roy. "Intelligence Agencies in Africa: A Preliminary Assessment." *Journal of Modern African Studies* 30, no. 4 (1992): 569–85.

Pennell, C. R. "Ideology and Practical Politics: A Case Study of the Rif War in Morocco, 1921–1926." *International Journal of Middle East Studies* 14 (1982): 19–33.

———. "Women and Resistance to Colonialism in Morocco: The Rif, 1916–1926." *Journal of African History* 28 (1987): 107–18.

Pool, David. "From Elite to Class: The Transformation of Iraqi Leadership, 1920–1939." *International Journal of Middle East Studies* 12 (1980): 331–50.

Popplewell, Richard. "The Surveillance of Indian Revolutionaries in Great Britain and on the Continent, 1905–14." *Intelligence and National Security* 3, no. 1 (1988): 56–76.

———. "British Intelligence in Mesopotamia, 1914–16." *Intelligence and National Security* 5, no. 2 (1990): 139–72.

Price, Roger. "Techniques of Repression: The Control of Popular Protest in Mid-Nineteenth-Century France." *Historical Journal* 25, no. 4 (1982): 859–87.

Provence, Michael. "An Investigation into the Local Origins of the Great Revolt." In *France, Syrie et Liban, 1918–1946: Les ambiguïtés et les dynamiques de la relation mandataire*, ed. Nadine Méouchy, 378–93. Damascus: IFEAD, 2002.

Rabinovich, Itamar. "The Compact Minorities and the Syrian State, 1918–45." *Journal of Contemporary History* 14 (1979): 693–712.

Rivet, Daniel. "Réformer le protectorat français au Maroc?" *Revue des Mondes Musulmans et de la Méditeranée* 83 (1998): 75–92.

Robinson, David. "French 'Islamic' Policy and Practice in Late Nineteenth-Century Senegal." *Journal of African History* 29 (1988): 415–35.

Rosenberg, Clifford. "The Colonial Politics of Healthcare Provision in Interwar Paris." *French Historical Studies* 27, no. 3 (2004): 637–68.

Satia, Priya. "The Defense of Inhumanity: Air Control and the British Idea of Arabia." *American Historical Review* 111, no. 1 (2006): 16–51.

Sayer, Derek. "British Reaction to the Amritsar Massacre, 1919–1920." *Past and Present* 131 (1991): 130–64.

Schor, Ralph. "Immigration familiale et assimilation: L'opinion des spécialistes (1919–1939)." *Revue de l'Occident Musulman et de la Méditerranée* 43 (1987): 67–71.

Sela, Avraham. "The 'Wailing Wall' Riots of 1929 as a Watershed in the Palestine Conflict." *Muslim World* 84, no. 102 (1994): 60–94.

Shearer, David. "Elements Near and Alien: Passportization, Policing, and Identity in the Stalinist State, 1932–1952." *Journal of Modern History* 76, no. 4 (2004): 835–81.

Sheffy, Yigal. "Institutionalized Deception and Perception Reinforcement: Allenby's Campaigns in Palestine." *Intelligence and National Security* 5, no. 2 (1990): 173–236.

Silvestri, Michael. " 'The Sinn Féin of India': Irish Nationalism and the Policing of Revolutionary Terrorism in Bengal." *Journal of British Studies* 39 (October 2000): 454–86.

Sirot, Stéphane. "Les conditions de travail et les grèves des ouvriers colonaiux à Paris des lendemains de la Première Guerre Mondiale à la veille du Front Populaire." *Revue Française d'Histoire d'Outre-Mer* 83, no. 311 (1996): 65–92.

Slavin, David H. "The French Left and the Rif War, 1924–25: Racism and the Limits of Internationalism." *Journal of Contemporary History* 26 (1991): 5–32.

Sluglett, Marion Farouk, and Peter Sluglett. "The Transformation of Land Tenure and Rural Social Structure in Central and Southern Iraq, c. 1870–1958." *International Journal of Middle East Studies* 15 (1983): 491–505.

Stafford, David. "Spies and Gentlemen: The Birth of the British Spy Novel, 1893–1914." *Victorian Studies* 24 (1981): 489–509.

Stoler, Ann. "Perceptions of Protest: Defining the Dangerous in Colonial Sumatra." *American Ethnologist* 12, no. 4 (1985): 642–58.

———. "Rethinking Colonial Categories: European Communities and the Boundaries of Rule." *Comparative Studies in Society and History* 31, no. 1 (1989): 134–61.

Stovall, Tyler. "The Color Line behind the Lines: Racial Violence in France during the First World War." *American Historical Review* 103, no. 3 (1998): 739–69.

Tauber, Eliezer. "The Struggle for Dayr al-Zur: The Determination of Borders between Syria and Iraq." *International Journal of Middle East Studies* 23 (1991): 361–85.

Teitelbaum, Joshua. "Sharif Husayn ibn Ali and the Hashemite Vision of the Post-Ottoman Order: From Chieftaincy to Suzerainty." *Middle Eastern Studies* 34, no. 1 (1998): 103–22.

Thomas, Martin. "Economic Conditions and the Limits to Mobilization in the French Empire, 1936–1939." *Historical Journal* 48, no. 2 (2005): 471–98.

————. "Colonial States as Intelligence States: Security Policing and the Limits of Colonial Rule in France's Muslim territories, 1920–1940." *Journal of Strategic Studies* 28, no. 2 (2005): 1033–60.

————. "Albert Sarraut, French Colonial Development, and the Communist Threat, 1919–30." *Journal of Modern History* 55, no. 4 (2005): 927–55.

Torpey, John. "An Analysis of Passport Controls in the French, Russian, and Chinese Revolutions." *Theory and Society* 26 (1997): 837–68.

Townshend, Charles. "Martial Law: Legal and Administrative Problems of Civil Emergency in Britain and the Empire, 1800–1940." *Historical Journal* 25, no. 1 (1982): 167–95.

————. "The Defence of Palestine: Insurrection and Public Security, 1936–1939." *English Historical Review* 103, no. 409 (1988): 917–49.

————. "Going to the Wall: The Failure of British Rule in Palestine, 1928–31." *Journal of Imperial and Commonwealth History* 30, no. 2 (2002): 25–52.

Vidal, Georges. "L'armée française face au communisme du début des années 1930 jusqu'à 'la debacle.'" *Historical Reflections* 30, no. 2 (2004): 283–309.

Vinogradov, Amal. "The 1920 Revolt in Iraq Reconsidered: The Role of the Tribes in National Politics." *International Journal of Middle East Studies* 3, no. 1 (1972): 123–39.

Warburg, Gabriel. "The Wingate Literature Revisited: The Sudan as Seen by Members of the Sudan Political Service during the Condominium, 1899–1956." *Middle Eastern Studies* 41, no. 3 (2005): 373–89.

Ward, Stephen R. "Intelligence Surveillance of British Ex-servicemen, 1918–1920." *Historical Journal* 16, no. 1 (1973): 179–88.

Warner, Carolyn M. "The Rise of the State System in Africa." In *Empires, Systems and States: Great Transformations in International Politics*, ed. Michael Cox, Tim Dunne, and Ken Booth, 65–89. Cambridge: Cambridge University Press, 2001.

Warusfel, Bertrand. "Histoire de l'organisation du contre-espionnage français entre 1871 et 1945." In *Cahiers du Centre d'Etudes d'Histoire de la Défense*, vol. 1, *Renseignement*, 13–40. Paris: CCEHD, 1996.

Watenpaugh, Keith D. "'Creating Phantoms': Zaki al-Arsuzi, the Alexandretta Crisis and the Formation of Modern Arab Nationalism in Syria." *International Journal of Middle East Studies* 28 (1996): 363–89.

Welch, David. "The Organizational Process and Bureaucratic Politics Paradigms: Retrospect and Prospect." *International Security* 17, no. 2 (1992): 112–46.

Willis, John. "Colonial Policing in Aden, 1937–1967." *Arab Studies Journal* 5, no. 1 (1997): 57–91.

Zubaida, Sami. "The Fragments Imagine the Nation: The Case of Iraq." *International Journal of Middle East Studies* 34 (2002): 205–15.

Zureik, Elia. "Constructing Palestine through Surveillance Practices." *British Journal of Middle Eastern Studies* 28, no. 2 (2001): 205–27.

INDEX

Text: 10/12 Baskerville

Display: Syntax

Compositor: BookMatters, Berkeley

Printer and Binder: Sheridan Books, Inc.